FOR REFERENCE

Do Not Take From This Room

THE OXFORD HISTORY OF THE NOVEL IN ENGLISH

The American Novel 1870–1940

The Oxford History of the Novel in English

GENERAL EDITOR: PATRICK PARRINDER

ADVISORY EDITOR (US VOLUMES): JONATHAN ARAC

Volumes Published and in Preparation

1. *Prose Fiction in English from the Origins of Print to 1750*, edited by Thomas Keymer
2. *English and British Fiction 1750–1820*, edited by Peter Garside and Karen O'Brien
3. *The Nineteenth-Century Novel 1820–1880*, edited by John Kucich and Jenny Bourne Taylor
4. *The Reinvention of the British and Irish Novel 1880–1940*, edited by Patrick Parrinder and Andrzej Gąsiorek
5. *The American Novel to 1870*, edited by J. Gerald Kennedy and Leland S. Person
6. *The American Novel 1870–1940*, edited by Priscilla Wald and Michael A. Elliott
7. *British and Irish Fiction since 1940*, edited by Peter Boxall and Bryan Cheyette
8. *American Fiction since 1940*, edited by Cyrus R. K. Patell and Deborah Lindsay Williams
9. *World Fiction in English to 1950*, edited by Ralph Crane, Jane Stafford, and Mark Williams
10. *The Novel in English in Asia since 1945*
11. *The Novel in Africa and the Atlantic World since 1950*, edited by Simon Gikandi
12. *The Novel in Australia, Canada, New Zealand, and the South Pacific since 1950*, edited by Coral Ann Howells, Paul Sharrad, and Gerry Turcotte

THE OXFORD HISTORY OF THE NOVEL IN ENGLISH

Volume Six

The American Novel 1870–1940

EDITED BY

Priscilla Wald and Michael A. Elliott

OXFORD
UNIVERSITY PRESS

OXFORD

UNIVERSITY PRESS

Oxford University Press is a department of the University of Oxford.
It furthers the University's objective of excellence in research, scholarship,
and education by publishing worldwide.

Oxford   New York

Auckland   Cape Town   Dar es Salaam   Hong Kong   Karachi
Kuala Lumpur   Madrid   Melbourne   Mexico City   Nairobi
New Delhi   Shanghai   Taipei   Toronto

With offices in

Argentina   Austria   Brazil   Chile   Czech Republic   France   Greece
Guatemala   Hungary   Italy   Japan   Poland   Portugal   Singapore
South Korea   Switzerland   Thailand   Turkey   Ukraine   Vietnam

Published in the United States of America by
Oxford University Press
198 Madison Avenue, New York, NY 10016

Library of Congress Cataloging-in-Publication Data
The American novel, 1870–1940 / edited by Priscilla Wald and Michael A. Elliott.
p. cm. — (The Oxford history of the novel in English; v. 6)
"The Oxford history of the novel in English; General Editor: Patrick Parrinder; Consulting Editor (US volumes):
Jonathan Arac" — Title page verso.
Includes bibliographical references and index.
ISBN 978–0–19–538534–2
1. American fiction—19th century—History and criticism. 2. American fiction—20th century—History and
criticism. 3. Literature and society—United States—History—19th century. 4. Literature and society—United
States—History—20th century. 5. National characteristics, American, in literature. 6. Transnationalism
in literature. I. Wald, Priscilla, editor. II. Elliott, Michael A., editor. III. Parrinder, Patrick, series.
IV. Arac, Jonathan, 1945– editor.
PS377.A545 2013
813'.409—dc23   2013022470
9780195385342

Contents

III: Genre Fiction and the Novel

IV. The Novel, 1915–1940

V: Critical Understandings

ACKNOWLEDGMENTS

We would first like to thank the many contributors to this volume. We refer not only to those scholars who actually penned the chapters of this book, but all of the members of the vibrant Americanist communities that sustain our reading and scholarship year after year. We feel fortunate to have so many gifted interlocutors, and we are constantly impressed with the intellectual generosity of our scholarly peers. The work contained here represents just a small introduction to a truly rich body of work on a period of American literary history that continues to fascinate us.

We also express our gratitude to Lynne Feeley and Sean Ward, whose labors on these essays and the list of works cited have made this book have made this book much better than it would have been otherwise. They repeatedly came to our aid with skill and speed. We are grateful as well to Patrick Parrinder and Jonathan Arac for inviting us to undertake this project and for their editorial advice and guidance. Likewise, we would like to thank Brendan O'Neill and his colleagues at Oxford University Press, both for their support of this series and the assistance that they have given us throughout this editorial process. Finally, we want to acknowledge the generosity of our institutions, Duke University and Emory University, for both the financial and intellectual support that made this project possible.

P. W. and M. A. E.

LIST OF CONTRIBUTORS

Jonathan Arac, University of Pittsburgh

Benjamin Balthaser, Indiana University, South Bend

Amy L. Blair, Marquette University

Gerry Canavan, Marquette University

Leonard Cassuto, Fordham University

Jeannine Marie DeLombard, University of Toronto

Michael A. Elliott, Emory University

Stephanie Foote, University of Illinois, Urbana-Champaign

Jonathan Freedman, University of Michigan

Jared Gardner, Ohio State University

Paul Giles, University of Sydney

Susan Hegeman, University of Florida

Lee Horsley, Lancaster University

Patrick Jagoda, University of Chicago

David Kazanjian, University of Pennsylvania

Betsy Klimasmith, University of Massachusetts, Boston

Caroline Levander, Rice University

John Michael, University of Rochester

Joshua L. Miller, University of Michigan

Michael Moon, Emory University

Gretchen Murphy, The University of Texas, Austin

Zita Nunes, University of Maryland

Orm Øverland, University of Bergen

Paula Rabinowitz, University of Minnesota

Elizabeth Renker, Ohio State University

Sonnet Retman, University of Washington

SARAH ROBBINS, Texas Christian University

AUGUSTA ROHRBACH, Washington State University

RAMÓN SALDÍVAR, Stanford University

MARK SCROGGINS, Florida Atlantic University

CLAUDIA STOKES, Trinity University

SHELLEY STREEBY, University of California, San Diego

SEAN KICUMMAH TEUTON, University of Wisconsin-Madison

JANE F. THRAILKILL, University of North Carolina, Chapel Hill

MIKKO TUHKANEN, Texas A&M University

CATHERINE TURNER, University of Pennsylvania

PRISCILLA WALD, Duke University

EDLIE WONG, University of Maryland

GENERAL EDITOR'S PREFACE

Unlike poetry and drama, the novel belongs entirely within the sphere of recorded history. Novels, like historical records, are written texts superseding the worlds of myth, of epic poetry, and oral storytelling. Typically they are commercial products taking advantage of the technology of printing, the availability of leisure time among potential readers, and the circulation of books. The growth of the novel as an art form would have been unthinkable without the habit of silent, private reading, a habit that we now take for granted, although its origins are much disputed among scholars. While novels are not always read silently and in private, they are felt to belong in the domestic sphere rather than in the public arenas associated with music, drama, and the other performance arts. The need for separate histories of the novel form has long been recognized, since the distinctiveness of fictional prose narrative is quickly lost sight of in more general accounts of literary history.

The *Oxford History of the Novel in English* is a multivolume series offering a comprehensive, worldwide history of English-language prose fiction, and drawing on the knowledge of a large, international team of scholars. Our history spans more than six centuries, firmly rejecting the simplified view that the novel in English began with Daniel Defoe's *Robinson Crusoe* in 1719. Fifteenth- and sixteenth-century prose fiction has, in fact, been surveyed by many earlier historians, including Ernest A. Baker, whose *History of the English Novel* appeared in ten volumes between 1924 and 1939. Unlike Baker's strictly chronological account, the *Oxford History* broadens out as it approaches the present, recognizing the spread of the English language across the globe from the seventeenth century onwards. The "English" (or British) novel becomes the novel in English. While we aim to offer a comprehensive account of the anglophone novel, our coverage cannot of course be exhaustive; that is a task for the bibliographer rather than the literary historian. All history has a commemorative function, but cultural memory is unavoidably selective. Selection, in the case of books, is the task of literary criticism, and criticism enters literary history the moment that we speak of "the novel" rather than, simply, of the multitude of individual novels. Nevertheless, this *Oxford History* adopts a broader definition of "the novel" than has been customary in earlier histories. Thus we neither focus exclusively on the so-called literary novel, nor on the published texts of fiction at the expense of the processes of production, distribution, and reception. Every volume in this series contains sections on relevant aspects of book history and the history of criticism, together with sections on popular fiction and the fictional subgenres, in addition to the sequence of chapters outlining the work of major novelists, movements, traditions, and tendencies. Novellas and short stories are regarded for our purposes (we would stress "for our purposes") both as subgenres of the novel and as aspects of its material history.

Our aim throughout these volumes is to present the detailed history of the novel in a way that is both useful to students and specialists, and accessible to a wide and varied readership. We hope to have conveyed our understanding of the distinctiveness, the continuity, and the social and cultural resonance of prose fiction at different times and places. The novel, moreover, is still changing. Reports of its death—and there have been quite a few—are, as Mark Twain might have said, an exaggeration. At a time when new technologies are challenging the dominance of the printed book and when the novel's "great tradition" is sometimes said to have foundered, we believe that the *Oxford History* will stand out as a record of the extraordinary adaptability and resilience of the novel in English, its protean character, and its constant ability to surprise.

—Patrick Parrinder

INTRODUCTION

By Priscilla Wald and Michael A. Elliott

In the aftermath of the Civil War, Americans faced the challenge of reimagining their nation. No less a figure than Abraham Lincoln understood the urgency and difficulty of this task, and his famous address at the Gettysburg cemetery attempted the oratorical feat of calling the modern United States into existence. Pronouncing impossible the task of dedicating, consecrating, or hallowing the field that had witnessed so much sacrifice, he called upon his listeners "to be dedicated here to the unfinished work . . . to the great task remaining before them." Unable to dedicate that ground, they had rather to dedicate themselves to this new nation—this new conception of a nation—"conceived in liberty and dedicated to the proposition that all men are created equal." Lincoln pressed upon his audience the idea of a nation founded not in a tradition so distant as to be wholly mythic, nor in a geographic space bounded by that distant tradition, but dedicated to a proposition—a concept—and propelled into an uncertain future by a community of *dedicated* believers.

The conceit was not new. In the crucial early decades of its history, the nation's politicians recognized the need for this new entity to be fashioned in letters as well as on the battlefield. Noah Webster called for an "America . . . as independent in *literature* as she is in politics, as famous for *arts* as for *arms*" (Webster 1953, 4), and America's early periodicals echoed the sentiment, calling for authors to show that "the spirit of Literature and the spirit of Democracy are one" (O'Sullivan 1842, 196). Anticipating what the theorists of decolonization would explain in the mid-twentieth century, these calls understood the incompatibility of the political independence of the United States with an artistic "colonial and provincial dependency on the old world" (Duyckinck 20.105: 165). The task of American literature was to show Americans how to imagine America.

The question by the middle of the nineteenth century, however, was "which America?" Political and cultural independence from England was considerably less than half the battle; political and cultural unity was proving much more of a challenge. Even as he commemorated the end of the war in his Second Inaugural Address, less than a year and a half after his Gettysburg charge, Lincoln could offer "no prediction" in regard to the nation's future.

The literary historical period represented in this volume begins with those years of uncertainty in which political and legal efforts to establish the terms and forms of national coherence, as well as the spirit of national unity, concerned the nation's literary figures as much as its politicians and lawmakers. Sectional strife was far from the only threat to national coherence. Urbanization and industrialization meant radically changing demographics, which contributed to the legacy of wartime uncertainties. Some public figures warned that statistics showed a concomitant rise in ethnic populations and decline in "white" (a notably unstable term in this period) Americans. The statistician Francis Amasa Walker observed this trend when he served as superintendent of the 1870 census, the first US census to count emancipated African Americans fully. In 1891, he remarked on the trends he saw: white couples marrying later and having fewer children, while immigrants and other marginalized populations were reproducing at higher rates. Walker warned that white Americans were committing "racial suicide," and later Theodore Roosevelt exacerbated those concerns when he made "race suicide" a refrain in public addresses both before and during his presidency. Barrett Wendell, Harvard University's first professor of American literature, confessed similar concerns about the impact of immigration on Americanism to his friend and former student, the German Jewish immigrant Horace Kallen; "we are submerged beneath a conquest so complete," he wrote in a letter to Kallen, "that the very name of us means something not ourselves. . . . I feel as I should think an Indian might feel, in the face of ourselves that were" (qtd. in Kallen, 1915, 194). For Wendell, the solution lay in "American literature," which, he believed, could communicate American values and serve as an antidote to the ravages of an encroaching world. He wrote of "literary contagion" and imagined literary works as sources of positive or negative infection; in both cases, literature mattered, and he designed classes and literary anthologies that he hoped would foster a healthy communicable Americanism.

* * *

Literary histories proliferated in this period, as historians sought to discover in the nation's stories some germ that might help in the project of imagining America. As Claudia Stokes, Elizabeth Renker, David Shumway, and others have described, the turn of the twentieth century witnessed the institutionalization of US literary history in the form of anthologies and college curricula. Every history encodes a new story, and this volume is an heir to that legacy of scholarly storytelling, building on the old stories and adding a new inflection. Then as now, literary histories are Janus-faced, at once recounting the past and looking toward the future. Readers of a national literature seek one of the most precious commodities to the process of nation-making: a usable past. And like all usable pasts, literary histories are subject to dramatic revision and rife with contradiction, depending on who is using them and to what purpose.

This literary history is focused on a specific genre—the novel—that became the dominant form of literary expression in the late nineteenth century in large part because of the claims the genre made as a form of representation, claims that its truth telling was as valid as history or the genres of the social scientific writing that were emerging during the same period. In "The Art of Fiction" (1884), Henry James made this point baldly, insisting that "the novel is history" and need not apologize for speaking with authority and precision about the reality of the social world. "The only reason for the existence of a novel," James insisted in the essay, "is that it does attempt to represent life."

James's verdict comes as close to a one-sentence summary of the history of the American novel from 1870 to 1940 as anything else we might craft. For several decades of this era, it was the reigning sensibility of the US literary establishment, particularly in the figure of William Dean Howells, an editor and author whose name recurs throughout the essays of this volume. As Howells explained in an 1887 "Editor's Study" column for *Harper's Monthly*, he believed that if fiction could "cease to lie about life," it could become more socially responsible, more influential, and even more democratic as an art form. Howells, moreover, was an ardent literary nationalist to a degree that James was not, so these principles translated for him into the representation of *American* life. However, the mimetic mandate to "represent life" created as many questions as it answered: Whose lives? How should they be represented? Where does truth stop and fiction begin? What, for that matter, is the relationship of truth to fiction? In her preface to *Hope Leslie* (1827), Catharine Maria Sedgwick had famously offered her fiction to "illustrate not the history, but the character of the times." Novelists writing in the years covered by this volume would have surely concurred, as they experimented with forms and styles that variously register the remarkable changes of a modernizing nation in its rapid emergence as a world power. Witnessing the end of a war that nearly terminated the nation, the abolition of racial slavery and rise of legal segregation (known as Jim Crow), the proliferation of urbanization and unprecedented immigration, the rise of Modernism and Hollywood, the closing of the frontier and two World Wars, these authors were living through a period of change, opportunity, and danger.

The literary debates that unfolded from the second half of the nineteenth century to the first half of the twentieth explored the promise and limitations of realism and abstraction, the relative merits of the popular and the highbrow, and the role of the literary as a vehicle for change or escape. In the last decades of the nineteenth century, social turmoil coupled with the rising prestige of journalism and emergence of the social sciences as well as the power and prestige of advocates such as James and Howells put literary realism at the center of those debates. But it quickly became as much a target as a guidepost. Characterized variously by its numerous advocates and detractors, literary realism was discredited by some for being too scientific and unimaginative; by others for focusing too much on the quotidian and vulgar; by later writers for being too genteel and not vulgar enough; and finally by high modernists for being too formal and overwrought. But what persisted throughout this period was a sense that the question raised in James's essay—about how the novel could and should "represent life"—remained urgent and nessary, especially in a nation that was struggling for coherence and self-definition.

As literary historians, we have been drawn to this period because of the urgency and complexity with which writers addressed these questions, and because of the variety of their responses. We were also drawn to this period because the "life" with which these writers wrestled seems to have so many threads connecting their time to our own and, at the same time, marking an astonishing distance. Questions fundamental to the articulation of the nation as well as to the creation of art and its role in the new nation—questions of race and citizenship; immigration and assimilation; gender and sexuality; nationalism and empire; the introduction of new media and technologies—reverberate throughout the novels written in the United States between 1870 and 1940/They continue to reverberate through the novels being written in the United States (and elsewhere) today, even while the demographics of authorship, the subject matter, and especially the form would astonish (for better or worse) most of the readers, writers, and, of course, publishers of the period covered by this volume, just as their works would have astonished their predecessors.

To take those questions on, as the essays in this volume do, invites two different kinds of criticism—both from those who worry about "presentism" coloring the writing of literary history, and from those who are concerned that an interest in social matters has overtaken the evaluation of literary merit. The chapters that follow offer their own refutation to these strands of criticism. For now, we will simply point out that the critics of the late-nineteenth and early-twentieth centuries leveled these same charges at the novelists working during their own time. From Mark Twain to Gertrude Stein to Richard Wright, many of these writers were accused of neglecting literary tradition and even abandoning literariness itself in pursuit of something else. And each helped in exciting ways to reshape the form of the novel and the very terms of storytelling in the United States.

This volume captures a range of ways writers during this period employed the novel as a form of thinking about the extraordinary changes they were witnessing, from the gritty realism and often clipped prose of former journalists such as Theodore Dreiser, Stephen Crane, or Ernest Hemingway to the poetic abstractions of Gertrude Stein and Djuna Barnes and the "cinematic grammar," as Patrick Jagoda calls it in his chapter for this volume, of Nathanael West and F. Scott Fitzgerald. In the preface to *The American* that Henry James composed for his New York edition in 1907, he stated that the "balloon of experience is in fact of course tied to the earth, and under that necessity we swing." No matter how "remarkable" the length of that rope, James continues, no matter how "commodious" the "car of the imagination," a novelist cannot cut that tie to the ground, or else the work becomes "at large and unrelated" to reality. To extend James's metaphor, we are interested in the arc and tangle of the tether, as well as the shape of the car that it ties to the earth. And to change the metaphor completely, we believe the literary historian to be twice-tethered—to the past and to the present—but with plenty of room to blow about in the winds of literary reading.

At a more literal level, the earth was changing a good deal during the period of James's literary career, and even more so during the full period that this volume covers, from 1870 to 1940. In the United States, this period is especially notable not only for the consolidation of the nation in the aftermath of the Civil War, but also for its subsequent—and astonishingly rapid—rise as a world power. An American born in 1870 would turn seven before federal troops completed their withdrawal from the former states of the Confederacy, and then at the age of seventy would watch the country prepare to fight in a global war across two different oceans. In telling our version of the literary historical story, we began with what is by now conventional: with how Reconstruction and the proliferating immigrations and migrations produced multiple and varied boundary crossings that were endlessly reshaping the composition and experience of the nation. Very little has been written, however, on the relationship of these changes to global transformations, and our goal for these chapters is to see how these global contexts might produce new insights into individual novels, as well as groups of novels, genres, and periodization. The following chapters emphasize the spatial reorientations and social transformations occasioned by changing networks of influence and world events as they are registered in and sometimes influenced by the literary production of the period. Throughout the volume, we are interested in how novels in the United States were shaped by, offer insight into, and affected social landscapes that were in the process of dramatic changes.

* * *

A governing assumption of this literary history is, as Gertrude Stein once put it, that "each of us [writers] in our own way are bound to express what the world in which we are living is doing" (Stein, "Portraits and Repetition," 1935). Fiction registers in unequal measure the pressure of everything from personal to global events, but it offers a unique insight into the past. Through its use of language, form, plot, and character, fiction records the unspoken inflections that give a moment its texture and the unrecognized assumptions that propel it: the character more than the factual history of its time. Novels register the silent changes that shape the possibilities of social interactions and form the earliest stirrings of the imagination, and they change as they capture the exquisite nuances that are the germs of the future. Artistic expression is always in flux, and "the novel" is no exception. "Novel," of course, means *new*, and it is a particular irony that any critical effort to define the form risks enshrining it in a static articulation to which it never quite conforms. It would be impossible to tell a single, definitive history of the novel during any one period, as generic boundaries are always markers of convenience that can be redrawn anew by each critical generation and are indeed always subject to debate even in their own moment. Therefore, we proceed with an attitude in accord with the philosophical pragmatism articulated at the turn the twentieth century, by recognizing that our own history is provisional, incomplete, and subject to further revision, much like the form of the novel itself.

The volume begins with three chapters on what we call "the fiction industry": the professionalization of literary production and authorship and the emergence of widespread literacy and a reading public in the United States. The post–Civil War decades saw the United States create and import many of the features of the literary marketplace that we now take for granted: the standardization and proliferation of book reviewing, best-seller lists, and the growth, simultaneously, of a professional, white-collar class of readers, a newly literate class of "mass" readers, and, especially with the rise of book clubs, a mediating "middle": middle-class and middlebrow. The commercial realm governing both author and text changed in significant ways, most crucially with the creation of international copyright laws, which were vociferously advocated in the United States by prominent writers such as Mark Twain and William Dean Howells. While authors on both sides of the Atlantic welcomed the creation of those laws, American authors in particular had long complained that they especially suffered from their absence.

A growing publishing industry in this period migrated from New England, the previous cultural center of the nation, to New York, its rapidly expanding business capital. Marketing, sales, and publicity all became specialized endeavors that affected how publishers regarded their novels and even how authors created them. Throughout literary history, publishers have been able to pressure their authors to produce novels that would meet the tastes of their audiences, often enforcing editorial standards at the expense of artistic material deemed inappropriate, but the late nineteenth century witnessed the emerging ability of publishing houses to assert their authority over particular sectors of the marketplace with confidence. Even as the reading public democratized, the changing literary marketplace fostered the rise of literary celebrity in the United States, most obviously epitomized by Mark Twain (easily the most recognizable American in the world for several decades), but also a label that would later apply to such authors as Jack London, Ernest Hemingway, and Gertrude Stein.

The changes even affected the increasingly amorphous reading public, as changes in publication and marketing strategies influenced reading practices. Readers could consume their novels as serials in periodicals, through subscription-based publications and tract publishing that aimed at particular readers, or through lending libraries, such as the Carnegie libraries, that spread throughout the nation, contributing to contemporary anxieties about the "massification" not only of literary culture, but of American democracy generally. The nation's changing demographics generated heated debates about the idea of "American culture," and transformations in the reading public were central to those debates.

Informing these changes were the legal, political, socioeconomic, and technological transformations that inevitably shaped the literary works. Although we call the second section "The American Novel 1870–1914," the chapters here expose the singularity of "the American novel" and the inclusive dates as somewhat fictive. The "novel" has always been a contested genre, and, indeed, the idea of genre itself is a classification, which means that it is always conventional and somewhat arbitrary. The language, form, storyline, structure, characterization, and other elements of fiction necessarily register a writer's efforts to negotiate the tension between cultural conventions and personal preferences and circumstances. As Jonathan Arac notes in his chapter, in 1935 Ernest Hemingway famously declared *Huckleberry Finn* to be the source of "all modern American literature." We begin with a chapter on Mark Twain's controversial 1884 novel, *The Adventures of Huckleberry Finn* (which, ironically, appeared first in England), in order to investigate not only the iconic place of *this* novel, but also of the concept of "modern American literature" that it emblematized for later writers as well as readers. The following two chapters explore the legal and political context that generated the controversies of Mark Twain's novel, which concerned racism and the institution of slavery. The Civil War Amendments had to perform the legal and political complement of Lincoln's rhetorical tour de force, turning "these united states" into "the United States," and the novels of the moment offer deep insight into the double helix of language and law in that process. They register as well the impossibility of that transformation, as they reflect the legal acknowledgement of racial difference and its concomitant hierarchies in the 1896 Supreme Court case of *Plessy v. Ferguson.*

While literary histories of a previous generation have tended to begin this period with a discussion of realism, we have preceded the discussion of that important literary movement with the chapters on legal and political debates in order to situate the emergence of "realism" in the context of rapid radical spatial and social transformations worldwide and in the conceptual shifts they engender as the impulse to document "the real." For its leading proponents in the United States, particularly William Dean Howells, the idiom of literary realism was a way of claiming a place for American fiction on a global stage, while at the same ameliorating class divisions and cultivating democracy. But, as critics have shown, the ostensible transparency of the realist idiom contributed to the naturalization of the hierarchies and power structures of the emerging world power. The chapters on journalism, geography, and religion offer discussions of how pressing issues of the moment prompted social and cultural engagements that complicated these tendencies of "literary realism" and emphasized its social dimensions at home and abroad.

The celebration and struggle with "America" for those inside and out is especially evident in the immigrant authors writing both in English and in their native languages, although the nature of both celebration and struggle varied depending on the authors' perception of their audiences (whether, that is, they were writing for "Americans" or for their countrymen). The acculturation processes documented by immigrant writers offered considerable insight for the emerging social scientific discussions of this period into the dynamics of collective identity as well as into the contours of "Americanism," and researchers in the nascent disciplines of sociology and anthropology made explicit use of novels in their work. Immigrant authors registered a range of responses to these processes, from appreciation for the opportunities afforded by their new surroundings to anguish at what they had lost and the difficulties and demands of the new life; their novels record their efforts to make sense of their experiences and of the difference between their expectations and the world they encountered.

The Spanish-American War exemplified the contradictions of democracy and imperialism. The war coincided with new forms of experimentation in storytelling, which in turn influenced the form of the novel, as authors struggled with the implications of those contradictions. Especially striking in these experiments is how the literary form of the novel manifested the importance of looking with new eyes—with, that is, attention to the way cultural forms conditioned individuals literally to perceive as well as to understand their world. The new interest in perception is evident in the observation of the philosopher William James, who authored a formative work in the new field of "psychology," that "Men have no eyes but for those aspects of things which they have already been taught to discern. . . . *The only things which we commonly see are those which we preperceive*, and the only things which we preperceive are those which have been labeled for us, and the labels stamped in our mind" (1890, I: 444).

New technologies complemented as well as influenced the political developments that led to those perceptual insights, and an understanding of that connection and its relationship to aesthetics infuses the work of William's brother Henry, the writer who typified the idea of cultural capital, and its particular confluence of tradition and innovation. But Henry James was far from the only writer to engage with the new media culture of his moment. In "Portraits and Repetition," Stein offered her observation about a writer's unwitting cultural recordings, as Jagoda notes, with particular retrospective attention to the influence of early cinema on her writing: "I was doing what the cinema was doing. . . . I of course did not think of it in terms of the cinema, in fact I doubt whether at that time I had ever seen a cinema, but, and I cannot repeat this too often any one is of one's period and this our period was undoubtedly the period of the cinema and series production."

Cinema exemplified how the new media and new technologies in this period shaped both perception and storytelling. Early cinema grew out of new visual technologies that were inspired by the recognition of literal blind spots in human vision. The medium at once called attention to the processes of perceiving and fashioned stories in accordance with its own limits and possibilities. It turned the everyday new and strange. Authors experimented with forms that would capture and complement cinematic technique as they came to terms with the insights afforded by the new medium—in particular, a heightened consciousness about the power of cultural forms to influence both awareness and sense making, as well as new forms of fantasy. Just as the narrative storytelling of the novel contributed to the development of narrative cinema, so too did the visual style of film affect the writing of fiction throughout the twentieth century.

The rapidity with which industrialization developed and introduced new technologies also led to new forms of consciousness and to a sense of limitless possibilities as well as countless dangers. The wider distribution of novels enabled by print technology, moreover, influenced the nature of the stories being told. A growing reading public clamored for stories commensurate with their lives and, even more, with their fantasies and fears. Utopian social movements proliferated following Edward Bellamy's influential 1888 novel, *Looking Backward*, which described a future world that the new technologies and social formations seemed to make plausible. Dime novels, serial novels, and the new category of the "best seller" responded to, and often shaped, the tastes of the ever-broadening reading public. In the early years of the twentieth century, the emerging genre of science fiction enacted the hopes and anxieties engendered by the new technologies and social relations they produced as well as by the geopolitics of a rapidly changing globe. Tales of adventure moved from the sea to the cosmos, and from the lawlessness of the western frontier to the crime of the inner city. Children's fiction expanded in scope as it catered to a larger segment of America's youth, which it socialized in accordance with the new relationships of their metamorphosing world. Among the most stylistically influential and innovative of the new forms, comics offered the readers of the nation's burgeoning newspapers a form of sequential and visual storytelling that complemented that of the early cinema.

* * *

Together, cinema and comics demonstrated the relationships among media that characterized the new international aesthetic movement of modernism. The early decades of the twentieth century witnessed a preoccupation, especially in the arts, with the question of perspective and an intense fascination with the senses as a way of knowing the world. An increasing anthropocentrism complemented a faith in science and technology that faltered, but did not shatter, when the First World War illustrated the destructive power of the tools that had been hailed for their utopian potential. Artistic production in the years between the wars grappled with profound philosophical questions about human nature and whether or not humankind could temper the capacity for destruction with the impulse to create.

Central to these questions was the subject of social relations—of how individuals interact to form a society and of how groups within that society behave. In 1895, the founding editor of the *American Journal of Sociology* had declared, "*In our age the fact of human association is more obtrusive and relatively more influential than in any previous epoch.* . . . Men are more definitely and variously aware of each other than ever before. They are also more promiscuously perplexed by each other's presence. . . . Whatever modern men's theory of the social bond, no men have ever had more conclusive evidence that the bond exists" (Small 1895, 1). That perplexity grew as revolutions in transportation and communication, as well as a World War and increasingly global economy, brought human beings into ever closer contact with one another. The change in consciousness inspired by that perplexity and the increasing cross-cultural encounters that fueled it found expression in the formal experiments of modernism, which exerted a formative influence on the shape of the twentieth-century American novel.

Among the most significant artistic revolutions in the first half of what Henry Luce famously dubbed "the American century" was what has become known as the Harlem Renaissance. W. E. B. Du Bois, a former student of William James, described what he called "double-consciousness": "the sense of always looking at one's self through the eyes of others, of measuring one's soul by the tape of a world that looks on in amused contempt and pity" (*Souls of Black Folk* [1903], ch. 1). In the 1920s and 1930s, Harlem served as a crucible that forged new thinking about the relationship of politics to art, and the works generated from that period have proven deeply influential, both in the United States and beyond, because of the complexity of that thinking. Equally important, the Harlem Renaissance converged with an artistic turn toward social realism occasioned by the crash of 1929 and the ensuing Great Depression. This era witnessed novelists from across the United States developing new iterations of the "folk," whether from urban slums or rural poverty.

The Harlem Renaissance is also crucial because it was a genuinely international artistic movement, its writers traveling to Europe and importing modernist philosophy and aesthetics. Literary critics are only now beginning to trace the ways artistic movements have traveled on global currents of exchange. Placing William Faulkner in the context of one such formation—the global South—demonstrates how such mapping might change our perceptions of one of the nation's most canonized writers and, with him, of literary history more broadly.

The culture industry in the United States was hardly oblivious to these global circuits; culture itself was increasingly conceptualized as an American export. If the beginning of the period covered by this volume witnessed the migration of the publishing industry from Boston to New York, the end coincides with an even more dramatic shift—from New York to California—which accompanied the rise of America's most representative, and most readily exportable, institution: Hollywood. As a geographical space and social concept, Hollywood is a distinctly American phenomenon, and very little better captures the ambitions and nuances of "American culture" than the story of the rise of Hollywood. Included in this shift are the stories of westward migration, of ethnic culture and the assimilation impulse, of the rise of a conspicuous culture industry, of new ways of thinking about space and climate, and of the rise of a new form of celebrity culture and new concept of entertainment. Such changes inevitably affected the "older" cultural form of the novel and help to explain the dramatic changes in that form in the United States in the second half of the century.

We have selected Richard Wright's *Native Son* as the topic for the final chapter of this section because his work so richly encapsulates many of the themes we seek to trace within this volume: the relationship of the novel to political activism; the documentary idiom of the novel; the ties between the novel and social science; and the growing recognition of the African American novel as central to literary expression in the United States. In addition, the novel's representation of Marxism, its stylistic echo of social realism, and Wright's own relationship to the Communist Party insist on the necessity of placing the novel within a transnational exchange of ideas.

The years covered by this volume constitute the crucible of American literary history, the moment when anthologies, critical studies, and university courses named the category of "American literature" and put in place many of the features of its narrative history that remain with us. Several of the final chapters in the volume explore the relationship of the novel to the emergence of "American literature" as a category in the academy, in public criticism and journalism, and in mass culture. These chapters make apparent the ways in which American institutions and cultures shaped perceptions of the novel and, in so doing, influenced the form of the novel itself. This perspective underscores the dynamic nature of the novel as a form and concept and, as such, its role in imagining and articulating a national cultural identity that is equally dynamic—that is, in effect, itself a work of fiction.

As we read these chapters together, it is clear that many of the most compelling concerns of the American novel from 1870 to 1940 are as urgent in the twenty-first century as they were then. The globalization of fictional narrative and the efforts to export American culture; the evolving relationships between the novel and other forms of media; the capacity of the novel to produce social representation—these are all major themes of this collection, but they could just as easily be the themes that govern an anthology of writing on the twenty-first-century novel. That is no accident. We have sought, like the literary historians before us, to create a usable past from the fiction of this period, and undoubtedly there will be new and contradictory uses that others will find in this period. In spite of decades of dire prediction that the American novel has been in decline, or on the verge of diminishing, the novel seems to us to remain a remarkable source of intellectual and creative energy. Even as critics predict that new technologies and media will make novels obsolete, the reading public has witnessed the incorporation of the new experiences and the new types of storytelling that these media and technologies have produced into new variants of the ever-changing form of the novel. We hope that collectively the chapters in this volume have not only documented the novel's remarkable capacity for metamorphosis but will also enable readers to reflect on the enduring power of the novel as a form of storytelling.

I

THE BUSINESS OF FICTION

TEXTUAL COMMODITIES
AND AUTHORIAL CELEBRITIES

BY SARAH ROBBINS

Between the end of the Civil War and the start of the Second World War, developments in the US marketplace had a profound impact on American literature's place in the larger culture. At the center of these shifts were writers themselves. With varying degrees of success, authors increasingly sought to perform a public role linked to career management. Two dimensions of this process involved writers' claiming their work as intellectual—and financial—property and carving out distinctive identities in the marketplace. These same decades saw the start of bestseller lists, widespread journalistic coverage of literary trends (with the launch of *Publisher's Weekly* in the 1870s one milestone), and the establishment of mail order book clubs as a distribution strategy. As Nancy Bentley has observed, the capacity that mass circulation brought for reaching audiences prompted anxiety that this floodtide would make literary distinction impossible. Ultimately, however, "[m]ass-produced fiction . . . had not lowered readers' tastes so much as turned popular tastes to the work of creating new readers in unprecedented numbers" (2009, 33). Because book reading was closely associated with becoming cultured, knowing about the writers of serious literature promised readers enhanced class status. Accordingly, a book of poetry could garner big sales, its author becoming widely known. Edgar Lee Masters's *Spoon River Anthology* (1915) was a bestseller over several years in the 1910s, and Edna St. Vincent Millay's *Fatal Interview* sonnets (1931) achieved a similar feat in the 1930s. But no literary form produced more celebrity figures during these decades than the novel. The novel was the dominant genre of the era—similar to memoir today. Indeed, narrative fiction was a major focus of such cultural sponsors as the Literary Guild (founded in 1927) and even of the more eclectic Book-of-the-Month Club (launched in 1926), which, Janice Radway reports, may have avoided literary modernism, but still aimed to promote "serious fiction" tied to "issues of everyday life" in its early years (1997, 278–79).

Novelists striving to manage their professional identities drew upon strategies increasingly available between 1870 and 1940. New tools in the literary marketplace could enable them to shape their own reputations in productive ways, even as gender, race, and social class could still constrain authorial identity. Analyzing this complex interplay of trends revises familiar characterizations of long-canonical writers, including Mark Twain, Henry James, Ernest Hemingway, and Gertrude Stein; it also illuminates figures such as Charles Chesnutt, Winifred Eaton, and Anzia Yezierska—writers whose efforts to claim renown during their lifetimes did not always translate into secure literary reputations.

Celebrity and Textual Ownership

A writer's quest for celebrity is not typically associated with asserting intellectual property rights, but these two agendas were closely related during this period in American literary history. Specifically, the efforts many writers exerted toward implementing international copyright and extending the length of time accorded to copyright within the United States were both consistent with the aim of carving out professional identities supporting permanent literary legacies. Thus, articles like a May 1881 *Scribner's Monthly* essay invoked financial as well as cultural registers to describe an author's intellectual property. That is, an author should "be in no danger of losing, in his old age, the fruits of his youthful energy," and "his children [should] not be beggars while others are profiting from the labor of his brains" ("Topics of the Times," 144–45).

As authorship became more a career and less an avocation, many American writers joined British counterparts in agitating for international copyright—as well as for provisions extending the time under which a text would be held back from public domain. Charles Dickens had complained during his trip to the United States in the 1840s that he found little support for an international copyright. Yet by the close of that decade, John Greenleaf Whittier was inviting literary colleagues to assemble in support of legislation. In the 1860s and succeeding decades, many American writers joined the campaign for legislation, with writer-editor voices such as William Dean Howells's and Charles Dudley Warner's chiming in.

At the heart of this campaign was an effort to convince legislators and the public that authors should "own" the products of mental labor, as distinct from other aspects of literary production (such as typesetting or bookbinding). Theories of toil aside, other motives behind the campaign included writers' wishes to control circulation of their texts and recognition that the lack of international copyright was certainly costing them money. Before the eventual passage of an international copyright law in 1891, a pirated edition of an English novel was far less expensive to produce than a book by an American writer, who would be paid royalties. Unsurprisingly, then, novels by figures like Sir Walter Scott and Charles Dickens outsold works by US counterparts, though British writers typically gained no profits themselves from these sales. On the flip side, by the time Harriet Beecher Stowe's *Uncle Tom's Cabin*

(1852) drew more readers in England than in the United States, without funneling revenue to Stowe herself, many of America's literary luminaries climbed aboard the international copyright bandwagon.

Writers like Samuel Clemens (Mark Twain) also agitated for extension of the copyright time frame to ensure future earnings for their heirs. Such attempts to delineate possession of literary products were bound up in writers' assertion of a business-oriented professional identity. These moves included trying to secure entry into high-status publishing venues and demanding prompt payment from publishers for accepted submissions (such as Jack London depicts through his protagonist-writer in *Martin Eden* [1909]). In this context, the term "textual ownership" embraces a broad range of agendas among writers seeking control over their own authorship. Such claims became increasingly desirable over the 1870–1940 decades, when managing one's textual production and circulation could bring substantial financial reward (as American literature increasingly became a commodity with potentially high returns).

Although the decades between the end of the Civil War and the start of the Second World War brought celebrity authorship and long-term reputation management to a pivotal stage in American literary history, these developments actually built upon trends from earlier in the nineteenth century. In the 1820s, James Fenimore Cooper laid the groundwork, through novels that brought a "first flush of celebrity," for a successful writing career, enabling him to support himself solely through authorship (Bell 2001, 82). Catharine Maria Sedgwick reveled in her novels' monetary success, carefully recording sales data in her journals, as well as readers' enthusiastic responses to narratives such as *Hope Leslie* (1827) and *Live and Let Live* (1837). Anticipating the arguments international copyright advocates would broadcast later in the century, Sedgwick was already grumbling in her journals about literary piracy. By the 1850s, the possibility of garnering both financial success and personal renown was evident enough that Nathaniel Hawthorne launched his famous complaint about his main competition in the literary marketplace, the "damned mob of scribbling women." In that vein, Sara Parton (Fanny Fern) captured an astounding income and celebrity status by writing with a shrewd eye for the periodical marketplace, then representing her own success as an author in *Ruth Hall* (1854). The careers of such forebears demonstrate that celebrity authorship was solidly in place before the Civil War. If *Uncle Tom's Cabin* is one hallmark, so too the inauguration in the late 1860s of Louisa May Alcott's novels on the March family, which prompted a parade of worshippers trying to catch a glimpse of her at home.

Despite the continuity between the 1870–1940 era and the decades beforehand, new features in American authorship emerged during the later period. Some of these evolved in fits and starts, whereas others extended over those decades. Overall, while recognizing that the careers of individual authors would overlap any divisions within this broad time frame, we can track stages in the evolution of textual ownership and authorial performance through three periods: (1) the 1870s to the close of the nineteenth century; (2) the early 1900s to the end of the First World War; and (3) 1918–1940 (sometimes dubbed the period "between the wars").

Nostalgia: Texts, Photographs, and Podiums

The years between Reconstruction's twilight and the start of the twentieth century produced new technologies with a broad reach. Advances in transportation supported cross-region book distribution. Technologies for producing print text and images for mass audiences expanded, facilitating the growth of periodicals, publishing syndicates, and marketing materials (such as advertising cards), as well as low-cost books. While these advances promoted a mass readership, they also nurtured specialized audiences that developed niche versions of celebrity.

Writers like Frances E. W. Harper achieved just such audience-specific renown by addressing the audience of African Americans cultivating middle-class status through their reading of targeted periodicals, such as the *Christian Recorder*, where several of Harper's serialized novels appeared. Newspaper coverage of Harper's lectures as she campaigned for racial uplift, temperance, and education in the South even drew the attention of some appreciative white readers. Meanwhile, although novelists like Albion Tourgée cast a critical eye on Reconstruction's failures, many white middle-class readers were drawn to narratives depicting cross-regional reconciliation through marriages linking North and South, thereby feeding shared nostalgia for prior national harmony more fictional than real.

One mark of nostalgia's lure was the shift in content within novels by Harriet Beecher Stowe, who increasingly capitalized on her lingering fame as the author of *Uncle Tom's Cabin* with narratives eschewing an activist focus on race. In *Old Town Folks* (1869), *Pink and White Tyranny* (1871), *My Wife and I* (1871), and *Poganuc People* (1879), Stowe returned to the domestic nostalgia more typical of her early writing than the politically charged assault on slavery evident in 1856's *Dred* or the boldly confrontational, protofeminist polemic of *Lady Byron Vindicated* (1870), where she had excoriated Byron's purported incest. The transatlantic energy evident in *Agnes of Sorrento* (1862) and Stowe's travelogue account of her first trip to Europe, *Sunny Memories of Foreign Lands* (1854), was replaced, in her late-career publishing, by *Palmetto Leaves* (1873), vignettes of her sojourns in Florida, blending enthusiastic descriptions of the southern flora with racist portraits of local black residents. This unsettling body of work from the later decades of Stowe's career disappoints us today, but it exemplifies her perceptive audience awareness. These books sold reliably, often capitalizing upon initial appearance as periodical serials. Stowe's celebrity status did not ensure that her reputation would survive the new mandates for novels in the next century, but for the final decades of the nineteenth century, it was sufficient currency for marketplace success.

Before the assertion of more masculinist models for literary excellence took hold, other women writers sought to assume Stowe's mantle, embracing the tradition of her feminized authorship. For example, Elizabeth Stuart Phelps's 1896 account of her own authorial career, *Chapters from a Life*, plays into popular nostalgia not only through its portrait of the author's New England upbringing, but also through a fond yet whimsical account of the monumental response to her own blockbuster, *The Gates Ajar* (1868). By envisioning reconnections in the afterlife, this novel addressed Americans mourning lost loved ones after the Civil War. As Phelps recounted in her memoir, "I wished to say something that would comfort some few—I did not think at all about comforting many . . . of the women whose misery crowded the land" (ch. 5). Seemingly modest protestations aside, her book sold close to 100,000 copies in the United States, and even more overseas—though, she reminded readers, the lack of international copyright meant that "all this foreign publication was piratical." Affirming the novel's striking success as a commodity, embodied in an "edition de luxe" brought out by Fields and Osgood, spinoffs abounded—including poster art, a "tippet, for sale in the country groceries," a sweet-tasting medicine, clothing, writing paper, and, it was rumored according to Phelps, "a Gates Ajar cigar" (ch. 6).

Overall, Phelps's autobiographical text resonates with a number of literary biographies from the turn of the century, honoring figures who had helped establish "American" literature. Here, again, nostalgia reigned supreme, as in books about Stowe's life by her son Charles and her good friend Annie Fields; Julian Hawthorne's *Nathaniel Hawthorne and His Wife* (1884) and *Hawthorne and His Circle* (1903); as well as the American Men of Letters series issued by Houghton Mifflin and edited by Charles Dudley Warner (comparable to the English Men of Letters series published by Macmillan, edited by John Morley, and including some US writers, such as Hawthorne). Produced in a period before American literature had coalesced as a field of research and teaching, such biographies avoided a critical stance. Instead, adopting a congratulatory tone, the American Men of Letters texts helped enshrine the first generations of US novelists, such as Washington Irving and Cooper, while simultaneously promoting literary celebrity itself.

Besides biography, another vehicle of literary celebrity making during this period was the photograph. Photographic technologies progressed from the daguerreotype of the pre–Civil War days to lithographed images that could be duplicated in newspapers, to *carte de visite* pictures of celebrities that could be sold by the thousands, further stoking the cult of personality. In the closing decades of the nineteenth century, professional photographers could draw a steady income from these images while enhancing the very celebrity of their subjects.

American writers took advantage of photography for self-promotion. One master of the form was Walt Whitman. Whitman is said to have grown tired of others making money by circulating pictures of him without paying royalties, but he understood the value he accrued from such images. David Haven Blake reports that

Whitman consistently "courted the camera, displaying himself like a show horse" (2006, 4). Thus, an 1877 staged portrait of Whitman holding an artificial butterfly helped shift his authorial identity from renegade to iconic elder of American literature. As Blake has noted, "The butterfly descends to us today as a testament to Whitman's remarkable merger of poetry and publicity" (3). For Whitman, photographs may have been more productive of reputation-shaping than money-making, but his concerted efforts to manage these images signal an astute awareness of authorship's potential link to celebrity identity.

Among America's novelists, no author better understood the power of the photographic portrait than Mark Twain, whose cultivation of celebrity cut across virtually every strategy for self-promotion available throughout his career. Twain circulated images of himself along with copies of his pen-name signature, another recurring element in his effort to achieve what several scholars have likened to a logo or trademark. Dressed in his white suit, with his white hair and mustache as visual complements, Samuel Clemens posed for photographs as Mark Twain in the same way that he posed on stage as a folksy lecturer, masking his rhetorical sophistication in homespun humor.

For Twain and others of this generation, the public talk also cultivated celebrity. With transportation systems improving, the traveling author would have found such promotional journeys less cumbersome than in earlier decades. Still, this work remained grueling, even if also energizing in its capacity to unite author with audience. Most American writers would never achieve the earnings from lectures of a Charles Dickens, who reportedly brought in more than $100,000 for his 1867 US tour, or reach the kind of celebrity status associated with Napoleon Sarony's 1882 photos of the traveling literary performer Oscar Wilde. Furthermore, women writers would be restricted in their ability to use this tool because of gender-based constraints on public presentations, leading Harriet Beecher Stowe to sit on stage while others read for her. But Stowe's Connecticut neighbor Mark Twain excelled at using the lecture format to bolster his income and his image.

As just one example of Twain's successfully integrating his lectures with other dimensions of authorial identity management, we can look to a short speech he delivered in Montreal, Canada, in December of 1881. Beginning with self-deprecating jokes, he shifted to a more serious point, the link between his visit to Canada and his campaign for international copyright: "I did not come to Canada to commit crime . . . but to prevent it. I came here to place myself under the protection of the Canadian law and secure a copyright. . . . This is a rather cumbersome way to fence and fortify one's property against the literary buccaneer, it is true; still, if it is effective, it is a great advance upon past conditions, and one to be correspondingly welcomed." Twain's commentary on copyright was leavened with jocular analogies, yet aimed at recruiting allies; he hoped "a day will come when, in the eye of the law, literary property will be as sacred as whiskey, or any other of the necessities of life."

The vocal techniques Twain employed so well in his lifetime are not retrievable in print today, but the adept navigation of tone, and his balancing accessibility with a challenge of the status quo, demonstrate why he was such a star author. Notes Twain, "In this age of ours, if you steal another man's label to advertise your own brand of whiskey with, you will be heavily fined and otherwise punished for violating that trademark; if you steal the whiskey without the trademark, you go to jail; but if you could prove that the whiskey was literature, you can steal them both, and the law won't say a word" ("Dinner Speech").

Though known for such vociferous support of copyright, Twain appreciated how piracy helped to disseminate his early writings, thereby garnering a wider audience for works like "The Celebrated Jumping Frog" (1865). Twain's strong late-career advocacy for perpetual copyright probably had more to do with concerns about his family's financial future than with a consistent philosophy. Thus, Twain's assertion of proprietary rights over his oeuvre near the close of his life can be seen as part of a larger, hands-on effort to claim textual ownership. He was effective for much of his career at shaping publication processes, including such decisions as who would illustrate his works. In that context, Twain's move to form his own publishing business, though a financial failure, could be seen as part of an ongoing effort to maintain textual control in an increasingly complex marketplace. Certainly, Twain did score the ultimate victory of long-term renown, as evident in responses to the 2010 release of his autobiography, which quickly climbed bestseller lists.

Undoing the Myth of "Art versus Business"

Scholarship on major authors from the turn of the century has often cast these figures as resisting the call of commercialization while committing to artistic vision. Modernism's elevation of the aesthetic object seemed to preclude a conception of the "best" writers as immersed in marketplace concerns. Narratives by authors like Henry James and European counterparts like James Joyce and Virginia Woolf—not to mention expatriate poets like T. S. Eliot and Ezra Pound—played into this dichotomizing of high art versus debased, commercial forms.

In James's case, many of his narratives directly criticized the literary marketplace in terms so forceful as to encourage contemporary readers (and later scholars) to equate characters' attitudes with James's own. Depictions of literary figures suffering at the hands of persistent interviewers or struggling to maintain some privacy in the face of intrusive, misguided fans have been interpreted straightforwardly as accounts of Henry James, the person, complaining about his own situation more than as astute engagement by Henry James, the author, with social issues of his day. Yet his repeated treatment of these topics—in works like *The Aspern Papers* (1888) and *The Death of the Lion* (1894)—not only contributed to an authorial identity setting him above commercial publishing's mere hacks, but also, ironically, helped attract readers, given the era's growing fascination with literary celebrities. James's own fascination with authorship has clearly resonated with many writers over the decades since, as evidenced by recent novels drawing on his persona, such as Colm Tóibín's *The Master* and David Lodge's *Author, Author* (both 2004).

Whereas Henry James's choice to live abroad for many years, and to set narratives in European locales, could be seen as a rejection of his homeland's uncouth and misplaced cultural values (as embodied, for instance, in his protagonist Daisy Miller), we should also recognize a market-oriented rationale for James's European settings. This, after all, was a period when European travel and study of European history and culture became a mark of social status within the United States. By locating himself abroad and setting novels there in the new century (for example, *The Ambassadors* [1903] and *The Golden Bowl* [1904]), James attracted a well-to-do audience who had either taken or aspired to the Grand Tour.

Recognizing connections between authorial identity as strategic performance and related strategies of textual production helps us see figures like James and his contemporary Edith Wharton as self-conscious navigators of the marketplace of their time. Meanwhile, the early decades of the twentieth century provided other would-be writers, less blessed with the class-based access of a James or a Wharton, with new tools for performing authorship. The rise of journalism—including investigative reporting, newspaper photography, and on-the-scene accounts like those associated with Jacob Riis's landmark *How the Other Half Lives* (1890)—dovetailed with the push to realism in literary culture, enabling a number of writers who began as journalists to cross over into the more literary novel form. As they had throughout much of the nineteenth century, magazines promoted the novel genre, particularly through initial serialization of forthcoming books. For well-known figures such as Henry James and William Dean Howells, in fact, serializing a novel could pay better than publishing in book form.

Periodical publication could be a minefield, however. Howells's *A Hazard of New Fortunes* (1890) chronicled challenges facing would-be magazine publishers at the turn of the century, especially those aiming to balance serious art and mass appeal. Jack London's 1909 novel, *Martin Eden*, highlighted difficulties facing would-be authors seeking to break into the periodical marketplace. London's hero encounters a litany of problems, ranging from glacially slow response to submissions to late payments for accepted pieces. Eden's working-class background provides rich material for his narratives, but it also blocks him from elite publishing networks. His love interest Maria (from a genteel, wealthy family) cannot understand his commitment to realistic narrative: "[W]hy do you persist," she wonders, "in writing such things when you know they won't sell? . . . Surely it will offend your readers, and surely that is why the editors are justified in refusing your work" (ch. 33). Predictably, Maria breaks off her relationship with Martin out of frustration with his unpragmatic approach to career-building. Later, once Eden's hard-won success is established, London's novel illustrates how celebrity authorship changes interpersonal relationships, as Maria tries to reaffiliate with Martin, now desirable because of his monetary success and his fame.

Although the narratives by Howells and London cast periodical publishing as a challenge for artists, some writers clearly benefited from this growing venue, including its connection to journalism. Even as Stephen Crane struggled to get his first novel, *Maggie: A Girl of the Streets* (1893), published, articles like his exposé "In the Depths of a Coal Mine" (1894), published in *McClure's Magazine*, generated reliable income while also building name recognition, laying the groundwork for literary success. Further, newspaper syndicates could jump-start careers when writers were unlikely to have their work accepted by top-drawer magazines such as the *Atlantic* or *Harper's*. Crane found an entrée into novelistic success via a syndicate: his submission of *The Red Badge of Courage* (1895) to *McClure's Magazine* was rejected, but the aspiring author had more success with Bacheller's syndicate.

Publishing with newspaper syndicates also had advantages for established authors. With their wide circulation, the major syndicates could pay more than even the most financially stable magazines, including the flush *Ladies' Home Journal,* led by Edward Bok. Famous figures from across the Atlantic, including Rudyard Kipling, Robert Louis Stevenson, and Arthur Conan Doyle, published with American syndicates. On the US side, Bret Harte and Mark Twain sold novels to syndicates. Besides providing cash, the syndicates brought turn-of-the-century novelists larger audiences. This scenario, in turn, could result in fuller access to high-tone magazines or a more lucrative book contract with a major publishing house.

Meanwhile, through both their selections for publication and their shaping of writers' manuscripts, the editors of elite American magazines exercised cultural capital, even when they could not outbid a syndicate financially. The series of editors at the *Atlantic Monthly* during this era had an especially significant impact on authorial careers. Positioning itself as a promoter of serious artists and thinkers, the *Atlantic* introduced its readers to a number of now-famous novelists, with its by-then regular practice of appending the names of writers to their publications just one example of how periodicals endorsed authors. While the *Atlantic* could be classified as holding more of a niche, high-culture position than other magazines during this period, many of those who published there are certainly celebrities of the curricular canon today thanks in part to the editorial strategies of Horace Scudder, Bliss Perry, and Ellery Sedgwick.

One particularly influential editor was William Dean Howells, who lived well into his eighties, and whose legacy in American literary history straddled the late nineteenth and the early twentieth centuries. Though Howells's own novels had only moderate sales and garnered uneven literary recognition, his performance of authorial identity was perhaps at its most enduring through his influence on other writers' careers. Howells had a ten-year stint as editor of the *Atlantic Monthly* (1871–81) and a longstanding position writing literary opinion columns for *Harper's* magazine (in the 1890s in "Life and Letters" and afterward under the brand-like title of "The

Editor's Easy Chair"). Howells's power as an unofficial broker can be marked by such anecdotes as Frank Norris finding his authorial star rising after Howells's positive review of *McTeague* (1899).

One of the most striking cases of Howells's influence was his involvement with Charles W. Chesnutt, whom the influential critic initially touted but later may have helped undermine via faint praise. When Howells wrote a 1900 essay for *Atlantic Monthly* entitled "Mr. Charles W. Chesnutt's Stories," he celebrated the aspiring African American writer's achievements in two short story collections, *The Conjure Woman* (1899) and *The Wife of His Youth and Other Stories of the Color Line* (1899). Selections from these works had already been published in periodicals, but to have both come out in book form and to receive high praise from the powerful Howells marked a turning point in Chesnutt's career. Howells further supported Chesnutt in the coming months by encouraging submission of a novel manuscript to Harper & Brothers.

But Howells's review misreads Chesnutt's novelistic *The Conjure Woman*, missing (or choosing to downplay) the radical underpinnings of Uncle Julius's relationship with the representative white audience for his stories (the rich, transplanted northerner John and wife Annie), while also ignoring the ways that Julius claimed authority over the local cultural space of the postwar South via a trickster rhetorical stance. Accordingly, we could position Howells as a stand-in for the character John, whose self-assured take on Julius repeatedly misses the point of the stories Annie hears with a more sensitive ear. Similarly, by encouraging readers to focus on the more accommodationist narratives in *The Wife of His Youth*, Howells suppressed resistant elements in that collection as well. Howells had grown up in an abolitionist family and had written a campaign biography of Lincoln; however, the turn-of-the-twentieth century was an era of reestablishing more positive relations with the so-called "New South" that had been touted by regional leaders like Henry Grady and Atticus Haygood. Later, Howells reviewed Chesnutt's novel *The Marrow of Tradition* (1901), which included an account of the famous 1898 race riots in Wilmington, North Carolina. Here, Howells's praise of Chesnutt's fiction is much more guarded. He calls the novel's direct assault on racism "bitter," and critics have speculated that Chesnutt may have been discouraged by the criticism of one of his champions. By the time *The Colonel's Dream* appeared in 1905, Chesnutt's self-positioning as an author would never again align with the expectations of his former supporter and the broader audience Howells represented. Forgoing his aspirations of literary fame, Chesnutt refocused his energies on the more reliable career of his stenography business while channeling his advocacy of racial justice into work through the NAACP.

Chesnutt's career as a novelist exemplifies challenges faced by writers seeking authorial success from a minority social position in the early twentieth century. Cultural arbiters like Walter Hines Page and Howells might embrace a self-affirming opportunity to assist such an author—on their own terms. Yet it would be a long time before a black male author could elicit a widespread positive response from white readers when presenting the kind of "bitter" critique of racism that Chesnutt mounted in *The Marrow of Tradition* and Richard Wright would revisit in an even more intense way later in the twentieth century, in *Native Son* (1940). (See "*Native Son* and Diasporic Modernity" in Chapter 32 of this volume.)

If a hard-edged orientation to racial difference was difficult for white middle-class readers to embrace in novels at the turn of the century, when W.E.B. Du Bois was voicing his assessment of the color line as the major challenge facing the nation, there were more palatable alternatives. One feminized and restrained examination of race differences emerged in the work of Winnifred Eaton, who carved out a liter-ary career by capitalizing on stereotypes associated with white Americans' visions of Asian cultures. Born in Canada, Eaton followed her older sister Edith (who wrote as Sui Sin Far) by simultaneously affirming some audience expectations and clev-erly tweaking others. In this respect, some might assess Winnifred Eaton's success as a novelist as capitulation—remaining within confines Chesnutt seemed to have accepted in the early stage of his career but eventually rejected. Another interpreta-tion, however, would foreground her rhetorical awareness, crediting her with astute manipulation of an available authorial role. In the latter view, we would attribute the decision to present herself under the Japanese-seeming pen name of Onoto Watanna, despite her own Chinese-Anglo heritage, to strategic career management. Similarly, her 1900 novel *A Japanese Nightingale* echoed the plot of John Luther Long's 1898 story of "Madame Butterfly" (also the inspiration for Puccini's opera), but with a more optimistic view of the cross-race romance between the white male hero and the Japanese heroine. The appeal of this novel, adapted for both stage and film, set alongside the authorial persona her text promoted, fed into continued success in the literary marketplace: the novel *Tama* (1910) became a full-fledged bestseller. Later, her memoir-as-novel *Me: A Remembrance* (1915) solidified her romantic authorial role by taking readers through a series of youthful adventures that accentuated her mixed-race identity and her femininity, even as it admitted to various infidelities. Eventually settling in New York to write screenplays, Winnifred Eaton anticipated the central role that the film industry would soon play in the literary marketplace. By accommodating her aspirations to the rhetorical frameworks most available for a woman of her background, she did not capture high-art renown, but she achieved a productive and celebrated authorial identity during her lifetime.

Between the Wars: Escaping and Embracing the Middlebrow

Much of the energy in US literary production throughout the nineteenth century was directed toward establishing the northeastern urban centers—particularly New York City—as the focal point for national-level publishing. But the period between the two World Wars in the twentieth century saw an expansion of that geographic focus in at least two directions: across the Atlantic to Europe and across the North

American continent to Hollywood. This period also brought increased cultural power to publications *about* publishing, such as book reviews and reports about celebrity authors.

By the 1920s, magazines, newspapers, and publishing houses' publicity machines were actively promoting individual authors as literary celebrities. Book reviews were a regular feature in mass-circulation periodicals, with columnists carving out their own distinctive personalities even as they directed consumers' reading habits. Previously, venues like the *Atlantic Monthly* and *Harper's*, using cultural arbiters like William Dean Howells, had aimed to shape a "high" literary culture. But by the 1920s and 1930s, periodicals with even broader-based readerships (such as *TIME, New York Evening Post, New York Times,* and *Chicago Tribune*) were providing influential coverage of newly published books, trends in the literary scene, and individual authors. The impact of these periodical-based constructions of authors' public identities could be so intense as to make writers feel they had little control over the process, as Anzia Yezierska would show in a satirical scene in her literary memoir, *Red Ribbon on a White Horse* (1950). Recalling a lunch she shared with one critic at the famed Algonquin dining room in New York, Yezierska described a series of critics claiming to have originated her characterization as a Cinderella of the tenements—and pulling out their own press releases to prove it.

Individual reviewers such as Edmund Wilson wielded enormous power in the 1920s and 1930s, writing for a range of influential publications. Wilson's treatments of novelists Sherwood Anderson, John Dos Passos, Thornton Wilder, and Princeton classmate F. Scott Fitzgerald shaped their authorial images. As Gordon Hutner notes, Wilson's "power as a tastemaker" was evident in pieces such as "The Emergence of Ernest Hemingway," which touted Hemingway as a worthy literary figure (2009, 53). On the flip side, Loren Glass observes, Wilson's 1939 *Atlantic Monthly* article, "Ernest Hemingway: Gauge of Morale," launched a critique of the author's celebrity persona as "personality for profit" embodied in Papa's "articles for well-paying and trashy magazines"—texts separating Hemingway-the-formerly-serious-writer from Hemingway-the-inflated-personality, a stance which Glass finds still haunts Hemingway criticism today (2004, 140; on the marketing of Ernest Hemingway, see Chapter 2 of this volume).

Colorful figures like Yezierska and Hemingway faced a particular challenge, trying to manage their own authorial identities while capitalizing on the allure of their public personas. Autobiography offered one tool for negotiating this challenge. Within these very public personal texts, we can see several celebrity authors of this period aligning themselves with settings that would contribute to the most positive self-image possible, such as Yezierska's self-portrayals as a daughter of the urban ethnic ghetto. For Hemingway, one fruitful setting was Europe—especially Paris—during the age of the so-called "lost generation."

Countering the kind of dismissive critique of staged bravado that Wilson had circulated, Hemingway used *A Moveable Feast* (published in 1964, after his death, and released in a "restored" version edited by grandson Seán Hemingway in 2009) to offer a serious version of his public identity. Hemingway pictures these years as a time when he savored interactions with fellow artists like Ezra Pound, James Joyce, Ford Madox Ford, Sherwood Anderson, and Gertrude Stein. He recalls a conversation tweaking Stein for having said, "All of you young people who served in the war" represented "a lost generation" (ch. 7). Hemingway resists that characterization with a portrayal of Stein's own salon as providing shared camaraderie leavened with intellectual energy, even as he limns himself as more dedicated to serious craft than some of his Parisian colleagues—particularly Fitzgerald. Depicting Fitzgerald as enslaved to alcohol and to a wife "jealous of Scott's work," Hemingway credits himself with striving to help Fitzgerald build on the foundation of 1925's *The Great Gatsby* (ch. 17). Meanwhile, Hemingway's self-portrait presents a disciplined figure, thriving on the Paris setting to extract himself from journalistic writing-for-hire. In one chapter set in a French café, Hemingway charts his determined progress through a story draft. Totally immersed in his writing, enabled by the modest café environment, Hemingway asserts: "I belong to this notebook and this pencil" (ch. 1).

Such vignettes in *A Moveable Feast* have generated the lingering mythology of a 1920s' expatriate band of American authors, seen as creating celebrity personalities along with their novels, whose sales, in turn, were spurred by readers' fascination with their autobiographical features. For instance, both *The Sun Also Rises* (1926) for Hemingway and *Tender is the Night* (1934) for Fitzgerald draw material from their authors' European stays. Thus, part of the attraction of these ex-pat authors arose from their blurring of the lines between personal experience and fiction, with versions of their own celebrity personas a key focus of their narratives. Hemingway accordingly notes in the preface to his Parisian memoir: "If the reader prefers, this book may be regarded as fiction."

His friend Gertrude Stein made a similar move to mark her own account of the European expatriate culture as a self-consciously crafted fiction linked to authorial role-playing and career management. While Stein's chatty 1930s' bestselling book anticipated Hemingway's later blend of celebrity-bashing anecdotes with appealing remembrances, it also drew hordes of readers through the conceit of being a narrative *about* the already-famous Gertrude rather than *by* her—as being *The Autobiography of Alice B. Toklas* (1933), Stein's secretary-lover. Referencing herself in the third person until the closing paragraph's saucy admission, Stein blurs and then clarifies point of view in the final lines of the book by having Toklas's voice explain that Gertrude had urged her companion to write an autobiography but finally had taken up the pen herself: "About six weeks ago Gertrude Stein said, it does not look to me as if you were ever going to write that autobiography. You know what I am going to do. I am going to write it for you. I am going to write it as simply as Defoe did the autobiography of Robinson Crusoe. And she has and this is it" (ch. 7).

With her playful reference to Defoe's authorship, Stein assumed the role of social historian, textual intermediary, life-writer, and novelist all in one. And with spicy personal anecdotes throughout her text, she capitalized on her audience's familiarity with her own celebrity status as well as their curiosity about the similarly famous figures in her social network. Although some have credited the huge sales success of this narrative tour-de-force with establishing the author as a celebrity, Stein was, in fact, already very well known in America when the book appeared.

In marketing and then capitalizing on the success of her self-portrait, Stein exemplifies yet another case of a "between the wars" writer linking performance of celebrity identity with savvy career management. Before its release in book form, substantial portions of *The Autobiography of Alice B. Toklas* were serialized in the *Atlantic Monthly*—a coup for Stein, who had long aspired to affiliation with that venerable periodical. Having the text selected by the Literary Guild had ensured solid sales among its decidedly middlebrow readership. The popular press stoked more interest in the book and in Stein by speculating about the figure of Alice, with some columnists raising doubts about her existence—which in turn prompted written responses from various readers who knew Toklas. Harcourt Brace fueled the frenzy by circulating ads asserting "Alice B. Toklas really exists," thereby feeding readers' curiosity about both Toklas and Stein (Leick 2009, 145–46).

Stein then tapped into her literary persona to promote *The Autobiography* in a 1934–35 lecture tour that brought her back to the United States for the first time in decades. She eagerly performed the witty and engaging personality that she had cultivated over the years for smaller audiences in her Paris salon. As Dickens had been in the previous century, Stein was greeted by crowds from her very arrival by transatlantic ship. As Twain had done, she produced pithy phrases whose repetition in the press further spread the cult of her personality. And unlike such role models, she could also draw on new media for rapid-fire access to audiences: the radio and the newsreel quickly circulated the sound of her voice and images of her activities nationwide. Stein's skilled performance of her own authorial role during the tour shifted the popular perception of her professional identity from a confusing writer of incomprehensible prose to a far more accessible figure, appealing both in her own right and for her clever insights into the cultural landscape of her day.

Stein's welcoming this public role and the media that enhanced it is just one example of ways in which numerous otherwise "highbrow" literary figures in the 1920s and 1930s embraced popular culture and its rewards. This era also marked the ascension of cinema in American culture, and a number of literary figures hitched their careers to the Hollywood star-making system—among them Anzia Yezierska, who turned to screenwriting to capitalize on the success of her novels (on Hollywood's influence on the novel, see Chapter 31 of this volume).

Film-making had begun to intersect with literary culture in the early twentieth century, when movies such D. W. Griffith's *The Birth of a Nation* (1915) demonstrated the power of the new medium to expand a novel's reach—in this case, Thomas Dixon's racist portrait of southern white "heroism," *The Clansman* (1905). In the 1920s and 1930s, the American film industry expanded. One way of measuring this progress is to track the growth of movie houses in major metropolitan centers, where new film palaces drew audiences in the thousands. Numerous factors facilitated the growth of Hollywood's financial and cultural power: economic (the emerging studio system), technological (the introduction of sound), and political (Europe's immersion in the First World War enabling the United States to become the major producer of movies and Progressive-era politics shaping the content of films themselves). But one underacknowledged catalyst supporting Hollywood's rise in American culture was its omnivorous absorption of popular literary texts and celebrity authors into the movie-making machine.

Throughout the 1920s and 1930s, Hollywood drew on literary classics for film scripts, as D. W. Griffith did for his 1920 production of *The Last of the Mohicans*, MGM for its 1926 version of *The Scarlet Letter*, and RKO for the 1933 *Little Women* (Anderson 1988, 100–101, 103). Adaptations of Shakespeare and of British novelists such as Dickens, William Makepeace Thackeray, Robert Louis Stevenson, Rudyard Kipling, and the Brontë sisters complemented the trend of filming nineteenth-century American novels. But material from contemporary US authors could be equally attractive to the studios, as seen in such speedy page-to-screen adaptations as Fitzgerald's *The Beautiful and Damned* (1922).

Some well-known writers were content to sell novels outright to the film industry, happily collecting both the windfall of screen rights and the royalties from associated increases in book sales, as Hemingway did with the 1932 film version of *A Farewell to Arms* and as Margaret Mitchell would do for 1939's blockbuster *Gone with the Wind*. However, others aggressively sought employment in Hollywood, either to adapt their own books or to try writing original screenplays. Novelists who worked in Hollywood between the World Wars included John Dos Passos, John Steinbeck, Tess Slesinger, and William Faulkner. Nathanael West found more success generating screenplays than he had selling his earlier 1930s' novels *Miss Lonelyhearts* (1933) and *A Cool Million* (1934), and F. Scott Fitzgerald spent his last years in Hollywood writing for the movies.

Yet some writers who had succeeded in other genres found the studio "committee" system stifling and the shift from print to cinematic storytelling challenging. In 1919, just as filmmakers were beginning to see artistic potential in what had previously been viewed as mere entertainment, Samuel Goldwyn created a company he called "Eminent Authors, Inc.," to help lift films to more highbrow status by commissioning artistic screenplays. The experiment failed, Tom Stempel explains, because the novelists and playwrights Goldwyn selected could not make the transition to collaborative work in the new form (1988, 52–53). Later, Dashiell Hammett's detective novels would generate popular films, such as the six-picture Nick and Nora Charles series based on the 1934 novel *The Thin Man*, but with other screenwriters' versions superseding his own botched adaptation efforts. A few writers became adept at bridging the two narrative forms—and even drew on the strengths of both, as Edgar Rice Burroughs did with Tarzan films, based upon (and promoting) his books while sparking a new career for Olympic swimmer Johnny Weissmuller in the title role.

Anzia Yezierska's Hollywood experience illustrates the complex forces then at play around literary celebrity and film as a mass culture medium. In her autobiography, *Red Ribbon on a White Horse*, Yezierska conveys how "going Hollywood" could enhance an author's celebrity persona while bringing stupendous financial success, but also how entering the movie realm brought dangerous challenges to self-concept and long-term financial stability. Yezierska's memoir begins in 1920 with her living in an urban Hester Street hovel, literally hungry after her *Hungry Hearts* (1920) book of stories has generated only two hundred dollars in royalties. She complains: "It had been praised by the critics, esteemed as literature. That meant it didn't sell," so she found herself "even poorer than when I had started writing." Almost magically, she receives a telegram from her agent, R. L. Giffen, telling her of bids for movie rights, which Yezierska recognizes could mean full-scale wealth. Despite the carping warnings from her father that she risks losing herself—even becoming " 'defiled' " as a " 'Daughter of Babylon' "—Yezierska heads west, already having received ten thousand dollars (which she dubs " 'riches for a lifetime' "), funds for her train trip to Hollywood, and the promise of work there as a Goldwyn studio screenwriter (1950, pt. 1, ch. 1).

Upon arrival in California, the memoir shows, Yezierska celebrates her good fortune, reveling in the surroundings of her Hollywood hotel. But discomfort rapidly replaces self-congratulation, as she "couldn't recognize [her]self" in the photos and planted stories of the immigrant catapulted " 'From Hester Street to Hollywood' " (pt. 1, ch. 2). She cringed at how her staged appearances at parties "exploited" a manufactured personality "to further the sale of *Hungry Hearts*," and struggled to accept a professional script doctor's imposition of a happy ending on her narrative (pt. 1, ch. 7). Although initially flattered by an invitation from William Fox to switch to his studio when her contract with Goldwyn expired, she explains, she could not bear to sign away three years of her life, even for payment almost beyond imagining. Why? She would lose control over her textual production processes, forfeit ownership of her own personal experiences, and, ultimately, give up mastery of her individual identity to the Hollywood machine.

Ironically, when she leaves Hollywood for what she assumes will be a reclaiming of her more authentic East Coast immigrant identity, she finds that the movie version of herself cannot be escaped. As the Depression hits, her autobiography asserts, she is repeatedly turned down for jobs because employers assume she couldn't possibly need funds to feed herself. After all, she's a cinematic celebrity. Finally finding temporary work with the Works Progress Administration (WPA) project, she is disillusioned by its emphasis on "make-work" writing, then both appreciative and jealous when her new colleague Richard Wright wins a special WPA award from *Story Magazine*. Watching Wright's victory, Yezierska anticipates his future successes while reliving the trajectory of her own rise and fall as a celebrity author. "I thought of Hollywood when I had been as intoxicated with the triumph over my handicaps as Wright was now, wresting first prize from a white world." But she credits Wright with more maturity than she had been able to muster: "he had the intelligence to take what he could get wherever he went and build with it. He would know how to take success for what it was worth and not become rattled by it as I had been" (pt. 3, ch. 10).

The closing pages of Yezierska's memoir reject her previous celebrity identity and the version of authorship that came with it, asserting in its place a patient laboring for authentic writing. Significantly, however, her daughter's "Afterword" offers a corrective note, alerting readers that much of the memoir is fabricated for thematic effect, that Yezierska has conveniently omitted episodes in her life after Hollywood that don't fit the clean line of her argument against celebrity as a writer's goal. Declares Louise Levitas Henriksen: "*Red Ribbon* is larded with many small and large fictions and exaggerations—too many to point to inclusively—because Anzia would invent whatever she needed to make her point." For Henriksen, the wish to make this 1950 narrative's "point" actually arose, at least in part, from Yezierska's longstanding frustration with others' moves to constrain her ownership over her writing and authorial persona, as seen in a *Cosmopolitan* editor's brutal cutting of elements from a 1925 magazine memoir. The edits had eliminated ways in which the Hollywood experience had separated Yezierska from a truer version of herself, "with the people she belonged to, the poor." For this daughter of a literary celebrity, her mother's final text represents recovery of the story Yezierska had wanted to tell before, on her own terms, a cautionary tale about the limits of authorship in the era of mass culture's growing influence.

Taking a cue from Henriksen, a reconsideration of textual ownership issues and authors' attempts at celebrity management over the decades between 1870 and 1940 should acknowledge the full range of responses that writers mounted to these intertwined cultural processes. If we marvel at the self-assurance with which Elizabeth Phelps looked back on her career at the turn of the century, and the skill with which Mark Twain enacted his highly marketable persona, we should also recognize the performative qualities in such self-representations and acknowledge the social forces that both enabled and constrained the stories authors told about their professional selves. As we join Yezierska in marveling at the confidence she saw in Richard Wright's WPA award-winning moment, we should remember that even a Nobel Prize could not prevent Hemingway's suicide, or the recurring interpretations of that act as a rejection of the stories told beyond his control and their impact on his private self. Taken together, these decades brought America's best-known writers an array of new tools for professional self-construction and self-promotion, but they also brought unprecedented pressures associated with authorial management.

2

THE BUSINESS OF PUBLISHING AMERICAN NOVELS

BY CATHERINE TURNER

Two advertisements in the early 1930s indicate the wide range of novels that had become critical to American publishers' business models and the variety of ways publishers appealed to consumers. As part of their publicity for Ernest Hemingway's *A Farewell to Arms* (1929), Charles Scribner's Sons placed an ad in the *New York Times Book Review* entitled "Who Reads an American Book" trumpeting that Hemingway had "taken England by storm." The advertisement included comments from British reviewers who called *A Farewell to Arms* "a most beautiful, moving and human book." Clearly chosen to indicate that Hemingway had moved past his reputation for unfeeling prose, these quotations also tie Hemingway's international stature to his nationality. For example, the London *Times* dubbed him "distinctively and absolutely American" (1930, 18). While celebrating the distance American literature had come since Sydney Smith sniffed at the inferiority of all American arts, this advertisement also announced the ways that the American-ness of the American novel had become an increasingly valuable and international commodity. Not incidentally, *A Farewell to Arms* was a critical and commercial success, cementing Hemingway's reputation as a writer whom smart people read and Scribner's reputation as a house willing to back new, radical authors with aggressive advertising (on Hemingway and celebrity, see Chapter 1 of this volume).

At the same time, Willett, Clark, and Colby, a relatively new publishing firm associated with *Christian Century* magazine, published Lloyd Douglas's *Magnificent Obsession* (1929). Their advertisements in journals such as *Golden Book Magazine* warned that Douglas had written "a book to beware of" because of its challenge to self-satisfaction and complacency. This advertisement promised readers less a chance to be up to date with international taste than a life changing, "vitalizing" experience. The advertisement also quoted a review from the *Saturday Review of Literature* claiming that, like so many other self-help books, this book promised "the idea of achieving a magnificent personality," without the commercial taint of similar books. To drive that implication home, the advertisement offered readers the chance to own the book for five days before purchase because its publishers "are confident you will not part with it for ten times the cost" (1931). Hence, even as the advertisement connected *The Magnificent Obsession* with other, more frankly commercial products, Willett, Clark, and Colby also asserted that the novel was not just another commercial bestseller.

These advertisements reveal many of the tensions that had marked American publishing since the 1870s. Although publishers had always advertised, and often quite heavily, these advertisements represented a concerted effort to develop a national canon for various tastes and give consumers a reason for buying books beyond entertainment, although that value remained important. They also show the publishers defining what made these books distinctive, attempting to influence what they meant in the marketplace. Finally, both advertisements show the efforts of publishers to define themselves and their calling as *beyond commerce* by focusing on the part books played in strengthening American character and American culture.

The two novels themselves show some of the range and deep divisions in the American market for fiction. While it might be useful to simply see one as a poorly written potboiler published only to make money and the other as a literary masterpiece published to secure its creator's reputation, publishers promoted both novels with quotations from serious reviews and with promises that the novels would be challenging. Scribner's did hope to change its reputation, from that of a stodgy, narrow-minded house to one that was more up-to-date with contemporary tastes and mores, but they also believed that Hemingway's novel would sell well. To gain these sales, they serialized *A Farewell to Arms* in *Scribner's Magazine* and promoted it heavily. Hemingway's attitude toward his book was equally commercial; he told his editor "it's something to sell" (qtd. in Leff 1997, 122). Douglas attempted to interest two commercial publishers in his novel before Willet, Colby, and Clark accepted it. As John Tebbel notes, they encouraged Douglas to revise his work, but they did not expect to have a bestseller. They did little to promote the novel until word of mouth sales demonstrated its potential. Late in 1931, because they lacked access to the distribution networks larger firms had, they sold the rights to Houghton Mifflin, a house large enough to create, ship, and distribute the nearly two million copies of the book that sold over the next six years (Becnel 2008, 62). Advertisements for these novels together demonstrate that houses defined critical reputation in ways that connected critical and commercial success.

Both novels were also exceptional because they made money and remain in print today. Technological change throughout the nineteenth century made mass publication of books like *A Farewell to Arms* and *Magnificent Obsession* relatively easy but demanded an initial capital investment in electroplates and, more importantly, in the author. The shift in manufacturing costs, authors' increasing demands for advances, and the growing importance of marketing all contributed to the rise in the number of sales necessary to pay for the costs of publication. In the 1880s, it took 1,000 copies to recoup the publisher's initial investment; by 1914 it had become 1,500 copies; just before the Second World War a book needed to sell 2,500 copies to break even. Publishers estimated that of every five new books published, three lost money, one covered its costs, and the fifth made money. Because that fifth book did not always make enough to pay for the costs of the three losers, publishers had to rely on the steady sales of their backlist to remain profitable. A spectacular seller like *Magnificent Obsession* was incredibly rare, impossible to predict, and its sales often subsidized the publication of dozens of other books. A book like *A Farewell to Arms*—selling well for another eighty years—was even more difficult to predict. Far more common, as Gordon Hutner has shown in *What America Read*, were the vast number of books aimed at the middle of the market (2009). These works of serious fiction have been recovered to some extent in recent scholarship on middlebrow readers by Joan Rubin, Janice Radway, Jaime Harker, Christina Klein, and Victoria Grieve. However, to publishers at the time it would have been difficult to know that Hemingway would continue to sell while Julia Peterkin, who won the Pulitzer Prize in 1929 for *Scarlet Sister Mary*, has been virtually forgotten.

Despite the difficulty predicting their success, novels were central to most trade publishers' business. *Publishers' Weekly* encouraged publishers in 1901, "keep publishing novels and you will be sure to strike some big successes. The book you bank on may fail, and the one you think the least of will go" (885). Such advice represents both the possibilities of publishing novels and the problems that publishers faced. The owners of publishing companies, like the owners of many other industries of the time, hoped to take advantage of wider distribution networks and mass marketing to increase their profits. As a result, many publishers issued a large number of different titles, so that many came to see publishing as a form of gambling in which publishers placed a large number of bets hoping that one of them would hit.

Trade publishers developed a number of strategies that they hoped would improve their chances. First, they created an image of themselves as genteel professionals, interested in art above profit. This claim allowed trade publishers to define themselves as the only legitimate conduit between authors and readers. Second, in this role, they lobbied Congress in support of copyright legislation that would help them control the investments they made in authors, manuscripts, and production but also, they argued, protect individual citizens and national culture. Third, they worked to control the prices at which literature could sell, in an attempt to ensure that a greater number of works could make a profit for publishers, authors, and booksellers. Fourth, and connected to all three of the above, they experimented with new ways to increase distribution through marketing schemes like book clubs and advertising, which helped publishers create a range of different canons. All of these activities allowed publishers to protect their investment in authors so that they could rely on their backlist to keep their firms profitable.

Publishers as Professionals

In his history of the firm of Harpers, Eugene Exman shows that the four found-ing brothers in the 1830s set type, ran the presses, and even bound the books they printed. On the other hand, Roger Burlingame's history of Charles Scribner's firm explains that Scribner took pride in never having set foot in the pressroom. These dif-ferent attitudes toward the craft of book manufacture illustrates the ways in which, as the nineteenth century progressed, publishers became middlemen who took an author's manuscript, negotiated with printers and binders, and distributed and sold the book to stores. Trade publishers found that in order to survive in the competi-tive market of publishing, they had to find ways to stamp the objects they had as legitimate literature and meaningful culture. This does not mean that books had to appear noncommercial to sell—sales figures appeared in many advertisements—but that the companies that sold books had to appear to be different from companies that sold other equally commercial products.

Changes in methods of production, distribution, and marketing affected pub-lishers in much the same way these changes affected other industries. As Michael Winship has pointed out, publishing shifted from small, family-owned concerns to larger corporations throughout the nineteenth century and innovations in mecha-nization and distribution networks allowed publishers to reach wider markets with more books. By the end of the nineteenth century most firms had specialized em-ployees who did one managerial task—such as reading manuscripts, editing, selling, design, or bookkeeping. Some firms could use their house's magazine to entice au-thors and to publicize their books. Often these same firms owned their own manu-facturing plants or served as wholesale or retail dealers. Winship notes several key changes in publishing throughout this period. First, in order to meet the need for capital many reorganized as public corporations. Second, the distribution of books became much more systematic, with the American News Company becoming the largest wholesaler of books. In addition, in 1873 Frederick Leopoldt published the first issue of *Publishers' Weekly*. This journal provided up to date, regular information about new publications and a forum for opinions and discussion throughout the book trades that connected publishers and booksellers. Such changes signaled that the publishing business, which had once been simply a small set of family-owned houses clustered largely in the Northeast, was becoming much more corporate, or-ganized, and national.

Donald Sheehan calculates that in 1900, *Publishers' Weekly* listed 1,000 firms that had issued books during the year; by 1913, that number had expanded to 1,512. How-ever, a small group of those publishers saw themselves as "trade" publishers and hoped to set the standard for what most consumers thought of as publishing. Janice Radway has pointed out that these trade publishers differentiated their firms from other types of publishers through their reverence for books and their desire to have their works appear elite and literary. Trade publishers insisted that their books were

"dignified objects" and asserted that they had the taste and judgment necessary to ar-
bitrate between novels of literary quality and those that were simply pulp (1997, 137).
In other words, by the turn of the twentieth century, a subset of publishers claimed
their firms added a nonmaterial value to the materials that went into making the
book (on the vexed relationship between critics and audiences and high and low
culture, see the discussion of literature and pulp in Chapter 3 of this volume).

Some of these trade publishers, such as Harper Brothers (1817), Ticknor and Fields
(1832, which became Houghton Mifflin in 1880), G.P. Putnam's Sons (1838), Dodd
Mead (1839), E. P. Dutton (1852), D. Appleton and Co. (1831), and Charles Scribner's
Sons (1846), had been in business since before the 1860s. Others, like Henry Holt
(1865), Doubleday and Co. (1900), and George H. Doran (1908), began publishing
in the second half of the nineteenth century after their founders apprenticed at older
firms. The set of trade publishers expanded in the early twentieth century to include
a new group of publishers who shared the reverence for the books that marked
more senior firms. These houses included Benjamin W. Huebsch (1902), Alfred A.
Knopf (1915), Boni and Liveright (1917), Simon and Schuster (1924), Viking (1925),
and Random House (1925). Historians sometimes differentiate between "old line"
houses, founded by Anglo-Saxon protestant families who frowned on experimental
or immoral literature, and these "new" houses, often run by Jewish entrepreneurs
with more adventurous tastes. This difference notwithstanding, both old and new
houses faced the same economic realities; both addressed those realities by defining
themselves as gatekeepers of American culture. While the definition of good literature may have differed slightly from house to house, all of these publishers, even
those with more "radical" tastes, hoped to create an image of themselves as public
servants, interested in improving the nation by providing its citizens with uplifting,
thoughtful literature that could both educate and entertain. This image allowed
them to control some of the risks of publishing and create a stable basis on which
their firms could operate.

Although the appearance of a trade journal like *Publishers' Weekly* in 1873 signified the increasingly businesslike conduct of the book trade, its editorial content
asserted that publishers were gentlemen first. Perhaps the most important element
of this identity was a publisher's commitment to "trade courtesy," a practice developed to give publishers the ability to compensate for the lack of international
copyright in the early nineteenth century. Trade publishers agreed that once a publishing house had advertised its intention to publish a work, that firm had exclusive
rights to that work. Along those same lines, once a house had published an author,
no other publisher should offer to publish other works by that author until the
original firm had declined the author's next work. As Henry Holt explained in his
memoirs, an honest publisher would not "go for another's author any more than for
his watch" (1923, 209). In its editorials *Publishers' Weekly* championed trade courtesy, arguing that those who respected it were legitimate trade publishers and those
who did not were dishonest pirates. Well into the twentieth century, a general sense

that real publishers were devoted to kindly business relations dominated publishers' sense of their profession. As a result, a wave of early twentieth century publishers' memoirs—including Walter Hines Page's, *A Publisher's Confession* (1905), Joseph H. Harper's *The House of Harper* (1912), George Haven Putnam's *Memories of a Publisher* (1915), and Henry Holt's *Garrulities of an Octogenarian Editor* (1923)—nostalgically remembered publishers in the nineteenth century as a set of noble men, celebrating that their "character and high tastes" were never swayed by the "brute force of dollars" (Holt 1923, 207). Such nostalgia covered up the fact that these publishers also competed with each other throughout the nineteenth century—bidding up advances for authors and aggressively marketing their own books.

"New" publishers in the twentieth century adopted trade courtesy and honored its importance as publicly as their predecessors had. In a piece originally published in the *New Yorker*, Geoffrey Hellman noted the fact that Alfred A. Knopf followed the courtesy of the trade rigorously. Early in Knopf's history, he wanted to reissue W. H. Hudson's *Green Mansions* (1904), which was no longer under copyright in the United States. Before going ahead with publication, Knopf asked for and received permission to publish from Hudson's earlier US publisher, G. H. Putnam. Beyond that, once the book's sales increased, Knopf voluntarily sent 10 percent royalties to the author's widow.

Just as *Publishers' Weekly* drew the line between legitimate publishers and pirates, its editorials attempted to define the difference between novels and pulp. Each year the trade journal reported on the general trends in the trade, and each year those reports deplored the low quality of the novels published. It complained that the novels of 1889 "were characterized by the feeblest indications of talent" and, what was worse, those written by women "were inspired by a motive so base, and illustrated with details so gross, as to put to the blush many famous French offenders in this line" (1890, 145). By 1904, its editorial staff complained that novelists had abandoned the "wholesome" historical novel to focus on novels with "even more coarseness than in the past" (Tebbel 1972, 695). Well into the twentieth century, *Publishers' Weekly* encouraged bookstores to avoid books "which are more likely to do harm than good," of which it was found there were far too many (Tebbel 1978, 56). The assertion that legitimate publishers and booksellers only sold what was beneficial for readers was critical to publishers' abilities to define themselves as culture brokers.

The value of separating publishing from commerce and novels from bad books had competitive advantages for trade publishers in the United States and for American authors. As scholars such as Janice Radway, Richard Brodhead, Thomas Strychacz, Lawrence Levine, Paul DiMaggio, and Gerald Graff have shown, a variety of different institutions set out to define the cultural canon during the late nineteenth and early twentieth century. This canon gave legitimacy to some artists and consumers at the expense of others. Policing the line between legitimate publishers and pirates allowed publishers to stabilize the terms of their gamble on fiction. If trade publishers could define their products as superior and their authors as worthy, those publishers could ask consumers to pay more for the works they sold. Once publishers no longer competed on the basis of price, they could more easily predict how to meet their fixed costs. Equally important, as publishers claimed that they refused to publish sensational trash, they could argue for the value of their enterprise to the individual and the nation.

Copyright

Peter Jaszi and Martha Woodmansee have noted that the late nineteenth and early twentieth century marked a transition in copyright that was critical to publishers' own business interests and to their efforts to define books as dignified objects and a measure of national greatness. They explain that notions of copyright shifted from a sense that the public had an interest in literary works, which outweighed the author's "ownership" of the work, to a sense that the author had property interests in her work, which outweighed the public's interest in free circulation of information and ideas. In 1891 the passage of international copyright legislation, known as the Chace Act, substantially improved publishers' abilities control the market in books. This federal legislation, like the other changes in copyright law, gave publishers greater control over authors and the stakes that they had in publication.

During the nineteenth century, as the price of paper dropped and technology lowered the costs of manufacturing, American firms published popular English novels by authors such as Sir Walter Scott and Charles Dickens in cheap paper formats often without offering payment to the author. In his *Cheap Book Production in the United States* (1937), Raymond Shove shows the disastrous consequences for publishers of the competition to issue popular works quickly and at the lowest prices. A publisher like George Munro, who both reprinted fiction and published dime novels, generated five and a half million books in 1886 alone. And Munro was just one of many; the year 1886 also saw 1,500 new titles issued in editions of various sizes by dozens of firms. These paper-bound, cheaply printed books could have cost as much as seventy-five cents, but price competition drove publishers to sell novels for as little as seven or eight cents. Trade publishers might have attempted to differentiate themselves from these "pirates," but they entered the fray as well. To compete with Munro, Harpers created the Franklin Square Library, Henry Holt created the Leisure Hour Series, and Appleton's created the New Handy Library. Price cutting consumed any profits that might have resulted from economies of scale. One of the reprint publishers reported in *Publishers' Weekly* that only one book in twenty repaid the cost of manufacture (1886, 556).

As such stories show, lack of international copyright protection made it difficult for publishers to control the risks they took on authors. Given their desire to present themselves as public servants, publishers had to word their arguments for copyright carefully, since copyright legislation would end this flood of low-priced books, which increased access to print literature. One writer, reprinted in *Publishers' Weekly*, celebrated the fact that he had seen ten- and twenty-cent editions of Thomas Carlyle, Walter Scott, Ralph Waldo Emerson, Homer, Goethe, Dante, and Shakespeare in backwoods Arkansas and in mining camps in Colorado, concluding that such a wide circulation of books made these people "more enlightened and intelligent" (1888, 884). This writer spoke for many Americans who believed the nation was strengthened by anything that provided citizens with worthwhile reading. A similar attitude led one of the "pirate" publishers to declare "We don't steal for ourselves; we steal for the public" (qtd. in Tebbel 1972, 639).

Trade publishers presented this issue differently. The *Atlantic Monthly*, a journal run by Houghton Mifflin, addressed the argument that these inexpensive books were good for the nation. The editor admitted that the books themselves were "not poor, as cheap literature is apt to be" but the project of reprinting them was no more to be commended than "the ingenious person who steps into your hall and gracefully appropriates your overcoat." In the eyes of this author these books "inflicted great wrong" on authors, publishers, and on readers' eyes. Readers hoping to get books inexpensively cheated "every man or woman in the United States who depends upon literary labor for a livelihood" and cheated themselves since the books were so difficult to read and full of errors (1877, 619–20). Trade publishers argued that consumers got cheapness, rather than culture, when they bought inexpensive books.

Supporters of copyright legislation also argued that inexpensive foreign works might overwhelm American literary culture. Poet and critic W. H. Rideing believed that pirated novels would act "like a rank weed in a garden" which chokes "all fiction of native growth" (qtd. in Shove 1937, 31). Although cheap books might seem a public good, ultimately the public suffered as low prices undermined the foundations of fine culture and American democratic ideals. *Publishers' Weekly* reprinted the *Boston Globe's* warning that "the great masses" of American readers were becoming "steeped" in English thoughts, views, and customs. Improving the situation "would quicken national life and educate and elevate the taste of the people" (1883, 522). While American readers suffered the imposition of British taste, American authors remained unprotected from piracy in other countries. Brander Matthews, among others, pointed out that American authors were not simply reprinted but their books were often altered as British publishers stole both their work and "their good name" (Matthews 1889, 25). The idea of fair dealing with authors and supporting the national culture galvanized publishers attempting to pass copyright law.

The passage of the Chace Act in 1891 ended unlicensed reprints and protected American authors' rights abroad. As a result publishers could stabilize prices and better predict the market. In addition, the inclusion of the "Manufacturing Clause"—which specified that only books manufactured from type set in the United States could be copyrighted—further protected the rights of American publishers and printing houses to control texts. Charles Scribner wrote to a friend in Britain, "we regard it as important that there should be no immediate increase of retail price on account of the passage of the copyright bill, but that publishers should rely upon the increased profit which would come from control of the market" (qtd. in Sheehan 1952, 217). While the business advantages were clear, the Labor Department's report on the 1891 copyright law, released in 1901, showed that the number of American novels published had increased but could not tie that increase to copyright. The same report, however, showed the extent to which arguments based on justice and morality, rather than competitive advantage, remained an element of the publishers' discussions of their businesses. Copyright, one publisher claimed, "was inherently just, and what is just ought not and cannot be detrimental to anyone" (qtd. in Wright 1901, 12). In this case, justice to the authors on both sides of the Atlantic allowed publishers to control the investment that they had in authors, keeping book prices relatively high.

Retail Distribution and Price

The Chace Act brought some regularity to the industry; however, the distribution of books remained a problem. Publishers knew that supporting booksellers would enable them to get the widest distribution but developing retail outlets that shared publishers' reverence toward books proved difficult. In fact, the number of retail outlets shrank throughout the nineteenth and twentieth centuries. In 1859 a survey by *American Publisher's Circular and Literary Gazette* found one bookstore per fifteen thousand inhabitants in the United States. A similar survey in 1914 by *American Book Trade Manual* estimated that there was a bookstore for every twenty-eight thousand people (Sheehan 1952, 189). In 1930, O.H. Cheney's *Economic Survey of the Book Industry* found a bookstore for every thirty thousand people. Bookstores were concentrated in urban areas and Cheney estimated that some 32 percent of Americans had no direct access to a bookstore (238).

Even as the numbers of bookstores shrank, publishers were able to develop a more systematic distribution system. Early in the century, publishers relied on large auctions known as "trade sales" to provide dealers with books. While these sales ended in 1891, throughout the late nineteenth century publishers developed more effective sales departments that would allow traveling salesmen to do the work of the trade sales more efficiently and effectively. While salesmen may have improved the distribution network, the bookstores they visited worried publishers. Just as *Publishers' Weekly* advanced a professional identity for publishers, the trade journal promoted the idea that good booksellers valued books as dignified, noncommercial objects. Its editorial pages celebrated booksellers who were devoted to selling "the best—not necessarily the highest, according to literary canons, but the best fitted for rational amusement or real instruction" (1876, 570–71). However, *Publishers' Weekly* complained that many books were bought in dry good stores where they were "sold like groceries." Clerks knew little more about books than any other product "not sold by the dozen or pound." Even worse, such stores frequently sold books at artificially low prices to lure customers into the stores. Such practices drove stores that focused on books out of business and undermined booksellers' and publishers' pretensions by suggesting that books were something consumers bought alongside eggs and soap rather than a special type of commodity to be bought from a reputable and knowledgeable bookseller (1885, 251).

Flush from their success in advocating for international copyright, publishers formed the American Publishers Association in 1900 with the goal of enforcing a net price system similar to the system that operated in Britain. The net price would be a price printed on the book below which it could not be sold. To police this system in the United States, publishers agreed to stop providing new books to any seller who sold net books for less than the net price. Not every book had to have a net price but as the advantages of the system became clear, publishers rushed to participate. According to Sheehan's figures, in 1909 only 10 percent of novels were listed as net; a year later nearly half of all novels had net prices, and by 1912 96 percent of fiction was net. *Publishers' Weekly* reported that implementation of the net price system did not raise prices significantly. In 1912 novels that listed for $1.50 had been sold, on average, at about $1.20. With the implementation of the net agreement the average price for books was about $1.23 (1912, 1547).

While many chain and department stores abided by the net agreement, R. H. Macy's refused. For example, Macy's sold Hallie Rives's novel *The Castaway* (1906) at eighty-nine cents, although Bobbs-Merrill, the publisher, listed the price as one dollar. Ralph Hower's *History of Macys of New York* explains that because the company was able to buy in volume, it still made twenty-nine cents a copy. While selling at net would have only increased profits, Macy's owners resented what they saw as a "Book Trust" controlling their store policy. After eleven years, nine court cases against the American Publishers Association, and five cases against Scribner's and Bobbs-Merrill, the Supreme Court ruled in 1914 that the net price agreement violated the Sherman Anti-Trust Act and assessed court costs that ended the American Publisher's Association. *Publishers' Weekly* consoled the trade by explaining, "Thirteen years ago price cutting was rampant . . . and the book business was fast falling into suicidal destruction." While net prices enforced by group coercion had been declared illegal, the experience showed that voluntary cooperation "brings trade solidarity, and makes prosperity, if not probable, at least possible" (Sheehan 1952, 235). This lesson reinforced publishers' inclination to see themselves as genteel tastemakers rather than cutthroat businessmen.

Tebbel shows that the collapse of the net price agreement did not necessarily lower book prices. Prices had started to fall even before the Supreme Court ruling, so that most novels cost about a dollar between 1912 and 1916. As costs for paper and labor rose before the First World War, prices for books also rose and continued to rise steeply throughout the 1920s. In 1918 the average book cost around $1.40. By 1928 a few publishers like Knopf, Little Brown, and Viking priced their novels

at $3. For consumers, these price increases made little sense. Although *Publishers'*
Weekly attempted to remind consumers that the 50 to 60 percent rise in book
prices did not keep up with what publishers estimated was a 75 to 80 percent
rise in costs, public complaints continued. Consumers might pay less for novels
depending on where they lived and how they got their novels, but until the Great
Depression first edition trade books were always expected to cost more than a
dollar, while reprints, issued after a book had recouped its initial costs, might be
priced at a dollar or less.

However, as the Great Depression increased concerns about both the price of
books and their place in American culture, a group of publishers experimented with
issuing first edition books at the price of a dollar. This group hoped that by lower-
ing prices, they would sell more books, but the response of the rest of the industry
showed what a threat price-cutting remained. In 1932, *Publishers' Weekly* complained
that the dollar book will "curtail the possibility of there ever being healthy sales,"
which will mean that publishers will no longer be able to publish the original that
allows for inexpensive reprints (1360). Alarmed that price-consciousness might
make book buyers equate books with other mass-produced items, another group
of publishers, with the help of public relations guru Edward Bernays, mounted a
national public relations campaign that asserted the virtues of books and the necessity of higher prices. Their press releases outlined the meager profits publishers
expected on books even when they were priced at $2.50 but argued that a publisher
had to issue books that might not sell in large quantities "if he is to maintain the
high standards of his calling." Only by publishing these "new authors and books of
outstanding merit" could the publishing industry prevent the national culture and
intellect from becoming "static and therefore sterile" (Haugland, 241). Concerned
about both price and prestige, publishers attacked cut-rate publishing for focusing
too much on profits at the expense of what they saw as publisher's duty to readers
and the nation.

Thus, publishers began the Great Depression still searching for the price stability
they had hoped to gain from both copyright legislation and net price agreements.
Early in the Depression, publishers asked O. H. Cheney to survey their industry
and provide a fair assessment of its problems. Cheney found that little had changed
in the publishing industry since the late nineteenth century. Publishers were unwilling to "reject any manuscript which contains even traces of merit or theoretical
sales possibilities." With so many books on the market "the competition between
books" made strong sales impossible. Nonetheless, Cheney could not imagine a sort
of "disarmament conference" where publishers voluntarily cut the sizes of their lists.
As a result, he felt that the industry would continue to suffer unless distribution
could somehow be improved (1930, 86–89). Despite the fact that large lists tended
to depress prices and limit the sales of individual titles, trade publishers still felt that
gambling on a large number of titles offered individual firms the best chance of
making a profit.

Creating Distinctions: Distribution, Advertising, and Culture

Cheney's report only reasserted a problem that the trade knew all too well. The inundation of books he described was especially true for novels which, as John Dos Passos told Malcolm Cowley, had limited sales because there were simply so many: "everything published goes down the same chute, out of the over bright glare of publicity into oblivion" (qtd. in Cowley, 281). Dos Passos's image, of books churned out via a conveyer belt into an undifferentiated mass spoke to the anxieties of both authors and publishers about mass production and its effect on cultural products. While publishers increased the size of their lists, they realized that they needed to find ways to differentiate individual titles from the mass of titles published. They addressed this problem in two ways. First, they used advertisements. Although publishers had always advertised, during the period from 1870 to 1940 they experimented with expensive advertising budgets and advertising. Second, as they developed these advertisements, publishers also participated in the larger process of creating cultural hierarchies through literary canons designed to define taste for consumers. These canons allowed publishers to assert the value of certain types of books—creating a sense that there were certain books that everyone who wanted to appear cultured and up-to-date ought to aspire to read. However, these canons also identified consumers at different levels of the cultural hierarchy. Thus publishers could both partially define tastes and exploit certain niche markets.

Often histories of publishing focused on the twentieth century depict "new" publishers as introducing more up-to-date methods of advertising and marketing. As Ellen Gruber Garvey has explained, trade publishers' restrained advertising reflected their commitment to the dignity of books and their conviction that "too frankly acknowledging commodity status threatened the prestige that [they] considered essential to success" (2009, 171). In 1889 appearance of a product named "Book Soap"—which promised "the great unwashed" a free book with a purchase of a fifteen-cent bar of soap and sold some 2 million novels—led to a series of complaints from publishers that books could not be sold like soap because books were not like other consumer goods (Shove 1937, 41–42). Nonetheless, advertising budgets spiked soon after. In 1880 Scribner's spent a little over $100 per book in advertising; in 1903 Scribner's spent close to $10,000 for one novel, Thomas Nelson Page's 1903 *Gordon Keith* (Sheehan 1952, 178). Publishers had used many of the advertising techniques associated with the 1920s throughout the nineteenth century. Bowen-Merrill (soon to be Bobbs-Merrill) hired a man in armor to ride the streets of Manhattan on horseback to advertise Charles Major's novel *When Knighthood Was in Flower* (1898). Newspaper editor Isaac Marcosson pioneered the idea of turning books into news as he promoted both Thomas Dixon's *The Clansman* (1905) and Upton Sinclair's *The Jungle* (1906) through syndicated articles. Even the idea of trying to turn the name of a publishing house into a brand was fairly common, as in 1894 when Scribner's used the slogan "When in doubt, buy Scribner's" (Tebbel

1972, 155–64). Despite publishers' claims that such gimmicky advertising reduced the dignity of their books, nearly every publisher used it.

The "new" publishers of the twentieth century insisted as much as "old" publishers that books could not be mass marketed. In fact, because publishers hoped to use the dignified status of books to sell books in their advertising, those publishers who spent most heavily on advertising asserted most loudly that advertising could not sell books. While Alfred Knopf attempted to turn his house into a brand, he also expressed doubts that "advertising does actually sell books" (1965, 47). Alfred Harcourt repeated the shibboleth that books could not be sold like soap to advertising agents at the J. Walter Thompson Agency when they invited him to speak in 1930. In 1932, Bennett Cerf took the book-soap theme a step further by advertising the Modern Library with a picture of a woman in the bathtub surrounded by floating books. The most important change that book advertising experienced, as historians Ellen Garvey, Richard Ohmann, Janice Radway, and Joan Rubin have shown, is that book advertising began to focus more on the "impact" a novel might have on a person's life. Advertisements asserted that novels could make a person more cultured, thoughtful, or successful. Horace Liveright, for example, consulted with Bernays to create advertising focused on psychological needs. So for the Hutchins Hapgood novel *Story of a Lover* (1919), Bernays devised advertisements with comments about love from movie stars like Mary Pickford and the Gish sisters that seemed to promise the novel could provide readers with insight into the glamorous experiences these stars represented.

By the 1930s, the range of personal qualities that a novel could offer a consumer had increased. In 1933, Farrar and Rinehart advertised Hervey Allen's *Anthony Adverse* with advertisements featuring images of duels and galloping stagecoaches, but they also promised that the book was "A World Classic of Our Time." They publicized Eleanor Roosevelt's comments on *Anthony Adverse* (she read it on a train journey from Chicago and claimed "I missed all of the scenery but none of the action") to suggest that important people were talking about the book. They ran a contest once the movie rights had been sold to MGM, offering a string of real pearls or a gown by a Hollywood designer, to readers who could correctly pick which stars would play which major characters. In short, *Anthony Adverse* became the center of a complicated set of qualities—from glamour to conversational ability to literary acumen—which consumers could gain by purchasing the novel. Farrar and Rinehart, however, remained conscious of the limits of merchandizing the novel. When Allen refused to do book signings because he feared that consumers would come to think of him as "that tall, blond Swede they met at Macy's one hot July afternoon while shopping for under drawers," they agreed. By the end of the 1930s, publishers continued to look for better ways to advertise novels and remained ambivalent about the usefulness of advertising for sales given the possible "harm" that commercialization could do to a novel.

Far more effective than advertising in distinguishing books from each other were the book series that academics and publishers created to distinguish outstanding, classic, or simply good books from the great mass of books. Such series had a long history. George Munro published a number of them, including the Seaside Library and the Fireside Companion. These late nineteenth-century series were pulled together because of the regularity of their publication rather than any coherent editorial choices. In the twentieth century, editors began to put together series of reprints that promised consumers the best previously published books. Eventually, as these series were increasingly successful, entrepreneurs began offering first edition books that promised readers the best choices among contemporary trade books.

While the association with dime novels made series like Munro's somewhat suspect, in the twentieth century series met with critical approval if they were run by publishers, sold at book stores, and focused on the classic and dignified qualities publishers hoped to connect to books. E. P. Dutton imported the classic reprint series Everyman's Library from Britain in 1906. While only thirty-five cents a book, this series featured editions of well-known works in clearly set type, quality paper, and well-designed covers. Everyman's Library set the stage for the development of the Modern Library, a series that combined older works with more recent "classics." Albert Boni and Horace Liveright began the Modern Library in 1916 to reflect and codify avant-garde tastes. Once Bennett Cerf bought it in 1925, he focused the series on providing "serious literature" to the "civilized minority" (Satterfield 2002, 119). Although these series announced their commodity status by offering inexpensive literature and advertising their low prices, they also promised that they were special commodities, inexpensive but well crafted, standardized in format but unique in their contents. Such series gave consumers and the series' publisher a way around the dilemma of mass produced literature by promising that their uniformity announced quality, not mediocrity.

Other series distinguished books on their lists for a different set of consumers and thereby led to critical consternation. In 1909 P. F. Collier began offering Dr. Charles Eliot's Five Foot Shelf of Books. Eliot, then the president of Harvard University, claimed that fifteen minutes of daily reading in the classics (including American novels such as Nathaniel Hawthorne's *The Scarlet Letter* [1850] and Henry James's *The Portrait of a Lady* [1881]) would provide people access to a full liberal education. Critics asserted that the advertisements for these books focused consumers' insecurities and put the classics into the service of getting jobs and romantic success. These critics feared that such a utilitarian attitude toward literature would cheapen the cultural value of literature even as such a set provided opportunity for many people to acquire culture.

Harry Scherman took Eliot's approach one step further with the Book-of-the-Month Club (BOMC). Scherman created a publishing sensation by cutting through the mass of books and using a set of judges to choose one "outstanding" newly published book each month. He also streamlined distribution by having that book sent by mail to subscribers. BOMC advertising appealed to consumers' fear of not keeping up but also directly addressed the issue of the overwhelming number of books they had to chose from: "You know that, out of the thousands of books published, there are only a few you are interested in. You want the outstanding ones. But what are they?" Scherman used these advertisements to appeal to middle-class readers, especially women. The BOMC ensured nearly automatic sales; as Joan Rubin has explained, the BOMC sold books before they were even published, creating "a new kind of cultural commodity," one that gained its value not from any of the qualities of the text but from the apparatus of the club and the assurances of the advertisements that surrounded it (Rubin 1992, 103). Much like the other series that preceded it, the BOMC organized a consumer's reading taste, but critics feared that its choices offered book consumers predigested, easy culture and BOMC choices came to constitute a canon of "middlebrow" taste.

Conclusion

While publishers may not have been fully able to control the market for individual titles or to save booksellers from competition, they were able to create a sense of distinction for novels. Hutner explains in his survey of what he calls "middle-class fiction" in the mid-twentieth century in the United States that even as radio and film came to dominate some of the public's attention, the "public sphere" remained "enmeshed in print culture." The novels he describes, often concerned with domestic issues and private life, performed "the liberal project of developing compromise, achieving consensus, resisting alienation, and participating meaningfully" that helped readers define how to live a good life and be a valuable American citizen. Hutner's study shows publishers' hopes that their industry and their work would become vital to the nation and its citizens had been realized, especially in the most mundane and ordinary works they issued. Publishers' strategy of gambling on a wide range of titles gave consumers of novels opportunities for self-culture, self-reflection and self-congratulation that they might not have had. Whatever business evils the strategy had engendered, it created a swath of novels that "set the boundaries of the country's political imagination" (2009, 184–86).

Publishers worked alongside the critics and scholars that Claudia Stokes describes in *Writers in Retrospect* to create a sense that great literature (however they chose to define it) written by a nation's citizens reflect the nation's greatness. More importantly publishers hoped to show that reading of all sorts would contribute to individual development and national power. American novels like *Anthony Adverse*, *A Farewell to Arms*, and *Magnificent Obsession* were clearly commercial and at the same time vital to publishers' efforts to create a set of American canons, defining and setting tastes for a wide range of consumers. Especially during the 1920s and 1930s, publishers issued increasing numbers of novels by American women and minorities, as well as novels from around the world. Ultimately, in order to assert their own essential role in American life publishers had to invest in authors and readers originally outside the canon.

In some ways, the changes that the industry faced in the late 1930s, especially the development and acceptance of paperback books, simply accelerated changes that were underway throughout the late nineteenth and early twentieth century. Because they allowed for the possibility of more sales and a wider range of retail markets, paperbacks increased the possibility of novels selling well and increased publishers' willingness to gamble. They also added additional reasons for publishers to promote their backlist and, because of the additional sales possibilities, eventually increased the advances paid to authors. Kathleen Winsor earned an advance of $30,000 for her first novel, *Forever Amber* (1944), but fourteen years later Vladimir Nabokov secured $100,000 for *Lolita* (1958). The development of paperback novels also drove publishers to continue to cooperate as Bennett Cerf pulled together a cartel of publishers to create Bantam Paperbacks in response to the department store Marshall Fields's efforts to buy Simon and Schuster and Pocket books.

John Hench has shown that the Second World War both accelerated the acceptance of paperbacks and solidified publishers' desires to see themselves as public servants who could strengthen the nation through their business efforts. Publishers formed the Council on Books in Wartime to provide servicemen with reading material and also to provide their industry with a serious, national purpose during the war. The Armed Services Editions that publishers created posited a canon for American readers dominated by fiction but that combined authors from Willa Cather to Zane Grey, and included classics such as an abridged version of Laurence Sterne's *Tristram Shandy* (1759) as well as more timely books like Joseph Grew's *Report from Tokyo* (1942). As a result, publishers may have ended the war facing similar business issues, but they had certainly strengthened their cultural position. As publishers entered the second half of the twentieth century, novels had become a key location for thoughtful Americans to think through ideas and an important reflection of America's power in the world.

3

AMERICAN READERS AND THEIR NOVELS

BY AMY L. BLAIR

In 1939, Charles Lee's *How to Enjoy Reading* presented advice to people wishing to improve their relationship to books, whether to learn how to read more profitably, or to appreciate the reading that they were already inclined to do. In a text liberally sprinkled with illustrations reminiscent of James Thurber, Lee counsels his readers that they are entitled to entertainment, and even escapism, from literature, as long as they do not wallow in "fifth-rate Cinderella distortions of actual life," and as long as their reading does not become "a perversion, a kind of ostracism, a magic carpet out of real or fancied inferiorities or defeats" (32–33). He provides a list of "What to Read," while cautioning that lists can easily become fetishized and offering blank pages for his readers to compose "My Personal Reading List." He praises the Pulitzer Prizes for the novel because "they represent a remarkably successful mingling of high-quality writing and universal appeal. [. . .] It is a compliment to the American taste that thousands of readers hailed many of these books before the Pulitzer Committee selected them for awards. Here, high art and wide reader acceptance frequently meet" (110–11).

Lee's careful negotiation of readers' desires to be diverted by their reading and his own desire to promote "the best books" nicely encapsulates the central debates around reading that dominated the period from 1870 to 1940. Each decade of this period witnessed significant developments in both local and global environments that contributed to profound changes in the constitution of the reading public and in the contexts in which people accessed and understood their reading. During this time, literacy increased as a growing professional-managerial class began to pursue both formal and informal educational opportunities. The proliferation of libraries made books accessible even to those who could not afford to purchase them. Magazines and newspapers were more numerous, had wider circulations, and were publishing more fiction than ever thanks to the new popularity of syndicates. Labor laws resulted in increased leisure time for a large portion of the US population, and a number of leisure activities battled with reading for attention.

At the same time, newly arrived immigrants brought to the United States cultures of reading that sometimes supplanted, and sometimes complemented or intensified, dominant cultural attitudes towards the material and social utility of reading. Newly freed slaves and other people of color, negotiating the economic and social frameworks of the rapidly industrializing United States, deployed literacy as a means of integrating into American society and of challenging their marginalization. Women, in particular—both white women and women of color—were active in reshaping reading culture during these decades, both formally through book clubs and informally through familial and social networks.

All of these demographic and material changes led to a high-stakes debate over the very nature of reading: What kinds of books do, or should, people read, and why? Who should read? How should reading for pleasure be balanced with reading for information? What, in short, is the *use* of reading? And, for that matter, what are its dangers? The answers that were offered to these questions continue to drive American attitudes towards reading, literacy, and the connection of both to the duties of citizenship through the present day. Overall, the story of American readers in the decades between 1870 and 1940 is one of increased access and a growing, if somewhat grudging, acceptance of the increased pluralism of readers and reading practices.

Who Read What?

Reading practices are, of course, both highly individuated and locally influenced; the primary challenge facing historians of readership remains balancing evidence of particular readers' behaviors and the temptation to generalize from them. Still, one can discuss general trends among readers and in reported perceptions of readerly practice—the latter of which are often a complex mix of observation and attempts to direct readers' behavior. The mid-nineteenth-century United States has been considered by some the "best-educated" nation in the world at that time—a distinction of course complicated by the stark disparity in education and literacy rates between the free and slave, or newly-freed, populations. While literacy and some experience of education were nearly universal in the free population, we know much less about the literary processes of the African American population, beyond the standard narrative of lack that accompanies the sparse evidence of technical literacy among blacks from the late nineteenth century through the beginning of the twentieth. For the most part, we can understand the spectrum of literacy at the beginning of our period as akin to Daniel and Lauren Resnick's notion of "industrial literacy," a two-tiered system "in which there is widespread rudimentary literacy across the population and a smaller elite corps of more extensively educated people with high literacy skills" (Kaestle and Radway 2009, 528). By 1940 education and literacy had expanded to the point at which high school graduation was a widely recognized rite of passage from youth to adulthood. There were many more tiers of industrial literacy by 1940, with all but a very few Americans completing school at least through the fourth grade. The steady increase in general literacy was influenced by, and in turn drove, the rapid spread of the periodical press from relative provincialism to national consolidation and cultural dominance by 1940, when 80 percent of the population claimed to read newspapers on a regular basis. Although only about a quarter of the population in 1940 would report reading books regularly, the presence of serial fiction in mass periodicals meant that novels were not solely experienced by that smaller group.

In the late nineteenth century, reading was not necessarily a solitary activity. Shared story reading was a principal form of entertainment in the household. Barbara Sicherman notes the influence a culture of domestic reading bestowed on women, in particular: "As both a sanctified activity and an approved entertainment—arguably *the* major form of entertainment for men and women of the comfortable classes and those who aspired to join them—this reading culture had unusual power and piquancy for the women who grew up in it" (2010, 251). The relatively well-to-do Hamilton family of Fort Wayne, Indiana, offers an example of one family's particularly intense engagement with books. The Hamiltons read to each other, cited texts as shorthand in letters to each other, memorized portions of novels and poems, and debated the boundaries of respectable fiction—"one person's trash was another's sensibility" (86–87). As in all family decisions, the issue of what to read was often contentious; Edith Abbott recalled that, growing up in the late nineteenth century, she and her siblings sometimes "rebelled when they reached their limits: the young Abbotts found the serialized stories in genteel magazines dull and implored their parents to postpone reading William Dean Howells's *The Rise of Silas Lapham* until they had gone to bed" (51). Familial reading was not practiced only by the comfortable middle class or by the native born. Rose Cohen, who emigrated from Russia with her family in the early 1890s, came from a tradition in which her grandmother told stories while knitting; in evenings on the Lower East Side, Cohen read aloud Yiddish translations of Dickens to her rapt family audience (Sicherman 2010, 201–2; Cohen 1918, 187–91). Cohen also recalls reading to her mother in English as she worked around the house; in immigrant families, where the younger members were more likely to have greater English fluency than their elders, such scenes were probably typical. Story-papers with titles such as *Fireside Companion* and *Family Story Paper* reflected and encouraged such reading among workers' families, both through their titles and through their publication schedules, timed for Sunday reading.

Groups outside the family circle also practiced communal reading. The workplace was also a site in which people read, either in groups during breaks or in idle periods, or even, as one female millworker recalled, at one's workstation from surreptitiously hidden clippings. In his fictionalized *Autobiography of an Ex-Colored Man* (1912), James Weldon Johnson recounts a scene in which his nameless protagonist becomes a "reader" at a cigar-wrapping factory, reminiscent of Samuel Gompers' own recollection of such activities. These, along with numerous other workers' autobiographical recollections of such practices, suggest that workplace reading was fairly common.

The phenomenon of commuter reading in the cities likewise grew to iconic status by the 1940s; cheap "railway editions" (long in print, and now perfect for intracity commutes) made it easier for workers to read in transit to and from work, and reading advisers often encouraged their charges to take advantage of this intermediate time for a rare moment of self-care in the midst of an other-directed life. As Hamilton Wright Mabie counseled in his May 1902 column for the *Ladies' Home Journal*:

> When you have formed the reading habit in the right way the time you spend on the street cars, in ferryboats, on journeys, in waiting for others, will constitute your chance for going to college, or of keeping up the education begun in college. Nine-tenths of those who are bewailing absence of opportunity are simply blind to the opportunities which lie within their reach; for the chief difference between men does not lie in difference of opportunity but in difference of ability to recognize an opportunity when it appears.

The message of this passage is clear: the willingness and ability to seize such moments could be the difference between ultimate success or failure, not just in reading, but in life.

By 1939, Charles Lee would still emphasize the social element of reading, although with an emphasis on influencing family and friends' tastes rather than enjoying a communal experience. "You are a center of people. You become a moral and mental significance to yourself and your circle as you assimilate the best that has been thought and said in the world" (13). Reading actually makes us "more interesting to ourselves. We become more interesting to others" (45). Books connect rather than isolate people. And when publishers began tracking the "bestselling" novels in the late nineteenth century through lists in *The Bookman* and *Publisher's Weekly*, the influence of popular taste threatened to dwarf that of professional critics. Edith Wharton worried in her 1903 essay "The Vice of Reading" about readers, particularly untrained readers, taking the reins of the marketplace; the mass reading public would, she feared, gravitate towards "the book that is being talked about, and [their] sense of its importance is in proportion to the number of editions exhausted before publication." The result of such popularity contests, she warned, was that the potential popularity of books to these philistine readers would become a more key consideration to publishers than their ethical and aesthetic duty to support "the best in literature." Wharton's concern was echoed by many literary critics in the mold of Matthew Arnold who strove to substantiate the difference between "quality" literature and "trash." As Nancy Glazener observes, in the latter part of the nineteenth century, "Books, periodicals, and their publishers became more strictly divided between those for the 'classes' and those for the 'masses,' and forums of high culture developed ever more elaborate criteria by which high and low tastes—or high tastes and low appetites, as they were usually characterized—could be discriminated" (1997, 20). Rather than grouping all novels together for condemnation, this new generation of critics carefully suggested that certain novels, but only a select few,

could be enlivening, uplifting, and informative. The ability to differentiate grades
of fiction became a marker of cultural capital for upwardly striving readers of all
stripes—genteel readers who hoped to maintain a hold on their cultural dominance,
middle-class readers who hoped to prove their legitimate claim to class through the
performance of good taste, and lower and working class readers, new immigrants,
and people of color, whose demonstration of culture became tantamount to a demonstration of fitness for citizenship and entrance into the economic system.

With so much at stake, readers gravitated to experts who would help them navigate the world of fiction, and professional critics gained notoriety even as they
lamented their perceived cultural obscurity. A dizzying array of volumes with titles
like *Books and Reading; Or, What Books Shall I Read and How Shall I Read Them?*
(1881); *What I Know About Books and How to Use Them* (1892); *Books, Culture, and
Character* (1906); *Open That Door!* (1916); and *What Books Can Do FOR YOU!* (1923)
offered themselves as guides for the prospective reader. Redeploying the rhetoric of
upward mobility commonly associated with success manuals, the authors of reading
manuals such as these increasingly counseled their audiences that all reading should
redound to the intellectual, professional, and emotional benefit of the reader. By
the second decade of the twentieth century, these texts came gradually to embrace
readerly desires for "escape" fiction, even as they tried to raise the profile and cultural capital of "serious fiction." This gambit was strategic; after all, if the reader had
become a consumer of fiction, the reading adviser's job, like any good marketer, was
to simultaneously cater to and direct the consumer desire. In *Middletown* (1929),
their longitudinal study of Muncie, Indiana, from 1890 to 1925, Robert S. and Helen
Merrell Lynd cited a local newspaper editorial penned by a "prominent citizen" as
evidence for the attractions of vicarious escape through fiction:

> And so we remain at home, go to the office at eight in the morning and depart
> from it at six at night, and we attend committee meetings, and drive the old family
> bus over the streets that we have traversed a thousand times before, and in general
> continue the life of the so-called model citizen.
>
> But these conditions need not fetter our fancy. In that realm we can scale the
> lofty Matterhorn, sail the sleepy Indian Sea, mine glittering gold in the snow-clad
> mountains of Alaska, tramp the Valley of the Moon, and idle along the majestic
> Amazon. (237–38)

These seekers after escapist fancy, not surprisingly, preferred "happy endings—or at
least endings that if not exactly happy still exalt you and make you feel that the world
is coming out all right" (238). The large majority of readers subscribed to periodicals
that serialized such novels, and checked cheerful books out from the public library,
even when cultural arbiters pressed them to leaven their more popular choices with
fiction from the realist or modernist schools. Thus by 1939, Charles Lee's ready abandonment of lists of "the classics," which perhaps serve best to "demonstrate that
'culture' existed thousands of years ago, that it is in a constant state of evolution (and

moments of devolution—should that perhaps be spelled devilution, with a nod to the Nazis?), and that it has flourished in more golden days than these" (90–91). The "nod" to the Nazis here signals one of the significant external influences explaining the sentiment against prescriptive lists; lists begin to smell of fascism, the dangers of which loomed large in the late 1930s. Even the bestseller lists threaten to "make Joneses of us all," and advance the trend by which "we have ceased to be self-reliant individuals" (95). By the late 1930s, it became more essential to make one's own book selections than to follow someone else's dictates, for reasons that went beyond aesthetics.

Serial Fiction

As Catherine Turner discusses in the previous chapter, the rise in cheap book production during the 1870s and 1880s created new markets for fiction and dramatically increased the number of fiction titles that could be offered on a continuing basis for purchase. This availability of affordable books, combined with the presence of fiction in periodicals, provided a number of venues in which readers could experience fiction. The primary trends in periodical publication at the end of the nineteenth century were expansion, differentiation, and increasing nationalization (for an extended discussion of serialized fiction, see Chapter 18 of this volume). In 1880, the Census Bureau's report on newspaper publication in the states and territories went it clear that local publication was the norm—newspapers were published in 2,073 of the nation's 2,605 counties. There were 971 daily newspapers in 1880, with a circulation of 3.5 million in a nation of population approximately 50 million. While much of the production of papers was local, there were also growing networks among newspapers; small-town presses could purchase "readyprint" pages from major city papers that dealt with national and international news stories, and a growing telegraph network transmitted news to the hinterland. By 1882, the Associated Press consolidated its reach nationally by finally uniting the last of the regional press associations under one banner. Readyprint publishers began including fiction in their offerings with serial installments of novels in 1870.

Charles Johanningsmeier offers an exhaustive description of the various processes by which the syndicates increased their clout with authors and publishers alike over the course of the late nineteenth century. The syndicates were profoundly significant for the dissemination of fiction. As Johanningsmeier writes, "One syndicate alone, McClure's Associated Literary Press, distributed 155 short stories and one serial novel in 1885 and 119 short stories and 16 serial novels in 1899, each of them to an average of 20 newspapers, from Boston to San Francisco, with circulation per newspaper ranging from 10,000 to 120,000 copies" (1997, 2). Such numbers are impressive enough alone, but after taking into account the general rule that each copy was shared among three readers, the significance of the syndicates is even more apparent.

Syndicates published for the most part fiction written by fairly well-known authors, but they are also considered responsible for introducing some significant authors— particularly British authors—to American audiences for the first time. Syndicates were able to offer established writers like Henry James and William Dean Howells venues for work that they could not place elsewhere, and sometimes their pay was more lucrative than the offers that could be made by individual newspapers or by struggling genteel monthly magazines. By the end of the nineteenth century, however, the rising clout of magazines and the declining prestige of newspapers led to the decline of syndicated fiction. Serial fiction of the "better sort" became largely confined to magazines, and dedicated story-papers took over the publication of serialized dime novels. Although their heyday was relatively short-lived, the newspaper fiction syndicates must be given credit for expanding the market for serial fiction beyond genteel and middle-class readers.

When we think of serial fiction, we generally think of monthly magazines, which had been the primary locus of such activity since the eighteenth century. Many of the monthlies jockeying for readership in the 1870s through 1890s had begun as house organs for book publishers—the *Atlantic Monthly, Harper's, Scribner's Monthly* (which became the *Century Magazine*), *Putnam's, Lippincott's,* and *Appleton's Journal* were all monthlies that functioned to advertise their house's list, to offer previews through initial serialization, and to brand the publishing company with particular characteristics that, publishers hoped, would lead to consumer loyalty. House magazines tended to be more expensive, selling for twenty to thirty-five cents an issue on the newsstand, and targeting more affluent and culturally enfranchised readers. As extensions of book publishing operations, these magazines had an editorial stake in promoting certain works or authors as their house's distinctive "brand"; Glazener has detailed how the *Atlantic* group (which included *Putnam's, Harper's,* and others) promoted literary realism and the careers of authors such as William Dean Howells, Henry James, and Charles Chesnutt.

By the 1890s, a host of new periodicals entered the scene competing for a wider, more budget-conscious audience; in 1893 a price war among *McClure's, Cosmopolitan,* and *Munsey's* resulted in a standard baseline newsstand price of ten cents, with a dollar-a-year subscription price. The *Ladies' Home Journal,* which had begun as a more exclusively domestic-issues periodical, increased its general content by 1900, when it became the first periodical to reach circulation of one million copies. Each of these general magazines relied to a great extent on the fiction they serialized each month as a continuing draw for subscribers; they offered novels as premiums for subscribing, and incorporated book chats that helped advise their more general readership on the kinds of books that would be "worth" reading, and the modes of readership that would be the most profitable. Over ten years, Hamilton Wright Mabie penned one hundred columns in the *Journal* that went far beyond current book recommendations, although they included plenty of them; he was just as concerned, though, with orienting his readers toward reading, helping them create a "habit of reading" that would allow them to embrace classic works, current elite literature, and reading for "entertainment" without prejudice or cognitive dissonance. Alongside other elite cultural arbiters, the advisers in the magazines worked to counsel readers about which books to read, and what they should be getting out of them.

Magazines also continued to serialize novels regularly, and while "elite" authors published in prestigious literary journals such as *Atlantic Monthly* and *Harper's*, and, by the 1910s and 1920s in "little magazines" such as the *Dial*, they could also be found in the pages of the *Ladies' Home Journal, Saturday Evening Post*, and *Good Housekeeping*. These magazines, as Christopher Wilson has pointed out, established their credentials as cultural arbiters by publishing for the most part already-established authors such as James, Howells, and Mary Wilkins Freeman, and drew readers in with more popular fare such as fiction by Kate Douglas Wiggin, Edna Ferber, and O. Henry. Wilson observes that the impulses of editors and publishers in the 1910s through 1940s were to professionalize authorship that produced fictions of "middling" America—and this because such were the fictions that the vast middle of the American population would buy, and read. By the 1920s, serial fiction was waning as a major form of publication for most significant authors. At most, periodicals would excerpt portions of text, or short stories, but entire novels were rarely serialized.

Subscription Series

1906 saw the first publication of books in the Everyman's Library series, which promised to make attractively bound copies of "classic literature" affordable for everyone. The sale of subscription series of books accelerated with the expansion of rural free postal delivery in 1902. One of the most long-lived of the bounded subscription book series is the Harvard Classics "Five Foot Shelf of Books," published with inspirational synergy by P. F. Collier from 1910 through 1961. As the previous chapter observes, the Five Foot Shelf combined a reading advisor sensibility with an impressively bound edition of the works themselves. One selling point of the Five Foot Shelf was its programmatic efficiency; in just "Fifteen Minutes a Day," following the daily reading guide in a bound pamphlet with this promising title, you could learn all you needed to know to succeed socially or professionally. The advertisements for the series reinforced consumers' desires and anxieties. One ad from 1921 pictures the interior of a train during the morning commute, seated men in business suits and fedoras (and one well-dressed woman), noses buried in their newspapers. (See Figure 3.1.) A lone standing passenger, eschewing the newspaper, is engrossed in a book. The banner caption crows, "Which Wins Out?" The book reader, it seems, will have a competitive business advantage over the newspaper readers because he is acquiring "'the essentials of a liberal education'—the power to think straight and talk well." A little over one month later, the reader of the *Times Book Review* would find a Harvard Classics ad appealing to a different set of aspirations. (See Figure 3.2.)

Which Wins Out?

Get FREE the booklet that tells what 15 minutes a day will do
to make a man think straight and talk well

WHICH wins out? The man who spends *all* his precious reading time with the daily paper? Or the more foresighted one who seizes upon every spare moment everywhere, to gain little by little, page by page, delightfully and easily that knowledge of the few truly great books which can lift men to distinction and success. What are the few great books—biographies, histories, n o v e l s, dramas, poems, books of science and travel, philosophy and religion —that contain "the essentials of a liberal education" — the power to think straight and talk well? Dr. Charles W. Eliot, from his lifetime of reading, study, and teaching, forty years of it as president of Harvard University, has answered that question in a free booklet that

you can have for the asking. In it are described the contents, plan, and purpose of

DR. ELIOT'S FIVE-FOOT SHELF OF BOOKS

Every well - informed man and woman should at least know something about this famous library.

The free book tells about it—how Dr. Eliot has put into his Five-Foot Shelf "the essentials of a liberal education," how he has so arranged it that even "fifteen minutes a day" are enough, how in pleasant moments of spare time, by using the reading courses Dr. Eliot has provided for you, you can get the knowledge of literature and life, the culture, the broad viewpoint that every university strives to give.

"For me," wrote one man who had sent in the coupon, "your little free book meant a big step forward, and it showed me besides the way to a vast new world of pleasure."

Every reader of this page is invited to have a copy of this handsome and entertaining little book, which is free, will be sent by mail, and involves no obligation of any sort. Merely clip the coupon and mail it to-day.

Send for this FREE booklet that gives Dr. Eliot's plan of reading

P. F. COLLIER & SON COMPANY
Publishers of Good Books Since 1875
BRANCHES AND REPRESENTATIVES EVERYWHERE

Fig 3.1 "Which Wins Out?" asks this 1921 advertisement for the Five Foot Shelf, a collection of books selected by Harvard President Charles W. Eliot.

Which of these two men has learned the secret of 15 minutes a day?

The secret is contained in the free book offered below. Until you have read it you have no idea how much 15 minutes a day can mean in growth and success. Send for your copy now.

HERE are two men, equally good looking, equally well dressed. You see such men at every social gathering. One of them can talk of nothing beyond the mere day's news. The other brings to every subject a wealth of side light and illustration that makes him listened to eagerly.

He talks like a man who had traveled widely, though his only travels are a business man's trips. He knows something of history and biography, of the work of great scientists, and the writings of philosophers, poets, and dramatists.

Yet he is busy, as all men are, in the affairs of every day. How has he found time to acquire so rich a mental background? When there is such a multitude of books to read, how can any man be well-read?

The answer to this man's success—and to the success of thousands of men and women like him—is contained in a free book that you may have for the asking. In it is told the story of Dr. Eliot's great discovery, which, as one man expressed it, "does for reading what the invention of the telegraph did for communication." From his lifetime of reading, study, and teaching, forty years of it as President of Harvard University, Dr. Eliot tells just what few books he chose for the most famous library in the world; why he chose them and how he has arranged them with notes and reading courses so that any man can get from them the essentials of a liberal education in even fifteen minutes a day.

The booklet gives the plan, scope, and purpose of

Dr. Eliot's Five-Foot Shelf of Books—
The Fascinating Path to a Liberal Education

Every well-informed man and woman should at least know something about this famous library.

The free book tells about it—how Dr. Eliot has put into his Five-Foot Shelf "the essentials of a liberal education," how he has so arranged it that even "fifteen minutes a day" are enough, how in pleasant moments of spare time, by using the reading courses Dr. Eliot has provided for you, you can get the knowledge of literature and life, the culture, the broad viewpoint that every university strives to give.

"For me," wrote one man who had sent in the coupon, "your little free book meant a big step forward, and it showed me besides the way to a vast new world of pleasure."

Every reader of The New York Times is invited to have a copy of this handsome and entertaining little book. It is free, will be sent by mail, and involves no obligation of any sort. Merely clip the coupon and mail it to-day.

Send for this FREE booklet that gives Dr. Eliot's own plan of reading

P. F. COLLIER & SON COMPANY
Publishers of Good Books Since 1875

Fig 3.2 Appearing in the New York Times Book Review, this advertisement ties literary self-improvement to masculinity.

A lovely woman sits at a dinner table, flanked by two men in evening dress. She has turned her back on one concerned-looking gentleman while she lavishes the other (the younger and more attractive of the two) with a winning smile. The headline asks, "Which of these two men has learned the secret of 15 minutes a day?" The ad continues:

> Here are two men, equally good looking, equally well dressed. You see such men at every social gathering. One of them can talk of nothing beyond the mere day's news. The other brings to every subject a wealth of side light and illustration that makes him listened to eagerly. [. . .]Yet he is busy, as all men are, in the affairs of every day. How has he found the time to acquire so rich a mental background? When there is such a multitude of books to read, how can any man be well-read?

The Five Foot Shelf is, of course, the answer to this conundrum, with its helpfully condensed and programmed plan for reading. This is "the answer to this man's success"—a success in this case not professional, but personal. By bringing a preselected slate of books right to your door, subscription series rendered the reading process more efficient; one had only to read, and the editors and publishers would perform the work of selection for you.

Public Libraries

Another cultural institution that stood at the junction of increased availability of fiction and the impulse to control reader access was the public library. In 1876, the year that the American Library Association (ALA) was formed, the federal government published a survey that counted 188 public libraries—free municipal institutions supported by general taxation—in eleven states. While the libraries were generally concentrated in urban centers and in the east, the ALA began to push for wider library coverage across socioeconomic and rural-urban divides. As Janice Radway points out, the meeting at which the ALA was founded in 1876 was also the occasion for Melvil Dewey's public unveiling of his system for organizing library collections, a system that "was reader rather than author driven" (1997, 137). The 1876 meeting was also consumed by a debate over which novels belonged in public libraries—if they belonged there at all. "Although all conference participants agreed that dime novels like the Deadwood Dick series and tabloids like the *Police Gazette* had no place in a 'public' library, they disagreed on novels of 'marginal quality' like *Lady Audley's Secret* (1862) by Mary Elizabeth Braddon and *Trial for Her Life* (1869) by Mrs. E. D. E. N. Southworth" (Wiegand 2009, 431).

The question of fiction was also a question about the very purpose of a library: was it an educational institution, or an entertainment venue? The answer to that question held considerable material significance for the future of librarianship, for the prestige of the librarian, and the professional requirements of the job. The librarian as gatekeeper to cultural values would require credentialing and would garner professional respect; the librarian as instrumental guardian of consumer-driven collections would need fewer skills. The slight consensus reached at the 1876 convention was that "the mass reading public was generally incapable of choosing its own reading materials judiciously. Libraries should intervene for the benefit of society by acquiring and prescribing the best reading materials for the public's consumption" (Wiegand 1986, 10). Melvil Dewey's ALA motto—"The best reading for the largest number at the least expense"—left open considerable room for debate on the parameters of "best reading." These determinations, which generally excepted dime novels and story-papers but were less clear-cut in cases such as E. D. E. N. Southworth, were left up to local librarians, although the ALA would come to offer guidance by way of a number of "best reading" lists. At the 1893 convention, held at the World's Fair in Chicago, the ALA displayed a "Model Library" of five thousand of the "best books" as selected by a committee of disciplinary experts, librarians, and library school students. Only 15 percent of the books in this collection were fiction, despite the fact that fiction accounted for 75 percent of circulation at most public libraries (Wiegand 2009, 436–37). The public's thirst for fiction thwarted the ALA librarians' desire for professionalization, although many hoped that fiction could become a "hook" for patrons who could form a "reading habit" and move on to more elevated material. The debates were largely waged in the realm of popular novels such as *Huckleberry Finn* and the works of "The Duchess" (Margaret Wolfe Hungerford). There was little debate about dime novels and story-papers, objections to which, as Michael Denning and Dee Garrison have observed, were lodged on moral, not aesthetic, grounds. Since "blood and thunder" stories had been cited as pernicious influences in several murder trials, they were considered dangerous reading for the young, and there was no assurance that parents would be able to keep them out of the hands of the innocents in their homes.

Small-town librarians, who were frequently closer to their patrons than the heads of the professional organizations, tended to be more accommodating of the public's tastes. In the Sage Public Library in Osage, Iowa, the most frequent users of the library were native-born, middle-class Protestants, presumably the same group most susceptible to the encomiums about "best reading" that were published in lifestyle magazines and in newspapers. And yet, the desire for more sensational or sentimental novels, of the sort that did not make the cut into the ALA *Catalog*, was only slightly diluted: Bertha M. Clay, "The Dutchess," and Miss Mulock rivaled the more ALA-sanctioned William Dean Howells, Walter Scott, and Wilkie Collins for popularity among that library's patrons. By 1923, roughly half of the citizens of Muncie, Indiana, had library cards, an increase from one-fifth of the population in 1890. Most of the books circulated from the library were fiction, although the Lynds note (with a slight note of reassurance) that, while in 1903 92 percent of the books taken out by adults were fiction, that number had decreased to 83 percent in 1923.

While libraries were public institutions, library infrastructure was largely funded through private philanthropy. Most donors gave locally, as when John Jacob Astor left $400,000 for a library in New York City, but Andrew Carnegie's legacy was national. Between 1880 and 1920, 1,697 Carnegie libraries were built in 1,400 communities across the United States. Carnegie's donations totaled more than $50 million, a largesse that served as a gesture of support for the culture of self-improvement to which he attributed his own success. He stated in 1900: "I choose free libraries as the best agencies for improving the masses of the people, because they give nothing for nothing. They only help those who help themselves. They never pauperize. They reach the aspiring, and open to these the chief treasures of the world—those steeped up in books. A taste for reading drives out lower tastes" (Augst 2001, 11). Mary Antin describes her young immigrant self viewing the public library as just such a refuge and an inspiration, as a "palace," but one that was built by civic funds: "Did I not say it was my palace? Mine, because I was a citizen; mine, though I was born an alien; mine, though I lived on Dover Street. My palace—*mine!*" (Sicherman 2010, 211; citing Antin 1912, 341). Immigrant children were frequently the most voracious patrons of the libraries in the major metropolitan areas, as Barbara Sicherman notes. The library offered a satisfying mix of guidance from librarians and ultimate freedom in the choice of books and in the possession of one's own library card. "In a study of twenty-six immigrant men and women educated in New York City public schools, '*Every* informant spoke lovingly of books and the library, and several recounted strategies they employed to up the two-book-per-visit quota'" (Sicherman 2010, 215; citing Brumberg 1986, 141). The pleasure of books became inextricably linked with a sense of national belonging through the use of public libraries, and prescription would ultimately not last long in the face of this heady mixture.

Not all of the potential patrons of public libraries were impressed by the civic and philanthropic largesse that hoped to direct and refine their reading; unions, community groups, and others who wanted to exert their own canons of taste inside their communities formed alternative libraries. In Alleghany, Pennsylvania, for example, workers "raised serious questions about who would control the library which Carnegie would offer the city" (Denning 1998 [1987], 50). Their skepticism was unsurprising given Carnegie's labor practices; surely it was difficult to imagine he had their best interests at heart when cornering the local market on print culture. Lacking conflict in their entertainment mission, union libraries frequently curated the kinds of collections eschewed by the public libraries: romance novels, sensation fiction, dime novels, and story-papers.

It would take a crisis requiring the entertainment of large numbers of citizens from all ranks of life to finally make the ALA similarly comfortable with the public library's hybrid function in society. The great fiction debate among librarians was resolved, for the most part, by default during the ALA campaign to provide novels to soldiers on the front during the First World War. While at home shelves were being purged of "questionable materials," such as German language texts and pacifist books, volunteers were donating scores of story-papers and light fiction for distribution to the military overseas. "Wartime experiences," Wiegand explains, "ultimately confirmed the American public library as a civic institution more in touch with popular reading tastes. Public library leaders finally came to accept the argument that the 'light' reading they had reluctantly provided for a half century to attract new patrons was, at worst, harmless" (2009, 448). The library, despite some of the efforts of well-meaning prescriptive librarians, had become a space for the profound democratization of reading.

Study Clubs, Political Clubs

One of the primary drivers of library patronage, according to the Lynds, was the ubiquitous ladies' civic book circle. Parodied in Sinclair Lewis's *Main Street* (1920) as the "Thanatopsis Club," book groups became popular social and intellectual outlets for women during the latter half of the nineteenth century. Elite white women had been meeting for book study in the United States since the early eighteenth century; such clubs were remarkable during the period between 1870 and 1940 primarily because of the increasing organization and institutionalization of the women's club movement. By 1906, five thousand clubs had joined the General Federation of Women's Clubs, and the actual number of regular meetings and study circles was clearly much higher. Barbara Sicherman and others have noted that such groups provided sympathetic companionship not always available in domestic reading settings; like-minded women could motivate each other to pursue intellectual projects that might be frowned upon at home. These clubs were also used as civic levers; women's clubs were active in voter registration drives, in movements supporting legislation significant to women, and, of course, in financing and maintaining civic literary and arts organizations. Libraries and magazines published lists of study suitable for women's clubs; many adhered to an order of business that saw one member responsible for leading discussion each week, writing a paper to present as oratory in front of the group. "Study" was a key word for women's clubs of this nature; even the fiction that came under consideration was read because of its cultural significance, and therefore the works suggested for such clubs tended not to be popular or recent offerings.

The guide to organizing a book club published in one issue of the *Ladies' Home Journal* in November, 1897, offers a glimpse into the more genteel and social manifestations of literary clubs. The author insists, "Long biographical sketches of authors, copied from reference books, and dry, critical essays, absorbed from other writers, with little or no individual thought, should be avoided. They give a semblance of literary study without the reality." Book clubs strove to offer women entrée into the world of serious intellectual work, during a period when "education was becoming especially important for middle-class Americans, yet women maintained a tenuous relationship to the institutions of higher learning" (Long 2009, 478). For women who were not able to complete high school, or to attend college, the book club was a welcome channel for intellectual energy. The intricate organization of women's clubs telegraphed the gravity of the endeavor to the often skeptical, even cynical, outside world; most clubs were conducted by Robert's Rules of Order, and many dispensed entirely with refreshments so as not to seem like social, rather than business, gatherings. In the late nineteenth century, white women's clubs were frequently engaged in reform work through either charitable outreach or political action; by the mid-twentieth century, such impulses had largely retreated in the face of external resistance. There are extensive extant women's club minutes available in local archives that are just now beginning to be mined for evidence of readerly activity; the resurgence of book clubs in the late-twentieth century offers a number of compelling parallels and contrasts to the work of white women a century ago. Unfortunately, the history of white women's book groups is frequently a history of racial exclusion, thus the necessity of separate treatment of African American women's groups.

Elizabeth McHenry's work on African American literary societies has emphasized the significance of communal reading for black Americans in the nineteenth and twentieth centuries. For middle- and upper-class blacks, such societies were "places of refuge for the self-improvement of their members" as well as "acts of resistance to the hostile racial climate that made the United States an uncomfortable and unequal place for all black Americans, regardless of their social or economic condition" (2002, 17). African American women's clubs were at the forefront of social justice movements during the Jim Crow era at the end of the nineteenth and beginning of the twentieth centuries. A well-documented example of such engagement is the Boston club, the Woman's Era, which was formed in 1893 and which published a nationally circulating newspaper. The *Women's Era* newspaper became an organ for connecting women's clubs across the United States, as it published the proceedings of far-flung clubs, enabled clubs to share tips for programs of study, and advertised the charitable work being done by women in other regions. The paper was both text and forum, embodying the ways that charity work and its publications were seen as integral parts of the total project of self-advancement through reading.

In 1895, the president of the Woman's Era called a convention in response to both a particularly vituperative attack against black woman's morality and to the exclusionary policies of many white women's clubs. This meeting, The Conference of Colored Women of America, eventually became the National Association of Colored Woman (NACW), and the *Woman's Era* became the group's national organ. Programs for the study of literature remained a central component of the work of NACW clubs. The newspaper often printed instructional guides and sample questions for the discussion of novels. The *Era* also had a literary columnist, Medora Gould, who sprinkled her text recommendations with literary gossip and encouraging words about the value of reading. While classic texts were central to this process, black women also contested the boundaries of what was considered "literature" by reading and promoting the work of African American and women authors. Although much of this reading, McHenry argues, "emphasized conformity to the dominant society's understanding of 'feminine sensibility' and its norms of manners and morals," this was not altogether negative, given the stereotypes against which her target audience had to signify. "A woman is most successful, Gould felt, when she transcends this conservative perspective and, through literary study, rises above the barrage of accusations of immorality and inferiority, and faces the complicated task of defining herself and her potential" (2009, 504–5). Carefully selected and conscientiously studied fiction, accompanied by judicious attention to history and biography, would achieve just such ennobling results.

The same impulses that created book clubs throughout the United States produced a club of a different kind in 1926, when Harry Scherman created the Book of the Month Club. The BOMC would act as both a filter and a procurer for the interested book purchaser who simply did not have time to do all of the careful research necessary to selecting the best books. Scherman would "manage the flood of books for his customers and thereby acclimate them to the hectic pace of modern life" (Radway 1997, 170). The BOMC recognized very explicitly the connection among reading, commerce, and culture, and proceeded from the assumption that anyone could acquire culture when given access to the right books. The BOMC's continued vibrancy through the last years of the twentieth century attests to the persistence of the ideals of reading and readership that were codified in the last half of the 1800s. As the general public came to imagine themselves as readers, and began to think of reading not as an activity exclusive to the elites, but useful for the instruction and betterment of everyone, the United States became a reading nation. Despite the myriad attempts to control and constrain readers' relationships to their novels, a concern about the potential reception activities of audiences tended to steer the marketplace, and to force accommodations on the part of the cultural arbiters who wanted to determine who should read and why.

Censors and Critics

The story of censorship struggles between 1870 and 1940 offers a thumbnail sketch of changing attitudes of and toward readers during the period. In addition to the informal means of attempting to direct reader behavior I have discussed above, there was an unspoken "gentleman's agreement" among the major publishing houses not to print "obscenities" that remained largely intact through the 1880s. As the publishing field opened to new companies, however, and as new philosophical and intellectual currents made their way to the United States from Europe and Asia, challenges to the genteel tradition that had not previously been able to achieve much exposure to the general public became more common. Even Hamilton Wright Mabie, in the pages of the *Ladies' Home Journal*, eventually came to accept some literary naturalism as acceptable reading; while he never conceded to Émile Zola, nor mentioned Theodore Dreiser, he did regularly recommend the gentler works of Frank Norris (*The Pit* [1902], if not *McTeague* [1899]) to his audience. After 1900, the bohemian intellectual tradition gained traction and readership; little magazines like *Little Review* and *Masses*, and H. L. Mencken's satirical *Smart Set*, entered the marketplace as countervoices to the large mainstream literary journals.

People concerned about the fate of the public's morals in the face of such challenges to cultural norms found a champion in Anthony Comstock and his New York Society for the Suppression of Vice. Comstock had begun the society in 1872, and lobbied Congress for the passage of the federal anti-obscenity laws that became known as the "Comstock Laws" in 1873. He was appointed a federal postal inspector, a post he would hold until 1905, and was initially quite successful in prosecuting censorship claims. While most of the objectionable texts were sexually explicit drawings and photographs, Comstock targeted unexpurgated editions of Continental writers like Balzac, Tolstoy, Rabelais, and even Ovid and Boccaccio. One notable action involved the federal banning of Tolstoy's *The Kreutzer Sonata*, which dealt with prostitution, in 1890.

Comstock was unable to suppress George Bernard Shaw's *Mrs. Warren's Profession* in New York in 1905 (it was closed in New Haven earlier that year), but his threats of prosecution prevented a British publishing house from printing Theodore Dreiser's *The Genius* in 1915. During the First World War, political censorship became more common after the passage of the 1917 Espionage Act and the 1918 Sedition Amendment, which targeted printed materials specifically. The Supreme Court upheld the two wartime acts in 1919, and Bolshevik and socialist movements in Eastern Europe continued to keep censors busy during the postwar years under the "clear and present danger" principle.

The 1920s became a battleground for censorship on a grand scale, with Comstock's successor, John Sumner, taking on fiction in particular with renewed energy. Although he failed initially to ban Radclyffe Hall's *The Well of Loneliness* (1928) in New York, he successfully prosecuted *Little Review* for publishing sections of the Nausicäa episode of James Joyce's *Ulysses* in 1918. After the *Little Review* published an excerpt from the book that included a masturbation scene, the New York Society for the Suppression of Vice took action to have the book banned in the United States; in 1921 at trial the text was declared obscene and was thereafter banned. Such successes emboldened the New England Watch and Ward Society in Boston, which, with the help of the Boston Police Department's clean books campaign, went after novels like Sinclair Lewis's *Elmer Gantry* (1927) and Dreiser's *An American Tragedy* (1925) (although the prosecution for the latter did not "stick"), alongside less-burnished titles like Elinor Glyn's *Three Weeks* (1907) and Floyd Dell's *Janet March* (1923). Although roundly criticized by the intellectual establishment, and by many publishers, the Watch and Ward and the police had the support of many nonacademic Bostonians. In 1929, the Watch and Ward successfully brought a case to the Massachusetts court that resulted in D. H. Lawrence's *Lady Chatterley's Lover* (1928) being declared obscene; objections to this ruling resulted in a liberalization of the Massachusetts obscenity statute in 1930, though it would take thirty more years for *Lady Chatterley* to be available in the United States.

The trend of legislative relaxation of censorship laws continued on the national level in the 1930s, when the Smoot-Hawley tariff included a provision for judicial review of all prior censorship rulings by the Customs Bureau in which works of "literary or scientific merit" could be returned to circulation. This set up the 1933 U.S. District case *United States v. One Book Called "Ulysses."* In a decision that termed the novel an "astonishing success" on formal and aesthetic grounds, Justice John Woolsey roundly rejected the Hicklin rule, which had been the prior standard for determining obscenity. The Hicklin rule had held that the work's effect on the most susceptible members of society should determine its evaluation; Woolsey countered that the effect on the average reader should be the determining factor. Where the Hicklin rule allowed for books to be judged based on isolated passages, Woolsey maintained that the work needed to be judged as a whole. Woolsey's reader response-centered decision concludes that the novel's overall impact is not prurient: "I am quite aware that owing to some of its scenes 'Ulysses' is a rather strong draught to ask some sensitive, though normal, persons to take. But my considered opinion, after long reflection, is that whilst in many places the effect of 'Ulysses' on the reader undoubtedly is somewhat emetic, nowhere does it tend to be an aphrodisiac. 'Ulysses' may, therefore, be admitted into the United States."

The significance of these censorship battles to the reader between 1870 and 1940 goes beyond the question of whether readers would have access to books, although that surely was one of the important considerations. Behind the shifting attitudes towards censorship were also shifting attitudes towards the "average reader's" ability to comprehend, evaluate, and interpret literature for her- or himself. Woolsey's decision, affirming as it did the average reader's sensibility, was likewise a reflection of a public becoming more accepting of the multiplicity of voices that comprised the national, and international, discourse.

II

THE NOVEL, 1870–1914

4

THE ADVENTURES
OF HUCKLEBERRY FINN

BY JONATHAN ARAC

Readers still love *Adventures of Huckleberry Finn* (1884), but this novel by Mark Twain first appeared as a leading part of a moment in history no longer ours. By the late nineteenth century, when *Huckleberry Finn* was published in Britain in 1884 and the United States in 1885, the novel in the United States was becoming a dominant cultural institution, which it had not been in 1850, when *The Scarlet Letter* was published. The novel as a genre took command of American literature: the lead in prestige and cultural authority shifted from orators such as Daniel Webster; historians such as George Bancroft; and poets, including Henry Wadsworth Longfellow and James Russell Lowell, to the novelist William Dean Howells. The later nineteenth century inaugurates what I call "the age of the novel" in the United States, which extends up till the middle of the twentieth century. This volume of the *Oxford History of the Novel in English* spans this age, and we live in its aftermath.

This American history of the novel is part of even a bigger picture. The novel in the West, especially Britain and France, became a going concern just as the term "literature" began to consolidate its modern meaning of imaginative belles-lettres (Williams 1976, 150–54). This was about 1830, right as print culture was becoming immensely more powerful. Ever since that time, the novel has taken up more space within literature, but since the early twentieth century, literature has become less important within culture as a whole, even in its elite sectors, as new media, including film, radio, television, and the e-world have rapidly risen to dominance. Twain's novel appeared when print was at its peak. For many admirers of *Huckleberry Finn* today, part of its power and charm arise because it reminds us of an age when literature counted, and novels were the heart of literature. When Ernest Hemingway asserted in 1935 that "all modern American literature" comes from *Huckleberry Finn*, Twain's novel was not yet a school text, and modern literature was a rebellious activity (*Green Hills of Africa*, ch. 1). The decades after the Second World War, when Twain's novel became almost universal in the classroom, from eighth grade through graduate school, were also the period when critics began to lament "the death of the novel." We know now that the novel did not die, but its total place in our lives changed, and *Huckleberry Finn* is the most widely shared souvenir of its earlier place.

Back around 1850, when Nathaniel Hawthorne, Herman Melville, and Harriet Beecher Stowe wrote their great novels, the novel as a form was culturally emergent; nowadays, it is culturally residual. Jonathan Franzen, whose novel *Freedom* (2010) was the biggest literary news in the United States of 2010–11, acknowledged in an interview that he writes novels for the limited number of people who like to read novels. It's just a niche. By contrast, in 1899, William Dean Howells, as America's most prolific and respected literary critic, a major novelist, and also one of Mark Twain's very closest friends, crafted a lecture on "Novel-Writing and Novel-Reading," which he took on tour to over fifty venues that year. Howells asserted: "Fiction is the great intellectual stimulus of our time. . . . It is ninety-nine chances out of a hundred that the book which at any given moment is making the world talk, and making the world think, is a novel. Within the last generation, I can remember only one book making the impression that a dozen of novels have each made."

From a different perspective, Henry James found a similar dominance. James was Howells's close friend and greatly admired fellow-novelist and critic, while Twain and James were not friends and did not care for each other's work. James wrote in his 1900 essay on "The Future of the Novel": "[T]he place occupied in the world by the prolonged prose fable has become, in our time, among the incidents of literature, the most surprising example to be named of swift and extravagant growth, a development beyond the measure of every early appearance. . . . The flood at present swells and swells, threatening the whole field of letters. . . . The book, in the Anglo-Saxon world, is almost everywhere, and it is in the form of the voluminous prose fable that we see it penetrate easiest and farthest."

James emphasizes not the novel's intellectual clout but rather its place within mass consumption, as part of a newly widespread literacy. Howells seems to be saying, "Good for the novel," while James, although himself even more committed to novel-writing than Howells was, expresses some alarm. But both concur on the centrality and dominance of the novel. This dominance may be seen in the extent to which even Twain—so much more at home in short or accumulative, unplotted forms, such as in *Innocents Abroad* (1869) and *Roughing It* (1872)—was drawn into the orbit of the novel, so that by the middle of the twentieth century *Huckleberry Finn*, a novel, had become the hyper-canonical work in Twain's corpus, not only the best known but also the most greatly admired, so much as almost to squeeze out anything else.

Unlike James and Howells, Twain did not devote much of his writing to literary criticism, but his most famous judgments on literature concerned the novel, specifically in his critique of the works most valued in literary culture at the time he was born. In *Life on the Mississippi* (1883) Twain passed severe judgment on what he considered the cultural power that had doomed the South to prefer empty pageantry to solid progress and clear thinking. The villain was the British novelist Sir Walter Scott. Twain concludes, "A curious exemplification of the power of a single book for good or harm is shown in the effects wrought by 'Don Quixote' and those wrought by [Scott's] 'Ivanhoe.' The first swept the world's admiration for the medieval chivalry-silliness out of existence; and the other restored it" (ch. 46).

Twain sees two novels as determining the fates of cultures. Never before the age of the novel would such claims have been made on behalf of this literary form. Twain condemns Scott even though, as Twain does not mention, Scott had pioneered the intensive fictional attention to nonstandard, backcountry cultures and languages that Twain glories in and delights us with. Scott lies behind Tom Sawyer's painfully foolish attempts to make romantic adventure out of freeing Jim but also behind Twain's goal of accurately depicting seven different varieties of American heartland dialect.

Huckleberry Finn requires its critics to think with multiple timescales. It lives in the twenty-first century, and it is also a historical relic from the age when the novel first began to dominate American culture. Twain's novel is now over 125 years old, yet it remains a vivid actuality in American life. As recently as 2011, a respected senior Twain scholar created controversy by producing an edition of *Huckleberry Finn* that replaces every one of the several hundred appearances of the word "nigger" (which has become a tabooed word in American culture) with the word "slave" (which no longer carries the force of abuse that marked its usage in the age of Shakespeare, or when the founders of what became the United States denounced British rule as slavery). This scholar hoped, according to *Publishers' Weekly*, to make the book accessible to younger readers, too immature to deal with the distress inflicted by the vulgar term of racial abuse. This is hyper-canonization at work: now it seems an important national goal to make sure young students read this particular novel; but long ago, *Huckleberry Finn* first appeared as a piece of entertainment sold by subscription. This move from commerce to canon is part of what Mark McGurl has called the "elevations" of the novel.

The prestige of *Huckleberry Finn* in turn stands behind continuing attention to the figure of Mark Twain himself. A century after his death in 1910, his unexpurgated *Autobiography* was for the first time published—though only the first volume of a promised three—and immediately rose to number two on the *New York Times* nonfiction bestseller list, where it remained for months. Why do people still care so much? Twain is a wonderful comic writer: from a cold start, any time he chooses, he can make you laugh in the space of ten lines. He is a savage satirist—it warms the heart to see fools and knaves so sharply skewered. And he writes sentences and sequences of astonishing beauty. He also was a leader in the mass commercialization of literature that James noted and feared. Samuel Clemens's pen name is not simply a pseudonym: it is a registered trademark. He founded a publishing company, Charles L. Webster and Company, headed by his nephew, to ensure maximal control over all aspects of the production and marketing of his work.

To understand the special power of *Huckleberry Finn* requires critical attention to Twain's success in placing the novel within a structure of national nostalgic self-conception. The novel depends on multiplied timescales: it offers the vivid immediacy of Huck's experience in the 1840s, but already when the book was published in 1884, Huck's world was a culture closed into the past by the Civil War, which had ended the regime of chattel slavery. Therefore, all readers have held an ironic relationship toward Huck: everyone who has read the novel knows things that Huck does not. Yet Huck seems to know something we do not; the novel seems to offer access to a wishful memory of earliness, not so much innocence as original primevality. The recovery of this earliness through *Huckleberry Finn*, over the long history of its reading, may foster a delusory complacency but it may also serve transformative purposes. This double action shows in the way Americans have responded to the issues of race in *Huckleberry Finn*. For some the book has provided an alibi, allowing the reader to feel that the nation had already solved the problems of race back in the 1880s, or even the 1840s, as shown by Twain's, or Huck's, commitment to freedom for Jim and gradual recognition of Jim's full humanity, across the barrier of color prejudice. Half-recognized feelings of this kind help explain why the period of the novel's hyper-canonization coincides with the rise of the Civil Rights Movement in the United States. On the other hand, some readers have been moved by the book's representations to take new and more capaciously egalitarian views than those in which they had been raised.

During Twain's lifetime, his book was quickly beloved but did not provoke much discussion. It readily sat within the emergent genre of the "boy's book," and it unsurpassedly evoked a lost way of life: small town, not city; steamboat, not railroad. Among the generations of writers born while Twain was still alive, who formed the literary culture of the United States in the first half of the twentieth century, *Huckleberry Finn* became an indispensable exemplar for two reasons. Ideologically it served the critique of the small town (as in Sherwood Anderson's *Winesburg, Ohio* [1919]) and of genteel philistinism (as in Sinclair Lewis's *Main Street* [1920]). Artistically, its prose became talismanic. Against Van Wyck Brooks, who understood Mark Twain as part of the genteel tradition, despite himself, because he compromised with propriety and capital, Henry Louis Mencken appropriated Twain for new values and Ernest Hemingway for a new prose. The claim for an American vernacular language, made far more stridently by later critics than Twain ever did himself, understood itself as democratic, in a popular-front way, but it also served less attractive exclusivist nationalisms. Even though Twain himself and in his work was in many ways antiracist, antinationalist, anti-imperialist, and cosmopolitan, the period in which *Huckleberry Finn* rose to transcendent standing within the culture of the United States coincides with the period of exclusionary restrictions on immigration (1924–65), and the claims for his vernacular stood against what has now become known as "ethnic modernism," practiced by immigrants or their children.

Because *Huckleberry Finn* has stood so high in American culture, scholarship has devoted extraordinary energy to analyzing every detail of its emergence. The Mark

Twain Project carried on at the Bancroft Library of the University of California, Berkeley, where Twain's literary remains are archived, has received funding from the National Endowment for the Humanities continuously since the mid-1960s. In recent years, a long-lost portion of Mark Twain's manuscript text of *Huckleberry Finn* came to light, and the standard scholarly edition has made available for easy study, in an inexpensive reading edition, the revisions by which Twain achieved his greatest effects.

The first words of *Huckleberry Finn* to appear in print in the United States, in December, 1884, were selected by Richard Watson Gilder, the editor of the nation's leading high-culture magazine, *Century Magazine*. This magazine illustrates what I mean by the age of the novel. In February 1885, along with its third excerpt from *Huckleberry Finn*, it was also running serializations of novels by James (*The Bostonians*) and Howells (*The Rise of Silas Lapham*). This is the novel burgeoning to fill the space of literature within the domain of culture. *Century* was highly popular—its monthly sales of some 200,000 far exceeded the number of copies Twain initially sold of his novel (around 40,000), let alone the sales numbers of Howells or James. Twain feared that serializing the novel would cost him sales of the complete work, but he gave Gilder the chance to read the novel in proof and to choose material to excerpt, while American publication of *Huckleberry Finn* was delayed because a craftsman in the print shop had obscenely altered an illustration.

Gilder decided to lead with the Grangerford-Shepherdson feud, but first he had to introduce the reader to Huck and Jim. Gilder removed the opening of chapter nineteen from its place following the feud and instead made it inaugurate the sequence. It illustrates a wonderful continuity in critical response that the passage Gilder chose is still considered one of the peaks of Twain's accomplishment, but it also shows the way in which Twain's work has been taken up in cultural battles not necessarily close to his own heart. Back in the 1950s, halfway between Gilder and us, the major Americanist critic Leo Marx chose the opening of chapter nineteen as the basis for claims concerning Twain's vernacular style—yet the passage had been first selected as the keynote of *Huckleberry Finn* by the editor most identified with the genteel tradition. Americans try to make Twain serve their arguments, but Twain's genius frequently puts him on both sides at the same time.

In *Century*, Twain wrote a brief head note to prepare readers for what followed. In Twain's note, he uses the polite term, not the rudely abusive term, to designate Jim's race, although the term is not capitalized, which by the mid-twentieth century would have made it, too, offensive: "The negro Jim is escaping from slavery in Missouri, and Huck Finn is running away from a drunken father, who maltreats him. The two fugitives are floating down the Mississippi on a fragment of a lumber-raft, doing their voyaging by night and hiding themselves and the raft in the day-time." So much for Huck's story; his voice is what lingers.

When the impending dawn forces Huck and Jim to pull over and hide, they:

> slid into the river and had a swim, so as to freshen up and cool off; then we set
> down on the sandy bottom where the water was about knee deep, and watched the
> daylight come. Not a sound, anywheres—perfectly still—just like the whole world
> was asleep, only sometimes the bull-frogs a-cluttering, maybe. The first thing to
> see, looking away over the water, was a kind of dull line—that was the woods on
> t'other side—you couldn't make nothing else out; then a pale place in the sky; then
> more paleness spreading around; then the river softened up, away off, and warn't
> black any more, but gray; you could see little dark spots drifting along, ever so far
> away—trading scows, and such things; and long black streaks—rafts; sometimes
> you could hear a sweep screaking; or jumbled up voices, it was so still, and sounds
> come so far; and by and by you could see a streak on the water which you know by
> the look of the streak that there's a snag there in a swift current which breaks on it
> and makes that streak look that way; and you see the mist curl up off of the water,
> and the east reddens up, and the river, and you make out a log cabin in the edge of
> the woods, away on the bank on t'other side of the river, being a wood-yard, likely,
> and piled by them cheats so you can throw a dog through it anywheres; then the
> nice breeze springs up, and comes fanning you from over there, so cool and fresh,
> and sweet to smell, on account of the woods and the flowers; but sometimes not
> that way, because they've left dead fish laying around, gars, and such, and they do
> get pretty rank; and next you've got the full day, and everything smiling in the sun,
> and the song-birds just going it!
>
> A little smoke couldn't be noticed, now, so we could take some fish off of the
> lines, and cook up a hot breakfast. And afterwards we would watch the lonesome-
> ness of the river, and kind of lazy along, and by and by lazy off to sleep. Wake up,
> by and by, and look to see what done it, and maybe see a steamboat, coughing along
> up stream, so far off towards the other side you couldn't tell nothing about her only
> whether she was stern-wheel or side-wheel; then for about an hour there wouldn't
> be nothing to hear nor nothing to see—just solid lonesomeness. Next you'd see a
> raft sliding by, away off yonder, and maybe a galoot on it chopping, because they're
> most always doing it on a raft; you'd see the axe flash, and come down—you don't
> hear nothing; you see that axe go up again, and by the time it's above the man's
> head, then you hear the k'chunk!—it had took all that time to come over the water.
> So we would put in the day, lazying around, listening to the stillness. (ch. 19)

Only after nearly a decade working off and on at the book did Twain figure out the
details it took to make Huck sound so natural (for this passage, the textual editors
Fischer and Salamo print facing texts of manuscript and final text). We care so much
about Mark Twain and *Huckleberry Finn* that huge investments have been made to
provide this new information, and the details are spectacular, perhaps none more so
than transforming what Twain originally wrote as "the sound, sharp and clear" into
a single word, which appears in no dictionary but electrifies the passage: "k'chunk!"

The second paragraph of the passage strikes a note that could be imagined as voicing a shrill denunciation from Huck's conscience: "lazy, lazy, lazy." But Twain makes the word *lazy* function—very unusually—as a verb, not an adjective, and each of its three usages in this paragraph was a late addition to the final text: "dream along" changes to "lazy along"; "nod off to sleep" becomes "lazy off to sleep"; "dozing, dreaming" turns to "lazying around." "Nod" and "dream" are perfectly ordinary verbs, but the stakes are raised by "lazy," which replaces each of them. It's a distinctively deviant usage; Twain deliberately repeats the same word twice with only a dozen words intervening, suggesting a writer unschooled in the rhetorical art of variation; and the term "lazy" introduces a moral frame. Like so much in *Huckleberry Finn*, this frame is there to be broken. "Protestant work ethic be dammed," Twain suggests, "this lazy life is the good life."

Twain greatly enhanced in his revisions Huck's freedom from the sound of the schoolroom grammar-teacher: with a shift still controversial among grammarians into the late twentieth century, "like" replaces "as if"; Latinate "forest" twice yields to the Germanic "woods"; "nothing" replaces "anything" to make a double negative, a grammatical shift that happens twice more through revisions in the second paragraph; "warn't" replaces "wasn't"; "off of" is more informal than "from" in the first paragraph and than simply "off" in the second paragraph. Perhaps most important are four major insertions: the added words not only fill in the scene but also strongly emphasize a language that follows different principles of construction from those of school rhetoric. Silence is broken by "only sometimes the bull-frogs a-cluttering, maybe." Beyond the backwoods diction of "a-cluttering," "maybe" duplicates the work of "sometimes," while creating a rhythmical effect signaled in print by its standing alone between a comma and a period.

The description of the streak and snag gains rhythm and punch. Twain's early draft of the passage read originally "see the ruffled streak on the water that the current breaking past a snag makes." The fancy word "ruffled," which condenses an impression, disappears, blown open into the materials from which the impression is composed: "which you know by the look of the streak that there's a snag there in the swift current which breaks on it and makes that streak look that way." Twain, as Huck, repeats "streak" twice in two lines, repeats "that" twice in four words, and adds three more active verbs—"know," "breaks," "look." The complexity of Twain's working with moral frames emerges through his adding in revision the wood-yard "cheats" and the stench of "dead fish." The insistence on "lazy" stood against conventional morality, but these new elements protect his scene from any simple idealization.

Huck responds in this sunrise sequence with all his senses: you can taste the fish for breakfast; smell the flowers, or the rotting gars; feel the cool water, or the sand underfoot; hear the quiet, broken by frogs a-cluttering, sweeps screaking, steamboats coughing, or galoots k'chunking; and above all, the many things he and Jim see. What might be summarized as a single, four-letter word—"dawn"—opens into an extended process, punctuated by emergences. First a "dull line," then a "pale place," next "little dark spots" and "long black streaks," before the "east reddens up" and images can at last be categorized more precisely as "mist" and a "log cabin." The process is registered through a second person narration: "you couldn't make nothing else out" but then "by and by you could see." Together with the "we" of Huck and Jim, the reader is invited also to share the experience of wonder and pleasure.

Mark Twain naturalizes, as part of the American frontier landscape taken in and uttered by an uneducated youth, the techniques of impressionist prose so important in Western art writing from his older French contemporary Gustave Flaubert to his younger Polish/British contemporary Joseph Conrad and beyond. The privilege of sensitive spectatorship is extended from the leisure class down the social scale, bringing to fulfillment an experiment that in the early nineteenth-century British poetry of William Wordsworth had met a far more mixed response. The risk, overcome by Twain, is that the supposedly natural perceiving consciousness will seem to be ventriloquized by the highly cultivated author. Marks of the authorial vocabulary and sensibility show up in the abstract nouns so important in composing the passage: "paleness," "lonesomeness," and "stillness."

The flow of language is the sign of Huck's voice, felt in his words and intonation, while the author has constructed the sentences, in all their intricacy. The second paragraph of the quotation above, beginning with "a little smoke," starts with a rather short sentence and moves through three sentences of increasing length, until concluding with the shortest in the sequence, "So we would put in the day, lazying around, listening to the stillness." The first paragraph features a Faulkner-length sentence 269 words long (starting with "the first thing to see" and running to the end), splattered with commas to set its micro-rhythms and built sequentially onto eleven semicolons, the punctuation mark most associated with high literacy.

Twain uses the story situation to motivate Huck's hyper-attentiveness. He and Jim are on the lam, danger lurks anywhere, so they need to notice everything. Hiding during the day enforces an idleness usually enjoyed only by rich people. The euphoric narration transfigures a state of deprivation ("nothing to hear nor nothing to see") into satisfying plenitude ("just solid lonesomeness"). To call an abstraction "solid" is quite a figure of speech—technically, catachresis—but who notices?

Huckleberry Finn stays in readers' memories, and it attracts critics' attention, not so much evenly or as a whole, but rather through its spectacular parts, such as this sunrise passage, or the sequence in chapter 31, discussed below, in which Huck broods over whether to help Jim or to try to return him to home and slavery. The novel does not have a plot in any Aristotelian sense. From the opening in Missouri, through the trip downriver, to the ending, some change of fortune occurs—Jim is freed, and Huck is liberated from anxiety about his alcoholic, abusive father. Yet the book's narrative economy muffles the process by which these changes occur. As in Shakespeare's comedies, both Jim's manumission and the death of Huck's father are revealed only in the very last pages of the book. They happened some time earlier and were concealed, Jim's freedom by Tom Sawyer so as to allow for the charade of

Jim's "evasion" from imprisonment, and Huck's father's death by Jim, for reasons left to the reader's speculation (ch. 39). So all that Huck did on Jim's behalf has not been essential to this plot. Jim was already free, and Tom Sawyer would in any case have arrived with the news at the farm where Jim was held.

The novel operates discontinuously, by repetition and difference more than by beginning, middle, and end. The strongest moments of the book, including the sunrise passage, are sublime, as defined by the ancient Greek critic Longinus. By sublime, Longinus does not mean highfalutin. The sublime may arise from the representation of silence and from terse, simple language. Longinus praises the opening of the Hebrew Bible: "'Let there be light,' and there was light." The sublime means simply the greatest literary experience. It does not depend on unity. Like a "whirlwind" or thunderbolt it tears up any smooth pattern or texture, so it stands out from the work in which it occurs. Longinus's key term in Greek is "*ekstasis*," or getting out of one's place, a "transport" into a new state or position.

This out-of-place-ness operates in several registers of the novel. Its title term, "adventures," suggests a picaresque novel, which involved roguery but also comedy. A "*pícaro*," in the earlier Spanish novel, was a social outcast and also geographically mobile, both characteristics of Huck. Huck's distance from the norms of his time brings him closer to us. His alienation from his society seems a strength rather than ground for pathos. There is also a trick here to flatter the reader: if Huck is uncultured, he is therefore, by a common logic, more natural, and if he is also more like us, then we allow ourselves credit for his good nature. Huck is not wholly formed by his culture, yet he is shown to believe in the social customs governing slavery, even though he breaks them in allying himself with Jim, and at several points acting to protect Jim. Readers applaud his actions and laugh at his self-doubts and self-castigations. The worse he thinks he is, the better we know he is.

Late in the book, this pattern of opposites stretches its farthest. Jim has been separated from Huck and betrayed; he is locked up on a farm way down river from his home in Missouri. Huck imagines sending a letter back to the owner Jim has run away from. That way, if he must be reenslaved, at least he can be reunited with his family and a familiar community. But then Huck realizes that if he returns home with Jim, he will be known as someone who helped a slave to escape. Huck's "conscience" kicks in, and his mind becomes a theater in which several versions of small town Missouri, and all-American, religious talk play themselves out. He feels compelled to write the letter, and afterward he purrs in the voice of revival testimony, "I felt good and all washed clean of sin for the first time." But Huck can't stay saved. Once he has written the letter, he remembers all that Jim meant to him on their travels together. As this string of memories unrolls, Huck decides to help Jim escape again. The language of this decision gains force from its sudden snap back to the discarded religious idiom. Huck concludes, "All right, then, I'll *go* to hell" (ch. 31). This moment has become talismanic for an important tradition of criticism.

Huck melodramatically, in a gestural extravagance equal and opposite to what he rejects, chooses hell over heaven, Jim over the society that enslaves him, and yet he does it in language that seems, to modern readers, racist. He calls Jim a "nigger." This term was not nearly so essential to Samuel Clemens's speech, in his adult life, as it is to Huck's. Over the course of the book, the term appears hundreds of times. The word is part of the historical and social distancing between author and character, and yet the word is not now a dead relic of slavery, nor was it when the book was written. Rather, the word did and still does active damage in the long working-through of a legacy of brutal inhumanity. Twain made great art out of dreadful history, and his work survives its time of writing, but it bears the scars of a racist society. Its language implies a literary world in which even so great a spirit as Mark Twain did not imagine that African Americans would form a consequential part of his readership.

The character of Jim presents some of the same problems. Jim is shown as a brave man and a good man, and at moments he and Huck are treated as equals. Yet the representation of Jim also draws on comic traditions that were highly disrespectful to the African Americans that made up their subject matter. In particular, American minstrel shows, an immensely popular form of entertainment from the 1840s through the rest of century, offered musical numbers and comic sketches in which white performers, in blackface makeup, masqueraded as African Americans.

Blackface minstrelsy underlies some of the way Jim appears (beyond Twain's prose, also in the original illustrations by E. W. Kemble), but worse trouble comes in the long sequence that ends the book. Tom Sawyer arrives from Missouri to the place where Jim is being held. Tom knows that Jim is now "free as any cretur that walks this earth" (ch. 42), because the woman who had owned him has died and emancipated him in her will. But Tom insists on staging elaborate schemes "to set a nigger free that was already free," casting Jim as a noble prisoner, and Huck and Tom as his rescuers (ch. "the last"). This scheming is not the book's best comedy, and it leads to "a raft of trouble": Tom gets shot and Jim risks his freedom to save him (ch. 42).

Huckleberry Finn contains tensions that arise from its compromises. This does not make it unique among novels of the United States or of the world. Novels are acts of communication and also items of commerce. They must answer to authorities different from those of the author. It is a wonderful, and yet rather puzzling, feature of liberal culture that America's most beloved novel, the most American of novels, savagely mocks life in the United States. Through Huck's narration, the small town decencies in Missouri seem confining, even pointless, compared to the pleasures of hanging out with friends or fishing. And on the river, Huck encounters no society, except Jim's, preferable to what he left behind. The Southern gentry life of the Grangerfords is appealing, until he realizes that they are caught up in a senseless and deadly feud with the Shepherdsons, and in Arkansas, which was in Twain's America a byword for rural idiocy, the riverfront life is not only murderous but also mean spirited. The King and Duke provide laughs, but they also sell Jim back into slavery.

The American institution that *Huckleberry Finn* most unremittingly attacks is the Christian church. Twice the novel stages false scenes of conversion, the pretense of a sinner redeemed, but Huck's pap and the King are just fooling the holy to make a buck. When Huck decides to go to hell, it is against the voices of religion. Far more than it fosters progressive interraciality, *Huckleberry Finn* attacks the social cowardice of the religion that was in Huck's 1840s and Twain's 1880s and that remains, in the twenty-first century, the core religion of the United States, a Bible-based Christianity committed to the drama of the individual soul choosing heaven or hell. Twain represents this religion as ignorant and, above all, selfish.

Huckleberry Finn glories in its power to make any venerated cultural institution appear ridiculous—from the Christianity of Sunday school, to the stuffy language of grammar school, to the funereal poetry of genteel society, to the excitements of romance fiction. Just as Twain mocked Scott, while also exploiting his heritage, so too with Shakespeare. The fraudulent Duke presents "Hamlet's soliloquy" with physical actions that butcher the text as badly as his memory does. He "strikes a most noble attitude . . . and then he begins to rip and rave and grit his teeth—and after that, all through his speech he howled and spread around and swelled up his chest, and just knocked the spots out of any acting ever *I* see before" (ch. 21). Huck quotes the speech, which mangles together *Hamlet* and *Macbeth*:

> To be or not to be; that is the bare bodkin
> That makes calamity of so long life;
> For who would fardels bear, till Birnam wood do come to Dunsinane,
> But that the fear of something after death
> Murders the innocent sleep,
> Great nature's second course,
> And makes us rather sling the arrows of outrageous fortune
> Than fly to others that we know not of. (ch. 21)

The nineteenth-century adulation of Shakespeare helped to make possible the age of the novel. It provided resources for the emergence of the novel by defining the characteristics of literature, which novels aspired to reach and then to transcend.

It is amazing that an English writer of playscripts, an actor and theatrical entrepreneur, became, centuries after he lived, an international model for what it means to be an author as a creative genius. This transformation of Shakespeare, moving him from the stage to the page, underwrites the modern Western idea of literature. The print monument of the first folio made this possible, after the folio was intellectually reprocessed into the scripture on which literature is founded, starting in the eighteenth century and running into the nineteenth. Shakespeare was canonized, nationalized, and universalized, as part of various larger cultural struggles for authority. This is why the Shakespearean travesty in the performance of the King and Duke is so hilarious. Everyone reading *Huckleberry Finn* has already learned that Shakespeare stands for the greatness of literature, and therefore the mockery of his immortal words thrills us by its transgression. It also allows us to glory in our cultural superiority to these backwoods buffoons who can't even keep straight the most famous passages. Through Huck, Twain asks: "You think Shakespeare is so great? Watch me pull monkeyshines on him." By fooling with Shakespeare's genius, Twain affirms his own, and we concur, keeping the novel alive.

5

THE NOVEL
AND THE RECONSTRUCTION
AMENDMENTS

BY JEANNINE MARIE DELOMBARD

Together, the Thirteenth, Fourteenth, and Fifteenth Amendments to the US Constitution (1865–70) sought to resolve questions that had been posed at the founding of the republic, debated throughout the slavery crisis, and reframed by the Civil War and Emancipation. What does it mean to be an American? What rights and duties attach to such a communal identity? Where does mutual accountability begin and end? How should responsibility for others be assessed and enforced?

A brief survey of the novels published between the Civil War and the First World War suggests that, rather than putting these questions to rest, the Reconstruction Amendments complicated them in new, often surprising ways. Whether written by African American clubwoman Pauline Hopkins, Yankee civil rights lawyer Albion Tourgée, or white supremacist Thomas Dixon, the romances of the period turn on questions of duty and obligation. With its penchant for long-winded intellectual debates and political speeches, the romance tended to propose explicit solutions to pressing social and political problems. But literary form did not follow political doctrine. Continuing the romance tradition of Harriet Beecher Stowe and John Pendleton Kennedy in the face of the more fashionable realism of William Dean Howells and Henry James, "novels of purpose" by Tourgée, Hopkins, and Dixon stymie any critical effort to align generic medium with political message. At the same time, even as they eschewed didacticism, realist and naturalist authors from Howells, James, and Edith Wharton to Theodore Dreiser and Frank Norris used the novel's intimate settings to cast what elsewhere appeared as predicaments of racial and national liability in personal and familial terms. Structuring the plots and preoccupying the characters of the era's fiction, uncertainties over individual and collective accountability cut across the contemporaneous formal debate over the novel.

This intersection was most visible in the pages of the monthly reviews, where serialized novels often ran alongside poetry, historical essays, and critical pieces (on serialized novels and monthly reviews, see Chapters 3 and 18 in this volume). Consider the remarkable volume of *Century Magazine* that spanned from November 1884 to April 1885. Introducing readers to Henry James's *The Bostonians* (1886), Mark Twain's *The Adventures of Huckleberry Finn* (1884), and William Dean Howells's *The Rise of Silas Lapham* (1885), the volume's greatest draw was its lavishly illustrated "Battles and Leaders of the Civil War" series. Immersing themselves in the new realist fiction while contemplating the ongoing debate over Reconstruction, readers of the January 1885 issue could turn from the Grangerford-Shepherdson feud and Silas Lapham's plans for his new Back Bay house to George Washington Cable's sober treatment of "[t]he greatest social problem before the American people to-day . . . the presence among us of the negro" ("Freedman's Case in Equity"). *Century* published "The Freedman's Case in Equity" just as Cable was wrapping up a lecture tour with Twain (in the person of Samuel Clemens) that was designed to consolidate his national reputation as the author of *The Grandissimes* (1880) and other romances of Creole life. Four months later, *Century Magazine* printed *Atlanta Constitution* editor Henry W. Grady's "In Plain Black and White. A Reply to Mr. Cable" on the page following the *Bostonians* installment in which reformer Olive Chancellor fatefully introduces her conservative Mississippi cousin Basil Ransom to Verena Tarrant. That politics and aesthetics were intertwined, if not clearly aligned, is suggested as much by local colorist Cable's polemic on behalf of African American civil rights as by the juxtaposition of Grady's laissez-faire defense of the New South with James's portrait of New England reform in decline.

Anxious lest the *Century's* readers had been "enchained by [Cable's] picturesque style," Grady commenced his attack on the Louisiana-born Confederate veteran's "repentant sentences" by noting that "in this article, as in his works, the singular tenderness and beauty of which have justly made him famous, Mr. Cable is sentimental rather than practical" ("In Plain Black and White"). It was a cheap shot: Cable's incisive Reconstruction essays would soon be collected in *The Silent South* (1885) and *The Negro Question* (1888). But launched from the pages of *Century*, Grady's verbal missile may have hit home critically as well as politically. The Howells, James, and Twain novels currently appearing in the magazine each championed the "practical" over the "sentimental," often by lampooning a "style" that, if not exactly "picturesque," was very much associated with Cable's preferred romance form.

Aesthetics circled back to politics when Cable's fellow "romancist," Albion Tourgée, criticized the irresponsible realism of "Mr. Howells and Mr[.] James" in short essays for *Forum* and *North American Review* ("The South as a Field of Fiction," "The 'Claim' of Realism"). Remembered today as Homer Plessy's eloquent lawyer in the landmark segregation case, *Plessy v. Ferguson* (1896), the white Union veteran and carpetbagging North Carolina judge was best known to contemporaries as the author of two widely read novels about Reconstruction, *A Fool's Errand* (1879) and *Bricks without Straw* (1880). Countering Henry James's attenuation of the novel's moral purpose in "The Art of Fiction" (1885), Tourgée deplores the realist rejection of any "appeal to sympathy" in the authorial endeavor of "rendering [life] 'interesting'" (Tourgée, "Realism"; James, "Art"). Having devoted his own fiction to what Cable had proclaimed "a moral responsibility on the whole nation never to lose sight of the results of African-American slavery until they cease to work mischief and injustice," Tourgée criticized the realist novel for actively discouraging just such a sense of accountability ("Freedman's"). Tourgée opposed this new form of prose fiction "not because it inclines men to do evil, but because it does an infinitely worse thing in inclining them to do nothing." (Stowe, recall, had concluded her anti-slavery classic, *Uncle Tom's Cabin* [1852], with the provocative query, "But, what can any one individual do?" [ch. 45]). In an 1889 *North American Review* essay, "The 'Claim' of Realism," Tourgée argued that the "idealist" author of romance may portray "degradation so terrible as to make his reader cower and tremble with disgust and shame" but does so "to leave the impression that it is not incurable; that vice exists because harmful forces have usurped healthy lives, and that the responsibility for social evils does not rest altogether with their victims."

Grady had commenced his *Century* essay by observing that the recent Supreme Court decision in the *Civil Rights Cases* (discussed below) had "deepen[ed] the responsibility of the South," requiring that "[w]here it has been silent, it now should speak." When, at the end of the piece, Grady's feminized white South does speak, "she" takes full responsibility for the national dilemma of Reconstruction, saying calmly but authoritatively, "Leave this problem to my working out." But this growing sense that "the Southern question . . . must be 'left to solve itself,'" as Cable put it his 1888 *Forum* essay, "A Simpler Southern Question," troubled both Cable and Tourgée. Three years earlier, in his 1885 *Century* essay, "The Freedman's Case in Equity," Cable had reminded his fellow Americans of their accountability for post-Emancipation racial justice, insisting that although "these responsibilities may not fall everywhere with the same weight . . . they are nowhere entirely removed." Whether it was the task of the novel to address or even assert such liabilities was precisely the matter in dispute between "idealist" Tourgée and realists like James and Howells.

Divided as they were in their views of politics, literature, and the correct relationship between the two, Grady, Cable, and Tourgée were united by their common focus on questions of responsibility. Taking this shared preoccupation as a point of departure, this chapter pursues a rather unconventional approach to the Reconstruction Amendments' legal and cultural significance by considering them in light of the contemporaneous development of tort law—in part as a replacement for Cable's increasingly outmoded "equity." ("A 'tort' is simply the Norman word for a 'wrong,'" notes legal historian Edward G. White, explaining that "'torts' have typically been distinguished from crimes and from 'wrongs' identified with contractual relations"; in short, "tort law . . . is concerned with civil wrongs not arising from contracts" [2003, xxiii].) Of particular interest will be Samuel D. Warren and Louis D. Brandeis's 1890 discovery of a tort "Right to Privacy." Articulated in their

Harvard Law Review essay as "the right to be left alone," Warren and Brandeis's brief against invasions of privacy resonated powerfully with the laissez-faire rhetoric many Americans deployed in response to questions of personal, racial, and national responsibility during and after Reconstruction. Viewing the Constitution's new civil rights regime from the perspective of the emergent legal field of civil wrongs elucidates a shared set of concerns about individual and collective answerability otherwise obscured by novelists' competing formal approaches and conflicting political positions. If in nineteenth-century American legal discourse "responsibility talk was at least as common as rights talk" (Blumenthal 2008, 185), novels published at the end of this era indicate that an important cultural effect of the Reconstruction Amendments was to translate the official, constitutional language of rights into civil law's idiom of responsibility and dignity. Intensifying the novel's generic predisposition to probe the most intimate spaces of personal and domestic life, the recent turn of American fiction to ever more elusive interior realms enabled the realist novel to privatize and denationalize questions of accountability left unresolved by the Civil War.

The Reconstruction Amendments

Originating in works by lawyer-novelists Royall Tyler, Hugh Henry Brackenridge, and Charles Brockden Brown, the American novel contributed to the popular legal consciousness that pervaded local as well as national culture. Noting in his 1835 *Democracy in America* that the "influence of . . . legal habits" extended well beyond law's institutions, authorities, and practitioners, French political observer Alexis de Tocqueville found that "all parties are obliged to borrow the ideas, and even the language, usual in judicial proceedings in their daily controversies," with the effect that "the language of the law . . . becomes, in some measure, a vulgar tongue" (ch. 16). As if to demonstrate Tocqueville's claim that "the spirit of the law . . . gradually penetrates . . . into the bosom of society, where it descends to the lowest classes" (ch. 16), formerly enslaved authors Frederick Douglass and Harriet Jacobs entered the antebellum slavery controversy by fashioning themselves as "eye-witness[es]" (Douglass, *Narrative,* ch. 6) and their autobiographical narratives as "testimony" (Jacobs, *Incidents,* Preface) against "the perpetrators of slaveholding villainy" (Douglass, *My Bondage,* ch. 23). While aggrieved slave victims and their abolitionist advocates appealed to the popular tribunal for redress, fiction writers contributed to the period's emergent rights discourse. Faced with the Constitution's failure to delineate the contours of US citizenship, novelists ranging from Nathaniel Hawthorne and Herman Melville to William Wells Brown and Harriet Wilson joined legislators and judges in "constituting Americans" (to borrow Priscilla Wald's apt phrase). In such a literary climate, to call the defeat of the Confederacy a "victory of LAW," as Herman Melville did in *Battle-Pieces* (1866), may have been an exercise in ironic overstatement, but, Deak Nabers contends, many of Melville's generation saw in the Reconstruction Amendments "a victory of legal process in general and American constitutional law . . . in particular" (2006, viii).

Commencing on January 31, 1865, with Congress's passage of the Thirteenth Amendment (abolishing slavery), this ambitious legislative endeavor culminated in the February 2, 1870 ratification of the Fifteenth Amendment (extending suffrage to virtually all adult male citizens, including former slaves). Read within the narrow margins of the written Constitution, the enactments did nothing less than transform human property into enfranchised US citizens. But read against the swiftly changing, often bloody, backdrop of late nineteenth- and early twentieth-century America, the Reconstruction Amendments were at once less transformative and more far-reaching than the brief lines of legal text would suggest. At the heart of this contradiction was the Fourteenth Amendment.

For many, the Fourteenth Amendment has come to epitomize Reconstruction as a political and social undertaking that was at once cruelly protracted and dangerously expeditious. By 1865 it had become apparent that any effort to rebuild the union must complete the process begun by Lincoln's Emancipation Proclamation (1863). To that end, the Thirteenth Amendment stated that "neither slavery nor involuntary servitude, except as a punishment for crime . . . shall exist within the United States." Typical of the initial, "Presidential" phase of Reconstruction, the amendment appeared to solve one of the nation's most pressing problems while creating countless others of equal, if not greater, urgency. Silent regarding the status of the newly freed people, the Thirteenth Amendment also neglected that of the larger African American collective, whose citizenship had been denied in *Dred Scott v. Sandford* (1857). More broadly, the amendment failed to address how abolition would transform the original Constitution, which had been tacitly constructed to accommodate slavery. Prior to the Civil War, political theorist Judith Shklar reminds us, membership in the polity was conceived in largely negative terms: "black chattel slavery stood at the opposite social pole from citizenship and so defined it" (1991, 16). By ending slavery, the Thirteenth Amendment made it necessary to voice the hitherto unspoken terms of a citizenship whose presumed locus had been the state, not the nation.

With the invisible prop of slavery kicked out from under it, the divided national house could not be reconstructed without some hasty retrofitting to shore up its suddenly shaky foundation. The Fourteenth Amendment offered just such a constitutional jack post. Ratified on July 9, 1868, after Congressional Radical Republicans had wrested control of Reconstruction from President Andrew Johnson, the enactment sought to resolve the above problems, as well as those of former secessionists' reintegration into the polity and liability for public war debt. "All persons born or naturalized in the United States, and subject to the jurisdiction thereof, are citizens of the United States and of the State wherein they reside," the first section began, continuing, "no State shall make or enforce any law which shall abridge the privileges or immunities of citizens of the United States; nor shall any State deprive any person of life, liberty, or property, without due process of law; nor deny to any person within its jurisdiction the equal protection of the laws." More than merely clarifying and extending the parameters of civic membership, the opening clause formally nationalized US citizenship for the first time in history. Shielding individuals from state as well as federal invasions of rights, the due process and equal protection clauses supplemented the Bill of Rights.

The enduring culmination of preliminary legal enactments, the Reconstruction Amendments also set in motion a still-unfolding legal and political process that would assign and often curtail their meaning in American life. Much as the Thirteenth Amendment superseded the Emancipation Proclamation, the Fourteenth Amendment embedded in the Constitution the extension of birthright citizenship provided by the Civil Rights Act of 1866. (Unlike that act, however, the amendment stopped short of guaranteeing citizens of color the same panoply of civil rights enjoyed by their "white" counterparts). As authorized by the amendments themselves, the Fourteenth and Fifteenth Amendments received federal legislative support in the form of the Enforcement Acts of 1870, 1871 (also known as the Ku Klux Klan Act) and 1875 (better known as the Civil Rights Act of 1875). Seeking to protect African Americans and Republican voters from violent Southern backlash, this legislation was subject to review by a recently expanded federal judiciary. Modifying the effects of the Fourteenth Amendment in particular, this litigation also yielded a largely unanticipated result: legal recognition of corporations as persons with constitutional rights. Thus, in a process that continues to this day, the amendment became central to the postbellum reconfiguration of the mutually constitutive relations among property, personhood, and civic membership.

In the decades immediately following ratification, the Supreme Court proceeded to limit the Fourteenth Amendment's impact on questions of racial equality. The leading case was brought not by African Americans but by Louisiana abattoir owners who argued that what was in effect a state-sponsored private monopoly constituted involuntary servitude and deprived them of their property without due process of law. After finding that the Thirteenth Amendment applied, narrowly, to "personal servitude," the Supreme Court in the *Slaughter-House Cases* (1872) went on to distinguish state from federal citizenship (rather than subordinating the former to the latter) in order to reserve to the states the power of protecting and regulating the civil rights of their citizens. Four years later another Louisiana case further disabled the new constitutional protection of civil rights. *US v. Cruikshank* (1876) arose from the horrific Colfax massacre, in which White League members murdered scores of black Republican militia men (including many who had surrendered) in a confrontation over the disputed 1873 Louisiana gubernatorial election. The court held that "the fourteenth amendment prohibits a State from depriving any person of life, liberty, or property, without due process of law; but this adds nothing to the rights of one citizen as against another." Taking up this ruling, the *Civil Rights Cases* (1883) declared unconstitutional the first two sections of the Civil Rights Act of 1875, which extended to "citizens of every race and color, regardless of any previous condition of servitude" the right to "the full and equal enjoyment" of "inns, public conveyances on land or water, theaters, and other places of public amusement." Justice Joseph P. Bradley held that "civil rights, such as are guaranteed by the Constitution against State aggression, cannot be impaired by the wrongful acts of individuals," which constituted, instead, "simply a private wrong, or a crime of that individual," demanding the appropriate civil or criminal redress under state, rather than federal, law. (It was this ruling that Henry W. Grady found to "deepen the responsibility of the South" while lessening that of the federal government.) With warring factions struggling for control of Southern state governments and African Americans daily exposed to discrimination and violence, the latter two rulings seemed to many what dissenting Justice John Marshall Harlan called an "abdication" of governmental responsibility. As Saidiya Hartman notes in a survey of freedpeople's primers and contemporary congressional debates, "[t]he ascribed responsibility of the liberal individual served to displace the nation's responsibility for providing and ensuring the rights and privileges conferred by the Reconstruction Amendments and shifted the burden of duty onto the freed" (1997, 118).

Even as the courts limited federal and state protection of African Americans' civil rights, they debated the applicability of the Reconstruction Amendments beyond the immediate context of slavery, emancipation, and abolition. Questions about the equal protection clause in particular surged in the wake of legislation affecting other non-white persons in state and federal jurisdictions, such as the Indian Appropriations Act of 1871 (which, denying sovereignty, effectively ended treaty-making between the United States and tribal governments) and the Chinese Exclusion Act of 1882 (which suspended "the coming of Chinese laborers to the United States" and mandated that "hereafter no State court or court of the United States shall admit Chinese to citizenship"). In *Elk v. Wilkins* (1884) the Nebraska Circuit Court upheld the constitutionality of Omaha registrar Charles Wilkins's refusal to register John Elk to vote on the basis of his status as an Indian: despite being born on US soil and having "severed his tribal relation," Elk could lay claim to neither birthright nor naturalized citizenship. Yet in *Yik Wo v. Hopkins* (1886), brought by a China-born San Francisco laundry owner, the Supreme Court ruled that the Fourteenth Amendment was "not confined to the protection of citizens" alone, but "all persons within the jurisdiction of the United States" (on *Yik Wo*, see Chapter 6 in this volume). Twelve years later the court found in *US v. Wong Kim Ark* (1898) that the Chinese Exclusion Act did not nullify the birthright citizenship of US-born children of resident laboring Chinese nationals. Offering a composite, blurry sketch of the "citizens of the United States" whom the Reconstruction Amendments had introduced into the polity, such litigation also posed new questions about the larger population of "persons within [US] jurisdiction."

At the turn of the century, the most striking of these questions was that posed by the corporation. Despite the popular tendency, then and now, to conflate persons with human beings, legal recognition of personhood has to do not with any claim to humanity but with the bundle of rights and duties that have historically represented legal standing. In *Dartmouth College v. Woodward* (1819) the Supreme Court had recognized the corporation as "an artificial person, existing in contemplation of law, and endowed with certain powers and franchises which, though they must be exercised through the medium of its natural members, are yet considered as subsisting in the corporation itself, as distinctly as if it were a real personage." By century's end, Morton J. Horwitz has shown, a new "theory of corporate personality" as a "natural" entity existing prior to, rather than created by, law succeeded in retroactively extending the Fourteenth Amendment's equal protection clause to corporations as persons through cases such as *Santa Clara Co. v. Southern Pacific Railroad* (1886) and *Pembina Mining Co. v. Pennsylvania* (1888) (1992, 67). Intensifying rather than ending battles over racial exclusion and civic membership, the Fourteenth Amendment would also become a valuable weapon in capital's war with labor. Citing the Fourteenth Amendment, judges thus expanded corporate power while contracting federal protection of the nation's new citizens.

Even before *Santa Clara*, the "paradox of paternalism" (in Avaim Soifer's phrase) had provoked protest from a dissenting Justice Harlan in the *Civil Rights Cases* (one of whose defendants was the Memphis and Charleston Railroad Company). "[W]hy shall the hands of Congress be tied?" the former Kentucky slaveholder asked his Supreme Court brethren, insisting that "the national legislature may, without transcending the limits of the Constitution, do for human liberty and the fundamental rights of American citizenship, what it did, with the sanction of this court, for the protection of slavery and the rights of the masters of fugitive slaves."

This judicial tendency to prioritize property over other "fundamental rights" was, of course, just what prompted antebellum literary abolitionists to place "slavery on trial" before "the bar of public opinion" (Douglass, *My Bondage*, "Editor's Preface"). But, as Harlan's dissent indicates, however much the Reconstruction Amendments may have heralded the victory of law, they did not, as so many had hoped, ensure the victory of justice. Quite the contrary. Nowhere was justice's tantalizing unattainability so cruelly apparent than in the decades following Reconstruction when the so-called "redemption" of formerly secessionist state governments accompanied the rise of violent white supremacist groups such as the Ku Klux Klan and their use of lynching as a form of racial terrorism. By the time the Colored Co-operative Publishing Company issued *Contending Forces: A Romance Illustrative of Negro Life North and South* in 1900, Pauline Hopkins's noble race-man Will Smith could bitterly affirm that the "[c]onstitutional amendments are dead letters." With "[c]onstitutional equity . . . a political fiction," the American novel once again became a capacious, revealing repository for what Wai Chee Dimock (1997) reminds us are the inevitable "residues of justice" (ch. 17).

Leaving Alone

"When a man has emerged from slavery, and by the aid of beneficent legislation has shaken off the inseparable concomitants of that state," Justice Bradley observed in handing down the 8–1 *Civil Rights Cases* decision, "there must be some stage in the progress of his elevation when he takes the rank of a mere citizen, and ceases to be the special favorite of the laws, and when his rights as a citizen, or a man, are to be protected in the ordinary modes by which other men's rights are protected." No mere rationalization of the federal abandonment of African Americans two decades after Emancipation, the ruling highlights the larger dilemma framing government response to each area of American life touched by the Fourteenth Amendment. From Reconstruction through the Progressive Era, whether they were discussing racial equality, the status of the South, or burgeoning corporate power, Americans debated the advisability of interventionist versus laissez-faire approaches to the nation's social, political, and economic problems.

Bradley's decision appeared in the same year as William Graham Sumner's manifesto, *What the Social Classes Owe to Each Other* (1883). Like naturalist novelists Norris, Dreiser, and London, Sumner found in the works of Herbert Spencer (coiner of the phrase "survival of the fittest") justification for his philosophy of ruthless competition driven by individual self-interest and unimpeded by government interference. Endorsed in its application to the South by the likes of Henry W. Grady, this view finds a mouthpiece in General Daniel Worth of Thomas Dixon's *The Leopard's Spots* (1902): "if the South is only let alone by the politicians and allowed to develop her resources," proclaims the former slaveholding manufacturer, "she will become what God meant her to be, the garden of the world" (bk. 1, ch. 9). Refusing to include blacks among the "2,000 hands" employed by his thriving cotton mills, Worth makes it clear that racial exclusion lies at the heart of his successful political economy (bk. 2, ch. 12). "I've simply let the Negro alone. Let others do the same," he explains to his future son-in-law Charles Gaston—whose redemption of the North Carolina governorship at novel's end promises to fulfill the General's white supremacist laissez-faire prophesy (bk. 2, ch. 12).

In a period when, as Soifer has found, careful judicial "avoidance of paternalism was an appealing surrogate for more explicit Social Darwinist rhetoric," the exact meaning of laissez-faire parlance lay in the ideology of the beholder (1987, 252). Responding, in 1865, to the perennial query, "What shall we do with the Negro?" Douglass admonishingly explained "What the Black Man Wants" to a Boston antislavery audience: "Let him alone! If you see him on his way to school, let him alone,—don't disturb him! If you see him going to the dinner table at a hotel, let him go! If you see him going to the ballot box, let him alone!—don't disturb him! . . . If you see him going into a workshop, just let him alone,—your interference is doing him positive injury." For Douglass, in stark contrast to Dixon's General Worth, to let the negro alone is to respect rather than deny his rights. Intervention is only required in default of such respect; it is triggered not by black incapacity but by the need to enjoin or redress the "positive injury" arising from racist "interference" that would prevent equal access to education, accommodations, suffrage, and employment. The bitter allegory of Reconstruction that concludes *The Adventures of Huckleberry Finn* centers on just such a refusal to let the "Black Man"—in this case, Jim—alone. Seizing the prerogatives of white supremacy, Huck and Tom Sawyer make the (unwittingly) emancipated but still physically captive adult slave the sport of their dangerous games, thereby literalizing Douglass' rebuke: "Do nothing with us! Your doing with us has already played the mischief with us. Do nothing with us!"

Fifteen years after Douglass suggested that to let the negro alone was, in effect, to "untie his hands" ("What the Black Man Wants") and three years before Harlan asked "why . . . the hands of Congress [should] be tied," Tourgée enlisted the same trope to challenge the colloquial definition of laissez-faire as a hands-off approach. In *Bricks without Straw*, Yankee schoolmarm Mollie Ainslee "blushe[s] with shame" at the "thought of the weak, vacillating nation which had given the promise of freedom to the ears of four millions of weak but trustful allies," then "appealed to them for aid to write the golden words of Freedom in its Constitution," only, finally, to have "taken away the protecting hand and said to those whose hearts were full of hate, 'Stay not thine hand'" (ch. 49). Inverting Douglass's figure, Tourgée leaves little doubt that, at this stage in Reconstruction, to withdraw the "protecting hand" of the federal government is to unloose the murderous hands of white supremacist officials and mobs. Focusing on class warfare rather than racial strife, Howells and Dreiser make a similar point through dramatic strike episodes in *A Hazard of New Fortunes* (1890) and *Sister Carrie* (1900). As allusions to actual incidents of repression such as the Great Railroad Strike (1877) and the Haymarket Affair (1886), these scenes illustrate laissez-faire political economics' dependence upon local authorities' brutal intervention in labor disputes.

What, then, does it mean to be left alone? For the next half-century, regardless of a given work's politics, the phrase would become the American novel's dominant refrain. "I am going to my room, now," Rhoda Ashgate, the orphaned tragic mulatta of Howells's passing novel *An Imperative Duty* (1893), coldly informs the weak-willed aunt who has finally revealed her racial heritage, "and whatever happens, don't follow me, don't call me . . . . I have a right to be alone" (ch. 7). Acceding all too readily to the injunction to let the Negro alone—as voiced by her racist white fiancé—Rhoda finally renounces a perceived "duty" to her enslaved "mother's people" in Louisiana for the equally "imperative" one of (presumptive) white wifehood abroad (ch. 13). Twain comes closer to Douglass's meaning when, in his novelistic travel narrative, *Roughing It* (1872), he wryly reassures anxious middle-class readers that the urban Pacific coast's "large Chinese population . . . are a harmless race when white men either let them alone or treat them no worse than dogs" (ch. 54). In *The Quest of the Silver Fleece* (1911), Douglass's successor, W. E. B. Du Bois, presents a monitory example of the sort of white intervention that, by providing relief, enables rather than limits black autonomy. With her family's cabin subject to constant invasion by white sexual predators, adolescent Zora finds welcome refuge when—eighteen years before Virginia Woolf's celebrated essay—her Yankee schoolmistress provides her with a room of her own to use "when you're tired and want to be alone" (ch. 11). Male intrusions upon similar female sanctuaries mark the climaxes of both *Contending Forces* and *Herland* (1915). In the latter, Terry, a Roosevelt-like American explorer, is expelled from Charlotte Perkins Gilman's feminist utopia for his unauthorized intrusion into his wife's (separate) home; he avoids lifelong imprisonment only by capitulating to the high council's demand not "to expose our country to . . . the rest of the world" (ch. 12). The novel closes with the assurance that Herland will, once again, be left alone.

In each of the above examples noninterference is exhorted on behalf of a collective: Southerners, African Americans, Chinese, women. Reverberating with sectional, racial, and gender tensions in the period's romances, entreaties to be left alone ring with a more personal anguish in realist and naturalist novels. Stripped of his successful practice by state licensing authorities, the eponymous self-taught "dentist" of Norris' *McTeague* (1899) wonders, "What had a clerk at the City Hall to do with him? Why couldn't they let him alone?" (ch. 13). Forced to sell his household effects at public auction, the unemployable McTeague remonstrates with his miserly, brutalized wife, "I don't want to be bothered. You understand? I want to be let alone" (ch. 15). At novel's end the man who on his wedding day had incongruously crooned, "No one to love, none to Caress/Left all alone in this world's wilderness," finds himself handcuffed to a dead man in Death Valley with only a sack of gold and a "half-dead canary" for company (chs. 9, 22). McTeague is not alone in being left, tragically, alone: the isolatos of James's *Roderick Hudson* (1875), Dreiser's *Sister Carrie*, Wharton's *House of Mirth* (1905), and London's *Martin Eden* (1909) all suffer unutterably lonely deaths. In the *Turn of the Screw* (1898), a shared yearning "to be let alone" seems to be the only sentiment uniting the members of the embattled Bly household: Miles and Flora's absentee uncle's "main condition" to their governess is that she should "take the whole thing over and let him alone"; the story climaxes when little Miles remonstrates with her, "ever so gently, 'To let me alone'"; and she, in turn, imagines him acknowledging a reciprocal desire "to be let alone yourself" (preface, chs. 17, 18). In the realist and naturalist novels of the period these countless separate appeals mingle in a single reprise, a chorus of defiant soloists all reluctantly striking the same note at once.

No proleptic wail of modernist alienation, the imperative demand bespeaks a distinctly fin-de-siècle sensibility. Consider Julian West, the morbidly isolationist Victorian gentleman who, at the beginning of Christian Socialist Edward Bellamy's wildly popular time-travel novel *Looking Backward: 2000–1887* (1888), literally walls himself off from friends, family, and society in a secret, underground sleeping chamber. Buried in the vault by a house fire and preserved in a mesmeric coma for 113 years, the excavated and resuscitated West—literally a relic of the nineteenth century—faces mental collapse whenever he is left alone in the modern, socialized America. ("How could we be aloner?" awkwardly wonders a bewildered Ellador, citizen of the similarly communal, utopian Herland [ch. 11].) Little surprise, then, that in James the impassioned cri de coeur often signals an outmoded Romantic posturing. There is the *Europeans'* (1878) shabby-chic Baroness Munster who, exiled to the American provinces, makes the Garbo-esque confession, "I wish very humbly your people here would leave me alone" (ch. 6). Or *The Aspern Papers'* (1888) reclusive Miss Boudreau, ancient lover of the titular Romantic poet, who sets the story in motion with her fruitless epistolary plea to be "let . . . alone" (ch. 1). Or tortured artist Roderick Hudson, who defiantly proclaims, "I am fit only to be alone! I am damned!"—just before pitching off an icy cliff to his solitary death (ch. 13). Even *Washington Square's* (1880) poor Catherine Sloper, who decidedly "isn't romantic," finds herself uttering the appeal first to her histrionic Aunt Penniman ("kindly leave me alone"; "why can't you leave me alone?") and then (via a servant) to her erstwhile fiancé ("I wish he would leave me alone"). Like Twain's Jim, Catherine becomes the reluctant victim in—and of—someone else's melodrama (chs. 2, 30, 35).

Instruments of Slavery

Lest the refrain lose its meaning in this turn-of-the-century hall of echoes, we would do well to attend to critic Kenneth W. Warren's assessment of Reconstruction's impact on literary realism. "When political claims for civil rights were apprehended as social claims," Warren observes, "the result was not a disappearance of the political but an investing of personal and responses and feelings with political, legal, and scientific weight" (1993, 42). With Warren's insight in mind, it is worth considering one final iteration from beyond the world of fiction: the epochal December 1890 *Harvard Law Review* article in which Charles D. Warren and Samuel D. Brandeis introduce "The Right to Privacy" as a means of "securing to the individual what Judge Cooley calls the right 'to be let alone'" (195). Taken from Thomas M. Cooley's *Treatise on the Law of Torts or the Wrongs which Arise Independently of Contract* (1878), one of the first books to mark torts' postbellum emergence as a distinct area of law, the catch phrase figures prominently in Warren and Brandeis's groundbreaking presentation of the invasion of privacy as a civil wrong. In a notoriously convoluted doctrinal argument based on unorthodox readings of copyright cases, Warren and Brandeis maintain that "[t]he common law secures to each individual the right of determining . . . to what extent his thoughts, sentiments, and emotions shall be communicated to others" (198). Struggling to extract a broader right to privacy from the intellectual property law in which they found it firmly encrusted, Warren and Brandeis maintain that "the principle which protects personal writings . . . not against theft and physical appropriation, but against publication in any form, is in reality not the principle of private property, but that of an inviolate personality"

(205). Framed as "the right to one's personality," the right to privacy is introduced as "a part of the more general right to the immunity of the person" (207).

Searching through recalcitrant Anglo-American case law for legal ground on which to rest their precarious argument, Warren and Brandeis did not pause to consider ratification of the Reconstruction Amendments as a precondition for the proposed right to privacy. But the concept of privacy was integral to a free American citizenship whose parameters had until very recently been delimited by race slavery. Indeed, the leading privacy case, *Pavesich v. New England Life Insurance Co.* (1905), cited the Fourteenth Amendment en route to affirming that with the invasion of an individual's privacy came the "realization that his liberty has been taken away from him . . . that he is, for the time being, under the control of another, that he is no longer free, and that he is in reality a slave without hope of freedom, held to service by a merciless master." Characterizing an advertiser's unauthorized use of an individual's photograph as "complete enthrallment," the Georgia Supreme Court trivialized the recent history of race slavery in the state and the nation even as it highlighted that history's role in defining liberty in terms of privacy.

Like *Pavesich*, "The Right to Privacy" joined a liberal tradition that traced membership in the polity to inalienable property in the person, or "possessive individualism" in the influential formulation of C.B. Mcpherson (1962). And, like the Georgia bench, Warren and Brandeis were members of a polity that had only recently reconstituted itself by revising its founding compact to abolish property in human beings and to extend political membership to those formerly deemed property. Since the nation's inception, its citizens had characterized intrusions upon privacy as, in effect, "instruments of slavery," James Otis' designation for the infamous 1761 Writs of Assistance ("On the Writs of Assistance"). Antislavery literature built on this revolutionary rhetoric associating Americans' privacy with their liberty to depict bound servitude as an invasion of privacy. Exhibiting not just the horror of slavery but themselves as its victims, famous fugitives gained a public hearing at the cost of the privacy that many Americans understood to be constitutive of their self-possession as free individuals.

It is against the backdrop of what Milette Shamir has called the abolitionists' "strategy of exposure" that we must view the newly national, insistently private, and still normatively white US citizen of the era's law and literature (2006, 128). For it was only upon the mass emancipation and official enfranchisement of African Americans that the entrenched racial boundaries around privacy needed to be sheathed with formal legal ones. With the Reconstruction Amendments' abolition of race slavery and extension of federal citizenship, the invasions of domestic and personal privacy that had long characterized the South's peculiar institution threatened to place a white American citizen like Pavesich in a state of "complete enthrallment." From James's *Portrait of a Lady* (1881), *The Bostonians*, and *The Tragic Muse* (1890), to Howells's *A Modern Instance* (1882) and *A Hazard of New Fortunes*, to Dreiser's *Sister Carrie* and London's *Martin Eden*, the era's fiction seeks, much like Warren and Brandeis and the *Pavesich* court, to disentangle property from personhood by probing the fraught interplay of privacy and publicity in the lives of individuals and families. Whether figured as Howells's egoistical Bartley Hubbard, James's irrepressible Henrietta Stackpole, or London's amoral "cub reporter" (ch. 38) prying fictional journalists personify Warren and Brandeis' fears about how the "newspaper enterprise ha[d] invaded the sacred precincts of private and domestic life" (195). Written in slavery's turbulent wake, these novels share with abolitionist print propaganda and the *Harvard Law Review* article a tendency to treat privacy as, in legal critic Jonathan Kahn's words, "the arena where the non-fungible aspects of the human spirit are protected from a debasing commodification" (2003, 383). With the invasion of privacy as a badge of servitude, the right to be left alone became the emblem of the new American citizenship. And nothing better revealed the racial content of that newly private citizenship than *Plessy v. Ferguson*. The case, which light-complexioned Homer Plessy initiated on behalf of New Orleans' Citizens' Committee to Test the Constitutionality of the Separate Car Law, marked the beginning of de jure segregation by upholding an 1890 Louisiana statute requiring railroads to provide "equal but separate accommodations for the white and colored races" and prohibiting passengers to occupy areas not assigned to their own group. Conflating the shifting boundaries of the "private" with those of the "social" (variously encompassing family, civil society, and/or the polity), *Plessy* endorsed the widespread perception of African American civil rights as incursions on private white space—even in such quasipublic facilities as railroad cars.

But what, beyond the right to be left alone, is privacy? Legal philosopher Richard A. Posner has defined it narrowly, as "the withholding or concealment of information" (1978, 393). Well-suited to the narrative requirements of extended prose fiction, privacy in this aspect drives the plot of novels as different as Constance Fenimore Woolson's *For the Major* (1883) and Stephen Crane's *The Red Badge of Courage* (1895). Central to the romantic entanglements of James's *Portrait of a Lady* and *The Golden Bowl* (1904) and Wharton's *The Reef* (1911), secret personal histories are indispensible to "color-line" fiction—novels such as Howells's *Imperative Duty*, Hopkins's *Contending Forces*, Frances Ellen Watkins's *Iola Leroy* (1892), and Charles Chesnutt's *The House Behind the Cedars* (1900), which explore American identity and cultural belonging across the racial divide. But privacy involves much more than secrecy. For to conceive of its invasion as a civil wrong is to make some crucial assumptions about the nature of civic membership.

Even without the "demeaning . . . commercialization of an aspect of personality" that so troubled mugwumps from James and Howells to Warren and Brandeis, Edward J. Bloustein contends in an influential essay, "personal isolation and personal control over the conditions of its abandonment [are] of the very essence of personal freedom and dignity" in Western culture (1964, 987, 973). Viewed in this light, "privacy does not refer to an objective physical space of secrecy, solitude, or anonymity," legal theorist Robert C. Post elaborates, "but rather to the forms of respect that we owe to each other as members of a common community" (1991, 651). Denial of such respect is a form of civic exclusion; tort proceedings enact justice by affirming civic membership. Crucially, however, whereas in criminal law "all power to prosecute infractions of important legal norms is concentrated in the hands of accountable public officials," Post explains, "the privacy tort devolves the authority of enforcement into the hands of private litigants" (1989, 966). If the privacy tort's role in redressing "violation[s] of social norms of civility" leads Kahn to remind us that "[e]qual protection is not the only way to approach identity-based harms," its civil law status should nonetheless give us pause (1996, 302). After all, the Supreme Court denied federal relief to the *Civil Rights Cases* plaintiffs by dismissing systemic racial discrimination as a "private wrong" arising from "the wrongful acts of individuals."

In the late nineteenth century, a significant cohort of African Americans responded to such disavowals of public accountability by recasting their demands for justice in the private idiom of torts. This newly defined area of law provided a vocabulary uniquely well suited to the psychic and physical injuries sustained as a result of federal and state government's failure to provide protection in the legislative and judicial aftermath of the Reconstruction Amendments. Faced with the everyday harms of racial segregation on public conveyances in the decades following the war, the vast majority of African Americans committed to the rule of law did not, like Homer Plessy and the *Civil Rights Cases* plaintiffs, mount federal constitutional challenges. Instead, they took the same legal route as their white fellow travelers who suffered from accidental injury and nervous shock in encounters with trolleys and trains: they sought redress through civil suits against the corporate and state defendants responsible for such quasipublic entities. Caught up (often with grim literalness) in the machinery of corporate power and industrial technology, female, immigrant, poor, and working-class plaintiffs quickly achieved proficiency in the language of civil injury. Equally adept in acquiring the lingo, a remarkable number of African American litigants likewise, historian Barbara Young Welke notes, "spoke to the rights of blacks in the language of injury" (2001, 301).

Not surprisingly, this popularized torts jargon followed more vernacular speech forms into the realist novels of Crane, Howells, James, and Wharton—where, according to critic Jennifer Travis, middle-class white men voiced their own emotional needs in the era's legally evocative "vocabulary of injury" (2005, 9). But as "Judge A. W. Tourgée" would argue in his 1888 *Forum* essay making his case for "The South as a Field for Fiction"—and against realism—"undoubtedly the richest mine of romantic material" lies in "[t]he life of the Negro as a slave, freedman, and racial outcast" precisely because "[t]he 'twice-told tales' of *his* childhood are animate with rankling memories of wrongs . . . . With the father's and the mother's blood is transmitted the story, not merely of their individual wrongs, but of a race's woe." From the realist novel to the romance, as in the era's ubiquitous tort proceedings, the new lexicon of civil wrongs offered another way to conceptualize and demand both legal and symbolic redress for individual as well as racial injustice in the face of the constitutional stalemate.

Individual Wrongs and the Race's Woe

"To view the novel through the prism of tort," Nan Goodman has suggested, is to access "ideas about responsibility in the new nation" (1998, 17). While novelists and polemicists in the renovated union debated responsibility for slavery's enduring harms and weighed the advisability of interventionist versus laissez-faire approaches to politics and the economy, one fiction writer, Pauline Hopkins, found torts a useful literary device for refracting unresolved constitutional questions of racial injustice. Read as an allegory of post-Reconstruction redress, the lawsuit that concludes *Contending Forces* encapsulates the shifts in legal and literary logic this essay has sought to trace.

The novel centers on the African American community that flows in and out of "Ma" Smith's Boston boarding house. As suggested by the title of chapter 3, "Coming Events Cast Their Shadows Before," the Civil War and Reconstruction do not mark a sharp temporal and psychic divide between slavery and freedom for these black Bostonians. Poised to enter the careers and marriages that betoken adulthood, Ma Smith's children, Will and Dora, find their romantic prospects—family friends John Langley and Sappho Clark—dragging them tragically into murky familial pasts.

In an era when "constitutional equity" has been reduced to a "political fiction," Hopkins's middle-class African American characters seem incapable of breaking out of slavery's narratives, those "twice-told tales" of remembered wrongs evoked by Tourgée. As members of fractured households, they struggle to retain individual and familial dignity in lives where publicity and privacy remain in antebellum disarray. Forced by the imperatives of the color line to perform her work as a typist at "home" in her boarding-house room, the light-skinned Sappho meets her fiancé Will as one of many paying lodgers in his mother's house (ch. 7). Sappho's efforts to veil in secrecy her childhood rape and resulting illegitimate son are defeated when well-meaning black orator Lycurgus Sawyer inadvertently exposes the details of her personal history in an impassioned public political speech. Delivered from a platform adorned with "[p]ictures of the anti-slavery apostles," the speech is a throwback, recalling both the content and setting of abolitionist accounts of female sexual exploitation (ch. 13).

In the end, however, *Contending Forces* pursues an alternative legal-literary path, different from that blazed by "the mighty host of anti-slavery fathers" (ch. 13). Commencing with the murder of Creole planter Charles Montfort and the theft of his estate from his young son, Jesse (Ma Smith's fugitive slave father), and culminating in the revelation of young Sappho's rape by her white state senator uncle, the novel joins the slave narrative and antislavery fiction in treating slavery's many crimes as just that—punishable felonies. Yet, set in the same year that saw *Plessy v. Ferguson* as the last of many rulings rendering the Reconstruction Amendments so many "dead letters," *Contending Forces* departs from its literary abolitionist forebears in demanding not public justice through criminal prosecution or a constitutional challenge, but private reparations via a civil proceeding. Thus the fortuitous eleventh-hour appearance of a "centenarian" ex-slave who had been present at Montfort's murder and Jesse's dispossession comes to nothing: rather than gaining a public hearing, the "eye-witness of the atrocious crime" dies in obscurity (ch. 16, 21). Indeed, "the case of Smith *vs.* the United States did not come to a public trial; it was heard privately before a court composed of the judges of the Supreme Court of the United States," resulting in the "sum of one hundred and fifty thousand dollars" being "awarded" to Ma Smith as "the last representative of the heirs of Jesse Montfort" (ch. 21). Significantly, however, the key word, "privately," cannot be read as a synonym for "secretly" here; we are told that "the case was a nine-days' wonder" that "startled society and all the world" (ch. 21). A well-publicized civil (or "private") proceeding, the suit offers symbolic redress of the race's woes in the form of monetary damages for individual wrongs—not unlike contemporaneous tort proceedings against streetcar companies and railroad corporations. In the process (quite literally), this private lawsuit likewise affirms the plaintiffs' standing as free people, legal persons, and US citizens under the Reconstruction Amendments. But if Hopkins's conclusion suggests a capitulation to judicial and popular efforts to privatize and thus denationalize responsibility for slavery's harms at the dawn of the twentieth century, it also offers a powerful fictional rejoinder to such efforts. For in contrast to constitutional or even criminal law approaches, *Contending Forces* suggests, torts ultimately offers inadequate recourse to racial injustice. Preempting the question of public accountability, the private proceeding reduces racial woes to individual wrongs, refusing to recognize them as instances of a collective injury that can only, finally, be redressed by the polity as a whole.

"Justice," Hopkins's post-Reconstruction novel trenchantly concludes, "was appeased" (ch. 21).

6

PLESSY AND THE NOVEL

BY EDLIE WONG

Before spearheading the landmark case of *Plessy v. Ferguson* (1896), described in the previous chapter, Albion Tourgée had embraced literature as a sphere of political action, authoring numerous novels in his crusade for social justice. Literature provided the testing ground for his legal argument, and the case, which upheld de jure segregation in the United States until *Brown v. Board of Education* (1954) overturned it, elucidates the relationship between legal culture and the development of the American novel. The doctrine of "equal but separate" established by the case captured the strange contortions of racial reasoning in the post–Civil War nation, as foreign immigration, industrial capitalism, and overseas empire began to transform the legal categories of "white" and "nonwhite." The African American Citizens' Committee of New Orleans engineered the case as part of a strategy to overturn the Louisiana Separate Car Act, among the many state-mandated racial segregation laws passed throughout the South in the turbulent years after Reconstruction. This law mandated "equal but separate accommodations for the white and colored races" (with the lone exception of "nurses attending children of the other race"), but neglected to provide a statutory definition of "white" and "colored," leaving racial sorting to the "officers, directors, conductors and employes [sic] of railway companies" (Lofgren 1987, 191, 153). The organization enlisted the aid of a white lawyer and novelist, Albion Tourgée, a former North Carolina judge who defended the rights of southern freedmen, and Homer Plessy, a light-skinned, mixed-raced Creole of "one-eighth African blood" agreed to be the test case. In an act of civil disobedience coordinated with the railroad company (unhappy with the high costs of separate cars), Plessy took passage in an intrastate white train car and was arrested when he refused to be removed. When Plessy's case came to trial, the Louisiana district court upheld the law, and Tourgée immediately appealed to the US Supreme Court.

Distinct among postbellum writers, Tourgée anticipated his *Plessy* brief in his bestselling novel, *A Fool's Errand by One of the Fools* (1879), in which he juxtaposes the social reality of ongoing slavery against its formal abolition. In the events that befall the naive carpetbagger Colonel Comfort Servosse, Tourgée offers fictional evidence of the disjunctive legal reality of southern life. "Slavery might be ended as a legal status by proclamation," the narrator tells us, "but as a living fact it could not" (ch. 20). Unwittingly drawn into Reconstruction politics, Servosse becomes, as Tourgée had been, an outspoken Union League organizer and freedmen's advocate. After his daughter heroically foils a Ku-Klux Klan plot to murder him, Servosse must accept that although "the *fact* of slavery is destroyed: the *right to enslave* is yet as devoutly held as ever" (ch. 18). In *A Fool's Errand*, its popular sequel, *Bricks without Straw* (1880), and the lesser-known *Pactolus Prime* (1890), Tourgée sought to convince readers of slavery's continuing hold upon the South, and the belated temporality of racial equality in social—if not legal—fact.

In the months after his *Plessy* arguments, Tourgée returned to literature, publishing a moving tribute to Harriet Beecher Stowe upon her passing. Reviewing Stowe's antislavery masterpiece, *Uncle Tom's Cabin* (1852), from the perspective of *Plessy* in an 1896 *Independent* essay, Tourgée reflected upon the literary past, and its enduring relevance to narrative production in the age of "Jim Crow," a term drawn from blackface minstrelsy designating this formative period of de jure racial segregation. "A nation can never bury its past," he cautioned in "The South as a Field for Fiction," challenging readers to complete the unfinished work of Radical Reconstruction. Chattel slavery "as an institution tolerated by law" might be abolished, in the words of Justice John Marshall Harlan's celebrated *Plessy* dissent, yet its power to curtail freedom would continue in the guise of "sinister legislation" like the doctrine of "equal but separate." A powerful reminder, as Tourgée noted, that slavery was not "a dead, unpleasant fact" of American life, *Plessy v. Ferguson* became a major "causative force" in shaping the form and content of the American novel, from the works of Mark Twain to William Faulkner, Richard Wright, Ralph Ellison, Toni Morrison, and Edward P. Jones.

This chapter brings a selection of novels to bear upon *Plessy v. Ferguson* to tease out the racial fictions and counterfactual imaginings embedded within the legal text of "equal but separate." In reading law with and against literature, it charts the fictional contexts and forms that directly (in the example of Tourgée) and indirectly shaped *Plessy* and the various literary challenges that the case subsequently provoked. Prominent novelists like Twain and William Dean Howells drew upon popular debates over "equal accommodations" from the 1880s, and anticipated the counterfactual syntax of *Plessy*'s legal arguments. Other writers, including Charles Chesnutt, Sutton Griggs, Frances Ellen Watkins Harper, Pauline Hopkins, Paul Laurence Dunbar, and Winnifred Eaton complexly registered the impact of the landmark case in color-line fictions organized around the plot of racial passing, in which mixed-raced characters attempt to assimilate into dominant white society. These fictions often emphasize overlapping subplots, racially indeterminate characters, and disjunctive temporalities, and serve as literary counterpoints to the popular plantation romances of Joel Chandler Harris, Thomas Nelson Page, and Thomas

Dixon and to the urban middle-class worlds of mainstream American realism. Often writing with, yet sometimes against the grain of American realism, political novelists like Tourgée and Chesnutt (who was also trained in law) sought to challenge and redraw the legal boundaries of race, giving expression to American realism's utopian desire to, in Amy Kaplan's words, "imagine resolutions to contemporary social conflicts by reconstructing society as it might be" (1988, 12).

In *Plessy v. Ferguson*, the Supreme Court deferred to the "established usages, customs, and traditions of the people" as a baseline for legal interpretation. Writing for the 7–1 majority, Justice Henry Billings Brown crafted a powerful "fiction of law and custom"—to use Twain's phrase from *Pudd'nhead Wilson* (1894)—to hold the Separate Car Law a "reasonable" use of state police powers (ch. 2). "[C]ustom is stronger than law," wrote Chesnutt in *House Behind the Cedars* (1900), "in these matters [of race] custom *is* law" (ch. 3). The *Plessy* court dismissed the idea that "equal rights cannot be secured to the negro except by an enforced commingling of the two races." On the one hand, the court refused to acknowledge the coercive role of law in the legacy of white supremacy, but on the other, it lent constitutional sanction to a racially tiered society. In affirming "equal but separate," the court artificially distinguished unenforceable "social rights" from the political rights protected by law and the Constitution. The Fourteenth Amendment extending citizenship to all black freedmen also mandated "the absolute equality of the two races before the law," but it did not intend, according to Brown, "to abolish distinctions based upon color, or to enforce social, as distinguished from political equality." *Plessy* thus subjected the "comprehensive Negro, black, brown, yellow, and white," in Chesnutt's words, to a "humiliating, insulting and degrading system" of "racial caste in the United States" ("The Courts and the Negro," 1908).

Contrary to Tourgée's legal and literary claims, the *Plessy* Court fashioned itself as a bulwark against the past. It embraced a temporal logic of linear succession, and dismissed Tourgée's argument that "equal but separate" violated the Thirteenth Amendment's ban against slavery and involuntary servitude, including the "badges of servitude" linked to the institution of slavery. Endorsing the restricted scope of the *Slaughter-House Cases* (1873), Brown asserted the Thirteenth Amendment's sole intention was to abolish chattel slavery, "as it had been previously known in this country," including "Mexican peonage" and "the Chinese coolie trade." He further dismissed Tourgée's brief for "running the slavery argument into the ground . . . to make it apply to every act of discrimination," citing Justice Joseph P. Bradley's opinion in the *Civil Rights Cases* (1883). Brown's majority opinion thus divorced slavery from the question of discriminatory segregation: a law implying a distinction between races did not reestablish a state of involuntary servitude or impose a "badge of slavery or servitude" upon African Americans.

In dissent, Justice Harlan, a former slaveholder, judged segregation a violation of the Thirteenth Amendment's mandate of freedom (from compulsion or coercion):

"Slavery, as an institution tolerated by law would . . . have disappeared from our country, but there would remain a power in the States, by sinister legislation, to interfere with the full enjoyment . . . of freedom." Endorsing Tourgée's argument, Harlan deemed segregation a modern slavery that placed "fellow-citizens . . . in a condition of legal inferiority." He predicted, "If laws of like character should be enacted in the several States of the Union, the effect would be in the highest degree mischievous." Only the past can generate the empirical evidence (or precedent) upon which law is adjudicated and based. Unlike law, fiction has the power to produce its own evidentiary reality. "Reason deals with facts," declares Donald Glover from Chesnutt's *The Quarry* (1928), but "[i]magination overleaps the boundaries of the known and soars into the empyrean of conjecture" (ch. 21). Turn-of-the-century racial passing novels by writers like Tourgée, Chesnutt, Griggs, and Hopkins experimented with the form and logic of *Plessy*, and used literature to reveal and combat the fictive qualities of the law and legal efforts to secure the explanatory power of race in America.

Attending to novelistic form offers us a key to understanding the contingency of judicial opinions, their buried texts, and complex relationship to historical precedent. Judicial opinions are often viewed as the culmination of a line of cases; yet courts—in response to evolving social norms—often return to and revisit prior holdings once they are thought to be out of alignment with the will of the people. Every opinion, as legal scholar Bret Asbury observes, "remains subject to future revision," and an evaluation of its impact must analyze "not just what it says, but the possibility of its being revisited and altered by future courts" (1999, 121, 123). Twain, for example, fashions the asynchronous tale of *A Connecticut Yankee in King Arthur's Court* (1889) as a palimpsest—"under the old dim writing of the Yankee historian appeared traces of a penmanship which was older and dimmer still—Latin words and sentences," which calls to mind the palimpsest-like qualities of the law: the contingencies between judicial opinions and their precedents and future re-evaluations ("A Word of Explanation"). Precedents, like the barely discernible "Latin words and sentence" under Hank Morgan's "old dim writing," do not go away, and they shape and inform the application of opinions. Thus Harlan analogizes *Plessy* to the infamous *Dred Scott v. Sandford* (1857), which declared blacks as outside the Constitution and bearing "no rights which the white man was bound to respect," just as Brown compares *Plessy* to *Yick Wo v. Hopkins*, revealing slavery and the threat of racial multiplicity as the buried text—the palimpsest's underlayers—of "equal but separate." Novelistic forays into *Plessy*'s divisive "race question" refracted and transformed the historical back-and-forth of judicial opinions and their openness to future reinvention. In both the popular mind and in the social enactment of segregation, these color-line fictions debunk a mistaken notion of the law's linear or successive temporality, recasting what Justice Brown dismissed as the "slavery argument" to reveal its troubling vitality at the dawn of the twentieth century.

White Skin, Black Masks

In an 1887 notebook entry, Twain sketched an idea—while crafting *A Connecticut Yankee*—for a never-realized story entitled "Prophesy." In this story, to be set in 1910, Twain wryly manipulates the counterfactual scenario that Justice Brown later invoked in *Plessy*: a world where blacks had superseded whites. In this future, the "colored brother has succeeded in having severe laws against miscegenation passed," and whites are forced to vote "as they are told, or be visited by masked men & shot, or whipped, & house burned & wife & d <stripped na[k]> turned out in their night clothes." Twain also imagines a scene in which "whites of both sexes" are forced to ride, for full fare, in smoking cars of trains since the "populous & dominant colored man will not ride with them." In "Prophesy," as in his later unfinished manuscript "Which Was It?" Twain uses a technique of counterfactual conjecture—imagining the interchange of black and white—to explore the question of racial inequity, particularly as it related to the racial sorting that occurred under the aegis of equal (but separate) accommodations. Twain fashions the kind of racial counterworld that black writers like Sutton Griggs and Pauline Hopkins explored in their speculative fantasies. "Prophesy" thus suggests a new way for us to understand the politics of *Connecticut Yankee* and its connection to the racial subject matter of Twain's novels set in antebellum Missouri (Cooper 2009, 70). Drawing details from Charles Ball's slave narrative, *Slavery in the United States* (1836), *Connecticut Yankee*'s anomalous time-travel narrative invokes a range of tropes intimately associated with the American slave narrative, such as Hank's embrace of literacy as the foundation of self-possessed individuality, the graphic depictions of the slave coffle and auction block, the grisly lynching of commoners, and the sentimental scene of familial separation. Specifically, Hank's extended analogy of the oppressed serfs to the "'poor whites' of our South" offers a powerful critique of the failed postbellum future in which social organization by inherited caste had supposedly given way to a modern society organized by contract and its promise of equal opportunities regardless of race (Thomas 1997c, 2).

One of the core constitutional issues at stake in *Plessy* was whether black and white railway cars were essentially interchangeable—whether "equal accommodations" could sustain the constitutional test of "equal protection." Arguments for either side, as Stephen Best argues, often used techniques of counterfactual conjecture to frame the formal equivalence between black and white. Defining counterfactuals as what has not happened, but might have, he notes that they find expression in a range of hypothetical "if-then statements or contrary-to-fact speculations" common to literary and legal hermeneutics and historical and philosophical inquiry (Best 2004, 210–11). Counterfactuals are common—even fundamental—to the rationality of liberal law, particularly in the post-Reconstruction "framework of contractarian thought," as Brook Thomas reminds us, dominant in the law at the time (1997c, 2). As a symbol of social relations, contract cloaked inequity in the language of free and equal interchange, particularly as its logic informed the Fourteenth Amendment's mandate of equality. From the vantage of the Constitution, blacks and white were interchangeable—in the language of the counterfactual—and therefore "equal" before the law. With *Plessy*, this rule of formal equivalence—what Neil Gotanda describes as "'formal-race' analysis"—became the standard of civic freedom and equality (Gotanda 1991, 4).

Twain's collaborator George Washington Cable's "The Freedman's Case in Equity" (1885) and the vitriolic response that it elicited from New South advocate Henry W. Grady most famously illustrate the counterfactual mode of these debates. In the issue of *Century Magazine* that also carried excerpts from *Huckleberry Finn* (1885), Cable and Grady both popularized the rhetorical forms that the *Plessy* Court later drew upon to legitimate segregation. Like Tourgée, Cable imagined black political equality in terms of whiteness, maintaining, in "The Freedman's Case in Equity," that "every interest in the land demands that the freedman be free to become in all things . . . the same sort of American citizen he would be if . . . he were white." In denouncing the "warping moral effect of race-prejudice," Cable asks his reader to feel "as if" he were in the other's circumstance. "Suppose, for a moment," he conjectures, "the tables turned." Without gainsaying white superiority, Cable imagines the interchange of white and black in the rhetorical effort to adjudicate equality: "Yet only read white man for black man, and black man for white man." Conversely, Grady argued that the white South should dictate the "race question." Ironically, his essay, "In Plain Black and White," exemplified the "domination of the white race" also by way of counterfactual conjecture: "If the blacks of the South wore white skins, . . . they would progress not one step farther towards the control of affairs." Countering Cable's empathetic injunction, Grady manipulates the figurative interchange of black for white to prove the consistency of white superiority and black inferiority even if "blacks . . . wore white skins" (on Cable and Grady's debate, see Chapter 5 in this volume).

Tourgée's "Brief for the Plaintiff in Error" (1896) embraced counterfactualism with similar dramatic aplomb when it asked the justices to imagine themselves as black men: "Suppose every member by some mysterious dispensation of providence should wake to-morrow with a black skin and curly hair." By posing this figurative interchange, Tourgée hoped that the justices might "feel and know" that discrimination "on the line of race was . . . intended to humiliate and degrade." Responding for the court, Brown imagined a different counterfactual scenario to dismiss Tourgée's claim that segregation branded "the colored race with a badge of inferiority." For Brown, viewing the Louisiana statute as a "badge of inferiority" was a matter of "choice" and not a formal element of the law, for

> the argument necessarily assumes that if, as had been more than once the case, and is not unlikely to be so again, the colored race should become the dominant power in the state legislature, and should enact a law in precisely similar terms, it would thereby relegate the white race to an inferior position. We imagine that the white race, at least, would not acquiesce in this assumption.

In turning to the "imagination," Brown invokes the counterfactual to test the consistency of the law's equity under a different set of historical conditions, namely, the inverted world of Twain's "Prophesy" sketch. However, the conclusion that Brown draws exists only in a formal vacuum shorn from the historical circumstance that it purportedly seeks to explore. As with Grady, white supremacy is an unchanging constant even in this counterworld where whites form the political minority. Assuming the impartiality of counterfactual conjecture, the court refused to look beyond the internal logic of the law to the larger social context. *Plessy* thus reestablished in law *Dred Scott's* "stigmatization" of blackness with slavery's inherited racial caste status and its "deep and enduring marks of inferiority and degradation." Brown's counterfactual imagination of a dystopic racial future—prefigured in Reconstruction's "bottom rail on top"—would find its most malignant literary redaction in the sinister "future of the new 'Mulatto' nation" in Dixon's *The Leopard's Spots* (1902), the first novel in his Ku Klux Klan trilogy, followed by *The Clansman* (1905) and *The Traitor* (1907) (bk. 1., ch. 10). A self-proclaimed corrective to *Uncle Tom's Cabin*, Dixon's *Leopard's Spots* romanticized white supremacy in portraying the Reconstruction South languishing under the "shadow of the freed Negro," and *The Clansman* later inspired D. W. Griffith's landmark film *The Birth of a Nation* (1915) (bk. 1, ch. 1).

By the 1890s, as Eric Sundquist notes, the pseudoscientific "one-drop" ideology of blackness had begun to transform race into an intrinsic and changeless entity signified by blood in American culture and law (1993, 248). Even though *Plessy* put aside the matter of racial classification, Brown inserted the seed of dissent into its final line when he conceded the possibility of future reassessment: "it may undoubtedly become a question of importance whether, under the laws of Louisiana, the petitioner belongs to the white or colored race." Thus the indeterminacy of race—embodied in Plessy's indiscernible "admixture of black blood"—stands as a legal remainder that undermines the racial logic behind the ruling's affirmation of the "enforced separation of the two races." Tourgée asked in his *Plessy* brief: "Who are white and who are colored? By what rule then shall any tribunal be guided in determining racial character?" This question of racial classification preoccupied novelists in the long nineteenth century, from William Wells Brown's *Clotel; or the President's Daughter* (1853), Frank Webb's *The Garies and Their Friends* (1857), and Harriet Wilson's *Our Nig* (1859) to the postbellum color-line fictions of Tourgée, Howells, Chesnutt, Dunbar, Griggs, Harper, and Hopkins and of later Harlem Renaissance writers, including James Weldon Johnson, Nella Larsen, Jessie Fauset, and George Schuyler. As Stephen Best observes, the counterfactual's conjectural syntax of what might-have-been structures these novels of passing; it asked readers to picture alternate racial histories.

Tourgée's experimentation with an unusual two-fold plot of racial passing in *Pactolus Prime* rehearsed arguments that found their way into his *Plessy* brief. The slave-born Prime passes for white after escaping slavery and joining the Union troops. Well after the Civil War, Prime undergoes another racial transformation when treatments of "nitrate of silver" for a gunshot wound produce a case of argyria that darkens his pigmentation so that he appears to be of pure "Negro blood" (ch. 4). Such a racial transformation would serve satiric fodder for Schuyler's *Black No More* (1931), in which a black doctor invents a process that turns "Negroes into Caucasians" as a solution to America's "Negro problem" (chs. 1, 3; for an extended discussion of Schuyler's *Black No More*, see Chapters 28 and 30 of this volume). Garbed in his "unnatural mask," the embittered Prime surreptitiously oversees the fortune he has painstakingly accrued for his "blue-eyed, fair-haired daughter" (ch. 24). Raised as white, Eva faces the difficult choice between "deception or the confession of inferiority" once she discovers her racial ancestry (ch. 28). Other color-line novels from Griggs's *Pointing the Way* (1908) to Faulkner's *Light in August* (1932) also depicted race as a matter "choice." Of "English, Spanish and Indian descent," Griggs's heroine Eina Rapona relocates to the Jim Crow South and finds herself in the "unique position of being allowed to choose [her] . . . racial home" just as Faulkner's orphaned antihero, Joe Christmas, drifts from one racial identity to another before his violent death in fictional Yoknapatawpha County Mississippi (Griggs, ch. 2). While Eina, like Glover in Chesnutt's *The Quarry*, voluntarily embraces the "colored" world, Tourgée's Eva evades the problem of "choice" by renouncing her white property and privilege to enter the convent as "Sister Pactola" in memory of her father.

The *Plessy* Court played an active role in protecting the exclusionary right to the privileges inhering in whiteness. The law had long established a property interest in whiteness as part of the legacy of legal slavery when whiteness defined a person as either freedman or chattel. By according whiteness legal status, the law, as Cheryl Harris argues, "converted an aspect of identity into an external object of property, moving whiteness from privileged identity to a vested interest" (1993, 1725). In making a violation of due process claim (for depriving Plessy of his "whiteness" as property), Tourgée forced the Court to consider the social meaning of whiteness in an argument adapted from *Pactolus*: "is it possible to conclude that *the reputation of being white* is not property? Indeed, is it not the most valuable sort of property, being the master-key that unlocks the golden door of opportunity?" Tourgée's argument that Plessy suffered a loss of white property baffled Brown, but its significance was not lost on Chesnutt, who later depicted the new-found white racial identity of his *Paul Marchand, F.M.C.* (1921) protagonist in terms of property theft: "he ha[d] been robbed, for all these years, of the sweetest things of life—a father's name, a mother's love—of gentle breeding, of honor and renown, of the companionship of his equals—robbed of them all" (ch. 9).

Tourgée and Howells held conflicting views on American realism, yet their passing novels shared a critique of the racial equality travestied in *Plessy*. In Howells's *An Imperative Duty* (1891), Rhoda Aldgate, raised as white, is shocked to discover that her mother was once the chattel of her grandfather who was an "old slaver, like those in Mr. Cable's book" (ch. 7). Howells recasts the concept of whiteness as property by depicting Rhoda's dramatic "loss of her [white] former self" in her grotesque efforts to "own" her blackness (ch. 8). In place of her lost whiteness, Rhoda finds a hideous vision of African chattel slavery: "a desert with a long coffle of captives passing by, and one black, naked woman, fallen out from weakness, kneeling, with manacled hands" (ch. 8). It is this "desperate retrospect" of black self-dispossession that shapes the "new present in which" Rhoda must "try to gain a footing once more" (chs. 13, 7). Faced with the "choice" of race like Griggs's Eina, Rhoda eventually overcomes her sense of racial duty to pass as white. In thus revisiting an earlier generation of inter-racial marriage plots—including Lydia Maria Child's *The Romance of the Republic* (1867), Rebecca Harding Davis's *Waiting for the Verdict* (1868), and Anna Dickinson's *What Answer* (1868), Howells discloses his meliorist stance on race reconciliation by resolving the novel in the successful interracial union of Rhoda and Dr. Edward Olney on Italian (rather than American) soil, thus repeating with a difference the prior generation's doomed interracial marriage.

The most successful of postbellum black novelists, Chesnutt dedicated his literary career to challenging *Plessy*'s legacy of racial inequity and legal violence. He lamented *Plessy*'s failure to elicit the public outrage of *Dred Scott* for it applied "to a class of rights which do not make to the heart and conscience of the nation the same direct appeal as was made by slavery, and has not been nor is it likely to produce any such revulsion of feeling" ("The Courts and the Negro"). Chesnutt addressed this failure of racial sentiment in a range of novels and unpublished manuscripts, from the pass-ing plots of *Mandy Oxendine* (c.1896–97) and *The House Behind the Cedars* and their inverted doubles in *Paul Marchand* and *The Quarry*, in which white protagonists reject the privileges of whiteness to identify as "black" to the penetrating insights into post-*Plessy* southern race relations in *The Marrow of Tradition* (1901) and *The Colonel's Dream* (1905). In challenging the boundary between the "white and colored races," Chesnutt's passing narratives drew from Tourgée's *Plessy* brief to dramatize the social meanings that accrued to "whiteness." A re-visioning of George Washington Cable's *The Grandissimes* (1880), a historical romance about slavery and racial caste, *Paul Marchand*—Chesnutt's only historical novel—was, in the narrator's words, a "social study" for a *Plessy*-era readership (ch. 17). Like Pauline Hopkins's *Contending Forces* (1900), Chesnutt sets *Paul Marchand* in antebellum Louisiana to emphasize the troubling continuity between slavery and freedom for the "privileges reserved by law or custom for white men only" in Marchand's time bear an uncanny resem-blance to the *Plessy*-era of legalized segregation explored in *Colonel's Dream* (ch. 2). Again adapting Tourgée's slavery argument, Chesnutt's Colonel Henry French sets off on a "fool's errand" to purge the New South of the "retrograde forces . . . of the spirit of slavery, under which the land still groaned and travailed" (ch. 13). Thus en-visioning his work as the "legitimate successor of 'Uncle Tom's Cabin' and 'A Fool's Errand,'" Chesnutt repeatedly returned to the form and substance of *Plessy* to ex-plore the relationship between law and Jim Crow society (qtd. in Elliott 2006, 220).

In an essay published in the *Boston Evening Transcript*, "The White and the Black" (1901), Chesnutt announced that he could "write a book about these [separate car] laws, their variations, their applications and curious stories that one hears continually concerning them." To illustrate his point, Chesnutt recounts a personal encounter aboard a Virginia-bound Jim Crow car—a nearly verbatim transcript of which appears in his final manuscript, *The Quarry*. Chesnutt plies an overweening train conductor—who mistakes Chesnutt for white—with barbed inquiries regarding his arbitrary power to sort the racial identities of passengers. "But suppose," Chesnutt counterfactually poses, "you should find in the colored car a man who had a white face, but insisted that his descent entitled him to ride in that car." The nettled functionary responds with a telling insight into the law's "pretense of equality": "Anyone that is fool enough to rather be a nigger than a white man may have his choice." A chronotope for American industrial progress *and* the racial inequity affirmed in *Plessy*, the Jim Crow car appears frequently in Chesnutt's writings, and *Marrow of Tradition*, the most controversial of his works, offers the best-known literary redaction of *Plessy*. Boarding the North Carolina-bound train at Philadelphia, Dr. William Miller—a representative of the New South's rising black bourgeoisie—shares the company of Dr. Alvin Burns, a white man, until they cross the former Mason-Dixon line. At the instigation of Captain McBane, an avowed white supremacist, the conductor separates Miller and Burns, deferring to the power of the law: "It's the law of Virginia, and I am bound by it as well as you." When Burns attempts to follow Miller into the "Colored" car, the conductor asserts: "white passengers are not permitted to ride in the colored car . . . the law will be enforced. The beauty of the system lies in its strict impartiality—it applies to both races alike" (ch. 5). The men are thus defeated by the "cunningly devised," as Harlan put it, yet selectively enforced law—for Miller's request that the conductor use the same logic of legal impartiality against McBane goes unheeded.

In *Marrow*, Chesnutt rewrites the infamous 1898 white supremacist "revolution" that overtook Wilmington, North Carolina—rooted in the overthrow of Reconstruction two decades prior—to address the continuity of slavery and racial segregation. The wife of a white supremacist, Olivia Carteret engages in agonizing counterfactual conjecture after she suppresses the legal documents affirming the legitimacy of her long-scorned mixed-race half-sister Janet Miller: "If the woman had been white,—but the woman had *not* been white, and the same rule of moral conduct did not, *could* not, in the very nature of things, apply as between white people! For, if this were not so, slavery had been, not merely an economic mistake, but a great crime against humanity" (ch. 30). A chain of conditional "ifs" emerges from Olivia's figurative exchange of black for white woman that leads her, albeit in a transitory flash, to ponder an alternate history—foreclosed by white domination—of legalized theft upon which her property and privilege was founded. *Marrow*'s unresolved ending further intertwines the two households as Dr. Miller, grief-stricken by the slaying of his own son, races to save the Carterets' only child and heir apparent to their white supremacist legacy. Chesnutt thus gives fictional form to Harlan's observation that "the destinies of the two races, in this country, are indissolubly linked together," while addressing the historical contingencies—the legislative history and discriminatory motivation behind Jim Crow—too often effaced in the counterfactual's principle of equality.

Unlike lawyer-novelist Tourgée, black polemicists like Chesnutt and Griggs approached the law as an instrument rather than a source of social change in their didactic fictions. Griggs moved away from the Howellsian realism initially embraced by Chesnutt to formally experiment with counterfactualism and its potential to "reopen received histories" and produce alternative narratives of the past (Bentley 2008, 286). Whereas the *Plessy* majority exploited counterfactual postulates to justify a specious formal equality, Griggs's self-published novels consistently resisted the idea of racial interchangeability, as in *Hindered Hand* (1905): "If through the process of being made white you attain your rights, the battle of the dark man will remain to be fought" (ch. 29). Moreover Griggs drew upon and critically recast *Plessy's* logic of formal equivalence in the racial parallelism and homologies that gave narrative shape to his most significant novel, *Imperium in Imperio* (1899). A secret black counterworld shadowing the US government, the Imperium has its own judiciary branch, deliberates on "every race question submitted to the United States judiciary," and records its decisions "side by side with the decisions of the United States" (ch. 16). This structural homology extends to the two protagonists, the light-skinned Bernard Belgrave and the dark-skinned Belton Piedmont whose stories—beginning in 1867—run along parallel, yet inverted tracks until they are first reunited before the US Supreme Court and again before the Imperium. In a key scene set before the passage of the Louisiana Separate Car Act, Belton runs afoul of southern custom for "the whites had an unwritten but inexorable law, to the effect that no Negro should be allowed to ride in a first-class coach" (ch. 12). The events that befall Belton after his violent ejection from the Louisiana railway facilitate the novel's drift away from realism towards counterfactual imagining. *Plessy's* historical antecedents thus produce an alternate path away from the Supreme Court's affirmation of white supremacy and towards the militant racial counterworld of the Imperium.

Such counterfactual imagining often filtered into the realist fictions grappling with *Plessy's* color line. In the year of the *Plessy* decision, Howells seized upon the publication of Paul Laurence Dunbar's *Majors and Minors* (1895) to advance his utopian vision of what he would later call the "republic of letters where all men are free and equal" ("Psychological Counter-Current in Recent Fiction," *North American Review*). "God hath made of one blood all nations of men," he pronounced in his 1896 *Harper's Weekly* column, "perhaps the proof of this saying is to appear in the arts, and our hostilities and prejudices are to vanish in them" ("Life and Letters"). In *Of One Blood* (1902–3), Hopkins embraced counterfactualism to fashion a fantastical reconfiguration of Howells's metaphor for racial equity. One of three novels Hopkins serialized in the *Colored American Magazine*, *Of One Blood* recasts the racial passing novel as speculative fantasy. Like Twain's *Connecticut Yankee*, Hopkins's novel compresses vast spans of historical time—ancient Ethiopia with industrial America—in Reuel Briggs's discovery of the hidden counter world of Telassar. An adaptation upon (rather than deviation from) the antebellum settings of her historical romances—*Contending Forces, Hagar's Daughter* (1901–2), and *Winona* (1902), Telassar is a gorgeous anachronism: an ancient Ethiopian antecedent that exists in the scientific advance of modern America, for its inhabitants have mastered the techniques of suspended animation. Like Griggs's Imperium, Hopkins's counterworld emerges from the racial histories of American slavery. The apparition of slave mother Mira is the indissoluble tie that binds together Aubrey Livingstone, Dianthe Lusk, and Briggs, marking each sibling with a birthmark in "the perfect semblance of a lily cut, as it were, in shining ebony" (ch. 21). History collides with and reveals this racial counterworld. Hopkins transforms the birthmark and its heredity status of slavery—blackness as the stigma or badge of inferior racial caste that *Plessy* reestablished in American law—into the mark of black sovereign power. "The slogan of the hour is 'Keep the Negro down!'" the narrator exclaims, "but who is clear enough in vision to decide who hath black blood and who hath it not?" (ch. 21). In rewriting the history of white domination, Hopkins formally elaborates the counterfactual's conjectural syntax in the annals of Telassar's alternative past, inscribed (like Twain's sketch) in "the language of prophecy" (ch. 17).

In a Foreign Tongue

In 1887, Florida enacted one of the first separate car laws requiring railroads to furnish Jim Crow cars for black passengers. Other southern states quickly adopted similar laws "separating the races in railway cars," including Louisiana where *Plessy* originated. That same year, sixteen-year-old James Weldon Johnson boarded the first-class car of the overnight train that would take him to Atlanta University. As he described it in his autobiography, *Along This Way* (1933), Johnson shared this momentous journey with his friend Ricardo Rodriguez, a Cuban who had been sent to the United States to "learn English" (ch. 6). Unaware of the new separate car law, the young men noted a "number of colored people had got on the train but we were the only ones in the first-class car." Johnson was baffled when the conductor gruffly asked the two to "get out of this car and into the one ahead." Sensing trouble, but uncertain of the conductor's words, Ricardo asked Johnson "¿Que dice?" The conductor's attitude changed when he heard the men "speaking a foreign language," and Johnson recalls how he "punched our tickets . . . and treated us just as he did the other passengers in the car." Presumed to be foreigners, the two men were granted the privileges of whiteness withheld from black citizens. Thus facing his "first impact of race prejudice as a concrete fact," Johnson concluded, "that in such situations any kind of a Negro will do; provided he is not one who is an American citizen" (ch. 7). Drawing attention to his racialized citizenship, Johnson's reminiscences illuminate another facet of the *Plessy* case that pivoted on the question of comparative rights and protections accorded to black citizens in relation to aliens and foreigners.

Harlan's dissent to *Plessy* disputed the constitutionality of black-white segregation, yet only by way of comparison to the alien status of the "Chinese race." It imagined an entirely different scenario of interracial contact as it hypothetically inserted a "Chinaman" into the white train car:

> There is a race so different from our own that we do not permit those belonging to it to become citizens of the United States . . . I allude to the Chinese race. But, by the statute in question, a Chinaman can ride in the same passenger coach with white citizens of the United States, while citizens of the black race in Louisiana, many of whom, perhaps, risked their lives for the preservation of the Union . . . and who have all the legal rights that belong to white citizens, are yet declared to be criminals, liable to imprisonment, if they ride in a public coach occupied by citizens of the white race.

In rejecting racial "caste" legislation, Harlan drew another line of demarcation between black and white citizens and Chinese aliens who were deemed politically inassimilable to the nation but not (it would appear) to the unstable legal category of "whiteness." By emphasizing Chinese difference as a "race" reclassified by the Chinese Exclusion Act (1882) as "aliens ineligible to citizenship," Harlan sought to combat the "sentiment of alienism," in Cable's words, directed against African Americans by enfolding black racial difference within the embrace of national identity. This romance of black-white national reunification came at the expense of another proscribed race. *Plessy* thus recast the dialectic of racial assimilation to the United States—here rendered in terms of black inclusion and Chinese exclusion.

Plessy's citation of what many legal scholars now view as the landmark equal protection precedent set in *Yick Wo v. Hopkins* (1886) may have provoked Harlan's scenario of Chinese alienism. As one of *Plessy*'s buried texts, *Yick Wo* emerged out of a contest between California and the federal government to control Chinese immigration. It involved a San Francisco police law prohibiting the operation of laundries in wooden buildings without the consent of the city board of supervisors. Convicted and jailed for laundering without a license, Yick Wo appealed to the US Supreme Court after losing his writ of habeas corpus. Although scholars continue to debate over the dicta and holding in the case, the unanimous Court broadened the construction of "equal protection" and "due process" (here, the economic right to pursue a lawful occupation) to "strangers and aliens" like the Chinese who were accorded a non-national status under the United States–China treaty that came into force in 1858 (amended in 1868 as the Burlingame Treaty). Unlike the "privileges or immunities" clause, the "due process" and "equal protection" clauses were not limited to "citizens of the United States," but applied to "any person." In *Yick Wo*'s most famous passage, the court determined that while the ordinance carried race-neutral language, its discriminatory enforcement violated equal protection. "Though the law itself be fair on its face and impartial in appearance," wrote Justice Thomas Stanley Matthews, "yet if it is applied and administered by a public authority with an evil eye and an unequal hand . . . the denial of equal justice is still within the prohibition of the Constitution." *Yick Wo* thus judged all persons "without regard to any differences of race, of color, or of nationality" within the scope of the Fourteenth Amendment although the Fourteenth Amendment's malleability—evinced in the counterfactual contortions of "equal but separate"—often enabled, as with *Plessy*, racial discrimination under the aegis of constitutional sanction.

Despite *Yick Wo*'s antidiscriminatory mien, jurists (until the Civil Rights era) generally interpreted the case for different ends. A decade later, Brown found *Plessy*'s segregated public accommodations "reasonable" and consistent with *Yick Wo*. He named *Yick Wo* as a glaring instance of the unreasonable exercise of state police power directed not "in good faith for the promotion for the public good," but for the "oppression of a particular class," namely the Chinese. For Brown, the *Yick Wo* precedent served as an example both of the Court's support for equal protection and "of a supposedly truer case of racial discrimination," according to Hoang Gia Phan (2006, 30). Unlike in *Yick Wo*, however, the *Plessy* Court refused to examine the legislative motivations behind the Louisiana Separate Car Act. Like the deceptive counterfactual invoked to test the consistency of the law's equity, Brown offers another form of interchange—between black citizen and Chinese alien—in counterpoising *Yick Wo*'s standard of misuse against *Plessy*'s reasonable use of police power.

Harlan urged the court not to abandon black citizens to Jim Crow in judging "equal accommodations" as somehow equal to the test of equal protection. Assaulting *Plessy*'s "thin disguise of 'equal' accommodations," Harlan marshaled the metaphor of color-blindness and its powerful logic of impartiality: "There is no caste here. Our Constitution is color-blind, and neither knows nor tolerates classes among citizens." Harlan borrowed this metaphor from Tourgée, who used the phrase critically rather than affirmatively in *Bricks without Straw* and later honed the idea of "color blindness" in his *Plessy* brief. Tourgée reminded the justices of Themis, the Greek goddess of justice: "Justice is pictured blind, and her daughter, the Law, ought at least to be color-blind." For Harlan, the Chinese alien—like the black nurse exception—troubles the distinction between "white" and "colored races" mandated by Louisiana law. Harlan lamented the diversion of the Fourteenth Amendment away from the protection of black citizenship, yet his call for constitutional "color-blindness"—one of the most enduring expressions of the ideal of racial equality in the United States—was at its heart racially particularized. In the following judicial term, Harlan's rejection of the native-birth citizenship claims of children born of Chinese parents on American soil in *United States v. Wong Kim Ark* (1898) offered a dramatic counterpoint to his celebrated *Plessy* dissent.

Both Chesnutt and Griggs captured in fictional form the differential racial logic at work in Harlan's dissent. In *Marrow*, Chesnutt offered a detailed restaging of Harlan's imaginary of Chinese alienism. Forced from the company of Dr. Burns and into the "colored car," Dr. Miller watches as "a Chinaman, of the ordinary laundry type, boarded the train, and took his seat in the white car without objection" (ch. 5). In *Imperium*, Griggs also plied Harlan's Chinese comparison to test the unequal measure of black civil rights, yet in his baroque fashion, multiplied the counterfactual variants: "An Italian, a Frenchman, a German, a Russian, a Chinaman and a Swede come, let us suppose, on a visit to our country." "Unable to understand our language," these various "strangers" are called upon to ask a black child to interpret the placard prohibiting the entry of "Negroes and dogs" into a public park built by the "unrequited toil" of African Americans (ch. 17). Without singling out the Chinese, Griggs's novel, like Harlan's dissent, sought to shift the question of equal protection from the axis of black-white racial identity to the axis of citizenship and national identity.

Unlike her sister who wrote under the pen name "Sui Sin Far," Chinese Eurasian Winnifred Eaton responded to the historical conditions of US anti-Chinese sentiment by passing herself off as Japanese. Using the pseudonym Onoto Watanna, Eaton set many of her early novels in a foreign Japan; yet their explorations of racial identity and miscegenation absorbed and refracted *Plessy*-era debates over the unstable categories of white and nonwhite, citizen and alien. The dilemmas faced by her racially indeterminate Eurasian heroines often implicitly recast, in the words from *Daughters of Nijo* (1904), the "turbulent, restless, troublous" quandaries of American race relations and national belonging in the plot of the romance novel (ch. 1). Howells, for example, compared Chesnutt's *Marrow* and its bitter "relations of the blacks and whites" to the "irresistible charm" of Eaton's *A Japanese Nightingale* (1903). The Eurasian Yuki, writes Howells, alluding to Chesnutt's polemical treatment of black-white miscegenation, is made "outcast from her own people—the conventions seem to be as imperative in Tokyo as in Philadelphia—because of her half-caste origin" ("Psychological Counter-Current in Recent Fiction"). Like other color-line fictions, Eaton emphasizes the construction of race as a social category, but further complicates it by recasting it in the figure of the foreigner. Eaton's use of Irish immigrant characters and her tendency to "whiten" her Japanese protagonists, as Gretchen Murphy argues, highlights the "plasticity of race" in an era when the distinction between the "white" and "colored race," as well as the boundary between citizen and alien (or the domestic and foreign), retained a measure of legal indeterminacy (2007, 33).

"Two Stories in One"

Published as *Plessy* moved through the Supreme Court docket, Twain's famously vexed narrative of mistaken racial identity, *Pudd'nhead Wilson* offers one of the most penetrating literary analogues to *Plessy*'s two-fold problematic of racial classification and national assimilation. First serialized in *Century Magazine*, Twain reworked *Pudd'nhead* and republished it with "Those Extraordinary Twins" as a single volume in 1894. As "two stories in one," *Pudd'nhead*'s allegorical tale of slavery and black-white race relations also addressed the growing unease over foreign immigration and racial multiplicity in post-Reconstruction America (Sundquist 1993, 227). Twain weaves a seemingly superfluous subplot chronicling the misadventures of Italian twins—identical in the tragedy, but conjoined in the farce from which the tragedy, Twain tells us, was born—to secure American citizenship into his wry exploration of race relations. The conjoined twins, loosely based on Chang and Eng, the "original Siamese Twins," allude to the other racial history referenced in *Plessy*'s *Yick Wo* precedent and Harlan's dissent. Well-known public figures, Chang and Eng first appeared in Twain's writing in an 1869 Civil War sketch to reemerge as *Pudd'nhead*'s buried text. Twain merged aspects of Chang and Eng with performers Giovanni and Giacomo Tocci to create the Italian "twin-monster"—the dark-skinned Luigi and the fair-skinned Angelo. A collective figure for the foreign, the conjoined twins appear monstrous in their lack of individuality, calling to mind both the specter of foreign masses and cross-racial "combination" promulgated in nativist propaganda. The representational disorder of Twain's "twin-monster" thus offers a "useful, albeit problematic trope" for testing the possibility of unity within a nation struggling to contain racial "difference and dissent" within its ever-expanding borders (Wu 2008, 34).

Judged to be equal, but conjoined before the law, the twins' corporate unity also challenges the *Plessy* Court's view of black and white as interchangeable and therefore equal before the law. Twain's Chang and Eng sketch had parodied interchangeability as a measure of equity in depicting a Civil War army court faced with deciding which of the conjoined twins had taken the other prisoner; it rules to "exchang[e] them." *Pudd'nhead* settles a similar legal impasse with the lynching of one the conjoined twins, thus killing the innocent along with the guilty. In this unsettling resolution, we might read a satiric riposte to *Plessy*'s ideological separation of social from political rights. Twain's "freak of form," as Susan Gillman puts it, dramatizes racial interchangeability in the tragedy while lampooning its formal failure—*Plessy*'s notion of a racially divided citizenship—in the comedy (Gillman and Robinson 1990, xii).

Two years after *Plessy*, the United States would begin its overseas empire with the annexation of Hawaii, and then Puerto Rico, Guam, and the Philippines in the Spanish-American War of 1898 as it brought into alignment white supremacy and imperial rule. For Dixon's *Leopard's Spots*, the Spanish-American War realized the "beautiful dream called *E Pluribus Unum*" for a long sectionalized "Anglo-Saxon" America (bk. 3, ch. 9). This fantasy of US race and empire found its critical counterpart in writers who envisioned (with mixed emotions) the articulation of black protest in the United States with colonial resistance abroad. Spurred by his reading of Chesnutt's *Marrow*, Howells exclaimed in a letter to novelist Henry Blake Fuller: "How such a Negro must hate us. And then think of the Filipinos and the Cubans and Puerto Ricans whom we have added to our happy family" (November 10, 1901).

In the Insular Cases (1901–22), the Supreme Court again reaffirmed the uneven, racialized application of the Constitution established by *Plessy* as it judged the subjects of these unincorporated territories US citizens in matters of discipline and taxation, yet ineligible to full protection under the Fourteenth Amendment. In *The Souls of Black Folk* (1903), W. E. B. Du Bois cast his color-line thesis within this two-fold context of race and empire: the "problem of the twentieth century is the problem of the color-line, the relation of the darker to lighter races of men in Asia and Africa, in America and the islands of the sea" (ch. 2). The modern era of US race relations inaugurated by *Plessy's* doctrine of "equal but separate" was not isolated from the global forces of colonization and racialization. The conjoined or "freak" form of *Pudd'nhead*, no less than the counterfactual imaginings of the other novelists discussed here, reflect even as they informed the wide-ranging debates about race, law, and literature of the post-Reconstruction United States (on race, expansion, and the novel, see Chapter 12 in this volume).

7

DOCUMENTING THE REAL

BY AUGUSTA ROHRBACH

Alfred Kazin once famously declared that without the political upheaval of the French Revolution, Americans lacked the philosophical basis for realism (*On Native Ground*, 1942). Clearly, Kazin did not consider the political dramas that Americans living through the slavery debates, the Civil War, and the labor unrest of the postbellum period had witnessed. Nineteenth-century Americans were no strangers to the political turmoil and social critique that inspired the most important literary movement of the period.

More recently, scholars have cast realism as a reaction to the sentimental fiction of the antebellum era. Antebellum writers such as Nathaniel Hawthorne and Herman Melville characterized the female-authored blockbusters of sentimentalism as both aesthetically inferior and emotionally cheap. From the late 1870s through the turn of the twentieth century, editor and author William Dean Howells inherited this tradition, offering realism as a mark of masculine professionalism and counter-weight to the emotional excess and melodrama of the sentimental novel, as in his derision of female readers of the imaginary novel, *Tears, Idle Tears,* in *The Rise of Silas Lapham* (1885). As editor of the *Atlantic* and *Harper's Monthly*, Howells occupied a platform that allowed him to formulate literary realism as a professionalized writing practice that could meet the approbation of institutional gatekeepers (on the business of literature created by authors and editors, see Chapter 2 of this volume).

This narrative of American literary history usefully emphasizes the business of literature created by a network of authors and editors who sought to professionalize literary writing in the late nineteenth century and who believed their doing so constituted a break with the recent practice of literature in the United States. Neither of these two conventional accounts, however, tells the full story of US literary realism—how it came to be and why it holds such an important place in US literary history. Both have overlooked the importance of the rhetoric of antebellum as well as postbellum radical reform movements in fashioning realism, which make it a partial legacy of rather than complete break with sentimentalism.

The Roots of Realism

Both the spread of reform movements and the development of realism in the United States stemmed from the rapidly expanding world of print. Technological advances ranging from moveable type, stereoscopic printing—two identical images printed side by side for a three-dimensional effect—and the development of photography made information rapidly available to large numbers of people. The influx of print media fueled discussion of contemporary topics of interests. As news and information circulated, the literary marketplace expanded to take advantage of a growing reading public and its political conscience. As documented elsewhere in this volume, these tumultuous decades witnessed a dramatic expansion of periodical publication as well as the creation of the "bestseller" as a recognized publishing phenomenon.

American print culture had long played a significant role in the national debate over slavery, emancipation, African American citizenship, and Reconstruction—and these connections influenced the rise of realism after the Civil War. The connection of both antislavery and sentimental writing to realism is evident in the writing of Harriet Beecher Stowe, whose 1852 novel *Uncle Tom's Cabin* was the second best-selling book in the United States, after the Bible. Stowe famously declared that "God wrote" the novel, yet she followed its publication with a nonfiction source book entitled *A Key to Uncle Tom's Cabin* (1853), designed to verify the facts upon which her bestseller was based. This moment in literary history epitomizes the intertwining of fact and fiction that characterized the period and forecast the terms of the realist novel with its impulse to document foundational details as a way to effect social change. Considering Stowe as a protorealist author makes visible an important debt that US literary realism has to both the political work and artistic legacy of abolitionist narratives.

In *A Key*, Stowe affirmed *Uncle Tom's Cabin's* debt to the slave narratives, thereby establishing a genealogy for several stylistic and thematic features that realism shares with them. Providing readers with sources, Stowe encouraged them to demand verifiable details in a fictional work. Using slave narratives as a source meant drawing on the lives of real people whose suffering had real consequences. The narrators of these accounts recognized their stories as necessary political tools, written and sold to help support those suffering under the bonds of slavery as well as to promote the abolitionist cause. William Lloyd Garrison, editor of the longest running abolitionist newspaper, *The Liberator,* affirmed that connection as he encouraged and published Frederick Douglass's 1845 *Narrative of Frederick Douglass, An American Slave, Written by Himself.* The popularity of the slave narratives both as propaganda and as works that freely circulated in the literary marketplace emphasized the power of literary mimesis. Central to their success was the incorporation of different forms of documentation, from the inclusion of author frontispieces and letters testifying to their authenticity to the many verifiable details that added drama as well as verisimilitude to these works. Authors of these works often noted the need to withhold details of their escape in order to avoid disclosing information that would compromise the efforts of those who sought to follow them from enslavement to freedom as well as those who aided them.

The historical connections between antislavery literature and American realist fiction are more than rhetorical, or even thematic. The two forms share a breeding ground: the *Atlantic Monthly*. Established in 1857, the *Atlantic Monthly*, which subsequently became known as the *Atlantic,* grew out of an acknowledged need for a national literature that reflected the professed democratic principles of the nation, quickly becoming the most significant print venue for literature in the United States. Calling itself "A Magazine of Literature, Art, and Politics," the periodical declared the interrelation of those categories, although "politics" animated the magazine from its outset.

A guiding principle of the politics of the periodical concerned the role of literature and the arts in building of a distinctly American culture. Along with other major figures of the period, the magazine's founding editor, James Russell Lowell, insisted in an essay written for the *North American Review*, that "our literature" should "give a true reflection of our social, political, and household life." American literature, he declaimed, "should be national to the extent of being free from outworn conventionalities and as thoroughly impregnated with humane and manly sentiment as is the idea on which our political fabric rests" (1849, 209). That sentiment, for Lowell, could not be reconciled with the institution of slavery.

Lowell was already an experienced editor, having served as editor of an abolitionist newspaper in Philadelphia. His politics played an important role in shaping the magazine, causing several contributors, Henry David Thoreau among them, to complain about his heavy editorial hand when it came to politics. Political essayist Parke Goodwin argued that his work was distorted and his reasoning cheapened by Lowell's editorializing, remarking that he did not intend "to write sensation articles for the news vendors." (qtd. Sedgwick 1994, 47). Yet, for models, Lowell looked to unabashedly political editors, such as Garrison, whom he described in *Words of Garrison*'s prefatory poem as having a "dauntless spirit and a press." *The Liberator*'s records show that the *Atlantic Monthly* under Lowell's editorship held not just one, but three subscriptions to the paper. Garrison's success with the paper—measured by its notoriety more than its balance sheet—was linked to his insistence that he be "as harsh as truth, and as uncompromising as justice," as he put it in the first issue of the *Liberator*. The number of copies circulating at the *Atlantic*'s office suggests Lowell's admiration for the paper both as a source of information and as an example worth sharing.

Like Lowell's demand that US literature be a "true reflection of our social, political, and household life," Garrison's aesthetic preferred examples from ordinary life. He tended toward the "real," even the "too real." He frequently reached for the uppercase so as to make his pages almost audible. "No! no!" Garrison exclaims: "Tell a man whose house is on fire to give moderate alarm; tell him to moderately rescue his wife from the hands of the ravisher; tell the mother to gradually extricate her babe from the fire into which it has fallen;—but urge me not to use moderation in a cause like the present." He concludes this explosive declaration of his devotion to the cause with: "I am in earnest—I will not equivocate—I will not excuse—I will not retreat a single inch—AND I WILL BE HEARD . . . " (1883, 1). His shrill use of typeface, varying font and size, was meant to affront a public that would become inundated with a steady flow of "the real," representations of the gritty details of life and death through the explosion of all forms of print media, and of photography in particular. With the advent of the daguerreotype, for instance, broadly circulating images of war showed the inglorious ends of young soldiers decomposing on the bucolic pastures that had become the battlefields of the Civil War. He broke with prevailing print conventions (and social norms) not to capture readers' money, but to move them toward his radical agenda for change. What some contributors experienced as editorial heavyhandedness was, for Lowell, a political legacy.

The *Atlantic Monthly* emerged from the widespread call for *American* authors who could articulate the democratic values of the nation, and for Lowell, those values were incompatible with slavery. They also entailed presenting American culture and custom without varnish. Lowell's editorial influence included his advocacy of stylistic experimentations, for which the *Atlantic Monthly* became known. In 1897, Henry James described Lowell as "the American of his time most saturated with literature and most directed to criticism" (James, 1897). Unlike many of his Harvard colleagues, however, Lowell was committed to a literature that represented the nation as it was, and among his most important experiments was a commitment to dialect.

A founder of the American Dialect Society, Lowell clearly saw dialect as a form of realism—a way to root his characters in place as part of his nationalizing agenda. His serialized satiric poems written in dialect under the title *The Biglow Papers* (1848) were an immediate success. Today his interest in dialect might seem incompatible with his abolitionism, since dialect literature has notoriously served to produce a virulent racism as a form of comedy, whether in the hands of the Southwest humor writers before the Civil War, or the plantation school of Southern apologists afterwards. Yet, for Lowell, dialect reflected homespun American wisdom. His plainspeaking titular character, Hosea Biglow, accurately captured Lowell's belief that language—especially when vernacular—is a meaningful reflection of natural intellect. What his character lacked in schoolbook learning, he more than made up for in cunning and sheer smarts.

Lowell used the venue of the *Atlantic Monthly* to promote writers who would expand the purview of his readers, and dialect and other regionalist markers appealed to his nationalizing streak as much as they seemed to represent a democratizing instinct. At least two of the major realists—Mark Twain and William Dean Howells—owe their interest and skill in dialect writing to Lowell's popular efforts. Of course, Twain's use of dialect is famous, causing Shelly Fisher Fishkin to speculate—in a news-breaking item on the front page of the *New York Times*—that the character of Huckleberry Finn might have been based on a young African American boy of Twain's acquaintance. Less has been said, however, about how dialect in the mouths of white characters and Yankees in particular reflects an effort to claim a kind of indigeneity that is typically associated with race rather than region in realist fiction. Stowe cleverly transferred the signifying power dialect had in her portrayals of African American characters in *Uncle Tom's Cabin* to New England Yankees in works like her 1869 *Old Town Folks*. In the tradition of Lowell's *Bigelow Papers*, Stowe marks the authenticity of her characters through their use of dialect.

Lowell helped to make dialect a convention of realism, supported in that venture by a frequent contributor who would become a well-known editor (of the *Atlantic Monthly*) in his own right. Hailing from well beyond the precincts of New England, Howells exhibited a "Western flavor" in the poems he sent in 1860, unsolicited, to the *Atlantic*. Lowell not only published several of these poems, but he also fostered the young writer as an emerging literary business professional. Upon Howells's arrival in Cambridge, Lowell provided him with letters of introduction to many of New England's most influential writers, including Hawthorne. It is not surprising that Howells would eventually become heir to the *Atlantic* editorship through his position as assistant editor (1866–71) and would continue to foster the "Yankee humanism" for which the journal had become known (Sedgwick 1994).

Like Lowell, Howells believed in fueling particular political agendas with the power of story. In an 1866 *Atlantic Monthly* review of M. L. Putnam's novel *Fifteen Days*, Howells wrote, "this is a work of fiction, in which the passion of love, so far from being the prime motive, as in other fictions, does not enter at all. The author seeks to reach, without other incident, one tragic event, and endeavors to make up for a want of adventure by the subtle analysis of character and the study of a civil problem." What makes this treatment subtle for Howells is the novel's approach. Placing little emphasis on romance as a fictional device or on slavery for its narrative tension, the author instead focuses on "the personal and social results of the system with incisive acuteness united to a warmth of feeling which at last breaks forth into pathetic lament" (Sedgwick 1994, 63). Howells's praise for the work stresses its realism as well as its politics.

These values were consistent with Lowell's successor at the *Atlantic*, publisher James T. Fields, whose editorial agenda is evident in the change on the magazine's front cover from the image of Shakespeare to the American flag. Abolitionist from its beginnings, the increased sectionalism that came along with the advent of the Civil War shifted the magazine's emphasis from New England to the country. When he took the editorial helm, Fields implemented strategies to promote and extend American culture beyond Lowell's stomping ground: New England. Now the magazine leveraged the sectional interests of the North to further feed its nationalizing tendency. The publication's continuing commitment to linking literature with politics resulted in a broadening range of topics that would appeal to people beyond the precincts of New England and that would contribute to the development of realism.

The Business of Literature

Like the abolitionists who preceded them, realists celebrated the power of literature as a political tool and as an emissary of social justice. Indeed, the particular brand of literary realism forming in the United States might find more accurate expression in the phrase "humanitarian realism." As abolitionists had before them, the realists turned to documentation to protect the ideological agenda of the work from being dismissed as mere fiction. The writers who took up these practices believed in literature as a likely catalyst for social reform, and many were drawn to the literary marketplace through journalism and other forms of civic engagement. Although no other realist of the nineteenth century would resort to the degree of documentation in, for example, Stowe's *Key*, authors who advocated realism favored subject matter that had a direct tie to contemporary social issues such as slavery, child labor, spousal abuse, labor unrest, housing conditions, even divorce and abortion—themes taken up by such authors as George Washington Cable, Ellen Glasgow, William Dean Howells, Henry James, Mark Twain, and Edith Wharton. Realist writers infused the relationship between form and content by using the minutiae of everyday life to engage a wide variety of readers.

As literary works sought an increasingly quotidian relationship with the world around them, however, some authors wondered if this mimesis came with a sacrifice of aesthetic achievement. Even Stowe mused in her introduction to *A Key* that the burden of "proof," if too exacting, might render a work "inartistic":

> Artistically considered, it might not be best to point out in which quarry and from which region each fragment of the mosaic picture had its origin; and it is equally unartistic to disentangle the glittering web of fiction, and show out of what real warp and woof it is woven, and with what real colouring dyed. (ch. 1)

A novel that emphasizes its real and verifiable basis, Stowe suggested, risks its classification as a work of art, snagging the "glittering web of fiction" on fact. The artist who drew on real life at the expense of imagination might not be seen as an artist at all. Yet the potent melding of fact and fiction attracted both writers and a growing number of readers to the genre from the outset. Whatever the risk, Stowe explained in the *Key*, "the book had a purpose entirely transcending the artistic one, and accordingly encounters at the hands of the public demands not usually made on fictitious works. It is *treated* as a reality—sifted, tried, and tested, as a reality; and therefore as a reality it may be proper that it should be defended" (ch. 1). Even though reality can demand a cost from the artist, Truth was its own form of Beauty, making the bond between politics and aesthetics an essential feature of the genre.

Realist writers tended to work from fact to fiction. Important examples of this practice are a pair of novels that virtually bookend Howells's writing career: his first novel, *Their Wedding Journey* (1872), and his later, more ambitious *A Hazard of New Fortunes* (1890). In the former, he eschews the dramatic story of courtship in favor of the postnuptials wedding trip taken by the main characters, Basil and Isabel March. Howells further defies traditional tastes for romance in literature by casting the Marches as older than the typical newlyweds, and thus lacking the dewy-eyed innocence of a young married couple. Unlike his contemporaries, Howells typically began his novels with marriage rather than ended them with a wedding. (When Howells does feature courtships in his novels, they can be deeply troubled by unconventional problems, such as the threat of racial mixing in his 1891 novel, *An Imperative Duty*.)

In a review of *Their Wedding Journey*, Henry Adams acknowledged Howells's skill at portraying the ordinary, but also worried that such an acute focus on the ordinary may be more useful for marriage advice than as the basis for art. Adams's highest praise, in the end, is for the book's peculiar utility: "It deserves to be among the first of the gifts which follow or precede the marriage offer. It has, we believe, had a marked success in this way, as a sort of lovers' Murray or Appleton; and if it can throw over the average bridal couple some reflection of its own refinement and taste, it will prove itself a valuable assistant to American civilization" (1872, 444–45). The homespun charm and down-to-earth approach Adams appreciates is epitomized by the Marches choice to avoid the glamor of a "honeymoon" and instead delay their trip until they could quietly slip away. The book is full of such clear-headed choices, offering a portrait of (a comparatively unromanticized) American life that many readers would recognize as their own. Adams accordingly justified Stowe's concern as he found the merit of Howells's novel in its social rather than aesthetic value.

For Howells, however, realism required representative protagonists in everyday scenarios, such as the increasingly inevitable sacrifices white, middle-class (and sometimes lower-middle-class) protagonists must make to earn a living. Howells returned to Isabel and Basil March in *A Hazard of New Fortunes*. One can only speculate on what Adams might have said about this novel concerning the relationship between money and motive, this time focusing on the now expanded publishing world that Howells himself helped to create. Isabel and Basil leave their home in Boston (a move that readers would know Howells himself had undertaken) to take a new position in New York. *A Hazard of New Fortunes* devotes several long chapters to their search for an apartment they can afford. No detail of their decision-making process is left out. Readers are privy to their finances, family concerns, and particular prejudices as they try to find an apartment that fulfills as many of their desires as possible, including affordability. Their ordinary struggles, coupled with the fact that they, along with Howells's devoted following of readers, have aged, make them perfect candidates for this foray into the pitfalls of late capitalism as it meets a thriving literary marketplace.

The fiscal worries of the Marches are characteristic of the dominant strain of literary realism that emerged in the late nineteenth century. Conflicts central to works in the realist vein often arise from financial exigencies, which is characteristic of both European realism and of antislavery writing of the United States. Literary realism in US fiction addresses the relationship between freedom and economy and focuses that relationship on a white, middle-class consciousness. Consider the beginnings of two paradigmatic novels: Uncle Tom is sold away from his home and family because of Mr. Shelby's debts in Stowe's novel. In Howells's *The Rise of Silas Lapham*, the reversal of fortune of the eponymous character is also set in motion by taking on too much debt, causing his family's downward spiral. Like Tom in Stowe's novel, financial exigencies lead the way to a new beginning. For Tom, whose story has its roots in the evangelicalism of the earlier period, the new beginning will be in heaven, and outside the limits of the novel. Lapham, too, ascends—not to heaven, but to a level of secular ethics. His epiphany signals a return to an earlier simpler time and place, relinquishing big-city Boston for rural New England. The novel brings together a critique of commercialism, post-industrial business practices, and the soul-sucking potential of big-city life. But at base, as different as these novels and the histories they describe are, they are all large-scale critiques of capitalism and the real-life suffering capitalism creates.

Realism used financial matters as both a quotidian detail and a major theme. In realist fiction, the reader often learns the precise cost of a home or a meal, the exact dollar figure of a wager or a debt. These references to money and finance helped produce an effect of social mimesis; some realist authors, moreover, used these details to gauge the relationship between social injustice and capitalism. In particular, Howells became increasingly vocal over the course of his career about the relationship between capital and social inequity.

Like the Yankee humanists who came before him, Howells believed that writing—and writers—mattered and could effectively address social conflicts. He joined a long line of author-activists who used print to heighten consciousness to the political issues of his time as Garrison, Lowell and Stowe had opposed slavery. Howells paid for his convictions; his outspoken opposition to the execution of the so-called Haymarket anarchists—eight men accused of planning a bombing during a Chicago rally in 1886—for example, earned him widespread scorn from the American press (on Howells and the Haymarket anarchists, see Chapter 33 of this volume). The sole literary figure to take on the imposed sentence of this landmark case, to stand both with organized labor and against the death penalty for political protesters, he was disappointed to see that his letter of protest had no effect on the outcome. But the impulse to defend labor against capital remained an important theme in his writing as well as his editorial work throughout his career.

As editor first of the *Atlantic Monthly* and later *Harper's Monthly*, Howells launched the careers of many writers known in their moment and into the present for their artfully realist depictions of social worlds to which mainstream America had little access: the worlds of immigrants, African Americans, and the impoverished. During his tenure as editor of the *Atlantic* (1871–81), Howells continued the project begun by Lowell—who famously published William Parker's "The Freedman's Story" in February/March 1866. Howells was the first to publish subsequently prominent nonwhite authors including Charles Chesnutt, Lawrence Dunbar, and Alice Dunbar-Nelson and to argue that their voices were essential to the creation of "American" literature. He promoted the socialist Yiddish writer Abraham Cahan and the indigenous writer Gertrude Bonnin (Zitkala-Sa). Howells bridged literary worlds, championing not only lesser known writers, but such luminaries as Mark Twain and Henry James.

A distinct difference between Howells's stewardship of the *Atlantic* and Lowell's, however, can be measured by the changes in the literary marketplace. Howells had to compete with a greater proliferation of periodicals than Lowell, including the attractive illustrated monthlies. Nevertheless, he successfully expanded the *Atlantic's* reader base to include middle-class readers. To capture those readers, Howells published material that considered social issues from a broader constituency than had his predecessors, opening the magazine to his progressive ideas about democracy. Howells put himself under the very same market pressures his readers experienced, as part of his own artistic process. In 1881, Johns Hopkins University offered him a lucrative professorship that he refused. A few years later, he was offered the prestigious position formerly occupied by Lowell at Harvard, and he turned that down, too. Howells clearly believed that his position as literary midwife to realism was best served not from the Ivory Tower, but rather from the editor's chair. He not only understood that literature is linked to the marketplace, but he dared to write about it in "The Man of Letters as a Man of Business," an essay published in 1893.

Money Matters

The link between business and authorship was an important theme for Howells's friend and fellow literary realist Samuel Clemens, also known as Mark Twain. Well known for his failed investment in moveable type, Twain subtly incorporated the link into his writing. At the center of many of the horrors and the hoaxes that prevail upon Huckleberry Finn are the conflicting values between capitalism and moral responsibility. Huck's famous declaration, "all right, then, I'll go to Hell" rather than turn his companion, the enslaved Jim, in to slave catchers, is just one example of how business (in this case, the business of slavery) violates the basic precepts of friendship and loyalty. Huck's father, Pap, is motivated to return for his son not from any paternal feeling, but to take his fortune from him. Held captive in a rude cabin by his drunken father, Huck tells readers that he "was all over with welts" and that Pap "got to going away so much, too, and locking me in" (ch. 6). Much of the comedy of the book derives from the money-making schemes of the imposter King and Duke—continuing a leitmotif of petty confidence men seeking easy gain that runs throughout Twain's fiction. *A Connecticut Yankee in King Arthur's Court*, Twain's tongue-in-cheek spoof of chivalry, offers a more substantial reflection on capitalistic production, with the main character moving from a job in a nineteenth-century factory to create a medieval one in Arthur's England. As Cindy Weinstein has observed, "Twain imagined the scene of writing to be inextricably connected to the scene of industrial production" (1995, 129).

Later realism, contrary to most sentimental fiction, cast doubt on the power of noble character to prevail against the ravages of finance and fortune. While early realist texts showed how capital could destroy the characters we care about the most, later realist novels refused to soothe readers even with the redemptive possibilities of a Christian afterlife. The death of Edith Wharton's Lily Bart in *The House of Mirth* (1905), for example, offers no clear moral redemption. Readers were devastated by Lily's demise. R. W. B. Lewis reports that one reader "said that when she read the final installment, she was so overcome that she telegraphed a friend, 'Lily Bart is dead'" (1975, 152). The outpouring of sentiment encouraged Wharton to account for her decision to kill her off. The novelist blamed artistic necessity and realism for the death of her character, explaining, "A frivolous society can acquire dramatic significance only through what its frivolity destroys. Its tragic implications lie in its power of debasing people and ideas" (Lewis 1975, 207). From naming Lily's bracelets "shackles" to depicting her dancing blithely to plantation music right before her final descent into poverty, Wharton aligns the debasing of human culture through capitalism with the brutalizing effect of slavery. Just as Frederick Douglass refused to participate in slavery's degrading exchange by purchasing his freedom, Lily refuses the opportunity to trade human virtue for capitalist value. Though Douglass was finally convinced to allow supporters to buy him out of slavery, his position registered a resounding critique of the pernicious effects of capitalism. Realists recognize—and condemn—capitalism as a corrosive force.

But while the slave narratives' critiques of capitalism centered on how slavery—as a form of capitalism—undermines spiritual or religious concerns, Wharton's focus on money is not about losing religion. Indeed, one of Lily's first—and most damning— faux pas occurs when she chooses to sleep in rather than attend Sunday church services with the other guests at Bellomont. This choice, in lock-step fashion, sets off a chain of events that begins with her losing her chance to wed the eligible (though horribly dull) Percy Gryce. This pattern intensifies in Wharton's 1913 novel, *The Custom of the Country*, the story of Undine Spragg. Money sets this plot in motion, and money brings it to a conclusion as Undine blackmails her former husband to obtain the necessary sum "to buy" an annulment and enable her to marry a Roman Catholic member of the French aristocracy. With *The Age of Innocence* (1920), Wharton becomes less interested in either capitalism or spirituality. Instead, the plot turns on the male protagonist, Newland Archer, who (naively) values the past for its traditions rather than recognizes its formidable purchase on the future. Through the interactions of the character Ellen Olenska, Wharton powerfully shows the narrow precincts allowed to members of the socially conscious upper classes, revealing an alarming lack of freedom amidst wealth and prestige. This novel registers a shift for Wharton that links her work more closely with the realism of her friend Henry James.

An ardent proponent of realism, James favored topics and themes that resonated more fully with those of his European counterparts. His novels are often set in Europe and feature Americans baffled by complex social circumstances that frequently overtake them. Howells would have agreed with James's assessment in "The Future of the Novel" (1899) that "the future of fiction is intimately bound up with the future of the society that produces and consumes it," but he believed fiction could actively *shape* society, while James was more interested in observing it. James began his career in the late 1860s at the *Atlantic Monthly* reviewing the literary works of the women writers (Stowe among them) who were dominating the literary marketplace at the time. From the outset, he was less concerned with capitalism as it pertained to slave labor than with the broader intellectual bankruptcy he saw plaguing culture both in the United States and abroad. Critics note James's interest in psychology—his brother William, a philosophy professor at Harvard, authored a defining work in that field—and in fact Henry James was referred to in his own time as the leader of the "scientific" or "psychological" school of fiction. His great subject—one that occupies center stage in almost all of his novels—is interiority.

In his review of James's *Portrait of a Lady* (1881), Howells captured an important difference between James and many of the writers that came before him: "it is the character, not the fate, of his people which occupies him; when he has fully developed their character he leaves them to what destiny the reader pleases" ("Henry James, Jr." 1882). Although money and finance are motivating forces in all of James's novels, they rarely concern themselves with the corruption of capitalism per se. From *Portrait* to his late masterpiece *The Golden Bowl* (1904), James explored states of consciousness and conscience. His 1897 novel *What Maisie Knew*, for example, focuses on the relative states of knowing available to the novel's title character, the child Maisie. Shuffling back and forth between her now divorced and morally bankrupt parents, Maisie witnesses more than a young girl should of her parents' indiscretions. Probing ever so delicately into the child's ability to discern what is going on around her, the novel explores her eroding innocence and knowledge acquisition. In the end, Maisie is given the choice between living with her stepfather or the paid governess, Mrs. Wix. Maisie wisely chooses Mrs. Wix, whose affection for the child is as genuine as is her professionalism. The realism of the novel lies in James's ability to portray Maisie's gradual awakening without didacticism.

James's novels develop a vocabulary—and an aesthetic—of intellectual processes, enhancing the realist focus on the quotidian details of everyday life with dramatic depictions of more cerebral preoccupations. The most dramatic events are decisions that evolve in complicated, even unconscious ways in the minds of his characters. For instance, *The Portrait of a Lady* is taken up by the various (and often nefarious) schemes of romance and marriage concerning the fate of Isabel Archer, the unmarried American traveling in Europe. Here, as in many of James's novels, the fate of the characters concerns their financial futures, but the actual attention to money and money matters is often less overt, as distinctions of class and culture occupy center stage.

James's more psychological focus manifests a move away from the earlier emphasis on concrete facts and details that had become a central feature of realism in favor of mood. As Jonathan Freedman discusses in his chapter on James in this volume, James's distinctive use of photography reveals the medium's more evocative qualities. He commissioned Alvin Langdon Coburn to take photographs for the New York Edition of his writings that demonstrate his refusal of the overly particularized quotidian detail of early realism. The blurry and impressionistic photographic plates he selected feature the actual location of the story, a bridge in Venice, for instance—yet with the least degree of realism. These photographs are not there for their documentary strength, but rather plunge readers into an interpretive quandary. They do not depict as much as they provoke, emphasizing the need to interpret mood, tone, and the other narrative challenges James poses for his readers. They also, rather famously, lack human subjects. The photographs, then, offer a view suggestive of the novel's setting without ever shedding light on any of its characters. Because his work is all about character, James guarded their development carefully, keeping the crucial interaction between reader and writer as much in his control as possible. From the absence of explicit financial references to the blurry scenes featured in his frontispieces for the New York edition, the move away from documentation epitomized in James's work also signals the beginning of a move away from realism.

Other Forms of Economy

James's turn toward interiority is one reason that he is rightly considered to be a transitional figure between nineteenth-century realism and twentieth-century modernism. His novels represent, however, only one of the directions that the shift away from literary realism took in the United States. *The Education of Henry Adams* (1907), which is a novelistic autobiography penned by the scion of the well-known Adams family, a man of letters, offers this powerful account of a general sense of rupture at the turn of the twentieth century:

> Satisfied that the sequence of men led to nothing and the sequence of their society could lead no further, while the mere sequence of thought was chaos, he [Adams] turned at last to the sequence of force; and thus it happened that, after ten years' pursuit, he found himself lying in the Gallery of Machines at the Great Exposition of 1900, with his historical neck broken by the sudden irruption of force totally new. (ch. 25)

Adams's meditation on "force" occurs in the well-known "Virgin and the Dynamo" chapter of *The Education,* and it climaxes in a figure of physical violence. Throughout this chapter, Adams manages to describe the scientific discoveries on display at the Great Exposition in Paris with cool detachment and also render the turbulence of his emotional state. "Force," as Adams represents it, is the source of revolutionary power, a turning from one world order (the spiritual order of the Old World epitomized by the Virgin) to another (the technological world of scientific discovery represented by the Dynamo). The "historian," as Adams calls himself, can grasp the outlines of this shift, but only in the crudest of terms. Instead, Adams realizes that the forms of historical knowledge he has at his disposal are no longer adequate. He had sought a history that could produce more coherent meaning than sequence, which could create order out of the "chaos" of his time. The turn of the century, however, unleashed forces that rendered this project impossible. The historian of the nineteenth century put himself at bodily risk in attempting to confront the twentieth.

Adams's reflections on the loss of agency register a radical change in outlook for the writers of the period. No longer convinced that literature could make change, many of these writers chose to depict the controlling power of forces with a brutal accuracy. The fragility and violence of a world driven by force became the subject of naturalist novels published in the United States at the turn of the twentieth century. "Among the forces which sweep and play throughout the universe, untutored man is but a wisp in the wind," Theodore Dreiser muses in *Sister Carrie* (1900). "Our civilisation is still in a middle stage, scarcely beast, in that it is no longer wholly guided by instinct; scarcely human, in that it is not yet wholly guided by reason" (ch. 8). Naturalist novelists depicted the unleashing of these primitivist forces in the world; they believed the forces of market capitalism existed as extensions of or arenas for this animality. Frank Norris titled the first part of his "Epic of the Wheat" trilogy *The Octopus* (1901), thereby designating the railroad an insatiable beast whose hunger cannot be subdued and whose will cannot be affected by human intervention. At the conclusion of the first chapter, a character imagines a passing locomotive as a "symbol of a vast power, huge, terrible, flinging the echo of its thunder over all the reaches of the valley, leaving blood and destruction in its path; the leviathan, with tentacles of steel clutching into the soil, the soulless Force, the iron-hearted Power, the monster, the Colossus, the Octopus" (bk. 1, ch. 1). The locomotive is not simply these things itself, but a "symbol" of them, for the true force that Norris seeks to reckon goes beyond any single object, but rather is elemental and universal; indeed, it extends to the land itself. The novel ends with an agent of the railroad, a speculator and land broker, buried in an avalanche of wheat: "a prolonged roar, persistent, steady, inevitable" (bk. 2, ch. 9). The wheat is greater than any person who would attempt to control it.

The emphasis on animality in Norris has a definitively masculinist cast, signaling another important way in which naturalism breaks with realism. The turn of the twentieth century was a moment in which white manhood was widely considered to be in jeopardy from both the emasculation of "over-civilization" and competition from nonwhite peoples. For this reason, just as fiction worked to expose the brutish nature of American men, Theodore Roosevelt urged them to engage in the "strenuous life," and groups such as Ernest Thompson Seton's Woodcraft Indians—and later the Boy Scouts—were founded to offer white children a symbolic connection to an earlier time through their identification with the figure of the (romanticized) American Indian. Jack London took this primitivist turn even further in his highly popular dog novels, *The Call of the Wild* (1903) and *White Fang* (1906). In the first, Buck is stolen from a California ranch and transported to Alaska, where he awakens to his primal memories of wild life and becomes transformed into the "Ghost Dog" of the wilderness. The latter novel reverses this movement by bringing a dog of the "savage, frozen-hearted Northland Wild" (ch. 1) into the civilization and domesticity of the south. In both cases, London's novels attempt to dramatize the power of social environment over their male, animal protagonists. Progress is measured through the lens of a violent evolutionism, and can only occur when the forces of nature—particularly masculine forces—are properly recognized.

Masculinity was hardly the only mysterious, powerful force at play in the novels of American naturalism. Kate Chopin's *The Awakening* (1899) chronicles the awakening of the protagonist, Edna Pontellier, as she comes to terms with her sense of constriction in the Louisiana creole community into which she has married. Unable to articulate what compels her to do what she does, she is thrown into turmoil by her own kind of call from the wild: "The voice of the sea is seductive; never ceasing, whispering, clamoring, murmuring, inviting the soul to wander for a spell in abysses of solitude; to lose itself in mazes of inward contemplation" (ch. 6). Edna listens to the voice of the sea, acting on the desires that it represents and then, when she comprehends the difficulty of achieving them, swimming out to the ocean in what most readers interpret as an intentional suicide. The ending registers a sense that modernity itself is incapable of assimilating the emotional and psychological currents that drive Edna Pontellier, another female protagonist, who, like Lily Bart, dies ambiguously.

By contrast, the eponymous protagonist of Theodore Dreiser's *Sister Carrie* contends much more successfully with the age of force. More than either *The Awakening* or *The House of Mirth*, *Sister Carrie* concerns itself with the emergence of new forms of urban, mass culture. The novel tells the story of Carrie's immersion in the commercial society of the metropolis, her extramarital relationships with two men, and subsequent success as an actress. In Dreiser's Chicago and New York, the very geography of the city streets is configured so as to produce an orgy of display for the masses who walk them. Plate glass windows extend down to the sidewalks, soliciting consumers for the commodities housed inside, and the pedestrians themselves participate in the making of spectacle. "To stare seemed the proper and natural thing," Dreiser's novel tells us of the Broadway promenade. "Carrie found herself stared at and ogled" (ch. 31). The education of Carrie Meeber shapes her into a font of longing for the material things that will enable her to succeed in this spectacular economy. "She did not grow in knowledge so much as she awakened in the matter of desire" (ch. 12). Introduced as "a waif amid forces" in the title of the novel's first chapter, Carrie finds synchronicity with the forces that otherwise overwhelmed Henry Adams, Lily Bart, and Edna Pontellier.

Dreiser figures this economy of desire most evocatively in Carrie's achievements as an actress. In a crucial passage in which the novel enumerates Carrie's talents, Dreiser describes his heroine as being in possession of a "sympathetic, impressionable nature" as well as "an innate taste for imitation" (ch. 16). Throughout the book, the question of which instincts and forces are "natural" and which are not recurs, and the genius of Carrie's thespian career seems to rest in her ability to walk a line: she is "*naturally imitative*" (ch. 11). In the final sections of *Sister Carrie*, Dreiser introduces Robert Ames, an inventor from the Midwest who seeks to instill in Carrie a proper sense of the value of things, as well as an aspiration for more serious drama than those in which she has appeared. However, if the novel intends Ames to provide a final (male) correction to Carrie's unfocused, constant (female) desire, then it is also deliberately ambiguous as to the possibility of success. While the idealistic inventor persuades Carrie to read Balzac, making her newly aware of the social injustices of the kind European naturalism portrays at the end of the novel, there are no indications that high literature will remake her acting career or the stage on which she performs; the penultimate chapter informs us that "the old, mournful Carrie—the desireful Carrie,—unsatisfied" remains (ch. 49). Literature, in other words, may be able to describe Carrie's desires, but Dreiser's novel is unclear on whether the literary narrative can satisfy the kind of yearning that drives the visual displays of mass culture.

Fiction in *Sister Carrie* had competition from another source of print culture: the newspaper. Dreiser was not unusual in having begun his career as a journalist. If realism was fueled by the political commitments of editor-writers, many of the writers who inherited and transformed their social reformist tendencies along more naturalistic lines similarly worked as reporters, including London, Harold Frederic, Stephen Crane, and Upton Sinclair. Newspapers offer an important contrast to—even competition for—the novel in *Sister Carrie*, as the source of information, entertainment, and sensation. As Betsy Klimasmith explains in her chapter in this volume, one of Carrie's lovers, George Hurstwood, whose decline is juxtaposed in the novel with Carrie's success, becomes enraptured by the newspapers, which he uses to learn about the local events that affect his search for employment. Eventually, the newspapers paralyze him, tempting him to read about rather than participate in the life of the city. Novelist and social reformer Upton Sinclair explains the appeal in *The Jungle* (1906), when his protagonist, Jurgis Rudkis, considers that a "most wonderful paper could be had for only five cents. . . . There was battle and murder and sudden death—it was marvelous how they ever heard about so many entertaining and thrilling happenings; the stories must be all true, for surely no man could have made such things up, and besides, there were pictures of them all, as real as life" (ch. 21).

The Jungle, of course, is full of its own "battle and murder and sudden death" in its grim account of the meat-packing industry in Chicago, and the purpose of this reform-oriented novel was to show that the horrors it detailed "must all be true." While occasional rumors of media corruption are floated through the novel—and in one particular episode Sinclair blames the newspapers for exaggerating the violence of a labor dispute—the newspapers generally serve as an ameliorative, if largely ineffectual, check against the capitalist excesses of industrial life. The novel mentions they have exposed the mishandling of waste, the canning of horsemeat, and the medical experiments on indigent patients at a hospital—the kind of muckraking with which Sinclair himself was famously identified.

Sinclair's novel confronts the forces of mass production in two different arenas: the making of meat out of the bodies of animals, and the making of members of the American working class out of immigrants. While the exposé of the former received more attention in Sinclair's time—influencing legislation regulating the meat industry—the link between these two processes is in fact the burden of the novel. Just as the meatpacking factory is designed so that the steers walk under their own power into the slaughterhouse, a combination of world economics and labor recruitment strategies brings unskilled, immigrant labor to Chicago to work there. Just as no part of the animal goes unused by the factory, all of the physical and mental energy of the workers is extracted by their labor—and by their constant effort to secure for themselves the barest material existence. Finally, just as the public prefers not to see how its sausage is made, it also turns a blind eye to the way that immigrant laborers are ground into the political process—led through the citizenship system and manipulated as voters by the bosses who run Packingtown.

Near the end of the novel, as Sinclair introduces his reader to the Socialist Party, he even includes a paean to its national organ, *The Appeal to Reason*: "It had a manner all its own—it was full of ginger and spice, of Western slang and hustle: It collected news of the 'plutes,' and served it up for the benefit of the 'American working-mule'" (ch. 30). *The Jungle*, in fact, does something different by collecting the stories of an immigrant family—"working mules," one might say—and using them to reflect on the working conditions created by the "plutes," or plutocrats. But what the novel shares with the propaganda newspaper as Sinclair describes it is a desire to circulate the truth among a public that can be prodded into action through literary representation, bringing print's purpose back to the reform-minded abolitionists and realists of an earlier era.

Uncle Tom's Cabin cast a long shadow over the half century that followed its publication in 1852. With its journalistic ethos of intense observation and its concluding call for a Socialist politics, *The Jungle* inherits and refashions a tradition of American realism that is motivated by a commitment to documenting the inequalities of American society. Whether in Stowe's *Uncle Tom's Cabin*, Howells's *A Hazard of New Fortunes*, or Sinclair's *The Jungle*, the forces propelling those inequalities are often overwhelming, truly awesome in their power and their reach. The work of the realist novelist is to contain them within the compass of narrative in a way that affords the reader a sense of possibility, to recover a belief in agency that can lead to substantive change. That optimistic sense of social purpose did not originate in the period covered by this volume, but it achieved a wider currency during the decades that this volume covers than at any other time in the history of the American novel, including the contemporary moment.

8

JOURNALISM AND THE URBAN NOVEL

BY BETSY KLIMASMITH

If a newspaperman working in the offices of Joseph Pulitzer's *New York World* happened to forget what his priorities should be, one glance at the banners plastering the walls would remind him: "The Facts! The Color! The Facts!" Although facts were necessary to newspaper writing, color was what had helped the *World* become New York's—and thus the nation's—dominant newspaper at the turn into the twentieth century. More than a ploy to sell papers, mixing facts and color in just the right proportions was something of an obsession for American writers at the time, whether they were reporting news or writing novels. Many were doing both, and given the overlap between novel writing and journalism at the time, we might read Pulitzer's motto as a snappier version of William Dean Howells's famous assertion that "realism is nothing more and nothing less than the truthful treatment of material" (1889, 966). Howells and James took great pains to differentiate the newspaper stories they considered lowbrow from their more highbrow literary realism, and the echoes of their distinctions still shape US literary studies. Yet the connections between the forms are far more illuminating than their differences.

If we cling to Howells and James's distinctions between high and low culture and separate novels from newspapers, we risk gravely misreading literary realism, and especially urban novels. Novels and newspapers sought to reflect everyday life, to animate reality through narrative. "Both forms of writing grew out of a common cultural milieu, and the imaginative and the journalistic drew upon each other in forming their respective stories" (Roggenkamp 2002, 21). The best stories were built on fact and fiction, and this fact-fiction dialectic powered newspapers and novels. And while it is tempting to see journalism as a training ground for realistic and naturalistic novelists, in reality almost no one followed a clear path from an "education" as a reporter to a "career" as a novelist. As the careers of Theodore Dreiser, Stephen Crane, and Edith Wharton reveal, identities as reporters and novelists overlapped and entangled just as tightly as fact and fiction were entwined in print.

The brief history of American journalism that follows unmoors some of the basic assumptions that shape how literary historians distinguish novels from newspapers. With notable exceptions, we tend to think of newspapers as objective, and often search newspaper archives for a sense of what "really happened" at the time a nineteenth-century novel was published or set. But journalistic objectivity is a fairly recent concept in the United States. While a drive toward "just the facts" journalism began in the 1890s with Adolph S. Ochs and the *New York Times*, objectivity began to resonate deeply as a cultural value for readers and writers after the First World War. This new emphasis on objectivity was shored up stylistically with terse, clean sentences—a style that bled into novels by literary modernists like Ernest Hemingway. If the style of objectivity was "less is more," urban realists before the First World War wrote in a journalistic milieu in which, simply, more was more.

Once we stop reading newspapers as vessels of "fact" and begin to appreciate how closely novels and the news were connected at this time, a trove of new writing and authors opens to students of the period. As Lennard J. Davis shows in *Factual Fictions* (1983), reading novels and newspapers as part of a connected matrix of print can teach us much about each form; in his case, about the rise of the novel in eighteenth-century Britain. Journalism historian Doug Underwood's *Journalism and the Novel* (2008) traces a similarly close relationship between forms in the American context. For literary scholars, newspapers offer much more than mere historical context; in many cases they are just as "literary" as their novelistic counterparts and can be productively analyzed alongside more literary texts. In the United States, as cities and their newspapers grew into national and eventually international forces, focusing on journalism and urban novels traces the long, messy evolution from a local to a national print—and urban—culture in the United States.

Urban Journalism in Nineteenth-Century America

Nineteenth-century journalism in the United States developed from the 1830s "penny press," which transformed newspapers from four-page journals mailed to elite mercantile subscribers (at six cents per issue) to one-cent papers aimed at a broader readership and sold by the issue by hawkers on the street. Journalism historian Michael Schudson claims that the penny press defined what Americans still consider "news." For the first time, newspaper editors hired reporters to cover local events. The dramas they concocted from events in "the courts, the commercial district, the churches, high society, and sports," became the first human-interest stories in the American press (1978, 27). The exciting local stories in the penny papers contrasted sharply with the commercial reports and foreign news that had dominated American newspapers before 1830, and readers responded enthusiastically.

Although the stories and images in the penny press were based in reality, verifiable facts were not nearly as important as the stories the papers wanted to tell. "Though the penny papers claimed to be 'the daily daguerrotype of the heart and soul of a modern republic,'" what mattered to readers and publishers was a good story, which meant that hefty doses of fiction animated the facts (Brown 1997, 14). A memorable hallmark of the penny press, newspaper hoaxes encapsulate the penny papers' impulse to produce the most engaging and compelling stories imaginable from the facts at hand.

Over the next few decades, newspapers changed and grew rapidly. By 1850, a 75 percent literacy rate, new publishing technologies, and speedier transportation built a large reading public and helped New York, Philadelphia, and Boston emerge as centers of print culture. From 1870 to 1900, the American population doubled and literacy rates rose. By the 1890s the operative word for printed material in the United States was *more:* more advertising, thicker papers, profuse multiplication of newspapers and magazines. By 1900, as Shelly Fisher Fishkin notes, there were six times as many daily papers as there had been in the 1860s, and more than three times as many weeklies (1985).

In the face of this expansion, connections between newspapers and literary fiction intensified. But the newspapers' commitment to juicy stories—what literary critic Michael Robertson calls a "fact-fiction discourse"—remained strong as the new century approached (1997, 6). A 1903 journalism textbook, Edwin L. Shuman's *Practical Journalism,* taught its readers that fleshing out bare facts with lively imaginative writing was "one of the most valuable secrets of the profession. . . . The paramount object is to make an interesting story. If the number of copies sold is any criterion, the people prefer this sort of journalism to one that is rigidly accurate" (123). Accuracy mattered, but it was more important that the sense of a story be accurately conveyed through imaginative writing than that the reporter cling to the bare facts of a case.

Facts still had their place. The Associated Press (AP) began as a wire service in 1848, and by the late nineteenth century it had become *the* source of facts for major papers. Eventually, having an AP membership became a prerequisite for any legitimate newspaper. Ironically, one benefit of relying on the AP for the facts was that it freed up reporters to do other work—that is, to tell stories. Joseph Pulitzer brought this approach to a mass audience with the *New York World*, and William Randolph Hearst developed it into its highest form. Hearst made it the policy of the *New York Journal* "to engage brains as well as to get the news, for the public is even more fond of entertainment than it is of information" (qtd. in Schudson 1978, 99). By the time Dreiser, Crane, and Wharton began writing novels, this dynamic was well established; newspapers simply *were* a mix of fact and fiction, of entertainment and information.

For Joseph Pulitzer, newspapers could offer readers something even more valuable—an American urban education. While the penny press and the older-style newspapers coexisted until the 1850s, after the Civil War, the mass-circulation press, led by Pulitzer's *New York World*, dominated the news business. A Jewish Austrian immigrant, Pulitzer had learned to navigate American politics from his adoptive

St. Louis, where his *Post-Dispatch* revolutionized journalism by adapting penny press strategies to make the city intelligible to its newest inhabitants, readers hungry to understand the bustling, fast-paced, confusing urban landscape. In a sense, Pulitzer's publishing career helped to move the industry from the local focus of the penny press—which the *Post-Dispatch* retained even after Pulitzer left St. Louis—and the mass appeal of the *New York World*. In Pulitzer's hands, the "local" news became the news of the nation.

From 1880 to 1925, New York was rapidly becoming the premier American metropolis, growing at an amazing rate with immigrants and native-born newcomers streaming into the city at an unprecedented pace. They all needed help to figure out how to live and possibly prosper in the city, and the newspaper was a relatively cheap, readily available, widely shared, and, especially in the case of the Sunday *World*, colorfully illustrated guide to the urban experience. New York *was* fact and fiction; both modes were necessary for writers who grappled with the metropolis.

Newspapers taught readers about the city's buildings and their inhabitants, the pleasures and dangers of the streets, how to dress (literally—the *World* published sewing patterns), speak, and behave. Newspapers allowed a shared experience to be internalized, enabling readers to encounter the city in a browsable, comprehensible, disposable form. Joseph Pulitzer made sure that his afternoon *World* was printed in a handy portable size so that people could unfold and read it while riding home from work elbow to elbow with their fellow New Yorkers on the streetcars. Hawked on corners by newsboys, condensing baffling experiences into readable narratives, teaching newcomers the ways and mores of the metropolis, offering membership—and making membership visible—to those who carried it, the newspaper's content and physical form signposted the urban panorama.

The approach that succeeded for Pulitzer in St. Louis was even better suited to New York, where there were more people creating and reading the everyday stories that were his specialty. As Pulitzer put it, the *World* should be "both a school-house and a daily forum—both a daily teacher and a daily tribune" (1891). In New York, countless new readers were eager to consume the cheap, colorful mobile lessons they found in the *World*, and they made Pulitzer the nation's first newspaper mogul. Other papers could offer rational and objective news to readers whose settled, successful lives already made sense. The *New York Times*, writes Schudson, "presented articles as useful knowledge, not as revelation. The *World* had a different feel to it; in tone and display it created the sense that everything was new, unusual, and unpredictable" (1978, 119). It took skilled storytellers to craft readable, coherent narratives from the tumultuous urban world. Pulitzer, and later William Randolph Hearst, felt that these writers were worth the investment.

Newspapers taught readers—and writers—to understand urban life through highly visual stories suffused with quotidian detail. Some literary historians argue that newspapers made realist fiction possible, while others claim that novelists generated the urban realism that dominated newspapers. What is clear is that for a few

decades, the two forms overlapped in mutually productive ways. Authors like Dreiser and Crane were not writing for the *New York Times* with its promise not to sully
the breakfast-table cloth. They wrote for publications with audiences who were still
working to establish their class and social identities, readers for whom stories were
the best way to convey the news and make legible the city they inhabited.

By the late 1800s, the fact-fiction mix that had characterized newspaper writing
since the beginning of the penny press in the 1830s took on new resonance and popularity, helping to nurture a new profession: the reporter. According to Schudson,
the "standard mythology" surrounding journalism in this period presents the "new
reporter" as "younger, more naive, more energetic and ambitious, college-educated,
and usually sober. He was passionately attached to his job and to the novels he felt
his experience as a reporter would prepare him to write" (1978, 69). Many novelists
of this era worked as journalists, including Theodore Dreiser, Jack London, Stephen
Crane, Frank Norris, Willa Cather, Abraham Cahan, Katherine Anne Porter, Sinclair Lewis, John Steinbeck, Eudora Welty, Richard Harding Davis, Joel Chandler
Harris, Harold Frederic, and Ambrose Bierce.

For some authors, journalism offered an apprenticeship in writing. Mark Twain,
Walt Whitman, and Ernest Hemingway began their careers as newspaper writers; as
Fishkin argues, their newspaper work had a profound impact on their imaginative
work, and indeed on American literature. Once these writers left journalism, she
notes, they were free to become artists: "These writers succeeded as writers of fiction
only when they returned, in new and creative ways, to material and approaches they
had first come to know as documenters of fact" (1985, 7). But the line between fact
and fiction was more blurred than Fishkin suggests. Her apprenticeship paradigm
only describes certain writers' careers; others took different paths, balancing journalism and novel writing in a variety of ways. Richard Harding Davis, whose obscurity
today matches the fame he enjoyed a century ago, played this dynamic perfectly,
parlaying newspaper articles into journalistic fame and fortune, using that fame to
attract book contracts, and, with the help of a continuing stream of long fact/fiction
newspaper stories (many concocted and told to convey maximum excitement from
minimal facts), make his novels, like *The Princess Aline* (1895) and *Soldiers of Fortune*
(1897), bestsellers.

Whether journalism prepared them to write novels or vice versa, "in their desire
to tell stories, reporters were less interested in facts than in creating personally distinctive and popular styles of writing" (Schudson 1978, 71). After all, novels and
news were both commodities, and prose writing, in whatever form, could help pay
the bills. The products were different; newspaper writing was published much more
quickly, the pay was far more predictable, the audience was guaranteed, and after the
advent of the byline in 1896 it became possible to gain fame as a celebrity journalist. Writing a novel demanded more time and patience and was riskier in terms of
return on time invested, but fiction allowed writers to create scenarios that might
have raised a newspaper editor's eyebrows at best or have faced censorship at worst.

But if novel writing was riskier than journalism, novels offered a literary cachet that newspaper writing did not. As Michael Robertson argues, in response to the "feminization" of literary culture that accompanied the rise of the "masculine" newspaper, Henry James and William Dean Howells used the means at their disposal—articles, editorials, novels, and memoirs—to promulgate a remarkably long-lasting disdain for the lowly newspaper and instill a veneration of literature, especially realist novels, as high culture (1997). Students and scholars of American literature have tended to repeat and reinforce this distinction. Moving beyond James's and Howells's formulations opens a new literary landscape to readers of urban realism.

Mining the Real: Theodore Dreiser and *Sister Carrie*

Theodore Dreiser's apprenticeship as a journalist clearly enabled his career as a novelist. Newspaper work helped to lift Dreiser out of poverty and exposed him to the extremes of urban life; his journalism also helped him develop his distinctive style and provided material for the plots and settings of his greatest novels. Dreiser began his career at the St. Louis *Globe-Democrat*, a paper that presented urban life as a series of contrasts. A member of the generation who grew up learning about the world from illustrated weeklies like *Frank Leslie's*, Dreiser had been raised on "pictures of the idealized city, sparkling with improvements and technological wonders (exemplified in the carefully charted construction and opening of the Brooklyn Bridge) . . . set against cautionary cuts depicting want and degradation" (Brown 1997, 192). Dreiser was primed to see the world as a set of binaries: rich and poor, old and new, success and failure, beauty and depravity. As he began his reporting career he deepened his reading of newspapers, and the combination only reinforced this worldview.

Newspaper work exposed Dreiser to a range of experiences that would indelibly mark his urban fiction. When he left newspaper work, Dreiser continued to publish articles in mass-market periodicals and founded a magazine called *Ev'ry Month* for which he wrote all the content. His continuing fascination with societal contrasts emerged in articles that "ranged from profiles of successful businessmen and of contemporary artists, photographers and musicians, to descriptive pieces about new developments in industry, transportation, education, and science, to discussions of the plight of the city's poor" (Fishkin 1985, 89). *Ev'ry Month* also included Dreiser's column "The Prophet," in which he mused on the subjects that he would later develop in his novels.

The theme of extremes existing in close proximity to one another, highlighting discrepancies of class and opportunity, connects Dreiser's newspaper articles, his editorials, and his novels. His journalism made the contrasts of the Gilded Age legible while keeping examples of success and failure always at hand for his readers. Dreiser animates this dynamic in his greatest urban novel, *Sister Carrie* (1900), through which protagonist Carrie Meeber rises while her counterpart Hurstwood falls. First, Carrie perceives societal contrasts from the position of a poor newcomer to the city—a position with which many of Dreiser's newspaper readers (and indeed Dreiser himself) would have identified. Carrie pursues an acting career in which she interprets and performs societal contrasts by embodying a range of emblematic characters on the stage, finally becoming an emblem of success emblazoned on the society pages of the newspapers. As the book progresses, scenes of Carrie's success and Hurstwood's failure are juxtaposed in much in the same manner that feature articles appeared in the newspapers and magazines that published Dreiser's journalism.

Dreiser's style was well suited to and honed to perfection by newspapers' demand for extended feature-length stories written in a wordy, leisurely style. His immersion in the "real world"—while growing up in a struggling, strict immigrant household, while on the job as a reporter, while moving from Indiana to Chicago to St. Louis to New York, as well as his absorption in newspaper depictions of "reality"—gave him access to the wealth of detail that he drew on in his journalism and his novels. When Dreiser began writing for the *Globe-Democrat*, his editor loved his grandiloquence and use of copious facts. It was a style that would stay with Dreiser as he began writing novels; in *Sister Carrie,* Dreiser's meandering style helps elicit powerful emotion and drama from the familiar stories he weaves together.

For Dreiser, "facts" meant more than names, dates, prices, addresses, events, or styles of fashion, though he mustered stores of such information in his novels. In the newspaper and in the urban novel, each form structured around a fact-fiction discourse, "facts" could also be common themes, familiar stories, or even widely shared feelings and desires. Dreiser based many of his novels on true stories, whether they concerned members of his family (*Sister Carrie, Jennie Gerhardt* [1911]), famous people (the Frank Cowperwood trilogy) or current events (*American Tragedy* [1925]). Though newspapers figure in all of Dreiser's novels, the newspaper plays its biggest role in *Sister Carrie,* in which all of the characters are drawn into the paper. We see Hurstwood becoming increasingly absorbed in the papers as he seeks first an investment opportunity, then a job, and finally nothing more than a warm hotel chair in which to read; the thrill Carrie gets when her picture is first published in Sunday paper; the casual bantering among Carrie, Ames, and the Vances about each other's celebrity. If Carrie and Ames "go in" to the papers—first as local and later as international celebrities—Hurstwood is sucked in much more destructively, first as a scab in the streetcar strike and finally as a tramp on a breadline. In both of these examples, Dreiser takes the newspaper-novel connection one step further by simply integrating Hurstwood into newspaper sketches he had previously published. Thus, *Sister Carrie* becomes a hybrid of fact and fiction, newspaper and novel.

Just as his characters step in and out of the newspapers, so did Dreiser as he assembled the novel's manuscript. As he wrote *Sister Carrie,* Dreiser actually glued newspaper clippings on to the manuscript's pages, so that when, for example, Hurstwood looks through his newspapers for a job, we are reading the very same items a "real" Hurstwood would have read. Dreiser built *Sister Carrie*'s urban world upon an assemblage of newspaper stories, and these stories, along with his attention to the names, places, and objects that surrounded his characters in the cities they inhabited, allowed Dreiser to balance the emblematic oppositions that structured city life with the specific details that made Chicago and New York distinct—and different cities.

Thanks to the practice and presence of newspaper writing, readers a century later can recognize Carrie's urban space as a faithful portrait of another historical moment—a realistic portrayal of Gilded Age cities. In juxtaposing glaring Gilded Age contrasts, loading on precise detail, and fact-checking to be sure of his accuracy, Dreiser used journalistic techniques to create believable local worlds for readers close or distant in time and space and, via his characters' engagement with mass culture, draw them into broader feelings and desires that transcend time and place. Dreiser's genius is to accrue the kinds of quotidian details that make readers at once know that while we do not want the actual *things* (the boots or the shirtwaists or toilet sets) that speak to Carrie, we understand her feeling of wanting—and to some extent feel that desire for or with her. The "facts" bring us into contact with the larger truths, or what Dreiser calls the "forces," that move the modern city: class, desire, justice, opportunity, decision-making, sex, money, and power. For Dreiser, the facts helped to tell the truths about society that he felt were critical for a writer—whether a novelist or a newspaperman—to convey.

Making It Real: Stephen Crane and Maggie, *a Girl of the Streets*

Unlike Dreiser, who used journalism to rise socially, Stephen Crane used journalism to shed his middle-class upbringing as a minister's son and gain experiences he had been forbidden in his youth. Perhaps because he was born into relative privilege, social standing and hierarchies of taste seem to have mattered little to him. "Unconcerned, both professionally and artistically, with the distinctions between literature and journalism, artist and reporter, high culture and low that were so significant to Howells and James," Crane moved easily in a variety of milieus and placed his work in all kinds of publications (Robertson 1997, 56). Crane's career calls into question the myth that journalism was a training ground for writers—an apprenticeship after which literary distinction could be attained. Because many of his best-known realist works, like *The Red Badge of Courage* (1895), describe experiences Crane himself had not yet had, Crane's career also raises the question of where to locate the "real" in realism.

Crane began his career reporting on religious meetings in Asbury Park, New Jersey, the seaside resort where he grew up. After a brief and undistinguished stint at Syracuse University, Crane moved to New York, where he continued to write, often generating material by embedding himself as a member of the lower class as a journalistic "experiment." Experiments like Crane's were a mainstay of urban newspapers in the Gilded Age. Elizabeth Cochrane, a.k.a. Nellie Bly, performed the decade's most famous and audacious experiment when she performed insanity in order to get herself committed to New York's public asylum and write a series of articles for Joseph Pulitzer's *World*.

Whether carried out in the newspaper or mined for material to write a novel, the experiment would seem a perfect fit for the realist writer, who could experience something, absorb it, and then use it to write an article or story so *true* that it would be the best possible fiction. Crane and Bly, however, redefined the experiment when they attempted to make fiction into reality. Bly's best-known experiment was her Pulitzer-funded race against Phineas Fogg's trip around the world in eighty days. Bly made it in seventy-two. Fogg, of course, was the fictional protagonist of Jules Verne's novel, but Pulitzer used the pages of the *World* to turn Bly's journey into a "real" race. "In framing Bly's journey as a race against an imaginary or fictional record, the *World* also framed a contest against imagination or fiction writing itself" (Roggenkamp 2002, 47). Journalism won that round, and fiction lost. Thanks largely to James and Howells, things changed. Today few students read Bly's newspaper reports in classes on American Literary Realism. We do, however, read Crane.

Like *The Red Badge of Courage,* which he wrote before he ever saw combat, Crane's urban fiction preceded his urban journalism. He wrote his best-known urban novella, *Maggie, a Girl of the Streets,* in 1893, before he had any significant experience in New York. Michael Robertson persuasively argues that *Maggie* must have been shaped by Crane's newspaper reading rather than his reporting. At times, Crane offers us images specific to Maggie's New York—the line of yellow convicts on Blackwell's Island, Maggie and Pete's dates at the beer garden and Central Park Menagerie, Maggie's final march toward death along the East River. But *Maggie*'s melodramatic "fallen woman" plot, its two-dimensional characters, and its diorama-like descriptions of urban space read more as emblems of the city than as a deep entanglement with urban lives. If Dreiser accretes enough detail in *Sister Carrie* to help us inhabit Carrie's cities, Crane flattens Maggie's New York enough to shut readers out. *Maggie* resembles one of Jacob Riis's urban photographs—the subjects holding frozen poses, the viewer struggling to develop empathy for the figures Riis's camera makes alien. And like Riis's photographs, Crane's urban fiction strains to make its point in a way that his urban journalism does not.

Maggie was a failure when it was first published. However, by the time *Maggie* was reissued in 1896, Crane was famous as a reporter, and the "experiments" he conducted among the lower classes in the city were some of his best-known work. Written richly and sympathetically, Crane's urban journalism is often better than his urban fiction. It is no wonder that readers assume that *Maggie* grew out of Crane's journalism. In a sense, *Maggie* became realism in retrospect.

While *Maggie* raises the question of whether Crane's lack of experience in the urban world makes the novel any less "real," the quality of his urban journalism argues for it to be read by students of urban realism at least as seriously as they read *Maggie*. As Robertson notes, "the fact-fiction discourse of the new journalism enabled Crane, whose narrative work has been praised by postmodernist critics, to consider the nature of narrative truth from the beginning of his career" (1997, 63). Crane, who wrote and lived among all of the permutations of the fact-fiction world, would probably not have cared very much about how to categorize his work. Yet his career, like Dreiser's, reinforces the importance for literary critics of understanding how closely journalism was entwined with fiction—and argues for attention to journalistic accounts of the city alongside urban novels.

Wharton: Tabloid Reality and *The House of Mirth*

A picture of journalism's relationship to urban novels in the Gilded Age would be incomplete without a look at the magazines that became hugely popular in the period. Illustrated magazines like *Frank Leslie's* had been part of the journalism scene since the 1870s, which saw the beginning, Brown argues, of the coexistence of printed word and image in American popular culture. "To many observers, 1870s America seemed obsessed with printed imagery; the range and breadth of illustrated periodicals had become excessive. . . . Newsstands and shops were filled with engraved books and weekly and monthly magazines; building exteriors were obscured by lithographed posters and advertisements; and homes were cluttered with chromolithographed prints, stereograph collections, and photographs" (1997, 8). By the 1890s, certain illustrated weeklies, such as *Harper's*, as well as monthlies including *Scribner's, Century,* and *The Atlantic* had carved out a highbrow niche to separate themselves from the newsstand hoi polloi. This position did little for the magazines' circulation—the decidedly middlebrow *McClure's* had a bigger circulation than the other four combined. But the literary weeklies allowed editors like Howells, who was intent on helping audiences distinguish between high and low culture, to maintain a foothold, however small, in the world of periodical journalism. And because the magazines serialized novels, they allowed writers an additional publication platform (and if they published in England, like Henry James, four separate copyrights—one each for the serial rights in England and the United States, two more for the British and American book rights—on their work).

As part of feminized high culture, the literary magazines seemed more refined than the average city newspaper intent on cultivating a tough, masculine image for their reporters and by extension, their paper. The weeklies published a number of women realist writers whose work would never have appeared in the rough and tumble world of new journalism. Rebecca Harding Davis, whose son Richard would become the most famous reporter of his day, published her fiction exclusively in magazines. She was not alone. Mary Wilkins Freeman, Mary Hallock Foote, Sarah Orne Jewett, Elizabeth Phelps, Sui Sin Far, and Edith Wharton are just a few of the American women realists who were mainstays in magazine fiction.

Edith Wharton is usually seen as a journalist only in connection with the reporting she did from the front during the First World War. But like almost every other author of her day, Wharton was connected with the periodical press from the beginning of her career. Wharton is not usually considered an urban writer. But the first short story she published, a tenement tale titled "Mrs. Manstey's View," appeared in *Scribner's* in 1891, marking the beginning of a long and fruitful relationship between Wharton and the publisher. Scribner would publish all of Wharton's New York novels, first in serial form and then as single-volume books. All of the New York novels, but especially *The House of Mirth* (1905), have important resonances with 1890s newspapers, capturing a moment when the newspapers balanced between local and mass culture, and showing how writers made New York legible to a simultaneously intensely local and increasingly international audience.

Unlike Dreiser and Crane, Wharton was very wealthy; Henry James's advice to write what she knew might seem to prevent her from writing urban realism. But the elevated social class into which Wharton was born fascinated readers; in her novels, Wharton satisfies readers' curiosity about the rich even as she offers an insider's critique of the symbiosis between newspaper publicity and the shifting world of New York's social elite. In *The Custom of the Country* (1913), Undine Spragg chooses her marital prey, judges her social successes, and quantifies the status of those around her according to the newspapers' valuations. She is aided in this pursuit by her manicurist, Mrs. Heeney, whose book of clippings serves as a veritable codex to the doings of the rich and famous. Undine is a more alarming version of Norma Hatch, a minor character in *The House of Mirth*. "Transplanted . . . from the scene of her first development to the higher stage of hotel life in the metropolis," Norma Hatch's image becomes "the recurring ornament of 'Sunday Supplements.'" Like Undine, Norma lives "in a haze of indeterminate enthusiasms, of aspirations culled from the stage, the newspapers, [and] the fashion journals" (bk. 2, ch. 9). More fully realized than Mrs. Hatch, Undine is the monster that newspaper culture creates—a mercenary woman who seizes on the desires that celebrity-focused journalism fosters in her, no matter who she may destroy in the process. Socialite Lily Bart is precisely the kind of celebrity Undine discovers in the Sunday papers she reads in her hometown of Apex, Kansas. Lily Bart might never travel to Apex, but newspapers allowed her image to journey to the hinterland. Simultaneously local and syndicated, "Lily Bart" is fact and fiction. She can inspire (or perhaps dredge up) someone like Undine to come to New York and attempt to join Lily's social world.

While newspapers are front and center in *The Custom of the Country*, they are woven more subtly into the background of *The House of Mirth*—yet they are crucial in that novel as well, serving as an accurate detail of Gilded Age life, a series of signposts (à la Hurstwood) of Lily's social demise, and most importantly, as a symbol of the dirty operations behind the scenes of upper-class society, operations in which Lily refuses to participate.

Early in the novel, newspapers serve as props for the social tableaux that Lily traverses effortlessly. After her tea at Lawrence Selden's house, Lily easily finds Percy Gryce on the train to Bellomont. Scanning the train car, "Her search was rewarded by the discovery of a very blond young man with a soft reddish beard, who, at the other end of the carriage, appeared to be dissembling himself behind an unfolded newspaper" (bk. 1, ch. 2). At Bellomont, newspapers are among the objects strewn about Judy Trenor's room. But for Wharton's wealthy, newspapers are far more than props.

The upper classes were not just readers; they were the subjects of the news, always conscious of being in the public eye. When Lily attends Gwen Van Osburgh's wedding, we see how thoroughly the press has made itself part of such social events. Later, Lily learns of Selden's departure for Havana and the West Indies from the newspaper, and in Europe, Lily and her entourage are followed around by "that horrid little Dabham who does 'Society Notes from the Riviera,'" a reporter intent on capturing every detail of the scene for his readers (bk. 2, ch. 2). For Lily, the lure of publicity is double-edged; she takes real risks in allowing herself to enter into the fantasy of publicity. In a novel whose plot revolves around secrets revealed and kept, Dabham makes visible the threat that sensitive information might escape the upper classes' control and become destructive, free-ranging publicity. By publicizing and making insinuatingly prurient Lily's late-night carriage ride with George Dorset, Dabham activates a chain of events that culminate in Lily's expulsion from high society and the newspapers that both propel and commodify it.

Beyond serving as a part of realism's backdrop and charting Lily's demise, newspapers expose the machinery that keeps upper-class society, and thus class divisions, alive. At the beginning of the novel, the charwoman, Mrs. Haffen, hands Lily "a small parcel wrapped in dirty newspaper," and Lily is repulsed (bk. 1, ch. 9). Fundamentally unclean, the newspaper is a fit covering for the dirty secrets it conceals. Lily refuses to participate in the sordid story Bertha Dorset's newspaper-wrapped letters might make possible. Yet these secrets, we are reminded throughout the novel, have the power to reshape upper-class society.

Resulting in part from the newspapers' unflattering, inaccurate publicity and her own unwillingness to make public the letters she holds containing secrets about Bertha Dorset, Lily's class position falls precipitously. Near the end of the novel, Lily has dropped out of the upper-class city and out of the papers that sustain it. Lily's working-class acquaintance Nettie Struther remarks that she hasn't seen Lily in the papers lately: "I used to watch for your name in the papers, and we'd talk over what you were doing, and read the descriptions of the dresses you wore. I haven't seen your name for a long time, though, and I began to be afraid you were sick, and it worried me so that George said I'd get sick myself, fretting about it" (bk. 2, ch. 13). This interaction happens at the end of the novel, after Lily has moved down many rungs in the social scale—and correspondingly down from her aunt's Fifth Avenue mansion to a dingy boardinghouse room near the elevated train tracks.

Given Dreiser and Crane's interest in such lower-class milieux, this seems like the "urban realist" section of the novel. But society reporting was also a significant part of the urban news. It was big business to keep readers of all social stations informed about the doings of the rich. And if we take our cues from the newspapers, we need to expand our definition of urban realism. Dreiser was certainly committed to including the world of wealth Carrie experiences as she gains fame and celebrity in *Sister Carrie*—and he shows how the newspapers have made this world part of Carrie's consciousness. Even before she visits the opulent restaurant Sherry's, "Carrie had read of it often in the 'Morning' and 'Evening World.' She had seen notices of dances, parties, balls and suppers at Sherry's. . . . The common run of conventional, perfunctory notices of the doings of society, which she could scarcely refrain from scanning each day, had given her a distinct idea of the gorgeousness and luxury of this temple of gastronomy" (ch. 35). The engagements and weddings, the dinners and parties, the yacht sailings and European travels that signpost the action in *The House of Mirth* are straight out of Wharton's experience, but straight out of the newspapers as well.

Although Lily begins the novel as a desirable subject for the newspaper, by the end of the novel, it is clear that Lily is not cut out for the world that journalism is making. By the end of the First World War, Wharton seems to have reassessed the newspaper. She made several trips to the front lines and wrote eyewitness accounts of the war. Unlike Stephen Crane, Wharton could never be a soldier, but she could bring the war to her readers. Only when newspapers became "clean" and objectivity became a value could Wharton contribute to their pages.

Journalism and the Urban Novel after the War

By most accounts, fact-fiction journalism, especially Hearst's brand of "journalism that acts," reached its peak during the Spanish-American War. And Stephen Crane was there, helping Hearst blur the "lines between fact and fiction, realism and romance, to manufacture once again a journalism that acted—and to create an entertainment that rivaled the most imaginative of texts" (Roggenkamp 2002, 91). If the Spanish-American War demonstrated journalism's power, the First World War dealt it a deathblow.

After the First World War, newspapers increasingly registered a norm of "objectivity," often signaled by a terse writing style. The standard bearer for objective journalism was the *New York Times*, which had actively resisted Hearst's brand of yellow journalism. If Dreiser, with his leisurely style and piles of detail, exemplifies a novelist parlaying Gilded Age journalism into the novel, Ernest Hemingway, who wrote for the *Kansas City Star*, shows what happens when the "objective" style works its way into fiction.

While Fishkin and others have convincingly linked Hemingway's style to his newspaper experience, other literary historians note that writers themselves were not always eager to do so. Despite the strong connections between newspapers' style and appearance after the First World War—a clipped, terse style; a new reliance on photographs—and modernism's aesthetic concerns—pared-down language; imagistic poetry—"modernists were loath to associate their writing with journalism, for they considered the latter a straight path to mass culture and thus to artistic death" (Roggenkamp 2002, 131). Between 1870 and 1915 newspapers and urban novels came together in a synergy that made both forms more successful and widely read; the urban novel would change radically as journalism and literature moved apart.

As the newspaper moved from local to mass culture, the fact-fiction discourse of the story faded in the move toward "objectivity." For modernists the "urban novel" was less compelling than it was for realists of one stripe or another. With the movement from realism to modernism, writers needed new artistic techniques to engage with the urban landscape and account for a world that seemed fundamentally destabilized. Modernist urban novels would have to be able to play with time and space in a way that conflicted directly with the demand for objective documentation that newspapers were making after the First World War. Individual cities (and the details that made them distinctive in realist fiction) became the realm of the newspaper; for literary modernists the city became an aesthetic object. Local meanings had to work differently to serve new artistic ends.

The city had changed, too, with the coming of the automobile. *The Great Gatsby* (1925), arguably a work of urban modernism, is largely set in the suburbs. Instead of walking through urban spaces, Fitzgerald's characters drive—and experience the city through the distancing frame of the car window. In *Gatsby,* elements of the "real" are shown to be blatant fictions. In Fitzgerald's hands, the sorts of objects that shore up Dreiser's realism—Gatsby's pile of shirts, his Montenegrin medal, and his photograph from Oxford—are hollow reminders that no quantity of physical objects can accrete to become "real." Gatsby's library is full of books with uncut pages; the house whose picture he sends home to his father is a rental. We never learn if the "facts" about Jordan Baker, who is in the news for her golf prowess and accusations of cheating are true. Daisy's society column marriage to Tom operates as a perfect cover for his affairs. Gatsby tries to use objects to undermine the stories that circulate about him—the new dress he sends to one of his partygoers signals that Gatsby wants to burnish his reputation—but any truth the novel might present is generated not through "fact" but through doubt. In the face of this doubt, the city is amalgamated into a series of images—the ash-heaps, the "city rising up across the river in white heaps and sugar lumps all built with a wish out of non-olfactory money,"

Nick's place at the window over Central Park "within and without, simultaneously enchanted and repelled by the inexhaustible variety of life" (chs. 4, 2).

As they moved beyond the fact-fiction discourse of Gilded Age journalism and realism, modernists grasped for a linguistic means with which to represent urban space. In *Manhattan Transfer* (1925), John Dos Passos drew on *Ulysses* (1922), *The Waste Land* (1922), and Sergei Eisenstein's films to create an experimental collage of modern New York. The novelists of the Harlem Renaissance drew inspiration from and set novels in urban spaces, but like modern novels these projects had far more in common with other artistic forms than with newly objective newspapers. Realism had its holdovers; numerous novelists depicted urban settings—especially immigrant or African American neighborhoods—in their fiction. But novels like Yezierska's *Bread Givers* (1925) or Jessie Fauset's *Plum Bun* (1928) remain distanced from the centers of literary modernism. The power of urban realism would resurface in Richard Wright's *Native Son* (1940), an homage to Dreiser that amasses newspaper stories, popular film, real estate maps, and boxing posters, among other quotidian details, to construct a portrait of Chicago that transcends the everyday. As Chapter 32 of this volume explains, Wright's depiction of modernity reminds us of what was lost in the transition to mass culture, objectivity, and aesthetics that separated novels from the news—namely, an interest in social and political justice.

Attending to the history of journalism with seriousness reinvigorates the urban realism of the Gilded Age for readers and literary scholars alike. Whether it appeared in novels or newspapers—or somewhere in between as the serialized content of high- or middlebrow periodicals—urban realism allows us to see cities becoming "the city," local culture coexisting with mass culture, fact keeping company with fiction. For students of the period, the question is not can we read urban realist novels and new journalism together—but how can they possibly be seen apart?

9

GEOGRAPHIC FICTIONS AND THE AMERICAN NOVEL

BY STEPHANIE FOOTE

There is a very simple question about literary maps: what exactly do they **do**? What do they do that cannot be done with words, that is; because if it can be done with words, then maps are superfluous.

—(Moretti 2005, 35)

Setting, Space, Narrative

In the question with which I begin this chapter, literary critic Franco Moretti considers why writers need the idea of the map, and asks how critics might use maps and mapping to track how literary genres rise and fall across literary history. By focusing on the idea of the map, Moretti's argument prompts us to linger over a question that seems so obvious as to need no explanation: how does literature define and represent the idea of place? Moretti's presentation and interpretation of both literary and conceptual maps as objects of narrative study lets him prise the map—that apparently most perfectly mimetic artifact for representing place—apart from a text's other strategies for representing place and its meaning, while at the same time allowing him to experiment with what it might look like to "map" a group of novels, to translate genre into spatial terms. In this exercise, maps are not perfectly mimetic; they have points of view, they are directed toward readers, they exclude certain objects. They work, in other words, like narratives, but what they narrate is a particular way of imagining place. The relay between maps and fiction in turn puts pressure on the map as a well-established and seemingly transparent metaphor in literary studies. Critics are certainly familiar with the map as a metaphor, routinely invoking cartographic rhetoric as they pursue interpretations that might have little or nothing at all to do with geographic place. We talk about the "literary landscape," to take a common example, or the "field of fiction," and often argue that novels "map" or "chart" or "guide" readers toward certain interpretations. But

Moretti's insistence that mapping is not merely a dead metaphor but rather a specific and quite singular mode of organizing information of special interest to some kinds of fiction and to some critical tasks asks us to step back and think about the larger issues of place and geography that inform how we think about the way narrative works, as well as how we imagine that particular novels represent space and geography.

It is nearly impossible to explain the relationship between geography and the American novel over the temporal span of the seventy years I shall cover in this chapter. The very conception of what geographic place is not only changes over time, but more importantly, it is at the heart of violent conflict between different social interests. Indeed, over these seventy years, the material area of the nation changed in large ways and small: territories were split into states; Native Americans were pushed from their land and into the new territorial formation of the reservation; dusty villages became small towns and cities; successive waves of immigration from the countryside to the city, and from a variety of European nations into cities, changed the demographics and the character of any number of places in the United States. Even the materiality of land itself—its reorganization into territories and states, its expropriation from its original owners, its sale and theft, its corporate use, its location as a lost and ideal state of being—cannot serve as a stable referent for a discussion of fiction, for the materiality of space is not merely a concrete fact that anchors the narratives social actors inscribe on it. Material space is always part of a set of literary, legal, and corporate stories that produce it as the site of conflict or identification for the social actors who are implicated in those stories. Place is not just important to fiction; it is itself a kind of fiction over which literary texts have struggled at different moments to make sense.

What then do we mean when we talk about place, or when we speculate about the role of place in fiction? Lawrence Buell has persuasively argued that we need to abandon a single definition of place and recognize instead what he calls its "nested" quality. "What counts as a place," he remarks, "can be as small as a corner of your kitchen or as big as the planet" (2005, 67). Affective attachments to place, he observes, are as constitutive of what place means as any "official" definition could be. Attachments to place are anything but linear; they move forward and backward in time, can be nostalgic and utopian, anchored in private memories or shared experiences. Buell's observation that places are always the product of narratives we tell about and through them follows the work of spatial theorists such as Henri Lefebvre and David Harvey who have looked at the contest of official and vernacular meanings of place, and at how different definitions of place are coordinated, sometimes uneasily, to produce the stories we tell about why some spaces are important and meaningful to us, while others, including those we might believe to be central to who we think we are, are merely names on a map, devoid of personal significance. In their shared emphasis on how place is narrated, cultural geographers and the literary critics influenced by them help us to see that if place cannot be described outside of human agency, neither can human agency be described outside of contests over what space and place mean to social actors. As a consequence, critics and historians interested in space (including, most recently, Ursula Heise, Hsuan Hsu, and Martin Bruckner) have challenged readers to acknowledge how the meaning of place, and the identities of specific places, have changed over time, and to understand how place has been the repository for both formal and ideological investments by a range of different texts and social actors.

But if the very idea of place is central to conflicting narratives about what people value and where they think they belong, how do we distinguish narratives that have a special relationship to "place" or "geography" from those that do not? Virtually every novel, after all, is set somewhere; it "takes place" in some moment and in some location or another. In some sense we might say that the novel form itself has a particular relationship to the idea of place because it unfolds its plots and represents characters in highly specific settings. But I shall argue that literary historians can rethink the relationship between high and low, local and national, domestic and imperial by examining texts and novels in which geographic place is under unusual pressure, achieving a centrality that exceeds "setting." In such fiction— some of which is conventionally identified as about specific place, like local color literature, and some of which is identified with abstract notions of place, like the Western—place is a circuit of meaning through which characters (and, as we shall see, readers) can build a sense of identity, navigate their fantasies of belonging, and assess different claims to membership in abstract and concrete communities. Geographic fiction is thus in close conversation with other historical narratives that also attempted to adjudicate claims of ownership, belonging, and community grounded in a particular idea of place. Geographic fiction focuses on the kinds of narratives that emerge when the competing stories that can be told about a place become central to the development of characters, to the unfolding of plot, and even to the larger archive of stories that have been told about a specific place or region. Place becomes both the "fact" that seems to guarantee and secure narratives of ownership or belonging as well as becoming in some sense the product of those narratives, and it is thus the pivotal category that can show us how different histories of places and spaces are put into motion in a text.

This chapter considers how conflicting stories about place have become part of a larger story that literary historians tell about the cultural work of the American novel between the Civil War and the beginning of the Second World War. I focus on selected genres that have taken geographical place seriously in multiple registers: as a problem of narrative form (how geographic place informs the narrative strategies a novel employs); as a problem of social belonging (how characters in a novel make affective investments in their community based on place); and as a problem of how extra-literary narratives inform texts (how competing stories about who has the right to define a given place shape a text). In my analysis, I follow the lead of literary historians such as Moretti who have looked at how the novel form changes historically, how it accommodates itself to new contexts and circumstances, how it in some ways tries to close the distance between affective and historical definitions of place. I shall also follow the lead of cultural geographers who have argued that we cannot ever really apprehend the seemingly pure referent of geographic place; what we understand as the pure fact of the land—a mountain, a pristine forest, a desert, a backyard—is always part of other narratives about socially embedded subjects' needs and desires, ambitions and hopes.

I have chosen to focus on three kinds of novels in this chapter: the late nineteenth-century genre of regional fiction; early twentieth-century modernist novels that anatomize the provincialism of community in towns and villages in the United States; and the popular genre of the Western. The list, as any reader who has a particular investment in a single geographic place can attest, is incomplete. American literary history can be narrated by aggregating the genealogies of discrete regions: the literary history of New England; the Middle West; the Southwest; California; or the South. Each of these regions has produced writers who have been classified as "regional" and identified with the areas about which they wrote, and many of these locations have coherent literary histories that have made them the subjects of articles, books, and entire courses of study at universities.

The South, in particular, has been a barometer of how race and region have been represented to the nation, and the tradition of Southern literature can be used to chart the fortunes of virtually every major literary genre from the Civil War to 1940, as well as the emergence of a self-conscious intellectual movement—the Southern Agrarians—that took seriously the shaping force of regional identity on intellectual production. Perhaps more than any other regional literature, that of the US South has been closely watched by cultural critics from Reconstruction until the present, and for good reason. Post-Reconstruction Southern fiction of the Plantation School, for example, deliberately superimposed a narrative of "the South" as a lost and idealized culture onto an economically and socially troubled territorial jurisdiction, making it one of the first examples of regional fiction that actively sought to create an aggressively mythical sense of place—a South that had never existed at all—in contrast to the official records and documents that were quite literally recreating the way that social actors in the South could claim a sense of citizenship and belonging. But I shall not tell that story here, in part because the South is a special case of the affective and administrative dimensions of place—what we might call the role of place in brokering emotional and political investments. And as I shall not tell a story of US literature that aggregates the traditions of each geographical location, I shall likewise not tell a completely linear story in which the idea of place changes in predictable ways across the nation and across the canon of fiction. Rather, it is my aim to use three broad examples to look at the way that place has been narrated in multiple registers to provide a broad overview of how place itself becomes a way to narrate key ideas in literary history, as well as how literary history shapes what we think geography does in culture.

Regional Literature of the Late Nineteenth Century

The geographic fiction most familiar to literary critics falls under the heading of regional or local color texts. Regional fiction was most popular at the end of the nineteenth century, and although many critics trace its history to the popular tall tales and humorous dialect fiction published in antebellum newspapers beginning in the 1830s, the regional fiction with which I am concerned here had all but lost its rougher edges by the time it began appearing in some of the most prestigious magazines of the day. As critics like Richard Brodhead, Amy Kaplan, and Nancy Glazener have argued, the regional literature of the late nineteenth century was as much an invention of publishers and literary critics as it was the freshly scrubbed and soberly attired literary heir of the frontier tales of miners or cardsharps. Stylistically, late nineteenth-century regional fiction was at least as indebted to realism's techniques of narration as it was to the oral tradition of dialect storytelling it often employed as a narrative device within its stories.

Late nineteenth-century regional fiction was published in periodicals such as *The Atlantic Monthly* and *Harper's*, and was championed by some of the most important editors and realist writers of the era, prominently William Dean Howells, who in many cases acted as a literary broker and mentor for emerging regionalist writers. From Sarah Orne Jewett's Maine and the New England villages of Rose Terry Cooke and Mary Wilkins Freeman, from Hamlin Garland's middle border, to Mary Murfree's Tennessee, George Washington Cable's Louisiana, and the idealized Southern world of Thomas Nelson Page, short stories focusing on the daily relationships between villagers and households became a staple of magazine fiction. The popularity of regional writing in the genteel periodicals of the day secured for its authors a cosmopolitan, urban, national audience, and critics have argued that its wide popularity as a genre among such readers was the result of their cosmopolitan desire to see the concrete fact of the local and the abstract idea of the nation as part of a single story. Literary historians have therefore argued that regional fiction was a nationalizing genre that presented local and rural cultures as commodities, evacuating regional differences of their potential political incompatibility with a national agenda by narratively transforming those local differences into mere cultural curiosities. Close descriptions of landscape and local, rural communities in regional fiction are less about geographic place, in this reading, than they are about creating a social place for the authentic, foreign, and strange in a culture grappling with immigration and Reconstruction.

This argument seems to gain traction when critics return to the work of one of regionalism's first champions, Howells, who in his influential column "From the Editor's Study," argued that the task of American literature should be to make the parts of the nation known to one another. That task was virtually guaranteed by regional writers, who as Nancy Glazener has pointed out, often saw their work published with a subtitle announcing the particular geographic section of the country in which they were set (1997, 190). Howells famously wrote, "A great number of very good writers are instinctively striving to make each part of the country and each phase of our civilization known to all the other parts; and their work is not narrow" (1887, 98). Howells's editorial judgment was crucial in helping local-color writers break into a national print market and find a national readership. But it was therefore also crucial in helping to shape what constituted regional writing, or writing about a specific place and its culture. In May of 1887, Howells similarly adjured the field of American literature in grand fashion: "Let fiction cease to lie about life; let it portray men and women as they are, actuated by the motives and the passions in the measure we all know . . . let it speak the dialect, the language that most Americans know—the language of unaffected people everywhere" (81).

Howells makes a double-gesture here that defines the contradictions of the genre and informs many of its future iterations, for he argues both that fiction should faithfully represent "everyday" life so that every reader might understand it and that it must focus on the particularities of everyday life unavailable to most readers. The regional fiction he celebrated, and that was championed by the contemporary high-brow periodicals, made the challenge of defamiliarizing the commonplace central to its formal and thematic method by arguing that the ordinariness of its characters lives was paradoxically shaped by the extraordinary locations in which they lived. The regional fiction most beloved by Howells and the readers of his literary columns not only sought to make the men and women of different geographic areas intelligible to educated urban readers; it developed formal methods for making cultural regions out of geographic regions, for making a sense of place out of distant spaces, constructing for various areas in the country systems of values, beliefs, social organization, language use, and social hierarchies that were uncannily nonnormative, or as Judith Fetterley has argued, "UnAmerican" (1994, 878).

In this reading, regional fiction does not construct place and the local cultures associated with it only in order to facilitate the urban elite's experience and consumption of local cultures. Rather, as feminist critics such as Fetterley, Stacey Alaimo, Sandra Zagarell, and Krista Comer have argued, regional texts negotiate concerns about who has a claim to membership in community, and who has a right to stake out a place in the local worlds regional texts describe. Such an observation, which as I shall describe, relies on a reading of the form and narrative of regional texts, is also motivated by regional fiction's particular print history. Stories about particular places, Richard Brodhead argues, enjoyed enormous popularity among upper-middle-class readers in part because their formal elements—including copious use of dialect and a scrupulous attention to the depiction of local customs—appeared to guarantee their authenticity. But if the genre's appeal lay in the implicit promise of authorial authenticity—that is, that local color stories were written by people who had intimate, insider knowledge of the places and people they were representing—its success among audiences also lay in the dual position of the writers themselves. Local color writers had to be sufficiently cosmopolitan to be able to address a national audience, but sufficiently provincial to be able to accurately depict the cadences of a particular place, sufficiently ambitious to want to enter the literary marketplace and sufficiently shrewd to see that the best way to do it was by converting their own geographic position into something like an authorial identity. This paradox, Brodhead argues, accounts for the fact that regional literature was an especially efficient genre for allowing women and minority writers to gain access to a national print culture.

If regional literature relied on the culture of a specific place to mediate between the rural and the urban, between the local and the national, between strangers and natives, it did so by using the formal strategies of realist writing. The texts often focused on the quotidian life of a small community in a predominately rural area, and generally employed a first person or omniscient narrator who used standard English while featuring the voices of villagers and rustics who spoke in meticulously rendered (and, as critics like W. P. James charged, sometimes tiresomely impenetrable) dialect. Many of the stories dealt with the intrusion of an "outsider"—often a sympathetic urban tourist in search of authentic, restful rural culture—whose perspective makes the commonplace rituals of the village seem strange and exotic. Many of the visitors are ostensibly in search of the recuperative powers of a rural area that seems to have been bypassed by modernity, but a few of the most evocative local color stories counteract the nostalgia that Raymond Williams has diagnosed as constitutive of much literature that positions the bucolic, timeless country village against the modern metropolis. Those stories thus work to portray the deep economic and social injustices that undermine the fantasies of village life as a rural idyll.

In stories like Sarah Orne Jewett's 1886 "A White Heron," for example, Sylvie, the nine-year-old protagonist, decides to withhold local knowledge from the urban visitor who comes to her region to hunt the rare white heron. Dazzled by the sophistication and enthusiasm of the young visitor, Sylvie is also tempted by the offer of a financial reward for whoever can lead him to the heron's nest. Wishing to please her visitor, and mindful that his money would alleviate her grandmother's poverty, Sylvie quietly tracks the heron one morning. Climbing a tree to watch the dawn break over the woods, she recognizes that she and the heron are sharing the moment, and understands too that she cannot give the heron's secret away and sentence it to death. If the story seems to follow the conventional dichotomies of rural versus urban ways of knowing, or authentic versus academic investments in the countryside, it also disturbs and rearranges that economy. Sylvie, the text's repository of local knowledge, is not a native of the countryside. She is a grateful refugee from the city who has come to love the country and feel at home there. Neither is the hunter a mere mercenary; he seems to have a feel for the countryside, and Sylvie discerns that he loves, even if he finally kills, the birds he claims to admire. Each of them occupies a complicated position in relationship to place, and neither position is more or less authentic, more or less accurate, or more or less affectively rich. Rather the text foregrounds how different ways of narrating the meaning of place define both the value of that place and how social actors will define themselves in relation to one another.

Indeed, the story's commitment to the narrative contest over what place means to different social actors is underscored by the scene in which a silent Sylvie, sitting at the top of a tree, can see the more of the countryside than she has ever seen before, and finds that she is perceiving it from the perspective of its rarest, wildest creature. It is not quite a local perspective, for it is a viewpoint that would be denied to virtually anyone who lived there. Neither is it an omniscient or even a global perspective, for Sylvie does not occupy a position that integrates her love of place with its value for a wider world of unknown urban people. The text's focus on different ways of apprehending the value of a place, a focus that drew sophisticated readers to the genre in the first place, helps it to embody what Glazener has described as the genre's ability to stir urban elite readers' interest in cultural difference as well as gratify their nostalgic emotional investment in the ostensibly primitive, pure worlds of rural places.

Regional literature's formal and thematic commitment to representing social and cultural difference and its complex staging of who is a native and who a stranger did more than allow women writers access to the literary field. It also helped to make it a favored genre for immigrant and African American writers who were attempting to break into the print market at the turn into the twentieth century. Indeed when William Dean Howells called for American writing to show readers that they were more alike than not, he was not merely making it possible for native born writers to depict exotic local color characters, their odd accents and outlandish customs, as if they were foreign and strange, he was also making it possible for immigrant writers to join a conversation about national identity by adapting the rhetoric of place to the rhetoric of community.

Abraham Cahan, for example, was a prolific journalist and publisher of the important Yiddish-language *Jewish Daily Forward* newspaper at the turn into the twentieth century, but his entrance into the national literary sphere was brokered by Howells once Cahan had begun to write stories that explored characters' longing for the place they once called home as well as their struggles to navigate the American places in which they were recreating their culture in exile. Borrowing from regional fiction's narratives of the affective investments different social actors make in the idea of place, Cahan's fiction pays special attention to how people create communities and preserve a sense of cultural tradition in places that are far from their homes. In narratives of immigrant life in New York such as *Yekl: A Tale of the New York Ghetto* (1896) or in short stories like "The Imported Bridegroom" (1898), Cahan describes the day to day life of the Jewish ghetto in New York, and like the regional writers focusing on village life, his stories are narrated in standard English while the characters speak in elaborately rendered dialect. If Cahan's characters have something in common with the fictional characters familiar to nineteenth-century middle class readers of regionalism, they also bear uncanny similarities to those readers who loved them. The stories detail the rich culture of the New York neighborhoods in which characters live, revealing the practices they used to create a community that could keep their traditions alive in exile. Yet the stories are also structured by a tone of loss and lament, for the Jews in Cahan's stories are exiles, and have been forced to immigrate (on Cahan and the immigrant novel, see Chapter 13 of this volume). The characters thus yearn for their "real" homes, for the places that seem to be the site of their most authentic and organic communities, for the places that they have lost by emigrating to the United States. Their stories about place revolve around commemorating the material spaces from which they have been exiled, but the stories in which they appeared focused on how their new neighborhoods in New York were becoming regions unto themselves.

Regional Literature of the Early Twentieth Century

If late nineteenth-century regional fiction was interested in the distinctive cultures of particular places, it was also invested in understanding how different kinds of people could make a place their own. For a genre widely dismissed in the first half of the twentieth century as "minor," regional fiction was especially good at developing narratives and rhetoric about how social actors could make claims to be citizens of various places and communities. Despite its prominence in the highbrow periodicals of the day, the genre of regional fiction exemplified by the work of Sarah Orne Jewett seemed to fall into decline in the first half of the twentieth century. This standard narrative of literary obscurity is not entirely accurate though, for the broad questions and techniques employed by regional fiction did not disappear. Rather they evolved in relationship to the changes in political and cultural conversations about place and community. The small towns and villages that formed the material for later nineteenth-century regional fiction continued to prove important to a select group of writers in the first part of the twentieth century who shared regional fiction's intense scrutiny of the relationships among place, individual identity, and community membership, but in the texts of what Carl Van Doren described, in the title of the second chapter of *The American Novel* (1921), as literature about "the revolt from the village," the crushing restrictions of local life were anatomized and indicted. Such fiction transformed one of regionalism's central interests—how place could sustain multiple narratives and commitments—into a darker question—how narratives of what it meant to live in or be from somewhere could converge into a single, monotonous, story about "who we are" and what "we" value? How, such fiction asked, could someone write their way out of a region or a place that no longer felt like home?

If the classic local-color fiction was written in an era in which waves of immigration seemed to some cultural commentators to be increasing the size and the character of major cities like New York, the modernist fiction of village life was written against a different historical set of concerns. By time of the publication of Sherwood Anderson's *Winesburg, Ohio* in 1919, post-Civil War Reconstruction and the national consolidation that was supposed to follow was no longer the primary concern of the government. The attempt to enfranchise African American men had largely failed, and racial segregation and Jim Crow dominated the South. The United States' entry into the First World War solidified its role in a larger geopolitical context. Similarly, in the teens and twenties, all major urban areas were expanding and smaller cities became important metropolitan hubs. While they did not usurp the cultural or financial power of Boston and New York, the rise across the United States of smaller cities with respectable presses, cultural scenes and local cultural elites who would not have recognized themselves in portrayals of quaint regional types meant that it was no longer possible to imagine a simple binary between country and city, nor to imagine life in a nation in which urban problems existed in a few East coast metropolitan areas. The geographic places that comprised the United States were much changed, as was the place of the United States in the world.

The category of place in literature was also under pressure; far from being a testing ground for diversity or community, rural or Midwestern regions began to seem provincial, moralistic, and suspicious of difference. In the work of writers like Zona Gale, Booth Tarkington, Edgar Lee Masters, Sinclair Lewis, and Sherwood Anderson, to take a few examples of "the revolt from the village" school of fiction, quaint eccentrics are not tolerated by their fellow villagers; they are despised and judged. Nor do their narrators present them as types of personalities worth celebrating for their resistance to the homogenizing rise of a national culture; they are presented as victims of a provincial culture that fears the diversity of urban areas. Mainly the work of Midwestern writers, "revolt from the village" texts rewrite small towns and villages not as havens from urbanization, but as self-satisfied enclaves of stagnant provincialism. And rather than describe a community of citizens trying to forge ethical relations, their work depicts the secrets that distort the interior lives of their seemingly most average and representative citizens.

In Anderson's chapter "Adventure," for example, Alice Hindman, approaching middle age alone in Winesburg, Ohio, "began trying to force herself to face bravely the fact that many people must live and die alone, even in Winesburg." In "Queer," Elmer Cowley dreams of getting out of the town that has both defined and repressed him. "He knew that a local freight train passed through Winesburg at midnight and went on to Cleveland, where it arrived at dawn. He would steal a ride on the local and when he got to Cleveland he would lose himself in the crowds there. He would get work in some shop and become friends with the other workmen. . . . He would not longer be queer and he would make friends. Life would begin to have warmth and meaning for him as it had for others." Elmer and Alice may be citizens of Winesburg, but their most secret selves are hidden from others, and are solitary and apart. Similarly, in Booth Tarkington's 1921 *Alice Adams*, set in an unnamed town in an unnamed state, Alice Adams, finds herself trapped in a town small enough for her to be invited to the parties of the daughter of the wealthiest man in town, but large enough for her to know that because she is the daughter of a working man, she will never really be part of the best social group. Her gradual recognition that she can never exceed the role her provincial little town has assigned to her is at the center of the text. For Tarkington, as for Anderson, Gale, and others, social place and geographic place conspire to enforce a dreary sameness that seems as much a parody of the social systems of the city as an extension of the elaborate folkways of the local color fiction of the late nineteenth century. As one critic summed up the movement, "the revolt is thus a revolt from mediocrity, from Philistinism, from dullness—in a word, from the Provincialism of America as revealed most typically by the small town of the Middle West. But this provincialism is not *confined* to the small town, nor is it confined to the Middle West. . . . A striking feature of this revolt is that . . . it has come, without exception, from American-born actual inhabitants of the villages" (Wann 1925, 299).

The "revolt from provincialism" waged by the writers I have discussed in this section was not, of course, the only kind of fiction that was dedicated to anatomizing the idea of place, to understanding the stories that could be told about it, or the narratives that emerged from competing claims over it. The writers of the "revolt from the village" fiction were prolific and well respected by their peers. They were widely and well reviewed, and often contributed reviews of contemporary fiction to journals like *The Nation*. Some, like Indiana's Booth Tarkington, even became beloved symbols and boosters of the Midwestern places much of their fiction criticized even though he had a national audience. It is worth noting that Tarkington, now remembered as a middlebrow provincial writer, was working at the same time as F. Scott Fitzgerald (to whom he was very well known), another Midwestern writer whose most famous narrator, Nick Carraway of *The Great Gatsby* (1925), was as anxious about how his Middle West upbringing limited his perspective as Tarkington's Alice Adams was about how it limited her social chances. (Carl Van Doren actually categorized Fitzgerald with the other "revolt from the village" writers). The writers in question, that is, were part of an emerging cosmopolitan elite that was increasingly suspicious of the danger of merely local points of view. In this way, despite the differences in their styles, work, and choice of subject matter, they shared with the urban writers of the Harlem Renaissance, an interest in investigating how the stories people told about places were also stories about their affiliations and identities.

The Genre of Open Space

In the previous sections, I focused on fictions of place that were organized around what Raymond Williams has called fantasies of "knowable communities." Those communities, though, were by no means *universally* known or knowable—indeed, much of the fiction of place I have looked at thus far staged conversations about who had the right to represent and claim knowledge of the interior life of a place— perhaps the most accurate way of describing how regional texts first understand membership in a community. The texts and genres I have discussed were deeply invested in carefully drawn portraits of small places—Winesburg, Ohio, or a small town on the coast of Maine—rather than "the Midwest" or "New England." When I discuss "The West," then, I invoke not just a specific geographic region but an abstract idea of region that seemed to transcend a definition of place rooted in a small, knowable, predictable community. I do not here mean to suggest the absence of literature associated with geographically discrete areas of the western states. Critics such as Lawrence Berkove, who writes about the Sagebrush school of Western literature, and Charles Crow, Kevin Starr, and Gary Scharnhorst who focus on California, have proposed careful genealogies of the relationship between specific geographic locations and the complex literatures that have arisen within and about them. And certainly, many great realist and naturalist novels understood the geographic space of the West as central to the development of their narratives; we might think here of Frank Norris's or Gertrude Atherton's depictions of both the fascinating, restless urban culture and the expansive, increasingly corporatized agricultural and ranching economy of California. My argument is rather that the kinds of attachments to "The West" as it was depicted in the genres of popular or dime Westerns, in manifestos and travel and nature writing, as well as in modernist novels set in western states such as those of Mary Austin and Willa Cather exemplify how this amorphously defined region gained cultural power as it become more purely textual.

If New England was understood by the first critics of place and region as the site of late nineteenth-century classic regional fiction, with its fantasies about what constitutes a community and membership in it, the West staged a fantasy about the individual's seemingly endless search to remake civilization entirely. The turn into the twentieth century witnessed an enduring fascination with the West, from Frederick Jackson Turner's 1893 paper "The Significance of the Frontier in American History" and Theodore Roosevelt's well-known admiration for the strenuous life to the emerging movement to create a national parks system and the nature writing of John Muir. All of these documents shared a sense that an underpopulated landscape could provide the means for a man to come to a more complete understanding of himself and his role in the world away from the vitiating influences of an overcivilized, feminized urban culture. The natural world, and the empty expanses of the western landscape, could connect men to a greater sense of purpose by bringing them into a purifying relationship to the harsh materiality and physicality of place. The West was, in this view, less a wide-open space of lawlessness than a place that was governed by the harsh, immutable laws of the natural world.

Critical to this ideology of purification and the recapture of masculinity and individuality was the genre of the Western. Unlike the other place-based literature

I have considered, Westerns were not part of the culturally consecrated publishing industry of the East Coast. They were far more popular and widely read, and far less critically acclaimed. Westerns were part of the dime novel tradition, and in the late nineteenth century, individual installments of its texts were often printed in serial form in newspapers and magazines, or as cheap novels from one of the large publishing syndicates. Formally, the Westerns did not have the same emphasis on authorship and originality as did the kind of regional fiction that has come to signpost late nineteenth-century literature about place; Zane Grey, for example, published well over seventy books over his career, rivaling the output of more critically esteemed writers like Howells, but most of these books relied on the same stock characters and lavish descriptions of deserts, sunsets, and native cultures. Yet Westerns were fantastically popular, in part because they were so formulaic, and gained in popularity as the regional fictions of the late nineteenth century seemed to fall into decline.

If the local color of the late nineteenth century mourned the loss of the local in the face of urbanization and immigration, and if it and its later iteration of "revolt from the village" fiction worried over the idea of enforced compliance with restrictive communities, Westerns manifested less interest in whether or not someone had an authentic right to be a member of a community than in how a community could maintain itself in the West without limiting an individual. Indeed, although Westerns represented characters in very schematic terms—they were noble or knavish, brave or cowardly, weak or strong—the West itself was the guarantee that the most cardboard character could paradoxically live out his or her freely chosen destiny. Any man, the novels argued, could find a community in the West to belong to, a place in which to feel at home, and any man, they argued, could just as easily decide to leave that community. The storied communities and preordained roles of the East did not exert the same normalizing pressure in depictions of the West, and the entrenched, unspoken social laws that ground down the characters in the fiction of Zona Gale and Sherwood Anderson were virtually nonexistent. Normativity, that is, was not as critical as individuality, no small irony in texts that adhered so strictly to among the most formulaic writing in the publishing industry.

But we should not make the mistake of seeing the Western as a paean to individualism at the expense of community; rather the Western is interested in brokering strategic, if often provisional, alliances between individuals and cultures. We can see how the Western grounds those alliances by explaining them in terms of a larger set of loyalties to the natural world. *Riders of the Purple Sage* (1912), for example, is set in the dramatic landscape of Utah, and centers on the conflict between Jane, a female ranch owner, and an exiled group of polygamous Mormons who are conspiring to raid Jane's ranch. After a series of increasingly dramatic events, including the rescue and adoption of a long-lost family member and the exposure of the degradation of polygamy for women, Jane and the novel's hero, a cowboy loner called Lassiter, deliberately close themselves off in a valley. There they will live in a virtual Eden, free from the depredations of other people. Like many Westerns, *Riders of the Purple Sage* explores why different people were drawn to the west and how they learned to adapt to the difficulties of the land. And like many Westerns, it returns repeatedly to the issue of how the act of settling a seemingly empty territory involves rewriting or assimilating the stories of those who have lived there before. The text certainly pays attention to the conflicts that arise over claims to vital natural resources like water, but it also gestures toward the violent history of settlement by including scenes of contact between Native Americans who are slowly losing their claim to the land and sympathetic white loners who eventually try to establish an authentic relationship to the land by establishing a relationship with a member of a Native tribe.

The instrumentalizing view of the disappearing cultures and customs of Native people and their utility for white men's blossoming awareness of the majesty of nature is critical to *Riders of the Purple Sage* as well as to its sequel, *The Rainbow Trail* (1915). In *Riders*, for example, a rancher comes upon a long-abandoned Anasazi cliff dwelling and the narrative pauses to imagine the scene from his perspective. "It had not been desecrated by the hand of man, nor had it been crumbled by the hand of time . . . it was just as it had been left by its builders . . . How many years had passed since the cliff-dwellers gazed out across the beautiful valley as he was gazing now? How long had it been since women ground grain in those polished holds? What time had rolled by since men of an unknown race lived, loved, fought, and died there?" (ch. 10).

Similarly, in *The Rainbow Trail*, Shefford, a demoralized but ambitious young man who wishes to escape civilization and who has come west because he has heard stories about the wild landscape (including the now legendary story of Jane and Lassiter's hidden Eden) tries to chart the impact of successive waves of escapees from civilized life on Native-American cultures. "The padre, the trapper, the trader, the prospector, and the missionary—so the white man had come, some of him good, no doubt, but more of him evil; and the young brave learned a thirst that could never be quenched at the cold, sweet spring of his forefathers, and the young maiden burned with a fever in her blood, and lost the sweet, strange, wild fancies of her tribe" (ch. 8). His, and the text's, romanticization of Native-American tribal life—in this case the Navajo—should not obscure that the narrative is organized not only around the regeneration of a middle-class white man, vitiated by his life in civilization through his fantasy of Navajo culture, but also through his recognition that he himself is part of that conquest.

Westerns' emphasis on how an authentic feeling for the land could be in part established through strategic, even culturally "outlawed" alliances with people perceived to have a more natural claim to the land does not, of course, preclude a triumphalist narrative about how that land could be turned to economic advantage by white settlers. In the Western, commercial success and spiritual renewal by no means preclude one another. The genre of the Western and the idea of the American

West have been so powerful and so popular not because they are transparent and uncomplicated but because they so efficiently narrate the difficult, contradictory, and perverse stories Americans tell themselves about where they belong. Indeed, the story of the West—its representation in literature, its position in the imperial designs of the nation, the ideological work of its landscape—has been the engine of a long tradition of literary and cultural histories about the United States, from Henry Nash Smith's *Virgin Land: The American West as Symbol and Myth* (1950) to Richard Slotkin's trilogy of histories about the cultural work of the frontier, from the groundbreaking feminist critique of Annette Kolodny and Stacey Alaimo, to new scholarship in the multiethnic histories of the West like that of Neil Campbell's *The Rhizomatic West* (2008). The West as a place still roots the narratives Americans tell themselves about their identities in part because it seems eternally to promise to remap personal identity in a new context, but for recent critics, an abstracted ideal of the West has provided the grounds for a reimagination of US imperialism as well. The West has thus been recognized as a geographic space that has been able to anchor fantasies of individualism and escape from civilization in part because the material histories of the other people who lived there were diminished in the most popular texts about it. The recent reevaluations of western literary traditions has, like the feminist recovery of women regionalists, focused attention on the literary and historical stakes of who defines the West and what kinds of communities emerge from those definitions.

Mapping the Futures of Place

Interdisciplinary scholarship in American Studies has made it possible for many literary critics to think about the global and globalizing ambitions of American literature. But if globalization has revealed that national identity is inextricably forged in relationship to fantasies about the nation's internal coherence as well as in relationship to other cultures, so too has it revealed that the same dynamic obtains in studies of the local. It is not, that is, just at the level of the nation that imperialism, to take one example, is staged; ideologies that seem to have everything to do with the official narratives of nation and empire work themselves out in surprising and often contradictory ways in studies of smaller neighborhoods, regions, and communities, imagined and otherwise. Place, as Eric Ball argues in "Literary Criticism for Places," is thus an increasingly vital category in new studies of the American novel, and three of the most important emerging fields of study in US fiction and culture—environmental or nature-themed writing, global or transnational literature, and ethnic literature—owe a debt to the pressure that the literary histories I have here discussed put on the category of place.

As I have argued in the previous sections of this chapter, the relationships among the different literary traditions in the United States that concern themselves with place are not linear; rather they are often associative and citational, drawing together various traditions, resuscitating some and rejecting others. The fiction that prioritizes the affective dimensions of place is also a fiction that seeks to understand how people have tried to suppress or assimilate the stories of other people's attachments to them. It can serve the aims of the nation, or can resist them. It can tolerate diversity or it can invoke an authentic, historical relationship to place as the grounds for violence and exclusion. Being able to invoke and claim a geographic place as one's home is arguably among the first identitarian warrants in the United States, and in a climate in which the romance of the striving immigrant has collapsed under the scandal of global refugees and displaced persons, being able to produce a claim to call someplace home continues to be among the most vexed ways to identify oneself.

SCIENCE, MEDICINE, TECHNOLOGY, AND THE NOVEL, 1860–1915

BY JANE F. THRAILKILL

Nineteenth-century science has received a bad rap: for evidence, one need look no further than the antebellum novels and stories of Nathaniel Hawthorne. Almost all of his characters who commit the unpardonable sin of violating "the sanctity of a human heart" are men versed in modern science, medicine, or technology (*The Scarlet Letter* (1850), ch. 17): Roger Chillingworth, the twisted "leech" who subtly tortures the man who cuckolded him; a researcher who performs fatal plastic surgery on his wife ("The Birthmark," 1843); a botanist whose toxic experiments destroy his only daughter ("Rappaccini's Daughter," 1844). The narrator of *The Blithedale Romance* (1852) equates science with vivisection: "if we take the freedom to put a friend under our microscope, we thereby insulate him from many of his true relations, magnify his peculiarities, inevitably tear him into parts, and of course patch him very clumsily together again" (ch. 9). Empirical study, by this account, is a cold, dissecting, third-person affair; it is the work of the man of letters to attend to the hot, relational, first-person aspects of experience.

Hawthorne wrote of his repugnance for scientific scrutiny in 1852; a scant decade later, the poet Emily Dickinson cannily made the opposite case, affirming the "prudence" of the clarifying vision provided by modern technologies:

> "Faith" is a fine invention
> When Gentlemen can *see*—
> But *Microscopes* are prudent
> In an Emergency—

Dickinson, writing on the cusp of the American Civil War, was aware of the ways that uncertain, turbulent times can outstrip the human capacity to comprehend them. Rather than eschew modern technologies, Dickinson likened her compressed, elliptical poems to "microscopes": small in circumference but powerful in their ability to magnify human insight. Science is here returned to its Latin root, *scientia*—knowledge gained through study, observation, and experience—making it the purview of the poet and biologist alike.

Although the years 1861 to 1865 were immensely productive for Dickinson, the same period witnessed a virtual moratorium on long narrative fiction in the United States. The most absorbing cultural story in the early 1860s, it appears, was the devastating one unfolding in real time. The next generation of US writers either were abroad (Henry Adams and William Dean Howells), turned to journalism (Samuel Clemens, Louisa May Alcott, and Walt Whitman), or were caught up in the antislavery cause and the war effort (Frances E. W. Harper, Thomas Wentworth Higginson, and John W. DeForest). Meanwhile, literary voices of the earlier period went all but silent. Herman Melville published his final novel, *The Confidence Man*, in 1857. Hawthorne followed with his last completed romance, *The Marble Faun*, in 1860 and died before the war was over. Ralph Waldo Emerson delivered his Concord neighbor's eulogy, as he had for Henry David Thoreau, who died of tuberculosis in 1862. (Not surprisingly, Emerson's first postwar publication was the elegiac poem, "Terminus," in 1866.) In the words of Louis Menand, "The Civil War swept away the slave civilization of the South, but it swept away almost the whole intellectual culture of the North along with it" (2001, x).

The decade of the 1860s, however, witnessed a flourishing of the natural sciences. The United States was entering the world stage, scientifically speaking: the internationally acclaimed zoologist Louis Agassiz founded the Museum of Comparative Zoology in Cambridge, in 1860, and by decade's end, the American Museum of Natural History had opened its doors in New York. The director of Harvard College's observatory, George Phillips Bond, in 1865 became the first American to receive the Royal Astronomical Society's gold medal. Cultivation and dissemination of scientific knowledge was fostered by the passage of the first federal land-grant college bill in 1862 and the publication of James Dwight Dana's *Manual of Geology* (1863), a milestone in the development of a specifically US-based physical science.

Technology also proliferated during the volatile war years. Following the founding of the Massachusetts Institute of Technology in 1861, the first successful oil pipeline was laid in Pennsylvania, George Westinghouse devised the air brake for use on railways, and the first commercially successful typewriter was developed (employing the QWERTY keyboard still in use today). Perhaps most significantly, in 1863 and at the height of the war, Abraham Lincoln signed the Act of Incorporation founding the National Academy of Sciences, creating a group of scientific elites who would serve as "advisers to the nation on science, engineering, and medicine."

If we looked solely at the institutionalization of science, the 1860s could be seen as a time of stately progress and steady development. The facts on the ground, however, evoke a more equivocal story. The Civil War plunged the United States violently into the modern era, with the overwhelming demand for artillery, ammunition, and transportation fueling industrial innovation. Advances in metallurgy and allied technologies gave rise to new classes of weapons unprecedented in their precision and firepower, including rifled guns, repeating weapons, and lightweight cannons. (Dynamite, barbed wire, the self-propelled torpedo, and the Gatling gun were all patented in the 1860s—though only the last saw use, albeit limited, on American battlefields.) The first clash of ironclad ships took place between the Union *Monitor* and the Confederate *Merrimac* in 1862, forever changing the nature of naval warfare. Meanwhile, the growing network of factories, railroads, and shipping routes provided the infrastructure to support an emergent corporate capitalism in the decades that followed.

During the war years, medicine, perforce, became a national concern. New technologies of destruction, when combined with older military tactics geared for less accurate armaments, produced unheard of damage to human bodies. Injured soldiers, in turn, formed massive patient populations, creating a pool of unwilling experimental subjects for desperate doctors trying to repair injured minds and bodies in hastily constructed field hospitals. Henry Adams's anonymously published work, *Democracy: An American Novel* (1880), articulated the difficulty of assimilating the monumental scale of modern carnage, as a young woman visiting Arlington National Cemetery

> found herself suddenly met by the long white ranks of head-stones, stretching up and down the hill-sides by thousands, in order of baffle; as though Cadmus had reversed his myth, and had sown living men, to come up dragons' teeth. She drew in her horse with a shiver and a sudden impulse to cry. Here was something new to her. This was war—wounds, disease, death. (ch. 9)

The scene at Arlington gestures to the terrible sublimity of violent cultural transformation by depicting a character groping for a way to assimilate the deadly consequences of monumental human aspiration when coupled with mechanical innovation.

The post–Civil War US novel reflected the paradoxes of progress that attended the United States' militant entry into modernity. The terrible toll of "blood and treasure" (to quote Lincoln's 1862 State of the Union Address) gave writers new license to represent the social fabric, and indeed human bodies, in tatters. There was also a felt imperative to reconstruct viable cultural narratives for changed conditions. The results were equivocal. The extension of human power embodied in new technologies was tempered—as writers such as Rebecca Harding Davis, Frank Norris, and Edith Wharton made clear—by a correspondent sense of diminished agency as individuals found themselves immersed in brutal factory systems, enfolded in anonymous city crowds, and buffeted by a volatile economic system. Evolutionary theory's challenge to religious precepts and traditional social structures triggered a vertiginous sense of dislocation that, as Hamlin Garland, Charles Chesnutt, and Kate Chopin would portray, led to naturalized, frequently invidious ways of sifting individuals into class, race, and gender hierarchies. As Oliver Wendell Holmes and Charlotte Perkins Gilman would document, the newly institutionalized disciplines of psychology and scientific medicine, which promised to ameliorate distress and shed light on the deepest recesses of human experience, also codified new ways of labeling and disciplining suffering human souls.

Formally, novels published after 1870 tended to mute the didactic moral voice associated with pre-Civil War prose and favor an impersonal or "objective" narrative perspective. In *Uncle Tom's Cabin* (1852), Harriet Beecher Stowe directly addresses her readers, "I beseech you, pity those mothers that are constantly made childless by the American slave-trade!" (ch. 45). By contrast, in *Sister Carrie* (1900) Theodore Dreiser deploys the clinical perspective of the budding social sciences: "When a girl leaves home at eighteen, she does one of two things. Either she falls into saving hands and becomes better, or she rapidly assumes the cosmopolitan standard of virtue and becomes worse" (ch. 1). Scholars such as Lawrence Rothfield have linked narrative objectivity with the detached, disembodied perspective associated with modern medicine (1994): "The observing gaze," writes French philosopher Michel Foucault, "refrains from intervening: it is silent and gestureless. Observation leaves things as they are; there is nothing hidden to it in what is given" (1963, 131).

As we will see, many late nineteenth-century novelists employed a particular form of narrative speech known as free indirect discourse, a modification of the clinical gaze Foucault describes. Free indirect discourse, familiar to readers since Jane Austen, is a stylistic device that combines a third-person perspective with aspects of first-person direct speech. It can be likened to literary laparoscopy in its capacity to snake inside and reveal the inner workings of different minds. Henry James further refined this narrative practice in *The Portrait of a Lady* (1881) by keeping the point of view closely identified with the "exquisite consciousness" of the protagonist Isabel Archer. Other writers also used free indirect discourse to extend their narrative range: in *The House Behind the Cedars* (1900), for instance, Charles Chesnutt gives voice to the unstated, barely conscious perceptions of a racist white character, who "felt a momentary touch of annoyance that a negro woman should have intruded herself into his dream at its most interesting point" (ch. 12). Chesnutt here presents bigotry from the inside, offering a glimpse of the private prejudices that propel individual action and that also underlie large social formations—in this case, the invidious system of racial segregation laws known collectively in the United States as "Jim Crow." Updated by writers at the cusp of the twentieth century, the technique of free indirect discourse was fertilized by novel theories about human psychology and the nervous system, modern technologies of observation, and wide-ranging modifications in the equipment of everyday life.

The post–Civil War US novel can itself be seen as an important technology for mediating—as well as meditating upon—the on-the-ground, in-the-mind, lived transformations of a rapidly modernizing United States. The first section of my essay will examine the interrelationship of technology and the novel, focusing on the literary embrace of the train and the telegraph, innovative devices that enabled human beings to fling themselves and their thoughts across vast distances. Novelists deployed a phalanx of physician characters, cultural and corporeal interpreters who also sought to ameliorate the stresses attendant on increased speed and mobility. Narratives about technology's perceived effects on individual bodies and minds promoted the new fields of physiological psychology and neuroscience, which affirmed a link between nervousness and "civilization" that helped secure the social standing of anxious, largely white middle-class Americans. The second section of my essay shifts from the micronarrative of the nervous individual to the macronarrative of the transformed and transforming human species, by examining the novel's assimilation of evolutionary theories. The novel, by providing a readymade form for stringing along causes and effects, was well suited to the narrative, accretive sensibility of the new biology. The third section further examines how the post-Civil War novel didn't just reflect advances in medicine or science but could itself be understood as a technology of visibility analogous to the photograph (in its realism) and microscopy (in its artifice). Before Rorschach tests and MRIs— and indeed, before the high modernist literary experiments of William Faulkner, H. D., and Jean Toomer—late-nineteenth-century US writers used the novel to explore the motions of human consciousness encountering a dynamic and changing world.

"A Network of Iron Nerves": Technology, Medicine, and the Novel

In Chesnutt's *The House Behind the Cedars*, a key plot point turns on a character's inability to get in touch with someone in a distant town, for "the train had gone; there was no telegraph to Patesville, and no letter could leave Clarence for twenty-four hours" (ch. 11). Following the Civil War years, the translation of military innovation into day-to-day civilian life was most visible in new technologies of transportation and communication. Lincoln had signed into law the Pacific Railway Act (1862–66), authorizing the creation of the first transcontinental railroad. The train and the telegraph, novelties in the antebellum period (think of Clifford's fantastical train ride in Hawthorne's *The House of the Seven Gables* [1852]) and then essential for transporting troop supplies and casualty lists, furrowed the national landscape in the decades that followed the war. Physician and novelist Oliver Wendell Holmes likened the newly technological nation to "a single living organism" connected by "a network of iron nerves" (the telegraph) and a "vast system of iron muscles" (the train) ("Bread and the Newspaper" 1861). Novels registered the presence of these prosthetic "nerves and muscles": the telegraph and train not only put the mark of modernity on natural settings, they also seeped into the mental and spiritual fabric of American life. In Willa Cather's *The Song of the Lark* (1915), the bone-chilling winds of rural Colorado send "the naked cottonwood trees against the telegraph poles and sides of houses," while an old lady huddled in an isolated church "made long, tremulous prayers, full of railroad terminology" (pt. 1, ch. 17). When characters in William Dean Howells's *The Undiscovered Country* (1881) hop on the wrong train, it speeds them northward toward a settlement of Shakers and sets in motion the novel's exploration of alternative faith communities in the industrial age.

These modes of transport took on lifelike animation in nineteenth-century novels, where they both figured and fueled the restlessness, speculation, and possibility of modern life. Here is Dreiser's memorable description of Carrie's physical and existential journey into a new urban existence populated by sentient-seeming technologies: "They were nearing Chicago. Already the signs were numerous. Trains flashed by them. Across wide stretches of open prairie they could see lines of telegraph poles stalking across the fields toward the great city" (ch. 1). By collapsing distance and speeding up travel, the railway became an effective plot device for novelists portraying the postbellum clash of cultures between rural modes and mores and those of the city. Train travel set in relief the political and cultural divisions between North and South, as when an African American physician in Chesnutt's *The Marrow of Tradition* (1901) is forced to switch to a segregated car once the train headed for North Carolina passes over the Mason-Dixon Line. Similarly, W. E. B. Du Bois inaugurates *The Souls of Black Folk* (1903) with a journey from the industrial North into the "Black Belt" below Atlanta. The geographical expedition by rail structures the spiritual passage of Du Bois as he seeks to give voice to post–Civil War, post–Thirteenth Amendment African American experience.

As vehicles of cultural change, trains at mid-century came under the scrutiny of scientists and physicians. The medical journal *The Lancet* in 1862 began a series of articles reporting on "The Influence of Railway Travelling on Public Health." Doctors worried about long-term nerve damage from the constant shaking and jarring; local authorities were concerned about catastrophic train wrecks brought about by single-track lines, insufficient signals, and poor braking technologies; insurance companies fretted over the lawsuits these crashes set in motion; farmers were troubled by increasingly powerful railroad monopolies; and commentators of all stripes puzzled over the effects of so much speed and motion. Oliver Wendell Holmes encapsulated a repeated concern in "Bread and the Newspaper," that "[a]ll this change in our manner of existence implies that we have experienced some very profound impression, which will sooner or later betray itself in permanent effects on the minds and bodies of many among us" (1861).

One can trace the technological, scientific, and medical aftershocks of the Civil War through the career trajectories of two men who found their vocations in the upheavals of the 1860s. Both S. Weir Mitchell (1829–1914) and William James (1842–1910) trained as physicians, though the two men weathered the war off the battlefield, the former in nearby field hospitals, and the latter in Cambridge pursuing his medical studies. Both helped to create new medical fields—Mitchell neurology,

James psychology—that sought to explain the effects of modernity on human minds and bodies. As a contract surgeon for the Union army, Mitchell saw the war's casualties up close, an experience that led quickly to two influential publications: "The Strange Case of George Dedlow" (1866), a story narrated in the first person, in which a physician describes the psychological and physiological effects of having all four of his limbs amputated, and the medical work *Injuries of Nerves and Their Consequences* (1872), an early contribution to the study of traumatic nerve injuries. Decades before British doctors described the distressing toll of trench warfare on soldiers' minds, and a century before post-traumatic stress disorder (PTSD) would enter the therapeutic lexicon, Mitchell had defined the contours of shell shock—a disorder he described in physiological, rather than psychological, terms.

Mitchell, a novelist as well as a physician, achieved notoriety for his work with patients suffering from neurasthenia, a specifically modern illness that came to be known as "American Nervousness." (Mitchell's rest cure for women suffering from nervous collapse, though maligned by prominent women such as Charlotte Perkins Gilman, attracted the attention of the young Viennese physician Sigmund Freud.) The founder and first president of the American Neurological Society, Mitchell drew a direct line between the modern industrial society and functional nervous disease in his medical treatise *Wear and Tear, or Hints for the Overworked* (1871): "The industry and energy" of the modern city, he affirmed, "are now at work to undermine the nervous systems of its restless and eager people."

Whereas Mitchell's neurological theories explained how technology transformed social conditions and shaped human bodies, the new psychology of William James drew on evolutionary biology to explain the embodied workings of the human mind. (Both James and Mitchell suffered from neurasthenia, the very nineteenth-century malady that their studies of the human nervous system helped to define and which Mitchell spent a lifetime treating.) James attended Harvard's medical school and in 1865 traveled with the anti-Darwinist scientist Louis Agassiz to Brazil; soon after this expedition, however, James parted intellectual ways with his mentor and began to formulate his own ideas about the importance of transformation and adaptation for understanding human psychology. James taught at the Lawrence Scientific School and in 1890 published *The Principles of Psychology*, which became the foundational text of the new physiological psychology. "A real science of man," James had written in an 1875 letter to Charles W. Eliot, "is . . . being built up out of the theory of evolution and the facts of archeology, the nervous system and the senses." As James's biographer Robert D. Richardson observes, "Since neither the pure physiologist nor the literary person who lacked firsthand knowledge of 'nervous physiology' could really do the job, James proposes 'a union of the two disciplines' in one man, a man such as himself" (2006, 157).

The ravages of internecine war left behind a dazed and weary population on both sides of the conflict, while the diseases and injuries related to poor urban sanitation and factory work also left their mark on people's bodies and psyches. In this context, the scientifically trained physician became someone able to make sense of, if not always to heal, the incursions of machine onto muscle. Doctors were frequent protagonists in novels written in the 1880s, where—contra Hawthorne—they signified social stability and helped to mediate new scientific theories, experiences, and dangers. Although antebellum literary physicians and scientists existed in the richly symbolic world of romance, those who populate novels such as Henry James's *Washington Square* (1881), William Dean Howells's *Doctor Breen's Practice* (1881), and Weir Mitchell's *In War Time* (1884) are professionals with specialized training. They are also ambivalent figures, vested with life-and-death responsibility but often confronted with the limits of their authority or power. James's Dr. Austin Sloper may be an acclaimed physician but he's a deeply imperfect parent, and he finds himself bested by the very daughter he found dull and weak. Howells's clever homeopath Dr. Grace Breen defers to a male "allopath"—a mainstream doctor—when she's unable to help a sick patient, eventually giving up her practice entirely to marry. And despite his talent for treating wounded soldiers in a well-equipped Philadelphia hospital, Mitchell's Dr. Ezra Wendell succumbs to avarice and money trouble.

Doctors become useful flash points for novelists seeking to register the clash of traditional values with new social imperatives; the physicians' decisions frequently point hopefully to a new moral order adapted to changing social roles, for African Americans and women in particular. In Frances E. W. Harper's novel *Iola Leroy: Or, Shadows Uplifted* (1892), a white physician wishes to marry his neurasthenic patient; but after discovering her mixed-race background, he urges Iola to pass as white. She instead marries a scholarly black doctor who has refused to pass, and together they move south to serve as teacher and healer to the black community. It is an African American physician, in Charles Chesnutt's *The Marrow of Tradition*, who embodies hope for racial reconciliation after white supremacists incite a rampaging mob against the local black community. Elizabeth Stuart Phelps's protagonist in *Dr. Zay* (1882), like the young Nan Prince in Sarah Orne Jewett's *A Country Doctor* (1884), negotiates gender norms for women; unlike Howell's Dr. Breen, these women refuse to sacrifice their profession for an offer of marriage. As Dr. Zay affirms, she is first and foremost committed to her career, and "such a woman demands a new type of man" (ch. 12). In Kate Chopin's *The Awakening* (1899), when a New Orleans physician is called in to explain the domestic rebellion of Edna Pontellier, he suspects that there is "a man in the case" but dispenses more reassuring, though less efficacious wisdom to her baffled husband: "Woman, my dear friend, is a very peculiar and delicate organism—a sensitive and highly organized woman, such as I know Mrs Pontellier to be, is especially peculiar" (ch. 22).

Cultural interpreter, consummate professional, and possessor of intimate knowledge of human psychology, the doctor protagonist often served as a figure for the novelist. "A writer can no longer expect to be received on the ground of entertainment only," Howells announced in *Criticism and Fiction* (1891), "he assumes a higher function, something like that of a physician or a priest[,] . . . bound by laws as sacred as those of such professions" (ch. 22). In some instances, the physician-as-priest is almost literal, as in Pauline Hopkins's serially published novel *Of One Blood, or, the Hidden Self* (1903). A brilliant African American medical student, fascinated by trance states and the work of the French psychologist Alfred Binet, tests out his theories about the subconscious on a beautiful young woman traumatized during a train wreck. He discovers that both he and the mysterious woman he saves have "hidden selves"—in this case, the reincarnated souls of royal Ethiopian ancestors. Psychology, for Hopkins, was always on the verge of returning to its religious and even occult roots—marking for her the deep compatibility between the science of the mind and the art of the novelist.

The late nineteenth century, as we've seen, witnessed the breaching of Hawthorne's romantic firewall between the man of letters and the man of science. The result, however, was equivocal: the figure of the doctor—the most visible cultural emissary from the realms of science—was demoted from a Chillingworth-esque agent of evil to a flawed, socially embedded character making provisional sense of human beings and their frailties. Intriguingly, the novelist, by contrast, achieved something of a promotion. Émile Zola, writing in 1880, famously equated the writer and the scientist, celebrating the work of French physiologist Claude Bernard (renowned for exposing inner workings of living bodies through vivisection) and the literary form he called, in a book of the same title, *Le Roman Expérimental.* Zola claimed the tools of objectivity, detachment, and the carefully constructed experiment for the writer: "Science enters into the domain of us novelists who are to-day the analyzers of man, in his individual and social relations" (ch. 1). The novel, by this account, was uniquely adapted to display, diagnose, and even to ameliorate the ills of individuals as they circulated within the larger, newly networked social organism that constituted the United States at the turn of the nineteenth century.

"Really, Universally, Relations Stop Nowhere": Evolutionary Theory and the Novel

Until recently, critical writing about post-Civil War American literature, influenced both by Hawthorne and by Zola, has emphasized the unholy alliance between science and the novel. Literary naturalism embraced "pessimistic materialistic determinism" (Becker 1963): human beings were driven by hereditary and environmental "forces" (Martin 1981); critics described the "determined fictions" of the 1890s (Lee Clark Mitchell 1989); bodies were aligned with machines (Seltzer 1992). In his introduction to *American Realism: New Essays,* Eric Sundquist sums up this position: "Reveling in the extraordinary, the excessive, and the grotesque in order to reveal the immutable bestiality of Man in Nature, naturalism dramatizes the loss of individuality at a physiological level by making a Calvinism without God its deter-mining order and violent death its utopia" (1982, 13).

Clearly, a crucial event in the naturalizing of "Man" was the 1859 publication of Charles Darwin's *The Origin of Species by Natural Selection*. Although he wouldn't spell out his specific thoughts about the human species until the 1870s, Darwin's potent alignment of transmutation (the capacity of species to change over large ex-panses of time) and natural selection (the mechanism by which traits best adapted to an environment are preserved) suggested that there was a natural history of human-kind akin to that of other life forms. Although Darwin, in an 1860 letter to Harvard botanist Asa Gray, affirmed that he himself did not believe that "this wonderful universe, and especially the nature of man" could be "the result of brute force," many commentators, both then and now, felt that evolutionary theories demoted human beings to the mud (1900, 105). For those who adopted this position, the literary modes of realism and naturalism seemed similarly base. Ambrose Bierce, for instance, defined "Realism, n." in *The Devil's Dictionary* (1911) as "the art of depicting nature as it is seen by toads. The charm suffusing a landscape painted by a mole, or a story written by a measuring-worm."

There has been, then, a narrative of declension that casts the influence of science on the post–Civil War novel as unidirectional and corrupting. Twenty-first-century literary critics, however, have increasingly attended to the ethical complexity and literary richness of the novel's encounter with evolutionary science. There is another story to be told, one that Darwin articulated in the first edition of *On the Origin of Species*. Worried about the moral, religious, and aesthetic implications of his theory, Darwin sought to draw out its transformational beauty by emphasizing the vital, expansive aspects of transformation as such:

> There is grandeur in this view of life, with its several powers, having been originally
> breathed into a few forms or into one; and that, whilst this planet has gone cycling
> on according to the fixed law of gravity, from so simple a beginning endless forms
> most beautiful and most wonderful have been, and are being, evolved. (ch. 15)

Using the mechanism of natural selection and the substrate of deep time, evolution-ary theory produced "just so" tales that yoked together the small, the common, and the insignificant with the immense, the myriad, the sublime. The emergent science of biology and the realist novel, as literary scholars have shrewdly discerned, have deep and reciprocal affinities. Darwin's tenet of change-over-time installs narrative as an essential aspect of natural history; in turn, the notion that small acciden-tal happenings can have potentially seismic importance becomes an increasingly central plot mechanism of the modern novel. Henry James tapped these dynamic connections when he wrote in the 1907 preface to *Roderick Hudson* (1875), "Really, universally, relations stop nowhere": it is up to the novelist—like the biologist, or sociologist—to delineate the relevant sphere of action and to cast the complexities of a changing world into a meaningful form.

In short, the science practiced by the most innovative, restless, curious investigators of the era fertilized the work of turn-of-the-century novelists, and vice versa. The new watchwords were experiment (rather than received forms); change (rather than stasis); contingency (rather than certainty); restlessness (rather than tranquility). Darwin's evolutionary biology helped to put human beings, at the level of the species, in motion; nineteenth-century writers, in turn, developed methods for casting insights based on immense stretches of time and vast numbers of individuals into that insistently individualizing form, the novel. As literary critic Wai Chee Dimock has observed, "The novel is, in fact, of uncertain dimensions. It can be bumped up to a much larger scale. . . . Scale enlargement here undoes human singularity and preserves it through that undoing" (2006, 88).

Oliver Wendell Holmes, Harvard professor of anatomy and man of letters, offers an early example of how the nineteenth-century novel became a venue for changing the scale for thinking about personal character and individual agency. His novel *Elsie Venner: A Romance of Destiny* (1860), updates Hawthorne's allegorical "Rappaccini's Daughter"—the tale of a scientist who transforms his beautiful daughter into a toxic creature—for a more materialistically inclined audience. Holmes's begins conventionally enough with an enigmatic young woman who has piqued the interest of her handsome teacher, who is also a medical student. A tale of courtship becomes a biological mystery as he conducts experiments to diagnose her snakelike, venomous qualities (a strangely hypnotic gaze, a desire to sun herself on rocks, a tendency to bite her enemies) and discovers that the girl was poisoned in utero when her pregnant mother was bitten by a rattlesnake. Dubbed a "medicated novel" by Holmes himself in his preface, *Elsie Venner* makes the case that, because a person's (seemingly) discrete identity in fact extends across generations, some flaws of character are akin to bodily illness rather than moral failings.

Holmes's novel includes the first literary reference to the theories of Charles Darwin. At one point the tale's narrator—a professor of clinical medicine, as was the author himself—breaks the story's diegetic frame to instruct his young female readers about the biological basis of courtship rituals: "Look you," he exhorts, "there are dozens, scores, hundreds, with whom you must be weighed in the balance; and you have got to learn that the 'struggle for life' Mr Charles Darwin talks about reaches to vertebrates clad in crinoline, as well as to mollusks in shells" (ch. 7). Alliteratively linking maidens and mollusks, Holmes playfully confirms that a young debutante's inflated sense of a party's importance is in fact a fitting affective index of the vast yet largely unseen drama of natural selection as it plays out on an intimate, girlish human scale. Anticipating Darwin's *The Descent of Man* (1871) by more than a decade, Holmes establishes an exponentially expanded family saga in which human beings and invertebrate sea creatures are distant cousins. In *The Education of Henry Adams* (1907), Henry Adams would extend Holmes's joke by referring to "his oldest friend and cousin the ganoid fish . . . with whom he had sported when geological life was young" (ch. 26).

To make visible the achingly slow work of natural selection, Darwin begins *The Origin* with the evolutionary equivalent of pressing a "fast forward" button, describing the infinitely quicker process of "artificial selection," the selective breeding of farm animals and the careful cultivation of flowers. These manmade transformations—a breed of cattle that gives more milk, a strain of orchid with an atypical blossom—were often visible after just a few generations. Author Jack London, in his dog stories *The Call of the Wild* (1903) and *White Fang* (1906), used the novel's scale-changing capacity to similar effect, first to rewind and then fast-forward the evolutionary narrative. *Call of the Wild* depicts the transformation of a house pet named Buck into a toughened sled dog and then into a primordial, wolflike creature after a series of adventures in the Yukon Territory. *White Fang* follows a wilderness-born wolf through a series of masters and a speeded-up civilizing process in which, by novel's end, the fully evolved, selfless animal sacrifices his life to save his master's. Frank Norris, in his posthumously published first novel, *Vandover and the Brute* (1914), folds evolutionary time into the human body, portraying a hyper-civilized young man whose debauched ways dampen his intellect "leaving only the instincts, the blind, unreasoning impulses of the animal" that lie dormant within (ch. 16). Vandover, it is revealed, suffers from bouts of "Lycanthropy-Pathesis"—a condition that sends him sliding back down the phylogenetic ladder, causing him to move on all fours and growl like a wolf.

Novelists succeeded in coiling (to invoke Dimock's term) evolutionary time into a literary form known for its attentiveness to the more intimate timescale of an individual life. The post-Civil War novel also accommodated and made visible the far-flung, abstract connections brought about by a globalizing economic system. In *The Octopus: A Story of California* (1901), the first installment of Frank Norris's (never completed) "Epic of Wheat" trilogy, the interests of corporate capitalism are condensed into one metonymic figure. In the eyes of the farmers being squeezed by the railroad conglomerate on wheat prices, the company's human representative—a man named S. Behrman—simply "*was* the railroad" (ch. 2, emphasis added). The novel then compresses the trope still further, casting the man as a tiny tool who nonetheless embodies the collective agency of the vertical monopoly: "S. Behrman was a screw." The almost thermodynamic potency of the "screw" is in turn likened to the evolutionary power packed into a tiny seed. The narrative voice addresses the reader directly: "Can you imagine the first—the very first little quiver of life that the grain of wheat must feel after it is sown[,] . . . the very first stir from the inert, long long before any physical change has occurred,—long before the microscope could discover the slightest change[?]" (ch. 6). Novels, in other words, could pick up tiny rumblings of future events that eluded more conventional technologies.

For authors writing after Darwin, the novel offered a narrative laboratory, in which slight alterations—like a trifling variation in the beak of a finch—could be shown to have seismic effects. Edith Wharton takes Norris's notion of a "sown seed" and plays it out in the plot of *The House of Mirth* (1905). In the first chapter, the lovely Lily Bart impulsively breaks with propriety and takes tea with an eligible bachelor at his apartment. This small act lies dormant for much of the novel, as the celebrated but impoverished Lily makes her way through New York high society, but her encounter was observed by another character who later tries to "cash in" on the knowledge of Lily's indiscretion.

Edward Bellamy's *Looking Backward: 2000–1887* (1888), a novel that is part social realism and part science fiction, tests out the narrative capacity to move both forward and backward in time, transforming "cause and effect" into "effect and cause" (on *Looking Backward* as science fiction time travel, see Chapter 23 of this volume). The central character, born in 1859, narrates the story from the temporal perch of the year 2000. A modernized Rip Van Winkle, the protagonist has slept through the social unrest and economic disparity of the Gilded Age. Upon awakening a century later he finds an efficiently run, egalitarian United States devoid of poverty. Bellamy used the novel as a form of time travel to call for sweeping social reforms. Similarly, the social activist Charlotte Perkins Gilman, whose disastrous experience of Weir Mitchell's rest cure for neurasthenic women is detailed in the short story "The Yellow Wall-paper" (1892), takes up the question of cultural transformation in her utopian work *Herland* (1912). Gilman in the novel argues that one can reform, literally and physiologically, women's agitated minds and bodies through the transformation of technology—the most striking of which involves a new mode of reproduction through parthenogensis rather than sexual congress.

Literary works during the Progressive Era were not in some way "opposed to" the emerging biological sciences. Instead, the novel as a literary form provided new ways of imagining and representing far-flung connections, of concatenating causes and effects, and of insisting on the dynamic, temporal nature of organic life. These compatibilities led writers to bring the very structure of evolutionary thinking into their literary productions, even as scientists such as Darwin were applying an evolving, contingent, narrative sensibility to entities, including the planet itself, once thought static and immutable. Novels, however, had the comforting ability to enclose and make coherent a world in motion, counterbalancing the unsettling scale of natural history, in which human beings (in the words of geologist James Hutton) could find "no vestige of a beginning,—no prospect of an end" (ch. 1, 1788).

A "Remarkable Interest in Mental States": The Novel and the Sciences of Mind

Along with changes in the scale, duration, and extension of human social existence, the new biology produced a radically altered understanding of individual consciousness. In his novel *Before Adam* (1907), Jack London again traverses the evolutionary timescale, though this time it is the human mind, and not the canine body, that encapsulates what he calls "race history." During sleep, the novel's narrator is imagi-natively transported to the "Mid-Pleistocene," where he has vivid, first-person ex-periences of climbing trees, building fires, and interacting with his prehistoric, tree-dwelling ancestors. "Evolution," he concludes, "was the key. It gave the explanation, gave sanity to the pranks of this atavistic brain of mine that, modern and normal, harked back to a past so remote as to be contemporaneous with the raw beginnings of mankind" (ch. 2).

Before we too quickly dismiss the crudeness of London's formulation, it is worth noting that Sigmund Freud and Josef Breuer in *Studies on Hysteria* (1895) had come to a similar conclusion about metaphors for strong emotions, such phrases as "stabbed to the heart" or a "slap in the face": "All these sensations and innervations belong to the field of 'The Expression of the Emotions,' which, as Darwin has taught us (1872), consists of actions that originally had a meaning and served a purpose" (ch. 5). The etiological narratives of novelists and scientists—hereditary accounts that traced the phylogenetic sources of domesticated dogs, atavistic dreams, and vehement passions—both drew on and seemed to confirm the evolutionary roots of human beings. The "atavistic brain," it appeared, might harbor insights into the most sophisticated modern mind.

Jonathan Kramnick has noted that, while "[n]o one literary form has a propri-etary stake in the mind, . . . as genres go the novel has since its inception taken remarkable interest in mental states" (2007, 263). Especially in the hands of Henry James, the late nineteenth-century novel expands the genre's formal alignment with the human mind. The depiction of consciousness in motion reaches its apex in his *The American Scene* (1907), a travel book that chronicles the aging author's impres-sions upon returning to the United States after decades living in Europe. It is, es-sentially, a novel with the narrator's consciousness as protagonist.

While certainly influenced by the new psychology, Henry James also developed his famously complex and allusive prose style in collaboration with a more me-chanical technology. After an injury made writing physically painful, James began dictating his novels to a secretary who tapped James's spoken words on a typewriter. Critics have claimed to locate the precise moment that the transition to the new technology took place, during the drafting of *What Maisie Knew* (1897), a shift made visible by the escalating complexity of James's sentences and the increasing inward-ness of his plots.

By centering so many novels on New World naifs set adrift in Europe (e.g., *The American* [1877] and *The Ambassadors* [1903]), James captures some of the cultural dislocation that many Americans felt closer to home. But *What Maisie Knew*, his only novel with a child protagonist, most vividly expresses the sense of a small, wonder-ing consciousness bumping up against a world of things and relations that appears both inscrutably vast and uncomfortably circumscribed (on the child protagonist in *What Maisie Knew*, see Chapter 19 of this volume). James uses free indirect dis-course to "stream" the narrative through the child, whose mind is the reader's portal to a tawdry milieu of neglectful and vituperative adults. Maisie struggles mightily to understand her father's plans for her: "while they sat there together, there was an extraordinary mute passage between her vision of this vision of his, his vision of her vision, and her vision of his vision of her vision" (ch. 19). This sentence is almost parodic in its depiction of "the meeting of two minds." The novel here becomes not just a medium for describing relations among characters; it serves, as critic Lisa Zunshine (2006) has argued, as a cognitive exercise machine for the reader, who (like Maisie) must send her mind ricocheting outward into multiply embedded, often conflicting perspectives. The child's eye view returns an anthropological strangeness—along with both humor and horror—to the everyday dramas of human relations.

At century's end, new scientific theories and technologies were revealing a world filled with odd mysteries and once-invisible entities that required careful scrutiny and cautious interpretation. This was especially true in the budding field of microscopy: Joseph J. Woodward and Edward Curtis, for example, in 1864 first used aniline dyes in the United States for staining slides; a decade later, scientist Robert Koch coupled this technique with photography to identify microorganisms, leading to the germ theory of disease and new insight into cholera and other epidemics that ravaged tightly packed communities. In the 1880s, incandescent bulbs were first introduced for street lamps, illuminating urban areas and bringing to light the denizens of the late-night city. Jacob Riis's camera, along with Stephen Crane's prose, made urban spaces visible for middle class eyes, as when readers of *Maggie: A Girl of the Streets (A Story of New York)* (1893, 1896) accompanied the novel's "street rats" into "a dark region where, from a careening building, a dozen gruesome doorways gave up loads of babies to the street and the gutter" (ch. 2; on *Maggie* as urban novel, see Chapter 8 in this volume). By the turn of the century, scientists had discovered electrons and X-rays, using the latter to take ghostly photographs of bones through human flesh.

While nineteenth-century geology and biology produced awareness of natural history's gradual accretion of infinitesimal changes, new visual technologies brought to consciousness everyday processes of modern life that were hard to see in real time. In the 1870s, the photographer Eadweard Muybridge was hired by a railroad magnate (and horseracing aficionado) named Stanford to settle a bet: did a horse in full stride at some point have all four hooves off the ground? Yes, was the answer provided by a series of split-second photographs captured by multiple cameras set in a row, each with a trip wire to take an image as the horse galloped past. While Muybridge used his cameras to break motion into parts, nascent film technology reversed this process, taking still images and setting them in motion. At the Chicago World's Fair in 1893, Thomas Edison displayed the Kinetoscope, a motorized proto-projector housed in a cabinet that produced moving images by passing strips of celluloid film in front of a magnifying lens backed by a bright light.

Writers after the Civil War used the novel in similar ways to magnify the small detail, picking up and tinting an important moment like a lab technician staining a slide. As Nicholas Gaskill has written, in the hands of Stephen Crane this metaphor proves close to literal (2009). Crane's manipulation of color in his novels condenses scenes to their essential elements, as in *The Red Badge of Courage* (1895) when the early morning battlefield slowly comes into focus for the waking troops:

> In the gloom before the break of the day their uniforms glowed a deep purple hue. From across the river the red eyes were still peering. In the eastern sky there was a yellow patch like a rug laid for the feet of the coming sun; and against it, black and patternlike, loomed the gigantic figure of the colonel on a gigantic horse. (ch. 2)

Crane's abstract use of color establishes the elements of battle yet strips the moment of the political positions and meanings (grey for the Confederacy, blue for the Union) of conventional war stories. Time itself, a human convention for situating human events into strings of causes and effects, befores and afters, is colorized and spatialized into an expanding splash of yellow as day breaks. Crane's novel unravels narrative temporality, distilling a series of events—soldiers waking, looking, planning, marching, fighting, dying, retreating—into a colorful tableau that takes on the logic of a chemical reaction: add a bit more yellow, and then purple will face off against red.

Crane also manipulates size in *The Red Badge*. In the passage quoted above, the morning horizon is condensed into a small "patch," while a man on a horse is "gigantic." What appears as a distortion linked to the young man's psychological immaturity—leading him to "magnify" the significance of his leader and "diminish" the background landscape—is in fact a novelistic method for quelling the mind's automatic perceptual adjustments for depth and distance. When the young soldier achieves a perch above the battle, the narrative depicts far-away objects without compensating for the effect of distance on magnitude: "Once he saw a tiny battery go dashing along the line of the horizon. The tiny riders were beating the tiny horses" (ch. 5). Crane's manipulation of color and size works to make visible the everyday aesthetic techniques (e.g., cause-and-effect narration, or one-point perspective in painting), as well as the unconscious processes of perception, by which our minds actively shape the raw material of the world into coherent and recognizable forms, rather than merely "finding" it that way. As the French thinker Hippolyte Taine put this point in his treatise *On Intelligence* (1870), "scientific experience comes in to contract or extend [our perceptions and ideas], to adjust their corrected dimensions to the real dimensions of objects" (vol. 2, bk. 4, ch. 1).

As we have seen, the same might be said of the novel. After the Civil War and before the full flowering of literary modernism, many US writers used the genre as medium for thinking about—and making visible—the ways that human beings were engaging with a rapidly changing world, both inside the skull and beyond the skin. Rather than construing novelistic concerns (e.g., historical events, social relations, and aesthetic experience) as opposed to scientific ones (e.g., biological theories, technological innovations, and medical practices), these writers were deeply interested in disciplinary cross-fertilization: in returning *scientia* to its etymological root in observation, study, and experience. The novel's representational elasticity made it both microscope and telescope, capable of revealing tiny truths as well as lending large-scale perspective, of attending—like the best scientists—to the strangeness and revelations residing in the everyday. In *The Gold Bug Variations* (1992), contemporary novelist Richard Powers writes that science is "a way of looking, reverencing," and that, above all, "the purpose of science was to revive and cultivate a perpetual state of wonder" (ch. 28)—a sentiment that writers from Emily Dickinson to Stephen Crane would surely affirm for the literary artist, as well.

II

THE RELIGIOUS NOVEL

BY CLAUDIA STOKES

Conventional literary historical wisdom dictates that American religious fiction reached its peak of popularity and influence in the mid-nineteenth century, with the flowering of sentimental novels, such as Susan Warner's *The Wide, Wide World* (1850) and Maria Susanna Cummins's *The Lamplighter* (1854), that depict the powers of Christian faith to abet female maturation and personal reform. The decline of this literary genre after the American Civil War, this story continues, coincided with the ascent of realism and naturalism as the late-century's premier aesthetic modes, a shift taken to signal the replacement of cloying literary piety with a tough-minded insistence on secular empiricism and documentary verisimilitude. However, to study the religious fiction of the late nineteenth century is to discern how faulty this enduring literary historical narrative really is. Sentimental novels remained popular well after the war, and, on the whole, religious novels actually rose in popularity in the late century, with novels such as Lew Wallace's *Ben Hur: A Tale of the Christ* (1880) and Charles Sheldon's *In His Steps: What Would Jesus Do?* (1897), which respectively sold copies numbered in the millions. Though nineteenth-century religious fiction is typically remembered as a genre composed largely by women for female readers, the most successful, respected writers working in the genre were in fact late-century men, such as Edward Eggleston and E. P. Roe as well as Sheldon and Wallace, whose fiction was oriented specifically to male readers. And though late-century religious fiction was predominantly Protestant in its leanings, it appeared within a variety of aesthetic modes, realism among them, and thus complicates the established narrative of late-century literary aesthetics. In all of these ways, religious fiction disrupts many of our received notions about the literary history of the late nineteenth century.

Harriet Beecher Stowe, perhaps the century's leading sentimental novelist, observed both the new pervasiveness of religious fiction after the Civil War and the particular appeal of this genre to male writers, quipping in her novel *My Wife and I* (1871) that "[s]oon it will be necessary that every leading clergyman should embody in his theology a serial story" (ch. 1). Here, she envisioned a future in which clergy from all denominations would regard the novel, and not the pulpit, as the premier medium for the salvation of souls. Stowe's prediction may have been sparked by the recent publication of *Norwood* (1868), the sole novel authored by her brother Henry Ward Beecher, the mid-century's preeminent minister, but her forecast proved prescient. By the century's end, the roster of bestselling American novelists included the names of such clergy as Edward Eggleston, George Hepworth, E. P. Roe, and Charles Sheldon, all of whom found considerable success writing novels narrating the rewards of a devout Christian life. But for every bestseller by Eggleston or Roe, there were countless lesser novels published by clergy eager to take advantage of this popular new medium, among them W. Boyd Carpenter's *Narcissus: A Tale of Early Christian Times* (1879), Henry Morgan's *Boston Inside Out! Sins of a Great City! A Story of Real Life* (1880), Thomas Bailey's *In the Pine Woods* (1893), and R. F. Bishop's *Camerton Slope* (1893). In addition to Beecher, some of the era's most prominent religious leaders tried their hands at novel writing, among them renowned Unitarian minister Edward Everett Hale with his novel *If Jesus Came to Boston* (1895), and Washington Gladden, a Congregationalist minister and prominent Social Gospel theologian, with his *The Christian League of Connecticut* (1884).

That Christian piety became so fruitful a subject of late-century novels is all the more striking in light of the fact that, until the mid-nineteenth century, novels were presumed by conservative Christians to be, at best, trivial amusements that fostered habits of idleness and, at worst, a moral contagion that endangered readers' souls by tempting them to emulate the worldliness, vanity, and licentiousness portrayed therein. Timothy Dwight, Lyman Beecher's mentor and one of the premier theologians of the Second Great Awakening, summarized this orthodox view of novels in his observation that "[b]etween the Bible and novels there is a gulph [sic] fixed which few readers are willing to pass. The consciousness of virtue, the dignified pleasure of having performed our duty, the serene remembrance of a useful life, the hope of an interest in the Redeemer, and the promise of a glorious inheritance in the favour of God, are never found in novels" (qtd. in Blodgett 1997, 11). Although the American Tract Society (ATS) issued conversion narratives that provided a literary precedent for later religious novelists such as Susan Warner (who had distributed such tracts among the urban poor), it was a particularly vehement opponent to novels. Thunderously exhorting readers to "PUT DOWN THAT NOVEL!" the ATS contended that novel reading led directly to unwholesome appetites, damnation, and even suicide (qtd. in Nord 2004, 118). This belief in an incompatibility between novel-reading and Christian piety would begin to dissolve in the mid-century at the hands of sentimental novelists such as Cummins, Warner, and Stowe herself, who would famously use the novel form to spark readers' conversion—both religious and political—in such novels as *Uncle Tom's Cabin* (1852) and *Dred: A Tale of the Great Dismal Swamp* (1856). Though works such as Warner's *The Wide, Wide World* often capitulated to traditional attitudes by including explicit warnings about the moral perils of novel reading, sentimental novels used narrative to depict the transformative effects of Christian conversion and in so doing reconstituted the novel from an agent of sin to a potential instrument of evangelism. If Susan Warner's many letters from newly devout readers are to be believed, these mid-century chronicles of piety and forbearance were indeed effective in prompting conversion in untold numbers of readers. This fact did not go unnoticed by clergy, whose sermons with increasing frequency adopted narrative over theological exegesis in accord with these changes. By the late nineteenth century, preachers such as Dwight Moody, T. DeWitt Talmage, and Reuben Torrey were famous pulpit raconteurs who could incite listener conversion with heart-rending tales of suffering and piety.

As theologians and ministers caught on to the potential persuasiveness and emotional impact of novels depicting conversion and piety, the religious antipathy toward novels began to seem increasingly outdated as the century wore on. In 1870, Noah Porter, Congregationalist theologian and president of Yale, sought to elucidate the complex relationship between faith and literature, observing that these presumed rivals were in fact conjoined by a mutual reliance on imagination and sympathetic projection. He wrote, "It is because the imagination is so nearly allied to faith that her power to hinder or help is so unlimited, and that literature itself becomes to religion either the deadliest foe or the most potent ally" (qtd. in Jenkins 1997, 5–6). Arguing that one could justifiably harness the imaginative powers of narrative to provoke conversion and inspire virtue, Porter confirmed that an automatic condemnation of novels was now a thing of the past. In the preface to his bestselling novel *From Jest to Earnest* (1875), E. P. Roe took the matter further by suggesting that it was incumbent upon the church to craft religious novels for impressionable young people, saving them from sin by proffering salutary works of fiction in place of morally questionable ones. He wrote, "If millions in the impressible period of youth, in spite of all that any can do, will read fiction, then it would appear a sacred duty in those who love their kind, to make this food of the forming character healthful, bracing, and ennobling in its nature. Earnest men and women, who hold and would transmit the truth, must speak in a way that will secure a hearing" (qtd. in Thorp 1961, 220). By the last quarter of the nineteenth century, novels of a religious character were fully accepted as a legitimate accompaniment to a devout life. Denominational organizations such as the American Baptist Publication Society conceded that some morally upright novels were acceptable, and religious periodicals such as the *Christian Advocate* and *Christian Union* reviewed novels, thereby determining for readers which novels were compatible with the Christian life. Opinion changed so drastically that, by the end of the century, religious novels would depict this reflexive conservative opposition to novels as the subject of mockery, taking it to denote a closed mindedness and a Pharisaical commitment to forms out of keeping with a modern Christian sensibility. For example, in his novel *Esther* (1884), Henry Adams characterizes the Midwest as hopelessly backwards when Catherine Brooke, a visitor to New York from Colorado, remarks that she'd been raised to regard novels as sinful, an oversight in her education thereupon corrected by the minister Stephen Hazard, an intervention that, in and of itself, signals changing clerical attitudes toward fiction. Likewise, in Helen R. Martin's novel *Tillie: A Mennonite Maid* (1904), the novel's eponymous heroine is cruelly beaten by her insular, pious father after having been found reading *Ivanhoe*.

Once they achieved a measure of acceptance and respectability, religious novels flourished, achieving extraordinary heights of popularity. One successful novel could spawn numerous imitators; for example, Florence Morse Kingsley built a career on literary spinoffs of *Ben-Hur*, among them *Titus, a Comrade of the Cross* (1895) and *Stephen, a Soldier of the Cross* (1896). Even Henry Van Dyke, a renowned poet, critic, and minister, published one such imitation, *The Story of the Other Wise Man* (1895), which, like its predecessor, focuses on an unknown witness to the life of Christ and became a bestseller. Elizabeth Stuart Phelps's novelistic inquiry into the nature of the afterlife, *The Gates Ajar* (1869), struck such a chord with readers that it spawned three sequels as well as a host of imitations, such as Louis H. Pendleton's *The Wedding Garment: A Tale of the Afterlife* (1894), which elaborated on her vision of heaven. Although William Dean Howells declined to review most of these works—thereby establishing the enduring critical indifference to popular American religious fiction—the predominance of this genre was such that it exerted visible influence even on Howells's own work, as with his novels *The Minister's Charge* (1887) and *Annie Kilburn* (1889), in which two separate ministers function as pivotal arbiters of literary taste, offering definitive literary opinions that provide much-needed moral clarity; both characters, Minister Sewell and Mr. Peck, speak to the ascent of ministers in this era to legitimate positions of literary authority, and the title of the former novel seems designed to appeal to current reader taste for novels about piety.

All of this is to say that religious novels occupied a central role in the literary late century, but have seldom received commensurate acknowledgment in the era's literary history, an omission that likely derives from a confluence of causes, foremost among them their marked divergence from the neat academic categories of periodization. The late century is typically demarcated as beginning in 1870, though the 1870s remain a gaping lacuna in literary scholarship, characterized, if at all, as merely the beginning stages of literary realism, which is typically anointed the foremost aesthetic of the 1880s, followed by naturalism of the 1890s. To review the offerings of religious novels in the late century is to see the insufficiency of this enduring assessment. In the first place, 1870 does not mark the emergence of late-century religious fiction, since a number of significant works were published in the late 1860s, on the border of the postbellum divide, and thus are lost in a literary no-man's land, left out of all standard historical groupings. H. W. Beecher's *Norwood*, Augusta Evan's *St. Elmo* (1867), Elizabeth Prentiss's *Stepping Heavenward* (1869), and Phelps's *The Gates Ajar* were all successful and important; Beecher's novel, for example, adapted the sentimental form by placing at its center male faith and religious experience, thereby paving the way for the many dozens of late-century novels about devout men, among them Margaret Deland's *John Ward, Preacher* (1888), Elizabeth Stuart Phelps's *A Singular Life* (1895), and Albion Tourgée's *Murvale Eastman, Christian Socialist* (1889). In this way, Beecher's novel—like its contemporaries by Evans, Phelps, and Prentiss—also illustrates that religious fiction proved a lasting home for sentimentalism through the nineteenth century, giving it a durability that outlasted the typical shelf life allotted to it in literary history. For example, literary histories have memorialized Susan Warner chiefly for *The Wide, Wide, World*, but she and her sister, Anna Warner, continued publishing for decades, each separately publishing a dozen sentimental religious novels in addition to two collaborative novels, *Wych Hazel* (1876) and *The Gold of Chickaree* (1876). Likewise, Harriet Beecher Stowe published such novels as *My Wife and I* and *Poganuc People* (1878), Martha Finley published several dozen novels in the Elsie Dinsmore series between 1867 and 1905, and E.D.E.N Southworth had extraordinary success with her blockbuster *Ishmael* as well as its sequel, *Self-Raised* (both 1876).

The literary historical void that is the 1870s was also a veritable golden age of religious fiction. As Frank Luther Mott notes, a great many bestsellers in that decade were religious novels, among them Southworth's novels; E.P. Roe's *Barriers Burned Away, Opening a Chestnut Burr* (1873), and *From Jest to Earnest*; Edward Eggleston's *The Hoosier Schoolmaster* (1871) and *The Circuit Rider* (1874). Scholarly inattention to the 1870s has thus obscured an important period in the continuation and evolution of the American religious novel. In the 1870s, male and female authors of varying statures, from the sensational Southworth to the eminent Eggleston, could all acceptably pen religious novels. The genre, moreover, expanded considerably in this period, adapting to such forms as the melodrama, the historical novel, or the *roman à clef*, and took up broader contemporary interests such as frontier history or topical events like the catastrophic Chicago fire of 1871, which inspired Roe to write *Barriers Burned Away*. In all of these ways, the religious novel went fully mainstream in the 1870s.

Nor was realism the dominant aesthetic mode of religious fiction of the late century. While novels agitating for social reform did employ the signature documentary methods of realism, other religious novelists, such as Albion Tourgée, were openly contemptuous of realism. Furthermore, with the exception of Harold Frederic's *The Damnation of Theron Ware* (1896), naturalism failed to leave much of an imprint on religious fiction; its pessimism and deterministic skepticism about human agency were unsuited to the innate optimism of religious fiction, which insisted on the everlasting power of faith to effect self-improvement and self-determination. However, religious novels were a particularly robust outpost for literary idealism, realism's chief antagonist and rival in late-century aesthetics. Although usually overlooked by literary historians, idealism was a significant force in late-century American letters, and its supporters included some prominent figures, among them Thomas Bailey Aldrich, editor of the *Atlantic Monthly* during the 1880s. Idealist critics such as Edmund C. Stedman contended that literary texts ought to provide inspiration amid a coarse and cynical world, and they frowned on realist texts that, to their mind, merely documented the quotidian and base, arguing that such works degraded literature and reified the ugliness of modern life. Instead, idealists maintained that literature ought to inspire and refine readers by depicting an idyllic world of beauty and moral clarity, and this aesthetic mode naturally complemented the interests of late-century religious fiction, which aimed above all else to inspire and edify the reader.

This aesthetic allegiance produced religious novels that often shunned formal innovation and hewed to simple characterization and predictable plots that modernized John Bunyan's *The Pilgrim's Progress* (1678) by narrating the struggles of contemporary Christians among worldly temptations and the consequent rewards for their piety, whether in material riches or a joyful death. A reader of such works may reliably expect the infidel love interest to undergo a conversion experience and the poor but honest Christian man to achieve professional success. While these elements certainly signal the idealistic allegiances of religious fiction, these scripted narrative forms openly admit their ideological foundations, for they were a strategic part of the religious novels' efforts to promote Christianity and inspire conversion in the reader. These formulaic conventional narratives offered reassuring evidence that Christianity could be relied upon to yield predictable results, regardless of the circumstance: self-betterment, comfort, and salvation. Likewise, the idealism of such novels suggests that Christian faith may simplify a complex world, rendering it manageable and apprehensible.

In support of this implicit promise, religious novels often deliberately adopt an artless, homely affect with marked nostalgia for a simpler time. As with such novels as Rev. George Hepworth's popular *Hiram Golf's Religion; or, The Shoemaker by the Grace of God* (1893) and its sequel, *They Met in Heaven* (1894), these works juxtapose modern cynicism and sophisticated disbelief with unpretentious, simple characters, whose unadorned piety and folksy wisdom render religious faith wholesome and accessible even to the most unlearned. In those two works, a sophisticated modern businessman visits a rural hamlet and finds himself embroiled in lengthy fireside discussions about Christianity with several local men, chief among them Hiram Golf, a plain-speaking but wise shoemaker. Although Golf is humble and inarticulate, his plain piety and simple faith offer the narrator much-needed inspiration, and the novels thereby implicitly reject modern sophistication and cynicism in favor of a faith undergirded by simple trust in scripture and the Lord. This crafted artlessness is also evident in religious novels' general distaste for theology, which is typically dismissed as an unnecessary intellectual appurtenance to faith. As Hiram Golf remarks in *They Met in Heaven*, "we've got too much theology in the world, and too little religion" (ch. 6); one may be a devout Christian and still be wholly ignorant of the nuances of abstruse doctrine.

The modest formal ambitions and idealism of much religious fiction no doubt contributed to the general impression that religious fiction was of lesser literary value and undeserving of serious critical attention. The career trajectory of Edward Egg-leston makes clear how aesthetic proclivity signaled literary import and prompted critical regard. In his preface to *The Circuit Rider*, which was based on his own experience as an itinerant Methodist preacher, Eggleston publicly differentiated his novel from the standard idealist fare of religious fiction and attempted to make a case for the compatibility of religious novels with realism. He wrote,

> no man is worthy to be called a novelist who does not endeavor with his whole soul to produce the higher form of history, by writing truly of men as they are, and dispassionately of those forms of life that come within his scope. . . . [T]his is not a "religious novel," one in which all the bad people are as bad as they can be, and all the good people a little better than they can be. . . . The story of any true life is wholesome, if only the writer will tell it simply, keeping impertinent preachment of his own out of the way. (Preface)

Presaging Howells's later essays in which he would argue for the inherent whole-someness of realist literature, Eggleston suggests both that religious literature need not be founded on idealist principles and that piety in no way necessitates that one shield one's eyes from the complexities of life (on Howells's wholesome realism, see Chapter 7 of this volume). It is in large part because of Eggleston's embrace of realism, as with his depiction of midwestern local culture, that he is among the few religious novelists to achieve critical esteem and inclusion in literary history.

While the idealism of religious fiction may make it seem naive and outmoded, it often betrays an uneasy suspicion that the sophistication of the modern world was inimical to faith. For example, many religious novels were historical in nature, set in earlier eras portrayed as simpler and more hospitable to religious belief, among them James Lane Allen's *The Choir Invisible* (1897), Edward Eggleston's *The End of the World* (1872) and *The Circuit Rider*, Annie Trumball Slosson's *The Heresy of Mehetable Clark* (1892), and Silas Weir Mitchell's *Hugh Wynne, Free Quaker* (1897). Their nostalgia implicitly bundles religious faith together with other long-vanished curiosities of the past, like the ill repute of Methodism or the eschatological terrors of the 1840s. Michael Kammen and T. Jackson Lears have examined the late-century climate of religiously infused nostalgia, which animated the Arts and Crafts movement as well as revived enthusiasm for more antiquated forms of Christianity, to argue that religious faith seemed increasingly impracticable in the late-century, a concern that religious novels would at times openly engage. For example, Henry Adams's *Esther* candidly questions the effectiveness and sincerity of modern Christianity. The main character, Esther Dudley, deprecates the decor of a new church and the fashionable society people commissioned to adorn it, commenting, "It has a terribly grotesque air of theater even now," and the painter Mr. Wharton replies, "It is a theater . . . . That is what ails our religion. But it is not the fault of our art. . . . I would like now, even as it is, to go back to the age of beauty, and put a Madonna in the heart of their church. The place has no heart" (ch. 4). In thus yearning for an

earlier time of beauty and simplicity, Wharton posits nostalgic idealism as more con-
ducive to religious faith and intimates that modernity has hopelessly compromised
religious belief. The anxiety that the modern world might not be hospitable to faith
also animates Arlo Bates's *The Puritans* (1899), which recounts the difficulties of two
Protestant seminarians in reconciling their faith with worldly ambitions; the novel
concludes with the decision of one of these men to leave the church altogether, while
the other elects to convert to a more antiquated form of Christianity in Catholicism
and retreats to a cloister. Set against this backdrop of late-century religious disbelief
and cynicism, the stylistic sincerity and ingenuousness of much idealist religious
fiction take on a different quality. Instead of appearing merely as the distinguishing hallmark of literary amateurism or talentless inability, it emerges as a defensive,
reactive counterclaim that optimistically refutes modern cynicism to depict faith as
a steadfast bulwark against skeptical sophistication.

One exception to this climate of religious nostalgia is the repeated enmity with
which late-century novelists portray Calvinist orthodoxy. Rather than treat this
once-pervasive form of Christianity with admiration or affection, late-century writers see in it both callous indifference toward suffering and a severity verging on
sinfulness. In James Lane Allen's popular novel *The Choir Invisible*, for example, an
Episcopalian priest compares Calvinism to "an uncorked inkbottle in a rolling snow-
ball: the farther you go, the blacker you get!" (ch. 18). In this formulation, Calvinism's belief in the utter depravity of human beings merely deflates and depresses its
adherents. Elizabeth Stuart Phelps famously began writing *The Gates Ajar* out of her
sense that Calvinism could not offer solace to the many women left bereaved in the
aftermath of the Civil War. The novel begins with the failures of Calvinist clergy to
console Mary Cabot upon the death of her brother, Royal, as they insensitively dispute Royal's salvation and characterize Heaven as a sterile, joyless place. Mary thus
sinks into a depression and renounces religion until the arrival of her aunt Winifred,
who challenges prevailing orthodoxy and offers an alternative view of heaven as a
sacralized home populated by reunited loved ones. Peter Van Brunt, the protagonist
of George Hepworth's novel *They Met in Heaven*, is similarly inconsolable upon the
sudden death of his wife and son. Raised by a severe Calvinist father who had characterized God as wrathful and the afterlife as brutal, Van Brunt is a bitter apostate
until the kindly interventions of shoemaker Hiram Golf, whose homely faith not
only converts Van Brunt but also enables Van Brunt's postmortem reunion with his
lost relatives. Calvinism likewise causes an irreconcilable rupture in the Ward family
in Margaret Deland's *John Ward, Preacher*, as minister John Ward, under pressure
from his stern orthodox congregation, refuses to reunite with his wife until she
accepts the doctrine of hell. It was not lost on observers at the time that Deland's
novel was published the same year as Mrs. Humphrey Ward's *Robert Elsmere* (1888), a
bestselling English novel that also depicted a growing modern disillusionment with
Calvinism, and the two were often cited together to betoken the waning influence
of Calvinism in a religious climate dominated by the Arminian belief that human

beings may take a more active role in their own salvation. It was abundantly clear to late-century novelists that the stranglehold of Calvinism was long gone, and these retrospective treatments of Calvinism implicitly celebrate a modern, meritocratic religious worldview in which faith reliably results in salvation and remains available to all, even in the very last moments of life.

The late-century culture of religious nostalgia found its greatest success with Lew Wallace's *Ben-Hur,* a historical novel about the adventures of a Jewish prince, Judah Ben-Hur, set against the backdrop of first-century Messianism. A sweeping epic, the novel follows Ben-Hur's adventures as he is falsely accused of attempting to assassinate the Roman governor, survives imprisonment on a Roman galley ship, and finds himself among a band of believers who eagerly await the fulfillment of Messianic prophesy. Along the way, he exacts revenge upon his accuser, the Roman Messala, in the novel's most famous scene, in which the two men fiercely compete in a heated chariot race. Although Ben-Hur is an ardent supporter of the man reputed to be the Messiah, Jesus only appears at the end of the novel, when Ben-Hur witnesses the crucifixion. While this delay mirrors the Christian belief that the faithful are rewarded for their loyalty with direct contact with their lord at the very end of life itself, Wallace would later admit that he had omitted Jesus chiefly for reasons of public relations: as he remarked, "The Christian world would not tolerate a novel with Jesus Christ as its hero, and I knew it" (qtd. in Carter 1991, 68). Wallace's own religious conversion became part of the book's legendary back-story. As a lawyer, Civil War veteran, and statesman (he served as governor of the New Mexico territory), Wallace claimed to have had no particular religious sentiments before writing the book: "I had no convictions about God or Christ," he remarked. "I neither believed nor disbelieved in them" (qtd. in Carey 1971, 93). The book, he maintained, was born out of a chance conversation with Robert Ingersoll, a prominent late-century orator and known agnostic. Deeply affected by Ingersoll's skepticism, Wallace embarked on the novel as an inquiry into religion, and he publicly claimed to have been converted through the process of writing, an assertion that no doubt contributed to sales as well as to Wallace's own reputation. The novel initially sold only modestly, and mainstream reviews largely dismissed it as an old-fashioned romance, but favorable reviews in Christian publications contributed to word-of-mouth publicity that led to an escalation in sales. By the end of the decade, the book had sold 400,000 copies, with lifetime sales estimated at between two and three million copies. In 1913, after Wallace's death, Sears Roebuck ordered a million copies of an inexpensive edition, and in 1936 it was added to the Modern Library. Because of its wide appeal and extravagant spectacles, the novel was adapted for numerous stage and film production, thereby sparking further sales with each production. Billy Sunday, the foremost revivalist of the turn of the century, gave his approval to one such production, proclaiming, "I wish 100,000,000 people could see the play, now running in New York" (qtd. in McKee 1947, 185).

As mentioned earlier, *Ben-Hur* spawned many imitators, among them *The Gladiators* (1891) by G. J. Whyte-Melville; *Come Forth!* (1891) by Elizabeth Stuart Phelps and her husband, Herbert Ward; and *John: A Tale of the King Messiah* (1896) by Katherine Pearson Woods. While this late-century fascination with novels set in early Christian history was clearly a literary trend inspired by Wallace's spectacular success, it also had a wider intellectual context that would have been readily recognized at the time. For most of the nineteenth century, Americans regarded the Bible as a factual, historical document that detailed the lives of real people and actual events. That belief came under considerable pressure when it was announced in 1870 that a transatlantic committee composed of scholars had begun work on a new translation of the Bible. In explanation for this mammoth undertaking, the editors published a series of essays in popular periodicals stating their rationale and methods, and in so doing they brought to American attention the significant advances in biblical historical scholarship. The "higher criticism," as it was called, emerged in Germany in the early nineteenth century and presumed the Bible to be a human-authored text rooted in cultural history and thus subject to historical, archaeological, and literary analyses. Although American seminarians and theologians had kept abreast of these scholarly advances, this new translation brought these findings and methods to a wider American public, among them the belief that the first five books of the Hebrew Bible had recognizable stylistic evidence attesting to composite authorship, thereby unseating the long-standing conviction that they had been authored by Moses himself. In addition, the public became aware that the translators had consulted more than five thousand separate Hebrew and Greek texts, most of them fragmentary and with uncertain authenticity. The Bible was thus exposed as a mutable, constructed text, a development that caused great excitement in some quarters and great anxiety in others. Modern Christian fundamentalism emerged in part from the discomfort caused by biblical historicism, as with the resolution of the Niagara Bible Conference of 1876 to maintain a strict belief in biblical literalness.

Publication of the Revised Version of the New Testament, which was finally released in 1881, was so heavily anticipated that it was preceded by preorders of a million copies. It went through thirty reprints in its first year, and in some cities its publication caused traffic jams. In such a climate, popular studies in biblical historicism also sold well, foremost among them Washington Gladden's work *Who Wrote the Bible?* (1891). That same year, Joseph Henry Thayer, a Harvard professor and member of the American Bible Revision Committee, reminded Americans that in reading the Bible they should always "Interpret *historically*. Remember that Palestine in the first century is not America in the nineteenth," an assertion that undermines the belief in a continuous biblical truth (qtd. in Szasz 1982, 34). Biblical historicism also sparked widespread interest in the historical Jesus, and revisionist biographies of Christ became a full-fledged international trend. Beginning with David Strauss's revolutionary *Life of Jesus* (1835), the 1860s saw the publication of both Ernest Renan's

Life of Jesus (1863), and J. R. Seeley's *Ecce Homo: A Survey of the Life and Work of Christ* (published in the United States in 1866). By the 1870s dozens of these works had been published. The biggest bestseller was Canon F. W. Farrar's *The Life of Christ* (1874), which derived from years of extensive historicist research that included a trip to Palestine in 1870. Even popular religious writers with no background in biblical scholarship found themselves inspired by this trend, including Henry Ward Beecher, whose *Life of Jesus Christ* appeared in 1872; Eggleston, whose studies *Christ in Art* and *Christ in Literature* were both published in 1874; and Elizabeth Stuart Phelps, who published *The Story of Jesus Christ* in 1897.

Harold Frederic depicted the disorienting and even disillusioning effects of the "higher criticism" on one believer in *The Damnation of Theron Ware*, in which naive Methodist minister Theron Ware undertakes to pen his own biblical biography. Motivated chiefly by his dire financial problems and utterly ignorant of historicist approaches, Ware embarks on a study of Abraham, only to learn from two sophisticated, learned men—the Catholic priest Father Forbes and the atheistic scientist Dr. Ledsmar—that Abraham had long ago been recognized by scholars to be merely a literary metaphor rather than an actual historical personage. Finding Ware's sincerity refreshing, the men lend him works of biblical scholarship, but they serve to undermine his already tenuous commitment to the church. Ware furtively and greedily reads one such work by Ernst Renan as if it were pornography, and his new knowledge inflates his vanity, causing him to regard with contempt the uncritical piety of his parishioners and to imagine himself above the traditional moral injunctions against adultery, theft, and deceit. While the novel does not suggest that the "higher criticism" is directly responsible for Ware's immorality or apostasy, it places this scholarship alongside the blatant showmanship of revivalism and the self-serving careerism of clergy as an equally significant contribution to modern religious cynicism.

Frederic's work was an exception, however. More typically, historical research in many novels about early Christian history vested religious novels with credibility. For example, Lew Wallace filled *Ben-Hur* with evidence of his extensive research in the Library of Congress, including innumerable details about first-century Middle Eastern mores, diet, flora, and architecture. Instead of undermining the credibility of the Bible, these details work to reify biblical narrative as historical truth: thus infused with researched data, Bible stories seem more realistic and lifelike, allowing readers to visualize more clearly the settings, contexts, and minutiae of biblical events. In the hands of novelists, that is, historicism largely revitalized biblical narrative and allowed writers such as Lew Wallace to restore the religious certitude that had been challenged by the "higher criticism."

As novelists embellished the tales of innumerable minor biblical characters in the vein of *Ben-Hur*, the biblical figure of Lazarus caught the attention of a number of writers—among them William Holcombe with *In Both Worlds* (1869), Elizabeth Stuart Phelps and her husband, Herbert Ward, with *Come Forth!* (1891), and Olla

B. Tolph with *Lazarus* (1895)—who retold the New Testament tale of his resurrection from the dead. While these novels about Lazarus dramatize the belief in the transformative powers of Christian faith, they do so by narrating a story of a man's conversion and its beneficial effects on his sisters, Mary and Martha. This narrative proved to be one of the cornerstones of late-century religious fiction, which is thoroughly overwhelmed by novels of male conversion, including Eggleston's *End of the World,* Hepworth's *They Met in Heaven,* E. P. Roe's *Opening a Chestnut Burr* (1874), Phelps's *Gates Between* (1887), and Louis Pendleton's *The Wedding Garment,* among many others, all of which depict conversion as the culmination of male maturation. Countering the presumption that religious men were credulous, gullible saps, these novels show that Christianity helps men to be more fully manly, giving them the inner strength to realize their ambitions and the character to honor their obligations to those dependent upon them. To illustrate that Christianity enables men to become bold leaders, these novels often have clergy as their protagonists, depicting them as iconoclastic heroes patterned after Christ himself, men whose character and commitment to Christian principles cause them to take valiant public stands against .a harsh, disbelieving public. As is evident in such works as Edward Eggleston's *The Circuit Rider,* Elizabeth Stuart Phelps's *A Singular Life,* Tourgée's *Murvale Eastman, Christian Socialist,* Charles Sheldon's *In His Steps,* and George Farnell's *Rev. Josiah Hilton* (1898), these novels seek to remake the public image of the Christian minister into a pillar of strength and fortitude.

This literary preoccupation with Christian masculinity was by no means an isolated development but derived from a larger late-century movement known as "Muscular Christianity," a term originally coined to describe the mid-century novels of English writers Charles Kingsley and Thomas Hughes, author of *Tom Brown's School Days* (1857). In the postbellum United States, Muscular Christianity came to denote a widespread campaign to invigorate Christianity by attracting male believers, an effort that informed the decision of the Young Men's Christian Association in 1869 to embrace athletics as a key part of its ministry in the hopes of luring more men. Muscular Christianity was permeated by an overt antipathy for the female-centered spirituality of sentimentalism and its attendant feminization of Christianity, and advocates protested that female influence contaminated every aspect of Christianity—from hymnals to images of Jesus to the ministry itself—and consequently made it inhospitable to men. In 1890 Methodist minister Howard Alan Bridgeman questioned whether men were welcome in the woman-dominated church, asking, "Have we a religion for men?" (qtd. in Kimmel 2006, 117). G. Stanley Hall, one of the era's foremost psychologists, denounced the "woman peril" that he believed afflicted American churches, while Billy Sunday, the leading revivalist of the late-century, directly aimed "to strike the death blow at the idea that being a Christian takes a man out of the busy whirl of the world's life and activity and makes him a spineless effeminate proposition." To counter this image, Sunday depicted Jesus as the "greatest scrapper who ever lived." In contrast with a "dainty, sissified, lily-livered religion" he deplored, Sunday characterized Christianity as a "hard muscled, pick-axed religion, a religion from the gut, tough, and resilient" and proclaimed that "the manliest man is the man who will acknowledge Jesus Christ" (qtd. in Kimmel 2006, 119).

Male religious novelists contributed to this effort to masculinize Christianity and sought to defeminize the literary medium altogether, an effort also undertaken by William Dean Howells and Mark Twain in their own respective efforts to differentiate themselves from literary sentimentalism. James Lane Allen, author of the *The Choir Invisible,* complained that literature had for too long been dominated by womanly influence, "producing a literature of the overcivilized, the hyper-fastidious . . . the fragile, the trivial, the rarified, the bloodless" (qtd. in Putney 2001, 31–32), and E. P. Roe agreed that "the day of prolix, fine, flowering writing" had ended, to be succeeded by more manly writing of "simplicity, lucidity, strength" (qtd. in Thorp 1961, 216–71). As one of the era's leading religious novelists, Eggleston actively supported the Muscular Christianity cause, publishing a series of articles in 1878–79 that lamented the sorry state of the ministry and urged ministers to assume greater manly strength: "Stand on your manhood and not on your office," he wrote in the 1878 essay "Parsons and Parsons" (qtd. in Randel 1962, 154). Eggleston aggressively recruited men to join his Brooklyn congregation by renaming it the Church of Christian Endeavor, which consolidated its association with manly striving and vigorous activity, and by adding a social center for working men. His novel *The Hoosier Schoolmaster* also visibly registers this influence, as with the resolution of newly converted Bud Means, a school bully, to stop fighting and save "his best licks for Jesus Christ," a statement that aligns Christian faith with manly strength and responsibility (ch. 15).

The novels of E. P. Roe are perhaps the fullest expression of the literary arm of Muscular Christianity. Although long forgotten, Roe was the nation's bestselling writer in the 1870s and '80s. Roe's novels typically portray the rise of a devout young man forced to begin his career at the bottom rung of the social ladder. For example, in the bestselling novel *Barriers Burned Away,* Dennis Fleet moves to Chicago to seek his fortune but experiences great difficulty landing a job suited to his education and talents. Although he'd planned to become a lawyer, he eventually accepts a humiliating job as a factotum in an art gallery, but his piety equips him with a strong work ethic that catches the notice of his employer and leads him on an upward path of promotion and achievement. Along the way, he succeeds in converting his disbelieving love interest, the haughty Miss Ludolph, helping to reform an alcoholic, and rescuing scores of people from the Chicago fire of 1871. Roe's novel *A Knight of the Nineteenth Century* (1877) similarly recounts the effects of conversion on a dissolute youth, Egbert Haldane, whose faith endows him with the fortitude to resist alcohol and a determination to serve others. This selflessness leads him to become a commander in the Civil War and a beloved, renowned physician. The Christian man in such narratives is typically heroic and willing to endanger himself for the good of others; these texts appeal to male readers by contending that faith imparts men with trustworthiness and a work ethic, both of which create opportunities and earn material rewards.

This depiction of Christianity as an indispensable accouterment to male professional advancement was seconded in this era by scores of self-help books designed for male readers. As exemplified by such texts as Orison Swett Marden's *Pushing to the Front* (1894), *Success* (1897) and *The Secrets of Achievement* (1898), these success manuals, as they were called, claimed to help men achieve their fullest potential, and many of them actively propounded Christianity as an essential vehicle for professional success because it helped cultivate a sound reputation and character, as well as a useful opportunity for networking. Many of these manuals claimed biblical justification for their advice, claiming that wealth corroborates virtue and that God desires prosperity for the faithful. Religious publishers issued many such works, and clergy were among the most successful authors of success manuals, among them Rev. Wilbur F. Crafts, author of *Successful Men of Today* (1883), and Rev. John Thain Davidson, author of *Sure to Succeed* (1889). Rev. Russell Conwell delivered an oral version of his popular *Acres of Diamonds* (1890), a text that began as a sermon, over six thousand times. Insisting that Christians have a "duty to get rich," he maintained that "[t]here is not a poor person in the United States who was not made so by his own shortcomings" (qtd. in Kimmel 2006, 59).

This unabashed materialism pervaded many late-century religious novels, especially ones that sought to appeal to male readers. For example, in Hepworth's *They Met in Heaven*, a minister applauds the narrator's business career, remarking, " 'Let me congratulate you . . . on the divine necessity of work. . . . Commercial activity means manliness. . . . The world of commercial transactions, the competitions . . . are God's university.' " He continues, " 'I have a notion that business and religion were intended to complement each other. . . . If religion is divorced from business, mankind suffer' " (ch. 1). But while novelists such as E. P. Roe averred that piety will bear fruit in material prosperity and business success, other writers such as Elizabeth Stuart Phelps and Albion Tourgée strongly questioned altogether the compatibility of capitalism with the Christian life. In so doing, they channeled into their novels the arguments and theology developed in the Social Gospel movement. Led by such theologians as Robert C. Ely, Washington Gladden, and Walter Rauschenbusch, the Social Gospel movement repudiated both laissez-faire capitalism and self-interested Christianity, and preached that Christianity should aim not for individual salvation but for the worldly betterment of all human beings through social reform, social justice, and activism. To be a true Christian, they maintained, one must imitate Christ fully and work on behalf of the poor and oppressed, rather than strive merely for personal financial gain and professional success, as supporters of Muscular Christianity had suggested. In their critique of capitalist self-centeredness, some supporters propounded socialism as a more faithful expression of Christian fellowship, taking the collective ownership of the Apostles, described in Acts 2:44–45, as a scriptural precedent for Christian socialism. This political affiliation would result in the Society of Christian Socialists, founded by Rev. W. D. P. Bliss in 1889, and the prominence of Christian Socialist George D. Herron in nominating Eugene V. Debs for president at the 1904 Socialist convention.

To be sure, the Social Gospel movement was never more than a minority opinion amid the blatant materialism promulgated by Russell Conwell and Wilbur Crafts, but it generated considerable attention and informed a great many religious novels that documented late-century social ills and agitated for Christian activism. In attending thus to the gritty realities of contemporary life, Social Gospel novels tended to be more recognizably informed by literary realism than by idealism and in that way diverged from more mainstream religious novels. Many dozens of Social Gospel works were published in the late century, among them Washington Gladden's *The Christian League of Connecticut,* E. J. Haynes's *Dollars and Duty* (1887), Edward Everett Hale's *How They Lived in Hampton* (1888), R. E. Porter's *The Union League Club,* Archibald McCowan's *Christ, the Socialist* (1894), and Marion Couthouy Smith's *Dr. Marks, Socialist* (1897). Occasionally, religious novels criticized the Social Gospel movement, notably Katherine Pearson Woods's *Metzerott, Shoemaker* (1889), which characterizes socialism as fully incompatible with Christianity.

The most famous Social Gospel novel—and the bestselling religious novel of the era—was Charles Sheldon's *In His Steps: What Would Jesus Do?* Sheldon was a Kansan Congregationalist minister who, as Stowe had predicted, used narrative fiction as a substitute for sermons. In an effort to lure his congregation to return to church for the second Sunday service, Sheldon read weekly installments of a lengthy narrative in lieu of a sermon, and it was thus that he wrote *In His Steps,* a novel that would be translated into dozens of languages and would sell millions of copies (Sheldon claimed that it sold 30 million copies, though later critics estimate that it likely sold closer to six million). The novel follows the transformation of a complacent, prosperous congregation after the minister, Henry Maxwell, invites them to spend a year attempting to imitate Jesus in every aspect of their lives. Inspired by this challenge, the town newspaper editor decides to cease publication on Sunday and to decline advertising from saloons, a railroad employee exposes company corruption, and an heiress resolves to use her wealth for social good. Through these examples, Sheldon depicts Christianity as a social practice that requires sacrifice and a commitment to the wider social good at the expense of individual profit or comfort.

Sheldon followed *In His Steps* with several sequels—*Jesus Is Here!* (1914), *In His Steps To-Day* (1921), and *In His Steps Today* (1928)—but none of them came close to the popularity of its progenitor. In fact, the unparalleled success of *In His Steps* was the climax of late-century religious fiction. The influence of the Social Gospel would continue into the first decades of the twentieth century, with the novels of Harold Bell Wright, author of *The Shepherd of the Hills* (1907) and *The Calling of Dan*

Matthews (1909), and Canadian writer Charles W. Gordon, whose novel *Black Rock* (1908) was a bestseller. Otherwise, religious novels waned in number and popularity in the first decades of the twentieth century, and the critique of capitalism staged by Social Gospel novels would be utterly routed by Bruce Barton's blockbuster *The Man Nobody Knows* (1925), which remained a bestseller for two years. Like many of its late-century predecessors, *The Man Nobody Knows* offered a revisionist examination of the life of Christ, and it likewise reconstituted Jesus in the spirit of Muscular Christianity, rendering him strong, hardworking, and tough-minded. And also like many of its antecedents, Barton's work characterized Christianity as the secret to business success, for it depicted Jesus as a kind of advertising executive whose entrepreneurial savvy enabled him to create, publicize, and organize an effective international corporation. Barton unabashedly upheld capitalism as a contemporary analogue to Jesus' ministry and, like E. P. Roe, envisioned business success as a worldly expression of Christian piety. According to Barton, Jesus is the "Founder of Modern Business," an assertion that thoroughly rejected the Social Gospel embrace of socialism while repackaging for a new century the capitalist sentiments of some late-century religious novels (ch. 6).

Religious fiction would remain a mainstay of popular publishing through the twentieth century, attaining particular prominence with such works as Lloyd Cassel Douglas's *The Robe* (1942), Leon Uris's *Exodus* (1958), Janette Oke's *Love Comes Softly* (1979), Frank E. Peretti's *This Present Darkness* (1986), and Tim LaHaye and Jerry B. Jenkins's *Left Behind* series (1995–2007). For the most part, however, religious fiction has been narrowly classified as a niche industry and thus seldom receives national press or attention outside of sectarian settings. Set against later American literary history, the late nineteenth century comes into view as the high-water mark of American religious fiction, an era before religious novels were marginalized as a special-interest genre and one in which they enjoyed both popularity and national visibility.

12

THE SPANISH-AMERICAN WAR, US EXPANSION, AND THE NOVEL

BY GRETCHEN MURPHY

In May of 1898, the United States entered Cuba's War of Independence. Cubans had been fighting for independence from Spain since 1895, but within one hundred days the United States won a decisive victory that ended the Spanish empire in the Americas. Only three hundred sixty-one US servicemen had died in combat, and although hundreds more would die in coming months from infections flourishing in unsanitary military camps, the seemingly easy victory swelled patriotic enthusiasm. As diplomat, antilabor novelist, and dialect poet John Hay proclaimed in a July 27, 1898, letter to Vice President Theodore Roosevelt, it was "a splendid little war, begun with the highest motives, carried on with magnificent intelligence and spirit, favored by that Fortune which loves the brave. It is now to be concluded with that firm good nature which is after all the distinguishing trait of our American character" (Thayer 1915, 337). But exactly how the war was to be concluded raised grave questions. When the Treaty of Paris was signed in December, Spain relinquished sovereignty over Cuba and ceded its other colonies, Puerto Rico, Guam, and the Philippines, to the United States in exchange for $20 million. (Cuba's independence had been stipulated when the US Congress ratified the decision to go to war.) If championing Cuban liberty was the "best of intentions" that drew the United States into the war, acquiring Spain's other colonies seemed to many to be an abrupt reversal in policy, a feeling that intensified a few months later, when the United States refused to recognize the new Filipino constitution and began fighting against Filipino nationalists in the Philippine-American War (1899–1902).

The Spanish-American and Philippine-American Wars thus sparked major debates about the nation's global mission, and these debates occurred in fiction as well as more traditional political discourse. As the first US war in which mass media played a major role in providing motivation and meaning for state action, the Spanish-American War offers a fascinating moment for studying the interrelation between fictional narratives and foreign policy. The first section of this chapter will examine the common portrayal of the Spanish-American War as either the cause or result of a crisis in national identity in which fighting is depicted as either a loss of or a return to true American identity. In both sorts of narratives, these debates over national identity engage domestic issues related to the woman question, economic equality, and African American rights as elements of national division and corruption that must be staved off by going to or avoiding war. The second section then considers the relationship of the war with the era's developing theories of popular culture and aesthetics of realism. Literary realists and anti-imperialists (two groups that sometimes overlapped) frequently blamed romanticism as a genre for the war fervor, developing an incipient argument about the power of feminized mass culture. Examining competing claims to realism, however, can offer a fuller picture of how genre and gender both played a role in the roots of the representational crises that would mark the dawning twentieth century.

Mark Twain argued in his anti-imperialist tract that taking possession of the Philippines represented a new entry into "the European game" of colonial conquest, leaving behind "the American game" of promoting democracy. But while Twain claimed that colonial conquest was a new departure, many authors used the form of the novel to argue for historical continuity between expansion across the United States and beyond. Those who agreed with Twain called themselves "anti-imperialists," but it might be more accurate to say that most denied the presence of empire in US history, including the wide-scale dispossession of Native Americans, territorial expansion through the Mexican American War, and gestures toward Caribbean and Pacific expansion dating back to the early days of the republic. By claiming that the outcome of the Spanish-American War marked an unprecedented departure, anti-imperialists promoted the historical myth of American exceptionalism. For the pro-imperialist writers who challenged this vision, recognizing and rewriting US history as a series of ongoing colonial ventures was an important goal in nonfiction and fiction alike.

For example, Stephen Bonsal authorizes Pacific expansion by linking it with national tradition in his epistolary novel, *The Golden Horseshoe: Extracts from the Letters of Captain H. L. Herndon, of the 21st US Infantry, on Duty in the Philippine islands, and Lieutenant Lawrence Gill, A.D.C. to the military governor of Puerto Rico* (1900). Bonsal, a journalist who promoted war with Spain through his testimony before Congress about the Cuban plight, poses as the "editor" of letters exchanged by his fictional characters, soldiers who first met during the famous battle of San Juan Hill and were subsequently reassigned to their respective posts in the new US colonies. The letters follow Gill's efforts to convince the doubtful Herndon of the rightness of the conflict in the Philippines. Gill's arguments center on a new understanding of empire in US history past and present. He writes to Herndon about an unknown incident from Virginia's early colonial days, in which a group of Virginia colonists refused to be "narcotized" by tidewater tobacco profits and instead fought to expand westward into the Blue Ridge Mountains. These westward moving Virginians took the sign of the Golden Horseshoe as their "insignia," a symbol of continuous mobility across North America and beyond (33). Figuring new colonial responsibilities as a similar heroic refusal of easy, domestic money-making, Gill claims himself to be a new member of the Order of the Golden Horseshoe, and he slowly wins Herndon to his way of thinking. Once in the Philippines, this historical continuity becomes obvious to Herdon as he watches the US military in action: "to see them you might imagine that they had come out a little way on a new road off the Santa Fé trail to build another army post and protect the white settlers; and, now that I think of it, that is about what they are come here to do" (292).

More than the historical continuity of expansion, Bonsal's legendary Golden Horseshoe depicts US history as a continual struggle between profitable complacency and the more noble, fraternal fellowship of violence. In this way, Bonsal promotes the popular notion that the war, instead of being a new departure, actually brought the United States back to its own traditions in the face of a crisis of identity. Historian Richard Hofstadter, in his influential 1952 essay "Manifest Destiny and the Philippines," argues that the United States' motivation for the war was not a desire for Cuban liberty, but rather a response to what he calls "the psychic crisis of the 1890s," the feeling that the bureaucratization of American business and the closing of the frontier line had dampened opportunities for competition and independent achievement, while domestic troubles such as economic depression, labor unrest, civic corruption in cities, and the failure to assimilate new immigrants suggested immanent national decline. Hofstadter contends that the war was sparked from the social psychology of the crisis, an argument that cultural historians and critics including Kirsten Hogenson and Amy Kaplan have reframed in gender terms by identifying the perceived "crisis" as one of manliness hemmed in by the feminizing threat of modern civilization, brought on by either an effeminizing "overcivilization" or the lack of strenuous, man-making opportunities for unskilled labor and middle management. The fear was not only that men were losing their energetic force, but also that "new women" threatened to usurp male social power. As more women entered public life, Hogenson argues, female reformers appealed to woman's supposed superior morality and preference for arbitration as a womanly alternative to war, an argument that provoked calls for war in terms of reaffirming besieged masculinity.

While gender politics in cultural representations of the war are more complex than this conflict between feminine pacifism and besieged masculinity, fictional narratives about the war did frequently represent it as resolving perceived crises of modernity. Edith Elmer Wood's lively society novel *The Spirit of the Service* (1903) is one of the better-crafted tellings of this crisis narrative, and it also signals the more variable terrain of gender politics in novels about the war. Its young heroine, Sue Ballinger, identifies the crisis and the route of return when she describes the military "spirit" that has vanished in modern US commercial life. While dining with officers on a naval base, she exclaims, "Now here we drop into a world whose ideals are purely military. I thought that spirit was dead and buried centuries ago, but here it is flourishing before my eyes." Fancying herself swept back into the Middle Ages, she says admiringly, "You people are an epic poem in the midst of an age of prose!" (ch. 2). This return to an invigorating, premodern martial spirit is also enacted in the plot. The novel tells the story of Major Julius Cartwright and his family; before the outbreak of the war, Major Cartwright is an officer in a New York naval shipyard that he tries to run with perfect military fairness, despite the corrupt machinations of a local Irish Democratic ward boss and petty partisan politics. Signs of an American decline, these divisive forces ultimately cause Cartwright to lose his post, and only his subsequent assignment in Dewey's Pacific fleet during the Battle of Manila can redeem his beset manly impartiality, a deliverance that he almost misses when an old maiden aunt (the female arbitrationist) tries to pull strings to "protect" him from war.

However, Major Cartwright's sense of honor is matched by the heroine Sue's dedication to her work in the settlement houses of San Francisco and Boston, and after the war ends, as a nurse in the fever camps of Santiago. Sue resembles the more active type of female heroine identified in Kaplan's study of the era's imperial romance insofar as she ratifies imperial power though her status as a liberated "new woman." But Wood makes Sue an equal bearer of "the spirit of the service," not a mere spectator. Indeed, Sue's suitor proves his worth to her not by fighting in battle, which he misses because of his humdrum military assignment, but by being the only character who sympathizes with her settlement house efforts to "bridge over the terrible chasm between the so-called upper and lower halves" (ch. 15). If Wood thus includes the foil of the sexless old maid unable to sympathize with the honorable, self-sacrificing war effort, she also is careful to outline a compelling space for female participation in a progressive vision of global mission. Wood, after earning a Columbia University doctorate in sociology, would turn from writing novels to a high-profile career in urban planning as a housing expert for federal and local government; her later works include *The Housing of the Unskilled Wage Earner: America's Next Problem* (1919) and *Slums and Blighted Areas in the United States* (1935). In her early career as a novelist, she offers urban reform and global mission as twin opportunities—for men *and* women—to reaffirm "service" in place of petty politics and financial self-interest.

Wood was not alone in representing the Spanish-American War as an act of service rather than commercial interest. As Hofstadter points out, big-business Republicans were initially cool about the prospects of intervening on behalf of Cuban revolutionaries, and "yellow press" newspapers typically employed Populist rhetoric to flame war sentiment. Richard Harding Davis, another war correspondent whose dramatic reports of Spanish atrocities in Cuba encouraged the war, criticized American commercialism in his short story "The Man With One Talent" (1900), in which a timid US Senator balks at publically supporting the war because powerful business interests bid him not to do so. The hero, a filibusterer whose graphic descriptions of acute Cuban suffering fail to persuade the senator, angrily addresses the senator and his colleagues: "[You] forget watching the money rise and fall, that outside the sun is shining, that human beings are sick and suffering, that men are giving their lives for an idea, for a sentiment, for a flag. . . . Can 'trusts' save your soul—is 'Wall Street' the strait and narrow road to salvation?" Here again a crisis of modernity in the form of corporate heartlessness threatens the soul of the nation.

Davis's bestselling novel, *Soldiers of Fortune* (1897), which, like his war correspondence, primed American readers for war with Spain, similarly casts commercialism as an obstacle to democratic liberation. However, rather than create a stark opposition between idealistic self-sacrifice and practical self-interest, *Soldiers of Fortune* carefully weaves these motivations together. The novel tells the story of Clay, an American civil engineer hired to run a US-owned iron mine currently under construction in Olancho, an imaginary South American nation beset by the twin threats of European monarchy and revolutionary instability. By the end of the novel, Clay has managed simultaneously to secure the interests of the US mining company and to restore Olanchan democracy by placing power the hands of Old General Rojas, the leader who, the Americans say, would be chosen as president by the Olanchans "if they were ever given a fair chance to vote for the man they want" (ch. 5). While the owner of the mine, a respectable but timid American capitalist, hesitates to interfere with Olanchan politics and promotes a policy of "non-interference," Clay learns to envision mining for iron and fighting for freedom as a two kinds of heroic global service. Joined by Hope, the capitalist's liberated daughter who, like Clay, casts off stifling bonds of tradition associated with mere money-making and respectable class status, Clay ends the novel looking forward to extending his service as civil engineer around the globe. Thus, far from promoting the humanitarian service of global liberation at the expense of "trusts" and "Wall Street," *Soldiers of Fortune* links democracy and economic development as compatible motives for a kind of beneficent US influence that did not require formal territorial possession.

We see a more exaggerated narrative reconciliation of profit and hemispheric democratization in the juvenile adventure tale *Under the Cuban Flag; or, the Cacique's Treasure* (1897), written by the naturalist and travel writer Frederick Albion Ober. While the US characters initially arrive in Cuba as part of enterprising money-making schemes (as treasure hunters and fruit merchant's sons), the search for a lost ancient Indian treasure causes them to fall in with Cuban revolutionaries, making the two campaigns (treasure hunting and freedom fighting) seem one and the same. The protagonists initially describe themselves in terms associated with US policies of isolationism: maintaining a "neutral attitude" and "keep[ing] clear of entangling alliances" (chs. 2, 9). But the Americans become so swept up in the Cuban cause that they vow to spend the fabulous treasure they unearth to fund future filibustering missions. This use of the treasure, which we learn was hidden from Spanish conquistadors in the days of Columbus, "at last avenge[s] the poor Indians of Cuba!" (ch. 30). Expelling Spain from the New World both frees up hidden resources (a topic that Ober would address more directly in his nonfictional *Puerto Rico and Its Resources*, rushed into press in 1898) and positions the United States as the executor to a hemispheric will for liberty.

Novelists like Davis and Ober used romance and adventure to rewrite national narratives of the US global mission for the twentieth century, instructing readers young and old in the new brand of neoliberalism that O. Henry would satirize a few years later in his composite novel *Cabbages and Kings* (1904). Set in an another imaginary South American country ("Anchuria") plagued by political corruption and instability, *Cabbages and Kings* consists of a series of interlinked short stories in which the US-owned Vesuvius Fruit Company aids a political revolution because the Anchurian government threatens its profits with a new tax on exported bananas. When a character naively protests that "a business firm does not go to war with a nation," a fruit company representative explains, "Oh, it is only a matter of business . . . and that is what moves the world of to-day" ("Rouge et Noir"). While Davis reassures readers that the United States could foster both democracy and economic development in its dealings with its southern neighbors, O. Henry's novel satirically mixes the languages of commerce and democratic revolution to show the reader a new, politically unstable (as in the "world-moving" Vesuvius), but perhaps inevitable state of affairs wherein democracy takes the back seat to informal commercial empire. Coining the now familiar phrase "banana republic" and ironically naming a US insurance company that benefits from Anchurian revolution the "Republic Insurance Company," O. Henry's pokes fun at the pretentions to democracy that thinly paper over commercial forces.

Constructing the meaning of the Spanish-American War as a return to true American identity often meant telling a story of national reunification, whether between workers and capitalists (as in Elbert Hubbard's frequently reprinted inspirational essay "A Message to Garcia" [1899]), or between regions. As Nina Silber explains in *Romance of Reunion*, patriotic rhetoric of the Spanish-American War stressed the reunion of North and South; once divided by the Civil War, northerners and southerners were seen as reconciling through international conquest. For example, Thomas Dixon depicts the outbreak of the Spanish-American War as a climactic moment for fusing white identity in his novel *The Leopard's Spots: A Romance of the White Man's Burden* (1902). As the narrator explains, the common purpose of world mission bound together fragmented factions of Americans: rich and poor, Catholic and Protestant, Northerner and Southerner. African Americans are significantly excluded from this nationalizing fusion: "Sectionalism and disunity had been the most terrible realities in our national history," Dixon writes, but "this hundred days of war had reunited the Anglo-Saxon race . . . and confirmed the Anglo-Saxon in his title to the primacy of racial sway" (bk. 3, ch. 9).

Not all stories of regional reconciliation followed Dixon in his baldly racist and imperialist agenda for projecting Southern white supremacy onto the global stage, but these stories tended to unite North and South at the expense of African Americans. For example, in John Fox's *Crittenden; A Kentucky Story of Love and War* (1900), the white Southern protagonist Clay Crittenden overcomes the lingering trauma of the Civil War through military service in Cuba, where despite the theme of racial unity, Clay and readers are assured of meek African American subservience and loyalty. Serving alongside Northerners and accompanied by his family's servant, the ex-slave "faithful Bob," Clay aspires to be "an American now, not a Southerner." Before going to Cuba, Clay felt repulsion at the sight of African American soldiers and feared a domestic race war, but fighting in Cuba inspires him with hope and tolerance. After his return he delivers a rousing speech explaining this transformation: the war "brought together every social element in our national life. . . . In the interest of humanity, it had freed twelve million people of an alien race and another land, and it had given us a better hope for the alien race in our own" (ch. 14). But this hope stems from the reassurance that in battle and at home, "alien" African Americans will reveal themselves to be loyal retainers in the tradition of the plantation novel, subservient to the white man's burden.

African Americans rejected such racist terms of national inclusion, but were divided on the question of whether to claim more equal participation in America's imperial mission or to affirm anticolonial unity with nonwhite peoples around the globe. The novelist Sutton Griggs explored this conflict in his three novels featuring the Spanish-American War: *Imperium in Imperio* (1899), *Unfettered* (1902), and *The Hindered Hand* (1905). For Griggs, the Spanish-American War marked a turn toward white supremacy in both domestic and foreign policies. Compelled "to force an unaccepted relation on an alien race" in the Philippines, white Americans were consequently more receptive to Jim Crow racism at home (1905, afterword). Charles Chesnutt identified a similar influence in *The Marrow of Tradition* (1901), his fictional retelling of the ascent of white supremacy in North Carolina. Chesnutt's narrator explains, "The nation was rushing forward with giant strides toward colossal wealth and world-domination, before the exigencies of which mere abstract ethical theories must not be permitted to stand. The same argument that justified the conquest of an inferior nation could not be denied to those who sought the suppression of an inferior race" (ch. 27).

Griggs explores the way this hostile environment divided African American loyalties in his novel *Imperium in Imperio*, which casts the Spanish-American War not as a catalyst for national unity, but as a crisis of national belonging for African Americans enduring the violence of the post-Reconstruction era South. The novel tells the story of the formation of an underground black nation, the Imperium, founded to protect African-American civil rights and foster racial unity. However, the outbreak of the Spanish-American War sparks a conflict within the group about its relationship with the US government. Some members want to fight with the United States on the side of Cuban liberty, especially since "Cubans were in a large measure Negroes," while others champion the more radical cause of seceding from the United States and forming a separate black nation (ch. 17). Neither side fully prevails, and the Imperium is divided by this crisis that represents, as Kaplan has argued, a "paralyzing and unresolved double allegiance" between race and nation (Kaplan 2002, 124).

A few black soldiers serving in the Philippines seemingly resolved the conflict of allegiance by deserting, a practice that Filipinos reportedly encouraged by creating placards affirming friendship between Filipinos and blacks and warning black soldiers that "white masters" want only "to make you the instruments of their ambition and also your hard work will soon make the extinction of your race" (qtd. in Gatewood 1975, 287). Other black soldiers affirmed more strongly their patriotic loyalty, which is the approach that Frank R. Steward seems to take in his short fiction about fighting in the Philippines. Steward published three short stories in the *Colored American Magazine* inspired by his service as a Captain US Volunteer Army during the Filipino-American War. Two of his stories share the same characters and the same subtitle, "A Tale of Laguna," suggesting that perhaps Steward had been planning a composite novel of linked local sketches. In the tales of Laguna, an unnamed and racially unidentified first person narrator allowed readers to imagine that race did not matter to the US soldier in the Philippines: black or white, the soldiers' task in the Philippines is to search out insurrectionists and explore the sexually charged potential of Americanizing a variety of seductive and repellant Filipina female characters. But arguably, even Steward's affirmative strategy breaks down in the context of divided African-American loyalties. When Steward employs the familiar trope of the tragic mulatta to characterize a mixed-race Filipina in "Starlik" (1902), he hints that racial hierarchy will prevent the benevolent assimilation of Filipinos, subtly reminding readers of parallels between racial divisions at home and abroad.

Fear of racial mixing in the Philippines was a major motivation for white anti-imperialists; with Thomas Dixon as a notable exception, Southern Democrats in the Jim Crow South largely opposed annexing the Philippines on the grounds that Filipinos were racially incapable of learning a democratic way of life and would, like African Americans, threaten white American purity by intimate proximity. This is the concern that Pauline Hopkins dismisses in her short story "Talma Gordon" (1900), which begins with a white character raising this threat in a discussion of US expansion. "Did you ever think," he asks, "that in spite of our prejudices against amalgamation, some of our descendents, indeed, many of them, will inevitably intermarry among these far-off tribes of dark-skinned people, if they become a part of this great Union?" The fear seems absurd in light of the rest of the story, which romanticizes unfairly stigmatized racial mixing among genteel blacks and whites in the domestic United States. On the other hand, fear of racial mixing is a concern animating Gertrude Atherton's anti-imperialist society novel *Senator North* (1901), which portrays the jingoistic call to war with Spain as a turn away from imagined American traditions of respectability and racial purity. The novel's protagonist, Betty Madison, a Washington, DC, socialite from an elite Kentucky family, experiences two crises that generate the novel's plot. In the first, Betty falls in love with a middle-aged senator from Maine whose name, Senator North, suggests the regional dynamics of reconciliation at work at work in their relationship. They meet in the spring of 1898 when war fever is mounting, and the Republican senator convinces Betty that cooler and more aristocratic heads must prevail against the young jingoes in Congress intent upon war. Betty attempts to aid Senator North in his lost cause against his own party by hosting political salons for measured discussion, all the while managing her secret love for the married Senator by high-mindedly waiting until his invalid wife dies before acting on their love.

This storyline strangely parallels Betty's second conflict. She learns that she has a half sister, Harriet Walker, born from her dead father's twenty-year-old-affair with an African American woman. At Senator North's prompting, Betty decides to take responsibility for Harriet, who looks white and whose tragic fate, the novel contends, is to belong nowhere. Betty helps Harriet to pass for white and introduces her to Washington society, but in doing so introduces her to Jack Emory, one of Betty's jilted suitors. Jack and Harriet fall in love, but when Harriet tells Jack about her ancestry, he kills himself, and then, wracked by guilt and grief, she commits suicide as well. Betty is left to ponder the tragedy she inadvertently created and has a realization that links the two plots: Nothing else but Harriet's death, Betty thinks, could have so clearly shown her the persistence of all acts: "It was this that made her hope more eager that the United States would be guided by its statesmen and not by hysteria, and it was this that made her think deeply and constantly upon her future relation with Senator North" (bk. 3, ch. 1). Betty links three illicit desires: the desire of white men for African American women, the "hysterical" desire of the United States to seek empire through war with Spain, and Betty's own sexual and romantic desire for a married man. Harriet's doom thus steels Betty's resolve to uphold ideals of chaste political and sexual restraint; she is determined to add no additional tragic victims born from the other passions she confronts: empire building and adultery. Like Steward and Hopkins, Atherton parallels race mixing in the Philippines with race mixing at home, but she uses that parallel to emphasize, like Thomas Dixon and John Fox, the alien intrusion of African Americans in a newly reunited North and South. Like Mark Twain, Atherton's anti-imperialist tactic represents war as a break with—rather than a return to—national tradition, but Atherton fears not joining the "European game" but descending into new extremes of liberal disorder and modern democratic leveling.

Many anti-imperialists echoed Atherton's opinion that unrefined tastes had demanded the war. They blamed, if not working class readers themselves, the forms of mass cultural reading that targeted them. In Raymond Bridgman's 1903 anti-imperialist novel *Loyal Traitors: A Story of Friendship for the Filipinos*, one character links American reading tastes with the United States war in the Philippines:

> Look in the bookshop windows. Note what are the most popular books. See what a rage there is now for "historical" novels. Enlarged drawings of the pictures are put in the windows; what do they set forth? Violence,—shootings, rapier-thrusts, fires, runaway horses, shipwrecks, assassinations, anything sensational in a grossly material way. . . . [T]he nation which has taste for such matters will in time show its character in actions. (ch. 1)

Here it is uncertain whether readers are guilty for their "gross" tastes, or bookstores and novelists of historical romances (the popular genre by British and American authors such as Marion Crawford, Charles Major and Anthony Hope) are guilty for pandering to them. However vaguely theorized, this often remarked upon relationship between popular reading and the war was an important early exploration of media, narrative, and US foreign policy at the dawn of the twentieth century. This convergence makes the Spanish-American War of particular interest to scholars interested in the power of narrative to shape mass consciousness and in the emergence of aesthetic theories accounting for this form of cultural power.

In the months leading up to the war, newspaper correspondents such as Davis and Bonsal employed the same melodramatic plots found in these bestselling romances to report on the Cuban conflict: aristocratic but brutish Spaniards assailed young Cuban maidens' purity only to be defeated by noble, heroic Americans. Through this narrative, US Americans could imagine declaring war as rushing to the rescue of a feminized Cuba. The story of Evangelina Cosio y Cisneros's imprisonment in a Spanish penal colony illustrates this powerful lens of melodrama and chivalric romance. A young woman from a wealthy Cuban family accused of aiding revolutionaries, Cisneros became in William Randolph Hearst's jingoistic *New York Journal* a heroine beset by Spanish villains. Sensational and lurid coverage speculated on the conditions of the penal colony, declaring that banishment there meant "dishonor first and death within a year" ("The Martyrdom of Evangelina Cisneros," 1897). Not content simply to stylize the story, Hearst staged its resolution as well: he hired a reporter to "rescue" Cisneros in an escape actually accomplished by bribing the guards. The staged rescue suggested a clear role for the United States. As Hearst's paper reported when she arrived in New York in late 1897: "We have freed one Cuban girl—when shall we free Cuba?" (qtd. in Hoganson 1998, 61; on Evangelina Cisneros as immigrant, see Chapter 13 in this volume). The famous—and possibly apocryphal—anecdote about the telegraph Hearst wrote to artist and war correspondent Frederick Remington ("You furnish the pictures, I'll furnish the war") suggests that some during this era possessed a high degree of self-consciousness about the press "wagging the dog" of state politics.

Julian Hawthorne, son of the famous American romancer, commented on the literary qualities of Cisneros's story in his introduction to her subsequently published autobiography, *The Story of Angelina Cisneros* (1897)—ghostwritten by Karl Decker. Noting that "the realist novelist" would eschew such material, Hawthorne claims that for the writer of romance,

> in its setting and background, in its *dramatis personae*, in its dash, intrigue, and cumulative interest, it is almost ideally perfect. The desirable component elements are all present. A tropic island, embosomed in azure seas off the coast of the Spanish Main; a cruel war, waged by the minions of despotism against the spirit of patriotism and liberty; a beautiful maiden, risking all for her country, captured, insulted, persecuted, and cast into a loathsome dungeon. None could be more innocent,

constant and adorable than she; none more wicked, detestable and craven than her
enemies. All is right and lovable on the one side, all ugly and hateful on the other.
As in the old Romances, there is no uncertainty as to which way our sympathies
should turn.

Lacking the ambiguity that literary critics have relished in Nathaniel Hawthorne's
romances, such romantic narrative conventions provided a clearly defined moral
role for Americans imagining their place in the world. Numerous fictional romances
about Cuba recycled these common generic elements, ranging from Wilson Gil-
let's lurid *Anita the Cuban Spy* (1898), to Isabella Witherspoon's sentimental *Rita
de Garthez: The Beautiful Reconcentrado* (1898), to Laura Elizabeth Howe Richards's
more chaste juvenile adventure *Rita* (1900), where the threat of rape is substituted
with the threat of life in a convent. From novels to newspapers and back again, melodramatic and chivalric narrative convention permeated not only the era's popular
novels but also the culture's most widely circulated accounts of international politics.
    Championing realism became, in this context, a response to romanticism's influ-
ence over the popular mind. Clarence Darrow's manifesto "Realism in Literature
and Art" (1893) identified war stories as tools for promoting state interests: "[The old-
time artists] painted war with long lines of soldiers dressed in new uniforms, looking
plump and gay. . . . One or two were dying but always in their comrades' arms and
listening for the shouts of victory that filled the air, and thinking of the righteous
cause that filled the air." Such material made it plain, Darrow writes, "which choice
a boy would make, and thus art served the state and king." Tolstoyan pacifist Ernest
Crosby satirized this kind of romantic mystification of war in *Captain Jinks, Hero*
(1902), in which the hapless title character goes to war with fond notions of glory for
himself and freedom for the "Cubapinos," a synthesis that allows no moral difference
between the two wars. All of the protagonist's subsequent experiences contradict
these patriotic ideals, such as when a war correspondent explains that the real reason
for the war was simply for newspaper syndicates to sell more subscriptions, but
Captain Jinks clings to his romantic ideals. The novel opens with the dawning of his
military passion: as a boy of five he opens a box of toy soldiers and becomes enam-
ored with one's white plume and colorful uniform; he keeps the lead figurine in his
pocket and calls it his "hero," "the talisman of his life and symbol of his ambitions,"
where it anchors his perceptions in the artificial world of childish fantasy (ch. 1).
    Of course, by writing satire, Crosby did not produce the kind of realist art that
Darrow and other critics, such as William Dean Howells and Hamlin Garland,
endorsed as romanticism's antidote. Satire was the most prevalent form for anti-
imperialist literature, as in the essays of Twain and Finley Peter Dunne, in George
Ade's serialized novel *Stories of Benevolent Assimilation* (1899), and in his musical
farce *The Sultan of Sulu* (1902). Both works mock the pretentions of Americans
intent on civilizing the Philippines; in the former, the significantly named Washington Conner eagerly explains his ill-considered mission to a polite and contented

family of Filipinos called the Kakyaks, who plainly want and need nothing America is offering in the name of progress or enlightenment. Perhaps a better answer to Darrow's call for more realistic accounts of war is found in the writing of Stephen Crane, both in his Civil War novel *The Red Badge of Courage* (1895), published before Crane became one of the most well-known correspondents in Cuba and Puerto Rico, and in his subsequent collection of war stories about the Cuban conflict, *Wounds in the Rain* (1900). While both works contain satiric elements, Crane conveys more ambivalence than consistent parody in his treatment of martial man making and heroism. Henry Fleming, the fallible protagonist of *The Red Badge of Courage*, may be vain and self-deluded in his maturation on the battlefield, but he is hardly the comic Don Quixote that Crosby provides in Captain Jinks.

Riding a similar line between glorifying and satirizing soldiers' accomplishments is *Wounds in the Rain*, Crane's last work (its dedication was written only a month before he died in June 1900 from tuberculosis). *Wounds in the Rain* contains nine fictional short stories (mostly reprinted from magazines and a few linked by shared characters), one of Crane's most dramatic newspaper reports, and an impressionistic memoir called "War Memories" that begins with the protomodernist assertion that representing the reality of war seems "impossible" because "war is neither magnificent nor squalid, it is simply life, and an expression of life can always evade us. We can never tell life, one to another, although sometimes we think we can." The volume's short stories attempt to convey this mixture of the squalid with the magnificent, with the result drawn between poles of satiric demystification and celebratory patriotism. The opening short story about the Battle of San Juan Hill, "The Price of the Harness," was originally titled "The Woof of Thin Red Lines" when it ran in *Cosmopolitan* in December 1898; the title change switches emphasis from the bonds among soldiers on the front to the costs they pay. The story clearly depicts the "price" of war when the four main characters, all privates, are wounded, suffering from fever, or dead at the end of the story. The new title also likens the soldiers to livestock in harness, an ambiguous image in light of the story's portrayal of horses. Horses in the story are far from dumb animals; the narrator pauses to praise equine virtue in a manner that resonates with the popular affirmation of service and chivalry: "the battery horses turned at the noise of tramping feet and surveyed the men with eyes deep as wells, serene, mournful. Generous eyes, lit heart-breakingly with something that was akin to a philosophy, a religion of self sacrifice—oh, gallant, gallant horses!" And yet, when a horse is later pitilessly dragged off the road where its death throes will not disturb passing soldiers, this "sacrifice" seems more gruesome than gallant. Similarly, when in the final scene two surviving soldiers reunite in a camp hospital and learn of the final fate of their comrades, the sense of patriotic honor through self-sacrifice is partially undercut by anti-sentimental and dark humor. A fellow sufferer "was wringing from the situation a grim meaning" by singing "The Star Spangled Banner" with "all the ardor that could be procured from his fever-stricken body." His fevered singing is a positive attribute—the narrator comments that the man was of a kind "always found in an American crowd, a heroic, implacable comedian and patriot, of a humor that has bitterness and ferocity and love in it." Yet it is also an ironic commentary on the difference between patriotic symbolism and the brutality of war. Crane conveys this sense of ambivalence throughout *Wounds in the Rain*, highlighting the difference between war's "grim meanings" and imagined ideals while still employing notions of gallantry and man making on the field of battle.

Also attempting a realist literature about war was William Dean Howells, who tried to eschew completely the narrative of heroic sacrifice in his anti-imperialist short story "Editha" (1904). His reluctant volunteer soldier, George Gearson, is summarily killed in Cuba in one flat sentence, placing the emphasis not on the scene of war but on the meanings assigned to his senseless death by his romantic-minded fiancée. Editha, who pushed Ralph to enlist by "parroting the current phrases of the newspapers" and insisting that he be a "hero, *her* hero," even looks to a romantic script after his death. As a widow, she "had the fever that she expected of herself" and refuses to rethink her ideal of military sacrifice even when confronted by the raw grief of George's mother, who plainly pins on Editha the blame for George's death. Yet Howells makes his censure of romanticism so clear (the story ends with Editha having her sketch drawn by an artist as willing to apply painterly "effects" to Editha's likeness as Editha is to apply the lens of romance to raw suffering) that the line between Howells's realism and Crosby's satire in *Captain Jinks, Hero* becomes blurred. Editha resembles Jinks's fiancée, Marian, a one-dimensional character who greets the news of his enlisting with effusive hope for his death: "I'd be in the first carriage, and the flag would be draped, and the band would play the funeral march. Oh, dear! how grand it would be, and how all the girls would envy me!" (Crosby, ch. 3). The fact that Howells employed a cardboard grasshopper—his own phrase for artificial literary types—suggests a problem that would linger through the twentieth century: how to represent the "reality" of war without glamorizing, sentimentalizing, or satirizing it.

Interestingly, the gender dynamics in Howells's story are precisely the opposite of those identified by Kristin Hoganson in her study of turn-of-the-century wars of American imperialism. Hoganson explains that during this period white men sought to reclaim social power from women who were elbowing their way into politics on the platform of moral authority against war. This gendering perhaps indicates Howells's awareness that women also claimed stakes in the new strenuous US foreign policy, but it simultaneously creates a narrative in which romance is feminized and "remasculinizing" means resisting the lure of feminized mass culture. Indeed, Howells had long associated romance with the feminine and realism with the masculine. Bridgman's account of the pernicious romances in the bookstore window shares this gendering; his character notes that it is primarily women who read such books, and who have "a great political influence, even if it is indirect" (ch. 1). Women today, claims this character (herself a girl named Faith, willing to stem the tide), lack wholly the feminine "tenderness" of earlier generations that once made them moral authorities against bloody warfare. Apparently for Bridgman, getting back to more domestic models of femininity and reading might cool the fires of war. Rather than the chivalric script in which men prove themselves men by going to war, anti-imperialists Howells and Bridgman implied that women, by refusing tender womanliness, had cast the nation into battle.

A female novelist who fits this profile of the outdated, "tender" female arbitrationist is Elizabeth Stuart Phelps, although her writing about war alters the gendered narrative that Howells and Bridgman employ. According to Carol Farley Kessler, Phelps wrote newspaper essays with titles such as "There Should Be No War" during the 1890s, and she adamantly opposed the war with Spain, a position articulated in gendered terms in her domestic novel *Though Life Us Do Part* (1908), which was first serialized in the *Woman's Home Companion* in 1907 before publication in book form. The novel, Phelps's last before her death in 1911, tells the story of the failure and rebuilding of a marriage. Dr. Chance Dane turns to alcohol and adultery before essentially deserting his wife by enlisting in the Spanish-American War, a choice rendered as a cowardly refusal to confront his marital problems. Phelps thus figures Hofstadter's "psychic crisis" in which war seems the solution to domestic discord, but she emphatically refuses Dane the resolution that other troubled male characters such as Fox's Crittenden or Woods's Major Cartwright achieve in battle. Dane's wife Carolyn takes his being killed as a matter of course: "From the first she had no delusions as to the outcome for herself of this latest and saddest of our national errors. . . . Women, who are the worst victims of war, whichever way we look at it, rapidly acquire its terrible lessons; and Carolyn in six weeks came to feel that she had been widowed sixty years by the blunders and brutalities of the governing sex" (ch. 11). Phelps's solution is to correct the "governing" sex, who are too slow in learning the lessons of war, not to blame women for falling from the domestic pedestal.

Phelps's novel could hardly be called realism. Through a preposterous series of events, Carolyn discovers that her husband has not died, that the body mistakenly buried under his name was his brother's, and that, most surprisingly, her husband—physically transformed from grief and regret—is the boarder who washed up on shore Odysseus-like a year later and lived with her for months under an assumed name before she realized his identity. And yet Phelps's novel conveys the experience of war for those who remained at home, distanced geographically and politically from the war, making it a contending force in the literary representation of war. Describing the glorious spring weather that accompanied the war in Cuba, her narrator remarks:

> The fields of New England—were they ever so fair? . . . . It was as if the spirit of peace, terrified and trampled, had fled to the sanctuaries of Nature for protection. On the hills a glory gathered. They interchanged signs solemnly: "There is no slaughter and no heartbreak. Who suffers? We enjoy. Who trembles? We stand. Who calls it War? We call it May." (ch. 11)

The beauty of a personified Nature on the untouched homefront belies the ugliness unseen but known by women. As with Phelps's earlier *Gates Ajar* series, written in the wake of her brother's death in the Civil War, finding meaning in women's experience of warfare requires a literary strategy attuned to the seen and the unseen.

In a November 1896 exchange with Howells in *McClure's Magazine*, Phelps agreed that the artist's purpose was "to tell the truth about the world he lives in," but insisted that her morally charged narratives, romantic plots, and idealized characters indeed reflected her vision of humanity. Reading the mostly forgotten Spanish-American War novels, one frequently finds such divergent claims to "realism," suggesting that the war itself became a contested terrain for claims to truthful representation on the eve of the century that would ultimately question any such authorial power. Throughout the twentieth century, experimental narratives by writers ranging from Ernest Hemingway to Tim O'Brien returned to the modernist problem of representing violence. While writers about the Spanish-American War maintained faith in the possibility of accurate representation, their multiple claims to truth and authority surrounding the war set the stage for these later, more philosophical inquiries.

One key question for debate was who had access to the reality of warfare in a conflict surrounded by layers of media representation. Soldiers who served in Cuba and the Philippines published numerous novels and short story collections, and their title pages often underscore the writer's firsthand knowledge by listing his rank, as in *Bamboo Tales* (1900) by Ira L. Reeves, 1st Liet. 4th Infantry, or Brigadier General Charles King's *Found in the Philippines: A Story of a Woman's Letters* (1899); *Ray's Daughter: A Story of Manila* (1900), and *Comrades in Arms: A Tale of Two Hemispheres* (1904). (Prolific juvenile author Edward Stratemeyer seized this strategy by publishing his numerous Spanish-American War novels under the pen name Captain Ralph Bonehill.) Popular adventure writer Will Levington Comfort launched his career with a book of stories based on his service in Cuba called *Trooper Tales: A Series of Sketches of the Real American Private Soldier* (1899); he boasts of their authenticity in his preface, claiming that even war correspondents and military officers cannot offer as much reality as the enlisted man, whose stories are "spattered with the mud of Puerto Rican hills, and are dark brown from the grisly pressure of Cuban sunshine." The characters in Israel Putnam's *Daniel Everton, Volunteer-Regular: A Romance of the Philippines* (1902) dismiss the limited knowledge held by their countrymen stateside—especially when it comes in the form of female temperance activists, Christian Scientists, and Red Cross workers meddling in a political and geographical context they don't know firsthand. These criticisms aim to discredit noncombatants such as Phelps, but they also point to the complexity of colonial intimacies; in *Daniel Everton*, new recruits arrive in the Philippines expecting to find a savage jungle and are surprised to discover an intriguing social scene of genteel Filipino landowners.

This claim to authentic knowledge of the Philippines is taken one step further in *Sarjint Larry an' Frinds* (1906) by Chauncey M'Govern, a former US Army volunteer who founded the Escolta Press in Manila. The preface (titled "Excuse") asks the reader to pardon deficiencies caused not only by the book's composition under the rough conditions of soldier camps and garrisons, but also by the fact that all the labor of setting type, proofing, and printing was performed by Filipinos, who nevertheless did their work so well that "the average American Guthenberger could not do better typographically with such limited facilities." *Sarjint Larry's* interlinked stories are generally sympathetic to Filipino nationalism, and although the Filipino printers did not write them, they do offer a more searching portrayal of the Philippines than the work of anti-imperialist satirists such as Ade or Crosby, whose comic depictions of Cubapinos and Kakyaks pointedly make no effort to engage cultural difference.

These renderings of cultural contact zones serve as reminders about the pervasively one-sided approach this essay has taken to the topic of the Spanish-American War novel. How did Filipinos or Cubans or Spaniards view the conflict, and should a discussion of the Spanish-American War novel comprise multilingual and multinational traditions? Perhaps, but seriously engaging with Cuban, Puerto Rican, Filipino, or Spanish literature underscores the different chronologies of the nationalist and colonial/postcolonial movements that converged in this state conflict. The year 1898 mattered greatly to US Americans contesting their own national narratives and identity, but not so much to Cubans and Filipinos for whom that year's events were part of larger, ongoing and multipolar struggles for sovereignty. These multiple histories are out of synch with the sense of abrupt historical crisis that, genuine or not, marked the experience the Spanish-American War for US Americans.

13

THE IMMIGRANT NOVEL

BY JOSHUA L. MILLER

In *The Rise of David Levinsky*, Abraham Cahan begins the narrative in the voice of its immigrant protagonist marking a radical divergence between spiritual and material developments in his life. After noting the "miracle" of his transformation from an impoverished Russian Jewish childhood into a millionaire New York manufacturer, he continues,

> And yet when I take a look at my inner identity it impresses me as being precisely the same as it was thirty or forty years ago. My present station, power, the amount of worldly happiness at my command, and the rest of it, seem to be devoid of significance (ch. 1).

Much of Cahan's melancholic portrait of immigrant commercial success-as-failure resonates with the literary and national narrative structures that preceded his novel—stories of economic uplift, self-making, immigrant displacement, cultural and religious assimilation, and so on—but what distinguishes his work is his artful revision of familiar conventions. In splicing together the American self-made individualist figure with a diasporic Jewish representative of disconsolate ambivalence for whom wealth accompanies a radical split from ethnic history and identity, Cahan draws upon both US and Jewish literary and aesthetic traditions, commenting on each from the vantage point of Levinsky's shifting perspective.

Cahan could engage in this project of revision because he knew how familiar twentieth-century readers had become with narrative structures, themes, and techniques in novels by and about immigrants written during the nineteenth and early twentieth centuries. As a subject of ongoing popular and scholarly interest, the "immigrant novel" has been understood as a tale of arrival to a New World, which includes trials of belief in the self and the new nation, optimism and obstacles, economic and social acceptance, and conclusions of disillusioned Americanism. Public views of immigrants were strongly informed by sociological assessments and emphases on particular immigrant groups, which contributed to ideas that certain patterns of social group assimilation were typical of immigrant narratives generally.

However, the archive of US immigrant novels written between 1870 and 1940 makes evident that fewer novels than we might expect conform to these conventions, and assumptions of uniformity—as Horatio Alger stories, as novels of proletarian striving, as representations of masculinity and femininity, as diasporic resettlement, even as stories of arrival—efface much of what distinguishes them within the history of the US novel.

In representing the lives of displaced characters and their communities who have to contend with official and informal policies of exclusion and inclusion, stigmatization, enforced acculturation, and whiteness, these works are often attuned to the tensions of citizenship policies and practices. Such portraits of ambivalent relationships to US nationalism suggest that we cannot refer to a single politics of immigrant novels, which articulate celebratory, accusatory, documentarist, and ironized declarations of belief in the nation. Many, if not all, of these modes could occur within the same novel, which may convey shock at unchanging structures of economic inequality and brutal violence in one scene and heartwarming paeans to American acceptance in another. Interwoven registers of seemingly inconsistent perspectives on the nation are present in a wide range of novelistic representations of immigrants' conflicted and contradictory beliefs in and experiences of the United States.

As examples of such multivalent perspectives, one might consider Lee Yan Phou writing in the years following the Chinese Exclusion Acts, Anzia Yezierska portraying patriarchial constraints during and after First World War-era nativism, or Michael I. Pupin commenting on the 1924 Johnson-Reed Act in his Pulitzer-prize winning autobiography, *From Immigrant to Inventor*. Each of these books, explicitly or obliquely, comments on the contemporary national scene through the viewpoint of recent arrivals. Not all or even most immigrant novels pursued political or social critique, but they frequently developed narrative innovations by portraying social histories of collective marginalization to the extent that even seemingly simple articulations of Americanism are suffused with productive forms of internal ambivalence, contradiction, and strategic silence.

Another feature common to most immigrant novels is that they heighten the qualities of mixture that theorists of the novel have long described as fundamental to the genre. As works straddling at least two national traditions, they innovate through overt translation and recombination of features from diverse sources. Within US conventional and experimental literary histories alone, immigrant novels appropriate a wide range of narrative structures and archetypes, including conversion and captivity narratives, folklore, Benjamin Franklin's self-made man (frugal, pragmatic, self-interested), vernacular tales, Westerns, Theodore Rooseveltian rugged individualism, autobiography, and many others. In this way, immigrant novels borrow from and adapt prior traditions in order to depict stories of transnational displacement and anticlimactic arrival. In addition to drawing on US intertexts, diasporic narratives through appropriated and translated European, Asian, Latin American, and African cultural forms is a common feature of immigrant novels.

Cahan's *Rise of David Levinsky* exemplifies this intertextual model of immigrant writing, as his title explicitly nods at William Dean Howells's *Rise of Silas Lapham*, while his narrative appropriates and revises themes and techniques of social realist labor novels, vernacular stories, and prominent autobiographies, such as Benjamin Franklin's, among others. Moreover, aside from US literary genres, Cahan also draws upon conventions in Yiddish and European literatures, including proletarian poetry, urban novels, the *Bildungsroman*, and narratives of corruption and decline. The immigrant novel was never a homogenous form, and its textual pluralism became particularly evident during this crucial period of demographic change.

The Demands of Acculturation in the Age of Expansion

When considering the historical transformations that took shape between 1870 and 1940, one structuring paradox is that powerful new nationalisms emerged simultaneous to the rise of new policies of racialization, exclusion, and citizenship restriction. In response to sanctioned and informal modes of anti-immigrant violence and stigmatization, many groups established civic organizations. The rise of immigrant institutions led to increased prominence of civic leaders within emergent ethnic cultures. Consequently, many nineteenth-century immigrant novels were written by, and sometimes to, elite members of these new diasporic communities.

Immigrant novels participated in the trends of US literary movements, such as realism and naturalism, while drawing upon the particular artistic, linguistic, and historical influences of their prior national traditions. Novels of European immigrants depicted nineteenth-century Westward expansion, new transportation technologies, and communities formed by native and foreign-born Americans. German-American novelists, some of whom were published in German, examined the processes and politics of acculturation, as in the works of Willibald Winckler, Nathan Meyer, Hugo Fürst, and Kathinka Sutro-Schücking. German-American authors who portrayed immigrants in multiethnic US environments include Georg Willrich's *Erinnerungen aus Texas* (1854) and Mathilde Franziska Anneke's *Uhland in Texas* (1866), both of which present German immigrants overturning slavery through alliances with African Americans in Texas; Adolph Douai's *Fata Morgana* (1858), representing a politically progressive German community in rural Mexico; and Rudolph Leonhart's *The Treasure of Montezuma* (1888), a further fictional extrapolation of German immigration to Mexico to establish a transracial community.

Early Irish-American novels similarly engaged the social and material challenges facing new immigrant groups. Emigration from Ireland grew substantially following the late 1840s famine. With the arrival of a new generation of Irish immigrants, the rise of the nativist and xenophobic "Know-Nothing" political movement, and limited options for work, the satiric and humorous topics of earlier Irish American literature were replaced by more overtly political and didactic themes in late nineteenth century novels. Such works included Peter McCorry's *The Irish Widow's Son, or The Pikemen of '98* (1869) and *Mount Benedict, or The Violated Tomb* (1871), which considers anti-Catholic mob violence, and David Power Conyngham's *The O'Donnells of Glen Cottage* (1874), which depicts an Irish family facing starvation, emigrating, and returning to Ireland. More than half of post-famine Irish-American immigrants were female, a trend reflected in McCorry's *The Lost Rosary; or, Our Irish Girls, Their Trials, Temptations, and Triumphs* (1870), John McElgun's *Annie Reilly, or The Fortunes of an Irish Girl in New York* (1873), and Bernard O'Reilly's *The Two Brides* (1879).

Although formally conventional in most cases, these novels draw on themes and techniques from widely varying sources—theological manuals, historical novels, Westerns, utopian fiction—and innovation emerges in the combinations of European and North American materials. Moreover, the plot structure that would become familiar in later immigrant novels was fully present in these works, including a departure from an oppressive life in the home country, a difficult sea crossing, an arrival marked by stigma and cruelty, ethical trials that distinguish the industrious from the miscreant, and a conclusion of moderately prosperous survival.

One of the most prolific of late nineteenth-century immigrant authors, Norwegian American Hjalmar Hjorth Boyesen, taught Greek and Latin before taking professorships in German at Cornell and Columbia Universities and publishing novels about Norwegian immigrants, the passage from Norway to the United States, and vice versa. He published twenty-five works of fiction, criticism, and poetry, including the novels *Gunnar* (1874), *A Norseman's Pilgrimage* (1875), *Tales from Two Hemispheres* (1876), *Falconberg* (1879), *Vagabond Tales* (1889), and *The Social Strugglers* (1893), which was dedicated to William Dean Howells, a recurring figure in immigrant writers' careers. Boyesen registered ambivalence regarding Americanness throughout his fiction, which frequently depicted conflicts between the desire to return to Norway and the magnetic pull of cosmopolitan European and American cities.

Chinese Americans in the nineteenth century were primarily male, as mandated by the 1875 Page Law, the 1880 revision to the Burlingame treaty, and the 1882 Exclusion Act that deemed Asians inassimilable and denied them the option of citizenship. The earliest English-language Asian American narratives were autobiographies marketed to white readers, including young adults and children. Publishers sought to capitalize on the exoticizing curiosity regarding new immigrant groups and, as a gesture of liberal humanist universalism, commissioned authors to narrate their childhoods and introduce global cultural traditions to Anglo readers. One such auto-ethnography, Yan Phou Lee's *When I Was a Boy in China* (1887), has been called the earliest Asian American novel, and critics have read it as navigating complex and competing demands of class, race, language, and nationality. Written from an elite position, Yan Phou Lee's book reflects what Elaine Kim has described as the "ambassadors of goodwill" aims of many Exclusion-era Asian American works, presenting

appealing, if mildly critical, visions of modern China and sympathetic portraits of
Chinese American immigrants (1994, 24).

Lee's formal mixture of autobiography, collective history, and ethnographic
explication is evident throughout the work in narrative shifts between first- and
third-person and descriptions of Chinese daily life. One such passage begins,
"Babyhood is the most enjoyable stage in the life of an Oriental. It is the only period
when his wishes are regarded and when demonstrations of affection are shown him"
(ch. 2). In what he presents as an objective account of Chinese domestic life and
hierarchies of familial and societal authority, Lee confirms a dichotomy that white
American readers may have presumed, that Chinese social structures emphasize a
"strict subjugation" that negates "freedom of action" during phases of childhood
development. However, narratorial shifts between third- and first-person disrupt
the veneer of detachment and disinterested observation. These shifts complicate
the position of the protagonist, who distinguishes himself from "the Chinese," as
when he follows a reflection on his own childhood—"often have I rued my impru-
dence in contradicting my parents, uncles or teachers"—with a generalization, "the
Chinese deem this method absolutely necessary for the preservation of authority"
(ch. 2). Such narratorial instabilities may strengthen or undermine stereotypical
views of Chinese-American immigrants, depending on the reader, but as a genre-
mixing formal strategy in the history of immigrant novels, it holds a crucial place
of innovation.

Chinese-American immigrant narratives published in the early twentieth century,
as Xiao-huang Yin points out, appropriated literary conventions to shape new narrative forms, for example, by producing autobiographies written with an awareness
of a Chinese literary tradition in which such works were "virtually unknown" (2000,
55). Auto-ethnographies tended to be constrained from directly engaging the dehumanizing daily oppression and violence that Asian immigrants faced in their daily
lives, so they were limited in tone and theme to optimistic and popularizing treatments. Finding ways to address painful realities within a constrained genre became
a productive textual challenge. In *When I Was a Boy in China*, Lee identifies "false
ideas" of China and Chinese Americans and counters such misapprehensions by
developing a culturally hybrid narratorial point-of-view, one that is simultaneously
Chinese and American (ch. 5). Moreover, the effacement of individuality that led
some of these and other immigrant authors to describe their own lives as "typical"
found echoes in later twentieth-century Asian American novels, such as those of
Carlos Bulosan and Maxine Hong Kingston, that controversially blurred textual
boundaries among individual memoir, collective history, and fiction.

Yan Phou Lee's book was the first in a twenty-one volume series illustrated "from
photographs" that its publisher marketed as the "Children of Other Lands Books"
through the 1920s, including Marietta Ambosi's *When I Was a Girl in Italy* (1892),
Sakae Shioya's *When I Was a Boy in Japan* (1906), Mousa J. Kaleel's *When I Was a Boy
in Palestine* (1914), Mercedes Godoy's *When I Was a Girl in Mexico* (1919), and New

Il-Han's *When I Was a Boy in Korea* (1928). Further reinforcing the ethnographic quality of these works, aside from an authorial portrait, each work contains interspersed photographs taken not from the life narrated, but generic images depicting cultural practices or sites referenced in the chapters. Much could be said about both strategic sophistication and simplification in these memoirs, but many conclude before or just after the protagonist departs for the United States, which suggests that they might be considered protoimmigrant narratives. Features they share with later works include an emphasis on rendering immigrant experience retrospectively through child's-eye-views, combinations of multiple modes of existing narrative forms, and attentive engagements to national sentiments.

Auto-ethnographies were not the only kind of works at this time that presented immigrant groups in a positive, if paternalistic, light. Immigrant novels were also written by authors who did not belong to the group they depicted, many of which drew on vernacularist techniques characteristic of the Gilded Age: literary realism, blackface and yellowface minstrelsy performance, and popular dialect literatures, such as Finley Peter Dunne's *Mr. Dooley* books and Montague Glass's *Potash and Perlmutter* stories. The relations among the rise of ethnography, literary realism, performance cultures, and discourses of ethnicity and race have been described by scholars such as Michael Elliott and Gavin Jones as infusing turn-of-the-century novels with tensions between ordering and disordering tendencies. Greek-American writing goes back at least as early as an 1851 memoir by Christopher Castanis, *The Greek Exile*, but one of the first novels centering on a Greek immigrant protagonist was penned by a non-Greek author, Jennette Barbour Perry Lee's *Mr. Achilles* (1912). Other immigrant novels were published under the assumption of insider knowledge, an appearance that turned out to be misleading. Writing under the pen name of Sidney Luska, Henry Harland claimed to be a Russian-born Jew though he was actually a New York Protestant, while publishing several novels about urban Jewish immigrants in the late 1880s.

As the immigration influx increased, incorporation anxieties rose as well, not merely among native-born Americans, but also among community leaders of ethnic groups who feared the effects of intermarriage and assimilation. Novelists explored these concerns from varied perspectives. Born in San Francisco to Alsatian Jewish immigrant parents and severely disabled by polio, Emma Wolf wrote her best-known novel, *Other Things Being Equal* (1892), at the age of twenty-seven. It was reprinted six times in less than a decade and revised for publication in 1916. A bourgeois, largely immobilized, unmarried advocate of both cultural Jewishness and interfaith marriage, Wolf's work celebrates intercultural exogamy, depicting love between Unitarian Dr. Herbert Kemp and "Jewess" Ruth Levice to validate both ethnic belonging and interethnic understanding among individuals of the same social class. Her novel *Heirs of Yesterday* (1900) and some of her later stories published in the literary magazine *The Smart Set* similarly consider how Jewishness is assimilated within the American scene. Though highly varied, immigrant novels that appeared during these decades share efforts to narrate ethnic difference and diasporic liminality. Their artistically innovative representations of characters who simultaneously experience national inclusion and exclusion both reflected and contributed to literary movements of realism and modernism.

Border In/Securities: Urbanism, Infection, and Social Reform

In a period dominated by incorporative movement inward and expansionary energies directed globally, historians have described the ethnoracial conflicts and fantasies underlying the purportedly origins-blind universalist Americanisms posited by political figures such as Theodore Roosevelt, industrialists such as Henry Ford, and writers such as Israel Zangwill in his play *The Melting-Pot* (1908). Though the views of these and their contemporaries diverged on citizenship and naturalization policies, their writings discuss the subjects of melting pots, literacy tests, public health inspections, language instruction, family structure, heteronormative masculinity, and hyphenated identities. In such programs and policies, these years witnessed some of the most visceral and explicit organized violence and exclusionary federal policies establishing what Rogers Smith has described as "ascriptive" hierarchies of citizenship to various racial and ethnic groups (1997, 347–409). Many authors documented such tensions, as James Oppenheim did in *Dr. Rast* (1909) and *Wild Oats* (1910), representing desperate health conditions of Lower East Side immigrants through the perspective of a German Jewish doctor. "We are slowly but surely awakening," writes Edward Bok in his Forward to the latter novel, "to a realizing sense that somewhere in the social body there is a festering sore that needs the surgery and cleansing process of the light of public discussion."

Politically radical unionist and socialist immigrant novels responded to anti-immigrant sentiments within nationalist movements. Journalist Edward King wrote travel narratives and novels, the last of which, *Joseph Zalmonah* (1893), centers on Jewish immigrants. King's novel anticipates muckraking social realism and the proletarian fiction of later immigrant novelists in its heroic dramatization of what a reviewer for *The Critic* called "the hottest . . . social question" of the day, "the condition of the Russian-Hebrew refugees in the 'sweating shops' of the East Side of New York City" ("*The Socialist*" 1893, 133).

Progressive-era novelists responded broadly to the discourse of immigrants as endangering social welfare by composing narratives that reversed the accusation. Instead of immigrants' presence harming native-born Americans, these works argued forcefully that US cities were harmful to vulnerable immigrants. They brought the lenses of social reform, documentary reportage, and anthropological empiricism to portray multiethnic urbanisms in New York, Boston, and Chicago. In addition to *How the Other Half Lives* (1890), the social reforming journalist Jacob Riis wrote several other books that drew upon elements of immigrant novel themes and techniques, including *Out of Mulberry Street* (1898), his autobiography *The Making of an American* (1901), and *Children of the Tenements* (1903). Riis's close relationship with Theodore Roosevelt in New York demonstrates the inclusion/exclusion dialectic so central to the era. Roosevelt's enthusiastic endorsement of other immigrant novelists' works cultivated public sympathy while maintaining and reinforcing boundaries of social distance and identitarian difference.

While the most famous example of this dynamic was Roosevelt's advocacy of Israel Zangwill's play, *The Melting Pot*, another telling instance was Dublin-born teacher and author Myra Kelly's popular novels portraying an Irish-American teacher in New York's Lower East Side schools populated primarily by "Hebrew youth." President Roosevelt wrote a July 26, 1905 letter of appreciation noting that as New York police commissioner he had been "immensely impressed" by the "good many Miss Baileys" teaching at a Houston Street public school and that what he saw "was very much like what your Miss Bailey has done" (qtd. in Heydrick 1920, 38). In works such as *Little Citizens* (1904), *Wards of Liberty* (1907), *Little Aliens* (1910), the narratorial perspective is a young, earnest female teacher, Constance Bailey, whose class is composed primarily of immigrant Jewish children with limited facility in English living in what an editor called "the most densely populated square mile on earth" (20).

In documenting complex interethnic classroom relations emerging within refashioned urban school systems, Kelly focuses attention on the compromised position of teachers, and, by association, the competitive positions of white ethnic groups in varied states of assimilation. The phonetically exaggerated vernacular draws upon the popular dialect literatures of the day, but what is most notable is Kelly's portrait of pedagogical difficulties in turn-of-the-century urban US schools. The noble teacher falls prey to both the ceaseless influx of new immigrants and a disciplinary school system that oversees teachers and seeks to professionalize superintendents into Progressive "new managers" by prioritizing empiricist teaching methodologies, efficiency, surveillance, and harsh punishments for departing from the corporate structure. Myra Kelly's stories anticipate the role of educational institutions in the governmental and industrial Americanization programs that took off during the second decade of the twentieth century. Exclusivist policies codified as citizenship restrictions in the 1906 naturalization act, state literacy tests, the 1917 immigration act, the first state language laws, and the 1921 and 1924 immigration acts centralized the instructional component of citizenship as "training."

Efforts to institutionalize naturalization processes and to associate US citizenship with the virtues of forgetting immigrant histories and languages in exchange for putatively American values of pluck, thrift, industry, pragmatism, and gumption run throughout the literature of the early decades of the twentieth century. As stories of struggle and survival told to engage a broader reading public sympathetically, many tenement stories were designed to soothe native-born Americans' fears of "greenhorns" bringing deadly infections, anarchist or antidemocratic politics, or loyalties to other countries. Immigrant novels were and remain subject to criticism that they overemphasize suffering to the point of depersonalizing a fuller range of experiences, allegorize individuals to present a social group as worthy of (patronizing, liberal, distancing) sympathy, and vernacularize dialogue to caricature and stigmatize rather than to accurately represent speech forms, among others. In adapting to the belief structures of Americanization and reflecting genuine desires to become citizens, novelists developed innovative literary techniques of appropriation, masking, vernacularization, perspectivalism, and narration.

Dilemmas of Inclusion: Translation, Masculinity, and Immigrant Interiorities

In his autobiographical narrative, *The Soul of an Immigrant* (1921), Constantine Panunzio relates the passage to the America of an incidental immigrant. Rather than presenting himself as desiring to live as an American, Panunzio's account is of a young shipworker who escapes an oppressive captain and finds himself alone and impoverished in Boston: "of immigration laws I had not even a knowledge of their existence; of the English language I knew not a word; of friends I had none in Boston or elsewhere in America . . . I had exactly fifty cents remaining out of a dollar which the captain had finally seen fit to give me."

Rather than an idealized arrival in America, Panunzio depicts one that is terrifying and traumatizing, but that also yields a political sensibility, "Those first five days in America have left an impression upon my mind which can never be erased with the years, and which gives me a most profound sense of sympathy for immigrants as they arrive" (ch. 4). Panunzio claims to document a "typical" immigrant's perspective, by which he means one who did not amass great financial wealth (unlike Pulitzer Prize winning immigrant autobiographers Edward Bok in 1921 and Michael I. Pupin in 1924), and he wrote on behalf of the mass of immigrants in the aftermath of wartime nativist attacks on "new Americans." Each of these narratives portrays an individual willfully crafting an American self, frequently presented in sentimental terms of devotion to the new land, as in Panunzio's concluding lines, "I love Thee, America, with manhood's strong love . . . I am of Thee; Thou art mine; upon Thy sacred soil shall I live; there I fain would die,—*an American.*" But such impassioned declarations of devotion convey different meanings within the various works in which they appear, as Panunzio has just noted that no matter how fervently he dedicates himself to Americanism, he is still rejected as a "foreigner," and he retains a "mystic" feeling of belonging to his "native land," Italy (ch. 20).

Many immigrant novelists sought to counter spurious accusations of ethnic otherness and treasonous binationalism by presenting immigrants as idealized or sympathetic new Americans who embodied national values more so even than native-born Americans themselves. Horatio Alger Jr.'s moralizing "boys stories" of earnest toil rewarded by mysterious aid and good fortune offered one narrative construct for national mythologies of uplift and class mobility as self-made men (and the vast majority were men). Immigrant authors such as Abraham Cahan drew upon the Alger narrative frame, but recast its upward trajectory as a Faustian bargain that entailed spiritual loss. In many immigrant novels, then, plots follow the logic of cutting cords from a collective past to strike a new path alone, conjoined with guilt and sorrow at the loss of meaningful history and group belonging (religious belief, familial relations, communitarian ideals) in exchange for material success that feels empty and a new identity that feels artificial and contrived. The protagonists of many works are complex, internally divided, refashioned selves alienated from both their past lives and the futurity of their children and descendants.

US nationalist rhetorics of voluntaristic inclusion carried an injunction to embrace a consensual amnesia in which individual pasts are shed in order to join the collectivity of US modernity. A melancholic structure of disavowed loss that remains unmourned appears within many early twentieth-century immigrant novels. Forgotten pasts provided a source for artistic innovation as experimental narrative representations of diasporic subjects' status, roles, and emotional lives. Novelists' portraits of immigrant interiorities as divided consciousness echoed William James's conception of stream-of-consciousness, Sigmund Freud's of the unconscious, and W. E. B. Du Bois's of double consciousness.

Gertrude Stein's early work, the posthumously published *Q.E.D.* (c.1903), *Three Lives* (1907), and *The Making of Americans* (1925), included techniques of linguistic reiteration, flat character types, and asymmetrical translation as aesthetic abstraction to render the isolation of immigrant, African American, and queer women's experiences. Her discomfortingly nonmimetic vernacular writing evokes interethnic identification, since, as contemporaries noted with annoyance, the narrative idioms representing her characters' speech forms and interior mindscapes are not recognizably distinctive as African American, Jewish, or German. Instead, the German-American Anna and the biracial Melanctha of *Three Lives* seem on the page more alike than distinct, thus ceding the particularities of social group histories, expressive forms, and experiences of Americanization. Stein's unsentimental representation of stultified women's lives within stilted prose became an important source of inspiration for later women writers of varied ethnic and racial backgrounds. The goal of presenting immigrant women's perspectives as worthy of literary treatment linked writers with little else in common. Although her aesthetics and affective register could not have been more different from Stein's, Mary Antin's widely read autobiography, *The Promised Land* (1912) drew upon nineteenth-century Romantic and Transcendentalist tropes and aesthetics as a spiritualist view of nature in order to make universalist claims for choosing to become Americans.

Rather than generalizing foreignness, other immigrant novels played upon techniques of translation and revision (and in rarer cases autotranslation) to emphasize cultural distinctiveness to multiple readerships at once. An early example is the "strange case" of Italian-American Luigi Donato Ventura's *Peppino*, which, as Mario

Maffi has pointed out, was published initially in French (1885) alongside works by George Sand and Guy de Maupassant; the following year *Peppino* appeared in an English-language collection co-edited by Ventura and a Russian author (1998, 166). This produced the unexplained anomaly that a key early Italian-American literary work exists only in French- and English-language publications. Other translated immigrant novels represented a cultural transition from previous generations of writers' relation to writing in English. In this respect, Ole Edvart Rølvaag's trilogy of Norwegian settlers in the Midwest has a distinctive historical role. After publishing seven novels in Norwegian, starting with *Amerika-Breve* [*Letters from America*] in 1912, his *Giants of the Earth* appeared in an English translation in 1927 and was followed soon after by *Peder Victorius* (1929) and *Their Fathers' God* (1931), as well as three earlier novels. Like many other immigrant novels, the trilogy traces a multigenerational family saga of arrival, frontier trials, acculturation, and alienation of the settlers from their descendants. (For more on Rølvaag, see Chapter 14 in this volume.)

Another well-known instance of immigrant works circulating in multiple languages is the work of Abraham Cahan. Religiously educated in his Lithuanian youth and a socialist from early adulthood on, editor and author Cahan was a central figure in the US Yiddish press during the first half of the twentieth century. With the support of William Dean Howells, he initially composed his novella *Yekl* (1896) for an English-reading public as a story of a "greenhorn" striving to become a "yankee." But Cahan's unsentimental and unappealing portrait of an ordinary, self-interested, and myopic Jewish immigrant did not fit the mold of valorizing immigrant novels editors had come to expect. Fearing it would go unread, Cahan translated the story into Yiddish for its initial publication and serialized it pseudonymously. Shortly after it began running, it was accepted for publication in English; however, the nearly simultaneously appearing versions are not identical, and Aviva Taubenfeld has shown that Cahan "reconstructed" the Yiddish version to address a different audience (1998, 144). Throughout these decades, many assimilation narratives unflatteringly portray a "typical" (to use Panunzio's term) immigrant's anticlimactic arrival in the United States and the challenges that arise in translating an old self into a new one.

Fictions of Immigrant New Women

Women's fiction from this era similarly drew on the tribulations of translated lives, as Gertrude Stein did, to complicate perspectives on belonging and the persistence of foreignness. They also merged forms from varied cultural sources, including life-writing, sentimental drama, epistolary novels, family sagas, and travel writing. Female authors also developed distinctive narratives through literary experiments with narrated exclusion and silence, vernacularized and multilingual dialogue, and characters navigating between ethnic traditionalism and the liberated "New Woman." Anzia Yezierska's autobiographical novel *Bread Givers* (1925) is structured around an intergenerational father-daughter conflict. Sara Smolensky seeks to escape from an anguished space between religious isolation in an urban ghetto and psychic isolation within an American modernity premised upon her marginalization. Immigrant women's fiction as a whole engaged such conundrums, emerging within what critics have described as a dual critique of ethnic patriarchy within the home and nativist national rhetoric that associated ethnic femininities with foreignness.

Born and raised in England and Montréal to a British merchant and a Chinese missionary, Edith Eaton (who wrote under the pen name of Sui Sin Far) and her sister Winnifred Eaton (Onoto Watanna) are recognized as pioneering Asian American authors. Edith Eaton became attuned to the systemic prejudice that Chinese Americans and Canadians suffered while working as a journalist during the 1880s. From the late 1890s until her death in 1914 she published stories in a wide range of periodicals and her short story collection *Mrs. Spring Fragrance* (1912). Americanization and translation are overt themes from the first sentence of the opening story: "When Mrs. Spring Fragrance first arrived in Seattle, she was unacquainted with even one word of the American language" (ch. 1).

Through ironic reversals, subtle shifts in narratorial point-of-view, and overdetermined dialogue, Edith Eaton's fiction undercut racialized expectations of Asian American difference. The stories in *Mrs. Spring Fragrance* counter prevalent views of Chinese immigrants as itinerant and lascivious male laborers by centralizing the perspective of an "Americanized," married, middle-class woman. Frequently in her work, the white characters are "mysterious, inscrutable, incomprehensible Americans," not Asian immigrants. In "The Inferior Woman," Mrs. Spring Fragrance voices a similar inversion that speaks to the larger project of immigrant fiction; she proposes to write a book on her observations of those around her. When a white female friend expresses surprise, she responds, "The American woman writes books about the Chinese. Why not a Chinese woman write books about the Americans?" She adds that her method will be reportage, "My book I shall take from the words of others . . . I listen to what is said. I apprehend, I write it down" (ch. 2). Her friend's son wishes to marry a woman she views as a less desirable daughter-in-law, but Mrs. Spring Fragrance's account of the "inferior" woman shows her to be an admirably independent "woman who has made herself," a feminine counterpart to the self-made man ideal. Narrating such tribulations and revelations, Edith Eaton's stories represent the lives of Chinese American immigrants as intricately interconnected with those of white Americans. While her work references dilemmas common to other immigrant groups, it emphasizes distinctive experiences of Chinese American exclusion and accusations of inassimilability, while portraying individuals striving for footholds in a nation that denied them citizenship. In several stories, she engages the taboo subject of interracialism through the experiences of biracial characters, as in "Her Chinese Husband" and "Its Wavering Image."

In the works of Edith Eaton, Winnifred Eaton, and their contemporaries, "becoming an American woman" is both a compliment and a source of unsettling anxiety, as when Mr. Spring Fragrance admires and fears his wife's autonomy and "cleverness" (ch. 1). A similarly delicate balance between ethnic femininity and Americanization runs through all of the works of one of the most prominent of 1920s female immigrant novelists, Anzia Yezierska, whose literary career literally took her from New York tenements to Hollywood. Her short stories brought her early recognition, including inclusion in Edward J. O'Brien's "Best Short Story" collection and his 1919 award for the best story. She drew on her friend Rose Pastor's relationship with philanthropist Graham Stokes, as well as her own with philosopher John Dewey in *Salome of the Tenements* (1923), a novel that portrays the pressures of assimilation within an interethnic love plot between a Jewish American immigrant and a prim Anglo-Saxon educator who is simultaneously magnetized toward and repelled by her. Though aesthetically quite different, Edith Eaton's stories portray white liberal reformers as patronizing at best and dehumanizing at worst. Yezierska's career-long fascination with self-made aesthetics—a "democracy of beauty" constructed from passion, fashionable clothing concocted with drab raw materials—challenges associations of ethnic ghettos with ugly, unhygienic, and depersonalized immigrants (ch. 5). That *Salome* concludes with the pair irreparably divided, yet longing for each other, aptly conveys Yezierska's sentimental cynicism regarding ethnic difference, which she essentializes as racial otherness, and the permanently incomplete promise of Americanization. ·

Although immigrant novels are frequently associated with urbanization, some of the most prominent and influential were those of regionalist and nonurban authors. In his 1929 introduction to Rølvaag's *Giants of the Earth*, for example, V. L. Parrington suggested that immigrant lives fit neatly within the structure of frontier and "middle border" narratives, which inhabited and extended conventions of immigrant novels. Drawing on techniques of "local color" stories and novels of domesticity, women's stories of immigrants and diasporic communities, such as those by Sarah Orne Jewett, Helen Reimensnyder Martin, Elsie Singmaster, and María Cristina Mena were published in magazines, journals, and anthologies. The frequency with which their works appeared during these years demonstrates wide interest among readers in how the writing of immigrant women's perspectives altered conventional narratives of diaspora.

Annexed Lands and Borderlands Immigrants

Autobiographical techniques and themes are present in many immigrant novels, but the novelistic framework allows writers to draw on and meld fictional and historical matter innovatively. Conversely, immigrant stories initially presented as factual have run into controversies regarding their verifiability, a trend that continues to the present day. Arguably no work stands more firmly at this nexus than that of Evangelina Betancourt Cossío y Cisneros, whose escape from a Havana jail on the eve of the wars of 1898 was trumpeted (and trumped up) into an international media event by William Randolph Hearst's *New York Journal*, as Gretchen Murphy also discusses in Chapter 12 of this volume. Although numerous aspects remain obscure, the sequence of events began with a young Cuban woman allied with the 1895 revolution against Spain who sought to surreptitiously free deported radicals, including her father. Captured and charged with treason and attempted murder of the commanding governor, Cisneros was imprisoned. The *New York Journal* began running sensationalist stories of the plight of a patriotic, beautiful, and wrongfully accused young woman epitomizing Cuba's struggle against Spain and engineered a petition drive to US women that reportedly received 15,000 supporters. When this mythical embodiment of national femininity was not released, Hearst sent a reporter to Havana to play the masculine role of American rescuer.

Soon after Cisneros found herself in front of a large, celebratory crowd in New York and at dinner with President McKinley. Her account, *The Story of Evangelina Cisneros* (1897), was published with illustrations by noted artists, including Frederic Remington, and introduced by Nathaniel Hawthorne's son, author Julian Hawthorne. Framed as a captivity narrative, a racialized national romance tale, and a celebratory immigration novel, Cisneros's work is highly mediated by the circumstances of its production. The contents of "her" narrative reflect the complexity of authorship in this case, as the volume includes a preface, a dedication, an introduction by Hawthorne, letters and petitions submitted on her behalf, "Mr. Decker's Story," "Miss Cisneros' Story," a history of Cuba, and a chronology; far less than half of the work is even attributed to her. As an exploitative pretext for war with Spain, her story succeeded in memorably portraying a distressed feminized Cuba in need of a militarized American masculinity to secure its virtue and morality. However, the narrative was clearly more useful to Hearst and remains best known as a media event. Moreover, after the din subsided, Cisneros married one of the men who accompanied her during her rescue and returned to Cuba.

If Evangelina Cisneros represents a spectacularly public story of immigration, the epistolary novel of Olga Beatriz Torres, *Memorias de mi Viaje* (1918), occupies an opposite affective register. A thirteen-year-old member of the displaced post-revolution Mexican gentry, Torres wrote letters to her aunt narrating her family's trip that were published in 1914 in *El Paso del Norte*, a Spanish-language newspaper founded by Mexican emigrés and then as a volume four years later. As a youthful, precocious member of "El México de Afuera," Torres's letters reflect her class privilege and racialist prejudices as well as a child's-eye-view of US modernity (transportation technologies, urbanization, industrialization, imperial expansion). Translator Juanita Luna-Lawhn cites Federico Allen Hinojosa's 1940 chapbook *El México de Afuera* to note that the community of Mexican Americans who moved to the United States during these decades viewed themselves as "having spiritually reconquered Mexican territories lost in 1837 and 1847 to the United States." This ongoing cultural protest against the US annexation of Mexican land identifies a significantly different vector of immigrant passage than those of individuals from European or Asian countries for whom the "Old World" was less geographically proximate.

In developing a plot through a series of letters from Olga to her aunt, Torres includes techniques of travel narrative, *Bildungsroman*, and border consciousness. The naive perspective of a youthful protagonist reflects her changing perspective as she encounters border towns and Texan cities. In the final pages of the work, the protagonist describes her inability to comprehend the Spanglish spoken by a housekeeper and hints at the painful liminality of Mexican Americans in Texas, a theme that also arises in other border novels of the period, including ethnographer, poet, and novelist Américo Paredes's *George Washington Gómez*, written in the late 1930s but unpublished until 1990. *George Washington Gómez* represents a range of borderlands identities of working-class Mexican Americans mindful that they live on annexed land that had previously constituted northern Mexico. Paredes defamiliarizes the central dichotomy of anti-immigration rhetoric in describing the protagonist as having been "born a foreigner in his native land" (ch. 2). Moreover, his formal innovations on the immigrant novel conventions begin with his protagonist's youthful binationalism, which he represents as both heterotopic and inherently conflictual in a "checkerboard consciousness" that recalls W. E. B. Du Bois's formulation of double-consciousness, as Ramón Saldívar has pointed out (2006, 145). Paredes's novel concludes devastatingly (or ironically) with the protagonist having been compelled to choose between Mexican American and Anglo American communities, though the panoramic work prior to that penultimate moment explores alternative pathways.

Diasporic and Ethnic Americanisms

The variety and range of immigrant narratives of the 1920s and '30s are characterized particularly by the work of second-generation US writers exploring the fitful ambivalence of their positions between worlds old and new. Their formal mergers— mixing avant-garde, proletarian, popular, abstractionist, everyday, utopian, and documentary techniques—are now pivotal to understandings of literary modernism, Depression-era cultures, and diasporic thought. As with their predecessors, they portray the quotidian events of immigrants' lives struggling the strictures of nativist nationalism, racism, sexism, and other institutionally sanctioned prejudices. The critical sensibility that I have suggested characterized earlier immigrant novels emerges more definitively in many these works as literary engagements with stigmatization and marginalization. Many still claim the mantle of Americanism (as citizenship, community, or philosophical ideal), but they do so mindful of ongoing hostility directed at new and old immigrant groups.

A useful starting point for tracing diasporic and ethnic immigrant novels is Gertrude Stein's transition from *Three Lives* to *The Making of Americans*. Nearly all of the themes of later immigrant novels are present somewhere in Stein's work: domestic labor, interethnic identification, intergenerational conflict (she famously begins *The Making of Americans* with a reference to father-son violence), unfamiliar speech, gendered and sexualized power relations, ambivalent assimilation, experiments with narration and dialogue, and unsatisfying conclusions. The characters of *Three Lives* are notable for being "foreign" and marginalized women whose dramas are quotidian, rather than epiphanic or sentimentalized, and taking shape in an experiential present tense, instead of in relation to immigrant pasts.

The masculinist cast of many interwar immigrant novels is well represented by those who castigated Stein, those who emulated her, and some who did both. Jamaican-American author Claude McKay's three novels—*Home to Harlem* (1928), *Banjo* (1929), and *Banana Bottom* (1933)—narrate the urban displacement of global black emigrants in New York, France, and Jamaica. His characters are identified less by nationality than by affinities derived from shared class and race experiences. James Farrell also mixed preexisting genres of dialect stories, Marxist anticapitalism, and immigrant naturalism. His *Studs Lonigan* trilogy (1932–35) received immediate recognition and wide acclaim. Coexisting tensely with a growing post-migration African American community in Chicago, Farrell represents Irish American masculinity as claiming Americanness via ethnic and racial competitive animosity. Aiming to crack the Horatio Alger-infused belief in individualist "rise of" narratives along with the gentility of prior Irish American literary cultures, Farrell's novels trace Lonigan from a working-class childhood to gang membership, a profligate young adulthood, and an early death (on the *Studs Lonigan* trilogy as a working-class epic, see Chapter 33 in this volume).

Several other immigrant novelists depicted diasporic disjuncture through "plain style" prose. Poet Charles Reznikoff's first novel, *By the Waters of Manhattan* (1930), uses a diptych structure to narrate two generations of a family's passage from the perspective of a mother and her son. The muted experimentalism of Reznikoff's novel subtly imported immigrant foreignness to the seemingly unadorned narrative idiom in a manner that reviewers commented on almost immediately and frequently thereafter. Like Gertrude Stein, Reznikoff used lexical simplicity to narrate cultural difference, an inheritance he made explicit in the closing lines of the first half of the novel voiced by the maternal character: "We are a lost generation . . . It is for our children to do what they can" (pt. I). Throughout the work Reznikoff plays with the Horatio Alger uplift narrative as well as the ambivalence of Abraham Cahan's revisions. Moreover, as a poet of "found words" drawn from biblical, legal, and testimonial intertexts, Reznikoff can be read as a model for appropriative, intertextual immigrant writing. Another adherent of the poetic plain style, trilingual William Carlos Williams (born to immigrants from England and Puerto Rico), published an immigrant novel trilogy—*White Mule* (1937), *In the Money* (1940), and *The Build-Up* (1952)—based on his wife's German-Norwegian family.

Reznikoff's *By the Waters of Manhattan* was published in the same year as Michael Gold's autobiographical *Jews Without Money*. While the two novels might be misunderstood as representing a schematic opposition between political and aesthetic commitments, their appearance in the hinge year 1930 indicates diverging cultural priorities at the outset of the Depression. *Jews Without Money* sold out multiple printings almost immediately, was translated into fourteen languages by 1935 according to Gold, and remains a landmark in politically engaged fiction (on Michael Gold and proletarian art, see Chapter 35 in this volume). Like McKay, Farrell, and many others, Gold employed narrative techniques of naturalism, vernacularism, and lyricism to adapt the immigrant uplift narrative into a story of emergence from ethnic origins to universalized communist sympathies with laborers of all social groups and nations. Another kind of ethnic awakening is plotted within Henry Roth's *Call It Sleep* (1934), which begins as a naturalist immigrant novel that reverses the usual linguistic hierarchy of US English (as instrumentally efficient and sufficient) and immigrant idioms (as foreign, distasteful, epiphenomenal). In its Joycean child's-eye-view of immigrant subjectivity, *Call It Sleep* follows David Schearl's interior consciousness from sexualized and violent familial domesticity to competitive street youth cultures and from traditional religious parochialism to cross-religious identifications and mimicry. The novel's narrative arc from ethnic particularism to interethnic contact and desire among immigrant groups in New York's Lower East Side parallels the author's mid-1930s shift from modernist experimentalism toward overtly political art. Roth's effort to maintain both political and artistic vanguardisms within an immigrant narrative is captured in an explosive maelstrom of voices, visions, and epistemologies in the penultimate sequence following the young protagonist's nearly fatal self-electrocution (on the modernist experimentation of *Call It Sleep*, see Chapter 24 in this volume).

A contemporary of Roth's who similarly drew upon both aesthetic and political vanguardisms was Chinese-American author, activist, and actor H.T. Tsiang. His first two works, *China Red* (1931) and *The Hanging on Union Square* (1935), were, he noted, "stubbornly or nuttily" self-published, the latter with a forward by Waldo Frank and blurbs by Granville Hicks, Louis Adamic, and Carl Van Doren. His last published novel, *And China Has Hands* (1937), narrates the perspectives of laundryman Wong Wan-Lee and Chinese-African American Pearl Chang in New York's Chinatown. Although less overtly experimental than his previous work, *And China Has Hands* contains puns, perspectival shifts, metafictional satire of the author's persona, nonsequential stories, stylized repetitions, and other hallmarks of literary modernism. As Floyd Cheung notes in his Introduction, Tsiang's novel draws on both Chinese and Anglo-American literary conventions in order to represent "the bicultural dissonance integral to the Chinese-American and, more broadly, Asian-American experience" (2003). The episodic narration conveys Wong Wan-Lee's daily encounters with customers, salespeople, a corrupt inspector, labor organizers, a sex worker, a loan shark, gamblers, and others. The intermittent, tragic-comic romance plot portrays tensions between recent Chinese American immigrants, like the protagonist, and those longer established, like the Southern US-born Pearl Chang. Wong Wan-Lee is taken with Pearl Chang's autonomy and beauty, but he considers her culturally bereft for her unfamiliarity with Chinese traditions, while she regards him as admirably knowledgeable and principled, but also alien, inflexible, and inept.

After initial, modest success in his business, Wong Wan-Lee finds himself mired in financial distress when the Depression, coupled with structural racism, forces him into debt. He has to sell his laundry shop, and the novel concludes with the American dream turned into a seesaw—the impoverished immigrant who worked his way up from being a restaurant busboy to an owner of a laundry shop returns to a busboy position. Pearl Chang ends up working in the same restaurant, and the novel concludes by unifying their disparate worldviews as they join in a labor strike that is broken up by violence. The penultimate utopian moment is followed by tragedy when a bullet strikes Wong Wan-Lee, and he dies in Pearl Chang's arms.

In relating the interethnic urban proletarianism of H. T. Tsiang to contemporary immigrant authors Gold, Roth, Daniel Fuchs, John Fante, and Pietro di Donato, Michael Denning has described the group as developing a "ghetto pastoral" novel form. Their novels foreground cross-racial contact and identification, left-wing political sensibilities, vernacular expression, and formal experimentation (Denning 1996, 240). Rather than pursuing the literary modernist aim of self-evidently "new" art, the ethnic immigrant novels mentioned in this section innovate intertextually by weaving together themes and techniques that appear in earlier works to create aesthetically hybrid mergers of autobiography, documentary, naturalism, and modernism. In this respect, diasporic authors of the 1920s and 1930s extend the cross-cultural, tradition-merging techniques of earlier immigrant novelists while bringing the political sensibilities that were more implicit in earlier works to the fore.

As a result of the diversity of seven decades of immigrant novels, few generalizations about them will be illuminating. Rather than hazarding such claims, this chapter focuses instead on the suggestion that immigrant novels during this period negotiate structural ambivalences—for example, the coexistence of celebratory and suspicious attitudes toward the nation—and the textual dynamics of formal and thematic mixtures. This approach centralizes seemingly contradictory impulses within the same work and detects political sensibilities underlying even avowedly apolitical narratives. A similar claim could be made about these diasporic novels' transnational intertextual relations to both US American cultural precursors and those originating in other national traditions. In these aesthetic and thematic domains, immigrant novels can be read as revisionary works in conversation with US American national rhetorics, contemporary events, and transnational cultural crossings.

14

THE AMERICAN NOVEL BEYOND ENGLISH

BY ORM ØVERLAND

The United States does not have an official language. It is nevertheless silly to argue that English is not the language of the United States. The history of the unrivaled cultural, social, and political position of English, however, is a troubled one. Native American languages and the Spanish of the inhabitants of the annexed provinces of northern Mexico as well as French in Louisiana have been actively suppressed in the political process of nation-building. There have been periods of nativist reactions to immigrant languages, peaking in the early twentieth century with the anti-immigration movement and the Americanization frenzy during the First World War, when particularly German was under attack. Later in the twentieth century the so-called English-only movement was mainly directed at the use of Spanish. Most languages other than English, however, have simply withered. Outside of such ethnic pockets as some Native American reservations languages other than English have rarely survived more than two or three generations of the processes of acculturation. English is now the native language of descendants of immigrants from Russia, Germany, and China as well as from Britain. The United States has been called the graveyard of languages.

Indigenous languages of the contiguous United States, Alaska and Hawaii became American languages through conquest, annexation and purchase of land, as did French and Spanish, two European languages with colonial roots in America. The official as well as the literary use of French in Louisiana came to a virtual stop with the restrictive measures of Reconstruction authorities. One of the few who continued to write and publish in French was Alfred Mercier in the pages of his journal *Les Comptes Rendus* and in novels such as *L'Habitation St. Ybars* (1881), a work that may be compared with the work of Thomas Nelson Page for its idyllic depiction of plantation life during slavery. Mexicans, of course, continued to use Spanish in Texas and in the large areas annexed in 1848. Ironically, it was the conquerors that provided the technology and capital for printing presses that made newspapers and books in Spanish possible. The first US novel in Spanish was written in 1881: Manuel

M. Salazar, *La historia de un caminante, o Gervacio y Aurora* [*The History of a Traveler on Foot, or Gervasio and Aurora*], that Nicolás Kanellos has characterized as "a colorful picture of pastoral life in New Mexico" (2005, 236). Others have followed but with such noteworthy exceptions as Daniel Venegas's 1928 *Las aventuras de don Chipote* [*The Adventures of Don Chipote*] and Tomás Rivera's remarkable story of boyhood in a migrant community, . . . *y no se lo trago la tierra* [. . . *And the Earth Did Not Devour Him*] in 1971, Hispanic American novelists have tended to use English for their published work.

No US languages, except of course the languages of captives from Africa, have been so systematically suppressed as the indigenous languages. Generations of Native Americans have been exposed to school systems with a policy of eradicating their languages and cultural traditions. This may be one reason why novelists with a Native American identity have tended to use English. There are traditional narratives in indigenous languages, such as the Hawaiian Moses K. Nakuina's *The Wind Gourd of La'amaomao* (1902), that may have deserved a chapter of their own. European immigrant groups with languages other than English, beginning with Germans in the colonial period, and Asian immigrant groups, mainly from China and Japan, have had flourishing literary cultures, particularly in the late nineteenth and early twentieth centuries until the first period of mass immigration came to an end with the legal measures against immigration in the late 1920s and the Great Depression in the 1930s. This chapter will focus on novels in what we may call American immigrant languages.

From a twenty-first century point of view the ethnic diversity of American novelists bears witness to the vitality and unifying force of English. Yet a volume on the US novel from 1870 to 1940—even in a series devoted to "the novel in English"— that did not pay attention to fiction in languages other than English would engage in historical misrepresentation as well as neglect works of literary excellence. In American libraries, however, fiction and poetry are placed according to language rather than country. In our taxonomy, American literature is a subdivision of literature in the English language; American novels in German or Chinese must be sought on the shelves for German or Chinese literature. This chapter seeks to place them where they belong: in the literature of the United States.

* * *

Frustrated at his inability to find a publisher for the English version of his first novel, *Yekl* (1896), even with the help of his mentor, William Dean Howells, Abraham Cahan decided to publish a serialization of a Yiddish version, *Yankel der Yankee*, in his newspaper *Arbeiter Tseitung* beginning in October 1895. On hearing of Cahan's decision, Howells expressed relief that the work thus published did not constitute an actual book, and he indeed went on to secure a publisher for the English language version, thus ensuring Cahan's reputation as an American novelist. Fully aware that significant numbers of Americans were reading newspapers, magazines, and books in a variety of languages, Howells nonetheless read the American landscape correctly: critics and librarians have in practice defined American literature as a branch of English language literature. Novels in languages other than English have, in effect, been invisible. Axel Nissen has characterized the 2002 translation of Drude Krog Janson's novel of 1887, *A Saloonkeeper's Daughter*, as "the end of its more than century-long, monolingual existence in a parallel universe of American literary history" (2009, 113).

Yankel der Yankee (1895), however, does not have a home in any other national literature. Even though he was from Vilna, now Vilnius in Lithuania, the author was an American and his intended readers were either Americans or immigrants on their way to becoming Americans. Its characters cannot be imagined in any other setting, nor does the language they and the narrator use have any other home than the United States. One of the objections raised to Cahan's Yiddish by more conservative users of the language was its profusion of Americanisms, making it unlike the Yiddish of Europe. Unavoidably, most immigrants who continued to use their native language in the United States were affected by the dominant language. In his monumental *The American Language* (1919) H. L. Mencken's preferred term for the majority language was *American* rather than American *English*. His eighty-page "Appendix: Non-English Dialects in American" is deliberately named. German American Mencken, who wrote the first edition of his work during the First World War and the heyday of antiforeign sentiment in the United States, was no friend of Britain; he insisted that not only English but all languages used in the United States had undergone such change that they must be considered American. As English had become American, German, Finnish, and Polish had also become American in the United States; they might have been called "dialects in America*n*," not, as listed in the table of contents, "dialects in America."

In a review in the literary journal *Kvartalskrift* [*Quarterly*] in 1920, Ole Edvart Rølvaag explained that he did not like the term Norwegian-American literature: "It would be more correct to call it American literature in the Norwegian language." For evidence, he suggested that his readers look through the many books of this kind and "see if you can find anything Norwegian about them. I read them and find nothing [Norwegian] but the language they are dressed in. This literature is about American life as we have experienced it on the plains and forest claims, in small towns and in prairie homes." There is a rather shrill defensive note in the insistence of both Mencken and Rølvaag that must be appreciated in a context where both Theodore Roosevelt and Woodrow Wilson were railing against the use of "foreign" languages. For us, a century later, there is no need to enter into an argument about who and what is American; we should simply accept that novels written in the United States, about the United States, and for readers in the United States are American novels regardless of language. We know that, because of a long history of migrations to and from the United States, answers to the question of the nationality of a literary text may be ambiguous. Is the late work of W. H. Auden or the early work of T. S. Eliot British or American? Both are included in *The Oxford Companion to American Literature*. Looking in another direction, Mariano Azuela's *Los de abajo* [*The Underdogs*], a novel based on the author's firsthand experience of battle in the Mexican Revolution, was written in El Paso, Texas, and serialized in the American newspaper *El Paso del Norte* in 1915. The author was a sojourner in the United States rather than an immigrant and after two years he returned to Mexico. Where does a novel set in Mexico but written and published in El Paso "belong"? Language is not the reason for such ambiguity of nationality.

Language has not been the only issue in defining the American novel. Even though Américo Paredes wrote his novel *George Washington Gomez* in English in 1936, it was not published until 1990. Howells, who had made the immigrants of New York a backdrop for the education of Basil March in *A Hazard of New Fortunes* (1890), had problems when he tried to promote a novel with immigrants at the center. Aviva Taubenfeld makes good use of Cahan's five-volume autobiography published in Yiddish in 1928 in her study of the two versions of his first novel. Here, she writes, "Cahan reports that the editor of *Harper's Weekly* returned the manuscript with a note saying 'the life of an East Side Jew wouldn't interest the American reader'" (1998, 147). The comment implies that neither the author nor his East Side Jewish characters were American.

Cahan and Rølvaag wrote at a time with a larger percentage of foreign-born and second-generation Americans than at any other time in American history. The fear of foreigners and their languages came to a peak in the early twentieth century when the population of many cities was dominated by first and second generation immigrants. Many Anglo Americans, who thought of themselves as "Native Americans," felt that their culture was under pressure. Harry Morgan Ayres concludes his chapter on "The English Language in America" in the 1921 third volume of *The Cambridge History of American Literature* concludes with reflections on the "serious problem" of achieving a "reasonable" standardization of American English with "Italian-American, Yiddish-American, Scandinavian-American, German-American yammering in our ears" (568). The movement to limit immigration, particularly from outside northwestern Europe, grew in the late nineteenth century, gained momentum with the Americanization movement during the First World War and the anti-"red" hysteria triggered by the Soviet revolution, and achieved political victory with the passing of several immigration acts in the mid-1920s.

Rølvaag may have been the first novelist to benefit from the temporary end to immigration anxiety brought about by the anti-immigration legislation in the mid-1920s. The American market for books in Norwegian was dwindling, and in 1924 and 1925 Rølvaag, for the first time, had a novel (in two parts), *I de dage* [*In Those Days*] and *Riket grundlægges* [*The Founding of the Kingdom*] published in Oslo, Norway, rather than in Minneapolis, Minnesota. Rølvaag was certain that this was his best novel and unsuccessfully tried to interest potential translators and New York publishers. His 1926 meeting with Lincoln Colcord, with whom he collaborated on the translation that was given the title *Giants in the Earth* (1927), was serendipitous. However, the consequent willingness of Harper & Brothers to launch an unknown Midwestern immigrant writer was surely inspired by their belief that the war against immigration had been won and that the reading public was now ready to appreciate a story about immigrants who no longer posed a threat.

American writers have used languages other than English for a variety of reasons. For many, of course, there was no other option: they did not master the language of their new country. Some wrote not only *in* a language but *for* a language—either in the hope that they were contributing to the establishment of a permanent alternative literary culture in the United States or, as in the case of Isaac Bashevis Singer, with the understanding that his work in Yiddish was a monument to a fading language. But publishing in a language other than English meant isolation from the literary establishment. Rølvaag had published four novels as well as other books in Minneapolis when Lincoln Colcord wrote to his New York publisher Harper & Brothers on March 9, 1926 about his discovery of a new and unknown American author: "He tells me that never before in his life has he been met on just this ground, or felt himself in touch with the publishing profession in America. Doesn't this seem incredible? Such is the lot of the alien in our midst. He simply has had no contacts." Members of minority-language cultures, on the other hand, are highly aware of the majority culture by which they are not only surrounded but in which they also spend much of their time. But they demonstrate as little interest in other minority-language cultures as do the establishment writers, publishers, critics, and readers.

Ironically, immigrant literary cultures have also been isolated from the literary cultures of their former home countries. Not only have their languages been influenced by life in the United States, but their themes, settings, and characters have been thus influenced as well. From the point of view of the literary world of European capitals, the immigrant newspapers where so many of the novels in languages other than English were serialized were hardly worth serious attention. Novels in languages other than English have remained obscure, also in their homeland, the United States. There is only one known copy of the serialized edition of Ludwig von Reizenstein's German-language *Die Geheimnisse von New Orleans* [*The Mysteries of New Orleans*] in the New Orleans newspaper *Louisiana Staats-Zeitung* (1854–55). Neither Reizenstein's novel nor Drude Krog Janson's 1889 Norwegian-language *En saloonkeepers datter* [*A Saloonkeeper's Daughter*] have until recently been included in discussions of gender or sexuality in American fiction. Unknown American novels may still exist on the crumbling pages of old newspapers in obscure archives while others have surely been lost along with the newspapers. They have been forgotten because the cultures that supported them were unstable cultures in transition from the language and culture of a European, American, or Asian homeland to full integration with the American majority language and culture. "We have become strangers," Rølvaag wrote in his first novel, *Amerika-breve* [*The Third Life of Per Smevik*] (1912), "strangers to those we left, and strangers to those we came to" ("1901: Losses and Gains").

It was difficult for many dedicated authors to accept that their literary culture was merely a phase in a development that gave their language and therefore their novels a limited life in the country of their choice. Some, like the Norwegian-American journalist and novelist Johannes B. Wist, were quite realistic about their transitional situation and function. In 1904 he characterized his ethnic group as a people that culturally speaking are "wandering nomads in transition from one nation to another" (qtd. in Lovall 1977, 39). This transition was more painful for some groups than for others. The Japanese American journalist and novelist Kyuin Okina could not himself become an American citizen since nonwhite immigrants could not be naturalized until after the Second World War. Nevertheless, he thought of his and other American writing in Japanese as a necessary transitional literature. In his preface to his short story collection *Ishokuju* [*Transplanted Tree*] (1923) he wrote about how, at the time he wrote these stories, he had been inspired by his conviction of the importance of creating a literature that reflected the immigrant experience. In 1923, surely aware that the Immigration Act that would be passed some months later not only spelled an end to further immigration from Japan but specifically defined the Japanese as "aliens ineligible to citizenship" (Daniels 2002, 283), he explained that the Japanese were in transition from seeing themselves as sojourners to becoming settlers: "From now on the Japanese people in America will stop living as overseas migrant workers [*imin*] and begin the life of permanent settlers [*ijumin*]. And, after the mid-twentieth century, we will have writers who write their stories in English—the world language—among our own descendants. Until their time arrives, we, as an intermediary generation and in the tradition of the Japanese race, must give expression to the emotional pain we suffer in an alien land" (Okina 1923, preface; translation by Teruko Kumel). Okina's second novel, *Akaki-hi-no-ato* [*A Trace of the Red Sun*] (1916), was, like his first, *Aku-no-hikage* [*Shadow of Evils*] (1915), serialized in the San Francisco newspaper *Nichibei shin-bun* [*Japanese American Times*]. The protagonist of his second novel is—like the author—a Japanese American writer who finds it difficult to adapt to life in the United States. He falls in love with the young second-generation Mieko Ichijo but realizes that she is different from him in belonging to "a new rising American generation, while he belongs to an old Japanese generation," and he explains to her several times that "old leaves fall off when new leaves are coming." In Japan his second novel was published as a book in 1928 with the title *Michi-naki-michi* [*Road without Road*], and Teruko Kumei has observed that the image of a road without road suggests the "trace of a boat which will remain only for a while on the water" (Teruko correspondence, 2007).

Transitional immigrant literary cultures have had a vital life and been important for their inhabitants as long as mass immigration from the homeland has continued. But cultures that depended on languages other than English could not have the continuity of the majority culture with its large publishing houses, recognized literary journals, and public libraries and archives. A Polish- or German-language newspaper could live for several generations but there would nevertheless be little continuity in its readership: while new immigrants depended on publications in their own language and also ensured a supply of editorial staff, the children and grandchildren of immigrants increasingly used English and preferred publications in that language. The German language has a long history in the United States, but there is little continuity in this history. The German intellectuals who immigrated after the failed revolutions in 1848 had little or no awareness of the German-language culture of the colonial and early republic periods, and German peasants and laborers who came in the 1890s probably had as little awareness of the literature in German in colonial Pennsylvania as of the literary culture of the German immigrants who had preceded them by a few decades. The isolation and transitional nature of the literary cultures in languages other than English has obscured them from the view of literary centers of their old and new homelands as well as from the descendents of those who wrote and read in the many languages that once defined their respective immigrant cultures. In this respect the American novel beyond English may rather be thought of as the American novel *before* English.

The isolation of a non-English literary culture both from the majority culture and from other minority cultures, however, is a main reason for one of the most important differences between ethnic literature in English and in languages other than English. It is also what gives literature in other languages its distinct value as a window onto ethnic culture. Generally, novelists are not considered representatives of their societies. But novelists who belong to and write about an ethnic minority in the language of the majority are read as minority representatives by readers who acquire much of their information about minority cultures from ethnic fiction. Consequently, members of ethnic groups will judge writers according to how "they" are represented. This is a point made by Xia-huang Yin in his comprehensive *Chinese American Literature since the 1850s* (2000). He explains that while "Chinese American authors who write in English . . . tend to present an image that fits the public's imagination . . . Chinese-language writers seek affirmation and recognition only from their own community " and concludes that those who write in Chinese "are more outspoken about problems, both in the Chinese community and society at large" (165). Although Yin only discusses Chinese-language novels from the period after 1960, his observation is also valid for earlier fiction in languages other than English.

The difference made by a writer's choice of language and, consequently, of audience is brought out in Taubenfeld's study of Cahan's two versions of his first novel: *Yankel der Yankee* and *Yekl: A Tale of the New York Ghetto*. When he rewrote his novel in Yiddish after failing to find a publisher for the English version, Taubenfeld explains that Cahan was "no longer a mediator between two cultures" (1998, 148). This is evident, she demonstrates, in the very different ways the two versions begin. While the English commences "with a third-person omniscient narrator describing a sweatshop and its inhabitants," the Yiddish starts with a first-person narrator telling the story of an acquaintance to a reader addressed in the second person: "telling it to you as if we were talking at a table." Neither the first person narrator nor his familiarly addressed reader can have a place in the English version. "'I' and 'the reader' can share the Yiddish text with the protagonists because all inhabit the same cultural and linguistic space" (1998, 149).

Cahan's English version of *Yekl* was attacked on two fronts, both regarding the author as a representative. Reviewing some of the reactions by Jewish critics, Tauben-feld observes that they "were tremendously concerned about the impression repre-sentations of their community would make on members of the dominant culture." A critic writing for *The Bookman* wondered whether the author wanted his readers to believe that his characters "are truly representative of his race" (1998, 146). Rølvaag had published negative portrayals of Norwegian Americans in several novels, but it was not until the success of the English language *Giants in the Earth* in 1927 that he received criticism from some Norwegian-American communities. Writing about a minority in a minority language and for a minority audience could give a novelist the same freedom of expression as a mainstream writer, a freedom often not enjoyed by ethnic or minority novelists writing in English.

Language may thus explain why American novels in languages other than English are distinctly different from ethnic writing in English. Any attempt to write a history of this fiction, however, must face several problems not usually encountered by liter-ary historians. The most obvious obstacle is the simple fact that no single person can possibly read all the languages of American novels. Another is the ephemeral char-acter of this body of fiction. Not only is there not a national repository of all Ameri-can literature regardless of language, there are no separate complete repositories for individual literatures in languages other than English (with the possible exception of Yiddish). No single library has all the books and publications of American literature written in the Norwegian language. Moreover, the descendants of those who wrote and read in these languages have no memory of a literary culture in their past. Many novels in languages other than English were serialized in newspapers and magazines, and most of these did not reappear as books. These transitional and ephemeral lit-erary cultures were also isolated both from the majority English-language culture and from the many other minority cultures. More than a continent separated the writers who gathered in Seattle's *Nihonmachi* [Japantown] to discuss literature from those who sought each other's company in the editorial offices of the Yiddish *Arbe-iter Tseitung* on Manhattan's East Side. Immigrant authors from Japan wrote with the awareness that the United States would not accept them as naturalized citizens because they were not considered "white." Authors who used German could write with the confidence that they belonged to the largest and—before the First World War—most respected non-English immigrant group. Writing about American lit-erature in Polish before the Second World War, Karen Majewski observes, "Polish-language immigrant literature, no matter what else it may be about, is nearly always about Poland" (2001, 112). But while Polish-American intellectuals imagined them-selves in their Polonia, the "fourth partition" of their divided European homeland, Norwegian-American writers imagined themselves in their American *Vesterheimen*, their peculiar Norwegian-speaking "Western Home" in the United States. United States novelists using Japanese, Yiddish, Polish, or Norwegian were separated both by their languages and their different relations to the United States as well as to a homeland, but they were all intensely aware of American society and its past and present literature and are related in creating a literature that reflects a wide range of American experience.

A book on literature in one of the American languages beyond English has a title that poses three simple questions that demand rather complex answers: *German? American? Literature?* (Fluck and Sollors 2002). The two first have been addressed above but the third one must also be considered: are the American novels beyond English worth the attention of present-day readers? Many of them are, of course, not. In this, American literature beyond English is much like American literature in general. Since there has been no long and established critical tradition of evaluation and selection of American fiction beyond English, however, there is no established canon of this fiction. With little available guidance a reader looking for novels in, say, Japanese or German may have to leaf through many books and newspapers before hitting upon works of fiction that come to life in the reading. An opening of the canon of American fiction to include texts written in languages other than English, however, must depend not only on a tradition of literary criticism and on the publication of liberal selections of texts in translation but also on an opening of minds to an American literature in many languages.

Ideally, chapters such as the present one will eventually be superfluous in histories of American literature. Similar chapters have appeared in several literary histories, beginning with the third volume of the first *Cambridge History of American Literature* (1916–21), that has two chapters on "Non-English Writings," one on German, French, and Yiddish (authored by three scholars) and one given the subtitle "Aboriginal." The second *Cambridge History of American Literature* comes closer than previous histories to an integrated discussion of American texts in both English and other languages in the chapter on "Ethnic Modernism" by Werner Sollors, while chapters such as "A Cultural History of the Modern American Novel," also in the sixth volume, might have benefited from a similar approach. Such expectations, however, are unrealistic in a situation where only a small selection of texts in languages other than English has been translated and where, consequently, there is no mainstream tradition of criticism and scholarship. In the following, some American novels in the Norwegian language are selected for a case study, not so much as examples of a little known part of American literature but as illustrations of how such novels may be integrated in thematic as well as chronological accounts of American literature—and perhaps change or modify such accounts.

* * *

American literature in Norwegian has been given considerable academic critical attention, beginning with the pioneering doctoral dissertations of Gerald H. Thorson

(1957) and Dorothy Burton Skårdal (1963, published 1974). Many other studies—dissertations, books, and articles—have followed. Most critical attention has, deservedly, been focused on Rølvaag, and his *Giants in the Earth* has been in print since its first publication in 1927, a result, perhaps, of the novel's place on high school and college reading lists until it was superseded by novels reflecting more recent immigrant experiences.

In comparison with immigrants from Germany and Ireland, immigrants from Norway have been a modestly sized group in American history. The majority of these immigrants came to the Midwestern states, and more of them than those of any other group settled on farms and in small prairie towns. Even though these immigrants came to the United States for material reasons, a surprisingly large number published literary texts in their own language in newspapers, journals, and books. Among the many who published plays, verse, short stories, and nonfiction, the bibliography of *The Western Home* includes ninety-seven novelists with 199 novels, most published in book form but some only serialized in journals or newspapers, a sufficiently large number to make canon-formation a meaningful critical and historical task.

The utopian fiction born of the class conflicts at the turn of the twentieth century and fiction influenced by the growing awareness of women's rights in a society where women could not vote in national elections before 1920 are two examples of central themes in United States literary studies that may benefit from the inclusion of writing in languages other than English. Ignatius Donnelly, Jack London, Frederick Upham Adams, and Edward Bellamy are merely some of the writers who would be considered in courses on political utopian fiction. But students of utopian fiction who cannot read Norwegian will miss Hans A. Foss's *Hvide slaver: En social-politisk skildring* [*White Slaves: A Social and Political Narrative*] (1892), Ole A. Buslett's *Glans-om-Sol og hans folks historie* [*Splendor-of-Son and the Story of His People*] (1912), and Emil Lauritz Mengshoel's *Øen Salvavida: Et samfundsbillede* [*Salvavida Island: A Social Portrait*] (1904) and *Mené Tekél: Norsk-amerikansk arbeiderfortælling fra slutten av det 19. Århundrede* [*Mene Tekel: A Norwegian-American Labor Novel from the End of the Nineteenth Century*] (1919). Without these and several other American novels in Norwegian, a study of American utopias and dystopias is not only incomplete in the sense that some novels are omitted but because these novels may add to our understanding of how such a central theme was not so much copied as it was further developed and differently expressed in a United States that was more multicultural in this period than most literary histories acknowledge.

Foss's first novel, *Husmands-gutten* (1885), translated as *The Cotter's Son* in 1963—about a poor boy held down by class differences in Norway who goes to the United States, becomes rich, and returns to marry his childhood sweetheart, the daughter of the wealthy farmer—was probably the most read of all American novels in Norwegian, but it was not considered "literature" by the immigrant group's literary elite. His 1892 novel, *Hvide slaver,* was published by the populist inclined North Dakota newspaper *Normanden*, which offered two contemporary novels as premiums for new subscribers, Bellamy's *Looking Backward* (1888) and Donnelly's *Cæsar's Column* (1891). Although these books influenced Foss, his novel of class conflict and its future solution is strikingly different. While Bellamy was unable to imagine a bridge between his sordid present and his imagined utopian future and Donnelly could only imagine an apocalyptic destruction of capitalistic society as the outcome of the social conflicts of his day, Foss was inspired by his basic faith in American ideals and the American system of government to imagine an outcome where the "white slaves," the working class, are set free thanks to revolutionary reform based on the radical platform of the People's Party. An immigrant American may not be as ready to describe his chosen country as a failure as were for instance the Populist Donnelly or the Socialist London. Populist-inspired *Hvide slaver*, as much about an immigrant's desire to belong to American society as about his wish to reform it, is a complement to mainstream radical fiction of the period.

Mengshoel was active in the Socialist movement and his first novel, *Øen Salvavida* (1904), was published in Girard, Kansas, where Julius Wayland, the publisher of the Socialist journal *Appeal to Reason* in which Upton Sinclair's *The Jungle* was serialized in 1905, had invited him to edit and publish the Norwegian-language journal *Gaa Paa!* [*Forward!*]. In Mengshoel's didactic utopian fantasy two different forms of social organization—the first based on self-interest, the second on socialist ideals—are tried out on two South Pacific islands by the shipwrecked crew of the ship *Sociedad*. This may seem an exotic setting for an immigrant novel but it all turns out to be a dream by the sailor narrator who has fallen asleep in a no less exotic setting, the salon of Madame Blawatskaja in the French port of Le Havre after having argued with her that egotism and self-interest are the cornerstones of civilization. The narrator, much like the narrator of *The Jungle*, is in the end inspired by an optimistic faith in the democratic road to a just and socialist society: "But out there in the breakwaters of the future Fridland is already rising up to meet us. There lies the course of society's hope."

By 1919, back in Minneapolis where he published his second novel *Mené Tekél* (1919), Mengshoel's outlook has become darker, influenced both by a growing anti-socialism and by divisions within the socialist movement. Mengshoel, like Sinclair, was a social democrat, convinced that education and the ballot were the most important levers for social change. The melodramatic plot of *Mené Tekél* provides settings in which the violent and self-destructive antihero August Varberg, a laborer, is tried and shown to be not only a failure but a danger to the socialist cause. He becomes an artist and his major work, the allegorical painting "Mené Tekél," is bought by Sir Aylcroft, who is both progressive and wealthy, and who commissions yet another allegorical work. In the cataclysmic conclusion, however, Varberg, under the influence of a Polish nihilist, throws a homemade bomb into a cathedral, bringing down the entire structure and killing all in it, including himself. "He gave them their Mené Tekél, all right!" exclaims the nihilist observing the wreckage. He is overheard by Sir Aylcroft who gives the concluding verdict: "with this mad terrorist action he again wiped out the writing on the wall. . . . For every such act of madness you strike a shaft through the hope for a just society" (epilog). A novel with an English aristocratic social democrat, a Polish nihilist, and a Norwegian terrorist may not have been written to promote a more favorable image of immigrants, but it may modify our view of both American radicalism and American ethnic fiction.

Many young writers looked up to Ole A. Buslett, a quirky autodidact and a prolific writer in many genres. His large body of fiction, drama, and verse cannot be our concern here, except to note that his several utopian as well as dystopian fictions may be seen as preparations for his best utopian novel, *Glans-om Sol og hans folks historie* [*Splendor-of-Sun and the Story of His People*]. Making this novel available in English would be a significant contribution to our understanding of American utopian and fantasy fiction. It is a remarkable novel inspired by the gold versus silver controversy initiated by the Populists, whose notion that the gold standard was the root of all social evil was taken up by the Democrats with William Jennings Bryan's "Cross of Gold" speech at the national convention of 1896. Buslett creates an alternate world with its own history, religion, and culture and at the center is a family descending from a prophetic figure, John, who are the bearers of long forgotten and recognizably Judeo-Christian ideals. The society where the action takes place is ruled by a priesthood who worship gold in the figure of an immense golden ox, Splendor-of-Sun. All effort goes into the mining of gold and the manufacture of golden objects for Splendor-of-Sun and his priests. The prophet John and his family are exiled but eventually his descendants return and a revolution topples the power of the priesthood and destroys Splendor-of-Sun. A new agrarian and egalitarian society is based on the prophetic advice of John, and the mining of gold is banned. But it is in no way safe from the machinations of the supporters of gold, and a second revolution, led by the granddaughter and great-granddaughter of the prophet, again gives victory to the people. To this optimistic ending, however, the author has added a warning postscript: "No terrible destruction has yet defeated him; no prophet has yet won over him; Splendor-of-Sun haunts the world, will always haunt the world!"

Matters of gender and sexuality have long been of interest to critics of turn-of-the-century US literature. Two very different novels by two very different writers may serve to illustrate both the social and cultural contrasts within an immigrant group and how an awareness of fiction in a language other than English may modify our view of American culture. Drude Krog Janson's *En saloonkeepers datter* [*A Saloon-keeper's Daughter*] was published in Copenhagen in 1887 before it was serialized in a Minneapolis magazine and then published as a book in Chicago and Minneapolis. Janson was a well-traveled and enlightened intellectual who counted Georg Brandes among her admirers, who in Minneapolis scared off the young and unknown Knut Hamsun with her direct sensuality, and was married to one of the then-best-known writers in Norwegian, Kristofer Janson. Dorthea Dahl, whose only novel, *Byen paa berget* [*The City Upon a Hill*], was published by a church publisher in Minneapolis in 1925, came to South Dakota with her immigrant parents when she was two and had no formal training in the Norwegian language. She had to leave college after a few weeks because of her poor health and that brief sojourn was her only away-from-home experience: she lived with her ailing parents first in South Dakota and then in Idaho, eventually living alone as a bookkeeper in a small Idaho town. As she explained in a letter to Rølvaag in 1916, she was "busy with the thousands of things that must be done in a home in addition to taking care of medication, massages, and poultices and whatever needs to be done for a patient." She wrote many stories in Norwegian and later mainly in English for Lutheran church magazines but was unsuccessful in her ambition to have a story accepted by the *Woman's Home Companion*. Dahl's world may seem limited, and the social worlds of small-town, immigrant women serve as the settings for many of her stories. And yet she is a fine short story writer, as may be experienced in the story translated in *The Multilingual Anthology of American Literature*, edited by Shell and Sollors (2000). With all their differences, the two novels by Janson and Dahl have potential as important contributions to American fiction. The former has attracted some academic criticism, while the latter remains untranslated.

In *A Saloonkeeper's Daughter*, Janson tells the story of Astrid Holm, the daughter of a Christiania merchant, a widower who flees bankruptcy and establishes himself as a saloonkeeper in Minneapolis before sending for his daughter and two younger sons to live with him in an apartment above his saloon in a squalid section of the city. Astrid is despondent but gradually accepts her new place in society. After much trial and error, including her engagement to a prominent and wealthy lawyer, she breaks away from both the expectations of her dominant father and her socially conservative immigrant group and becomes the companion of Helene Nielsen, a physician. After further trials she enters a Unitarian seminary, and after graduation she and Helene establish themselves as a family that includes Astrid's younger brother and her family's elderly maid. In keeping with popular fiction, Janson's novel ends with the heroine at the altar, but the occasion is not her wedding. It is instead her ordination to the Unitarian ministry. From the altar she will embark on a life of challenge, not on a life of subjection to a husband's rule. *A Saloonkeeper's Daughter* may be read in many contexts of the American novel, but perhaps most profitably in the female *Bildungsroman* tradition in the second half of the nineteenth century, as described by Nina Baym. Three features in combination mark a significant departure from other late nineteenth century novels. There is no male relationship that makes the protagonist waver in her choice of profession; Astrid and Helene together form a stable nuclear family, and their relationship is quite explicitly also a physical union. To Nissen, "Janson ventures beyond any previous writer . . . in the period in the explicitness of her description of the two women's physical attraction to each other" (2009, 130).

A Saloonkeeper's Daughter and *Byen paa berget* were published in Norwegian and have woman protagonists and immigrant settings. Beyond these similarities, however, the contrasts between them are more readily apparent. Indeed, Dahl's novel of 1925 seems a throwback compared to Janson's of 1887 in its imagined scope for a woman's thwarted ambitions. Dahl wrote in response to a literary competition for serialization in the Iowa newspaper *Decorah-Posten*. But her plotless and uneventful story of a marriage in a small South Dakota town did not fit the format of the serialized novel and was turned down. It was accepted by her church publisher in Minneapolis, but neither contemporary reviewers nor later scholars have thought highly of it. Indeed, the story of the life and marriage of Frederikke Lervang, the city upon a hill of the title, may be more remarkable for all that does not happen than for what does. We first meet the protagonist as a self-centered and aspiring young woman fresh out of college and spending the summer of 1883 on her parents' farm in Minnesota. The slow-moving seven opening chapters (out of in all twenty-seven) set the stage for the courtship of Frederikke and Otto Lervang, a theological student. While Astrid in the earlier novel realized her ambition to be the pastor of a Unitarian congregation, Frederikke has a more modest vision of her Lutheran future: "In her dreams she had always seen herself in a vicarage—now taking leave of Otto when he was off on a journey, now jubilantly welcoming him on his return. And at other times she would be with him on visits to members of the congregation, taking part in ladies' aid meetings, and playing the organ at services while he was officiating at the altar" (Dahl 1925, ch. 9). But this is not to be. An eye disease forces Otto to leave school, and his decision to become a storekeeper in a small frontier town in the Dakota Territory is as disturbing to the high-minded Frederikke as is the door closing on her future as a pastor's wife. She goes off alone to her husband-to-be, changing trains in one frontier town after the other. The two meet to be wed in the county seat, which has a Lutheran pastor, decidedly not an occasion where she has use for her wedding gown. The baptism of their first child seems the occasion to bring it out, but the child dies after a hasty home baptism. As the years go by and Frederikke's thoughts of what might have been grow fainter, the never-to-be-used wedding gown becomes a symbol of her unrealized dreams and ambitions. Dahl, perhaps realizing that it is easier to create a convincing portrait of a woman faced with adversity than of a woman increasingly blessed with somewhat idealized children, focused most of her novel on the early years. The last five chapters present sketches of significant events, the move from the rooms above the store to their own house, the war with Spain, their silver anniversary, 1917, the year of the war that takes the life of a son, and the Spanish flu, which takes Otto's. Primarily a short story writer, Dahl wrote an unusual yet fine novel that reflects her own modest ambitions in a life in retreat, reminding us that our view of American fiction in the 1920s may be different if seen from a small town in Idaho and a church publisher in Minneapolis rather than from wherever you write for Scribner's in New York.

The best American novels in Norwegian were published as anti-immigration sentiment was flourishing, eventually leading to the legislation to restrict further immigration in the 1920s. This was the death knell for the long period of vital immigrant

literary cultures in languages other than English. The two most highly regarded novelists, Waldemar Ager and Ole Edvart Rølvaag, despairing of an American market,
began to publish their work in Norway in the 1920s, while others accepted that the
market for books was shrinking and that newspaper serialization had become the
main publishing form for novels. This chapter cannot be a history of the American
novel in languages other than English nor even of the fiction of one such language.
As a further illustration of how including fiction in languages other than English
may complement and expand our view of the American novel this chapter will conclude with brief readings of two little known novels by Ager and Rølvaag.

Ager's literary skills are apparent in his first proper novel in 1910, *Kristus for
Pilatus*, translated as *Christ before Pilate* in 1924, about the conflicts between a well-
meaning clergyman and his congregation. Immigrant churches were typically based
on ethnicity rather than on social class, and Ager's congregation includes the entire
social spectrum of the urban ethnic community, the unskilled laborer as well as
the bank director. With considerable skill Ager describes the social, cultural, and
political tensions in this community and his novel compares favorably with a better
known novel about a clergyman in a similar setting, Harold Frederic's *The Damnation of Theron Ware* (1896). A main difference between the two is similar to the difference between Cahan's English and Yiddish versions of *Yekl*; while Frederic gives
an observer's view of Theron Ware for outsider readers, Ager identifies with the
clergyman and his world.

Rølvaag is known mainly for his bestselling *Giants in the Earth* (1927). His second
novel, *Paa glemte veie* [*On Forgotten Roads*] (1914), has yet to be translated. He chose
his third, *To tullinger* [*Two Idiots*] (1920) for revision and translation as *Pure Gold* in
1930. It is a remarkable novel in the American naturalist tradition beginning with
Frank Norris and continued by such novelists as Theodore Dreiser and Richard
Wright. Like Norris's *McTeague* (1899) it explores the destructive and dehumanizing
force of "greed," as Erich von Stroheim titled his striking film version of Norris's
novel. As so many other contemporary writers, Rølvaag explored the consequences
of the loss of identity and the rootlessness and isolation of individuals without a
sense of community. It is this quintessential American theme, a theme expressed
through such diverse characters as Henry Sutpen, Jay Gatsby, and Bigger Thomas,
that also gives *Pure Gold* its compelling power. The novel opens around 1890 at
threshing time on a Minnesota farm where two young people fall in love, marry, and
settle on a farm of their own. From this warm, sensuous, and happy beginning the
story has the downward movement to be expected in naturalist fiction: avarice turns
the two country people into grotesques with hardly a vestige of humanity when they
eventually freeze to death one on each side of a locked door in lonely desperation and
terror. They are buried as paupers and their ragged and dirty clothes and belongings,
including their homemade canvas money belts packed with $72,000, are thrown on
a bonfire: "The paper which had been wrapped around the clothes and the clothes
themselves gave a cheerful flame. The belts went more slowly. But gradually they too

changed into slender columns of blue smoke which mingled with the calm, deep night and was gone" (ch. 5). The novel that began with the music of sensuous and youthful dreams ends in a vast and silent emptiness. Rølvaag's *Pure Gold* is one of the fine American naturalist novels that awaits a new generation of readers.

* * *

While previous histories of American literature have included chapters on literature in languages other than English, there may never be a literary history that fully integrates this body of American literature with that in English. The pioneering immigration historian, Marcus Lee Hansen, may have explained why in 1940: "The student of the future who is willing to conceive of American literature in more than a parochial sense must be the master of at least ten or a dozen languages" (1964, 138). Although the future imagined by Hansen has not yet arrived, it may be that we now have a Mount Pisgah view of its approach. Several publishing programs—including Editions Tintamarre at the Centenary College of Louisiana, the Arte Público Press in Houston, and the Longfellow Institute at Harvard University—are behind a growing number of translations that are making the multilingual literature of the United States available to readers who are more or less monolingual. It may be, however, that translations alone will not move this literature from the library shelves for Japanese, French, or Finnish literature to those where we find Fante, Farrell, Faulkner, and other American novelists. It may be that the prevailing concept of an American literature as a branch of English literature will have to make way for a concept of American literature as a national literature in its own right, regardless of language.

15

HENRY JAMES, THE NOVEL, AND THE MEDIASCAPES OF MODERNITY

BY JONATHAN FREEDMAN

In 1904, Henry James returned to America for the first time in thirty years. As he records in the lambent, flowing, circumlocutionary prose of his "late manner," the country had been transformed in his absence, and nowhere more so than New York. Skyscrapers towered over his beloved Trinity Church; the city was filled with strange faces (mainly "Hebrew") betokening "a human movement that affected one even then as a breaking of waves that had rolled . . . on this very strand from the other side of the globe" (*The American Scene* 1907, ch. 5); the entire town seemed gripped not only by hubbub but by a desire for "the last revelation of modernity" (ch. 4). In the 1930s, Carl Van Doren sneeringly referred to James's work as a "homesick hegira" (1921, 192). But, to the contrary, James's American journey was strikingly unsentimental. He fully depicts the lineaments of a transforming America: the vitality of its immigrants; the ascendant capitalist order the skyscraper symbolized; and the persistent urbanization that not only created regional metropolises like Chicago and Cleveland but transformed New York into a global city. This urban setting was a transatlantic mercantile hub, a center of world finance, a node of national and international communications, and a publishing capital: "the last revelation of modernity," indeed.

These elements revolutionized the life of the nation and also the world. But what might seem in retrospect to have been the most enduring transformation was the explosive growth of new media, novel forms of communicative exchange and production that utterly transformed the ecology of expression. James witnessed in his lifetime the rise of cheap pulp paper and the perfection of lithographic technologies that, combined with an increase in literacy, led to a vastly expanded mass market for print. Other developments during this time included the invention of the telephone, the typewriter, the gramophone, the radio, and the laying of transatlantic telegraph cable. New technologies such as rolled film and the easy-to-use Kodak camera altered photographic methods, replacing the tedious process of daguerreo-typing. Throughout this period, theatre grew into a mass urban entertainment, with vaudeville, music halls, arcades, circuses, and immigrant theatres. And, famously, this was a time when film technology was adumbrated and perfected, fashioned into spectacle, and transformed into narrative that would first reach working-class-centered nickelodeons and later, middle-class-friendly movie palaces.

Taken together, these developments created a new, increasingly transnational media culture. Most relevant to James is this quality of transnationality. James assumed the lead in transmitting the latest developments in British and Continental fiction to the United States via his on-site reviews in England and the Continent. He wrote about authors great (Gustave Flaubert, Honoré de Balzac, George Eliot) and not-so-great (Charles Reade, Guy de Maupassant)—and sometimes the down-right mediocre—for similar venues in England and America. Later, his prefaces to the New York edition helped define the novel as a serious art form for English and American writers alike. What James thereby helped to accomplish was relevant to more than just the internationalizing project. His critical work assured the transmis-sion of the historically vagrant form of the novel into a new environment, guiding its safe arrival in a newly emerging zone of high culture. So too did his fiction, with its powerfully dialectical relation to the emergent mass culture of the era. James's work was antagonistic toward yet at the same time inclusive of existing forms such as sentimental fiction and melodrama, and uncannily prescient with newer ones like photography and film. Indeed, I want to suggest here that James crafted a tex-tual response to modernity in its many manifestations—to the new senses of space and time and novel sensual engagements with the world, all generated, heightened, transmitted by the rise of new visual, aural, and print media. All these he placed, compellingly, at the very heart of the newly forming art of fiction, in ways that were revolutionary for his own era and that continue to reverberate in ours.

James, the Novel, and the Trials of Cosmopolitanism

Novel-writing did not come easily to James. He worked up to it through a series of five-finger exercises, many of them in the mode of his first great precursor, Nathaniel Hawthorne, and most dabbling in the form of romance. His first novels—*Watch and Ward* (1871), *Roderick Hudson* (1876), and *The American* (1877)—bore the signs of his apprenticeship, although with each successive fiction he gained greater control over his medium. With the latter two emerged a significant Jamesian motif that scholars have dubbed the "International Theme," that is, the intricate patterns of collusion and collision between Americans and the values of the Old World. These themes were central to his bestselling novella *Daisy Miller* (1879), in which the contrasting strands of a putative American innocence and a quite literally diseased Old World are woven into a tragic tapestry. The narrative traces the disastrous interaction of a soon-to-become Jamesian staple, the so-called American girl—young, leisured, beautiful, innocent—with the corrupt world of Europe. Daisy's desire to access experience in Rome leads her to a disastrous flirtation with an Italian, Giovanelli, who complies with her desire to see the swampy Colosseum. Soon after, Daisy contracts malaria and dies. The story is filtered through the viewpoint of another American expatriate, aptly named Winterbourne, who is both attracted to Daisy and stands in chilly judgment of her ingenuous unconventionality, ultimately deciphering the riddling "ambiguity of her behavior"—is she a naïf? an American flirt? an innocent?— with the verdict that "she was a young lady whom a gentleman need no longer be at pains to respect" (pt. 2). When Daisy dies insisting that she is innocent of Winterbourne's suspicions, her pleas direct the reader to question Winterbourne's judgment as thoroughly as he has questioned her virtue.

Although thematically the tale enacts the collision between an innocent America and a diseased Europe, formally it represents the marriage of Old World and New World narrative modalities: if the lesson taught by *Daisy Miller* is the incompatibility of American and European, its narrative apparatus accomplishes their union. Technically, James describes the tale as "that loved form, the *nouvelle*"—a form somewhere between the long short story and the novel, which was developed, James asserts, in France by the likes of Flaubert and de Maupassant. But of course the form is not exclusively French; what else is Herman Melville's *Billy Budd* (1888)? Moreover, James marries *Daisy Miller* to a distinctive Anglo-American form of narration. Winterbourne, the cruel, judgmental focalizer, can trace his origins to Emily Brontë's cruel, repressed narrator Lockwood in *Wuthering Heights* (1847), or to Miles Coverdale in Hawthorne's *Blithedale Romance* (1852). The tale enacts one of the multidimensional strands of cosmopolitanism—the mixing of material deriving from different national traditions—that its narrative argues is tragically impossible.

Daisy Miller is cosmopolitan in a more consequential sense, as well; the story is complex and sophisticated about the ways we know and judge other people. The narrative allows us both to enter into a limited mind and to transcend that mind, to see Daisy as an innocent unprepared for the Old World while also showing Winterbourne's perspective of Daisy in a provincial, Protestant light. This multiperspectivalism—this perspective *on* perspective—puts readers in a position to make a judgment and to distance themselves from the process of judging itself, to adopt the urbane, tolerant attitude that is nowhere available in *Daisy Miller*, but which James is attempting narratively to craft for his readership. The international success of the book suggests that audiences on both sides of the Atlantic learned the lesson.

Not until *The Portrait of a Lady* (1881), however, did the new, transnational guise for the novel truly become a part of the formal apparatus in James's fiction. Here James draws on the traditions of the English courtship novel, that form that centers on the question of the wooing, winning, and marrying of young women. Such narratives convey the notion that through love and marriage, a young woman may exchange judgmental naiveté for a deeper form of knowledge—whether that involves moving beyond prejudices like Elizabeth Bennett in Jane Austen's *Pride and Prejudice* (1813), or tempering idealism like Dorothea Brooke in George Eliot's *Middlemarch* (1874). In *Portrait*, we are presented with a beautiful, impetuous woman making just such a transition. Lively, nineteen-year-old Isabel Archer is confronted with not one but four suitors: a rich English Lord, an American inventor, a winsome and affectionate cousin, and an expatriate aesthete, "the man with the best taste in the world" (vol. 2, ch. 42). Each of these men bears with him a set of narrative precedents—and James quickly distances himself from them. Lord Warburton is a failed version of Austen's Darcy—a handsome, leonine Liberal, he seems an ineffectual anachronism. Isabel's unhappy marriage to Osmond, the aesthete, resembles Gwendolen Harleth's union to Grandcourt in Eliot's *Daniel Deronda* (1876), except that Osmond is a petty sadist rather than a grand one, and in the absence of a convenient drowning Isabel returns to Rome to fight for her step-daughter, Pansy. The possibility raised just before then—that Isabel might find a life of passion and fulfillment with the American Caspar Goodwood—is encoded in terms resembling Dorothea's embrace with Will Ladislaw near the end of *Middlemarch* (though James's lightning-and-thunderbolt theatrics are internal, not external). But James's sources are not entirely British. The very possibility that Isabel would remain in a marriage to a cold manipulator aligns the novel with the originary adultery text of nineteenth-century America, *The Scarlet Letter* (1850), as does Isabel's Hester-like decision to return to the locus of her trial and pain rather than make a new life in England.

In *Portrait*, as in *Daisy Miller*, James is crafting a transnational role for the novel itself, one that brings together British, European, and American traditions and creates new ones by their melding. But here, too, his interventions are not merely thematic; James's experimental regraftings reshape the form of the novel itself, pushing beyond precursors like Eliot to create something entirely new. Like Dorothea, Isabel serves as the filter through which we witness events, but at particularly crucial moments we are given access to her thoughts. One example of this is the famous scene from chapter 42, when Isabel muses over her misbegotten marriage. In an extensive interior monologue, Isabel's memories mix with her play of intellection to create a layered effect of re-presentation—a narrative of past events shaped by present consciousness. This form grows into the method of James's "late manner" in ways that raise deeper narrative questions; the form also grows into the modernist novel of Virginia Woolf and James Joyce, extending the technique to the breaking point. But within the context of James's career, this scene is noteworthy for pointing in directions that define his subsequent endeavors. One is toward the valorizing of a self-reliant consciousness willfully separating itself from the world—a translation into literary terms of the philosophy of Emerson or the dreamy mysticism of his Swedenborg-influenced father. Another gestures at a consciousness that acknowledges its embeddedness in a compromised social sphere. When Isabel takes a ride on the Roman campagna after learning of Madame Merle's role in "making" her marriage, she recognizes that it was "a place where people had suffered" and connects her own pain with the grief of those who had gone before her (vol. 2, ch. 49). Rome—the pestilential site of the failed cosmopolitan venture of *Daisy Miller*—becomes the site of a richer vision: one that connects the history-less American to a historically imbricated world of others given shape in Rome and by extension, Europe. Form— the union of British, Continental, and American novelistic traditions—and matter become one. James's fiction both enacts and argues for a cosmopolitan vision made possible by and finding expression in the transatlantic print culture he responded to, and in so responding, remade.

The Middle Years: Henry James, the Novel, and Late-Victorian Media Culture

James remained in England for the rest of his life, with the exception of brief trips back home to America and frequent visits to the Continent. But his work continued to engage with the expanding media culture of the late nineteenth and early twentieth century, reckoning with while taking advantage of new forms of production, communication, and representation. That engagement began with an increased interest in traditional forms, especially theater and visual arts, but broadened to include new visual media as well as new forms of information transmission which the telegraph and typewriter made possible. All of these went into the making of the late-phase Jamesian novel, the experimental audacity of which led the way not only to modernist practices, but new forms of cultural expression emerging even now.

Consider the case of drama. While the theatrical world James commented on as a critic (and sought to enter) was by and large the world of bourgeois theater, his early experience was with American melodramas like those of Dion Boucicault or the travelling company of *Uncle Tom's Cabin*. And James identifies these qualities as the essence of the art, claiming in *A Small Boy and Others* (1913) that the form's representational intensity stayed with him throughout his life. More than a half-century after observing the staged version of *Nicholas Nickelby* (1839), a production "that gracelessly managed to be all tearful melodrama," James makes a startling claim: "in face of my sharp retention . . . who shall deny the immense authority of the theater, or that the stage is the mightiest of modern engines?" (ch. 9).

James's trope of "the mightiest of modern engines" is significant, for in addition to endowing the theater with the force of the modern, the expression also assigns a role to the stage in the construction of modernity. Indeed, popular theatrical venues serve as a problematic backdrop in many of James's midcareer fictions. Set in resolutely urban locales such as Boston, New York, or London, as well as the perpetually fascinating Paris, these novels address hot-button topics such as the women's movement and anarchism. Their casts of characters run the social gamut from shop girls and Socialists to faded nobility and art-dabbling aristocrats. But they also identify public performance as an integral part of the new urban landscape. In *The Tragic Muse* (1890), the maniacally self-shaping Jewish actress, Miriam

Rooth, embodies the dedication of one's life to art, though she ultimately finds success in the popular theater. The climactic scene in *The Bostonians* (1886), when Basil snatches Verena from her feminist friends and leads her toward an uncertain future, takes place in the Boston Music Hall, a venue for public events where, Basil fears, Verena's oratory will transform her into a popular icon. In *The Princess Casamassima* (1886), working-class life, popular entertainments, and radical politics merge. Mr. Vetch, the "friend" of the woman who raises Hyacinth Robinson, plays violin at a music-hall when not attending anarchist cell meetings; Christina Light (the eponymous Princess) slums in both; and, in a crucial scene in the novel, Hyacinth escorts Millicent, the shop-girl, to the theater for the melodrama *Pearl of Paraguay*. Once there, Millicent exemplifies the close link between spectatorship and urban experience. Even while she is lost in the drama her eyes wander to the house, and when she tells Hyacinth that it is a "'shime' to bring a young lady to the play when you hadn't as much as an opera-glass for her to look at the company," she means by "company" the audience, not the actors (bk. 2, ch. 7). Both absorption and scoping reach their apogee at the same moment, as she is moved to tears by the spectacle but simultaneously points Hyacinth to a box in which appear the Princess and her sinister companion, Colonel Sholto, pointing back to him. Absorption and distraction are fully compatible for Millicent because for her, the action onstage and the social drama enacted in the stalls are one, the melodramatic panorama of urban modernity.

Thereafter, the stage—both as a stage and as a metonym for urban modernity—become staples of the Jamesian canon, and the reversal and breaking down of the barriers between them one of his most compelling subjects. In *The Ambassadors* (1903), for example, Lambert Strether encounters Chad Newsome at the Comédie Française, noting there the dramatic change in his character as well as the line between theatre and social worlds. Parisian melodrama and "Chad's own private stage" become hazy, at least for poor Strether (bk. 2, ch. 2). At the same time, as Leo Levy, Jacques Barzun and Peter Brooks have argued, melodramatic plot devices, action, scene framings, and hyperbolized moral bifurcations enter into the great later fictions like *Wings of the Dove* (1902), with its plot of a dying, innocent woman deceived by her best friend and her lover, or *The Golden Bowl* (1904), where the struggle of Maggie to save her marriage is rendered in scenes of great dramatic intensity as well as metaphors drawn directly from the melodramatic tradition. James's invocation of melodrama represents a tendency Brooks has called "the moral occult," the replacement of sacralized injunctions and prohibitions with new ones registered in theatrical and literary performance (1977, 6). But such a tendency also speaks to James's recognition of human experience mediated by a world of mass entertainment. When he famously wrote H. G. Wells in defense of his own literary practices that "it is art that *makes* life, makes interest, makes importance, for our consideration and application of these things, and I know of no substitute whatever for the force and beauty of its process" (July 10, 1915), he anticipates Marshall McLuhan's assertion that "the medium is not just the message, it is the massage." That is, expressive forms reshape our experience through the "force" as well as "the beauty of [their] process" (1967).

The truth that drama represents—the mediated, media-made quality of experience in modernity—is also operative for James in other venues such as visual art. Indeed, responses to art illustrate for James both the nature and consequences of a mediated vision. James's references to art works are not only frequent; they offer a metaphor for his own practice. We have already seen some examples: *Daisy Miller* is subtitled "a study," an artistic sketch not unlike the ones young Henry and William James composed in their early, Ruskin-dominated days of artistic education; *Portrait* takes its title from a finished version of the artistic study. But an even more extensive version of the collapse of life into visual art can be found in a later fiction, when Milly Theale of *The Wings of the Dove* recognizes her own mortality as she contemplates a Bronzino portrait of a long-dead Princess (Figure 15.1). When Strether in *The Ambassadors* spends a day in the country, it feels to him like entering a painting

Fig 15.1 Bronzino, Agnolo. *Portrait of Lucrezia Panciatchi.* 1540. Uffizi Gallery, Florence. Photo Credit: Scala / Art Resource, NY.

Fig 15.2 Lambinet, Émile. Chemin de halage à Bougival. 1860. Private Collection.

by Lambinet (Figure 15.2). Anticipating the famous argument of art historian E. H. Gombrich, James understands that the seemingly naive eye is trained by forms of representation as it seeks to know and comprehend its world. And anticipating Walter Benjamin, James understands the ways in which such a trained perceptual apparatus aestheticizes the world.

Anticipating but also going beyond these critics, the persistent lesson of James's work is that the world is *not* a work of art, and that approaching reality as such is a mistake of the first order. Milly's recognition of her own existential predicament in Bronzino's dead Princess ignores what is also salient in that portrait to her condition—the Princess's wealth and power, represented in the painting by the subject's red velvet dress and exquisite jewelry. These are precisely the assets and qualities the impecunious lovers Densher and Kate desire as they gull Milly. Strether's entry into a Lambinet is spoiled when he recognizes that the figures he thinks of as objects in the painting are actually Chad and Madame de Vionnet out for a day in the country, hence, their "virtuous relation" is a fraud. Perception understood as spectatorship, these works tell us, leads to deception, gulling, error, and delusion. This tendency may make James's poetics appear closer to those of a trompe-l'oeil painter like his American contemporary William Harnett rather than Hawthorne's or Balzac's—all the more so, perhaps, because Harnett's illusionistic art reaches its apogee in the making of trompe-l'oeil money (Figure 15.3), just like Gilbert Osmond, who is last seen in *Portrait* sketching a gold coin. By that same token, it makes the Jamesian writer—the master manipulator behind the scenes—closer to P. T. Barnum than

Fig 15.3 Harnett, William Michael. *Still-Life Five Dollar Bill.* Oil on canvas, 1877. 8 x 12 1/8 inches (20.3 x 30.8 cm). Philadelphia Museum of Art: The Alex Simpson, Jr., Collection, 1943.

Gustave Flaubert. Certainly, the fates of Strether and Milly Theale suggest in ways either melancholy or heartbreaking that there's a sucker born every minute.

James, the Novel, and the New Media of the Twentieth Century

As in the case of drama and melodrama, James does not just reference visual art; rather, he understands the medium as a catalyst for human perception and uses spectatorship as a metaphor for the glories and fallibilities of that perception. This interpretation suggests affinities between James and emerging forms of visual representation—the "new media" of his day: photography and film. In all of these, we can see James actively working alongside these media—sometimes incorporating them, sometimes paralleling them—to explore perceptual possibilities opening up in the nineteenth century and exploding in the first years of the twentieth century.

As far as the first is concerned, James had a complex relationship with the photographic image, particularly the sort most popular in his youth: the portrait. James devotes a number of loving and beautiful pages in *A Small Boy and Others* to the day he spent at age eight being photographed with his father by the first truly celebrated American photographer, Mathew Brady (Figure 15.4). Although he sometimes expressed distaste for photography, James was frequently photographed himself. The walls of his home at Rye and the desk in his study in London were filled with photos of his friends, and some of his most beautiful lines to his young friend Henrik Anderson are devoted to enumerating his glorious appearance in a photograph. Nevertheless, his work manifests ambivalence regarding the powers of photographs to capture a veridical sense of the world. When the Antiquario comes to visit Maggie in *The Golden Bowl* and sees the photograph of Amerigo and Charlotte, the image allows

Fig 15.4 Brady, Mathew. Daguerreotype of Henry James Sr. and Henry James Jr. 1854. University of California, San Diego, Matthew Brady Papers.

him to make the identification Maggie has intuited and offer the final break in the fantastical relationship in which they are enmeshed. The function of the photograph in this case, and indeed, of the ones listed above (to use the terminology of James's family friend C. S. Pierce), is indexical rather than iconic. The uncanny power of the photograph—the real light falling on the real image of the real human—points to what James refers to in his short story of the same title, "The Real Thing" (1892).

But the lesson of this story is anti-mimetic: the aristocratic couple who pose for a painted portrait are less successful models than the lower-class, raffish substitutes who replace them. In this scenario, the "real thing" is best represented by something that only looks real, and thus illusion proves to be an indispensible part of the mimetic agenda. No wonder, given James's interest in simultaneously deploying and expanding the notion of "the real," that he should have picked the young American photographer Alvin Coburn to provide the frontispieces to the *New York* edition of his work (Figure 15.5). Coburn was not only distinguished by his wonderful eye, his fine portraits, and his engaging way with distinguished older men, he was an avid participant in an emerging school of photographic theory that deemphasized

Fig 15.5 Coburn, Alvin Langdon. Photographic portrait of Henry James. 1906. *Courtesy of George East-man House, International Museum of Photography and Film.*

the indexical quality of the photographic image in favor of metaphoric, evocative qualities—the image's "iconic" possibilities, again in Pierce's terminology. This school was emerging in the first years of the twentieth century and superintended by Alfred Steiglitz, who stood in relation to photography as James did to the novel: an advocate of the proposition that a resolutely popular form could indeed serve as a form of finished and self-conscious art. An avowed Stieglitzian—to Stieglitz's own eventual contempt—Coburn was interested in using the techniques of soft focus, telephoto lenses, and manipulation of the print itself to create a photographic image that supplemented its indexical function. Supplemented rather than replaced, since, at James's own direction, Coburn shot the precise spots the author felt would best illustrate moments in his works: a corner telegraphist's shop for *In the Cage* (1898); the front of the Comedie Française for *The Ambassadors*; and a bridge over the Tiber for *Portrait*. The photographs Coburn produced, however, were determinedly non-referential. They present enigmatic, decontextualized scenes and objects bereft of human forms and social context—and this in novels that buzz and hum with social interaction. And they illustrate the books obliquely, at best—consider the frontis-piece to volume two of *The Golden Bowl* (Figure 15.6).

Fig 15.6 Coburn, Alvin Langdon. Portland Place. 1906. *Courtesy of George Eastman House, International Museum of Photography and Film.*

The shot exemplifies Coburn's commitment to a pictorialist aesthetic. It artfully places a cab off-center in the photograph but fully in the center of the vanishing point of the street. The scene is veiled by a London fog that creates a soft-focus effect in the background, which is complemented by the sharp focus of the cab and cab-driver in the foreground. Both qualities—blurring and revealing—are evident in the relation of the photograph to the text, as well. In discussing his and Coburn's efforts in the preface of *The Golden Bowl*'s New York edition, James writes that "the reference of [the frontispieces] to the Novel or Tale should exactly be NOT competitive and obvious, should on the contrary plead its case with some shyness, that of images always confessing themselves mere optical symbols or echoes, expressions of no particular thing in the text, but only of the type or idea of this or that thing." But even when considered as "type or idea," the question of reference is as misty as the background of the picture. To exactly what idea or typical thing does the image refer? The fog in the background bespeaks a romantic view of London (not the Prince's, all shops and commerce); the scene is evocative of Maggie's loneliness in the face of her odd marital situation; and there is the occasional metaphorical reference to carriages in the text. Just as the photograph does and does not refer to the real spot where the picture is taken, the image does and does not refer to the volume it illustrates. And so doing, the image is made to straddle the line between indexical and iconic, referential and metonymic, the "real" thing and the fictitious re-presentation that both James and photographers were exploring at this particular moment.

I have dwelt on these issues not merely to suggest how rich was the collaboration between James and Coburn, but also how inventively James entered into dialogue with the new technologies of his time. The turn of the century debate about the status of the photograph is one that James not only invokes but embeds in the capacious form of the novel. The very question of reference is constantly being raised, dramatized, and problematized, not only in James's criticism but in the method of the late fiction, in which the narratives circle around crucial but mysterious facts (Millie's health, Chad's relation to Madame de Vionnet) or objects (the golden bowl). These facts or objects are constantly being interrogated, interpreted, yet at the same time veiled from the novel's characters as well as the reader. James's medium, of course, was words rather than images, but the problems he was working out in his own fictional practice paralleled those of an emerging visual culture in which issues of visibility and appearance were pushing to the forefront. I will develop this parallel further, by thinking through James's concerns with those of form with which, unlike drama, art, or even photography, he had little contact: cinema.

Henry James went to the movies—occasionally. He mentions taking his niece to a variety show in London in 1900, which included an "Actuality"—a scene from the Boer War. He saw the famed, seventy-minute-long film of the James J. Corbett-Bob Fitzsimmons fight of 1897. In his 1909 story "Crapy Cornelia," James describes the approach of the title character's black hat to a cinematic close-up: "it grew nearer and nearer, while it met his eyes, after the manner of images in the kinematograph." Although critics like David Trotter have attempted to make a good deal out of these intersections—especially the last—surely the point to be made here is that out of all the possible conjunctures between James and film, there are so very few. This dearth is all the more striking in that the rise of the cinema paralleled directly the development of the Jamesian novel. From approximately 1895 to 1907, the years when Edison and the Lumière brothers were developing film technology and when early films were moving from novelty items as entr'actes at variety shows to entertainment staples, James was undergoing his trial by drama and refashioning the novel into the form of the "later phase." Indeed, during this time the film industry was frequently developing in physical proximity with James: Biograph built a studio in 1907 on Fourteenth Street and Fifth Avenue, six blocks up from James's beloved Washington Square; a number of filmmakers gathered in Hove and Brighton—not forty miles from James's Lamb House in Rye—to form an essential cog not just in the British film industry, but in the development of cinema itself. Drawn to Sussex by the light, and working in tandem with each other, the so-called Brighton School created an "English Hollywood" via figures like the American Charles Urban, who rose to be the head of the international arm of Edison's motion picture operations; inventor-tinkerer-filmmakers like Theodore Brown, Esmé Cowlings, Alfred Darling, and, most prominently, George Albert Smith, a magic-lantern performer, lecturer, and hypnotist who turned to writing and directing a number of short films between 1898 and 1903.

Smith's films are whimsical, bizarre, complex, and amusing: they display to a full extent the agenda Tom Gunning has described as that of the "cinema of attractions," that is, the tendency of early cinema to celebrate "film's ability to show something" rather than tell stories, to present an audience with a view or a vision that solicits ocular and somatic rather than narrative excitement. Gunning notes in his article "The Cinema of Attractions: Early Film, Its Spectator, and the Avant-Garde" that this is an "exhibitionist cinema" rather than a voyeuristic one, "a cinema that displays its visibility, willing to rupture a self-enclosed fictional world in order to solicit the attention of its spectator" (2006, 271). Smith's rupturing of the "self-enclosed fictional world" is remarkable. Consider for example *Grandma's Reading Glass* (1900), in which a boy puttering with his grandmother picks up her reading glass and explores her room (Figure 15.7). Intercut are insets of the things he is peering at: a parakeet, a kitten, and—in the very middle of the film—his grandmother's eyes, twitching and revolving in anatomically impossible ways, making them visibly grotesque (Figure 15.8).

Fig 15.7 Cinematic still from *Grandma's Reading Glass*. Directed by George Albert Smith. 1900.

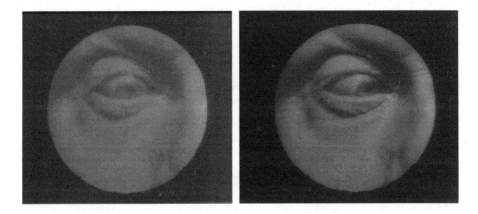

Fig 15.8 Cinematic stills from *Grandma's Reading Glass*. Directed by George Albert Smith. 1900.

This rendering of the act of vision grotesque is also the central labor of James's works of precisely this time: *The Ambassadors* and the shorter work that he was finishing when he took niece Alice to the movies, *The Sacred Fount* (1901). In the latter, a nameless narrator spending a weekend at a country house becomes obsessed with a pattern of relations he thinks he sees in which partners either flourish or decline in diametrically opposed relation to each other, draining the other's "sacred fount" while augmenting their own. Led to this belief by observing changes in his fortyish friend Mrs. Brissenden—who suddenly looks twenty-five—and her thirty-ish husband—who appears prematurely aged—the narrator visually interrogates his fellow guests, peering, prying, and scoping to discover who is draining themselves for the flourishing but seemingly unattached man, Gilbert Long, and by what mysterious means this act is being accomplished. To this end, the narrator enlists an artist, Ford Obert, and none other than Mrs. Brissenden herself, to whom he confides his fantastical theories based on his increasingly fervent observations—especially those of a beautiful unattached woman, May Server. At the end of the novel, Mrs. Brissenden—tired of his obsessive ranting or worried that he will dis-cover a secret passion—tells the narrator that he is crazy, at which point the narra-tive abruptly ends.

Read in isolation, *The Sacred Fount* is a comic meta-commentary on Jamesian fiction, a monitory parable about overinterpretation, a self-indictment of someone who was, after all, a fussy, celibate bachelor. Read in the context of James's moment, the story portrays a world governed by the logic of visual apprehension. Amidst social ambiguity, the narrator attempts to know and understand the configurations of desire through its effect on human appearances. Despite the explicit warning of the figure who should know best, Ford Obert (one consonant away from "overt"), the narrator's fervent theorization based on direct observation becomes increasingly ludicrous, making him seem less the gentleman and more the prurient voyeur. At the very end, he is left in this very position, reduced to helplessly "watching [Mrs. Briss], though the lighted rooms, retreat and disappear" (ch. 14). After speculations fold in on themselves, the narrator is left in a visual void, deflated and punished by the very means he has taken so much pleasure in exploring.

There is an analogue to this movement in a short film of Smith's, which was shot on a public street in Brighton where James might well have walked. Titled *As Seen Through a Telescope* (1900), it shows a middle-aged gentleman dressed in a morning coat and top hat gazing through a telescope while a young couple walks a bicycle behind him. As the couple pause, the gentleman turns the telescope directly at them, crouching as if he were stalking wild game, at which point we see as if through the lens a close-up of the young man adjusting the young woman's ankle-sock, then caressing her ankle in a gesture at once furtive and public. The film then cuts back to the gentleman gleefully putting down his telescope—he all but rubs his hands in pleasure—convinced that he has been unobserved. But his complacency is undone when, while passing behind him, the male bicyclist knocks him over and departs, leaving the middle-aged voyeur flat on his rump (Figure 15.9).

The similarity between James's novella and Smith's film lies in the narrative patterns that define both. In each case, everyone—viewer and viewed, spectator and object of action—is involved in some form of transgressive behavior, the activities of the observed framed by the tools of the respective media. The furtive public lovers in the former are isolated by the shot that appears to be taken from the telescope; the hyperactive couples in James's novel are foregrounded by the speculative observations of the first-person narrator. But the dynamics of scoper and scoped also mirror each other. The telescoper thinks he can spy unobserved just as the bicyclist thinks he can safely fondle his sweetheart in public; the married and unmarried lovers' own relations with each other are mimicked by the narrator's own discursive word flow, which establishes his own relation to Lady Brissenden, who, after all, is one of those whose intimacy he is observing. Both texts, moreover, are involved with the power, real or assumed, of their eye- or insight, whether augmented by the apparatus of the telescope or through the process of discussion, interpretation, and narration. In each case, the pleasure of the observer lies in his ability to peer beneath the surface to the facts of erotic connection, whether the surreptitious but thrilling ankle-pat rendered visible through the lens, or the "facts" of intimacy discerned by the narrator. Finally, in both cases those pleasures are offered to us as the spectator or reader: as we experience the telescope shot (which occupies roughly two-thirds of the film) or hear the narrator's fervid observations, we are led to share their joy at their penetrative vision—and then, comically in both cases, are deflated along with them as they are physically or verbally cuffed for their overweening pride in their own powers.

Both James and Smith explore the extensive and ramifying dynamics of pleasure and punishment that open up in what Martin Jay would term an ocular-centric culture; indeed, in both cases, text becomes something of a machine

Fig 15.9 Cinematic stills from *As Seen Through a Telescope*. Directed by George Albert Smith. 1900.

designed to produce these mingled effects in us, the reader or the viewer—and with prescient results. If, as I have suggested earlier, *Portrait* anticipates modernist narrative experiments, *The Sacred Fount* anticipates the postmodern in its exploration of limited point-of-view, narrative monomania, and most particularly in its radical undecidability. As for Smith's film, it is prescient, too. *As Seen Through a Telescope* is one of a number of early silent films in which people look through a keyhole at sexual shenanigans, usually with the result that they get physically punished for their voyeuristic activities. This is a tendency central to films like *Rear Window* (1956), not to mention less highbrow fare such as *Porky's* (1982), in which voyeurism is punished as women discern and taunt the men who are staring at them through a peephole (Figure 15.10). We seem to be a long way from Smith and even farther from James, but this node of narrative possibilities is the logical culmination of their shared sense of the alluring possibilities and punitive consequences experienced within the emerging visual culture of the twentieth century.

Fig 15.10 Cinematic still from *Porky's*. Directed by Bob Clark. 1982.

James and Hypermedia

But what about James and other emerging forms, especially those more infrastruc-
tural, like the telegraph and the typewriter? I would like to conclude with these
because his relation to them shows what I have been trying to argue, which is that
James's art and example are best to be thought of in the context of his engagement
with new media cultures, and that it is in this context that we might best reassess his
contribution to the unfolding fate of the novel.

James's fascination with telegrams has been abundantly treated in recent criticism, for which *In the Cage*, James's story of a female telegraphist, has played the role
that the Major Phase novels did in earlier criticism: as a mini-parable of Jamesian
artistry itself. The mediating or relaying role of the unnamed telegraphist; her status
as a woman in a profession increasingly devoted to people of her sex; the amazing
ability of this lower-class service worker to retain the coded messages along with the
romance-novel driven fantasies that also possess her: these serve as metaphors for
the imbrication of writing not only in the new technologies of telegraphy itself, but
as a sign of the new social relations generated by the information economy at large.

But where does the Jamesian artist fit within this new order, with its emphasis on
the commodification of language and its strings of socially puissant but meaningless code and vapid mass fiction? Surely it is significant that even as telegrams come
to play a role in James's fiction his style itself becomes ever the more untelegraphic,

as if to register a silent protest at the ways in which the compression of the form reshapes social intercourse. But James was no Luddite. He remained thoroughly engaged with new technologies and the social relations in which they were embedded. Beginning in 1898, his hands and wrists fatigued by arthritis, James began dictating his novels and continued this practice for the rest of his life, employing private secretaries such as William McAlpine, Molly Hale, and most famously, a highly educated woman named Theodora Bosanquet. Critics have not failed to notice the implications. As media theorist Friedrich Kittler notes in *Gramophone, Film, Typewriter*:

> In 1907, Henry James . . . shifted his famous, circumlocutionary style of novel writing toward Remingtonese. He hired Theordora Bosanquet, a philosopher's daughter who had worked for the offices of Whitehall and who learned to type for James's sake. . . .
>
> So it went for seven years [until] James had several strokes in 1915. His left leg became paralyzed, and his sense of orientation in space and time was impaired; only the conditioned reflex of pure, intransitive dictation remained intact. Writing in the age of media has always been a short circuit between brain physiology and communications technologies—bypassing humans or even love. Hence, James ordered the Remington, along with Theodora Bosanquet (not the other way around), to his deathbed, in order to record the real behind all fiction. Henry James had become emperor and dictated: a letter to his brother Joseph, the king of Spain; a decree specifying new construction at the Louvre and in the Tuileries; finally, some prose on the death of the royal eagle. . . . From 1907–17, a typewriter and its female operator produced the modern American novel. From that, imperial eagles died. (1986, 216)

What is striking here is Kittler's insistence on the "short circuit" (in all senses) between "brain physiologies" and "communications technologies" by which the humanness of the human is rendered null and void. His techno-determinism ignores the ways James actively made transcription respond to his own human needs. The new technologies that James adopted did not just help produce the text of the late novels. Through the dictation method, James was physically enabled to create his distinctive late style: the flood of words that constituted his normal speech were able to proceed directly onto the page free from exigencies of writing itself, much less the further elisions necessitated by his badly cramping hands. The crucial ingredient here is voice, traditionally the means of expression most fully connected to the body and with the idea of presence, plentitude of meaning, and vatic authority. To be sure, voice at James's moment was being rendered both proliferative and subject to mechanical reproduction with the advent of the gramophone and the telephone. And, as we have seen, the voice speaking these texts is subject to multiple forms of mediation, human and technological, expressed in the very word "typewriter," which could designate either the machine or its operator. That being said, we miss something crucial about James's audacity if we forget that these works might not only be viewed as authoritative novelistic texts, but also as written records of a verbal descanting that merge or cross over between forms of writing and speech.

Consider the first work James produced via dictation, *The Turn of the Screw* (1898), which possesses one of the most intricate framing devices of any fiction I know. The story begins, famously, with a nod to the power of the spoken. A verbally narrated "story held us, round the fire, sufficiently breathless," which is followed by the promise of another guest, Douglas, to top it and give the story "another turn of the screw." But the tale that follows, the tale of *The Turn of the Screw* itself, is Douglas's performance of the written manuscript "read with a fine clearness that was like a rendering to the ear of the beauty of his author's hand" (pt. 1). The story thus mimics the process of its own production, presenting itself as an unstable amalgam of speech and writing, transcript and original, never making up its mind as to which is primary, the text or the voice, the spoken or the written tale or the recreated performance of it. And this ambiguity mirrors that of the narrative, in which the exact nature of the ghosts is rendered undecidable. (A product of the governess's imagination? The children's? Or "real" spirits?) The point of the story and frame is to question the notion of narrative authority—both a concomitant of James's writing practices and a logical extension of them.

Taking seriously James's composition practices suggests that we recognize the radical experimentalism of his work. Theodora Bosanquet once observed that James could only dictate to the sound of one particular typewriter, the Remington, suggesting that, like Douglas, he was attuned to the sonic dimension of his own work. Accordingly, we might think of his texts in a performative sense, as a kind of lied to typewriter accompaniment. This would make James appear more like his contemporary, the wildly popular opera singer Jenny Lind, also known as "the Swedish Nightingale," than a writer like Charles Dickens who made a second career of public readings. Alternately, given James's early engagement with the form, it might be thought of as impassioned dramatic speech to musical accompaniment—in short, melodrama. Or we could think of the texts themselves as being like early phonograph recordings, the technology of which (impressions made on tinfoil, one-time reproduction only) involved many of the same questions of presence and absence, immediacy and authority, as did James's late work.

Or perhaps James's mode of production might be best seen as being more in tune with our own multimedia forms than with the novel as he himself found it, or even the novel as he left it. The point is not that one should think about James's novels as, say, proto-multimedia-blogs, or console game environments, or MP3-player enabled texts, as enticing as those prospects may be. Rather, in his attempt to merge voice and writing, presence and textuality, precisely at the point of their seeming estrangement, James speaks to our own condition as we seek to guarantee a place for humanness in an environment that is advancing well beyond human agency. His openness to a multiplicity of media technologies, traditional and innovative; his acceptance and indeed conscious exploitation of the necessarily mediated quality of expression; his productive response to the opportunities opened up by the new media of his moment even as he sought to shape them in ways that allowed for the affirmation of embodied being: these are not merely indices of James's crucial role in the remaking of the novel, but a guide and a goad to creators of our own moment, poised on the threshold of a media transformation as all-encompassing in its nature and as revolutionary in its effects as the one James faced a century ago.

16

THE NOVEL AND THE EARLY CINEMA

BY JOHN MICHAEL

Film Adaptation and Novel Form

In 1926 MGM released a film version of *The Scarlet Letter*. Directed by Victor Sjöström, written by Francis Marion, and staring Lillian Gish as Hester, the film spends its first half investigating a budding romance between Gish's girlish Hester and the straight laced minister Arthur Dimmesdale (Lars Hanson). This courtship, of course, forms no part of Hawthorne's novel. The film also documents, often for comic effect, a host of ersatz Puritan courting rituals and ritual punishments including ducking stools and neck stocks that either have no place in Hawthorne's 1850 novel or appear there with vastly different effect. The movie's depiction of Hester and Dimmesdale falling in love seems more like later Hollywood comedies, such as *Bringing Up Baby* (1938), than Hawthorne's austere historical romance. Things in the film do finally turn serious when Chillingworth (Henry Walthall), Hester's long-lost husband, appears and rapidly brings the film to its crisis on the town scaffold. Even here, however, the film comes to a wholly satisfying melodramatic resolution that seems very unlike the novel's famously ambiguous end.

Early films often adapted American novels and were notorious for playing fast and loose when doing so. 1926 also saw an ambitious film version of Herman Melville's 1851 *Moby-Dick* (not as well known then as now) appear as *The Sea Beast*. Directed by Milard Webb, written by Bess Meredyth, and starring John Barrymore as Ahab, the film features some remarkable innovations. Ahab, it seems, has an evil brother, Derek (George O'Hara), who, consumed with sibling and sexual jealousy, precipitates Ahab's accident with the whale by pushing him out of the boat and into Moby Dick's maw. He then returns to Nantucket and claims Ahab's young girl friend (Dolores Costello) as his own, telling her that Ahab loves her no longer.

Misunderstanding his lover's attitude and maddened by his failure as suitor rather than his injury, Ahab dedicates himself to vengeance on the whale. After some remarkable sequences depicting the laboring men of the whaling industry—scenes that capture Melville's fascination with whaling very well indeed—the movie arrives at a surprisingly happy ending. Ahab, learning of Derek's treachery, regains his senses, renounces his quest for vengeance on the brute and avenges himself on his brother instead. Finally, he happily returns to Nantucket to marry his lover and live his days in happy domesticity.

Then as now, film adaptations of novels elicited howls of protest from literary-minded critics. Writing in *The Wall Street Journal*, August 12, 1926, James Metcalfe gave this assessment of *The Scarlet Letter* in an essay called "What the Movies Do to Classics":

> Not having lived in the early Colonial days we lay no claim to exact knowledge of the general correctness of the production but we have read Nathaniel Hawthorne's *The Scarlet Letter* and feel entirely competent to say that this movie drama is not Nathaniel Hawthorne's tragic and austere romance but more in the nature of a burlesque of it. The adapters of the tale to the screen have not been content with destroying the atmosphere created by the author but have man-handled the plot in a way to make it almost unrecognizable.

Similar criticism might be made of other, later adaptations of American literary classics, including Roland Joffé's 1995 remake of *The Scarlet Letter* with Demi Moore as Hester and John Huston's magnificent 1956 version of *Moby-Dick* with Gregory Peck as Ahab. The many versions of *Last of the Mohicans* (1826), beginning with Maurice Tourneur's 1920 version and including Michael Mann's impressive 1992 edition, depart significantly from Cooper's tale in plot, character, and action.

Anyone who has studied film adaptations—indeed, anyone who has seen a film based on a novel with someone who has read (or worse, taught) the original—is familiar with such criticisms. More so than adaptations of novels to the stage or the opera—to take two examples—adaptations of novels to film have provoked criticism, polemics, and theories. Can film do justice to novels? Is there a fundamental incompatibility between novelistic and cinematic forms of narration? Do differences in the media assure that film adaptations of novels will always be inferior to their originals? Film has generally come off rather badly in studies of adaptations. Thirty years ago, Seymour Chatman's widely influential account of the different narrative potentialities of novels and films set the tone for many adaptation studies to follow. In Chatman's view, film cannot describe, it can only depict, it cannot represent interiority but only action, it cannot show ideas or concepts but only people and things. The novel has free indirect style and omniscient narration; film has, early on, only the cumbersome intrusions of intertitles or, later, the equally clumsy intrusiveness of voice over narration. Yet long before Chatman and contemporary adaptation theory, some of the most acute observers of the new medium noted its remarkable formal affinities with the nineteenth-century novel. Considering Sergei Eisenstein's view of these affinities will help bring into focus the way in which the desire to formulate a national narrative, often associated with nineteenth-century American novels, especially books like *The Scarlet Letter* or *Moby-Dick*, translated quite easily to the early films based upon them, however much those films may alter the details of the novels on which they are based. Film adaptation poses many interesting questions beyond the critical carping that simplistic notions of fidelity tend to encourage.

Eisenstein's work as a film theorist was almost as important to the history of early cinema as the tremendously influential films he made. In "Dickens, Griffith, and the Film Today" (1949), Eisenstein began a detailed consideration of developments in film technique by returning to Dickens's *The Cricket on the Hearth* (1845). Nothing, he says, seems less cinematic than the story's opening phrase: "The kettle began it . . . ." And yet, he argues, the tale's opening is intrinsically visual and essentially cinematic. We have, he points out, seen D. W. Griffith use precisely this technique: "As soon as we recognize this kettle as a typical close-up, we exclaim: 'Why didn't we notice it before! Of course this is the purest Griffith. How often we've seen such a close-up at the beginning of an episode, a sequence, or a whole film by him!' (By the way, we shouldn't overlook the fact that one of Griffith's earliest films was based on *The Cricket on the Hearth*)" (1977, 199). Such moments—in which something that seems purely cinematic turns out to have its origins in the nineteenth-century novel—abound in Griffith's pioneering films and become parts of the film language he helped establish. As Eisenstein notes, these moments function not only as techniques of exposition (the traditional function assigned to establishing shots), but also as modes of characterization through "atmosphere." "A close-up [the same Dickensian tea kettle] saturated, we now become aware, with typically Dickensesque 'atmosphere,' with which Griffith, with equal mastery, can envelop the severe face of life in *Way Down East*, and the icy cold moral face of his characters, who push the guilty Anna (Lillian Gish) onto the shifting surfaces of a swirling ice-break" (198–99). Griffith recognizes that visualization, which Chatman would say was film's forte, derives from novelistic techniques of characterization through atmospheric settings, like Dickens's description of Dombey's parlors in *Dombey and Son* (1848) as a way of characterizing Dombey himself. In *Way Down East*, as Eisenstein sees it, "the print of cold lies on everyone and everything—everywhere." In both novels and films, he argues, "'Atmosphere'—always and everywhere—is one of the most expressive means of revealing the inner world and ethical countenance of the characters themselves" (199). In this light, interiority may be represented at least as well on film as on the novel's page. Eisenstein makes us see how "optical" (his term) the nineteenth-century novel already is. He writes at length on the visual nature of Dickens's writing. He even edits passages from well-known novels to demonstrate how he borrowed the technique of montage, for which he is famous, from the novelist's art.

Literary critics, long convinced that film's formal qualities make successful adaptations of novels impossible, should be intrigued by Eisenstein's argument. If the

formal innovations of early narrative films—including pictographic characterization and montage (the composition of a narrative sequence from scenes separated in
space or time and then edited together)—originate in the technical innovations of
the nineteenth-century novel brought to the screen, then prejudices privileging the
literary that remain evident in many adaptation studies may need to be rethought.
As Eisenstein says, "strange as it may seem, movies also were boiling in that kettle.
From here, from Dickens, from the Victorian novel, stem the first shoots of American film esthetic . . . " (195).

Griffith himself, in a newspaper article that Eisenstein cites, bore witness to the
origins of parallel editing (an early form of montage) in the plotting of Victorian
novels, especially Dickens:

> Mr. Griffith . . . found the idea . . . in Dickens . . . [H] e might have found the same
> idea almost anywhere . . . The idea is merely that of a 'break' in the narrative, a shift-
> ing of the story from one group of characters to another group. People who write
> the long and crowded novels that Dickens did, especially when they are published
> in parts, find this practice a convenience. (qtd. in Eisenstein 1977, 205)

Making a composition of parallel plot lines may have been a convenient way of handling the complexities of long novels, but it becomes the signature effect of early film
narration and the essence, as Eisenstein says, of American film aesthetics.

One can make too much of such analogies between media. As Eisenstein himself
notes, "Analogies and resemblances can be pursued too far—they lose conviction
and charm" (1977, 213). But tracing Griffith's invention of an important syntacti-
cal component of modern film language back to innovations in characterization
and plotting associated with the nineteenth-century novel suggest that fidelity of
adaptation to the original may be more difficult to assess than commonly thought.
So, though I will give some attention in what follows to the traditional questions of
fidelity that adaptation studies usually pose, my interest lies less in adjudicating the
differences between film and novel that have occupied adaptation studies for a long
while than in considering a certain continuity of form and purpose that runs from
novels in the nineteenth century to cinema in the twentieth and is reflected both in
the cinematic text and in some remarkable early commentary on it. These continuities might be more evident if we take a hint from Eisenstein and consider filmed
versions of novels as translations from one kindred storytelling language to another
rather than as adaptations across incompatible media.

Film Translations and Artistic Vision

Considering filmed versions of novels as translations rather than adaptations does
not, of course, make fidelity an uninteresting question, though it does redefine
the terms in which that question might be considered. Considering the fidelity of

adaptations as an aspect of their character as translations refocuses attention on the complex issue of what one expects a successful adaptation to be faithful to. Emily Apter has argued in *The Translation Zone* that a concept of translation that moves away from mechanical questions of fidelity or felicity and toward an analogy with genetics and codes might end arid debates and pointless criticism. Adaptations, like translations, often achieve fidelity not to the surface characteristics of the original (never a possibility, in any case, since those surface characteristics are the properties of the original language or medium) but to the deep structure or code, the artistic impulse or aesthetic effect manifest in or by the original work.

Film historians have known this for a long time. In contrast to many students of adaptation, who fixate on the incompatibility of these media, film historians have often sided with Eisenstein and recognized the ways in which the novel and film seem to be made for each other. As Tom Gunning puts it, "Across the chasm between showing and telling the two narrative discourses seem to signal each other" (2009, 393). But even when a film seems faithful to the formal details of its original, interesting problems of fidelity can arise. Consider a widely recognized moment in the history of the novel when the form of narration reaches a significant peak of formal complexity, the scene of the agricultural fair in Gustave Flaubert's *Madame Bovary* (1857). This is an appropriate example because, as Robert Stam has argued, *Madame Bovary* is "proto-cinematic" in its exploitation of point-of-view and what Stam calls the "feel" of seeing (2005, 144). For Stam, Flaubert's novel marks "a moment in the history of literature and of the visual arts when a kind of mobilized regard crystallizes the altered perceptions associated with modernity" (155). Flaubert helps us see the formal affinities that allowed nineteenth-century novels to come so readily to the screen. Moreover, Vincent Minelli's 1949 adaptation of the novel, and particularly its attempt to render the scene at the fair on film, suggests ways in which the fidelity of an adaptation is more than merely a question of compatible or incompatible media.

Flaubert worked on this scene a long time. In it Emma and Rodolphe sit on a balcony overlooking Yonville's agricultural fair. While a local official delivers a bombastic speech on duty and the glory of a life spent in rural labor ("You! Farmers and Workers of the Countryside! You peaceful pioneers of civilization! You men of progress and morality!"), Rodolphe is hard at work himself, seducing Emma (pt. 2, ch. 8). As he presses his point in the room above, the official below begins to the award prizes for crops and fertilizer and livestock. Flaubert arranges these simultaneous but spatially disjunctive scenes so that they interrupt and reflect upon each other:

> "What chance has dictated that we should meet?" Rodolphe asked. "Like two rivers that run over miles of distance to combine, we have found our way toward each other."
>
> And he took her hand; she did not withdraw it.
>
> "Prize for the overall maintenance of cultivation!" cried the president.

"As soon as I saw you at your house, for example . . . ."

"To M. Bizet, de Quincampoix."

"I somehow knew that I would be with you . . . ."

"Seventy francs"

"A hundred times I tried to leave, but I followed you. I stayed."

"Manure [*fumiers*]." (pt, 2, ch, 8, author's trans.)

The ironic intercutting of these scenes reaches a comic climax when Rodolphe declares his helpless devotion and the official says "Manure" ("fumiers" in French suggests not only "shit" but a low-life "bullshitter," like Rodolphe, as well). Flaubert's intercutting of these two levels of action undercuts both the official sentimentalization of peasant virtue and the romantic banalities of Rodolphe's lovemaking. Moreover, Flaubert achieves these mutually corrosive ironies by deploying a mode of disrupted action and parallel editing akin to those proto-cinematic techniques that Eisenstein found in Dickens. Flaubert's novel—and especially this scene—seems ready for the screen.

But the film adaptation of the novel demonstrates how even when the mechanics of form in a given novel seem to lend themselves to cinematic realization, serious pitfalls remain. Robert Ardery's screenplay does faithfully follow the plot and effectively mimics some of the formal devices in the book, with one important exception. He frames the novel (as have some of the most interesting recent critics of the novel) with the proceedings of Flaubert's obscenity trial, following fairly closely that language used by the imperial prosecutor, Ernest Pinard, and assigning Flaubert's attorney's defense to Flaubert himself (James Mason). In the film, Flaubert in court retells his novel, with occasional voiceovers, as a morality tale about the evils of poor education and an over active feminine imagination. Thus, like Flaubert's attorney, the film settles for moralizing melodrama that fails to translate the novel's unsettling and finely etched acidity.

This comforting moralizing of the film (as opposed to the novel's disquieting ironies) is evident even in Minelli's fairly faithful transcription of the scene at the agricultural fair. Like the novel, the film depicts Rodolphe (Louis Jordan) and Emma (Jennifer Jones) in an empty room overlooking the town square. In the film, as in the novel, one overhears the official talking about "Manure, manure, we must have more manure." But because the film's scene remains focused on the lovers, "narrativized," as it were, through Emma's overheated imagination and bodice-heaving passion, and, most important, because the film shows the characters reacting to and commenting on the speech's absurdity, smirking with superior disdain, the scene in the film achieves a very different effect from the scene in the novel. Like the whole movie, it lacks Flaubert's ironic and destabilizing distancing achieved in the novel's construction by the careful juxtaposition of voices, without commentary from the narrator or the characters to direct the reader's reaction. In the film, the scene becomes less an ironic evacuation of both Emma's romantic yearnings and Yonville's quotidian realities and more certainly an example of what Emma wants to escape. In the film, rather than being held at a distance, the audience identifies with Emma. In short, Minelli's film supplies what Flaubert worked hard to avoid—a comfortably identifiable moral center or significance that stabilizes and limits irony's destabilizing play. Thus, while following Flaubert's "proto-cinematic" novel with considerably more fidelity than film versions of novels usually achieve, Minelli's *Madame Bovary* still fails to bring Flaubert's vision to the screen.

This film's failure has little to do with any intrinsic differences between the media of novels and films. Moreover, cinematic adaptations of literary works can also be stunningly equal to and sometimes arguably superior to their "originals," but when this occurs, the superiority of adaptation to original also has everything to do with the incalculable problematics of translation as an art and little to do with any simple or mechanical idea of fidelity.

Consider Eric von Stroheim's 1926 film *Greed*, for which June Mathias and von Stroheim wrote the screenplay. This film offers a complicated case because there is a lost original, an eight-hour attempt to take fidelity to the text—Frank Norris's novel *McTeague* (1899)—to an extreme. The director's ambitions were thwarted, however, when the studio, driven by commercial considerations, cut von Stroheim's masterpiece, sacrificing entire subplots (Old Grannis and Miss Baker, Zerkow and Maria) and many scenes, to a more normal running length of just over three hours and retitled the remainder *Greed*. Despite the deviations from Norris's plotting and design that these edits entailed, *Greed*, focused on the story of how McTeague's wife Trina's $5,000 lottery windfall destroys the couple and their erstwhile friend Marcus, remains a remarkably faithful adaptation of Norris's novel. There is a happy consonance between the author's insistence on the "truth" of his tale and the filmmaker's insistence on location shooting, even in the grueling environment of Death Valley, to capture the novel's grisly ending. Beyond its realism and fidelity, however, Stoheim's film, arguably, realizes Norris's vision of truthful objectivity far better than the novel does.

Norris, for example, cannot hide his distaste for his characters. The opening paragraph of *McTeague* typifies the novel's method:

> It was Sunday, and, according to his custom on that day, McTeague took his dinner at two in the afternoon at the car conductors' coffee-joint on Polk Street. He had thick gray soup; heavy, underdone meat, very hot, on a cold plate; two kinds of vegetables; and a sort of suet pudding, full of strong butter and sugar. On his way back to his office, one block above, he stopped at Joe Frenna's saloon and bought a pitcher of steam beer. It was his habit to leave the pitcher there on his way to dinner.

McTeague then returns to his "Dental Parlors," removes his coat and shoes, crams his little stove full of coke, drinks his beer and reads the paper "while his food digested; crop-full, stupid, and warm" (ch. 1). This is fine writing, closely observed, topographically accurate, and atmospheric. Yet Norris's inability to refrain from editorializing adjectives applied to the hero's food and conduct underscores the disgust he feels and expects his readers to share. Norris's narrator intrudes his judgments throughout the novel and creates an effect strangely at odds with the author's claim to naturalistic objectivity. The narrator always seems to be slumming on Polk Street.

By contrast, Stroheim's cinematography of Polk Street and its environs realizes Norris's promise to make this a "tale of San Francisco" and by making full use of film's documentary capacities to present the residents of Polk Street with more resolute neutrality than Norris. But Stroheim's "truth" lies not in his projected fidelity to Norris's text, nor in his less judgmental presentation of the novel's characters. *Greed* offers its own poetic editorializing, notably realized through Stroheim's use of montage. In fact, sometimes Stroheim seems to realize Norris's naturalist vision best when he departs by design from strict fidelity to the novel. For example, Norris mentions McTeague's past as a cart boy in the gold mines in a brief digression after the novel describes its hero's Sunday routine. Stroheim's film begins more elaborately and focuses not on McTeague but on gold, not on character itself but on the impersonal forces—economic as well as hereditary—that determine it.

Greed begins—as many film adaptations of books do—with a photograph of a book. In this case, however, it is not the novel but a paragraph of Norris's prose, from his essay "The Responsibilities of the Novelist" (1902), printed on an open book's page: "I never truckled; I never took the hat to Fashion and held it out for pennies. By God I told them the truth. . . . They liked or they didn't like it. What had that to do with me? I told them the truth, I knew it for the truth then, and I know it for the truth now." After cast lists and credits, the film's beginning opens an iris on yet another text localizing the first sequence in time and space: "The Big Dipper Gold Mine, Placer County California 1908." The iris closes and reopens on yet another text, a bit of doggerel: "GOLD-GOLD-GOLD-GOLD / Bright and Yellow, Hard and Cold / Molten, Graven, Hammered, Rolled / Hard to Get and Light to Hold / Taken, Borrowed, Squantered-Doled." The film irises in and opens with a high-angle establishing shot of the mine, then cuts to men tending heavy hydraulic hammers, then to a close-up that shows mechanical sledges that break the ore to extract the gold from it. A close-up shot of muddy hands scooping and straining the pulverized slurry containing the bright flecks of gold in it follows. Next comes a sequence of shots of men laboring up from the mine's mouth with heavy rail carts laden with large chunks of ore. In this way, Stroheim documents the work required to get the gold before individualizing one of the laborers pushing the carts in a medium close up. This, of course, is McTeague (Gibson Gowland). The film then shows in more detail than the novel McTeague's life in the mines, his enormous strength, his mawkish sentimentality, and his uncontrollable rages. In one sequence, he rescues a wounded bird and when another miner smacks it out of his hand he throws the man off a trestle—the intertitle reads, "Such was McTeague."

In the novel, Norris deploys gold as an overt, stylized matrix of symbols that sometimes seems overly literary. Gold appears, for instance, in the huge, gilded sign shaped like a tooth that marks McTeague's dental parlors and defines the limits of his professional aspiration. Gold leads to madness: mad Maria Macapa repeatedly invokes a gold dinner service that her family once possessed; it comes to obsess Zirkow, finally driving him mad as well, as do the gold pieces that Trina wins, and fondles, and hoards. Gold leads to Trina's death and to the deaths of McTeague and Marcus as well. Stroheim's film takes the logic of this conceit a step further by suggesting that gold as a commodity as well as a symbol is precious and cursed because of the amount of brutal and brutalizing human labor required to extract it from the earth. The heavy pounding of the mine's machinery not only documents the extraction process, it symbolizes as well the irresistible forces of greed—rooted not only in hereditary frailty but in an impoverishing environment as well—that ineluctably destroy each of the film's main characters the way the hydraulic hammers crush the ore. The juxtaposition of this sequence with the film that follows it comments poetically, as Eisenstein would have it, on the stark, dispassionate, documentary realism of the film's shabby setting and increasingly desperate action, a realism that Norris advocated but which his own frequently stylized and editorializing version of naturalism doesn't quite attain. Stroheim, unlike Norris, shifts attention away from judging the characters toward exhibiting the forces that produce them. In this way, his "adaptation" seems a better version of Norris's naturalism than Norris himself could make. Even when Stroheim departs from Norris's novel he is, arguably, more faithful to the novelist's aspiration to achieve a compellingly naturalist vision combining poetry and realism than was the novelist himself.

That a major film by a mature artist at the peak of power should be better than a minor novel by a young writer who began it while still in school should surprise no one. But the way in which Stroheim's film realizes Norris's vision suggests why adaptation might better be thought of as a process like translation if one understands translation as something that cannot be adequately described in terms of fidelity to an original. The film *Madame Bovary*, for all its mechanical fidelity, seems less true to Flaubert's vision than von Stroheim's reworking of Norris's novel, which, paradoxically, departs from its original but seems truer to the author's naturalist vision of dispassionate "truth" than the novel itself. Even bizarre adaptations such as *The Sea Beast* or *The Scarlet Letter*, which invent characters and plots that Melville and Hawthorne never imagined, capture something of the erotic tensions and passionate transferences, the fascination with human labor or with historical visualizations that inform the novels. Attending to what is gained (while not forgetting what is lost) when novels are translated into films allows us to appreciate not only the particular power of the new media but also some of the hopes and anxieties that attended its ascendency as well.

National Hopes, Historical Anxieties, and *The Birth of a Nation*

Artists and intellectuals have often looked to aesthetic forms like novels and films to embody the ideals and history of the nation. Despite the irreducible cosmopolitanism of early Hollywood—*Madame Bovary* was only one of many European novels adapted for the American screen and Stroheim was only one of many foreign artists working there—popular film seemed perfect as a medium for national identification. Benedict Anderson has taught a generation of literary scholars that the emergence of the nation state as an "imagined community" at the end of the eighteenth century depended upon the existence of media such as newspapers and the novel to forge the affective links upon which any community depends. With the advent of film in the first decades of the twentieth century, intellectuals and artists believed they had found a more perfect medium to unify the nation and express its character. Film audiences responded to spectacular visualizations of the nation's history just as novel readers a century earlier had responded to imaginative reconstructions of it. Historical novels were a ready source of imaginative grist for the early cinematic mill. And intellectuals witnessing the rapid rise of this popular new means for evoking the national narrative and provoking identifications with it were filled not only with hope, but also with apprehension. Two intellectuals passionately committed to a belief in American exceptionalism and to celebrating, castigating, and promoting the new media of film as a vehicle for and a threat to national culture were Gilbert Seldes and Vachel Lindsay. And the film most revered and reviled as an imaginative reworking of the nation's past was D. W. Griffith's translation of Thomas Dixon's *The Clansman* (1905) to the screen. *The Clansman*, one of three historical romances Dixon wrote tracing the reassertion of white supremacy as a form of national healing in the postreconstruction south, offers a sentimental portrayal of America as a nation unified by its Anglo-Saxon heritage and troubled only by the presence of unassimilable racial others who become the occasion for the fraternal struggle of the Civil War and the sectional strife of the postwar period. *The Birth of a Nation* (1915), Griffith's adaptation of Dixon's vision of the United States, was not only Hollywood's first blockbuster, it was also the first major work of cinematic art that programmatically set out to reunite the nation's people by presenting them a version of their own history meant to heal the wounds of sectional discord and Civil War. The effect of Griffith's translation of Dixon's racist romance was, of course, somewhat different.

Not everyone thought that the new medium should lend itself to spectacular stagings of national narratives. Seldes, who was a popular essayist during the first half of the twentieth century and among the first widely read writers on movies, in his best known early book, *The Seven Lively Arts* (1924), championed the anarchic energies of early cinema—especially slapstick comedies—as an antidote to what George Santayana had castigated as the "genteel tradition" in American culture. Max Sennett's Keystone Cops were, for Seldes, a truer expression of America's character than D. W. Griffith's *The Birth of a Nation*. Seldes disliked film adaptations of novels in general, not because they did violence to their literary originals but because they imported "the whole baggage of the romantic and sentimental novel and theatre" (13), epitomes of the genteel tradition, and in doing so turned their back on their more revolutionary "Rabelesian" potentials. He detested the melodramatic narratives, opulent spectacles, and costume dramas—frequently borrowed from literature—that came to dominate the movie scene after D. W. Griffith's adaptation of Thomas Dixon's novels made historical spectacle a Hollywood staple. Seldes manifests a certain vanguardist sensibility (his favorite novelist was his friend James Joyce), but he also shows a deep appreciation of the new medium's vast potential to move mass audiences and to upset middle-class commonplaces and complacencies. Film, Seldes admonished no less a personage that D. W. Griffith himself, is merely "movement governed by light" (2001, 324); and while he admired the director's early work he excoriated—on purely aesthetic grounds— Griffith's seminal *The Birth of a Nation*. "[N]early all your absurdities began about this time," he complained.

Seldes rebelled against precisely the sensational and sentimental propensities in narrative films that attempted to embody ideas about the nation and its people. From "*The Birth [of a Nation]*," he wrote, "sprang the spectacle film" and the spectacle film, while it may have been "intrinsically all right," vitiated both Griffith's gifts and the industry's potential and helped to establish the film as, sadly, "a genteel intellectual entertainment" with its reassuring moral complacencies and political pieties (331). If the nation were to find itself in the movies, Seldes believed, it would not be in the soaring sentiments of the historical romance but in the pratfalls of slapstick comedy that captured the visceral anarchy of the American people.

While Seldes's distaste for the genteel tradition was widespread among intellectual elites during the first half of the last century, his belief that film realized its highest potential with the Keystone Cops was a minority position. Vachel Lindsay, a popular poet who—among other achievements—composed verse narratives on national themes like John Brown and Daniel Webster, was more typical in his belief that film's combination of history and spectacle might fulfill what many felt was a longstanding American need. According to Lindsay, nineteenth-century writers tried but failed to present the nation's people with democratic representations of themselves, and the nation with an image of its own unifying identity. Film, he hoped, could succeed where literature had failed.

Like Eisenstein, Lindsay recognized a formal affiliation between novels and films. He developed a scheme of film types that included categories such as the Action Picture, the Intimate Picture, and the Crowd Picture. But film, he adds, also tends to mix these genres and modes: "You will not be apt to find a pure example of the Intimate" or any other photo-play form, he notes (1970, 57). Like the nineteenth-century novel, popular films combine a bewildering assortment of discourses and modes—romantic tales, historical spectacle, sociological observation, travelogue and fantasy, and more. The most powerful, popular pictures of the early period combine elements of historical drama, romantic or domestic intimacy and intrigue, spectacular crowds, authentic settings, and personalized portraiture. The popular narrative film comes to mix elements of the earliest cinema of attractions which, as Tom Gunning notes, tended to produce exhibits, with narrative film's tendency to reveal, combining public spectacle with the voyeur's gaze. The narrative film, in Gunning's account, orients its spectators as voyeurs while the cinema of attractions—the rendering of things and events as spectacle—constructs them as an audience (2006).

Lindsay's commentary indicates that after Griffith, film began to take over the nineteenth-century historical romance's project of making the national narrative powerfully appealing to a popular audience, often by adapting historical novels for the screen. The combination of spectacular historical recreation and intimately realized quotidian details (including intimate views of historical personages) is often what critics mean when they speak of novels or films that bring history to life. Intellectuals have often believed that modern nations, especially the United States, require national narratives that live to forge their unity. They believed that early film narratives, often with borrowed plots and settings from novels such as *Last of the Mohicans* or *The Scarlet Letter*, could help to forge a national narrative and identity. The personalized elements of private life these tales exposed to the public frequently serve as points of popular identification with the national history they exhibit, frequently by provoking and assuaging anxiety. Watching a white woman pursued through the woods by painted Indians and finally rescued by a virile and handsome Natty Bumpo in Maurice Tourneur's *Last of the Mohicans* (1920), the audience should feel personally implicated in the nation's history and its perils unfolding before their eyes.

Lindsay believed in the spectacular potentiality of such films to forge a national identity. "The possibility of showing the entire American population its own face in the Mirror Screen," he announced, "has at last come" (93). That mirroring, for Lindsay, involves two things that he believed film did especially well: representing history in the form of personal memory and capturing the omnipresence of the crowd, that quintessential topic of modern art. The experience of the crowd was also at the root of the experience of the nation. For as Whitman famously observed, the United States was a teeming nation of nations best realized in the multitudinous anonymity of its bustling city streets. "Note how easily," Lindsay instructs his readers about film's relation to history, "memories [in film] are called up, and appear in the midst of the room. . . . The dullest hero is given glorious visualizing power" (65). Moreover, what gets bodied forth on the visual plane of Hollywood's magic screen is not only historical time in the form of personal recollection, but also a determinately middle-class view of history itself as personal experience. Lindsay brings together formal analyses of film elements with an appreciation for film's ideological power. He seems, at such moments, like an American precursor to the German critic Walter

Benjamin, whose better-known meditations on film and politics would come a decade later. While Benjamin saw in film the possibility of a truly democratic art, one that could appeal to and mobilize the masses without the intercession of priestly acolytes to polish its aura, Lindsay saw in movies the possibility of linking people imaginatively to the democratic state. Unlike Benjamin, who had the example of fascist propaganda before him, Lindsay expresses few anxieties about such a political instrumentalization of aesthetics, and Griffith becomes for Lindsay the first and best example of the new medium's potential to present the nation to itself.

In his chapter on "Patriotic Splendor," Lindsay writes, "We must have Whitman-esque scenarios." Moreover, he continues, where the poet only brought the "idea of democracy to our sophisticated literati," and could not persuade "the democracy itself to read his democratic poems," here at last was a medium capable of carrying the message of democracy to the masses (93). "The photoplay," as Lindsay puts it, "penetrates in our land to the haunts of the wildest or the dullest. The isolated prospector rides twenty miles to see the same film that is displayed on Broadway . . . [T]he people's message will reach the people at last" (94–95). Thus, Lindsay imagines film taking over and completing the unfinished project of the novel, in its form, its content, and its nature as a popular medium forging the imagined community of the United States.

The reality of early film as an instrument of national unity was, of course, a little different. Despite Lindsay's optimistic upsurge, both regional conflict and disputes about what national belonging might practically mean have characterized the United States from its beginnings. These disagreements were as prevalent in the first decades of the last century as they are now. In a period defined by regional and racial strife, it is not surprising that the first full-length Hollywood blockbuster should be a spectacular historical romance, retelling the Civil War and its aftermath. *The Birth of a Nation*, as its title suggests, attempts to forge national unity among the nation's white population, north and south, by demonizing and abjecting black Americans.

By translating Dixon's popular racist romances into a spectacular historical film (Griffith himself worked on the screenplay and expanded its scope to include stirring battle scenes and a moving portrayal of Lincoln's assassination not included in the novel), Griffith hoped to give white supremacy and lynch law the present and persuasive immediacy of visual demonstration: audiences in the movie theaters would be able to see debased African American characters for themselves and witness the outrages they perpetrated upon white Americans in the south during Reconstruction. White audiences would see for themselves that the preservation of the nation's identity—the nation that Lincoln and so many soldiers gave their lives to save—required the ruthless subjugation of blacks. When the Klan rescues the white heroine from the clutches of her black pursuer and restores order by expelling upstart blacks from the beleaguered southern town, the appropriate conclusion—that not only Elsie Stoneman and the town but the nation itself has been saved—is meant to seem self-evident. Vachel Lindsay, while he deplored the film's "poisonous hatred of the negro," was enthusiastic about Griffith's powerful evocation of national feeling:

> [I] n the Birth of a Nation, which could better be called The Overthrow Negro Rule, the Ku Klux Klan dashes down the road as powerfully as Niagara pours over the cliff. Finally the white girl Elsie Stoneman . . . is rescued by the Ku Klux Klan from the mulatto politician, Silas Lynch (impersonated by George Seigmann). The lady is brought forward as a typical helpless white maiden. The white leader, Col. Ben Cameron (impersonated by Henry B. Walthall), enters not as an individual, but as representing the whole Anglo-Saxon Niagara . . . . As a result this rescue is a real climax, something the photoplays that trace strictly personal hatreds cannot achieve. (75)

Griffith sought to put film's concrete visual power and the imaginative resources of sweeping historical spectacle and suspenseful parallel editing to work demonstrating the origin of and the solution to the nation's problems. If all the troubles of the United States, including the tribulations of the Civil War (the film's most impressive sequences are its panoramic recreations of battles), originate with the arrival of Africans on these shores, and if the most pressing threat to the nation in the present day was the sexual threat black men posed to white women and the political threat black lawlessness posed to civic order (like Dixon's novels the film is obsessed with specters of rape), then the solution was the restoration of whites—through law and through terror—to their rightful place as rulers.

But Lindsay's and Griffith's hopes for national unity were doomed to be disappointed. Rather than healing the nation's divisions, the reception of *The Birth of a Nation* revealed deep disagreements in the United States about history and race. While President Woodrow Wilson endorsed it as history "written in lightning," dissent was led by, but not limited to, African American critics and intellectuals writing in the African American press. Public figures such as W. E. B. Du Bois and Jane Addams attacked the film's vision of the United States and its past. To take a typical example, Lester Walton, editor of *The New York Age* and later US ambassador to Liberia, responded to descriptions of *Birth* as "the greatest piece of work done for the film by American producers," by noting that only a white American could make such an assessment. Do "we Americans," he writes, "share the views of Germans" when it comes to triumphs of German arms? From his perspective, the problems attending the film's presentation of spurious history as visual fact were more than apparent:

> If at any time during the Reconstruction Period colored members of the legislature walked about in their bare feet, drank liquor and committed other acts of indiscretion during the session of the legislature as described by the film . . . we would highly appreciate [the] favor if facts were published. . . . The Chicago Tribune says: "The sin of the film is its effectiveness." We say the sin of the film is its viciousness— its distortion of history and its uncalled [for] assault on a race that was loyal when

such men as Thomas Dixon opposed the North which he now cunningly seeks to win over (qtd. in Everett 2001, 79–80).

Certainly the film's effectiveness was part of the problem. This film, like historical novels at the beginning of the nineteenth century, seemed, to concerned intellectuals, to pose a risk to historical knowledge precisely because, even more viscerally than the novel, it seemed to recreate historical experience as a distortion of historical fact.

Walton was perfectly correct to assert that Griffith hoped to reverse the results of the Civil War and to win the North over by cinematic means. Representing the Civil War as a misunderstanding among white brothers about the proper status of blacks, Griffith and Dixon hoped to promote white supremacy as the key to national unity. To a degree, despite protests by concerned intellectuals, they succeeded with their mass audience. As Russ Castronovo says, "the campaign of legal terror against black people, promoted by literature such as Thomas Dixon's romances of the Klan, justified in film by D. W. Griffith, and accepted by the mainstream press, was in accord with national taste" (2007, 118). In David Blight's assessment:

> In *The Birth of a Nation*, Griffith and Dixon gave their well-plied audiences the message not only that blacks did not want their freedom, but also that emancipation had been America's greatest and most dangerous disaster.... The lasting significance of this epic film is that by using powerful imagery, buttressed by enormous advertising and political endorsement, it etched a story of Reconstruction that has lasted long in America's historical consciousness.

The war, in this view had been noble on both sides, but reconstruction was a perilous nightmare of deranged Northern radicals and sex crazed southern blacks who threatened white womanhood and the family, imperiling the "very lifeblood of civilization," and against whom only the perpetration of a "reign of racial terror," saved the day (2001, 395). The film brings widespread racism and pervasive anxieties to a spectacular and focused point. W. E. B. Du Bois attributed the increase in lynching in 1915 to this film's enormous popularity and to its depiction of lynching as a heroic act.

In Griffith's translation of Dixon's romance into the language of narrative film, especially in his famous use of parallel editing, the audience experiences the imminent danger to the nation—to return to the most film's most famous sequence—as the threat to a beautiful white woman menaced by a hulking mulatto brute. By intercutting scenes of Lynch pursuing Elsie throughout her house with shots of the drunken mob of blacks looting the town and stirring images of white hooded Klansmen riding to the rescue, Griffith offered white American audiences a forceful representation of their own anxious sense of an imperiled national existence. In the technique Griffith pioneered, a technique Michael Paul Rogin has called "an art of simultaneities and juxtapositions rather than traditions and continuities," the temporal and spatial sweep of the nineteenth-century novel are translated into a new medium, and the disjunctions and the anxieties of the modern nation find a powerful mode of expression. Rogin quotes Griffith, "We had had all sorts of runs-to-the-rescue in pictures and horse operas. . . . Now I could see a chance to do this ride-to-the-rescue on a grand scale. Instead of saving one little Nell of the Plains, this ride would be to save a nation" (1991, 346). Though it realized this ambition with more visceral potency than the novel on which it was based, *The Birth of a Nation* did not, in fact, heal the nation's wounds nor save America from its persistent anxieties about the nature and limits of national belonging. No film and no novel ever has. Like the historical novel that preceded it, film adaptations of historical novels, early and late, become moments in America's long conflict with itself.

III

GENRE FICTION
AND THE NOVEL

17

THE DIME NOVEL

BY DAVID KAZANJIAN

> As soon as the word "genre" is sounded, as soon as it is heard, as soon as one attempts to conceive it, a limit is drawn. And when a limit is established, norms and interdictions are not far behind . . . [But] what if there were, lodged within the heart of the law [of genre] itself, a law of impurity or a principle of contamination?
>
> —Jacques Derrida, "The Law of Genre" (1980, 56–57)

> This similarity of plots, together with the absence of an international copyright agreement until 1891, made for a kind of "world literature" as sensational novels were translated back and forth from English, French, German and Yiddish, translated not to be faithful to the "original," but . . . to be adapted to local names, geography and customs.
>
> —Michael Denning, *Mechanic Accents: Dime Novels and Working-Class Culture in America* (1998 [1987], 37)

The cleanest and most systematic way of describing the classic US dime novel would be this: it was a genre of melodramatic literature, akin to but more sensationalist and affordable than the sentimental novels of the nineteenth century, that began in northeastern US publishing centers in 1860, spread to other parts of the country, and thrived until the 1910s; it was made up of a number of subgenres, such as the dime Western, the mysteries of the city, detective tales, and tales of romance; and its decline led to the rise of related genres such as pulp fiction, noir fiction, and the modern Western. The problem with this account is that it too hastily cleans up the messy origins, unruly development, and fitful legacy of the genre.

Dime novels, nickel novels, story-papers, pamphlet novels, novelettes, red-backs, yellow-backs, yellow-covered literature, paper-covered literature, railroad literature, broadsheets, libraries of adventure, cheap libraries, working-girl stories, adventure stories, domestic romances, Western tales, pulps, trash . . . The sheer number of monikers used during the nineteenth and twentieth centuries to name the genre addressed by this essay suggests that as soon as we attempt to conceive "the dime novel," we encounter "a law of impurity or a principle of contamination," to borrow terms Jacques Derrida uses in my first epigraph. Indeed, it was not until well after the genre's heyday had passed that "dime novel" effectively eclipsed other monikers like those listed above, such that today "dime novel" is often used broadly as a name for sensational literature in general. The term "dime novel" itself began simply as a brand name used by the Beadle and Company publishing house for their series of cheap, paper-covered works of sensationalist fiction measuring about four inches by six inches and running barely over one hundred pages. Yet even the often cited origin of the term—the first volume of Beadle's series, *Malaeska, the Indian Wife of the White Hunter* by Ann S. Stephens (1860)—was a modified reprint of a tale published well before "dime novel" even existed as a popular expression: a short story called "The Jockey Cap," first published in April 1836 by the *Portland Magazine* and then expanded as a serial in a story-paper called *Ladies' Companion: A Monthly Magazine* during February, March, and April of 1839. The literature we have come to call the dime novel, then, ought to be understood less as a coherent genre with an enumerable set of formal features and more as an historically specific but *unruly* body of popular culture that indexes the social conflicts, transformations, and potentials of the nineteenth and early twentieth centuries.

This unruliness was expressed in a number of ways, four of which I will discuss in this essay. First, as a *genre* the dime novel developed out of eighteenth- and early nineteenth-century serialized fiction that drew wide audiences in Europe and early America. Not only were many dime novels reprints of those earlier, serialized fictions, but also US publishers pirated European popular fiction as it was published, just as Europeans pirated US popular fiction (on serialized fictions and piracy, see Chapter 2 of this volume). Even texts that were not pirated usually drew their narratives from the most exciting and shocking newspaper stories of the day. From its origins in the nineteenth century through its decline in the 1910s, then, the dime novel was something of a stolen literature. What is more, as we will see, these illicit and unruly cultural flows ran north and south, throughout the Americas, as much as east and west. All this traffic in sensational culture produced texts that both conformed to *and* transgressed generic "norms and interdictions."

Second, the *conditions of production* of these texts were—like other early industrial capitalist ventures—at once cutthroat, chaotic, and highly regimented. The dime novel enterprise was spurred by technological revolutions in printing; organized by sharp divisions of labor; driven by publishers' insistence on speed and quantity; and forced into cycles of bust and boom by fluctuating postal rates as well as regular global and national economic crises. Those booms and busts led to periodic disorganizations and reorganizations of the literature's production, distribution, and consumption processes and, coextensively, of the very shape of the genre itself.

Third, the *practices of reading* these texts did not conform to the images usually associated with nineteenth-century bourgeois culture: families gathered around a living-room fireplace listening to uplifting literary recitations, or an individual with leisure time huddled close to a candle or gaslight, poring over sentimental stories of adventure, tragedy, and hope. Rather, thanks to mass circulation, the rise of lending libraries, and relatively high literacy rates resulting from burgeoning, compulsory mass education, poor and working people avidly consumed these "Books for the Million!" (as *Beadle's Dime Novels* series loudly proclaimed on its covers) not only in their homes, but also in workplaces, in public spaces, and en route from place to place. What is more, reading sensational fiction has long been an ideological flashpoint that set bourgeois culture against popular culture. The dime novel was decried throughout the nineteenth century and romanticized in the twentieth.

Finally, and perhaps most spectacularly to today's readers, the *content* of these novels was, to say the least, unruly. Full of scenes of violence, cross-dressing, miscegenation, crime, sex, and other underworldly activities taking place along frontiers, across national borders, and in the grimiest corners of America's immigrant-filled cities, dime novels show us how far sensational fiction strayed from the related but more genteel realm of popular, sentimental fiction. The dime novels are still great reads, and still cry out for contemporary interpretation, because they continue to unsettle presumptions and test taboos we share with the nineteenth- and twentieth-century reading masses.

Throughout this essay I will also pay particular attention to one feature of this putative genre that has been relatively neglected in contemporary scholarship: its transnational character. In my second epigraph, Michael Denning's classic 1987 study *Mechanic Accents* aptly refers to the dime novel as "a kind of 'world literature.'" The US dime novel was continually influenced by, and asserted its influence upon, sensationalist fiction written in Yiddish, Spanish, German, and French, among other languages, by immigrants to the United States as well as writers throughout Europe and the Americas. Denning's worldliness manifests figuratively, too, in the US dimes' frank and shocking depictions of race, class, sex, and violence that broached multiple borders and taboos.

My hope is that, by the end of this essay, the convenience of the genre's name will have become as flimsy and frayed as the cheap paper on which this unruly literature was printed, and as untrustworthy as the absurd and ingenious disguises so often donned by the novels' most memorable and scandalous characters.

Genre(s) of the Dime Novel

The dime novel was not invented tout court in 1860 by plucky, enterprising US publishers or by a handful of savvy American authors with their fingers on the pulse of the American people. Which is to say, the emergence of this genre confounds rather than confirms enduring nationalist myths about American culture's exceptionalism and autochthony. The eighteenth- and early nineteenth-century serialized fiction out of which the classic dime novel developed—and from which it often liberally borrowed—was a transnational, multigeneric, and multilingual phenomenon, as was the late nineteenth- and early twentieth-century dime novel itself.

Seventeenth- and eighteenth-century Europe and the American colonies were awash in sensational broadsides and pamphlets about crime, particularly confessional narratives by and about criminals sent to the gallows. At the same time, so-called captivity narratives about white settlers kidnapped by Indians enthralled the reading public on both sides of the Atlantic. These profitable genres presaged the nineteenth-century boom in sensational literature. Notably, in the early 1800s French newspapers started publishing inserts or supplements of simple folded sheets of paper printed on both sides called feuilleton, which offered true crime and fictional tales as well as analysis of important news items, cultural criticism, and social gossip. In short order, this form of publication spread throughout Europe and the Americas. As an index of this popularity, the term feuilleton was widely adopted in England, but was used to refer more specifically to a serialized work of fiction. (Indeed, the term is still used today among French speakers to mean what in Spanish is called a telenovela and in English a soap opera.)

During the 1830s, this sort of serialized fiction was quickly expanded from the supplement format, and publications devoted primarily to publishing serialized fiction sprung up throughout the Atlantic world, going by names such as "story-papers," "the penny-press," and "weeklies." Relatedly, in the United States, the popular "police gazettes" catered to "true tales" of crime and justice. Through the 1850s New Orleans had a lively feuilleton or story-paper culture in its numerous French-language newspapers as well as popular fiction serialized in Spanish-language papers, while dime novel scholars long ago established that American cities in the northeast had multilingual papers that serialized original and pirated fiction in Italian, Yiddish, and German. Although many of these serials offered genteel fiction that catered to people with means, other less expensive papers presented more sensationalist tales that were extremely popular among the poor and working classes. Indeed, the story-papers would continue to thrive alongside the classic dime novel into the twentieth century, contaminating the dime's generic purity by continually feeding it plotlines and characters.

Expanding on the success of the feuilleton and story-papers, during the late 1830s and throughout the 1840s and 1850s European and American publishers began publishing longer stories in fewer, stand-alone installments and, eventually, in complete editions under one paper cover. One of the most popular genres of such early fiction was the "mysteries of the city," which offered tales of the crime and justice, poverty and luxury, scandal and debauchery that readers liked to imagine filled the period's ever-growing urban centers. Most famous among these texts was Eugène Sue's *Les Mystères de Paris*, which began as a serial published by the conservative Paris paper *Le Journal des Débats* from 1842 to 1843. A popular sensation—and a huge money-maker for the paper despite the antagonism between its politics and Sue's socialism—the serials were quickly gathered and published in book form by 1843, and in less than ten years sold over sixty thousand copies. *Les Mystères de Paris* was immediately translated into multiple languages and republished throughout Europe and the United States. Celebrated by many socialists of the day for its exposé of the ravages of capitalism, and rigorously critiqued by Karl Marx in *The Holy Family* (1844) for the limits of that very exposé, *Les Mystères de Paris* revealed a vast market for the consumption of socially conscious, gritty urban fiction at a time when urban masses throughout Europe and the Americas were organizing and agitating for radical social transformation.

As *Les Mystères de Paris* struck a chord with readers, clones such as F. Thiele's *Die Geheimnisse von Berlin* [*The Mysteries of Berlin*] (1845) and George W. M. Reynolds's *The Mysteries of London* (1844) soon appeared. In the United States, the "mysteries of the city" genre was adapted to local contexts and conjunctures: Osgood Bradbury published his *Mysteries of Lowell* in 1844, and Ned Buntline (whose real name was Edward Zane Carroll Judson) made one of his earliest attempts at sensational fiction with *The Mysteries and Miseries of New York* in 1848. George Lippard, who along with Buntline would become one of the most prolific and well known of US dime novelists, made a splash in 1845 with *The Quaker City, or the Monks of Monk Hall: A Romance of Philadelphia Life, Mystery, and Crime*. Reminding us that nineteenth-century circuits of popular culture ran both east and west, *The Quaker City* was immediately pirated in Germany and England, appearing in Leipzig under translator Friedrich Gerstäcker's name as *Die Quakerstadt und ihre Geheimnisse* [*The Quaker City and its Mysteries*] (1846) and in London under Lippard's own name as *Dora Livingstone, the Adulteress; or, the Quaker City* (1848). As Denning and David S. Reynolds have importantly added, German immigrants to America even wrote their own, German-language "mysteries" in the United States, such as the messianic antislavery tale *Die Geheimnisse von New Orleans* [*The Mysteries of New Orleans*] by Baron Ludwig von Reizenstein and Emil Klauprecht's *Cincinnati; oder, Geheimnisse des Westens* [*Cincinnati; or, Mysteries of the West*] (1854).

Klauprecht's novel in particular underscores that this early period of cheap, sensational US fiction was by no means devoted exclusively to eastern urban themes. Mid-nineteenth-century Cincinnati was a crossroads between northern and southern, eastern and Western, as well as rural and urban North America, and thus was the perfect setting for Klauprecht to stage an "impure" hybrid between the "mysteries of the city" genre and another extremely popular genre of sensational fiction in the United States: the dime western or frontier novel. The latter proliferated after the 1860s, and provided many of the plot structures and themes that thrived in twentieth-century westerns both on the page and, eventually, the silver screen and television. Dime Westerns drew on centuries of fascination with, and advocacy of, white settler colonialism in North America, particularly on genres such as Indian captivity narratives, travel narratives, and historical romances like Sir Walter Scott's *Waverley* (1814) and James Fenimore Cooper's *Leatherstocking Tales* of the 1820s and '30s.

Alongside the "mysteries of the city" and the dime Western, we can place another extremely popular—if today less well remembered—genre of the early dime novel, one that surely influenced texts like *Cincinnati*: the US-Mexico War novelette. Thanks to advances in dispatch technology, war correspondents on or near the front lines of the 1846–48 US–Mexico War were able to send reports to their papers' offices in major US urban centers in a matter of days. Such was the appetite among US readers for news of the war that a handful of the period's most entrepreneurial publishers rushed to produce scores of inexpensive, paper-covered, one-hundred-page novels full of the nationalistic exploits of a heroic US military against "savage" and "rapacious" Mexicans. For critics today, US–Mexico War fiction reorients our understanding of the streams of sensationalist culture from the familiar east-west or Europe–United States flow to a south-north flow.

In addition to these immediate predecessors to the classic dimes, from the late 1830s through the 1850s there appeared a number of sensationalist literary works that have long escaped the attention of critics and that defy generic classification. In fact, contemporary literary historians are still discovering these long-lost gems, suggesting that we have more work to do to flesh out this period of sensational fiction, work that will further contaminate the clean story of the classic dime. For instance, Kristin Silva Gruesz has brought our attention to Victor Séjour, a French-speaking Creole who at nineteen left his native New Orleans for Paris, where he wrote and published *Le Mulâtre* [*The Mulatto*] (1837), an antislavery and antiracist tale of race-mixing set in prerevolutionary Haiti. Rather than being American, Haitian, or French, Séjour's sensational novel is thoroughly transnational, participating *in* without belonging *to* particular national literatures.

When Ann S. Stephens's *Malaeska, the Indian Wife of the White Hunter* was published in 1860 as the first volume of *Beadle's Dime Novels* series, then, it did not so much bring the dime novel genre into existence as it began an especially popular and lucrative chapter in the longer story of the genre I have briefly sketched above. After moving from Buffalo to New York City in 1859, the brothers Irwin and Erastus Beadle immediately began churning out an entire suite of cheap advice books priced at one dime: as they announced loudly on their covers, *Beadle's Dime Book of Dreams: their Romance and Mystery; Beadle's Dime Song Book; Beadle's Dime Cook Book; Beadle's Dime Book of Beauty.* As Bill Brown observes, when "the standard working-class wage amounted to six dollars a week," the dimes fit into the means of their audience much better than the one to two dollars a work of sentimental fiction typically cost (1997, 20). Other American publishers such as George Munro, Norman L. Munro, Frank Tousey, Francis Scott Street, and Francis Schubael Smith soon jumped into the successful wake of Beadle's dime enterprise.

Neither the United States nor the English language, however, had a monopoly on the late nineteenth-century dime. As W. H. Bishop wrote in his 1879 *Atlantic Monthly* review of what he called "story-paper literature": "The taste for cheap fiction is by no means confined to this country . . . not a daily paper on the continent of Europe, in any language, but has its scrap of a continued story, its feuilleton, in every issue" (383). Consider just a few examples of this world literature of sensation. In the 1880s, a genre of Yiddish sensational fiction called *shundromanen* thrived in eastern US cities among Jewish immigrants from Europe and Russia. The best-known author of these shundromanen was Shomer, the pen name of Nachum Meir Shaykevitsh, who trafficked in tragic tales of romance between rich and poor. Like many participants in the enterprise of sensational fiction, Shomer weathered the withering critiques of more genteel writers—in his case, especially high-culture Jewish writers—who saw his brand of sensation as debased. Around the same time, as Ronald A. Fullerton has explained, the 1870s saw a boom in "*colporteur*" or "ten Pfenning" novels in Germany. Drawing on oral traditions of folk tales recorded and published by the Grimm brothers, and taking advantage of 70 percent literacy rates as well as the *Gewerbefreiheit* or "free entry into trades" legislation established in the North German Confederation in 1869, a new generation of ambitious publishers gave the poor and working classes serial novels in affordable, eight-to-twelve-page installments that could run over two-hundred pages and were sold door-to-door (hence their name, as a colporteur was traditionally a traveling book peddler). Often repurposed French novels or retold tales of ghosts, knights, bandits, and romance, the colporteur novels were also distinguished by their violence and by their attention to the scandals of the elite.

In Mexico, serial novels (*folletines* or *novelas de entregas*) such as Justo Sierra O'Reilly's *Un año en el hospital de San Lázaro* [*A Year in the San Lazaro Hospital*] and *La hija del judío* [*The Jew's Daughter*] began to appear in Yucatán during the 1840s. During the 1860s, there was a miniboom of folletines published about the Caste War of Yucatán, a decades-long Maya uprising that started in 1847, such as *Los misterios de Chan Santa Cruz: Historia verdadera con episodios de novela* [*The Mysteries of Chan Santa Cruz: A True History with Novelistic Episodes*] (1864), written by leading Yucatecan creole Pantaleón Barrera under the pen name Napoleon Trebarra. Largely forgotten novels such as these were more popular than the now classic sentimental novels of the period, such as Ignacio M. Altamirano's *Clemencia* (1869). They were also precursors to sensationalist novels like Eduardo Castrejón's tale of sexual polyphany and policing in Porfirian Mexico, *Los cuarenta y uno: Novela crítico-social* [*The 41: A Novel of Social Criticism*] (1906), about a real-life police raid on a drag ball in Mexico City that resulted in the deportation of those arrested to the Yucatán itself.

By viewing the classic US dime novel of 1860–1910 in the context of both its transnational antecedents and its contemporaries in the world literature of sensational fiction, we confound rather than confirm enduring presumptions about the coherence of the genre, and even of the idea of genre itself. As Derrida suggests in "The Law of Genre," the very word "genre" promises that we can determine a unique set of discernable features belonging to certain texts that are distinct from other unique sets of discernable features belonging to other texts: "If a genre is what it is . . . then 'genres are not to be mixed;' one should not mix genres, one owes it to oneself not to get mixed up in mixing genres. Or, more rigorously: genres should not intermix" (1980, 57). Yet the very idea of genre itself oddly refuses to participate in this law of genre. That is, while the law of genre orders us to go about classifying objects within particular sets, "genre" itself is not part of any classifiable set. As the order to classify, it stands outside the law it nonetheless incites. "Genre" as such, then, has its own law, "the law of the law of genre," the law of "participation without belonging" (59). Derrida thus challenges us: what if, like the very notion of genre itself, genres could also be said to participate without fully or finally belonging to their proper sets. What if "every text participates in one or several genres, [what if] there is no genre-less text; there is always a genre and genres, yet such participation never amounts to belonging" (65). For Derrida, this suggests that *boundaries* between genres be thought instead as *folds*. Such an account of genre has, in its most far-reaching sense, "inundated and divided the borders between literature and its others" (81).

Thinking in the spirit of Derrida's unruly folds, we might consider how the dime novel folds into other popular cultures of the nineteenth and early twentieth centuries. Drawing on Linda Williams's work, Shelley Streeby has remarked that sensational fiction shared with other forms of melodrama—such as blackface minstrelsy, Barnum's freak shows, and the popular theater—an ensemble of generic conventions which "emphasizes temporal coincidences, stages moments of truth that expose villains and recognize virtue, and tries to move its audiences to experience intense feelings, such as thrill, shock, and horror" (2004, 180). Perhaps we ought to push this insight even further and notice how these features persist today in popular films, viral videos, and queer performances in *zona rosas* around the world. Were we "to get mixed up in mixing genres" in this way, we might say that what we have come to call the dime novel is, rather than a lawful set, a genre characterized by "a principle of contamination, a law of impurity, a parasitical economy" (Derrida 1980, 59): an unruly genre, or the unruliness of genre itself.

Making Dime Novels

This unruliness manifests too in the very material practices that created sensational fiction. While many dimes were authored by individual writers, much of the industry preferred a more factory-oriented production process in which teams of workers (typically women and girls) would read newspapers, clip out exciting stories, and pass along rough outlines of plots to professional writers (often moonlighting journalists and anonymous middlebrow writers) who would draft the narrative according to strict principles such as page limits, copious scenes of sex and violence, and romantic resolutions. A number of political-economic shifts during the first half of the nineteenth century created fertile conditions for the rise of this fiction factory system. First, advances in the processes of pressing and of stereotype printing—or the use of metal plates cast from molds of composed type made from materials such as papier-mâché or clay—at once drove many artisan printers out of business and created new opportunities for larger, entrepreneurial publishing houses. These publishers both innovated their own businesses and bought up other, failing papers to which they applied new technologies and popular tastes. Second, low postal rates for newspapers helped to foster the *feuilleton* or supplement and story-paper styles. Then, when rates for mailing papers increased in 1843 and rates for books decreased in 1845, conditions favored the rise of dime novels. Third, as Denning has remarked, three global economic crises—the Panics of 1837, 1857, and 1873—were followed by sensational fiction publishing booms, suggesting that low cost enterprises faired best when higher cost enterprises (such as the traditional book and newspaper trades) struggled. Fourth, the labor market during the period was flooded with a diverse pool of urban workers—including large numbers of immigrants, children, and women—who drove down wages and created conditions ripe for mass production.

In an 1892 article in *Publishers' Weekly*, reprinted from the *Boston Journal*, the accomplished nineteenth-century editor Edward W. Bok offered perhaps the most famous account of the dime novel's production process:

> This literary factory is hidden away in one of the by-streets of New York. . . . It employs over thirty people, mostly girls and women. For the most part these girls are intelligent. It is their duty to read all the daily and weekly periodicals in the land. These "exchanges" are bought by the pound from an old-junk dealer. Any unusual story of city life—mostly the misdoings of city people—is marked by these girls and turned over to one of three managers. These managers, who are men, select the best of the marked articles, and turn over such as are available to one of a corps of five women, who digest the happening given to them and transform it to a skeleton or outline for a story. This shell, if it may be so called, is then returned to the chief manager, who turns to a large address-book and adapts the skeleton to some one of the hundred or more writers entered in his book. . . . Now the most remarkable part of this remarkable literary manufactory to me was that manager's address-book of authors. . . . There were the names of at least twenty writers upon that book which the public would never think of associating with this class of work—men and women of good literary reputation, whose work is often encountered in some of our best magazines. . . . The idea of "literary factories," if we are not mistaken, originated in Berlin immediately after the success of the translations of Sir Walter Scott's novels. [There was also] a similar institution in London. . . . (231)

Bok finds "the manager's address-book of authors" the most "remarkable" aspect of the "literary manufactory" in part because the address-book foregrounds what he considers a certain class irony of the system: namely, that "men and women of good literary reputation" would deign to write trashy dime novels. However, his account actually undermines the import of the traditional, individual author by foregrounding the collective if segmented work of girls and women. Indeed, Bok offers us rare insight into the gendered division of labor in this industry. Clearly, as gender and labor historians have been pointing out for decades, early nineteenth-century working-class women and girls were not confined to the so-called private realm. Though the pay was low and the conditions difficult thanks to the publishers' oppressive insistence on productivity (meaning speed of output and long working hours), we ought not jump to the assumption that these women and girls were merely victimized cogs performing rote labor in a fiction machine. Mass-production workplaces have historically been sites of both exploitation and struggle, where the very collectivization that facilitates the owner's efficient extraction of surplus value from the workers *also* creates opportunities for workers to forge collective bonds and take collective action.

As Bok's article makes clear, many dime "authors" were pseudonyms for what were, in effect, writing workforces. Consequently, the dime novel's conditions of production unsettle one of the persistent features of literary culture: the principle of the author as individual creator and imaginative genius. While well-known dime authors such as Ned Buntline and George Lippard have gotten the most critical attention—perhaps in part because of the very comfort of the author-function—how much attention should we grant them over the work of the anonymous women and girls Bok goes out of his way to describe as "intelligent"? Consider a fictional author like "Bertha M. Clay," a name the New York publishers Street & Smith lifted from the *New York Weekly*, which had invented it during the 1870s as the "author" of tales it pirated from actual English author Charlotte M. Brame. Street & Smith used "Bertha M. Clay" for decades on their dime novels after Brame's own death in 1884, as Denning, William Noel, and Ralph Adimari have all explained. How might we understand the labor of authorship Street & Smith concealed beneath its authorial fiction?

The dime novel genre prompts us to theorize a diffuse form of authorship, one with only a fictive sovereign at its center, one in which the qualities usually associated with the individual writer—creativity, imagination, even genius—were dispersed among workers whom we might otherwise be tempted to think of as manual laborers without such qualities. When Bok describes the fiction factory girls and women as "intelligent," might we come to understand that intelligence as the source of the exuberant creativity and imagination that bursts forth from sensational fiction? Might we think of these girls and women as communal geniuses who focused the attention of "the Millions" on such gender transgressions as cross-dressing, on such racial taboos as interracial sex and marriage, and on the scenes of violence that typify—but are often censored from nationalistic accounts of—war and social conflict? Could it be that in the United States—the putative land of individualism par excellence—a radically collectivist practice of authorship thrived in the most unruly of popular culture genres? And not only in the United States, for as we learn from Bok's *Publishers' Weekly* essay, Berlin and London had their own writing workforces. As such, dimes can be said to have foreshadowed subsequent collective culture industries like Hollywood.

Reading Dime Novels

Nineteenth- and early twentieth-century readers consumed their sensational fiction wherever they could: in groups, during solitary moments, at work, on the way to and from work, at home, in public places. Such mobile musing explains some of the popularity of this cultural form. Newspaper supplements, story-papers, and lightweight novels all have portability in common: they are affordable texts that can be read on the go. Anyone familiar with today's subway and bus systems knows that such reading practices are still alive and well; paperback literature, tabloid papers, and now computer tablets are ubiquitous, even viral, on public transportation in part because they are so well suited to traveling consumption.

Reading practices are not just practical affairs, however; they are also highly charged ideological scenes. One can glean a hint of that charge in Bok's description of the "literary factory" I discussed above. Elaborating on his surprise at seeing in the manager's address-book authors "which the public would never think of associating with this class of work," Bok relates this exchange: " 'Not such a bad list of authors, is it?' laughingly said the 'manager,' as he noted my look of astonishment. I was compelled to confess it was not" (231). Bok's assumption about "the public's" sense of the class distinctions among types of literature, his "look of astonishment" at the address-book's authors, and his reluctant if quasi-penitent acknowledgment of the manager's boast together convey the deep disdain with which many among the elite and middle-classes regarded dime novels. Indeed, throughout the nineteenth and early twentieth centuries, while the masses avidly consumed dimes on the go, the vast majority of the published discussions of sensationalist fiction amounted to relentless criticism of its power to debase and degrade its readers.

Perhaps the most spectacular manifestation of such criticism was the vigorous censorship campaign of Anthony Comstock and his Society for the Suppression of Vice, founded in 1873. While the 1873 Comstock Law is most remembered for its criminalization of the mailing of contraceptive materials, it was also aimed at literature regarded as immoral, and sensational fiction was a prime example (on the Comstock laws and censorship, see chapter 3 of this volume). Anxieties about the dime novel's potential to subvert social norms shaped struggles over the creation of public libraries; over literacy and the expansion of compulsory public education; and over efforts to alleviate poverty by "reforming" the morality of the poor. While most elite critics blamed this popular literature for an array of social ills, a few others did defend it. Yet even those defenses were typically tinged with reluctance, if not outright embarrassment. As W. H. Bishop haltingly concluded in the remarkably detailed and sympathetic review of story-paper literature he published in the *Atlantic Monthly* in 1879: "The story-papers, then . . . are not an unmixed evil" (393). Presaging Derrida's "law of the law of genre," Bishop suggests that dime novels indeed get mixed up in mixing their presumptive purity, be it pure evil or pure good.

A striking scene from a novel I mentioned above—Emil Klauprecht's genre-mixing *Cincinnati; or, Mysteries of the West*—offers insight into the wider social import of these anxieties over the value of popular culture. During a social gathering of visiting European elites and homegrown white American settler-colonists, a "sweet," "charming," and "enchanting" performance of Beethoven's "Adelaide" by the beautiful German singer Johanna immediately puts the audience of American "pork aristocrats" to sleep. When Johanna deftly switches to a rousing rendition of "Yankee Doodle," one of the aroused Americans roars with approval: "'Splendid! Magnificent!' old Zacharias cried when Johanna was finished and all the gentlemen clapped their approval so that the walls shook. 'Our Yankee Doodle beats all of Beethoven, Mozart and other whatsits from the field with bells. Such a lamenting tone is good for church and camp meetings, but I myself prefer a healthy *nigger*-song.'" In the debate that follows between those at the party who prefer the European masters of high culture and those who, like Zacharias, extol popular American music, one of the novel's protagonists, Mr. Filson, challenges the old Westerner with a critical genealogy of sorts:

> It is national pride . . . which swells your spirit with the playing of this song. Yankee Doodle is our Marseillaise, it helps drive away our enemies and thus these crude sounds of Basque Gypsies is a harmony which excites the ear of a patriot. . . . Yes, sir, the melody came from Spain to Cuba and Mexico, and from there we have derived our national hymn. We're very involved in taking over foreign melodies. You would be amazed if you traveled in Germany to hear all the tunes which here accompany the texts of our church hymns being used in student hangouts and the lowest bars as drinking songs and dirty ditties. (bk. 3, ch. 13)

Mr. Filson's intervention undercuts Zacharias's rough and racist brand of nationalism with a cosmopolitan attention to transnational flows of culture, as well as a hint of anti-imperialism: "We're very involved in taking over foreign melodies." Crucially, Mr. Filson emphasizes a south-north flow of culture—the tune for Yankee Doodle came from Spain through Cuba and Mexico to the United States—rather than a Eurocentric flow from east to west, or an American exceptionalist flow from the United States to the rest of the world. However, Filson's elitist preference for the European masters, which becomes even more pronounced as this chapter unfolds, ultimately amplifies old Zacharias's easy racism by turning his idea of "a healthy *nigger*-song"—a song whose black authors Zacharias disdains even as he happily appropriates their culture—into "crude sounds" and "dirty ditties" that have no place in culture's proper parlor rooms.

That Mr. Filson delivers his elitist, anti-imperial racism in the midst of Klauprecht's own "dirty ditty" dime novel only complicates *Cincinnati*'s representation of the relationships among racism, nationalism, imperialism, and the high/low culture divide. Part "mystery of the city," part "dime Western," with liberal borrowings from themes raised by the US–Mexico War novelettes and even Cooper's *Leatherstocking*

Tales, Cincinnati at once practices sensational fiction's unruly potential for generic contamination; dramatizes the nineteenth-century debate over the dime's impure influence on its readers; and self-consciously foregrounds its own powerful if popular cultural status. It shows both how the anti-imperial politics of Mr. Filson fit easily with an elitist cultural racism, and how the racist nationalism of Zacharias presupposes cultural imperialism.

The often volatile, nineteenth-century debates over the supposed immorality of sensational fiction gave way, in the twentieth century, to a certain romanticization of the genre. As if confident that the genre's heyday had passed, critics spent less time worrying about the dime's dangers and more time extolling the scene of reading dimes as exemplary of a lost age of communal innocence when there were still frontiers to explore and urban mysteries to uncover. The political and cultural transformations that accompanied this shift in part explain it. The massification of literature that produced the dimes spread to other forms of culture in the early twentieth century—including the rise of the popular music industry in the 1910s, the dawn of radio in the 1920s and of television in the late 1940s—each of which was met with the anxiety associated with the heyday of sensational fiction. Among critics, reading quite suddenly became a more generalized, organic, and wholesome pursuit, one that could be contrasted favorably to newer forms of popular culture.

It was during this period that the term "dime novel" came to the fore as a generalized name for all such fiction, and much of the volatility of the genre was forgotten. The dimes' most shocking and unsettling aspects—such as the racial and sexually violent scenes of war from the United States–Mexico novelettes, or the raw class struggles depicted in the "Molly Maguire" series—were replaced in the critical imagination by the more family-oriented tales of humor and sports typical of the Munro's *Fireside Companion* series, the romance of dime Westerns, or the bucolic and wholesome images characteristic of the story-papers and dimes directed at young readers.

An important index of this revisionist history of the dime novel is the effort by a handful of twentieth-century literary historians to create archives of what were then scattered and rapidly deteriorating texts. By emphasizing Western, urban detective, and children's dimes from the 1860s–1910s rather than foreign language dimes from the 1850s, for instance, these historians artificially shaped the genre. These early archives, in turn, led the first wave of mid-twentieth-century critics to focus on what turned out to be a too-narrow segment of the genre. The nucleus of Stanford University's archive of sensational fiction came from Oakland postal inspector P. J. Moran's collection of thousands of story-papers and dimes for boys. The University of Minnesota's archive was seeded by George Hess, who focused his collection efforts on Beadle's novels. And the famous O'Brien collection of Beadle's novels—gathered by Frank O'Brien, donated to the New York Public Library, and sold to the Huntington Library in the 1920s—gave focus to Albert Johannsen's important history of "The House of Beadle" as well as Henry Nash Smith's seminal work on dime Westerns, both of which were published in 1950.

Thanks to more recent recovery efforts, critics have been able to sketch a fuller picture not only of the dime novel, but also of the wider field of sensational fiction and popular culture into which the classic dime fits. Consequently, both the practices *of* and the ideological struggles *over* reading this literature during the nineteenth and early twentieth centuries now appear to us in a fuller and more complex—which is to say a more contaminated and impure—light.

Interpreting Dime Novels

As contemporary readers, our interpretations of sensational fiction are exercises in both literary and historical analysis, because the texts we interpret are indices of their period's unruly social and political struggles. This unruliness is expressed by dime novels in their relentlessly exuberant focus on scandalous content. To present a finer-grained feel for the hermeneutics of this content, I'll offer brief interpretations of two scenes from two remarkable dime novels separated by fifty-six years.

As I mentioned above, the 1840s and 1850s saw a boom in one of the earliest forms of the dime novel: the US–Mexico War "novelette." One of the most violent and salacious of these texts is Charles E. Averill's *The Secret Service Ship: or, the Fall of San Juan D'Ulloa* (1848), though we must remember that Averill's nominal authorship is haunted by the workforce of women and girls Bok described as "intelligent." Set in 1846 during the US siege of Veracruz, *The Secret Service Ship* centers on the relationship between a US naval officer called Rogers and the "radiant" daughter of a Mexican general, Isora la Vega. As the novelette opens, Rogers saves Isora from rape at the hands of a Mexican officer with a "black heart," General Ampudia (ch. 1). Soon thereafter, however, Mexicans "ruffians" working for Ampudia capture Rogers, cast him into a cell, and tie him to a bizarre "death-couch" that sways "from side to side," emits a narcotic odor, and plays "wild and ravishing" music—all of which somehow puts Rogers to sleep, although he eventually escapes (chs. 6, 8). Isora turns out to have a cross-dressing alter ego, Lorenzo Larasca, who leads a band of honorable Mexican fighters against both the US invasion and the corrupt Mexican military, particularly Ampudia. Though he is heroic and honorable throughout, and he eventually marries Isora, midshipman Rogers is never quite in control of the sensational events that unfold around him. Indeed, one gets the impression that even the most innocent and good-hearted American can get caught up in a war that is difficult to justify and whose sides—Mexican and American, just and unjust, male and female—are constantly bleeding into each other, often quite literally. *The Secret Service Ship* thus offers both a panegyric to American heroism *and* an index of the ambivalence with which many Americans viewed this war.

Two of the most vivid characters of the novel are Ampudia's evil deputies, Juana and Geronimo, whom the novel calls "twin Patagonians." As Geronimo describes himself and his sister: "the Cannibal blood of Patagonia flows in our veins! we are, both she and I, of the race of giants,—the race which scorns connection with the poor pigmy populace of the world, and loves to feast upon the paltry mannikins' blood and revel in their misery!" (ch. 21). Rogers and Isora eventually kill Juana and Geronimo, overcoming the latters' uncivilized and reckless violence with their own, putatively refined violence learned from their respective national armed forces. Condensed into the sensational figures of Juana and Geronimo are a host of mid-nineteenth-century antagonisms over race, nation, gender, and empire. For instance, the novel was written during and set within the first period of popular interest and enthusiasm over archeology in the Americas. In 1841 and 1843, John Lloyd Stephens published his *Incidents of Travel in Central America, Chiapas and Yucatan* and *Incidents of Travel in Yucatan*, which were multivolume travel narratives and archeological reports complete with meticulously imagined etchings of Mayan ruins Stephens had "discovered." The popular and critical success of these narratives shows that Americans were eager to hear tales of what Stephens represented as a vanished empire, one characterized by great power and great violence. Readers also learned from Stephens of the degeneracy of the descendants of that great civilization, the nineteenth-century Maya who, he claimed, did not appreciate the value of the ruins in their midst and who could barely take care of their own quotidian needs. Of course, these were the very Maya who did much of the labor of "discovery" for Stephens, and with whom he negotiated for control of Mayan ruins and artifacts, and from whom he stole antiquities that still reside in US museums. Indeed, in 1847 Americans also began reading newspaper accounts of a massive uprising of those very Yucatec Maya against the creole population of the Yucatán peninsula during what would come to be called the Caste War. In *The Secret Service Ship*'s "twin Patagonians," then, one finds a condensation of assumptions and anxieties about native peoples in the Americas, assumptions and anxieties that would fuel US imperialism for decades to come. At once degenerate and powerful, violent and crafty, the figures of Juana and Geronimo allow the novel to differentiate an abject, extra-national native population both from Rogers's US whiteness and Isora's Mexican "fairness." As became clear during the US Congress's debate over, and ultimate rejection of, President Polk's 1848 proposal to annex the Yucatán, Americans were largely confused about the racial identity of Mexicans: were they Spanish, Indian, white, or black, many congressmen wondered quite explicitly. Bloodthirsty figures like Juana and Geronimo work to clarify this confusion by marking "fair" Mexican and white US nationals off from the Indians in their midst.

In 1904, *Dr. Quartz II, at Bay; or, A Man of Iron Nerve* was published in the December 3 issue of the *New Nick Carter Weekly*. The character of New York detective Nick Carter had been first created in 1887 for three novels nominally authored by John R. Coryell and published by Street & Smith in their *New York Weekly*. In the 1890s, the detective reappeared for a number of stories and novels that ran serially, and in the twentieth-century Carter popped up in the theater, movies, comics, and radio dramas. Hard-boiled and driven by a passionate and practical desire to defeat crime, Carter is always smarter than his fellow police officers and always more re-sourceful than his criminal antagonists. In *Dr. Quartz II*, readers find Carter locked in a battle of wits with a brilliant, serial-killing villain who turns out to be the brother of Carter's dead nemesis, the original Dr. Quartz. Just as the two Dr. Quartzes echo Averill's "twin Patagonians," *Dr. Quartz II* has its own version of *The Secret Service Ship*'s narcotic, band-music-playing couch: a chair in Dr. Quartz's house in which Carter fatally sits, only to be pierced by needles embedded in the armrests, needles "tipped with the most delicate poison" that renders him unconscious, but from which Carter eventually recovers in time to hatch a plan to defeat the evil doctor (ch. 5). Unlike the confusingly described and deafeningly loud narcotic couch, how-ever, Dr. Quartz's chair is rendered with mechanical precision, its soporific effect surgically and silently achieved. And unlike the raw and savage violence of the "twin Patagonians," Dr. Quartz's madness is a scientific genius he consciously abstracts from morality. As the doctor himself explains, "I am wedded to science, my dear Carter, and the most interesting of all sciences is the study of humanity itself"—a "study" he intends to conduct by performing vivisections on humans in a special laboratory he plans to set up on an "island in the Pacific" (ch. 6). Finally, unlike the "refined" violence with which Rogers and Isora defeat Juana and Geronimo, Carter couples his own psychological knowledge of Dr. Quartz's fatal flaw, his egoism, with a crafty, crime-fighting intelligence that is more practical than the doctor's elaborate evil, and that never loses track of morality. *Dr. Quartz II* thus offers its readers the promise of clear moral lines between good and evil and the hope that Carter's Ameri-can know-how will control the excesses of Dr. Quartz's cold, scientific rationality—all this, in the midst of an early twentieth century replete with vigorous debates over the risks and possibilities of science itself.

In each novel, the hermeneutics of sensation function at once to blur and to re-inforce presupposed distinctions. In *The Secret Service Ship*, the boundary between Mexicans and Americans is breached by the relationship between Rogers and Isora, and yet that very breach is made possible by the production of a common Indian enemy. Isora's cross-dressing breaches norms of masculinity and femininity, yet that breach is sealed by her ultimate marriage to Rogers. In *Dr. Quartz II*, scientific reason is shown to hold both evil and just potential, in the form of the doctor's medi-cal knowledge and Carter's knowledge of psychology and logic. Only Carter's ability to exercise a clear and practical moral vision holds reason back from its criminal potential.

Perhaps it is here that we can make our final use of Derrida's suggestion that "every text participates in one or several genres, [that] there is no genreless text; there is always a genre and genres, yet such participation never amounts to belonging" (1980, 65). For in the dime novel's sensational excesses and its long, genre-mixing history, we encounter the thrillingly equivocal practice of boundary drawing and boundary busting, a practice that continues to offer readers a certain experience of participation without belonging.

18

SERIAL FICTION AND THE NOVEL

BY JARED GARDNER

While we continue to organize our literary history of the novel around the book, with its unified text, discrete boundaries, and single author, the fact remains that from 1870 to 1914 a vast amount of novel reading took place serially, not in books but in magazines, newspapers, and story-papers. This reading of course includes a broad range of popular novels not often found in survey syllabi: urban mysteries, swashbuckling adventures, and sensational romances. However, readers today are often surprised to learn how many canonical novels began life published serially in periodicals. For example, Henry James's *The Portrait of a Lady* was serialized in the *Atlantic* and *Macmillan's* (1880–81); William Dean Howells's *A Modern Instance* (1881–82) was serialized in *Century*, as was Mark Twain's *Pudd'nhead Wilson* (1893–94); and Sarah Orne Jewett serialized *Country of Pointed Firs* (1896) in the *Atlantic*.

In each of these cases, readers read the novels—and discussed their merits, made predictions for future chapters, and even wrote in with advice to the authors—in monthly intervals. Edith Wharton, one of the later authors of the period to achieve both literary and financial success through serialization of her novels, was launched into the public eye through the phenomenal response to the serialization of *The House of Mirth* in the pages of *Scribner's* in 1905. As she described later, it was the experience of writing this novel under the publishing timetable of the month magazine and an engaged and demanding readership eager to offer advice as to the fate of her heroine, that transformed her "from a drifting amateur into a professional" (qtd. in Benstock 2003, 132). As a reviewer in the Kansas City *Star* put it, "This is one novel properly read as a serial since the strength of it held one keenly expectant in the long year since those opening chapters printed in the January Scribner's, and each month's allowance has provided so many features for thought and discussion" ("The Kingdoms of Vanity" 1905). One of the most important and lasting American novels of the period was shaped both in terms of its production and its reception by its serialization, and yet so foreign is serialization of novels to us today that trying to imagine the original scene of serial reading and writing is a challenge.

In many ways, the serial novel reached its high point in the period at which this volume begins and then slowly begins a decline into the twentieth century, such that by the end of our period of inquiry—1940—the serial novel was almost entirely associated with juvenile fictions. It was a slow, uneven transformation, and one that involved fierce contests over an expanding literary marketplace, changing economies of cultural capital, and the rise of new narrative media and new serial narrative forms in the twentieth century. Well into the new century, even authors who actively sought out a "literary" readership and reputation occasionally would serialize a novel. Willa Cather's *The Professor's House*, for example, was first serialized in *Collier's* in 1925, and F. Scott Fitzgerald serialized *Tender is the Night* in *Scribner's* as late as 1934. Today, of course, despite occasional attempts to revive the form, the serial novel is an extreme rarity, associated with the potboilers of the past, with sensational fiction devoted to the cliffhanger. But for several decades and especially in the late nineteenth century, novels as diverse as Howells's *The Rise of Silas Lapham* (1884–85), *The Gun-Maker of Moscow* (1856) by Sylvanus Cobb, and Pauline Hopkins's *Of One Blood* (1902–3) were published serially in weekly or monthly periodicals.

What these novels shared can therefore not be reduced to plot devices, audience, or characterization. Rather, what united them was the unique practice and pleasures of serial production and consumption, which invited an ongoing and interactive relationship with readers and required the consumption of the serial novel in conjunction with a range of periodical paratexts around a series of scheduled deferrals and interruptions. Alongside the serial novels were always other features, equally important to the reading experience, including illustrations, historical essays, and editorial columns—all of which necessarily affected the experience of reading the serialized fiction. For example, the concluding installment in *Scribner's* of *House of Mirth* is followed by a poem by W. J. Henderson that speculates on the nature of the "Hereafter," a meditation that the reader heartbroken over Lily Bart's fate would likely read in relationship to the novel's tragic conclusion. And this poem in turn is followed by an essay by the economist J. Laurence Laughlin on "The Hope for Labor Unions," which an attentive reader might well connect to Lily's own final experiences working in the hat factory. The serial novel, that is, was always a messy, interactive, and cacophonous affair.

While the serial novel, or "magazine novel," reached its heyday during the period covered by this volume, it does have a prehistory. A rapturous 1869 survey of "magazine novels" in *Galaxy* goes so far as to suggest that instead of seeing serial novels as a modern bastardization of "true" novels, we might understand the form as one that traces its origins back to the households of ancient Rome, where bards told their "continued stories" in occasional installments to their masters ("Magazine Novels" 130). It is certainly true, as the author suggests, that many novels of the eighteenth century were themselves published in parts over extended periods of time.

In the United States, while English novels had been imported and reprinted for decades, a novel written by an American in conventional book form did not emerge until after the nation itself was established and the Constitution ratified (William Hill Brown's *Power of Sympathy* [1789] is most commonly acknowledged as the "first" American novel). Nonetheless, in the struggling magazines of the early republic we can find earlier examples of serial fiction. "Amelia: or, the Faithless Briton An Original Novel, Founded upon Recent Facts," for example, was serialized in the *Columbian Magazine* in 1787, where Jeremy Belknap's satirical novel *The Foresters* was also serialized, incompletely, in nine installments between June 1787 and April 1788. Both of these works are potential candidates for the title of "first American novel," even as both have been denied the claim for different reasons: "Amelia" because of its relative brevity, *The Foresters* because it was not published as a complete text until 1792.

Other experiments with serial novels can be found intermittently in American periodicals throughout the subsequent decades. Beginning in 1792 Judith Sargent Murray experimented with weaving a serial novel (often retitled by modern critics as "The Story of Margaretta") into her ongoing column, "The Gleaner," in Isaiah Thomas's *Massachusetts Magazine*. Eventually, the instability of the magazine forced Murray to continue the narrative in book form, which she published in 1798. Charles Brockden Brown, the nation's first would-be professional novelist, attempted to publish an unfinished serial novel, *The Memoirs of Stephen Calvert* (1799–1800) in his *Monthly Magazine*; ultimately, however, the pressures of editing the struggling magazine, which folded at the end of 1800, left the text incomplete. A few years later, Susanna Rowson published an epistolary novel, *Sincerity* (1803–4), in the *Boston Weekly Magazine*, where she was engaged in editorial duties while simultaneously running her own boarding school. *Sincerity* would be published in book form a decade later as *Sarah; or, The Exemplary Wife* (1813), and it would remain the only one of her novels to appear first in serial form.

As these examples suggest, the serial novel did not thrive in the early decades of the republic primarily because there was no stable periodical form in which it could develop and circulate. Magazines before the 1820s were almost certain to fail within a few years—many lasting just a few months. Further, all of the periodicals of the early republic struggled not only financially but also with securing suitable contributions such that in many cases the magazine's editors were also the primary contributors, as in the case of all of Brockden Brown's periodical enterprises. Of course, the novel in the early republic faced other challenges in terms of finding a stable home in periodicals. Until the nineteenth century, the novel remained a source of anxiety for many, and in many magazines of the period editorials on the dangers of novel reading vastly outstripped serial fictions or even reviews of novels. The early magazine was a social form, designed to be shared by the entire family, and the novel, it was widely understood, had no place in respectable parlors.

Even once novels became respectable and magazines at last financially viable, the serial novel did not emerge immediately. For example, James Fenimore Cooper, the first writer in the United States to make a successful career as a novelist, did not begin serializing his novels until the very end of his career. Of the various forces which converged to make possible the development of the serial novel in the United States, the most important was surely Charles Dickens's phenomenal success with serial fiction in the late 1830s, first with *Pickwick Papers* (1836–37) and then, more fully, with *Oliver Twist* (1837–39), which appeared in monthly installments in England in *Bentley's Miscellany*. Almost immediately, *Oliver Twist* surfaced on the other side of the Atlantic: in *The Museum of Foreign Literature, Science, and Art* and the *Pennsylvania Inquirer* beginning in May 1838, and in the *Albion* beginning in June of that same year. *Nicholas Nickleby*, serialized in 1838–39, was even more enthusiastically received in the United States than in England. The reason for this interest is not surprising. As the *Baltimore Sun* reported in 1838, "It is stated that not less than 30,000 copies of Nicholas Nickleby are sold monthly in London" (December 6). And without an international copyright law, such phenomenal circulations were ripe for the picking in the United States. While some publications remunerated Dickens for access to advance sheets on the ongoing serial publications, many more openly pirated his novels in whole or in part.

Such piracy was especially practiced by the new penny-press that emerged in the United States at this same time, and that constitutes the second important force that leads to the rise of the serial novel. Up through the 1820s, the early American newspaper had been dominated almost exclusively by business and political interests. Most newspapers were sponsored by political machines and linked into a network of exchanges that resulted in remarkably homogenous news. As Alexis de Tocqueville observed following his 1831 visit to the United States, "nothing but a newspaper can drop the same thought into a thousand minds at the same moment" (*Democracy in America*, bk. 2, ch. 6). The traditional six-penny paper of the 1830s was a ponderous affair, putting forth the political talking points of the moment and detailing the facts and figures of trade and commerce of interest to the predominantly elite readers who made up its regular subscribers.

Benjamin Day's *New York Sun* in 1833, however, introduced a very different vision of the American newspaper, one that would become increasingly influential in the second half of the century. Day's paper was sold for a penny, hawked on the streets to ordinary people, and focused on the ongoing daily life of the city instead of political clippings from party bosses and shipping news unlikely to be of interest to ordinary readers. The penny-press as it was epitomized by pioneering papers such as the *Sun* and James Gordon Bennett's *Herald* (1835) for the first time "told stories of ordinary people confronting life in the big city" (Huntzicker 1999, 1). And in "going beyond the official sources and following up on a story," the penny-press made news—and especially the news of crime, a staple of the new newspapers—a *continuing*, serial story (Stevens 1991, 41).

Since the penny-press relied on advertising revenue instead of political patronage, the 1830s and 40s witnessed a series of circulation wars among the growing number of penny-papers in major cities across the country. In 1835, Day struck first against his would-be rivals, experiencing a tremendous increase in circulation following the serial story of the discovery of manlike creatures on the moon. By the time the hoax was revealed to the reading public, Day could boast a circulation of almost twenty thousand. The following year, Bennett's *Herald* would work similar magic with the story of a murdered young prostitute named Helen Jewett, a case that first attracted widespread notice less because of the nature of the crime (tragically common in 1830s New York) than the novelistic aspects of the victim's life. As the story was told, Jewett was a beautiful and educated young woman who had been seduced and cast out of her family home in Maine. Instead of transcribing police and court records as had been the practice up to that point, Bennett secured access to the crime scene and interviews with the victim's family, and he then described all he saw and learned for his readers. The *Herald* transformed a seemingly open-and-shut case into a "mystery yet unrevealed," and as the story unfolded serially over the coming weeks the circulation of the paper tripled, allowing it to supplant the rival *Sun* (April 14, 1836).

In many ways the serial novel found its audience in the penny-press of the 1830s and '40s, and especially in the stories of crime and violence in a rapidly growing city of strangers. And so it was perhaps inevitable that these new papers were quick to exploit the success of Dickens by pirating his early serial novels in the United States, most commonly in tabloid-sized weekly "supplements" designed to tap into a growing market for cheap novels. Printing the pirated novels as "supplements," *Brother Jonathan* and the *New-World* were able to beat the big presses at their own game, securing copies of new installments of Dickens right off the boat and publishing them serially and then in whole in newsprint "supplements" more cheaply than established presses such as Harper's could hope to. Further, the papers were able to take advantages of a loophole in the postal codes that allowed them to send these densely printed quarto editions in the mails at reduced newspaper rates, enabling them to reach inexpensively through the mails a growing audience outside of the urban centers.

Following his visit to America in 1841, Dickens complained that in the United States the English writer is not only pirated with impunity, "but he cannot even choose his company. Any wretched halfpenny newspaper can print him at its pleasure—place him side by side with productions which disgust his common sense—and by means of the companionship in which it constantly shews him, engenders a feeling of association in the minds of a large class of readers, from which he would revolt, and to avoid which he would pay almost any price." As this complaint makes clear, what dismayed Dickens even more than the loss of substantial income from the reprinting of his novels in the United States was the practice of reprinting his work in periodical formats that violated distinctions of genre and taste and that allowed the author no control over the presentation of his texts or the company they kept.

Yet this tendency for unlikely juxtapositions and cacophonous circulations clearly defined a good deal of the pleasure that early readers of these serial novels took in the new form. By the early 1840s new periodicals emerged from the penny-press devoted entirely to publishing serial fiction and newspaper novels in "supplements," such as *Brother Jonathan* and the *New World*, the most successful periodicals of their day. Committed almost entirely to pirated reprints of serial novels, these periodicals capitalized on the tremendous appetite for this material, and at least part of the success lay in the miscellaneous nature of the publication itself. *Brother Jonathan* and the *New World* were the ancestors of a more respectable new periodical form that would emerge in the 1850s, the story-paper. Like the first wave of such publications in the 1840s, the story-paper, as epitomized by Robert Bonner's *New York Ledger* (1856), focused primarily on original publications by American authors. Bonner especially paid handsomely for exclusive arrangements with the most popular authors of his day and then used his remarkable skills as a promoter to transform his stable of authors into literary celebrities. Within a short time Bonner achieved circulations that dwarfed those of his contemporaries.

We see a useful example of how serial fiction in the story-papers both capitalized on and differentiated itself from the formulas developed in the penny-press in the work of Sylvanus Cobb, Jr. Cobb was one of the most reliable of Bonner's serial novelists, not least because of his ability and willingness to extend a story to ensure that two serials did not end at the same time or to quickly wrap one up if the public attention waned. But like all of Bonner's writers, Cobb was also possessed of the ability to combine the sensations of penny-press seriality with moral lessons and closure the penny-press inevitably could not provide. His "Rosalind Hubert; or, the Hillside Tragedy," serialized in the Ledger in 1858, provides a good case in point. After first describing in salacious detail how a criminal executes and justifies the murder of his guardian and the subsequent kidnapping of his guardian's heir, Rosalind, we then see how our villain effectively covers his tracks, making his crime undetectable by the police and the press. The reader is thus given access into the workings of the criminal mind and invited to apply these insights to the other "true" crimes found daily in the penny-press.

The rest of the novel then describes how the reader—or her surrogate within the story—can bring about the justice that eludes both our heroine and the institutions dedicated to protecting the innocent. As with so many serial fictions in the *Ledger*, mistaken identities, disguises, and cross-dressings of various kinds abound in "Rosalind Hubert." But while our heroine sees through some of these disguises, she is unable to penetrate the criminal's deeper designs on her life and her fortune. About midway through her dizzying adventures, Rosalind meets another lost girl in the city, Jane, who tells a familiar story of seduction and abandonment, providing Rosalind with an excuse to tell her own tale (and the new subscribers with an opportunity to catch up on the complicated story). But, of course, Rosalind does not know all the details of her own story, having been fooled by her "parents" into believing she had accidentally murdered her "husband." And thus it is Jane who is shocked by Rosalind's tale, and not vice versa, as the conventions of the seduction tale would lead us to expect—shocked, that is, by Rosalind's bad reading of her own life, allowing herself to be so easily duped and manipulated. From this point on, it is Jane, the good reader, who assumes the disguises and brings about the vengeance that will help rescue Rosalind, our modern urban heroine, from the forces conspiring against her.

In this way we can see how in the *Ledger* "true crime" is solved by serial fiction, allowing the readers of these serial fictions to become different kinds of detectives than those promoted by the penny-press—not, that is, taking to the crime scenes to examine the body or search for evidence, but using the lessons of sensational fiction (the power of sympathy, the unreliability of appearances, the invariability of the profit motive, and the need for transparent communication) to gain epistemological command over an increasingly unstable and unreliable world. Bonner routinely celebrated the certainty the *Ledger* brought to an uncertain world, in opposition to the uncertainty and chaos inherent in the serial crime narratives of the penny-press. For example, in an editorial entitled "Crime," the *Ledger* describes the world Bennett and his colleagues made: "No one can read the daily papers of our great cities . . . without being painfully convinced that we have fallen in an evil day, socially. Theft, robbery, arson, murder, and every other species of crime are stalking about with bold and bloody front, bidding defiance to every well-established principle or rule of social order" (September 25). And what gives encouragement to the growing population of the criminal class is "uncertainty of punishment," an uncertainty that the daily papers both profited from and helped facilitate. But while gruesome subjects and sensational crimes are the subject of some of the serial fictions in the *Ledger*, here at least the reader can be *certain* of punishment and justice.

But if the story-paper initially held up its serial novels as an antidote to the amorality of the penny-press, by 1860, serial fiction had become so popular in the United States (especially following the tremendous success of Harriet Beecher Stowe's *Uncle Tom's Cabin* [1851–52] and E. D. E. N. Southworth's *The Hidden Hand* [1859]) that anxieties about the impact of this new mass serial reading became regular features in elite publications. The *Scalpel* for example saw "our weekly story-papers" as constituting a threat to the health of the nation, preying on weak minds and providing "powerful incentives to an unhappy state of mind" ("Suicide and Civilization"). More immediately, the monthly literary magazines worried over the explosion of "Bonner's *Ledger* and half a dozen 'story-papers' for the circulation of the cheap 'sensational' novels" at the expense of "the higher class of literary journals" ("New York Newspapers," *Littel's Living Age*).

In fact, the rise of the serial novel coincided with the emergence of a distinction between high- and popular-literature, between what we today often term highbrow and lowbrow, in the second half of the century. As appetites for serial fiction expanded, the format and frequency of serial publication began to be identified as a marker of an increasingly meaningful distinction in an emerging cultural economy. As *Lippincott's* put it in 1868, "the New York *Ledger* and all story papers are well patronized" by the lower classes, while even among the poorest fishing villages "the marks by which good breeding is distinguished will show themselves" in the "very class of literature they purchase, and the books from the library which they peruse" ("An American Fishing Port"). What you read and where you read it came to be a marker of cultural capital, with "the weeklies" marked as lowbrow literature for the masses and the monthly "literary journals" serving as signs of "higher class."

By 1870, with serial novels now regularly published both by story-paper weeklies and by "quality" monthlies, the distinction had widened into something of a literary class war. As one commentator put it in 1874, in an age when "authorship finds periodicals rather than books its best medium, both for reaching a wide audience and for earning a livelihood," "when it comes to what is more distinctively literature, there . . . remains a distinct field for the monthly" ("Monthlies and Weeklies," 475). In the years following the end of the Civil War, the struggling magazine industry had recovered quickly and opportunities for publication in monthly literary magazines expanded with the founding of *Harper's* (1850) and *Atlantic* (1857) and subsequently *Galaxy* (1866), *Lippincott's* (1868), *Scribner's* (1870), and *Century* (1881). And all of these magazines regularly published serial novels. Indeed, by the 1870s it was commonplace, even expected, for novels to appear first in serial form. Many of the "quality" magazines continued to privilege English serial novels. For example, in 1872, *Harper's Monthly* serialized Anthony Trollope's *The Golden Lion of Granpère* (1867), and Wilkie Collins's *The New Magdalen* (1873).

In part because of an ongoing predilection for English serial novels, the increased number of venues for serial novel in the 1870s and '80s did not necessarily result in more opportunities for US writers. Further, most of the American novelists who published in these elite magazines failed to generate the kind of interest in their works that, say, Stowe had received in 1852 with the serial publication of *Uncle Tom's Cabin* in the abolitionist newspaper *The New Era* or that many of Bonner's celebrity authors were regularly achieving in his story-paper. And even as circulations rose overall for the quality literary magazines, payment for authors at these magazines did not keep pace with the rising cost of living, as increased competition among the monthlies dampened profits. The result was that by the end of the nineteenth century, the enthusiasm for seriality among those who aspired to literary laurels was beginning to wane. Indeed, even Henry James, who perhaps more than any other author of the period successfully exploited the serial novel form, worked to reframe his legacy and achievement away from the periodical origins of most of his works by producing the New York Edition of his novels (1907–9). After James and his friend Edith Wharton, very few American novelists who sought the approval of the literary establishment would consider founding their career on the basis of serial publication.

The story of how we get in such a short time from the near-universal popularity of Dickens in the late 1830s to the rapid decline of the serial novel's reputation in the twentieth century is a familiar one. We see similar transformations at work in other cultural spheres; as Paul DiMaggio has argued, "The distinction between high and popular culture, in its American version, emerged in the period between 1850 and 1900 out of the efforts of urban elites to build organizations that, first, isolated high culture and, second, differentiated it from popular culture" (1982, 3). While DiMaggio focuses on the establishment of the Museum of Fine Arts and the Boston Symphony Orchestra as a means of securing an art apart from the popular entertainments of the masses, the discrediting of serial novels and their readers is part of the same larger seismic shift in the cultural landscape that would open up meaningful fault-lines between "literature" and "magazine novels." As the *Harper's* editors noted approvingly in 1915, "readers of to-day" were no longer "as slavishly addicted to the serial habit as they were fifty or sixty years ago" ("Editor's Study"). Here as elsewhere, serial readers are defined as addicts incapable of the self-control and mental disciplines necessary to wait patiently for the whole work to be presented for private contemplation. *Harper's* identifies such an "exceptional reader who refuses to take ten or a dozen bites at his cherry" as a "very exceptional person rejecting the serial tradition" and imagines a rising "class of him." Implicitly, therefore, the weekly serial reader is he who cannot control himself, the child who cannot stop nibbling at the cherry.

Such distinctions served to define as mature, proper, and disciplined—as *civilized*—the aesthetic practices of idealized (white, male) readers of a certain class, marking as immature, tempestuous, and uncontrollable the aesthetic tastes and passions of other readers who openly read, discussed, and shared serial novels: female, working-class, immigrant, and African American readers. Ultimately coalescing into the New Critical insistence on treating all texts as self-contained and all good readers as freed from the fallacies of emotional attachments and projections, from the late nineteenth century on the professional institutions of literature worked to reify a notion of the literary which, like the ideal of art in the Museum of Fine Arts and music in the Boston Symphony Orchestra, requires physically and emotionally disciplined responses on the part of the right sort of readers.

Of course, such attitudes did not spring into being suddenly; a stigma circled around serial fiction from the start. As Michael Denning's *Mechanic Accents* and David S. Reynolds's *Beneath the American Renaissance* have both demonstrated, as early as the 1840s serial novelists such as George Lippard were associated with working class readers, and Stowe's achievement with *Uncle Tom's Cabin* in an explicitly abolitionist newspaper concretized a link between the serial novel and social activism. Indeed, it was in part the impact of Stowe's novel that strengthened the anxiety regarding the kinds of attachments and communal responses serial fictions were capable of eliciting. A novel read in the privacy of one's room might inflame, but a novel read and discussed socially and over shared periodical time had a much great likelihood of spreading the fires stirred up by the novel. *Uncle Tom's Cabin* had been profoundly shaped for and by a serial audience, and as the publisher of the *National*

Era suggested to Stowe, the tremendous response to the novel to follow had every-thing to do with the collective practices fundamental to serialization.

The very qualities that made this first generation of serial novels so immensely successful and influential—their didacticism, their emotionalism, their appeal to an emerging mass readership, their open embrace of the pleasures of the collective reading experience and the shared anticipation and speculation enforced by serial publication—were also precisely what would contribute in the final years of the nineteenth century to the rapidly declining critical respect accorded to the serial novel. A good example of this phenomenon can be found in the career of E. D. E. N. Southworth. The most widely read novel of the second half of the century was quite likely Southworth's *The Hidden Hand*, which told the story of young Capitola's triumph over such adversaries as the notorious highwayman Black Donald and the villainous aristocrat Le Noir. Stitching together numerous genres including melodrama, comedy, adventure, plantation romance, and even military drama, the novel was serialized three times (1859, 1868, 1883) before being finally published in book form in 1888—all three times in Bonner's New York *Ledger*, which in 1870 boasted over 370,000 subscribers. Knowing that periodicals passed around a household and a community to additional readers, we can conservatively assume that over the course of its three serializations *The Hidden Hand*, in whole or part, reached well over one million readers, considerably more, for example, than the book publication of *Uncle Tom's Cabin*.

Unlike *Uncle Tom's Cabin* or the serial novels of George Lippard, *The Hidden Hand* was not an activist text, and as Christopher Looby has demonstrated, it seem-ingly goes out of its way to avoid engaging the moral and political crisis that domi-nated all aspects of American life in 1859. Yet if it was not her explicit message that critics found threatening, it is undeniably the case that many critics early on viewed Southworth with anxious disdain "because of her frank depictions of men's abuse of women, her prodigious output, and her unprecedented popularity, none of which they could control" (Naranjo-Huebl 2006, 142). If serial readers would increasingly be portrayed as incapable of controlling their appetites, their curiosity, and their pas-sions, popular serial authors were threatening precisely because they themselves pos-sessed a power that could not be regulated, garnering audiences and even fortunes that did not depend at all on the literary establishment.

But the miscellaneous form of the story-paper was itself a source of concern for its critics. If Dickens worried that at the hands of the penny-press his fiction could be made to keep very low company, in the story-paper the diverse makeup of the contents of individual issues was a significant part of the experience of reading serial fiction. For example, a new serial novel would often begin on the front page for a few weeks, but then move to the inner pages of the weekly to make room for the beginning of a new serial. Readers were therefore reading not only one novel each week, but often three or four in various stages of development. The successful serial novelist had to be prepared to speed up or draw out the pace of their narrative to coincide with the beginnings and conclusions of other serial novels being published in the same publication. And the letters from the readers themselves served as a regular forum on the popularity of an individual feature to which the novelists were expected to respond attentively. Thus the weeklies established a larger community, one in which the readers were invited to see themselves as active participants, not only in the correspondence columns but in the public understanding that the success of an individual author depended on the positive response from readers. This response was most directly communicated in the form of increased subscriptions, and Bonner, for example, regularly reported to his readers as if they were joint stock-holders, detailing the fortunes of individual authors in his stable based on changing subscriptions.

Further, like the penny-paper from which it descended, the weekly story-paper was designed to be taken out in the street, folded in back pockets, or secreted in school bags. It was shared and circulated freely and often read in public on the day of publication so that readers might participate in the discussion of the week's serial installments at work or school. Where the monthly magazine was aimed at family reading in the middle-class home, the weekly story-paper circulated openly in public spaces and workplaces, encouraging shared reading and public interpretative communities far outside of the control of the academy or the literary establishment. Thus, even as the majority of popular serial fiction published in the weeklies and story-papers was *not* explicitly political or radical, seriality itself came to represent for many readers and institutions a meaningful threat, to both the mental hygiene and the political stability of the nation. Writing in the *New York Times* in 1897, Harry Thurston Peck summed up the feelings of many in the literary establishment:

> In the old days, say fifty years or less ago, the writing of a book was a very serious affair. An author thought over his subject perhaps for years. . . . It was thus that the greatest works in our own literature were written, and the desire of those who put them forth was, first of all, to give their readers the best of all their thought enshrined in the most appropriate medium of expression. A book was not a pot-boiler, a hit-or-miss bid for public approbation. It was the choicest product of a human mind, sent forth to influence in some way other human minds.
>
> The magazines and the syndicates have changed all this, for the magazines and the syndicates have turned authorship into a purely commercial and money-making affair. The "serialization" of every novel, . . . the speculative spirit that urges a writer to make the most of his popularity while the sunshine of public favor lasts—these things have converted the author into a literary huckster and have flooded the world with a sort of writing that is doing endless harm both to the persons who produce it and the persons who feel bound to read it.

"The result," Peck concludes, "is seen in the vitiation of literary taste, the confusion of literary standards, and a general loss of the power to discriminate between what is bad and what is good" (1897, BR4).

Even amidst the growing concern on the part of the literary elite, there were voices who defended the serial novel as a uniquely democratic form, one that opened up new possibilities of characterization and readerly agency. In 1885, for example, Charlotte Porter defended the "serial story" against its critics, with the argument that the "'installment' method . . . defends . . . against the demands of the market by making it harder than ever for any but the fittest novels to survive the passing purpose of filling a leisure hour," shifting the balance of power from author to reader (1885, 812). Perhaps more surprising, given current assumptions about the serial novel, Porter argued that the serial form opens up the "life within" literary characters—allowing the reader to speculate about characters' inner lives in a way that the traditional novel does not afford. Porter argued that the serial form and the investments it encouraged in its readers was especially invaluable to finally bringing psychologically complex female characters to literature.

Nonetheless, by the 1890s defenses of the serial novel from the literary establishment were increasingly few and far between. And the backlash against the serial came from several fronts. For example, postal reform legislation, proposed by Senator Eugene Loud in 1897, sought to curb the flow of serial novels through the mails. Within the quality magazines a subtle but eventually distinct shift began to occur at the same time away from the serial novel and toward the short story, as celebrated by Brander Matthews in his influential 1885 essay (expanded in 1901 into a book of the same name), "The Philosophy of the Short-story." For Matthews, the short story was to be cultivated because it provided opportunities for the author to attend to "symmetry of design," "compression, originality, ingenuity," and of course "philosophy," all qualities understood to be impossible to achieve in the novel form as it has been bastardized by serialization (which Matthews patriotically blames on English influence, and not American taste) (1901, 72). In 1892, Thomas Wentworth Higginson similarly celebrated the short story as a form that relieved the author from the corrupting influence of serialization; for Higginson, the "justification of the short story" lies in its freedom from serialization: "there is no sub-division of interest; the author can strike directly in, without preface, can move with determined step toward a conclusion, and can—O highest privilege!—stop when he is done" (4). For the proponents of the short story, which would rise significantly in the early decades of the twentieth century, the form freed the author from the taint of commerce and the demands of the masses and elevated the reader to contemplate form, originality, and philosophy otherwise trampled under the pressures and demands of the serial novel.

There is in fact a submerged but vital racial rhetoric that runs throughout the celebration of the turn from serial novel to short story—as there was in the postal reforms dedicated to protecting Americans from the serial novels invading their homes and leeching off the government. If the short story represented restraint, aesthetic perfection, and originality, the serial novel was defined metaphorically as the sprawling mob with its insatiable appetite and inattention to any quality save attention itself. And it is hard not to contextualize the othering of the reader of serial literature at this time with the rising tide of immigration from eastern Europe and great emigration of southern African Americans to the northern cities that served as the base of the literary establishment. Everything about the serial novel—its communal and necessarily unruly reading practices, the passionate attachments of its readers, the celebrity of its authors, and especially the fact that "writers and publishers of substantial works rarely grow rich, while producers of [serial] fiction often amass large and rapid fortunes"—marked the serial novel and its reader as increasingly aligned with what many commentators at the end of the century perceived to be a rising and threatening "tide of color" ("Novels and Fiction," *Ladies' Repository* 30, 1870).

At the same time, even as the serial novel was being driven from the mails and from the pages of the "quality" monthlies, it continued to thrive for precisely those authors who would have had little access to the established book publishers or literary magazines. For African American novelists, in fact, the highpoint of the serial novel coincides almost exactly with the beginning of its excommunication from "polite" literary circles. Its origins, however, go back to the early years of the form. For example, Martin Delaney published *Blake: or, Life Among the Lowly*—at once a response to Stowe's *Uncle Tom's Cabin* and a radical call for a pan-African revolution—in 1859 and 1862 in the *Anglo-African Magazine*. At the time there were few opportunities for novels by African Americans to be published in the United States (an earlier African American novel, William Wells Brown's *Clotel*, had been published in London in 1853), which was certainly one reason Delaney sought out serial publication of his novel. But the novel's radical vision of pan-Africanism—as Katy Chiles puts it, its mapping of "a contingent and kaleidoscopic world where the local, the regional, the national, and the diasporic overlie one another"—was one ideally suited to the serial form (Chiles 2008, 348). The serial novel, which presented each installment in a complex—sometimes deliberate, sometimes accidental—relationship with a wide range of other texts and voices, local and global, was ideally suited to Delaney's larger arguments in *Blake*.

Ultimately, Delaney's serial novel remained unfinished in the pages of the *Anglo-American Magazine*, its final chapters lost, interrupted by the Civil War, by Delaney's travel to Africa in preparing a plan for mass emigration, and by the instabilities of periodical publication. It would wait for Pauline Hopkins to fully develop the potential of the African American serial novel in three works she published in the *Colored American Magazine*: *Hagar's Daughter: A Story of Southern Caste Prejudice* (1901–2), *Winona: A Tale of Negro Life in the South and Southwest* (1902–3), and *Of One Blood: Or, The Hidden Self* (1903), the last of which specifically addressed many of the same challenges and questions raised in Delaney's *Blake* over forty years earlier. While Hopkins' shift from publishing her first novel, *Contending Forces* (1900), in book form to publishing her next three novels serially obviously owes a great deal to her responsibilities as editor of the *Colored American Magazine* during this time, the demands of the serial form allowed her to break with the racialized sentimental traditions that governed her first novel; as Augusta Rohrbach puts it, "Hopkins's use of the serial format creates opposition to white notions of racial supremacy embedded in the novel form" (Rorhbach 1999, 483).

While Hopkins remains the most prolific and visible African American serial novelist of the period (and there are reasons to suspect she wrote other serial novels under pseudonyms), serialization continues into the early years of the new century, especially in African American newspapers. Charles Chesnutt's *House Behind the Cedars* (1900) was serialized in 1921–22 in the Chicago *Defender*, bringing the book back into print and to the attention of the pioneering African American filmmaker Oscar Micheaux, who would adapt the novel to film in 1927. The fiercely independent George Schuyler continued to use serialization as late as 1938 in the Pittsburgh *Courier*, which published his satire of black nationalism in general and of Marcus Garvey in particular, collected many years later as *Black Empire*.

It seems significant that the first and last major serial novels by an African American both dealt with the subject of pan-Africanism and black nationalism, although from very different periods in history and from authors of very different political sympathies. After Schuyler, however, it is hard to find any African American authors who deployed serialization as a means of addressing such overarching political issues, or to secure audience, reputation or remuneration. The major African American novels of the next decade, from *Native Son* (1940) to *Invisible Man* (1953), would not be serialized. Most certainly it is vital to recognize that all of these examples of serialization, from Delaney to Schuyler, took place in African American magazines and newspapers, which allowed for the circulation of novels and authors not necessarily embraced by the white-owned periodicals and publishing houses.

Of course, by the 1940s serialization of novels was increasingly rare, not only in literary monthlies but in more popular media as well. Following a brief explosion of popularity with the newspaper serial—a tie-in with the movie serials of the 1910s and '20s—periodical serializations of novels decline steadily. Even pulp magazines that had once regularly serialized novels began to advertise in the 1930s and '40s new policies favoring "complete novels" in a single issue.

The decline of the serialization of popular fiction, however, was ultimately less the result of the cultural sea change in the attitudes of the literary establishment at the end of the nineteenth century than with the rise of new narrative media that began to claim serialization as their own. Beginning with the rise of open-ended serial comic strips such as *The Gumps* and *Gasoline Alley* in the late 1910s, the comic strip would popularize a new form of daily seriality that made even the weeklies seem slow by comparison (on serial comics, see Chapter 22 of this volume). At the movies in the 1930s, a new wave of serial adventure films at the Saturday matinees captured the former audiences of science fiction and Western pulps from the previous decade. On radio, the serial soap opera launched with *Guiding Light* in 1937, and countless other serial dramas filled the airwaves throughout the '30s and '40s. And by the end of the decade, television would bring another—and ultimately the most powerful—new media player to lay claim to serial narrative.

In other words, while we associate the serial novel today with melodramas of a bygone age, the serial novel in fact has distinct and vital genealogical connections to all of the new narrative media of the twentieth century—and indeed, the twenty-first, as we see the resurgence of the serial novel today within Internet culture. In a sense then, while the serial novel has a fairly discrete history within American literary history, its longer history is one that suggests an ongoing and vital form of storytelling whose story critics have only just begun to tell.

19

FICTIONALIZING CHILDREN, CHILDREN'S FICTION

BY CAROLINE LEVANDER

What do we make of the fact that the book hailed by many as *the* classic American novel of all time, Mark Twain's *The Adventures of Huckleberry Finn* (1884), has a child at its center? Not only does *Huckleberry Finn* track the adventures of a child who lives in the small Mississippi riverfront town of Hannibal, Missouri, but it also explores his need to escape from the community that tries but fails to protect him. Whether it is the abusive drunk father who beats Huck for learning to read, the cloying and ineffectual efforts of adults to provide such children with sufficient nurture, or the slave system's institutionalized infantilization and violence against African Americans like Jim, *Huckleberry Finn* insists that youthful resourcefulness, creativity, escapism, and rambunctiousness are as much a function of grim necessity as a sign of a halcyon world of childhood freedom from life's weightier realities.

Just as the child protagonist of *Huckleberry Finn* seems to be an uneasy mixture of childhood innocence and adult responsibility, so too do the readers of the novel straddle adult and child worlds, collectively reflecting the complex and enduring interconnections that link these seemingly separate stages of life (on *Huck Finn* as a crossover novel, see Chapter 4 in this volume). *Huck Finn* has, from the start, drawn its healthy readership from both demographics. It is the ultimate "cross-over" novel, appealing equally to readers of eight and of eighty years of age. Thus from its subject matter to its continuing reception among readers, Twain's novel reminds us that clear distinctions between "adult" and "child" can be highly arbitrary and that categories such as children's literature and adult literature fail to represent the full range and complexity of American reading publics. Indeed, it is precisely the imaginative opportunity that readers of novels like *Huck Finn* have to blur the boundaries between adulthood and childhood that is one of the novel's most powerful allures. Adult readers of the late nineteenth and early twentieth centuries found within the pages of many American novels ample opportunity to immerse themselves in nostalgic recollections of childhood, while a growing population of late nineteenth-century child readers, conversely, turned to such novels for training in dominant narratives about what it meant to be a child as well as for insight into necessary steps for achieving successful maturation.

Nowhere is the American novel's engagement in this reflexive project of reaching across generational divides more apparent than in the writing of Louisa May Alcott. As the titles of *Little Women* (1868) and *Little Men* (1871) suggest, Alcott foregrounds the points of contact between childhood and adulthood as the starting point for her fictional portrayals of American life. With novels that insist upon the complex inter-weaving of adult responsibility and childish impulse, Alcott has captivated readers of all ages. Her most popular little woman, Jo March, quickly became an enduring icon for highly successful professional women, and noted feminists like Catherine Stimpson and Carolyn Heilbrun, among many others, continue, over a hundred and fifty years after *Little Women*'s publication, to cite Jo March as a foundational feminist role model. Yet Jo's choice to marry Professor Bhaer rather than her childhood friend Laurie elicited equally strong responses from the novel's many child readers, and upset children sent countless letters of protest to Alcott in the hopes that she might reconsider the kind of adult world she fashions for Jo.

Regardless of whether or not adult and child readers applaud or object to the transition from child to adult world that Alcott ultimately scripts for little women like Jo, a significant part of the novel's appeal has to do with the domestic world in which the girls live and grow. It is a world of relative safety, humanity, and camaraderie that richer children who are lonely in their luxury (like Laurie) want to join and to which indigent children who are troubled by disease, poverty, and want (like the Hummel children) remain largely peripheral.

In subsequent novels such as *Little Men*, Alcott focuses directly on those individuals who are biologically children but who have not been treated as such because of their marginal place in society. Such children would increasingly interest late nineteenth- and early twentieth-century social workers, philanthropists, and artists, from the photojournalist and author of *The Children of the Poor* (1892), Jacob Riis, to prominent child-welfare reformer and Illinois governor John Altgeld, who advocated for progressive child rights, and women such as Jane Addams, who created benevolent institutions like Hull House, or Louise Rockford Wardner, who promoted legislation such as the 1879 Industrial School for Girls bill. Influenced by Charles Darwin's theories of natural selection and evolution as well as new theories of social environmentalism, many late nineteenth-century writers and thinkers began to recognize that children were not only born pure, innocent, and close to God, but were also raw human material, shaped by circumstance and driven by primal, possibly antisocial urges (on the influence of Darwinian evolutionary theory and social environmentalism, see Chapter 10 in this volume). As such they posed a potential threat as much as a challenge to direct their development such that they could become contributing members of society.

In her fictional portrayal of such children, Alcott explores in meticulous detail the capacity of even the most indigent and abandoned children living at the social margins to be made into productive members of society. Published the same year as Charles Darwin's *Descent of Man* (1871), *Little Men* relies heavily on emerging scientific theories of evolution and natural selection to show children's seemingly infinite capacity to transform themselves from wild animals into little men fit to rule rather than ruin society. The small boarding school that Jo Bhaer runs with her husband takes in the boys that no one else wants and aims to teach them "self-knowledge, self-help, and self-control" (ch. 2). In order to do so, Mrs Bhaer accepts that the "robins who stray into her nest" are nothing other than untamed animals, and she shapes her educational agenda with this fact clearly in mind. Through watching a family of crabs that seem to be "settled in their new house" quickly turn on each other, the biggest crab "eating one of his relations in the coolest way," the children receive a powerful lesson that natural savagery can destroy family order and nurture, if left unchecked (ch. 10). Each boy, therefore, must tame the urges that threaten to undo the little ecosystem at Plumfield, which depends upon the idea that "we all help one another" (ch. 3). As part of this re-generative lesson, each boy is given a cookie in the shape of the beast or bird that most clearly characterizes him. In the eating of his pig cookie, Stuffy, for example, comes to accept that he acts like a pig—that his sloth and gluttony need to be counterbalanced with restraint and industry. The child who acts like a dog "must be treated like a dog" and is tied up to stop Nan's "growl[ing] and grovel[ing] on the floor" and to instill better manners (ch. 12). The most difficult boy to tame is reclaimed through the power of science itself. By rewarding his enduring interest in the natural world with the creation of a natural science museum which he will curate, mother Bhaer is rightly convinced that she will see in "the pebbles, mosses, and gay butterflies" that Dan collects and organizes "good resolutions carried out, conquered faults, and a promise well kept" (chs. 10, 7). The science of success-fully teaching this "wilderness of boys" to be upstanding citizens, therefore, clearly trades in the science of the day—showing readers that the evolutionary models that potentially threaten the idea of innate childhood innocence and purity can be the very means by which to ensure adult civic responsibility in the most wayward of children.

Alcott's novel fuses contemporary science and fiction with the aim of answering a pressing question of the day—how to ensure that the children that no one wants will not attempt to destroy the society that fails them. But other scientific discourses, such as the burgeoning field of American psychology, also featured the child as the privileged object of scientific inquiry, and American novels were integrally engaged in exploring how the child's mind might elude easy observation. Earlier in the nine-teenth century, Nathaniel Hawthorne had observed that the child's "beauty of in-nocence" and that early phase of life widely understood as "shining angel infancy" might be less straightforward than many thought. Even as he wrote stories for chil-dren, such as *Tanglewood Tales* (1853) and *A Wonder Book* (1852), and novels that featured children like Pearl in *The Scarlet Letter* (1850), Hawthorne was troubled by the child's capacity to seem at one moment "a holy thing" and at the next "a spirit strangely mingled with good and evil" (qtd. in Hawthorne 1903, xv).

This fluctuation between the "elfish" and the "angelic" became a focal point for scientists of the mind during the 1890s. Princeton psychologist James Mark Baldwin, for example, asserted in *Mental Development in the Child and the Race* (1895) that the child is the perfect subject of study for those who wish to chart the genesis and development of the "true self" because the child is malleable and has not yet "learned its pedigree" (4). Child development specialist Granville Stanley Hall agreed. Hall's *The Contents of Children's Minds* (1883) was one of the earliest serious scientific attempts to examine the psychology of the child, and as chair of the new psychology department at Johns Hopkins University, Hall developed a psychological laboratory grounded in his European training and focused on child development. In his seminal text *Adolescence* (1904), Hall concluded that "the years from about eight to twelve" "constitute a unique and particularly perilous period of human life." With such a declaration, one of the leading figures in American scientific and intellectual life argued that "children live in an essentially different world than adults" and thereby led "the way into [the] unknown territory" of the child's mind (9).

As scientists were identifying childhood as the pivotal period of individual development and the child subject as the key to unlocking the mysteries of the self, they were also keenly aware of the importance of novels to this process. In his 1919 "A Child is Being Beaten," Sigmund Freud, for example, makes marked reference to the constitutive role that reading and the novel play in the formation of individual psychosexual consciousness, when he notes: it is "almost always the same books"—books such as *Uncle Tom's Cabin*—"whose contents give a new stimulus to the beating-phantasies" of his patients. The child's impulse to "compete with these works of fiction" by "producing his own phantasies [of the] wealth of situations and institutions in which children were beaten" forms a pivotal moment in the child's psychosexual development, according to Freud. If the novel looms large, according to psychologists, in child maturation, American novelists like Henry James also identify the novel's founding importance for the development of childish imagination. In *A Small Boy and Others* (1913), James observes that, for a child audience in particular, Stowe's novel was "much less a book than a state of vision," requiring young readers to "wal[k] and tal[k] and laug[h] and cr[y]," but never merely read, the novel (ch. 12).

In his own writing Henry James featured child protagonists to begin to explore the complexity of the human mind and to tease out the shape, texture, and final content of child knowledge. In *What Maisie Knew* (1897), for example, James explores the circumstance of a child who, though biologically young, has already, by the second page of the novel, had the words "poor little monkey" inscribed on "the epitaph of the tomb of [her] childhood" (preface). What seems to be left is Maisie the "ready vessel for bitterness"—the child who has value for her parents only to the extent that she can be used to harm one another; she is "a deep little porcelain cup in which biting acids could be mixed" for the other's injury. And yet this child, precisely because she is forced "to see much more than she at first understood," becomes a subject of particular interest and complexity for James. As the title suggests, the question of what this child actually does know is the novel's abiding concern. Does she understand the complex, Machiavellian machinations of the adults who surround, and act as surrogate or real parents to, her? Because she is taken into adults' confidence and made confidant to their adult "passions," her "little world [becomes] phantasmagoric" (ch. 1). But to what extent does Maisie understand the sexual liaisons of those who claim to nurture her, and to what extent can she manipulate as well as be manipulated in the game in which she is an unwitting player?

While *What Maisie Knew* ends with these questions still unanswered, James's novella *The Turn of the Screw* (1898) explores child psychology in even more minute detail. His brother, the prominent American psychologist William James, had given a series of immensely popular lectures in 1895, which he subsequently published as *Talks to Teachers* in 1899. This work focused on how to train, teach, and govern children in the throes of developmental stresses of the kind that Hall and Baldwin described. According to William James, the most "proper pedagogic moment" to teach "useful habit" is exactly when children are most volatile, but teachers and governesses must have and use innovative tools in order to successfully harness the child's potentially disorderly energy (ch. 7). By triggering forgotten or buried memories and feelings teachers can capture and usefully direct the attention of children whose minds have developed irregularities and who have been "sifted out of school for both its good and their own" (ch. 4). Henry James made his own fictional contribution to this ongoing conversation about teaching, child development, and psychological modeling of individual identity formation with *The Turn of the Screw*. Featuring two children and a twenty-year-old governess, the story explores the complex psychological dynamics of pedagogic authority and child development. More specifically, it contemplates the interconnections, vanishing points, and murky borders between child and adult—the moments when generational boundaries do not hold and role reversals occur.

The task confronting James's governess is to unravel the seeming conundrum of her innocent charge's dismissal from school. From Miles's appearance—his "sweetness of innocence" and the general air and "look" of him—she finds it impossible to believe that he could "carry a bad name" (ch. 3). Yet this seeming incompatibility becomes the puzzle that she must solve. Much like Hawthorne, the governess finds unnerving the possibility that "the most beautiful child[ren] [she] had ever seen" might also be the worst (ch. 1). Like one of William James's teachers, she undertakes to win Miles and Flora's confidence and to encourage their memories of past traumatic events in the hopes that she will be able to eradicate the corrupt elements that might be lurking beneath the surface they present. The story is comprised of her attempts both to "save" the children from the corrupting influences that surround them and to identify the extent of their corruption. When Flora is directly confronted about what she knows, "her incomparable childish beauty" suddenly vanishes, and she becomes "hideously hard," "almost ugly" (ch. 20). Interior and exterior states finally aligned, Flora speaks "horrors," and her "appalling language" reveals the full extent of her psychological disorder (ch. 21). Henry James may track a governess' attempts to reclaim children at precarious points in their development, but it is not entirely clear that these pedagogic interventions are finally beneficial. The novella ends with a similar confrontation with Miles that may force the child to identify his inner passions but also causes his "little heart" once "dispossessed" to "stop" (ch. 24). In these final, equivocal words, James seems to be suggesting that the very inner states that can disrupt children's public educability may not be worth eradicating—that the cure may be worse than the malady.

But James's novella also blurs the very distinct lines between adulthood and childhood upon which the novella seems to depend. From the perspective of scientists like Hall or William James, the governess is herself still in the late stages of adolescence—a period of time, according to Hall, that commences between the years of eight and twelve but that extends into the early twenties. Her perceptions, like her charges', therefore, may be as susceptible to the false visions, intense new sensations, and psychic disturbances that characterize child development. Certainly her description of her first encounter with the children's uncle and her relocation to Bly, the country estate where she will reside with them, suggests the emotional swings that Hall and others claim are experienced by young adults. The "succession of flights and drops, a little see-saw of the right throbs and the wrong" that marks the beginning of the governess's adventure at Bly, as well as the "bewilderment of vision" she experiences when she first sees the ghost of Peter Quint (chs. 1, 3), indicate that the governess may be subject to the hallucinations, hysteria, and general emotional and mental turbulence that Hall asserts trouble individuals during that "unique and particularly perilous period of human life" when children begin the process of becoming adults (1904, ix).

As we have seen thus far, much of the late nineteenth-century American writers and readers' fascination with the child had to do with the very permeability of the category of childhood—the difficulty of determining where childhood stopped and adulthood began, the difficulty of itemizing the distinctive features of childhood, and the impossibility of identifying children's unique experiences, feelings, and characteristics. Whether it is the unconscious workings of the individual child's mind or the social threat and possibility for regeneration posed by marginal American children, American writers saw in the child a rich array of opportunities to explore the inner workings of the individual's relation to the social structures that comprise American culture. American readers, likewise, turned to these novels with relish because they represented many of the abiding concerns and interests of Americans—nostalgia for the halcyon days of childhood innocence, concern for the nation's future, and fascination with the meaning of contemporary scientific thought and technological innovation for individual development and human capability.

Yet in addition to these important facets of social inquiry and popular debate, children became particularly powerful representatives of another urgent social issue facing the nation during the late nineteenth century—race relations. Earlier in the century, child protagonists such as little Eva in Harriet Beecher Stowe's *Uncle Tom's Cabin* (1852) had powerfully stirred up readers' sympathy for abolition, and the regenerative power of the pure, angelic, and Anglo-Saxon Eva's love to transform the unruly slave child Topsy into a model of Christian virtue is a centerpiece of the novel's abolitionist message. But *Uncle Tom's Cabin* also advocated for abolition by likening adult slaves like Uncle Tom to children and, in so doing, took part in a long-standing tradition of infantilizing the enslaved, even while invoking the Christian purity of the little child.

In the postbellum era, the child once again became a powerful representative of Americans' complex and contradictory feelings about racial equality and racial justice. Take, for example, the emergence of what has become known as the "black baby myth" in much late nineteenth-century and early twentieth-century fiction. The plethora of novels, stories, and tales that featured a white woman's birthing of a black baby reflected the racial hysteria of a period that has subsequently come to be identified as, arguably, the worst in terms of racial violence in the United States. Thomas Dixon's *The Leopard's Spots: A Romance of the White Man's Burden* (1902), for example, declares that "a man or woman of Negro ancestry, though a century removed, will suddenly breed back to a pure Negro child" by way of justifying racial segregation (ch. 7). Robert Lee Durham's *The Call of the South* (1908) depicts a white woman who goes mad when her marriage to a seemingly white mulatto produces a black baby. But racist white authors were not the only ones to use the black baby myth to sway readers to their racial agendas. The African American novelist and minister Sutton Griggs, for example, reverses the racial dynamics of the black baby myth in his important novel of racial equality, *Imperium In Imperio* (1899). Both African American male protagonists in Griggs's novel must struggle with the legacy of miscegenation: one abandons his African American wife when it appears that she has given birth to a white child and the other loses his fiancée, who kills herself rather than contribute to the degeneration of the race by marrying and procreating with a man who is of mixed race. These revisions of the black baby myth challenge the assumption that it is only whites who fear the "taint" of racial otherness and suggest the multiple ways that racial tensions can cut.

Mark Twain's popular novel *Puddn'head Wilson* (1894) takes the child's special capacity to indicate and transmit racial identity to an ironic extreme, and, in so doing, Twain challenges the very racialist logics in which black baby myths trade. The novel features two children. One is the offspring of Roxy, a slave woman who is one-sixteenth white and who bears a child who is "thirty one parts white" but a slave, despite his "blue eyes and flaxen hair," because of the "fiction of law and custom" in which all children follow the condition of the mother. The other child is the offspring of one of the prestigious white families in the small town of Dawson's

Landing. Despite these children's different legal status—one free and one a slave—they look so similar that "even the father of the white child" is unable "to tell the children apart" (ch. 2). The infant switch that Roxy implements because she is afraid that her son might be sold away from her is effective, and all the town is convinced of the children's false identities until the children become men. Each, in turn, grows up thinking that he is the race of the other.

The question that Twain uses this story of two interchangeable children to ask is none other than the question of race itself: is there such a thing as racial difference? Is race innate, as the proliferation of racial scientists writing at the end of the nineteenth century argued, or is race a social construct, which is to say an idea that has been generated over time to normalize social hierarchies but that is not actually real? Twain's fictional portrayal of children who unwittingly pass as the race of the other, therefore, engages with urgent questions of the day. Anna Tolman Smith, a US Bureau of Education specialist and author of numerous sociological and educational studies of children, summarized a prevailing view of race and child development in her 1897 *Popular Science Monthly* article, "A Study of Race Psychology." She concludes that "the negro child" is "psychologically different from the white child," and that it is this essential difference that explains the "inferior developmental state" of African Americans (362). Her view was not unusual but was articulated in such social scientific treatises as James Mark Baldwin's *The Mental Development in the Child and the Race* (1894). Against the backdrop of this contemporary thinking about race and individual development, Twain writes his commentary on racial essentialism. Given the prominence of children to these scientific accounts, his decision to locate his critique of American racism in two child protagonists who represent the vanishing point of racial difference is no accident. With these child protagonists, Twain is able to suggest that racial identity isn't racial destiny. In fact, he insists on this important assertion by highlighting how the children assume the attitudes, behaviors, and figures of speech that Dawson's Landing associates with each of the races, in direct proportion to how the children are racially identified within the community.

It is precisely this commitment to the idea that racial identity doesn't determine social destiny that prominent race men of the late nineteenth and early twentieth century used the child to emphasize. Such key political and literary figures as W. E. B. Du Bois and José Martí not only advocated, respectively, for African American and Cuban social and political equality, but they often did so through recourse to images of and publications for children. Both men edited children's periodicals as part of their commitment to social justice for all races. Du Bois's children's magazine *The Brownie's Book* (1920–21) as well as the *Crisis* Children's Number (1912–34) highlighted the important role that children played in the movement for black social progress, while Martí's 1889 children's periodical, *La Edad de Oro*, propounded a similar pedagogic purpose of Cuban children. Just as Martí declares, in the preface to *La Edad de Oro,* that "children are the hope of the world," so too does Du

Bois comment, in his novel *Darkwater* (1920), that "all our problems center in the child"—if "democracy is a failure" we can make it succeed by "turning our attention to the child" (ch. 8). In *The Souls of Black Folk* (1903) Du Bois had mourned the death of his son in a chapter entitled "Of the Passing of the First-Born." The child he loses is a child of great innocence and infinite possibility—a child graced with "olive-tinted flesh and dark gold ringlets," eyes "mingled blue and brown," and "perfect little limbs" through which coursed "the blood of Africa." Yet this child, Du Bois contemplates, would all too soon experience the violence of living in "the Land of the Color-line"—a land that will identify him as black and therefore lesser. The child's temporary state of innocence is one in which he remains ignorant of this fact, one in which he knows "no color-line," and so "in his little world walked souls alone, uncolored" (ch. 11). It is therefore with a mixture of grief and relief that Du Bois beholds his dead son. "Not dead, but escaped; not bond, but free" are the words he whispers by way of consolation. But twenty years later, in *Darkwater*, Du Bois turns to the child to envision alternatives to the inevitable violence experienced by African Americans because of the color-line. It is "in the treatment of the child" that, according to Du Bois, "the world foreshadows its own future and faith." Therefore "all words and all thinking lead to the child—to that vast immortality and wide sweep of infinite possibility which the child represents" (ch. 8). It is just such possibility with which Du Bois's late-career novel *Dark Princess* (1928) ends. The child born by the Princess Kautilya is understood to be "the Messenger and Messiah to all the Darker Worlds" (pt. 4, ch. 19). In a scene that reenacts the nativity, three Brahmin emerge, like the wise men, to celebrate and to train the child. Thus, just as Du Bois's early vision of the most vulnerable victim of racism is a child, so too is his final vision of the most successful advocate for social justice a child.

In addition to being featured within the pages of much adult writing that aimed to effect dramatic social change, children were also encouraged to read fiction so that they would internalize the social ideals that writers from Du Bois to Alcott espoused. Advice writers throughout the late nineteenth and early twentieth centuries increasingly saw the twinned acts of reading and writing as integral to the development of successful citizens. As affluent children spent less and less time as their parents' helpers and apprentices, their leisure time expanded, and the question of how effectively to employ their minds and imaginations became an urgent one for adults. Worried that young middle-class girls would squander their newfound freedom from domestic chores, the advice writer William Thayer proposed that their mental development and religious improvement could be effected if girls read ideally a hundred pages a day. Advice writers and religious leaders had expressed concern about girls reading fiction throughout the early nineteenth century, but reading became elevated to a defining and central component of affluent girls' lives as the century progressed. By 1901 the advice writer Heloise Hersey estimated that girls between twelve and twenty-one, on average, read over an hour every day and so devoted over a year of full-time work to the occupation of reading. As printed materials became more affordable and readily available, children's literacy rates increased and, by 1880, 90 percent of the native-born American public and 80 percent of the nation's non-native born populace claimed to be able to read.

This dramatically expanded reading public corresponded to the proliferation of public libraries. In 1876, a government report listed 3,682 public libraries, but by 1900 that number had increased to over eight thousand. The increasing availability of books sharpened attitudes about appropriate fiction for juvenile audiences. If the Bible and *The Pilgrim's Progress* (1678) were mainstays of earlier reading genera-tions, the proliferation of novels, often sensational, caused alarm for advice writers like Harriet Paine. In *Chats with Girls on Self-Culture* (1900), Paine lists appropri-ate writers for young readers as including, among others, Charles Dickens, Alcott, and Sir Walter Scott. Social reformers' concern about the negative influence that popular sensational fiction by authors such as E. D. E. N Southworth and Wilkie Collins might exert on young readers led the American Library Association (ALA), in 1881, to consider imposing uniform censorship on public library collections. The ALA compiled a list of sixteen novelists who should be excluded from public collections because of the deleterious effect of their writing on young minds, but got no further in their efforts to shape the young minds of the American people (on increased literacy, the ALA, and censorship, see Chapter 3 of this volume). Despite the attention that adults devoted to dictating the reading habits of chil-dren, the journals of young readers suggest that they were powerfully drawn to novels, often sensational in nature. The journals of avid late nineteenth-century child readers like Margaret Tileston, Agnes Hamilton, and Lucy Breckinridge sug-gest that the challenge was not to read a sufficient amount but rather to limit their reading time each day. Their journals describe resolutions to limit the time they devoted to reading and the frequency with which these resolutions failed. They admit shamefacedly that they often stayed up throughout the night to finish such favorite novels as Jane Austen's *Northanger Abbey* (1817) and Augusta J. Evans's *St. Elmo* (1896).

Young readers' insatiable appetite for fiction, coupled with the widespread accep-tance of the idea that reading was a central part of childhood led to the burgeoning of literature written specifically for children. Authors like Frances Hodgson Burnett exemplify the emergence of children's fiction as a genre. Her publication of *Little Lord Fauntleroy* in 1886 propelled her into the national eye. Originally intended to appeal to a child audience, the novel became most popular with middle-class mothers, who saw the child protagonist as a model for the sons they wanted to raise. Just as children were encouraged to read in order to see themselves as heroes and heroines, so too did adult readers of Burnett's novel take every aspect of the fictional child's appearance and manner as a powerful model for child-rearing. The name "Cedric" became a popular boys' name for decades, the signature Fauntleroy velvet suit with lace collar was a popular fashion statement on children of the affluent, and the fictional child's long curly locks could be seen reproduced on the heads of boys in family photos for a generation to come. But as importantly, women readers found in Cedric's close relationship with his mother, whom he calls "Dearest," a compelling depiction of maternal power and a model for mother/son relations. Cedric's protection of his mother and the intimate domestic world that they create together after the death of Cedric's father suggest close links between adult and child sensibilities and the seductive allure of this intimate world for adult readers. While the distinctions between children and adult fiction were still somewhat fluid in the late nineteenth century, as *Little Lord Fauntleroy*'s reception suggests, the early twentieth century witnessed a proliferation of fiction written explicitly for and about children. Burnett's *The Secret Garden* (1911) exemplifies this key shift in reading sensibilities. The early twentieth-century children's novel for which Burnett is best known today is one in which children must learn to survive and thrive without parents and with minimal adult influence or care. The novel features two children who have been orphaned or abandoned by parental figures and who learn how to flourish on their own and through the influence of other children. The child world that the two children create together in the secret garden that Mary discovers is one that is regenerative for both of them, but they find and nurture it in spite of their parent and guardian, who refuses to give them access to it or knowledge of each other. In a world devoid of the kind of parental presence that Cedric's mother "Dearest" exerts, these children learn how to cope in a world largely of their own making.

Just as *The Secret Garden* depicted a world occupied almost exclusively by children and modeled explicitly for child readers, so too did the proliferation of children's and young adult fiction subordinate the world and influence of adults, often narrating a dramatic break with adult expectation as a part of child life. Though written by adults, often out of concern for the successful maturation of girls and boys into autonomous women and men, this fiction depicted the important lessons of young life as ones that were primarily peer-taught or self-taught. Take, for example, progressive-era girl's fiction. The writings by a host of women writers who aimed to validate the importance of women's communities focused on the adolescent years in which girls were making important choices about their future lives. While much writing had described girls' progress from parental home to marital home, an outpouring of writing depicted young girls making the radical choice to defer marriage in favor of college. Although that choice was embraced by like-minded peers, it provoked heated opposition from adults and parents. Thus built into the fabric of progressive-era girls' college novels was a radical view of American girlhood that refuted mainstream adult expectation.

The heroines of Helen Dawes Brown's immensely popular *Two College Girls* (1886), for example, are temperamentally and socioeconomically opposites, but they learn to put aside their differences and support each others' ambitions. When they read a passage from Henry James's *The Portrait of a Lady* (1881) they become infuriated at the image of femininity that James depicts, and denounce "women [who] do with themselves nothing at all; [who] wait, in attitudes more or less gracefully passive, for a man to come their way and furnish them with a destiny" (ch. 1). Rather than be that kind of woman, these two Vassar girls, acting together, model a different kind of female maturation. Brown's novel represents a sea change in gender expectations for young girls, but it also generated a half-century revolution in girls' fiction. *Two College Girls* not only went through numerous printings, but it spawned hundreds of books written by women activists, club members, and social reformers who recognized the power of fiction to alter future generations' expectations of what they could achieve for themselves if they refused to capitulate to traditional expectations.

This explosion in girls' and boys' fiction extended from the 1890s through the 1940s and ranged from the college novel to the detective novel and outdoor fiction. These genres were often pitched to insatiable readers in serialized form, as evidenced by Rachel Sutton's *Judy Bolton Mysteries* series (1932–67), and written by publishing syndicates, as evidenced by the Stratemeyer Syndicate's *The Hardy Boys* (1927–present) and *The Nancy Drew Mystery Stories* (1930–2003). *The Rover Boys Series* (1899–1926), and *The Bob Chase Big Game Series* (1929–30) propounded outdoor adventure for young boys as an antidote to fears of the decline of Anglo-American boyhood. But outdoor adventure was not the exclusive prerogative of boys. Books such as Irene Elliott Benson's *How Ethel Hollister Became A Campfire Girl* (1912) and Lilian Garis's *The Outdoor Girls of Deepdale; or Camping and Tramping for Fun and Health* (1913) sold tens of thousands of copies and made millions by advocating independence, action, and physical exercise as mainstays of American girlhood. Lilian Garis was a college-educated journalist and advocate for women's rights. With her husband she worked for Edward Stratemeyer on numerous series such as *The Bobbsey Twins* (1904–79) and *The Blythe Girls* (1925–32). These series shared a few common features that ensured sustained profitability: they left parents out of the mix while featuring mystery and physical activity. *The Outdoor Girls* motivated girls from many towns to form like organizations, and Garis received mail from girl readers telling of the Outdoor Clubs they were setting up as a result of reading her book.

Though many of these series began in the first decades of the twentieth century, some have had remarkable longevity and continue to be popular with readers of both genders today. Edward Stratemeyer created the *Hardy Boys* series in 1927, and the series was so successful that he decided to create a similar one for girl readers in 1930. Ghost-written by a number of authors but carrying the pseudonym Carolyn Keene, the *Nancy Drew* series featured the intrepid Nancy Drew and her female friends Bess Marvin and George Fayne, who solve numerous mysteries with the occasional help such remote male figures as Nancy's attorney father Carson Drew. While it might be easy to dismiss these novels as less than "great literature," they have shaped the thinking of generations of girl readers. Prominent women from Supreme Court Justices Sandra Day O'Connor and Sonia Sotomayor to Secretary of State Hillary Rodham Clinton and former First Lady Laura Bush have cited Nancy Drew as a formative influence, while feminist literary scholars have variously analyzed the girl protagonist as cultural icon, mythic girl hero, and representative of conflicted feminine codes. The Nancy Drew series influenced girl readers for seven decades until the series formally ended in 2003. However, Nancy's character, updated for a new century, can now be found in a new mystery series. In the *Girl Detective* series (2003–present), Nancy drives a hybrid car rather than her signature red convertible, and uses a cell phone, but many have commented that the real character has not changed much and that her ongoing appeal among twenty-first century juvenile readers shows no sign of abating.

Most of these juvenile literature series and most children's literature tended to feature Anglo American protagonists, but there have been some notable exceptions. Both Amelia E. Johnson and Emma Dunham Kelley-Hawkins were pioneers in the field of children's literature, writing to promote self-esteem among African American children. Johnson's first children's book, *Clarence and Corinne; or, God's Way* (1887), was tremendously popular, receiving strong reviews in mainstream newspapers, and *The Hazeley Family* (1894) was equally well received. Kelley-Hawkins's *Megda* (1891) and *Four Girls at Cottage City* (1898) provided young readers with African American characters who formed girls' communities that are committed to helping their members develop strong senses of self. By the 1910s, '20s, and '30s, children's literature written specifically for and about African American youth became a crucial component of social uplift and, increasingly, a key element of the Harlem Renaissance's investment in community activism and racial pride. The increase in African American education at the elementary, secondary, and university levels created a sharp generational divide between African American children and their parents, and many New Negro texts written for children overtly call on their progressive child readers to reform backwards parents. Thus the children's literature written during the Harlem Renaissance not only sought to create a New Negro child but to remake all the generations comprising African American communities.

While Du Bois's *The Brownies Book* had highlighted the child's special place in black social progress, subsequent writings for African American children sought to correct the ongoing damage that traditional textbooks' incipient racism was doing to African American youth. Founder of the Associated Publishers (1921), which published African American children's literature from 1931 to 1951, Carter Woodson devoted much of his energy to rebutting racist textbooks, building race pride in child readers, and helping the next generation claim the rich heritage of their racial identity. Books such as Jane Dabney Shackelford's *Child's Story of the Negro* (1938) and Helen A. Whiting's *Negro Art, Music, and Rhyme* (1938) emphasized an African American heritage and history that was essentially different from that which child readers were, too often, getting in school. These writers sought to protect this new generation of publicly educated African American children not only from the ongoing racism that they were encountering in school but also from the traumatic story of their past. In Shackelford's text, for example, she has a chapter entitled "How Africans Came to America," in which she does not vilify US slavery but rather suggests that, because slaves already existed in Africa and because America required labor, slaves were doing a patriotic duty for the country. In this effort to insulate her child readers from the systematic, institutionalized exploitation that their race had been subjected to, Shackelford and other writers sought to ensure that the next generation was not as damaged by their African American past as had been prior generations.

In addition to this social mission, much writing for and about children during the Harlem Renaissance found in children a rich imaginative source for an emergent African-American aesthetic tradition. Langston Hughes's children's poetry collection *The Dream Keeper* (1932), for example, helped Hughes cultivate a national literary reputation. His collaborations with Arna Bontemps generated a remarkable amount of children's literature, ranging from *Popo and Fifina: Children of Haiti* (1932) to *The Pasteboard Bandit* (1935). *Popo and Fifina* was the first book that Hughes published after returning from Haiti, and it emphasizes the quiet beauty, simplicity, and humanity of Haitian working-class life. It was on Macmillan's prestigious list for more than two decades and was translated into numerous languages.

The story begins with Popo and Fifina walking behind their parents, Papa Jean and Mamma Anna, from their rural village to Cape Haiti, where Papa Jean plans to become a fisherman. The children's world is comprised of a combination of play and work—indeed the relation of one to the other is an abiding theme of the story. Papa Jean takes time from his job to make the children a kite that they want. It is "red with trimmings of yellow and green paper," and, as his fishing boat passes the shore, Papa Jean waves his arms proudly in the air as he sees the children flying the kite. Yet the work of his hands becomes the prey of another kite—"a dull brown thing" that reminds Popo of "a hawk swooping over a smaller bird." While Popo's "big red star kite" is threatened by "the big brown hawk-kite," Papa Jean's son has confidence that the homemade kite will defeat the kite that is trying to cut his string with its seeming greater strength. He is right that "his big star-kite was a match for any hawk," and it is "the hawk" that finally falls "to the earth like an evil bird with a broken wing" and the "big red star [that] climbed to the sky proudly, a true conqueror" (ch. 8). An activist for a number of Communist-sponsored causes at the time of the story's writing, Hughes clearly embeds in the kite story a critique of labor practices and of American economic policies.

Just as the kite episode suggests the value of anticapitalist forms of labor and production, so too is Popo's introduction to the world of adult work one that emphasizes the importance of the laborer's relation to his or her labor. Popo is apprenticed to his Uncle Jacques's woodworking trade, and this family business refuses the dehumanizing effects that characterize other kinds of labor. Every design that Uncle Jacques etches on the tables, trays, and other pieces of furniture that he makes carries his personal feeling. As he tells Popo, "you have to put yourself into the design[;] . . . what I am inside makes the design. The design is a picture of the way I feel. . . . The design is me. I put my sad feeling and my glad feeling into the design. . . . And when people look at your design . . . they will feel as you felt when you made the design. . . . That is really the only way that people can ever know how other people feel" (ch. 9). When it is time for Popo to make his first tray he puts his happiness into the design, and it is "precious" as a commodity because a part of his identity inheres in the object that he has made—the object carries and transmits part of the laborer, rather than deprives the laborer of his identity (ch. 11).

As this story suggests, writers of both the Left and the Right saw children's literature as the key to the future. Social transformation was a significant component of much progressive educational philosophy, and leftist writers of the 1920s, '30s, and '40s, influenced by John Dewey's educational philosophy, Sigmund Freud's psychoanalytic models, and Karl Marx's political writing turned to children's literature because they saw in the artistic and creative aspects of childhood a model for social liberation. Writers like Lucy Sprague Mitchell, for example, applied the ideas of progressive education to children's literature to produce such classics as *Here and Now Story Book* (1921), which she targeted to seven-year-olds and aimed at helping children learn how things that they needed were actually produced. Much like *Popo and Fifina*, *Here and Now* narrates the relationships between human beings and industrial processes and focuses on concrete lived experience rather than fantasy worlds or escapism. Translated into many languages and especially popular in the Soviet Union, *Here and Now Story Book* aimed to provide informational literature for children and helped to spawn other educational children's books. *Diggers and Builders* (1931), *How the Derrick Works* (1930), and *A Steam Shovel for Me!* (1933), for example, focus on the strength of manual laborers and explain how laborer and machine interact. A number of these stories also highlight the racial identity of laborers and labor relations between the races, and some, like *The Dutch Twins* (1911), *The Eskimo Twins* (1914), *The Japanese Twins* (1912), and *The Pickaninny Twins* (1935), focus on fostering mutual respect and understanding among people of different nations and races.

Throughout the late nineteenth and early twentieth centuries, American writers and readers consistently turned to the pages of American fiction to form and to find stories about children, the relations between children and adults, and to understand the nation's future as well as its past. As we have seen, American writers have always had a deep and abiding relish for fictionalizing children—for scripting them as the carriers of various kinds of social, scientific, spiritual, and psychological knowledge. With the turn into the twentieth century, these writers became increasingly interested in writing to and for children as a distinct reading demographic. In the act of scripting child protagonists, authors with a range of interests, politics, and priorities fictionalized children in order to generate a distinctive children's fiction, and, in so doing, they created a series of complex fictions about, for, and featuring children that we continue to unravel today.

20

THE AMERICAN BESTSELLER

BY LEONARD CASSUTO

What is a bestseller? The question is worth asking, even though—or perhaps especially because—there's no easy or objective way to answer it.

Yet the question has rarely been asked in scholarly circles. The idea of the best-seller, despite its obvious importance to how we think about books, has received very little academic scrutiny over the years. (It has received more attention from authors who believe that they belong on the lists, and who have challenged them.) Books tend to be called "bestsellers" by scholars who find anecdotal evidence of very high sales, multiple printings, and other evidence of wide circulation. There are ways to get specific figures on some older titles, typically by consulting publishers' records, but the data are patchy, and scholars apply the term "bestseller" pretty casually. Even so, the categorization of bestsellers is widely understood as a science of formulas and absolute values—even though it turns out that the numbers are incomplete and not always trustworthy, and the formulas are arbitrary, tendentious, and often secret.

But the sketchiness of the numbers is probably not the reason that literary schol-ars have stayed away from bestsellers. Part of the academic aversion to bestsellers surely stems from the literary critic's self-appointed task, which is to separate good books from bad ones. A bestseller is a book about which the buying public has al-ready rendered a verdict, and that judgment amounts to a kind of competition with the critic who is trying to persuade the reader to pick up a book, or leave another one alone. This competition for the reader's interest points to the much-vaunted and inconsistently permeable boundary between so-called high and low culture. Critics represent high culture, while bestsellers are typically seen as low. But high and low culture define each other, so we should look closely at the antagonism—it helps to show us why bestsellers matter.

Bestsellers build community by involving readers together in shared thought and emotion. The literary canon, a group of books deemed worthy of special praise and study, is supposed to do this too (and books later deemed great usually started out as commercial successes). Bestsellers are in this respect a low-culture version of canon—a different kind of literary community. Oprah Winfrey's twenty-first century efforts to unite the high and low from her unique position as the head of the world's largest book club make this comparison especially clear.

In the pages that follow, I will explore the distinction between novels that sell a lot of copies and "bestselling novels" in order to pursue two main arguments. First, I will suggest that while bestselling novels readily embrace topical controversies, they do so only after the issues have settled into discernible opposing positions, and they do so in ways that reflect these positions. Or to put it differently, a novel that engages a widely known social debate is more likely to become a bestseller if it appears after the sides for that debate have already been drawn.

Second, I'm going to propose two main ideas that provided structural support for bestselling novels during this period: sentimentalism and evolution. These two ideologies were often in dialogue with each other during the period under discussion. I don't mean to suggest that all of the bestsellers of the period focus on sentimentalism or boil down to evolution. Instead, I am arguing that sentimentalism and evolution provided ways of looking at the world that gave a narrative skeleton to many of the most popular stories of the time.

The Bestseller in American Print Culture

A raft of books that purported to teach inexperienced readers how to read a book began to appear in the 1870s, with titles like *What to Read, and How to Read* (1870), *How to Read a Book in the Best Way* (1873), and *The Best Reading: Hints on the Selection of Books* (1877). These books were published at the same time that the book industry was shifting into a new commercial gear, with publishers exploring new forms of advertising and branding. Many (though not all) of these How-to-Read books grew out of the efforts of publishers to establish their own highbrow credibility and thus gain authority to market their wares, and they amounted to a form of regulation as well as marketing.

The overarching idea of the early How-to-Read books was to raise literary sensibility by teaching readers how to read for something other than entertainment. The ideal of intellectual enrichment fit comfortably with the new commodification of upward mobility and personal advancement. Charles H. Moore, for example, in *What to Read, and How to Read*, counsels readers to bear in mind that "a book of real worth not only pleases during its perusal, but leaves the reader wiser and better" (1870, 11). Numerous references to schools, workplaces, and money suggest that the implied reader of these new manuals was a new member of the middle class. These How-to-Read books met a larger need for guiding novice readers through an increasingly confusing literary marketplace, as bestseller lists would later do. As such, they participated in a struggle for power and control of readers and their reading material that was also being played out in publishing houses, libraries, and government (whose workings were harnessed by censors like Anthony Comstock, about whom more later). In *How to Read a Book in the Best Way*, George P. Philes describes the printing press as "a great power, which, when uncontrolled, broods over a murky wilderness of ink, and floods each brain with a shapeless mist of thought" (1873, 11). The reader evidently needed guidance to struggle out of the mist—and there was no shortage of volunteers for the task.

We may presume, I think, that good reading habits were being commodified and put into the service of upward mobility precisely because many people felt upward mobility to be difficult to achieve. Horatio Alger's hugely successful upward mobility novels (which the author began publishing in quantity during the mid-1860s) and the How-to-Read books were of a piece in that they both offered the reassurance that people could get ahead if they worked hard and applied themselves, and applying themselves meant reading properly. The implication, of course, was that reading bestsellers was an example of *not* reading properly—and that implication endures to this day.

The bestseller therefore represents a new way of thinking about books in context—and that context was, at least at the beginning, distinctively American. The idea of the bestseller is a socially constructed one, and also a cultural symptom. As such, it does important cultural work. Bestsellers are anointed books, and the title confers meaning within its larger surrounding.

That larger surrounding was, between the end of the Civil War and the beginning of the Second World War, in dynamic flux, as the United States underwent rapid and dramatic social and industrial change. The nation urbanized rapidly after the Civil War: In 1860, only 20 percent of Americans lived in cities. By 1900, the figure had climbed to 40 percent, and the 1920 census marked the first time that a majority of the American population was urban. The population of New York City rose from under a million in 1870 to nearly seven-and-a-half million in 1940, a more than sevenfold increase. The total population of the country more than tripled during the same period, from thirty-eight to more than 132 million people, a rise fueled in significant part by increased immigration; more than twenty million new Americans arrived from Europe alone during the period 1865–1914. Increased growth brought both increased wealth (including the rise of monopolistic trusts) and increased poverty: about 40 percent of the U.S population lived below the poverty line in 1900, a ratio that remained constant through the early twentieth century. The period saw the rise of progressivism, populism, and reform movements of all sizes—including socialism (which reached its American apex during the 1910s), suffragism (which triumphed in 1920) and women's rights more generally, modern hygiene reform, labor reform and trade unionism, and anti-imperialism (which followed the rise of imperialism). Race relations entered a new era; the NAACP was founded in 1909 after decades of lynchings that were as horrifying for their regularity as for their grotesque brutality. The telephone, the car, the radio, and the electric lightbulb were invented during this period, resulting in a revolution in transportation and communication, catalyzed by the lower costs of printing and distribution that allowed printers and publishers to "hurl words across great distances" (Kaestle and Radway 2009, 10) to create a "culture of print" (Kaestle 2009, 24).

The book trade modernized rapidly as this new print culture came into being. Literacy increased greatly with the availability of public high school in the early twentieth century, and libraries multiplied to serve legions of new readers. Newspapers and magazines proliferated, and many of them serialized fiction. More and more novels were written and published for this growing market, using new technologies (such as "hot type" machines) that made book production faster and cheaper, and thus more affordable for this expanding universe of consumers. Beginning in the 1880s, book publishers fell in with what cultural historian Alan Trachtenberg describes as "the incorporation of America." The book became a carefully marketed product, part of a complex system driven by distribution, pricing, and the search for new marketing possibilities such as subscriptions and catalog sales. Commercial publishers experimented with different business techniques to create brands to attract specific audiences, such as series, catalogs, and the creation of genres for marketing purposes. The genre of local color writing, suggests Nancy Glazener, originally arose from marketing imperatives rather than authorial innovation (2011, 347). Publishers also attempted regionally based price fixing, but were defeated in the Supreme Court in 1901, freeing retailers to offer discounts. From these transformations was born what book historians call the "commercial book," a necessary prelude to the bestseller.

The Bestseller and the Bestseller List

So what is a bestseller anyway? F. Scott Fitzgerald's *The Great Gatsby* sold twenty-one thousand copies at two dollars apiece as a Scribner's frontlist title in 1925. The figure was a great disappointment to Fitzgerald and his publisher. Fitzgerald received a 15 percent royalty for *The Great Gatsby*, so he earned—and spent—something over six thousand dollars for its initial sales run, along with another twenty-six thousand dollars that he received for stage and screen rights to the novel. (The first paperback edition of *The Great Gatsby* did not appear until 1945; the paperback revolution lies largely outside the chronological boundaries of this volume.) As a backlist title, though, *The Great Gatsby* currently sells 500 thousand copies per year, just in English. Consider as well that the majority of those half-million copies presumably sell in September and January (that is, at the beginnings of new semesters), and the concentration of sales at those times would make *The Great Gatsby* one of the nation's top sellers—yet the novel never appears on the bestseller list.

Frank Luther Mott defines a book as a bestseller if its sales figures reached the equivalent of 1 percent of the US population during the decade within which the book was published. This definition is reasonable, but it's also arbitrary—as have been definitions by other scholars like James D. Hart (who focuses on sales immediately following publication) and Robert Escarpit (1966), who tries to thread a way between the Hart's "fast seller" and Mott's "steady seller." The whole idea of a bestseller originated in the United States, where it emerged in the postbellum period—along with the word itself. The first recorded use of "bestseller" (or "best seller") came in an offhand reference in the *Kansas Times and Star* in 1889, but the second recorded instance of the term, by the *New York* trade magazine *The Bookman* in 1895, is particularly telling in that it traces the early usage of the term to the publishing business (*OED* 2.141). *The Bookman* published the first monthly bestseller lists beginning the same year, 1895.

So "bestseller" is both an American concept and an American word. The concept dovetails with the development of the "commercial book" which I noted earlier. Not surprisingly, the United States is where the practice of celebrating a big-selling book began. It is also unsurprising that the idea of calling attention to big-selling books emerged during a period of highly self-conscious, largely unregulated industrial capitalism in the country. Bestseller status, after all, came about as a form of marketing, and from there it quickly became a form of advertising—and the advertising industry grew exponentially and took on its modern form during the same period. As Trachtenberg notes, spending on advertising increased tenfold to over five hundred million dollars between 1870 and 1900 (1982, 136). It's also of more than passing significance that lots of novels about big business—both pro and con—were published during the period when the concept of the bestseller emerged.

The word "bestseller" has always been a marketing tool above all. Bestseller lists are like IQ tests. They both measure what they measure—but what they measure is not exactly what they purport to measure. IQ tests, according to the oft-repeated criticism, measure IQ, not intelligence itself, the nature of which remains much debated. Bestseller lists arise from an implied understanding of "bestseller," but any actual definition of that term is nearly as elusive as "intelligence." The lists are compiled in order to sell books. I mentioned the novels of Horatio Alger earlier; Alger's books remain familiar precisely because they circulated so widely that Alger's name became a cliché in the upward-mobility lexicon, with a meaning understood by people who have never read his books. Yet Alger never appeared on a bestseller list even though the last decades of his career—when he was an established success— overlapped with them. (The lists weren't around when he started writing.) Alger's books didn't make the bestseller lists because publishers didn't want them to. That's because bestseller lists were never designed simply to record which books were selling the most. Instead, the lists were designed to bring attention only to certain books from among that group.

A few words about how bestseller lists do and don't work: First, they have never worked by keeping track of a book's sales, at least not exactly. Even with twenty-first century technology, there is no way to keep a running tally of how many copies of a book sell from week to week. You can't simply tally copies printed; just because a copy of a book is manufactured doesn't mean it will sell. Just because it is shipped to a store doesn't mean it will sell either. (Beginning in the 1930s, bookstores were permitted to return unsold stock to publishers.) Second, bestseller lists have never collected figures from all stores. The *New York Times* bestseller list, the one with the greatest authority with the general public today, collects information from representative booksellers and chains, and compiles it according to formulas that (amazingly) remain a trade secret. Their practice is generally consistent with the one established by *The Bookman* magazine in the first bestseller lists more than a century ago. Third and most important, as the Alger example shows, the lists never have been value-neutral.

Keeping that last point in mind, let us consider the example of the dime novel. As David Kazanjian discusses in his chapter in this volume, dime novels were a massive publishing phenomenon that started around 150 years ago and lasted into the early twentieth century. They were published not by old-fashioned publishing "houses" but by "fiction factories" such as Beadle and Company and Street and Smith. The authors—some of whom were extraordinarily prolific—wrote to specified formulas for plot and word length, and the books were mass-produced using cheap materials (including wood pulp in the paper, hence the term "pulp fiction").

In this respect, the dime novel presaged the mass-market paperback, and dime novels played a shaping role in the development of popular genres like the Western and the detective story. Puzzle-like detective novels sold very well through the late nineteenth century and into the twentieth, with Metta Fuller Victor and Anna Katharine Green as pioneer bestsellers who handed the baton to Mary Roberts Rinehart later on. But the emergence of the hard-boiled detective story between respectable hardcovers in the 1930s—with bestselling authors like Dashiell Hammett, James M. Cain, and Raymond Chandler, all of whom were originally published by the high-toned publisher Alfred A. Knopf—is scarcely explainable without factoring in the influence of dime novel detective stories and their rugged heroes in shaping the characters and conventions of this important genre offshoot. (For more on this connection, see Lee Horsley's chapter in this volume.)

Unlike paperbacks, dime novels were rarely sold in bookstores. They were marketed through the mail, and in local shops, newsstands, and the like. Dime novels sold a lot of copies, hundreds of thousands in the case of more successful titles. They attracted wide disapproval from moralists who feared that they were corrupting children (who were the targeted readers of many dime novels) and from literati (who saw them as corrupting taste more generally). Powerful bureaucrats like Anthony Comstock, head of the New York Society for the Suppression of Vice and a postal bureaucrat, used mail regulations (most notably the infamous "Comstock Law," passed in 1873) to restrict the circulation of objects (not only books but also birth control paraphernalia) that he deemed objectionable. He made a specific effort to suppress dime novels. (Here too we may draw an implicit connection with the goals of the How-to-Read books.) Comstock did his fundraising among the upper classes—people who didn't read the books that they were helping to ban. (For more on the Comstock Law, see Chapters 3 and 17 of this volume.)

Not surprisingly, dime novels did not appear on bestseller lists. The people who made the lists didn't want them there. Dime novels are an exception that shows the lists to be incomplete guides to the literary marketplace, but the omission of the dimes provides a revealing look at the ideology of that marketplace and the place of the bestseller list—and the "bestseller"—in enforcing that ideology. The lists are valuable resources in the end, but we shouldn't completely trust them on their own terms. I therefore use the term "bestseller" to refer in general terms to a book that sold well in its own time. Many of the books that fit that criterion appeared on best-seller lists—but not all of them.

The Anatomy of a Bestselling Novel, and the Problem of Race

What turns a novel into a bestseller? There are many causes, both known and unknown. Some of these are not very complicated, but let's not overlook the obvious: readers like ripping yarns. In particular, American readers have gravitated toward historical romances since the days when pirated copies of Sir Walter Scott's *Waverley* (1814), *Rob Roy* (1817), and *Ivanhoe* (1819), among others, dominated the literary market of the early American republic. The bestselling book of 1900, for example, was *To Have and to Hold*, a now-obscure historical romance by Mary Johnston set in colonial Jamestown. The popularity of *Gone With the Wind* (1936) has many explanations, but one of them is that it follows a long-established American taste for romances with sweeping historical backdrops. Terence Martin has observed that the early American novel was dominated by "the historical and the sentimental" (1957, 73). These two categories were always hard to fully separate; think, for example, of James Fenimore Cooper's *The Last of the Mohicans* (1826), one of the biggest selling novels of the 1820s, which combines historical action with the spectacle of threatened virtue and assaulted family ties, sentimental themes which I will discuss in more detail later on. Gretchen Murphy argues that "the genre of heterosexual romance binding together and/or excluding disparate elements into a historically symbolic family" helps to organize "the racial and international conflicts" that historical romance so often displays (2011, 566). Helen Hunt Jackson's hugely successful *Ramona* (1884), the story of a doomed interracial romance against the backdrop of the competing national claims for California by whites, Native Americans, and Mexicans, is one of the more prominent novels that bear out Murphy's claim.

These examples, along with *Gone With the Wind*, show that by the postbellum era, sentimentalism and historical romance had thoroughly blurred together. Historical fiction, like science fiction, is always about the present in which it is written, and as such it will reflect its times in different ways—but the historical romance story has always been a popular vehicle for American novelists to convey their thoughts about the world around them.

Bestsellers can also result when novels reimagine the conflicts of previous stories in ways that make them more palatable. Consider the examples of two pairs of upward mobility narratives. Edith Wharton's *The Custom of the Country* sold well when it was published in 1913, but when Anita Loos remade the story of a canny and ruthless social climber into a comedy in *Gentlemen Prefer Blondes* (1925), the result far outsold Wharton (who may have been seeing her own reflection in Loos's book when she called it "the great American novel"). Theodore Dreiser's *An American Tragedy* (1925) was released the same year as Loos's comic satire, and the book received great acclaim and sold well. But the story of a young man who yearns for wealth and position and is willing to sacrifice other people to get it received a satiric makeover from Budd Schulberg in *What Makes Sammy Run?* (1941), which far outsold Dreiser's masterpiece. Schulberg's portrayal of a man who is only ever on the make is, for all its scabrousness, much funnier than Dreiser's powerful novel, and that may have made it easier for the reading public to digest.

A novel may become a bestseller (or it may return to bestseller status) when it's adapted into a successful movie. Lew Wallace's *Ben-Hur*, a religious story which sold sluggishly upon its publication in 1880 before it gained traction in the marketplace, burst onto bestseller lists again in 1925 and 1959, both times as a result of the popularity of movies made from the novel. Such resurgences are both understandable and even in some cases predictable, for a profitable film provides the best possible advertising for the novel that inspired it. But the success of *Ben-Hur* also reflects the consistent popularity of religiously themed novels in the most religious of the western democracies—as Claudia Stokes explains in her essay in this volume.

Controversy, we know, sells books. Mark Twain was a bestselling author before there were bestseller lists, beginning with his first book, the travel account *Innocents Abroad* (1869). *Tom Sawyer* (1876) was one of the bestselling novels of the 1870s. Well aware of his own value and substantial following, Twain sought ever higher royalties and finally decided, in an age of branding, to become his own brand. So he self-published *The Adventures of Huckleberry Finn* in 1885. The novel generated a high advance sale of forty thousand copies and continued to sell well after its publication, but its sales rocketed when it was banned in Concord, Massachusetts. Louisa May Alcott declared that "If Mr Clemens cannot think of something better to tell our pure-minded lads and lasses, he had best stop writing for them"—to which Mr Clemens reportedly cackled, "That will sell 25,000 copies for us sure" (qtd. in Hart 1963, 150). The example of *Huckleberry Finn* proved that banning a book in the United States nearly always rebounds against the censor.

Upton Sinclair's *The Jungle* (1906) generated large sales because it publicized the unsafe and unsanitary practices of the nation's meat manufacturers, practices that Sinclair rendered in gruesome detail. The book catalyzed the passage of the Pure Food and Drug Act of 1906, one of the few times that a novel has so concretely affected social policy. Even so, this result disappointed Sinclair, whose goals centered on the plight of factory workers and not the food industry as such. "I aimed at the public's heart," he famously lamented, "and by accident I hit it in the stomach." The author failed to rake the muck that he targeted—because the food industry proved much simpler to argue about than unregulated national labor markets and growing economic inequality.

Most novels can't be compartmentalized as neatly as *The Jungle* was in the public mind. Race, for example, is not so easily elided. As a result, even though it's an issue that has consistently stirred American public debate, race is conspicuously under-represented in American bestselling novels between 1870 and 1940. Many novels were of course written about "the Negro question" after the Civil War and through the opening decades of the twentieth century. But despite the earlier colossal success of Harriet Beecher Stowe's *Uncle Tom's Cabin* (1852), postbellum novels that spot-lighted racial inequality did not sell exceptionally well.

I want to underscore the distinction in this case between novels and other forms of literature. Writing about race sold and circulated widely in the United States in the decades following the Civil War, but novels about race did not gain the same purchase in the marketplace as other literature about the subject did. Ida B. Wells, for example, wrote pamphlets denouncing lynching that were read and debated ex-tensively, but Wells served up her propaganda harsh and raw, while bestselling novels arise from a longer preparation that gently braises their subjects for easy consump-tion. That cooking takes time.

To put it more literally, a novel about race could only become a bestseller once the racial divide was unambiguously worked over and marked out. Michael Korda (2001) says in *Making the List: A Cultural History of the American Bestseller 1900–1999* that the history of American bestsellers shows that the national reading public likes for its assumptions to be challenged, even attacked, but bestselling novels do not generally bear out this assertion. Instead, novels more readily become bestsellers when they follow social debate rather than starting it.

Without clear sides in the racial debate, it seems that a story could not deliver suf-ficient reassurance to deflect the anxiety generated by the volatile open-endedness of the issues themselves. Charles W. Chesnutt's *The Marrow of Tradition* (1901), for example, a novel based on a race riot in North Carolina, honors the ambiguous com-plexity of the issues that led to the white terrorism that erupted in Wilmington—and we read the novel today because of the author's refusal to accept simple answers to complicated social problems. But despite Chesnutt's high hopes that his novel would bridge the color line and achieve mass success, it sold "fewer than four thou-sand" copies in its first two years of release (Crisler et al. 2002, xix).

Thomas Dixon's *The Clansman* (1905), on the other hand, emphatically divided the two sides of the issue from a white point of view. The novel successfully captured and firmly resolved racial anxiety for a large white readership in the years following *Plessy v. Ferguson*, when segregation had beaten back its most serious legal challenge and was now enshrined as the law of the South (on *Plessy* and *The Clansman*, see Chapter 6 of this volume). *The Clansman* consequently became that rarity in American publishing: a bestselling novel about race relations. An origin myth of the Ku Klux Klan imagined by an unflinching white supremacist at a time when lynching was near its historical peak, *The Clansman* accepts the end of slavery without nostalgia, but denounces Reconstruction as a corrupt and criminal occupation that brings about "a sovereign Negro state" (bk. 3, ch. 8), filled with leering Negro politicians—rendered essentially as rapists in finery—installed by venal Washington politicians in positions of power over victimized Southern whites. Only the violent terrorism of the Klan restores whites to their proper place atop the social order as "an unconquerable race of men" (bk. 4, ch. 1). This victory, writes Dixon, is "racial destiny" (bk. 3, ch. 10).

D. W. Griffith translated the visceral racism of Dixon's novel to the screen in a 1915 film adaptation that gave the book a second bestselling run. Though purportedly a history of past events, Dixon's story spoke clearly to the concerns of his present—and his Manichean plot delivers a resolution comfortably telegraphed from early on.

Dixon's novel had its imitators, but it did not expand the bestselling possibilities for race-themed novels, just as *Uncle Tom's Cabin* had spawned no further bestsellers when it appeared a half-century earlier. Not until Richard Wright's *Native Son* (1940) did a novel about race gain the spotlight that *The Clansman* had—and as Clare Eby shows, Wright used "Dixonian logic" in his construction of the "fantasy of the black beast" (454, 451) . *Native Son* (discussed in more detail by Mikko Tukhanen in this volume) redirected the race debate toward ambiguity, which would seem to contradict my theory that bestsellers arise at the sites of clear ideological oppositions. But the success of *Native Son* highlights an important corollary to that rule: the role of book clubs and prize committees in the creation of bestsellers.

Native Son gained its prominence—and its high sales and wide readership—with the material aid of the Book of the Month Club, which made the novel a main selection. Wright and his publisher dearly wanted this designation and sought it avidly—so avidly, in fact, that Wright proved willing to make some significant cuts in the manuscript to make it less objectionable to white readers. A few years later, Wright would for the same reason make even more sweeping cuts to his 1945 memoir, and agree to change its title from *American Hunger* to *Black Boy*—and it became the first book by an African American author to reach number one on the bestseller list.

Prize sponsors have proved no less self-interested than book clubs. For example, the Pulitzer Prize committee, in only the fourth year of its existence, voted to give the fiction prize to Sinclair Lewis for *Main Street* (1920), a critical portrait of small-town America that clearly reflected the new primacy of cities in the United States. The novel was the first of many bestsellers for Lewis, and it established him as a gloves-off social critic of American middle-class life. However, the Columbia University trustees overruled the prize committee and directed the award to Edith Wharton for *The Age of Innocence* (1920), a much more genteel bestseller. In so doing, they showed that literary prizes, like the How-to-Read books, act as carrots that promote culturally approved reading habits, while efforts at censorship like the Comstock Law serve as the sticks. The marketing evolution of the bestseller implicates the class distinctions embedded in all of these practices, and enforces the standards that they enshrine.

Of course a book may also become a bestseller on the basis of an author's track record. Once Lewis established himself with *Main Street*, it was surely easier for his subsequent efforts, including *Babbitt* (1922), *Arrowsmith* (1925), and *Elmer Gantry* (1927), to achieve bestseller status. Jack London's books sold consistently well during the first decade and a half of the twentieth century because (as Jonathan Auerbach (1996) has persuasively demonstrated) London succeeded in branding, even trade-marking, himself as the author of a certain kind of story, and he created a relation-ship with his reading public based first of all on his identification with the Yukon. So a London book would typically sell a lot of copies because London's fan base would eagerly reach for the author's latest with a set of narrative expectations in mind. The more compelling question in this case, therefore, is: what made London's 1903 breakthrough book, *The Call of the Wild*, into the success that enabled this self-marketing campaign?

The real mystery behind a bestseller arises when its popularity cannot be readily explained by an author's popularity—as with London's *Call*. What made English-man George du Maurier's *Trilby* (1894), the story of how a character named Svengali makes a star out of young singer named Trilby, such a hit in the United States, for example? *Trilby*, which brought the word "svengali" into English, was one of the first books ever marketed as a bestseller, and was the top-selling book in America in 1895. The book clearly touched a collective nerve of some kind—but which one? The source of the electric connection of a book to many readers at once remains the great mystery of book publishing.

The Twin Pillars of Sentimentalism and Evolution

The alchemy of a bestseller is bound to be inscrutable, but we can certainly trace specific patterns among notable American bestselling novels. For one thing, gender conflicts evidently underwrite bestselling novels more readily than racial conflicts do. American bestselling novels have addressed gender issues in many ways over the years, but all of these grow from a sentimental stem. Most of the biggest-selling novels in the decades before 1870 were sentimental novels—stories about life "in-relation" (Dobson 1997, 267), which often follow the maturation of a young woman. In the bestselling *The Lamplighter* (1854), for example, Maria Cummins tells a tale of an orphan girl who is cured of her obstreperous wildness by the love of an old man and a blind young woman who separately teach her respect for others, and for God. Stereotypically female, white, and middle-class in their outlook and driven by a nondenominational Christian evangelism, sentimental stories celebrate the reliable and nourishing social ties that result when people extend sympathy to others around them, beginning with home and family.

Sentimentalism as a literary genre began to decline in popularity after the Civil War, but its central ideas did not weaken so much as disperse. The history of the U.S literary marketplace displays the continuing power of sentimental narrative conventions to shape the form of the American bestseller. In other words, the novel-buying public continued to read sentimentally even after they stopped reading specifically sentimental novels—and sentimentalist storytelling thus undergirds many important American bestsellers well into the twentieth century. Dixon, for example, alternates portraits of black men with "the gleam of the jungle" in their eyes (bk. 3, ch. 2) with sentimentally inspired renderings of white women possessing "a simple ideal that finds its all within a home" (bk. 3, ch. 9).

The other major idea that underwrote many American bestselling novels after the Civil War was evolution, an idea that immediately escaped the scientific arena, and which continues to provoke anxiety and debate in the United States. Charles Darwin published *The Origin of Species* in 1859, and that monumental and controversial book, which showcased the theory of evolution by natural selection, focused a continuing discussion about the origins of life on earth. The phrase "survival of the fittest" belongs not to Darwin, however, but to Herbert Spencer, a philosopher whose grand theories encompassed not just the natural world but also the evolution of social and cultural life. The scientific and social debates exchanged ideas and rhetoric with each other beginning in the late nineteenth century, so that Darwin's later work, such as *The Descent of Man* (1871), found him arguing in decidedly Spencerian teleological terms, while Spencer and other cultural theorists became known as "Social Darwinists." Both progressive and conservative thinkers employed the logic of evolution to promote the social policies—ranging from laissez-faire capitalism to socialism—that they favored.

Evolution quickly became both a compelling subject and a powerful metaphor in American literature, following the widely translated example of Émile Zola, whose "scientific" novels heralded the literary use of evolutionary logic for human behavior (2004 [1868], 4), and whose *Nana* (1880), a novel about a courtesan that pushed the decency standards of the time, sold "like hotcakes" in the United States (Kaestle 2009, 41). Naturalism, a label originally suggested by Zola, flourished in American literature around the turn of the century, with writers like Frank Norris and Theodore Dreiser showing the influence of Darwin and Spencer in novels that in turn influenced writers after them. (For more on the influence of Darwinian evolution on postbellum bestsellers, see Chapter 10 in this volume.)

The evolutionary metaphor expressed the anxieties of a rapidly changing society, particularly over the need for rapid adaptation to social and economic environments. For example, the first of Ellen Glasgow's many bestsellers, *The Deliverance* (1904), tells the story of the fallen South in terms of an "old order" that has been supplanted by a new one (bk. 3, ch. 2) (represented by an old overseer turned New Southern parvenu—a type borrowed by Margaret Mitchell thirty-two years later). The former Southern aristocracy (symbolized by the once-regal plantation matriarch, now blind, demented, and living in the past) subsists in genteel poverty, cared for by her children because she is unable to adapt to the changed environment. Glasgow's story of the postbellum South thus reflects the new evolutionary imperative: adapt or die out. This worldview is on display at least as far back as James Fenimore Cooper's portrayals of vanishing noble savages, but in this instance it's implicated with the pressing scientific issues of the day.

Edgar Rice Burroughs's *Tarzan* series (beginning with *Tarzan of the Apes*, first published in book form in 1914) reflects the anxiety that accompanies this imperative in the form of an action hero who utterly lacks any such adaptive anxiety. Tarzan masters every environment he enters, from the jungle to western civilization: he's equally adept at killing a lion, learning languages on his own without ever hearing them, and driving cars without ever having seen them before. *Tarzan of the Apes* was first serialized in pulp magazines in 1912, and many readers of those magazines, as Erin A. Smith has shown, were immigrant members of the working classes, a group that would have harbored considerable anxiety about adapting to the demands of their new country. Unlike his readers, Tarzan faces the hardships of adaptation without a qualm—he's an immigrant reader's dream man who fits perfectly wherever he wants to. No wonder the Tarzan series (which stretched to over twenty novels) sold so well, even though its associations with pulp fiction barred it from consideration for the bestseller lists.

Edward Bellamy's *Looking Backward: 2000–1887* (1888) exemplifies the persistence of sentimentalism and the turn toward evolution together. An updated Rip Van Winkle story in which the protagonist, Julian West, falls asleep at a time of domestic ferment and awakens more than a century later in a perfectly, peacefully organized socialist paradise in which everything and everyone fits in assigned places, *Looking Backward* was an enormous bestseller, not only selling over half a million copies in its first few years of release but also spawning "Bellamy clubs," and a magazine, *The Nationalist*, with a Nationalist movement to match. *Looking Backward* inspired numerous other utopian novels by such writers as H. G. Wells, William Dean Howells, and Jack London, while Mark Twain also tried time travel—in the other direction— in *A Connecticut Yankee in King Arthur's Court* (1889) as a way to change the context for social debate.

Looking Backward adopts evolution as the lingua franca for talking about social change—especially the labor strife (strikes, poverty, inequality) of the time. *Looking Backward* is a talky novel in which very little happens. The Rip Van Winkle conceit provides a forum for debating "the labor question" which, the protagonist's host informs him, "solved itself . . . as the result of a process of industrial evolution" (ch. 5). Crime is seen as "atavism" (ch. 19), while religion achieves "a new phase of spiritual development, an evolution of higher faculties" (ch. 26).

The involved explanation of humanity's "golden future" (ch. 5), resulting from its "moral and material evolution" (ch. 13), mainly takes place in a future home that possesses the same sentimental virtues that had such currency in Bellamy's present. As in the home, so in society writ large: "a complex mutual dependence becomes the universal rule" and everyone belongs together to "one human family" (ch. 12). Sentimental sympathy assimilates protagonist Julian West into the new society, especially that expressed by his love interest, Edith Leete, whose "sympathy was the vital breath which had set me up in this new life" (ch. 28). This talk of sympathy culminates in a formulaic sentimental ending centering on the revelation of blood ties: West discovers that Edith is a descendant of his fiancée from his life a century before. Like Stowe, Bellamy uses the sentimental family plot as a delivery vehicle for a specific social message.

The value of that sentimental vehicle was well known in the publishing industry. Historian Marc Aronson recounts how Edith Wharton complained to her Scribner's editor, William Crary Brownell, about the marketing of her early books, including a 1904 short story collection suggestively titled *The Descent of Man*. Brownell rebuked Wharton for avoiding sentiment, "the one emotion readers craved," and he chastised her for not "lifting a finger" to court her readers (qtd. in Aronson 1994, 8). The editor challenged the author to write a book that readers would not be able to ignore. Wharton's next book, *The House of Mirth* (1905), traces the decline and fall from social grace of her heroine, Lily Bart, in New York high society. The story advances an evolutionary explanation for Lily's failure to adapt to the demands of her surroundings: "Inherited tendencies had combined with early training to make her the highly specialized product she was: an organism as helpless out of its narrow range as the sea-anemone torn from the rock" (bk. 2, ch. 11). *The House of Mirth* was Wharton's first bestseller.

Edna Ferber likewise combined sentimentalism and evolutionary thinking in her first bestseller, *So Big* (1924). The first part of the book is a sentimental bildungsroman about a young woman exiled from the city to a hardscrabble farming existence when she is abruptly orphaned. Further chastened by circumstance when she is widowed with a young child, she learns to find beauty in her harsh surroundings, and in her son, Dirk. The second part of the novel, which spotlights Dirk's business career, resembles the business novels—such as Dreiser's *The Financier* (1912)—that proliferated in the age of naturalism. By playing the sympathy-driven sentimental worldview against the Social Darwinian economics of business, Ferber follows a similar recipe to Wharton's, with similar results: *So Big* made the bestseller list and won the Pulitzer Prize. Like Wharton, Ferber followed this first commercial success with many others, starting with *Showboat* (1926, soon adapted into a classic musical) and *Cimarron* (1929), a story of the Oklahoma land rush.

The examples of Wharton and Ferber suggest a new way of looking at gender that developed as the twentieth century progressed, a combination of sentimentalism and naturalism that reflected on the lives of both men and women. Jack London's stories of charismatic outdoor masculinity, beginning with the popular *The Sea-Wolf*

(1904), combined frontier adventure with sentimentalized romance. Such stories followed from the bestselling popularity of Rudyard Kipling's works in America during the previous decade, and typified a variety of such novels by now-forgotten authors like Rex Beach, whose publishers once claimed sales of over three million copies of his books (Hart 1963, 215). Gender, sentiment, and evolution clearly provided ingredients that could be combined into highly palatable bestselling fictions.

The Western

Nowhere was masculinity turned more painstakingly on the literary lathe than in the genre of the Western. John G. Cawelti, one of the pioneers in the serious study of the Western, suggests that Westerns originally offered a way of sorting out the clash of civilizations on the frontier—and this is very much the case with early frontier stories such as Cooper's Leatherstocking tales. Dime Westerns, central to the development of the genre, draw on European-Native American oppositions popularized by Cooper, with the homegrown American genre of the Indian captivity narrative also influencing these portrayals.

The Western reinvented itself at the turn of century, as the genre embraced the gender issues that became more urgent around that time. If earlier Westerns asked, "What is an American?" these later ones asked, "What is a man?" Owen Wister's enormously successful *The Virginian* (1902) stands as both archetype and avatar of this change, and Wister understood the place that his book came to occupy. In a 1928 preface to a reissue of the novel that he titled "A Best Seller," the author noted that *The Virginian* "suddenly created the popular taste which has demanded westerns ever since" (xxxii). Wister had earlier called his novel "an expression of American faith" (1911, xliii)—but faith in what, exactly?

The Virginian exalts the cowboy as a masculine ideal, "a gentleman without cultivation" who nonetheless possesses "true nobility" and "heroic stature" and reflects the individualistic ideal of "true democracy" (ch. 2, 3, 13). "Magnetically" charismatic (ch. 16), the Virginian is "a man who was a man" (ch. 34). The Virginian wins over the novel's male narrator so that he declares, "had I been a woman, it would have made me his to do with what he pleased" (ch. 21). The Virginian's love interest, Molly Stark, proves less immediately pliable, but she too comes to recognize the Virginian as "her worshipper still, but her master too" (ch. 35)—despite his practice of the frontier justice that she despises. Their marriage therefore symbolizes her acceptance of male violence, and "*The Virginian*," says Lee Clark Mitchell, "offered a muted resolution to the crisis over women's suffrage developing at the turn of the century" (1996, 114). Accordingly, dangerous Indians remain offstage, the business of capturing them left to the US military.

Zane Grey's *Riders of the Purple Sage* (1912) likewise has no truck with Indians. Inspired by Wister, Grey became perhaps the most successful of all Western writers, a perennial bestseller who also recognized early on the lucrative potential of the film industry to adapt his books. *Riders* was Grey's breakthrough book, the one that brought him to widespread attention, and that gave him the market capital to brand his name.

Bestsellers happen at the site of issues where the sides are defined, if not settled—and *Riders of the Purple Sage* draws its villains from "The Mormon conspiracy" and its victims from women who are stifled by either Mormons [a "terrible creed" (ch. 4)] or cattle-thieving outlaws. The controversial New Womanhood of the time is evoked by the destabilizing spectacle of a young girl, Bess, who's forced to pose as a man, and a wavering but resistant Mormon woman, Jane Withersteen, who lives under threat of losing her property by being forced to become a Stepford wife of a polygamist.

These distressed damsels are rescued and brought to conventional womanhood by two different manly heroes, each of whom owes something to Wister's earlier example. Lassiter, a gunslinger "without fear" (ch. 2), must "soften to a woman's grace and beauty and wiles" (ch. 6) and give in to his "child hunger" (ch. 11) in order to win Jane, while the younger Bern Venters, who is not yet battle-tested, "[drinks] a rider's sage-sweet cup of wildness to the dregs" and finds a remorseless strength in himself (ch. 17) that allows him to protect Bess. These two converge at the strong and compassionate example of Wister's hero.

Jane Tompkins argues that "The Western answers the domestic novel" almost point-by-point, with sentimentalism acting as the "real antagonist" of the Western genre (1992, 38–39). *The Virginian* and *Riders of the Purple Sage* both maintain this antagonism in suspension. Each novel ends with sentimental domesticity in nature, with Wister's couple making beds and washing dishes on a remote island, and with Grey's two couples each escaping the Mormons. Lassiter turns out to be Bess's "Uncle Jim" (ch. 21), and he and Jane rescue Jane's foster child and seal themselves in a canyon to create the ultimate domestic seclusion.

These eccentric resolutions typify the flexibility of literary sentimentalism between the Civil War and the Second World War. This unusual flexibility is also clear in two of the biggest bestsellers of the 1930s, Pearl S. Buck's *The Good Earth* (1931) and John Steinbeck's *The Grapes of Wrath* (1939). Buck's novel has been rightly held up as a commentary on China's twentieth-century feudal legacy, but it may also be read as a commentary by an American expatriate author on the economic Depression that had overtaken her native country. Buck's family-centered tale of the striving Wang Lung and his suffering wife O-lan analogizes Wang's desire for land and prosperity with the American dream (a phrase that was coined during the Depression), a dream that fell under siege in a country where the average family income dropped by 40 percent between 1929 and 1932.

Buck's Wang Lung seeks security in land. It brings him wealth, but not the certainty he seeks. Meanwhile, in the United States of Buck's birth, uncertainty extended to the earth itself. "Land is the only thing in the world that amounts to anything," says Gerald O'Hara to his daughter Scarlett in *Gone with the Wind*, a novel of the Depression as well as of the South. "'Tis the only thing in this world that lasts!" (ch. 2). In *The Grapes of Wrath*, the land literally disintegrates in the dust-bowl disaster that uproots the Joad family from Oklahoma and turns them into migrant workers. Michael Szalay (2000) has observed how the Joads's plight activates a new kind of male-centered New Deal sentimentalism run by male bureaucrats, not home-centered mothers, and such federal intervention carried its own threat to the ideal of the self-made American man. As Sonnet Retman shows in Chapter 30 of this volume, the Depression shook the foundations of male and female identity in the United States and rebuilt them with government assistance. The bestsellers of the time reflect the anxiety that accompanied these changes, expressed in some new sentimental forms.

Coda

In 1940, the philosopher Mortimer Adler published *How to Read a Book: A Classic Guide to Intelligent Reading*. It included a list of 137 writers and books, and became a foundation stone for the Great Books Foundation that Adler established a few years later with Robert Maynard Hutchins, a still-extant organization dedicated to the creation of reading communities that, according to the home page of their website, "value intellectual growth and civic discourse" (greatbooks.org). Adler presumably appreciated that the high-toned Ernest Hemingway made the bestseller list for the first time with *For Whom the Bell Tolls* during the same year that Adler's latter-day How-to-Read book came out. But nothing much had changed since the 1870s, when an earlier group of intellectuals tried to set the American reading public on the straight and narrow. The bestselling book of 1940, Ellery Queen's *The Adventures of Ellery Queen*, grew proudly from its roots in pulp magazines and dime novels. And onward it goes.

21

CRIME AND DETECTIVE FICTION
AFTER THE GREAT WAR

BY LEE HORSLEY

Carroll John Daly's "The False Burton Combs," published in the December 1922 issue of *Black Mask*, is arguably the first American hard-boiled crime story. Daly's nameless protagonist begins by locating himself in relation to the roles available to a man of action:

> I ain't a crook; just a gentleman adventurer and make my living working against the law breakers. Not that I work with the police—no, not me. I'm no knight errant either. . . .

The adventurer, the working man, the scourge of law-breakers, the criminal, the cop, and the knight errant all function at one time or another as protagonists in the detective and crime fiction written between the wars. In Daly's other *Black Mask* stories, the narrator often reflects on where exactly he belongs—on where he stands in relation to criminality and to the ethical and legal codes of his society. Daly's preoccupation with such questions was characteristic of early hard-boiled crime writing, and his influence was formative. His "Three Gun Terry" (1923) introduced the first wise-cracking hard-boiled private eye, a hero who, like his earlier "gentleman adventurer," uncovers crime from a position halfway between the crooks and the policemen. These liminal investigative figures, soon appearing by the dozen, became so popular that they are often taken to be a defining element in the hard-boiled tradition. Their centrality is indisputable. At the same time, interwar crime writing is a much more complex phenomenon, with private eyes, transgressors and victims, strangers and outcasts all playing a part. Hard-boiled crime fiction recurrently shades into noir, in which pulp writers create a gallery of unheroic characters, ranging from downtrodden victims to violent criminals. Many of these protagonists act without any semblance of an honorable ethical code, and others, particularly in the 1930s, lack the capacity to act at all—their struggles exemplifying the human cost of a brutal modernity.

Pulp Publishing and the Transformation of American Crime Writing

No publication was as crucial in encouraging and marketing the new kind of crime story as *Black Mask*, which belongs to the great era of pulp publishing—of magazines printed on cheap paper stock, bound between coated covers offering boldly painted, action-packed illustrations. As Jared Gardner explains in his chapter on "Serial Fiction" in this volume, pulp magazines had been gaining in popularity since the 1880s, but the market expanded greatly from the turn of the century. Fiction aimed at a popular market was also being published in hardback form. Several crime writers published directly in hardback (e.g., James M. Cain, W. R. Burnett, Armitage Trail), and some publishers made notable efforts to reach a wide audience: A. L. Burt, for example, had a reputation for reprinting affordable hardback editions of popular fiction, including mysteries and adventure stories; the Literary Guild of America published and promoted (as a book club) hardback fiction on a huge scale, generating sales of a million books a year at the time it was acquired by Doubleday in 1934; and Knopf had, by the late 1920s, begun to give increasing attention to the publication of popular detective fiction, with Blanche Knopf editing the Borzoi mysteries. Hammett's *Red Harvest* (1929) was the first hard-boiled novel to be reprinted by Knopf (from *Black Mask,* October 1927–January 1928), and in 1930–31 Knopf sold over ten thousand copies of *The Maltese Falcon* (1930). Hammett's hardback sales figures, however, were small in comparison to those he achieved by writing for *Black Mask*, which had climbed to a circulation of 103,000 in 1930.

Until the advent of mass-market paperbacks in the 1940s, the pulp magazines had no equal as purveyors of original popular fiction. In their heyday in the 1920s and 1930s the pulps were displayed in hundreds on newsstands and in drugstore racks, snapped up by "a faithful readership in the tens of millions each month" (Server 1993, 9). Originally just a description that referred to the wood pulp paper used, "pulp" came to stand for stories that were mass-produced, affordable, and aimed at an urban, working-class audience. In comparison to the more sophisticated "slicks" (magazines like *Cosmopolitan, Colliers, The Saturday Evening Post*), the pulp magazines opened the way for a freer approach to popular literary forms and to engagement with contemporary urban life. Pulp magazines offered romance, fantasy, and escapism, but also, especially in the pulps devoted to crime fiction, they registered the anxieties of the time. Being rapidly and cheaply produced, they allowed space for innovative ways of writing, most importantly for the hard-boiled style. At first looked down on as "publishing's poor, ill-bred stepchild," the pulps "had to make do with imagination and the power of the written word. This, as it happened, was their glory" (Server 2002, xiii–xiv). Many of the writers of the time never rose above the status of pulp hacks and are long forgotten. But the hard-boiled style, which soon crossed over into more mainstream fiction, became one of the most recognizable of the twentieth century. As the new kind of crime fiction established itself, several of the stories published in *Black Mask* made the transition from the pulps to the slicks (stories, e.g., by Erle Stanley Gardner, Frederick Nebel and Dashiell Hammett) and others from magazine to hardback novel publication. Knopf repackaged the fiction of Hammett and Chandler, as well as that of less well-known figures like Nebel and George Harmon Coxe. The "lowbrow" pulp origins of their crime writing, however, remained essential to their impact: "The appeal of this fiction for educated readers was, in part, that it came out of worlds that did not include people like them" (Smith 2000, 36).

Black Mask was founded in 1920 by H. L. Mencken and George Jean Nathan, who were also the editors, from 1914 to 1923, of *The Smart Set*, which was noted for introducing readers to a wide range of writers. They sold the magazine to its publishers, however, after only eight issues, and *Black Mask* is generally seen as coming into its own under the editorship, beginning in 1926, of Captain Joseph T. Shaw, who encouraged a high standard of colloquial, racy writing, favoring "economy of expression" and "authenticity in character and action" (qtd. in Pronzini 1995, 9). Even before Shaw took over, *Black Mask* had established a reputation for featuring tough, realistic action, with material ranging from tales of adventure and Westerns to early noir crime stories. As the circulation of *Black Mask* grew, other pulp crime magazines (for example, *Action Detective, Dime Detective, Detective Fiction Weekly, Black Aces*) entered the market. There were over fifty other detective magazines by the late 1930s, but *Black Mask* retained its supremacy. It expressed cultural energies and tensions in a way that exerted a huge influence on interwar culture. As Christopher Breu argues in *Hard-Boiled Masculinities*, the ideological impact of *Black Mask* is evident in gangster fiction and films, in the urban fiction of Damon Runyon and Ring Lardner, in the tough-guy journalism of Walter Noble Burns and in the literary modernism of writers like Hemingway and Faulkner. Half a dozen of the writers included in this survey of interwar crime fiction were regular contributors to *Black Mask:* Carroll John Daly and Dashiell Hammett, Raoul Whitfield, Paul Cain (George Sims), Horace McCoy, and Raymond Chandler. The form of writing inaugurated by *Black Mask* was captured in Chandler's famous description of Hammett's seminal influence in his 1950 essay, "The Simple Art of Murder": "Hammett wrote at first (and almost to the end) for people with a sharp, aggressive attitude to life. They were not afraid of the seamy side of things; they lived there. Violence did not dismay them; it was right down their street."

It was a period characterized by deep postwar disillusionment. There was growing evidence of illicit connections between crime, business, and politics in American cities; the folly of Prohibition and its attendant gangsterism were all too evident. In the 1930s, as unemployment and poverty worsened, crime fiction increasingly served as a vehicle for protest against an unjust economic and social system; criminal-centered narratives figured the failures of capitalism and developed a range of strategies for challenging, mimicking, and reproaching a society that had ceased to operate in a legitimate way. The world represented was one in which there seemed to be no escape from hostile economic forces, where, as Benjamin Appel writes in his short story "Red Mike, Mabel and Me" (1935): "It was all hard facts for them, for all the people in the West Side. It was sweat and blood and the poor-house. . . . They just didn't have the money, the chance in life to keep the facts from getting to them." During the creative boom years of the pulp magazines, such crises helped to generate what Chandler, in "The Simple Art of Murder," described as the "smell of fear" in crime stories that responded seriously to the modern condition: "Their characters lived in a world gone wrong. . . . The law was something to be manipulated for profit and power. The streets were dark with something more than night."

Chandler's essay puts forward the most articulate defense of the complex, often contradictory practice of hard-boiled crime writing. First published in *The Atlantic Monthly* in 1944, the essay emphasizes Hammett's creation of a language capable of expressing "the seamy side of things" and of protagonists tough and aggressive enough to cope with the city's criminal milieu. This radical revision of the traditional detective genre makes it possible to expose the truth about urban corruption, dishonesty and moral cowardice—about what is "not a fragrant world, but . . . the world you live in," as Chandler puts it. A key part of Chandler's generic foundation myth is his belief in an opposition between American and British forms of detective fiction. He exaggerates the opposing characteristics to make his case, but the broad lines of the contrast are evident. The hard-boiled protagonist, who, as Daly says in "Three Gun Terry" (1923), occupies "the center of a triangle, between the crook and the police and the victim," is never aloof from action and danger. There is much more attendant risk and moral uncertainty than there is in the orthodox detective story, with its puzzle-solving sleuths analyzing clues and providing rational solutions. In the work of "Golden Age" writers like Agatha Christie, Dorothy Sayers, or S. S. Van Dine, detectives are detached and insulated from the crime they investigate. In the characteristic *Black Mask* story, every case becomes part of an ongoing sequence of violent events. Suspense in the American genre is more important than mystery, and the hard-boiled private eye is keenly aware of the qualities demanded by the threats of a hostile environment: "He finds no way out. And so he is slugged, shot at, choked, doped, yet he survives because it is in his nature to survive" (Ruhm 1977, xiv).

The earlier model of detection manifestly influenced emergent hard-boiled fiction. In the first Hammett *Black Mask* story, for example, "Arson Plus" (1923), the narrative is introduced with: "This is a detective story you'll have a hard time solving before the end. Form your ideas of the outcome as you go along and then see how near you guessed it." Alongside the classic whodunit structure, however, there are many traits that are more indebted to American circumstances and literary traditions, most obviously to the dime novel adventures, the Western, and frontier stories that themselves continued to provide much of *Black Mask*'s fare. Nineteenth-century traditions of popular fantasy were transplanted to an urban environment, and stories about outlaws, frontiersmen, and vigilantes were recast to create a new version of determined, rugged masculinity—the man who struggles "to maintain autonomy in the face of an entrapping society and a wilderness to be conquered" (Smith 2000, 39). For *Black Mask* readers, this iconic male self-assertion was unquestionably an important element in its appeal: as Phil Cody, the second editor of the magazine, said in a January 1926 *Black Mask* editorial, "*Black Mask* gives its readers more real, honest-to-jasper, he-man stuff . . . than any other magazine." The hard-boiled tough guy comes closest to the earlier mythic figures when his survival instincts are allied to an individualistic core of values that ultimately distinguishes him from "a guy with a gun . . . on the wrong side of the fence" (Chandler, *The Big Sleep*, 1939, ch. 23).

Many of the *Black Mask* writers—for example, Frederick Nebel, Carroll John Daly, and George Harmon Coxe—based their appeal on this recycling of traditional "he-man stuff," creating a gallery of breezily macho action heroes. The character of the romanticized lone male is, however, modified in numerous ways both in pulp fiction and in the work of the other contemporary crime writers, many of whom lead readers into the despondent, doomed, transgressive world of noir. In the novels of Hammett, Paul Cain, Raoul Whitfield, James M. Cain, W. R. Burnett, and Armitage Trail, protagonists are deeply implicated in corruption: they acknowledge their own anarchic tendencies and capacity for violence; at best they are morally compromised investigators, at worst gangsters and criminals. In other novels of the time, heroic masculinity is undercut by a feminization of the protagonist. In *Hard-Boiled Sentimentality*, Leonard Cassuto argues that the infusion of hard-boiled attitudes with intensity of feeling led to the emergence of the sentimental action hero, particularly as the tradition developed in later decades (for example, in the work of Ross Macdonald). In the fiction of the interwar years, we recurrently see masculine toughness softened by feminized qualities. This is particularly evident in Chandler's creation of Marlowe—a tarnished, often ineffectual knight-errant who eschews the aggressive violence of earlier hard-boiled heroes and whose underlying sentimentalism arguably weakens his "potent male subjectivity" (Abbott 2002, 28). In many noninvestigative texts as well, the hard-boiled protagonist's masculine, self-interested individualism is replaced by a feminine ethos, leading to a loss of agency and an inability to venture into the world or to withstand its threats. Home, where virtue resides in the sentimental novel, becomes an ignominious refuge: in Horace McCoy's *I Should Have Stayed Home* (1938), for example, it signifies resignation, defeat, listlessness, and immobility.

Daly, Hammett, and the Early Years of *Black Mask*

The most popular detective hero of the 1920s was the epitome of manly self-sufficiency. Race Williams, created by Carroll John Daly, first appearing in "Knights of the Open Palm" (1923). He embodied a cultural fantasy of masculine prowess—violent, insubordinate, tough talking, and semiliterate. His all-conquering, two-fisted action carried him through over fifty *Black Mask* stories and eight novels between June 1923 and November 1934. The first hard-boiled series detective, Race can be regarded as "the true progenitor of the American private eye" (Geherin 1985, 10). He has little use for clues or chains of reasoning and few talents as a detective. Occupying a territory between legitimacy and illegitimacy, he fearlessly tackles brutal gangsters and master criminals, dispensing rough justice when the situation seems to demand it: "Call it murder if you like—a disregard for human life. I don't care. I'll run my business—you run yours" (Daly, "The Flame" (1931)).

In his work for *Detective Fiction Weekly* from August 1931–April 1936, Daly introduced an even more disreputable, morally ambiguous protagonist, wreaking vengeance in stories that often gesture towards his infernal namesake—e.g., "Satan Sees Red" (1932) and "Ready to Burn" (1935). Satan Hall is a man who actually wears a police badge but whose methods isolate him within the force and whose hatreds have become a twisted fixation. The series was published at the height of the public preoccupation with gang warfare and city corruption. In comparison to the Race Williams stories, the nature of the crimes portrayed has shifted towards contemporary relevance. Instead of concentrating on devious criminal masterminds and foreign villains, Daly focuses on the corruption of local politics. Society is shown to be at war because the forces of destabilization and threat are within. The predecessor of later avengers like Mike Hammer and Dirty Harry, Satan has to go into the dark doorways and dismal streets, keeping "close to the gutter" and dispensing his own form of justice: it might be murder in the eyes of the state law but not in the light of "The criminal's law. Satan's law" (1932, ch. 5).

Daly carried on writing crime fiction until the 1950s, never much altering his style and gradually fading from favor as pulp audiences declined. There is no doubting his immense impact on this phase of American crime writing. In a limited sense, he popularized some of the most recognizable ingredients of hard-boiled fiction: William F. Nolan, in *The Black Mask Boys*, said of Daly's earliest story, "This pioneer private eye tale is remarkable in that almost every cliché that was to plague the genre from the 1920s into the 1980s is evident in *Three Gun Terry*" (1985, 43). Daly did not, however, develop the means by which the mode affected a wider range of works, and his fiction had nothing like the lasting impact of the complex, innovative stories of his *Black Mask* contemporary, Dashiell Hammett. Hammett only wrote crime fiction for about a dozen years. His first contribution to *Black Mask* was "The Road Home" in December 1922; his last was "Death and Company" in November 1930. *Red Harvest* (1929), *The Dain Curse* (1929), *The Maltese Falcon* (1930), and *The Glass Key* (1931) were all published first as *Black Mask* stories between November 1927 and June 1930. After he left *Black Mask*, he published only a handful of stories in other magazines and his last novel, *The Thin Man*, which appeared in novel form in 1934. In his short career, however, he did more than anyone other than Chandler to transform American crime fiction, writing in clean, colloquial prose that was unsparing in its representation of contemporary American life.

Having served as a Pinkerton operative, Hammett was one of the few pulp writers to have had any firsthand experience of the criminal world about which he wrote. For eight years off and on, employment as a detective had been part of his daily experience. When he turned to writing fiction he was able, more effectively than any other writer of the time, to create a convincing representation of the workaday world of the most ordinary of detectives. In his October 1923 story for *Black Mask*, "Arson Plus," he introduced the Continental Op, "a fat, middle-aged, hard-boiled, pig-headed guy" who works for the Continental Detective Agency in San Francisco. The Op appeared in some three dozen of Hammett's stories and two novels over the next eight years. We never know his name, and readers at first didn't know Hammett's name either. The earliest of his *Black Mask* contributions (including "Arson Plus") were published under the byline of Peter Collinson. As Hammett explained, "Peter Collins" was slang for a "nobody," so that his byline meant "nobody's son." This explanation aligns his work with the long tradition of picaresque fiction, and it underscores the anonymity setting the Op apart from poseurs in the genteel tradition of detective stories, like Christie's Hercule Poirot or Van Dine's Philo Vance. The absence of individual identity goes with a morality detached from any traditional familial or social ties and with an absence of the stereotypical heroic traits that would make him "somebody" in the world of self-promoting masculinity. A commitment to the work itself is all that matters: as an agent ("Op" is short for "Operative"), his function is to adhere to the code of his job. As the Op says in "The Big Knockover" (1927), "Now I'm a detective because I happen to like the work. . . . And liking work makes you want to do it as well as you can. Otherwise there'd be no sense to it. . . . I don't know anything else, don't enjoy anything else, don't want to know or enjoy anything else." His work ethic constitutes its own form of integrity. Similarly, Sam Spade, at the end of *The Maltese Falcon*, articulates a simple code of professional responsibility, which is all that gives any semblance of meaning in a morally chaotic time: when Effie asks him if he sent Brigid O'Shaughnessy to jail, Spade replies, "Your Sam's a detective" (ch. 20).

Dedication to getting the job done is one of the only fixed points in the unstable world that Hammett creates. The Continental Op stories set the pattern. Tough when necessary, the Op never glorifies toughness: he admits that there is a certain attraction in brutality, but is self-doubting enough to be worried by this. As in all of Hammett's novels and stories, we see the protagonist's male sufficiency but also his weaknesses and self-distrust and the limitations of his agency. His complete commitment to the task at hand does not mean that he ends by accomplishing what he set out to do. He often has to cope with obstacles that undermine his strength and competence. In "The Gutting of Couffignal" (1925), for example, the protagonist's loss of masculine effectiveness is figured in his lameness—a defect for which he compensates by stealing a crutch from a cripple. It is possible to see the Op as occasionally manifesting chivalric qualities (for example, in his more compassionate moments in *The Dain Curse*) but on the whole he is deliberately created as the antithesis of a knightly hero. The moral ambiguity of the Op is apparent from the outset. In "The Gutting of Couffignal," when the guilty woman confesses, the Op, unable to pursue her, shoots her in the leg: "I had never shot a woman before. I felt queer about it. 'You ought to have known I'd do it!' My voice sounded harsh and savage and like a stranger's in my ears. *Didn't I steal a crutch from a cripple?*'"

Much hard-boiled fiction aims to expose the falsity of public discourse and to bring out the hidden connections between the criminal and the official. Hammett goes further, creating narratives in which lying and deceit erode all human relations and all of the fictions sustained by respectable society. His protagonists turn out to have their closest alliances with those who are most guilty and who have the most to conceal. Duplicity and betrayal are ubiquitous, and those who hold power maintain their position by creating intricate lies to conceal their exploitation of everyone associated with them. In *The Glass Key*, for example, Senator Henry betrays his daughter by using her attractions to secure the support of Paul Madvig, and, having killed his own son, shows himself willing to kill Madvig so that he would carry the blame for the earlier crime. Children cannot conceive of the treachery of their fathers.

The society Hammett represents is one governed by force and driven by greed, with widespread collusion between government and big business. The sources of conflict and betrayal are irremediable, and his protagonists most often find themselves powerless to achieve any restoration of order. In *Red Harvest*, the Op's position is hopelessly compromised, and we see both the underlying causes and the "cultural costs" (Breu 2005, 57) of an increasingly detached, amoral and instrumental ethic. The novel centers on a representative town, run as the personal property of a man so corrupt that crookedness and violence have spread like a toxin through the body politic. "Personville," which has been renamed "Poisonville," is emblematic of the ills of American society. The Op, himself infected, plays rival factions off against one another, establishing a structure that carried over into such cinematic versions as Akira Kurosawa's *Yojimbo* (1961), Sergio Leone's *A Fistful of Dollars* (1964), and Walter Hill's *Last Man Standing* (1996). Hammett's protagonist abandons himself to the violent atmosphere in full awareness of the corruption of his own character and motives: "It makes you sick, or you get to like it" ("Laudanum"). The end of the novel appears to bring resolution, but it is a brief point of equilibrium after which things will return to the same sort of conflicts that set the plot in motion. Personville is "all nice and clean and ready to go to the dogs again" ("Blackmail").

The Criminal Protagonists of the Depression Years

In *The Glass Key*, Hammett chose as his protagonist a man of dubious values and cloudy motives, a gambler and the henchman of a prominent racketeer and politician. Half-gangster himself, Ned Beaumont works for a man who in turn works for the murderer. It was a piece of fiction that *Black Mask*'s editor, Joseph T. Shaw, thought to be in need of defense. In his September 1930 "Letter to the Editor of *Writer's Digest*," he argued that the novel, the only *Black Mask* serial in which "the gangster was in any sense 'the hero,'" was justified as a representation of the alliance between corrupt politicians, public officials, and organized crime. It was a demonstration, he said, of "one of the most serious illnesses, to put it mildly, that our body politic has ever suffered from."

Many of the *Black Mask* writers of the late 1920s and early 1930s continued to create versions of heroic, hard-boiled self-sufficiency. But it was a time when the gangster (both real and imagined) had become one of the most easily recognizable emblems of the changes afflicting America. Newspaper headlines gripped the popular imagination with stories of organized crime and urban violence, bootlegging, gambling, and prostitution. During the course of the Thirties, in *Black Mask* and elsewhere, the use of criminal or semicriminal protagonists became increasingly common in narratives of both private and public crimes, with many writers publishing crime as opposed to detective fiction. It was a period in which hard-boiled fiction shifted markedly in the direction of noir, with its damaged, defeated protagonists and fatalistic downward spiral of events. Some narratives introduced investigative figures immersed in the corrupt milieus being investigated, such as the ex-cons and the hard-bitten strong-arm men to be found in the work of Raoul Whitfield and Paul Cain. Others abandoned an investigative structure altogether, taking as protagonists doomed gangsters, petty crooks, and outlaws on the run.

Raoul Whitfield wrote nearly one hundred stories for *Black Mask* between 1926 and 1933, including the Jo Gar stories he wrote as Ramon Dacolta. Starting in December 1929, he published "The Crime Breeders," a story sequence reissued in 1930 as a novel called *Green Ice*. Although Whitfield's ex-con narrator, Mal Ourney, has criminal connections, he is not a crook in comparison to those "inside" the criminal fraternity. A crusader of sorts, his methods are unscrupulous, even if his purpose is not. Whitfield shares what was, in the Depression years, a common conviction that the source of many social ills lies in the exploitation of the small and weak by the large and greedy. The object of Ourney's crusade is to bring down some of the big crooks who are "using a lot of other humans as they wanted, then framing them, smashing them. . . . I'd like to smash some of the ones who use the others up" (chs. 3, 6).

A couple of years after the publication of *Green Ice*, a new recruit to *Black Mask*, Paul Cain, established his reputation as "the hardest of the hard-boilers" (Nolan 1985, 199). Cain wrote seventeen stories for *Black Mask* between 1932 and 1936, creating criminal protagonists who are even more closely involved with the corruption they investigate. Cain had, as Captain Shaw said, "a grim sense of realism in its hardest texture" (Nolan 1985, 198). The omnipresent criminality of Cain's stories epitomizes the imbalance and social ills of Depression America. His writing is notable not just for its sheer toughness but for the unsettling, disorienting use it makes of morally equivocal perspectives. In "Black" (1932), for example, the narrator, very much like

Hammett's Op, controls the unraveling of guilt and stage-manages the punishment of a town's corrupt controlling interests. In Cain's story, however, the narrator is not employed as an investigator but as a hired gun who has been sent by his boss to take revenge. He exposes secret connections and offers to work for the rival factions, ironically proposing that he accept money from both and kill them both: " 'I'm auctioning off the best little town in the state . . . ' I was having a swell time."

The hallmarks of Cain's writing are black humor and a laconic manner, the stylistic equivalent of the blunt vision and methods of his protagonists. His distinctive voice was established from the outset, in the first five of his *Black Mask* stories, published as his only novel, *Fast One* (1933), one of the most savage and compelling of the unheroic gangster novels. The events of *Fast One* change direction so rapidly that the effects are dizzying and surreal. Betrayals, tersely presented violence, and random deaths seem like bizarre accidents glimpsed from the corner of the eye while speeding past. Gerry Kells has a background of war, drug addiction, and criminal convictions—though in a novel abounding with false narratives, we can never be sure that his story is entirely to be believed. What is clear is that his duplicity and toughness are not enough to ensure survival in a brutal world. The plot has elements of the rise-to-power gangster novel, but Kells is also a wrongly accused victim and an ill-fated investigator. As events overtake him, he becomes increasingly unhinged and vengeful. Kells is a sympathetic but also a very disturbing figure, and we see in his behavior the capacity of violence to destabilize: "a kind of soft insanity came into his eyes"; "the grin was a terrible thing on his bloody face" (ch. 2). Having "helped eliminate a lot of small fry," Kells meets his end in final pages that are among the grimmest of any noir narrative: "He wanted to be alone in the darkness. . . . Still he crawled on, dragged his torn body over the broken earth" (ch. 5).

Readers of the 1930s were fascinated with the perspective of the criminal, and the *Black Mask* stories of Whitfield and Paul Cain emerged in the same period that saw the publication, in hardback rather than pulp magazines, of the gangster sagas of W. R. Burnett and Armitage Trail. Many types of criminal, from the urban gangster to the poor farm boy turned bank robber, acquired, in the Depression, cross-class and cross-ethnic appeal. The myth of the rapid rise and sudden catastrophic fall of the ambitious gangster had great resonance at the time of the Crash and its immediate aftermath, and these transgressive figures acted both as symbols of rebellion and as parodic reflections of legitimate society. The criminal big shot could be seen to mimic and ironize the American dream of success; the deposed gangster or the small-time crook (really just an average man trying to avoid ruin) acted out the failures of laissez-faire capitalism, falling victim to an economically determined reality. As Burnett said, "if you have this type of society, it will produce such men" (qtd in McGilligan 1986, 46).

Burnett saw himself as the writer most responsible for the shift towards depicting crime from the point of view of the criminal himself. *Little Caesar*, a Literary Guild hardback published in 1929, was, he said, "the world seen through the eyes of the gangster. It's commonplace now, but it had never been done before then. . . . The criminal was just some son-of-a-bitch who'd killed somebody and then you go get 'em" (qtd. in McGilligan 1986, 46). Filmed in 1930 with Edward G. Robinson as Rico ("Little Caesar"), Burnett's book was the most influential of all gangster sagas. It was imitated in dozens of early Thirties films and novels, among them Trail's *Scarface* (1930). Like Burnett's novel, *Scarface* was based on the life of Al Capone and created a protagonist obsessed with scaling the heights of power. Both writers analyze the qualities that enable their heroes to rise. In comparison to Trail, however, Burnett gives closer attention to the flaws and insecurities that bring about the protagonist's downfall, a preoccupation that also distinguishes his novel from most gangster films of the time, in which heroes "of dynamic gesture," strutting and posturing, are "awe-inspiring, . . . grand, even in death" (Shadoian 1977, 59–60).

In *Little Caesar*—and in such later novels as *High Sierra* (1940) and *Nobody Lives Forever* (1943)—Burnett's gangsters are driven by a sense of social inferiority. In these later novels, the rise to power is viewed from the perspective of criminals entering a period of decline, worn down by years of struggle and filled with nostalgia for a past when they had the energy to hope for the success of the big-time. Criminal failure is a particularly strong theme in the hard-boiled writing of the time. Representations of the small-time criminal owe something to the *Black Mask* stories of the early 1920s, which created what Breu calls "sociological noir," centering on "yeggs" or no-account crooks who, unlike the protagonists of gangster sagas, did not belong to organized crime and completely lacked the glamour that characterizes "gutter Mac-Beths" like Rico and Scarface (2005, 39–41). By the mid-1930s, such downtrodden figures had become a much more familiar variant of the heroic gangster saga, most notably in the work of Benjamin Appel and Edward Anderson, whose stories of the failed underside of criminal enterprise captured the despair of the Depression years.

Benjamin Appel, many of whose stories were published in non-genre magazines such as *Esquire* and *Colliers*, was one of crime writing's hardest-hitting social critics. His *Hell's Kitchen* stories of the late 1930s all center on the weak and dispossessed. In a 1935 short story ironically titled "Movie of a Big Shot," Appel constructs a condensed version of the rise of gangsterism from 1916 to the mid-1930s. Underworld activities replicate the injustices and vicissitudes of American economic life, with its illusions of upward mobility, its preoccupation with image building, and its hierarchy of exploiters and exploited. The myth of the heroic gangster is presented as a dream of success beyond the grasp of most ordinary men. Instead, vulnerable, poverty-stricken young criminals are driven by hardship into a world of organized crime where they are remorselessly destroyed. Anderson's *Thieves Like Us* (1937), adapted for the cinema by Nicholas Ray in 1948 as *They Live By Night*, and by Robert Altman as *Thieves Like Us* in 1973, uses the figure of the outlaw to explore the social origins of crime and the economic disparities that produce it. The fate of the small-time crook acts as the measure of "respectable" society—of its criminality, its want of humanity, and its failure to recognize that this society itself is constituted by "thieves like us." The choice of bank robbers as protagonists is, in the context of the time, a way of generating sympathy, since hostility towards banks, which were often blamed for the Depression, was widespread in the 1930s. Anderson underscores the irony of the poor allowing themselves to be persuaded that small-time criminals are deserving of punishment in a system in which the masterminds never go to prison at all. These characters are destined to be fleeced not only by respectable society but by the bigger crooks as well, an emblem of the defeat of the small man.

Horace McCoy and James M. Cain: American Existentialists

The ordinary citizens whose lives are laid bare in the novels of James M. Cain and Horace McCoy are not part of criminal subcultures, but routinely stray into transgression and disaster. Both Cain and McCoy wrote genre novels that modify and transcend the conventional form, focusing Depression-era social criticism through individual tragedy. Dismissed as pulp novel hacks by many American critics of the time, both writers were treated by European critics as the equals of Hemingway and Faulkner and were cited as influences by French existentialists. They were seen as anticipating absurdist themes, representing isolation, alienation, loneliness, and dread. They chose insignificant protagonists under sentence of death, struggling to make sense of a random and unstable world, epitomized in Los Angeles, with its "population of strangers drifting about, surrendering to heedless impulse" (Schickel 1992, 30).

McCoy, who started writing stories for *Black Mask* in 1927, was a contributor contemporary with Hammett, Paul Cain, and Chandler. He depicted decent, gullible, ineffectual protagonists, ill equipped to cope with the world. There are interesting affinities with Burnett's later novels: although McCoy's narratives are in most respects very unlike Burnett's gangster sagas, they are echoed, for example, in an early 1940s novel like *High Sierra*, in which violent death constitutes a form of choice and freedom for a protagonist who finally "crashes out" of life when travel in the "hopeful" westward direction is no longer possible, and in which the condemned criminal is seen as far less brutal than those who organize so unjust a society. Like Hammett, Anderson, and the proletariat writers of the Thirties, McCoy probes the socioeconomic factors producing the world he describes. He starkly captures the deprivation of the time, embedding his wider themes in the life of Thirties America. The dance marathon of *They Shoot Horses, Don't They?* (1935), for example, is an absurdist parable, a picture of a deadening and dehumanizing contest so self-enclosed and denatured that contestants are disqualified for opening a door to the outside. Futile repetition is interrupted only by random violence, like the shooting that closes down the marathon, or Gloria's suicidal decision to get off the "merry-go-round." At the same time, the novel is a protest against the casual viciousness of American society, and against the pursuit by so many in the Thirties of illusory goals, only to end by having their fragile hopes (that they might, for example, be discovered in Holly-wood) worn away by weariness and defeat.

In the novels of James M. Cain, the protagonists more deliberately commit murder, not quite with professional skill, but successfully and with intent. In spite of their murderous scheming, his transgressors—bums, drifters, seedy salesmen—are sympathetically drawn. Cain, who did not write for *Black Mask* or the other crime pulps (publishing instead with Knopf), described his novels not as genre fiction but as tragic depictions of the "force of circumstance" driving characters to commit some "dreadful act" (Hoopes 1982, 551). Although he does not offer sustained social criti-cism, the Depression years are taken as given, a constant determinant in characters' actions and movements. *The Postman Always Rings Twice* (1934) opens with Frank Chambers, who is bumming along the California roads, thrown off of a hay truck he has sneaked a ride on; *Double Indemnity* (1936), as Cain says in his preface, "really be-longs to the Depression," as does *Mildred Pierce* (1941), in which the iron resolution of Mildred is embodied by her assertion that " 'I can't take things lying down, I don't care if we've got a Depression or not' " (ch. 1). Cain presents his characters as victims of a society traumatized by national economic disaster but nevertheless driven by myths of limitless opportunity, success, and unhampered self-determination. They follow the ignis fatuus of the American dream, and when they have (opportunisti-cally) attained their wishes they find that all they have really secured is defeat and entrapment. As Frank says to Cora towards the end of *The Postman*, "We thought we were on top of a mountain. That wasn't it. It's on top of us, and that's where it's been ever since that night" (ch. 15). *Double Indemnity*, too, ironically echoes the American dream of mobility. Walter sits on the steamer, sliding by the coast of Mexico, and, in the final twist of the plot, his feeling that he isn't "going anywhere" is confirmed by the realization that he is accompanied by Phyllis, an intimate of Death who knows with certainty that " 'There's nothing ahead of us' " (ch. 14). Among the most im-portant literary models for film noir, Cain's novels allow their protagonists little by way of redemption.

Chandler's Marlowe: "a quality of redemption"

The proliferation of transgressor-centered narratives in the 1930s was counterbal-anced by the emergence of the most honorable of all hard-boiled private eyes. Chan-dler concluded his essay "The Simple Art of Murder" by describing at length the "quality of redemption" secured by a detective capable of confronting the mean streets without himself being mean—a man "who is neither tarnished nor afraid. . . . He is the hero, he is everything. He must be a complete man and a common man and yet an unusual man. . . . He must be, to use a rather weathered phrase, a man of honor. . . ." Tinged with sentimentalism, this description applies most obvi-ously to Chandler's own Philip Marlowe. Alongside his defense of Hammett's crucial contribution to the creation of a distinctively American form of crime fiction, Chandler also observed, in a October 13, 1945 letter to Charles Morton, that "Old Joe Shaw" might have been right when he said that Hammett "never really cared for any of his characters." As Sean McCann argues, Chandler in contrast creates a hero who feels things intensely and who infuses the hard-boiled idiom with "longing and sensibility," turning hard-boiled fiction into "a powerful vision of the conflict between romantic idealism and an existing world of squalor" (2001, 52–53). Strongly influencing such later writers as Ross Macdonald, Robert B. Parker, and Walter Mosley, Chandler's Marlowe is the consummate example of the "knight-errant" that Daly banished from his prototypical hard-boiled story, spawning a new breed of "tough guys who get passionately involved in what they're doing" (Cassuto 2009, 99).

Chandler started writing for *Black Mask* in December 1933, the same month that Hammett's final novel, *The Thin Man*, appeared in condensed form in *Redbook* magazine. Although Chandler is rarely as direct in his engagement as Hammett, the early *Black Mask* stories, published between 1933 and 1939, contain significant elements of sociopolitical critique. "Finger Man" (1934), for example, does little to develop the character of the private eye, focusing instead on the machinations of "a big politico" who is willing to go to great lengths to fix things in his territory. Another short story, "Guns at Cyrano's" (1936), ultimately reveals the consequences of the unscrupulous behavior of "that thin cold guy," a corrupt state senator. And in "Trouble is My Business" (1939), the real villain of the piece is old man Jeeter, who ruined people during the Depression "all proper and legitimate, the way that kind of heel ruins people," driving them to suicide while never having "lost a nickel himself."

The crimes of power-hungry politicians, the clandestine alliances of government officials with gangsters and the criminality of "legitimate" business, often supported by brutally corrupt policemen, are preoccupations to be found in Chandler's novels as well, where such themes provide a public dimension to the narrative. Chandler has not always convinced readers of his serious commitment to exposing corruption in high places. Brian Docherty, for example, argues in *American Crime Fiction* that the bosses—the corrupt businessmen and political manipulators—are often perceived by Marlowe as presentable and decent, Chandler perhaps being more inclined to exculpate gangsters than to imply that all businessmen are gangsters themselves. It is certainly true that, in comparison to Hammett, the reader is not immersed in a sense of nightmarish urban corruption, and figures like Eddie Mars and Laird Brunette do remain civil and presentable. It might be said that the key word here, though, is "presentable." Part of the point about his smooth businessmen-gangsters is that they retain their façade of gentlemanly respectability, and having succeeded in this they do, in fact, go unpunished, because that is the nature of the society portrayed. Chandler's emphasis on the personal dimension of his narratives perhaps "tilts the plot away from the kinds of criminal reality that Chandler argued for in 'The Simple Art of Murder'" (Knight 2004, 119), but one should not underrate the disturbing elements in his narratives or the underlying darkness of his vision. Such elements clearly did not escape the notice of his early reviewers, who found much to object to in his representation of contemporary sleaze and corruption. In *The Big Sleep* (1939), for example, personal degeneracy (psychotic drug-taking, nymphomania, pornography, and homosexuality) is situated in a wider world of exploitation, blackmailing, racketeering, police corruption, and murder. The critical view, Chandler lamented in a 1939 letter to Knopf, was that he had written a novel characterized by sheer nastiness, "depravity and unpleasantness" (qtd. in Hiney 1998, 107–8).

There were other qualities as well, however, which would in due course begin to attract critical attention. Chandler created fictional worlds mediated by the voice of a protagonist who combines honorable conduct with penetrating judgment and self-mocking humor. Freed from the restrictions of writing pulp stories, Chandler used the more leisurely pace of the novel-length narrative to give more nuanced substance not just to his creation of the different strata of Los Angeles life but also to his narrator, establishing at the outset his characteristic tone of witty, ironic aloofness, his chivalric qualities, his moral makeup as a man of honor "good enough for any world" (Chandler's phrase in "The Simple Art of Murder"). From the first page of the first novel, Chandler's trademark style establishes the character of his detective. Marlowe introduces himself with self-deprecating wit: "I was neat, clean, shaved and sober, and I didn't care who knew it" (1939, ch. 1). As he surveys the Sternwood mansion, his reflections on a stained-glass knight who is "not getting anywhere" trying to rescue a lady create a sense both of his own honorable intentions and of the limitations of his agency. When Marlowe has at last completed his investigations, he feels that some of his answers must be kept from the dying General Sternwood, in a Conradian "saving lie" that is evidence of Marlowe's knightly qualities, but also of the extent to which he feels futile and compromised: "What did it matter where you lay once you were dead? . . . you were sleeping the big sleep[,] . . . not caring about the nastiness of how you died. . . . Me, I was part of the nastiness now. . . . But the old man didn't have to be" (ch. 32).

This act of gallantry is entirely in keeping with Marlowe's character and with the protective stylistic presence that he establishes. The tone of his narrative acts to evaluate and to distance the moral disorder of the society he investigates, if not ultimately to counteract it. When Hammett's Op is shot in *Red Harvest*, he issues a declaration of war on Poisonville and on "fat Noonan," the chief of police: "'Now it's my turn to run him ragged, and that's exactly what I'm going to do. Poisonville is ripe for harvest. It's a job I like, and I'm going to do it . . . . I've got a mean disposition. Attempted assassinations make me mad'" ("A Tip on Kid Cooper"). This mood of aggression, leading the Op to fight the corruption in Poisonville by means of violence and brutality, provides *Red Harvest* with the distinctively noir element of immersion in a world gone wrong. It is very unlike Marlowe's response to extreme provocation. In *Farewell, My Lovely* (1940), for example, when he tries to make Anne Riordan see the rottenness of Bay City, he says, "'Sure, it's a nice town. It's probably no more crooked than Los Angeles. But you can only buy a piece of a big city. You can buy a town this size all complete, with the original box and tissue paper. That's the difference. And that makes me want out'" (ch. 28). The effects of this quip are characteristically double. We see the realities of local corruption, and we understand Marlowe's weary cynicism about the deceptiveness of decent appearances and the ease with which powerful coalitions can buy and sell influence. Marlowe's humor and his ironic tone also, however, act to hold him apart from the brutal scene just experienced. He engages far less in physical violence than the prototypical hard-boiled private eye introduced by Daly. He takes more abuse than he doles out and proves himself to be tough and resilient. However, his superiority to his environment is not a matter of physical prowess but of a subtle intellect that can manage a self-deprecating joke even when he's been sapped and imprisoned and "shot full of dope and locked in a barred room" (ch. 27). Unlike the Op, Marlowe would never "go blood-simple." He exemplifies a sentimental virtue that was an important element in Chandler's writing from the outset: as the pre-Marlowe protagonist, Carmady, is told in "Guns at Cyrano's," "You think you're hard-boiled but you're just a big slob that argues himself into a jam for the first tramp he finds in trouble."

Chandler continued to publish crime novels until the mid-1950s. But by the time the fifth Marlowe novel, *The Little Sister,* was published in 1949, the landscape of American crime fiction and film had been transformed. The heyday of the pulps was over. The years immediately following the end of the Second World War marked the start of a crucial phase in the creation, definition, and popularizing of both literary and cinematic noir. From the early 1930s, when the talkies came into their own, there had been a clear feedback loop between the cinema and popular fiction— evident in the great gangster sagas of the 1930s and even more important in the increasingly numerous noir crime narratives of the 1940s. Films released in America just before the end of the war, such as Billy Wilder's *Double Indemnity* (1944) and Edward Dmytryk's *Murder, My Sweet* (1944), were taken as evidence, when they appeared in France, that "the Americans are making dark films too" (Chartier 1996 [1946], 25). At the same time, American publishing was being transformed by the introduction of the paperback. The content, authors, and even the cover artists of the pulp magazines crossed over into the new mass-market paperback format, which had emerged towards the end of the 1930s (following the success of Penguin in the United Kingdom, Simon & Schuster launched Pocket Books in 1939). By 1946 there were over 350 softcover titles in print (three times as many as in 1945), with Pocket Books, Avon, Popular Library, Dell, and Bantam all publishing in the paperback format and replacing the pulp magazines on the newsstands. Both the films noirs and paperback crime novels of the American mid-century were deeply indebted to the hard-boiled investigative novels and the transgressor-centered noir of the 1920s and 1930s. The interwar crime writers laid the foundations for the paperback originals that revolutionized American publishing in the late 1940s and 1950s— the work, for example, of David Goodis, Jim Thompson, John D. MacDonald,

Mickey Spillane, Charles Williams, and Gil Brewer. They provided, as well, the basis for some of the most memorable of early films noirs: along with *Double Indemnity* (1944) and *Murder, My Sweet* (1944) (based on Chandler's *Farewell, My Lovely*), the early to mid-1940s saw adaptations of Burnett's *High Sierra*, Cain's *The Postman Always Rings Twice*, Hammett's *The Maltese Falcon* and *The Glass Key*, and Chandler's *The Big Sleep* and *Lady in the Lake* (1944). And Bogart's performances as Sam Spade in *The Maltese Falcon*, and as Marlowe in *The Big Sleep* established him as the iconic private eye, uniting two writers who did more than any others to define an American tradition of crime writing, and whose work embodied the hugely varied possibilities it contained—together creating a form that, as Stephen Knight says, "exhibited at once the personal aspirations and the painful limitations of contemporary American manhood" (2004, 121).

22

COMICS AND THE NOVEL

BY MICHAEL MOON

When William Faulkner arrived in Hollywood in 1932 to take up his job at MGM, he informed his new boss that he believed he should be assigned to work on one of the only two kinds of "film" he liked, newsreels or Mickey Mouse cartoons, and that he already had an idea for one of the cartoons. Head writer Sam Marx patiently explained to the newcomer that Mickey Mouse was a project of the Disney studio and that what MGM had in mind for Faulkner as his first project was a film starring two-fisted Wallace Beery. Marx ushered Faulkner into a screening room and a projectionist started showing him Beery's latest film. After a short while, as Faulkner biographer Joseph Blotner recounts, Faulkner signaled to the projectionist to stop the film and left the studio, not to return until nine days later (1974, 772).

This anecdote about Faulkner's alleged interest in working on scripts for Mickey Mouse has been retold often, but to my knowledge no one has given it much further thought—perhaps because of a ruling assumption that the novelist could have only been joking about his interest in working on something as trivial and ephemeral as an animated cartoon. But as Marxist cultural historian Esther Leslie has reminded us, Disney's Mickey Mouse had, to begin with, been a heroic and exciting figure to some of Faulkner's most brilliant peers in the first wave of international modernism, such as Sergei Eisenstein and Walter Benjamin, for whom, Leslie writes, "Disney's cartoon world [was] a utopia" (2002, 86). In using the new technologies of film and sound recording to produce what these artists and intellectuals took to be the most aesthetically and technically advanced as well as the most popular work in the emergent field of animation, Disney seemed to them to be sending the whole realm of performance and visual representation in mass culture in genuinely new directions.

Leslie also reminds us that the Mickey Mouse of the late 1920s and early '30s was not the squeaky-clean idol of the nursery that he would later become. Initially, Mickey was a fairly raffish character who smoked, drank, and relished his own aggressive behavior. One aspect of early Mickey Mouse that might have been largely lost on his European admirers but that would have likely struck an American, and perhaps especially a Southerner such as Faulkner, as a central feature of the character's persona was its roots in minstrelsy. For many American filmgoers around 1930, part of the fun or thrill of Mickey's raucous "performances" must have lain in the variety of pleasures that this latest embodiment of the contradictions of minstrelsy had to offer, as it skipped rope over highly charged lines between behaviors human and animal, admissable and shameful, defiant and abject. The black face with its "banjo" eyes and outsized grin, the white-gloved hands and black body, by turns singing, dancing, whistling, gesticulating, laboring, and openly engaging in the milder forms of violence and taboo-breaking: all of these would have struck an American audience of circa 1930 as thoroughly familiar elements of minstrel theater, albeit ones given new energy by its translation into the novel animated cartoon form. As what Nicholas Sammond calls a "vestigial minstrel" (2012, 170), the early Mickey Mouse was an animated hieroglyph of the spectacle of racialized performance at a watershed moment both in the history of relations among races in the United States and among the institutions and technologies of mass entertainment. Embraced by the masses as well as by the mandarins, his rowdy, jazzy performances, joyful and insolent, made the early Mickey Mouse lovable, laughable, and, at the same time, slightly dangerous.

Faulkner had published his most pungently southern-gothic novel, *Sanctuary* (1931), only months before he first arrived at MGM. It tells the story of Temple Drake, a "fast" coed, and her captivity, rape, and placement in a Memphis brothel by a sexually impotent gangster known as Popeye. Popeye the Sailor first appeared and rapidly rose to comics stardom in E. C. Segar's strip *Thimble Theatre* in 1929, the year that Faulkner wrote much of *Sanctuary*, but whether or not the novelist had the Man of Spinach in mind when he named the ratty gangster in *Sanctuary* "Popeye," cartoon considerations (as we shall see) were apparently not absent from his mind. Hollywood, acting from its chronically divided heart, quickly bought up the rights to Faulkner's "scandalous" novel and then set about determining how it could both reap the financial benefits of the book's reputation as a grotesque, possibly pornographic shocker, and at the same time clean it up sufficiently so as to satisfy the rigid censorship requirements of the newly established Hays Office. Memos circulating among Paramount Studio executives during the time the film was being planned reveal that the casting of the character of Faulkner's Popeye was the focus of much anxiety—unsurprisingly, perhaps, since the novel made the character's sexual dysfunction a key element of his behavior, and also rendered his presumptive race in some ways ambiguous. One memo suggests that George Raft, one of the studio's emblems of young white-male virility, be cast as Popeye, but early drafts of the screenplay rename "Popeye" as "Mex," in an apparent attempt to resolve the sexual anxiety around the character by making him nonwhite. (The Popeye character in the film that Paramount eventually released is rather desperately called "Trigger.") When Faulkner was himself asked if he had any idea about who could play the tricky role, he is said to have responded—for reasons that I hope may by now seem overdetermined—"Mickey Mouse" (Binggeli 2009, 105).

In our time, after a century and more of "funny-animal" comic strips, comic books, animated cartoons, toys, dolls, and theme parks, Faulkner's association of Disney's Mouse with an impotent and sadistic thug may strike us as bizarre or absurd. But through the (by Faulkner's time) long-established practice of political cartooning, readers and viewers of the opening decades of the twentieth century had no trouble associating animals in drawings—often although not always comic ones—with various forms of human depravity. The kind of convergence of "high and low" that we see between Faulkner in his major phase as an exemplary modernist novelist and his involvement in screenwriting, and especially in his intermittent fascination with Disney's Mickey Mouse, is one that in our time has been most commonly associated with "postmodernism." But as the much-enriched history of the novel of the past couple of decades keeps reminding us, fictional narrative has frequently from its inception been a site on which new ways of conceiving of the social and the psychological—and new ways of exploring and refashioning aesthetic forms—have productively interacted with the popular, the "vulgar," the "low," the childish, the scandalous, and the obscene. And as the histories we are considering in this chapter make evident, the impact is strong in both directions between, say, an ostensibly lowbrow practice such as cartooning and the middle- to highbrow practices of writing and reading novels. Faulkner's formation as a literary artist and also as a connoisseur of drawing and cartooning provides a rich illustration of how these various modes of representation simultaneously reinforced and revised each other throughout the late nineteenth and early twentieth centuries. He had been a talented and productive amateur cartoonist as a young man—an assiduous imitator of the then-new elegant and "decadent" manner of Aubrey Beardsley. The keen eye that he had developed then for cutting-edge visual styles and rapidly changing visual technologies may have helped him see Mickey Mouse not merely as a figure of fun in the realm of popular amusement, but also as a culmination of sorts of a series of dynamic developments over the previous half-century in the increasingly overlapping fields of political and social cartooning, caricature, and satirical writing and drawing.

So the convergence between visual and verbal forms of narrative was hardly new to the Hollywood of circa 1930, although it was certainly in a highly combustible and creative state there at that time. But so it had been in the New York City of fifty or sixty years before, when cartoonist Thomas Nast had emerged as one of the most politically influential figures in the United States, reviving with renewed force the ancient art of animal fable and allegory by means of the art of the engraved and printed visual-image-with-caption. An icon-maker of a magnitude comparable with Disney, Nast established the visual conventions of some of the modern United States' key images: it was he who made Santa Claus fat, and gave Uncle Sam his distinctive goatee. Nast, from his bully pulpit in the pages of *Harper's Weekly*, was more than an illustrator of national holidays. By means of his political cartooning, he was considered to have played an instrumental role in bringing down Boss Tweed

and the corrupt syndicate that had been ruling New York City, and to have strongly
influenced the outcome of a series of US presidential elections.

Richard Brodhead has compellingly argued that the great increase in both the
quantity and quality of newspaper and magazine production around the turn of
the twentieth century had made it possible, and perhaps inevitable, for many of the
most influential new novelists of the time to emerge not from the book-centered
literary culture of Boston and New York, but from the more widely diverse (and
more heavily capitalized) new industry of periodical publishing. In illustration of
his thesis, Brodhead discusses the example of the emergence of Theodore Dreiser the
novelist from the world of magazines—tracing the in some ways seamless transition
from his editing the lavishly illustrated fashion magazine the *Delineator*, which offered sewing patterns to a vast readership, to his authorship of *Sister Carrie* (1900), a
novel impelled by (in Brodhead's words) "rapidly processed communication, minute
attention to contemporary appearances, and deep knowledge of the desires created
by commodities: the concerns, that is to say, of the magazine world of the 1890s"
(Brodhead, "Literature and Culture," 1988a, 477). In a somewhat different register at
a slightly later time, Faulkner's characteristic preoccupations in his fiction with grotesque and abject forms of relation between persons and communities seems in some
ways an outgrowth of his lifelong fascination with the dynamically shifting practices
of caricature and cartooning in the political and humor magazines of his childhood
and youth—including the so-called little magazines that had begun featuring the
graphic work of such aesthetes as Beardsley.

The publishers of the large-circulation magazines in the United States that had
begun to come into existence in the 1850s appear to have felt (judging from the
ways they tended to advertise their wares) that to begin with they had little to offer
their newly constituted mass readerships beyond serialization of the latest novels
from Charles Dickens and William Makepeace Thackeray. In their second decade,
however, their intensive coverage of the Civil War, and especially their use of new
printing and engraving technologies—as well as their employment of a network of
combat reporters and sketch-artists of the caliber of Winslow Homer—established
the illustrated periodical press in the United States as the primary medium of the
post–Civil War public sphere (on the relation of the periodical press to the Civil
War, see Chapter 1 in this volume). For several decades following the war, such
large-circulation pictorial magazines as *Harper's* (in both its racier *Weekly* and more
dignified *Monthly* forms), *Scribner's*, and others provided a heady combination of
political analysis, editorial cartooning, and humorous and satirical work. Henry
James, in his early critical monograph *Hawthorne* (1879), made a famous catalog of
the many social types and institutions allegedly "missing" from the American scene
of Hawthorne's time in comparison with the European one ("no country gentlemen, no palaces, no castles, nor manors, nor old country-houses, . . . no novels, no
museums, no pictures, no political society, no sporting class"). James then goes on
to opine (in a relatively rarely quoted sentence) that although the American reader

may protest that many other things remain to fill this putatively null category of "American life," exactly what these things are must remain "his [i.e., the American's] secret, his joke," "his national gift, that 'American humour' of which of late years we have heard so much" (ch. 2).

One may suspect that for James, the reason the characteristic American types and institutions, both in the decades before the Civil War (in Hawthorne's day) and after (in the present in which James is writing), must remain in some sense "secret" and a "joke," albeit a widely shared one ("his national gift . . . 'American humour'"), is that social classes and political institutions in the United States continued to exist in (to James's mind) an intolerably high state of tension relative to each other—one that rendered impossible the development of anything approaching the kind of "settled" or "established" society and culture on the European model for which the James of 1879 appears to long. In its place, the United States after the failure of so-called Reconstruction provides only a landscape of gaps and a culture of gaffes, of complacent joking and satirical jabbing. Fifty years later, Faulkner could perhaps have imagined the hilarious and truculent "joke" of Mickey Mouse helping himself and his contemporaries in the United States—just on or just over the verge of the Great Depression—draw near to but also draw back from the abysses that still (possibly more than ever) seemed to set at intractable odds black and white "races," workers and bosses, rebels and respectables. In the intervening half-century, it had become even more richly evident than it had been to James that it was to be the enduring role of "American humor"—political, editorial, "gag," and narrative cartooning, a proliferation of verbal and visual forms of social satire and comedy across print (and eventually film and radio) media—both to expose and to cover over the shifting but volatile range of gaps in "American life."

Ten years later, in 1889, James published "Our Artists in Europe" in *Harper's Monthly*—one of the first full-dress critical essays on the burgeoning printed pictorial journalism of the time. "The illustration of books, and even more of magazines, may be said to have been born in our times, so far as variety and abundance are the signs of it; or born, at any rate, the comprehensive, ingenious, sympathetic spirit in which we conceive and practice it." Several of the half-dozen visual artists whose careers James discusses in the essay worked at a consistently high level across the fields of newspaper and magazine cartooning and magazine illustration, as well as portrait and landscape painting. No longer the emblematically sad and isolated young American artist that James had earlier depicted Hawthorne as being, several of these men are expatriate Americans who live in London or Paris but sell much of their lucrative work to US newspaper, magazine, and book publishers. Far from arousing his pity, these American artists strike James with, he admits, both awe and envy, for the power and ease with which they appear to him to imagine, produce, exhibit, and sell their work. But even as he envies them, James implies that something about their shared success and virtuosity troubles him, or at least makes him wonder about their possible cost to the artist and his vision. Wouldn't these artists, he asks, "quite as soon" draw or paint "one thing as another?" And does not this "absence of private predilections" perhaps preclude these artists' having precisely the kind of strong inclination toward some subjects and away from others that are the very basis of the most stylish and expressive art? What he had seen as the very narrowness and localness of Hawthorne's world had earlier made James appear to marvel at the fact that Hawthorne had been able to produce beautiful art at all; only a decade later, he worries that cosmopolitan circumstances and highly developed and rewarded forms of artistic facility and virtuosity across media may actually deprive an artist's work of genuine feeling and style.

The terms in which James attempts to specify what the particular nature of the threat to this kind of artist are telling ones, as when he wonders if the artist in Charles Reinhart's (or, implicitly, at least to some degree, his own) situation, does not find himself, "amid the mixture of associations and the confusion of races, liable to fall into vagueness as to what types are?" Apparently, a sense of strong clarity about "what types are" is indispensable to what James sees as genuinely artistic work, and what is needed to guarantee and underwrite such clarity are habits of unmixed associations and well-differentiated, one might even say segregated, "races." The reader of the "pictorials," *Harper's Weekly, Harper's Monthly*, and of the new (and extremely popular) "humor" magazines that came into existence in the mid-1870s and after, such as *Puck* and *Judge*, was quite unlikely to "fall into vagueness" about "what types are," for the mass-production and mass-circulation of a vast verbal and visual image-repertoire of national, racial, ethnic, and gendered "types" were among the primary activities and effects of the new illustrated-periodical press. The flighty young woman of fashion, the suffragette, the street urchin, the fraternity man, the supercilious aesthete, the mincing pansy, the "counter-jumper" (i.e., retail sales clerk), the American tourist abroad, the flinty New England farmer, the backwoods-man (later the hillbilly), the fat girl, the large immigrant family, the mistress of the house and her "colored" or Irish maid, the "Negro" laborer (or layabout), the happy hobo, the sullen American Indian, the wily "Chinaman"—these and dozens of other "types of the day" constituted an entire verbal-and-visual language that was for de-cades vigorously cultivated and spoken, with varying inflections and meanings, by legions of readers, writers, and cartoonists.

This tradition of popular illustration would soon have a much more respectable companion in the academic science of sociology, which took the observation and analysis of social types both in themselves and in their dynamic relations to each other as one of its main concerns. Like their scientific counterparts, popular il-lustrators furnished a flourishing language of types (and for a substantially larger audience) through caricature, sketch-portraiture, and brief sequential narratives— the evolving forms of the "comics" or "funnies." Some of the most illuminating cultural-studies scholarship has taken as its focus the apparent paradox between (on the one hand) the commitment of many of the leading novelists of the time (e.g., William Dean Howells, Mark Twain, Henry James, Edith Wharton, Charles

Chesnutt) to the projects of literary realism and (on the other) the ubiquity in their culture (and in the very magazines which several of them edited and to which all of them frequently contributed) of caricature and cartoon. A work such as Henry B. Wonham's *Playing the Races: Ethnic Caricature and American Literary Realism* makes evident that the hard-fought battle for literary realism was not and could not have been fought in a realm "disinfected" of stereotype, caricature, and cartoon, ethnic and otherwise; rather, the novelists whose work he analyzes were in various ways all (whether they liked it, or we like it, or not) native and highly fluent speakers of the verbal-visual vernacular that dominated public discourse in the late nineteenth and early twentieth centuries. "Stereotypes" were taken up by both visual and verbal artists at the time and deployed and redeployed with a wide range of intentions, meanings, and affective associations.

An Austrian immigrant named Joseph Keppler became the co-founder and presiding graphic genius of *Puck* magazine, and soon succeeded Thomas Nast as the most widely acclaimed political cartoonist of the time (proving his mettle on a graphic satirist's dream, the corruption of the Grant administration). At its peak (from the late 1870s to the mid-1890s), the magazine was edited by Henry Cuyler Bunner, arguably the most innovative literary and political editor in the late nineteenth-century United States. On the visual side, Keppler contributed to the rich image-pool that continued to form during those years not only his own work but also the training of some of the most accomplished members of the succeeding generation of graphic artists. Of these, another Austrian immigrant, Frederick Burr Opper, proved one of the most versatile as well as one of the most enduring (see Figure 22.1). Opper not only was a top contributor of sketches and cartoons to *Puck*; he also became a leading illustrator of books of several of the bestselling humorists, as well as, eventually, the creator of one of the first hugely popular newspaper comic strips, *Happy Hooligan* (1900). He has come to be considered by historians of US popular arts to have been one of the key transitional figures between the highly elaborate graphic style of political cartooning of the color-lithograph era and the relatively simple and improvisatory-looking manner that dominated the newspaper comic-strip page.

As this new vernacular sociology represented it, American cities were, for decades after the Civil War, a babel of dialects. So, for that matter, were the backwoods of the South and the farming counties of New England and upstate New York. Marietta Holley, in her long series of "Samantha" novels (1873–1914), presented a country wife "argifying" with her husband and others about the changing rights and responsibilities of women—all in elaborately accented regional speech. Holley's writing, along with fellow humorists Joel Chandler Harris's *Uncle Remus, His Songs and His Sayings* (1880), Twain's *The Adventures of Huckleberry Finn* (1885), George Ade's "Stories of the Streets and of the Town" in the Chicago *Record* (1893–1900), Finley Peter Dunne's "Mr. Dooley" columns (eventually gathered into eight books, 1898–1919), Charles Chesnutt's *The Conjure Woman* (1899), and

Fig 22.1 Frederick Burr Opper excelled as a political cartoonist, book illustrator, and creator of some of the first and longest-running newspaper comic strips (e.g., Happy Hooligan, 1900–1932). Image courtesy of the G.T. Maxwell Collection, the Ohio State University Billy Ireland Cartoon Library and Museum.

Alexander Posey's "Fus Fixico" letters (on Mvskoke Creek tribal affairs in the forming state of Oklahoma, 1903–8), produced a remarkable array of voices and "accents." The illustration of many of these works involved some of the most accomplished and versatile graphic artists of the time. Opper of *Puck* produced the illustrations for Holley's *Samantha at Saratoga* (1887) and Dunne's *Mr. Dooley's Philosophy* (1900). Influential editorial artist John T. McCutcheon, who came to be known early in the twentieth century as "the Dean of American Cartoonists" (having inherited the title from Opper), regularly contributed the images to Ade's story-column about the denizens of "small-town Chicago." Twain not only praised Ade's writings but went on to declare of McCutcheon's work that "for once" the illustrator was perfectly matched with the author. In the previous decade, Twain had enthusiastically contracted E. W. Kemble, who was already well known for his minstrel-style caricatures of blacks, to illustrate *Huckleberry Finn*, but Joel

Chandler Harris later complained about having had Kemble imposed on him by his publishers as illustrator of his *On the Plantation* (1892). For *Uncle Remus and His Friends*, published the same year, Harris succeeded in obtaining the services of illustrator A. B. Frost, whom he lauded for freeing his characters from what he saw as the tired conventions of stage-derived "coon"-style caricature, which Harris of Atlanta associated with "northern" styles.

Perhaps the most highly fraught relations between verbal and graphic text in this period has been uncovered by Henry B. Wonham in his work on Chesnutt's earliest writing and its relation to ethnic caricature. Many critics have treated Chesnutt's career as having begun in earnest only with the publication of his story "The Goophered Grapevine" in the *Atlantic Monthly* in 1887, but Wonham, as only a few critics had done before him, went back and reexamined the early sketches that Chesnutt was publishing around the same time in such popular illustrated magazines as *Puck*. There he discovered that some of these writings had shared page-space with caricatures of African Americans, some of which reproduced the most egregious features of the Kemble-style "Coon" character. How potentially explosive such images remain was brought home to me when, in consulting my university library's on-line database of late nineteenth-century US periodicals, which includes a full run of *Puck*, I discovered that in the process of transferring the magazine into digital format, someone had "eliminated" some of the very images that Wonham discusses. The important point that Wonham makes in discussing the appearance of work such as Chesnutt's amidst such images is that the depictions of African Americans in the pages of the turn-of-the-century humor magazines actually varied considerably in style as well as in political and affective charge, and, for the most part, cannot be simply and belatedly sorted out into two piles, "sensitive" and "offensive." As Wonham writes of *Puck*, "the sheer abundance of exaggerated ethnic signifiers within its pages produced an almost chaotic impression of racial mobility, an impression oddly compatible with Chesnutt's conception of human identity" (2004, 153).

Toward the end of the seven-year period in the 1890s when the young George Ade was producing his "Stories of the Street and of the Town" about various types of new arrivals to Chicago, he began publishing the tales as books about the characters who had turned out to be the main foci of the tales: "Artie Blanchard," a boy who had risen from humble origins on the South Side to become a young model businessman; "Pink Marsh," an outgoing black shoeshine boy who eventually marries a widow and becomes a Pullman porter; and "Doc Horn," a broken-down gentleman who entertains a motley assortment of mostly younger men with grandiose tales of his personal past. Since for the most part Ade did little revising of the daily pieces he had written for a deadline as he compiled them for book publication, he may have been surprised when the "novels" he produced in this manner were praised as important new realist literary work by the likes of Twain and William Dean Howells. Howells invited Ade to contribute his next novel to a new series that was designed to showcase the fiction of the twenty most distinguished English and American novelists of the time. Flattered as he must have been, Ade never composed the realist novel, what he called the "long . . . photographic" account of midwestern life, that Howells had attempted to elicit from him; instead, Ade turned to writing the long series of brief, racy, burlesque "Fables in Slang" that made him rich and famous. He kept meaning to go back and write a great American realist novel, he would comment years later, but every time he reminded the owner of the newspaper syndicate that distributed his column of his solemn intention, the man would remind him that the latest volume of "Fables in Slang" had sold four million copies, and Ade would go back to his office and write some more of them. In 1963, James T. Farrell would publish a laudatory preface to a University of Chicago Press edition of Ade's early *Artie* and *Pink Marsh* "novels," but what is striking when one looks back from Farrell's *Studs Lonigan* trilogy (1930–35), which depicts the life and early passing of a young man growing up in Chicago's Irish ghetto, to earlier writing such as Ade's is how much stronger the affinity of *Studs Lonigan* is with the feisty, wiseguy, at times overtly comic-strip attitudes of "Fables in Slang" than it is with the somewhat fast-fading "realism" of Ade's earlier work that Howells had rated so highly. Howells politely deprecated Ade's jazzy "Fables" in print, but H. L. Mencken recognized that if one were not put off by their novel and brash surface, there was about them "an artfulness infinitely well wrought" (Brenner 1966, 200–206). Meanwhile, to reread *Studs Lonigan* after several decades of irenic "multiculturalism" is to be reminded of the considerable (and by multiculturalists generally disavowed) degree to which ethnic group-identity has tended to be grounded in interracial conflict and rivalry, but also of what a divisive and contestatory thing ethnic identity can be among the members of a single ethnic group: being "Irish-American" means a violently different range of things to Studs, various of his pals, his mother, and his Jewish sister-in-law. Ade's work a generation earlier had similarly pulled few punches about how it was the differences not only between but within ethnic groups that kept people in his society moving from the country to the city (and sometimes back again) and from one part of the city to another.

The violence of difference as it made itself apparent between and within ethnic groups provided much of the matter of the newspaper comic strips that began appearing in Joseph Pulitzer's New York *World* and William Randolph Hearst's New York *Journal* in 1895. The two newspaper magnates were locked in a circulation war at a time when new technologies were just beginning to make it possible to produce splendid four-color images on newsprint, so each of their respective papers soon boasted of a new Sunday color-comic supplement. In one of the first of these comics, *Hogan's Alley*, Richard Outcault purveyed a jaundiced child's-eye view of the teeming life of the slums through the figure of the bald and be-nightgowned little "Yellow Kid." Reading this foundational comic today, one can imagine Stephen Crane's Maggie's toddling little brother Tommie, who dies early in her story (*Maggie: A Girl of the Streets* [1893]), gaining a new lease on life in his reincarnation as Outcault's "Mickey Dugan," beginning in 1895.

The first generation of newspaper comic-strip creators—which included, besides Outcault and Opper, other remarkable artists such as Lyonel Feininger and Winsor McCay—immediately took the visual level of the new medium to its first great heights, but with regard to narrative, the comic strip long tended to organize itself along the short and predictable lines of the gag, the joke, and its punch-line. A new kind of strip began to develop along quite different, much more sustained narrative lines in the years just after the First World War. In the so-called continuity strip a second generation of newspaper cartoonists began to develop a mode of verbal and visual storytelling that, while being relayed in microunits of only three or four panels per day, was shaped to accumulate into much longer story arcs, usually of around four to six weeks' duration. Many of the most popular of these strips ran for decades. Fans like Chicago "outsider artist" Henry Darger began clipping their favorite strips every day and pasting them into scrapbooks—in the process becoming the first readers to realize the potential of the continuity strips to develop over long stretches of time into a new kind of popular saga-novel or epic of everyday life.

The first and in many ways the most widely influential of the continuity strips was Sidney Smith's *The Gumps* (1917). The Gumps were a lower-middle class family, depicted as ordinary to the point of caricature: a married couple named Andy and Min (Minerva) with a young son, Chester, and an annoying maid. The family's single departure from the norm was their Uncle Bim, who was exceptional only insofar as he was very rich; otherwise he was a Gump through and through. The Gumps are all homely (as drawn, Andy Gump has no chin, no lower face at all below his moustache), but, as Stephen Becker pointed out in his early study, *Comic Art in America*, every member of the Gump household, from rich Uncle Bim to Tilda the maid, exhibits the kind of scrappy and independent drive that was considered the bedrock of national character in the United States in the years between the World Wars. Andy was a scheming blowhard, cowed by no one except his sharp-eyed wife, but endlessly vulnerable to the get-rich-quick schemes of others. Would Uncle Bim be hornswoggled into marrying the "conniving" Widow Zander, thereby diverting the natural route of inheritance of his vast fortune away from his Gump relations? Millions of newspaper readers wanted to know.

The Gumps was so successful that it made its effects felt not only on the comics page but in other media. As the newspaper cartoon strip was finding its serial-narrative legs in the early-to-mid 1920s, the infant broadcast industry was still desperately casting about to come up with feasible programming formats beyond the uplifting talks and symphonic concerts that had so far failed to galvanize mass audiences. The promotions manager of the Chicago *Tribune* and the station manager of its fledgling radio station, WGN, decided that what radio needed was *The Gumps*, and they approached comedy duo Charles Correll and Freeman Gosden about possibly headlining a *Gumps* radio serial. Freeman and Gosden decided not to take on *The Gumps*, fearing that the strip would not allow sufficient play of the kind of male-male cross-talk humor on which they had built their success, and counterproposed a program designed to feature their strengths, to be called *Amos 'n' Andy*. As *The Gumps* had done in its newspaper context, *Amos 'n' Andy* soon became the first runaway success among radio programs, and the narrative radio serial in both its comic and melo-dramatic genres (including the first soap operas) began to proliferate immediately. To fill out their scripts, Elizabeth McLeod explains, Correll and Gosden sedulously imitated the convoluted web of often overlapping romantic and financial schemes that had first been perfected in *The Gumps* (2005, 25).

Sidney Smith drew *The Gumps* and, by common consent, did a fine job of it, but he had not created the pathbreaking strip and did not exercise full editorial control over it. It was actually the creation of Joseph Medill Patterson, co-owner and editor of the Chicago *Tribune* and founder of the New York *Daily News*, the first daily tabloid in the United States. In his socialist youth, Patterson had written and pub-lished several novels about American social problems, and he brought a novelist's sense of plot, character, and genre to bear on the continuity strips he midwifed in his newspapers (which soon came to include *Dick Tracy* [1931–77] and *Little Orphan Annie* [1924–2010] as well as *The Gumps*). Young cartoonist Frank King's *Gasoline Alley* (1918 to present) had puttered along on the comics page of the *Tribune* with moderate success for several years as a strip about a fat and appealing young man named Walt Wallet who spent most of his leisure hours making "car talk" with his male neighbors. Patterson decided at that point that King's comic needed develop-ment and told him to add a baby to the strip. Soon afterwards, an infant boy was abandoned on Walt's doorstep, and Walt brought him inside and named him "Skee-zix" (cowboy slang for "motherless calf"). Walt eventually married and took his little family on epic cross-country road trips, and little Skeezix was kidnapped not once but twice. Walt and Skeezix and their by now numerous descendants have contin-ued to age in real time in the strip down to the present moment of writing. Unlike the Gumps, comics historian Robert C. Harvey explains, Walt and Skeezix and their family and neighbors are not caricatures, or they are caricatures of a friendlier, small-town midwestern kind (1994, 92–115).

By the end of the 1920s, the dialect-saturated style of comics that had predomi-nated to that point began to show signs of reaching a radical limit. During the same week as the Wall Street Crash in late October 1929, Lynd Ward published *Gods' Man: A Novel in Woodcuts*, the first of six entirely wordless picture-novels that he would produce in the ensuing decade, dealing with such highly charged topics as the heritage of slave-owning and the ethics of bringing children into a world that appeared to be succumbing to fascism. *Gods' Man*, in 142 black-and-white images of relentless expressionist intensity, tells a Faustian story of a young artist corrupted by the city and mammon who, through suffering and the love of a good woman, is subsequently restored to a kind of innocence only to have that cut short by his early death—part of the unholy deal, it turns out, that he had struck with the forces of darkness in exchange for artistic success. Milt Gross, who had achieved fame as the leading exponent of Yiddish-English cartoon humor in a succession of strips and subsequent books based on them, such as *Nize Baby* (1926), *Dunt Esk!!* (1927), and the old Clement Clarke Moore favorite, *De Night in de Front from Chreesmas* (1927), was stimulated by Ward's *Gods' Man* to produce his own three-hundred-page wordless parody, *He Done Her Wrong: The Great American Novel and Not a Word in It* (1930). In focusing the book's humor on a "woodcutter," Gross satirizes Ward's reappropriation of the medium of the woodcut (supposedly outmoded since the printing advances of the mid-nineteenth century) for his wordless novels, in favor of what Gross sees as the pen-and-ink wit and immediacy of the thoroughly modern postwoodcut cartoon which is his own medium. Ironically, the story Gross's "Great American Novel" tells is otherwise largely nostalgic in its loyalties, testifying to an encyclopedic knowledge on his part of the conventions of both the slapstick comedy of silent film (just coming to an end at the time with the release of the first sound films) and the verbal formulas and plot devices of the earlier popular American melodrama of the barnstorming variety. In his account of the cultural politics of Yinglish in twentieth-century Jewish American literature, historian James Loeffler calls for Gross to be recognized by literary historians as a missing link of sorts between such pioneering fiction as Abraham Cahan's novella *Yekl: A Tale of the New York Ghetto* (1896) and such (at the time of its appearance) controversial early writing of Philip Roth's as his 1959 story "Epstein" (2002, 133–62).

George Herriman, in his acclaimed comic strip *Krazy Kat* (1913–44), took the development of a kind of neo-stage-Yiddish *über*-dialect to unexpected places, both artistically and geographically. As a person of mixed-race descent, Herriman may have been particularly aware of the rich texture of ethnic interaction in the United States of his own day. Umberto Eco and other admiring critics have routinely called his strip's landscapes "surrealistic" and "lunar," but viewers familiar with the rock-formations of Monument Valley, Utah, which figure importantly in the Westerns directed by John Huston and many others, will recognize familiar landmarks in *Krazy Kat*'s desert landscapes. In the "Tom Outland's Story" section of her novel *The Professor's House* (1925), Willa Cather famously retold the story of cowboy Richard Wetherill's accidental sighting of the ruins of the Anasazi Cliff Palace in December 1888. Around the time that Cather visited the Wetherills in 1915, the family also began to host for extended stays some of the period's most noted painters and cartoonists, such as Rudolph Dirks (of *The Katzenjammer Kids* [1897–present]), Frank King (of *Gasoline Alley*), and Jimmy Swinnerton (of *Little Jimmy* [1904–58]). Herriman joined the expeditions early on and returned for them annually for twenty years or so, and southwestern desert landscapes began to appear in his work just before he launched *Krazy Kat* on its thirty-year run. In something of the way that J. R. R. Tolkien is said to have written the *Lord of the Rings* trilogy in order to have some place to exhibit Elvish and the several other languages—grammar and syntax as well as vocabulary—that he painstakingly invented, Herriman spoke of having loved Navajo country so much that he made the "Indian names" of the area "fit" into the strip, "somehow[,] whether or not the readers understand their meanings."

The traces of the Navajo language and his drawings of the southwestern landscape were, along with "the characters themselves"—Ignatz Mouse, Officer Pupp, and the ungenderable Krazy Kat—for him the most important things about the strip (McDonnell 1999, 68–69). As Eric Gary Anderson has pointed out, positive comparisons of Herriman's art to the painting of Joan Miró and other canonical modernist "masters" have had the effect of distracting readers from its vital relations to "local, cross-cultural, southwestern American contexts, particularly . . . the Navajo [ones]" (1999, 149–50). But strong traces of both verbal and visual motifs from Navajo culture appear frequently in *Krazy Kat*, as in the Sunday strip for November 11, 1938, when Officer Pupp, characteristically lying down to nap, engages in an extensive paraphrase (beginning, "Today my world walks in beauty," and concluding "So—I'll nap in beauty") of the best-known lines of the Navajo Night Chant ("With beauty may I walk"; qtd. in McDonnell 1999, 74–75).

At the end of the 1920s, with the advent of swashbuckling spaceman Buck Rogers and foreign-adventurer Captain Easy, along with the movement of Edgar Rice Burroughs's Tarzan from the pulp magazines to the funnies page, the comics took on an exotic and erotic charge that was for the most part new to them. Patterson of the *Tribune* and the *Daily News* responded to this latest trend by luring a promising young cartoonist named Milton Caniff to work at the Chicago paper, telling him that he wanted him to create a kind of male-romance adventure comic in which a virile and mature man and his boy sidekick would have adventures on the East Asian coast, and the older man would become emotionally entangled with a series of beautiful and sexy but sometimes treacherous women—in other words, *Terry and the Pirates* (1934–73). Caniff was intrigued but unsure at first how he should go about putting together this new kind of comic strip. Patterson suggested that a couple of books that might help him come up with material: a recent pulp novel entitled *Vampires of the China Coast* (1932)—and *Wuthering Heights* (1847), which Patterson recommended for its atmosphere of intense and protracted but somehow unconsummatable desire. Robert C. Harvey notes that young Caniff read both books with great absorption (as the strip he rapidly produced shows), supplementing them with Pearl Buck's *The Good Earth* (1931) and recent writing of Somerset Maugham and Noël Coward about Asia (2007, 198).

In Caniff's meticulous account of the conversation, the name Hemingway is not mentioned, but in retrospect, one may find it hard not to see the tough-white-guy heroics and sentimental misogyny that give both Hemingway's novels and Caniff's strip their predominant atmospheres as working in parallel with each other. Some of Hemingway's most perceptive early readers among his fellow novelists saw the common sources and effects of newspaper comic-strip culture on such characteristically American products as *The Sun Also Rises* (1926) and the Nick Adams stories. Virginia Woolf commented in 1927 on Hemingway's strategic use of flatness of characterization and sparsity of dialogue, and Joyce Cary observed in 1952 that "it has been said" that Hemingway "belongs essentially to the world of the strip cartoon" (Meyers 1997, 103–4, 416).

One doubts that Hemingway would have ever proposed that a Hollywood film producer cast Mickey Mouse, or even Caniff's brooding hero Pat Ryan, as the tough-but-tormented Jake Barnes (Tyrone Powers played the role when the novel was finally filmed in 1957), but other leading novelists of the day enthusiastically took up the comics as an avowed model for a new kind of satirical fiction, as Nathanael West did when, in his working notes, he subtitled *Miss Lonelyhearts* (1933) "A Novel in Comic Strips." John Dos Passos and his publishers reached far back into the history of US graphic narrative when they persuaded Reginald Marsh, an accomplished painter of New York City's seedier side (the burlesque houses and Coney Island) who had also been a frequent contributor of cartoons to both the *New Yorker* and the *New Masses* throughout the 1930s, to provide images for a 1946 illustrated edition of Dos Passos's *U.S.A.* trilogy (see Figure 22.2). By Marsh's account, he excitedly produced upwards of five hundred mostly small-scale drawings for the new project within about a month, almost all of which duly appear in the illustrated edition of

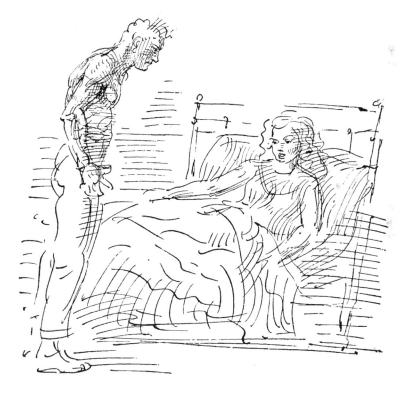

Fig 22.2 One of the *New Yorker*'s first cartoonists, Reginald Marsh made hundreds of illustrations for a 1946 special edition of John Dos Passos's *U.S.A.* This characteristic image captures the tense relations between men and women that pervade the trilogy. Illustration by Reginald Marsh from *U.S.A.* by John Dos Passos. Reprinted by permission of Houghton Mifflin Company. Copyright 2012 Estate of Reginald Marsh/Art Students League, New York/Artists Rights Society (ARS), New York.

the novel. The drawings, continually dropped into the text between its lines, casual and notational in appearance, provide a radical contrast with the kind of high-gloss, Raeburn Van Buren-style full-page illustrations with which the *Saturday Evening Post* had long ornamented the stories of such top authors of theirs as Mary Roberts Rinehart and F. Scott Fitzgerald. In their improvisatory and unpolished appearance (Hemingway found them "absolutely atrocious"), Marsh's drawings make *U.S.A.* seem far more like "the novel in comic strips" that West had envisioned than *Miss Lonelyhearts* does. In *Dos Passos and the Ideology of the Feminine,* Janet Galligani Casey compellingly argues that what March's illustrations consistently emphasize in Dos Passos's text is the trilogy's sympathy with the unease of many of its characters, especially its female characters, with the dominant tone of emotional and sexual relations between men and women in the society the novel depicts. Marsh's sketchy and often somewhat grotesque cartoons of men and women lingering in darkened doorways or getting into bed together are the antithesis of the kind of glamorous, painterly illustrations that had long graced the slicks—but that style was perhaps already beginning to look a little dated when Nick Carraway, in the closing pages of *The Great Gatsby* (1925), approaches Jordan Baker for their final kiss-off conversation and thinks as he catches sight of her, regretfully but somewhat dismissively, "She looked like a good illustration" (ch. 9).

Drawing on a tradition of humorous newspaper sketch-writing involving such comic personae as Finley Peter Dunne's "Mr. Dooley," George Ade's "Pink Marsh," and Alexander Posey's "Fus Fixico," Langston Hughes, working through the 1940s, produced his highly acclaimed series of "'Simple' Stories" about an African American Everyman named "Jesse B. Semple" ("Just Be Simple"?). William Empson defined the pastoral mode of representation as "the putting of the complex into the simple" (1974 [1935], 22), and a gathering critical consensus (focused by Donna Akiba Sullivan Harper's exemplary editorial and critical labors over Hughes's "'Simple' Stories") has credited Hughes with doing precisely that in conveying so much of the complexity of African American life in the 1940s in the "simple" tales told by and about his Jesse. Realizing midway through writing the series what a successful persona he had devised, Hughes is said to have toyed with the idea of producing a comic-strip version of the work. Carl Van Vechten urged him to start publishing the newspaper columns as books (they eventually appeared in five volumes), and Joseph H. Johnson, founder of *Ebony* magazine, a brand-new venture at the time, began negotiating with Hughes about possibly publishing a popular book-version of "Simple," perhaps with illustrations by the leading African American cartoonist Oliver Harrington. But nothing came of the plan, and several successive "Simple" volumes appeared in 1950 and after without benefit of illustration of any kind. When Hill and Wang finally published *The Best of Simple* in 1961, they grudgingly bought and reproduced some of the illustrations (not very satisfactory ones) by Bernhard Nast that the publishers of a German translation of some of the stories had commissioned; half a century later, this is still the only illustrated volume of the "Simple" stories in print.

Hughes had known Oliver Harrington since early adulthood; the cartoonist had been famous among African American newspaper readers since 1935, when Harrington started producing his single-panel comic *Bootsie* (1935–62), which featured a widely beloved "average black guy" who was an important predecessor and parallel to Hughes's "Simple." In the 1950s, Harrington joined Richard Wright and other distinguished African American artists in the expatriate community in Paris and became Wright's closest friend there. With the recovery of extensive amounts of work such as Harrington's, and of his female counterpart Jackie Ormes, whose publication of *Torchy Brown in "Dixie to Harlem"* strip in 1937 and *Patty-Jo 'n' Ginger* in 1945 is described in a recent biography by Nancy Goldstein, it has become possible to tell the story of African American narrative fiction across media more fully than it has so far been told—just as the ongoing republication of *Gasoline Alley* and *Terry and the Pirates* and other massive accumulations of continuity strips is making it possible to tell fuller versions of other, integrally related histories of US narrative fiction, including those of verbal-visual forms and formats. We are still at the beginning of the vast project of recovering the common roots in the popular graphic prints, the newspapers and magazines of the nineteenth and twentieth centuries, which continue to reveal the many ways that Mickey Mouse, "the Yellow Kid," "Fus Fixico," *The Gumps,* and *Bootsie* constitute indispensable elements of many of the same histories, literary and otherwise, that we are in the process of re-composing about *The Golden Bowl* (1904), *The Making of Americans* (1925), *The Professor's House,* and *Native Son* (1940).

23

SCIENCE FICTION IN THE UNITED STATES

BY GERRY CANAVAN

“To be modern,” Marshall Berman writes in his seminal work on the intertwined origins of modernity, modernism, and Marxism, *All That Is Solid Melts into Air,* “is to find ourselves in an environment that promises us adventure, power, joy, growth, transformation of ourselves and the world—and, at the same time, that threatens to destroy everything we have, everything we know, everything we are” (1988, 15). In that work Berman shows how the cultural and political forms that emerge out of the conditions of modernity can be arrayed along a dialectic between “thrill and dread,” between the “will to change” and a “terror of disorientation and disintegration, of life falling apart” (13). Although Berman pays little attention to the emergence of science fiction in that work, the genre might have been his best example of the tension he identifies as the crux of modernity and the engine of literary and artistic modernism. Virtually every science fiction story ever conceived oscillates between the promise of utopia and the threat of apocalypse.

The origins of science fiction as a genre have been traced from the early twentieth-century pulp magazines that first coined the term back through the Gothic novels of the early nineteenth century to the imaginary voyages and “Oriental Tales” of the early modern period, even as far back as the religious and mythological foundations of culture itself: the Bhagavad Gita, the Epic of Gilgamesh, the Book of Genesis. In this way the spatial and temporal constraints of this volume that might initially flummox us—how to begin to talk about the emergence of science fiction without reference to More, Swift, Shelley, Poe, Verne, Wells, Čapek, or Zamyatin—can also come as something of a relief; if nothing else they spare us from any impulse towards a total history of the emergence of the genre and allow us to focus instead on the indelible stamp left by American writers on the formation and early history of science fiction.

The term itself—science fiction—was coined surprisingly late, emerging only in the late 1920s out of the pages of Hugo Gernsback's *Amazing Stories* as the consensus name for a genre that previously had been variously described as “scientific romance," fantasy, or "weird tales." In practice the name "science fiction" quickly came to function as a principle of exclusion as much as inclusion. Whereas once all manner of imaginative and speculative fantasies might have seemed of a piece—and indeed would have appeared comfortably together in an earlier publication such as *Weird Tales*—Gernsback's intervention established a generic divide between science fiction and other modes of fantasy that continues to vex critics.

Likewise, the far-flung consequences of the Gernsback revolution remain alive in the divide that still separates the SCIENCE FICTION & FANTASY shelf from FICTION & LITERATURE in contemporary bookstores. While before *Amazing Stories* such literary authors as Mark Twain, Edgar Allan Poe, Nathaniel Hawthorne, Jack London, and Charlotte Perkins Gilman could write stories of improbable experiences and fantastic inventions that appear in retrospect to be science fictions, after Gernsback science fiction was situated primarily in the pulps, the sort of juvenile indulgence a "real writer" ought to avoid. This divide between the "mature" and "serious" character of literature and the allegedly juvenile and frivolous speculations of science fiction is highly naturalized today, but the history of its development can be traced across our period.

Most contemporary readers of Twain would be surprised to discover, for instance, that when Huck Finn announces his intent to "light out for the Territory ahead of the rest" at the end of that quintessential American novel (ch. 43), *Adventures of Huckleberry Finn* (1885), his frontier destination turns out to be not California, Texas, or Oregon, but *Africa* in *Tom Sawyer Abroad* (1894), and his unlikely mode of transport neither raft nor transcontinental train but a hot-air balloon ripped from the pages of Jules Verne. The contemporary conspiracy of parents, teachers, scholars, and critics to pretend *Tom Sawyer Abroad* was never written reflects, in miniature, what happens to the creative practices that make up science fiction between 1870 and 1940. Beginning the period critically unrecognized but firmly in the literary and cultural mainstream, science fiction entered 1940 as an established community of discourse at the cost of a newfound marginality, a tradeoff that has haunted the genre for decades.

Science Fiction and Utopia

Few have captured the difficulty facing critical analysis of science fiction as well as Everett F. Bleiler in his mammoth compilation of the emergence of science fiction, *Science Fiction: The Early Years,* where he notes the central paradox of science fiction studies: everyone knows what science fiction is, but no one can satisfactorily define it (1990, xi). Darko Suvin offered the definition that has most nearly approached consensus when, in 1972, he defined science fiction as the literature of *cognitive estrangement*—and even this definition is less consensus than the starting gun for decades of arguments.

Unpacking the two terms, we have *cognition*—including "not only natural but also all the cultural or historical sciences and even scholarship" (1979, 13)—and *estrangement*, derived from the *ostranenie* of the Russian formalists and Brecht's famous V-effect to denote the opening of the mind to previously unimagined alternatives, which, in turn, cast new and unexpected light on everyday life (6). Consequently, Suvin and the science fiction theorists influenced by his approach have approached science fiction through the relationship between cognitive estrangement and utopia, with Suvin fond of describing science fiction as both daughter and aunt of utopian literature to suggest the extent to which each genre encompasses the other (2010, 39, 43).

We find both these genres at work in the best studied of the proto-science-fiction novels of turn-of-the-century America, Edward Bellamy's 1888 utopia, *Looking Backward: 2000–1887*, whose mammoth popularity and outsized cultural influence would demand special attention in any study of the period independently of the science fiction context. Within just two years of its publication, the book had already sold more than two hundred thousand copies, as Phillip Wegner notes in *Imaginary Communities*, and ultimately was only the second American work of fiction to sell more than one million, making it not only the most popular and influential of the proto-science-fictions to be published in the pre-Gernsback era but arguably the most important work of fiction of its day. Translated into twenty languages, *Looking Backward* spawned a wide host of imitators and detractors both domestically and overseas, almost singlehandedly launching a craze in Utopian fiction that would last for decades and even spawning a real-world political movement dubbed "Nationalism" that was promulgated by the springing up of "Bellamy Clubs" nationwide. In terms of circulating and popularizing socialist ideas, *Looking Backward* is arguably second in influence only to Marx's *Capital*.

Looking Backward exemplifies the electric charge of novelty and possibility that Berman identified as characteristic of the modern world—a world that not only *can* change, but *is* changing, day by day, in fundamental and irreversible ways. The novel is the story of Julian West, a privileged scion of Old Boston who goes to sleep in the year 1887 only to awaken 113 years later in the transformed America of the year 2000. West never returns to 1887, and the book is presented as if it has been published in the very future it depicts—rendering the mere act of reading the novel at all an impossible temporal paradox. The last chapters further highlight the inaccessibility of *Looking Backward*'s utopia in a clever twist on the already clichéd "dream ending" of speculative fiction: West's narrator briefly reawakens near the end of the novel back in the nineteenth century, finding himself alienated and alone in an inequitable social context he now recognizes as a nightmare—only to reawaken a *second* time, safe and secure in the year 2000, forever separated from his 1888 public by the unnavigable gulf of time.

The book was published with a preface from the "Historical Section of Shawmut College" dated December 26, 2000, which seeks to assure the disbelieving readership of utopia that, yes, things had really been this bad just one century earlier: "How strange and well-nigh incredible does it seem that so prodigious a moral and material transformation as has taken place since then could have been accomplished in so brief an interval!" (preface). Life in Bellamy's utopia synthesizes the classless communism that culminates Marx's historical materialist theory of history with the productivity and creativity of capitalism through a unique bloodless revolution. The ever-growing trusts, syndicates, and monopolies characteristic of American capitalism are finally merged into a single monolithic "Great Trust" that employs every worker and provides every good, and as a consequence becomes indistinguishable from the state. In such a context the profit-centered competitiveness that had previously organized capitalist expansion no longer has any meaning, allowing capitalism unexpectedly to transform itself in the service of the public good. In Bellamy's utopia private luxury has been abolished; all workers are paid an equal wage and have an equal share in the proceeds of their collective endeavors. The citizens of this army of labor are motivated not by greed or self-interest, but by "service of the nation, patriotism, passion for humanity" (ch. 9), a transformation of values so complete that such seemingly essential human vices as dishonesty and deception are now anachronistic.

Contemporary readers have been starkly divided on the desirability of the utopia *Looking Backward* describes, with many (Darko Suvin and Fredric Jameson prominent among them) much preferring British author William Morris's more traditionally socialist retort, *News from Nowhere* (1890). Raymond Williams acknowledged the widespread anxiety about Bellamy's reduction of social relations to a well-ordered mechanism by noting its "overriding rationalism" and calling the book a utopia "without desire" (2010, 101); David Ketterer goes further still in calling Bellamy's future America "a dystopian society in which the citizens have evolved, or rather devolved, into machines" (1974, 113). Even contemporary critics more favorably disposed to Bellamy are not without their reservations; Paul K. Alkon attributes common "misunderstanding" of the book's proposals to "Bellamy's inability to show vividly the superiority or even the existence of the art, music, and literature that we are assured abound alongside mechanical inventions in his twenty-first century" (2002, 112).

In an analysis that extends beyond Bellamy to the utopian form as such, Marc Angenot reminds us that utopian texts like *Looking Backwards* are always, by their nature, "equivocal and ambiguous," and must be read as cognitive estrangements—as critiques of what already exists—rather than genuine predictions of the future or positive platforms for change (2000, 110–11). But the temptation to quibble over the details proved as impossible to resist in Bellamy's contemporaries as in his later critics; Bellamy's work divided its contemporaneous readership, inspiring as many as it horrified. There were numerous responses to the work, many of them fictional treatments often employing Julian West himself as the main character, including Bellamy's own sequel, *Equality* (1897), intended to shore up points he felt were lacking in the original.

Many of these dreams of the future have now been entirely forgotten. Richard C. Michaelis's procapitalist retort *Looking Further Forward* (1890), for instance, rejects both the thesis that capitalism *will* be overturned and the thesis that it *should* be. Instead, Darwin's theory of evolution—evoked by Bellamy as a scientific grounding for his prognostications—is employed in the other direction: "Inequality is the law of nature and the attempt to establish equality is therefore unnatural and absurd" (ch. 3). Similarly reactionary replies include Arthur Dudley Vinton's racist *Looking Further Backward* (1890), an early Yellow Peril story in which the Chinese invade the utopia of *Looking Backward,* which proves completely unable to defend itself, and J. W. Roberts's anti-utopian *Looking Within* (1893), which sought to explicate the "misleading tendencies" of *Looking Backward* through the experiences of James *North,* who discovers that by 2025 Bellamy's utopia must revert to capitalism in order to escape the corruption that has come to plague it. Former US Congressman Ignatius Donnelly's *Caesar's Column* (1890) takes Bellamy's basic recognition of an America divided by class in a much more dystopian direction, with the class struggle between capitalist oligarchs and exploited workers culminating not in paradise, but in the "Caesar's column" of the title: an immense mass grave, filled in by oppressors and oppressed alike and covered over with cement to stand forever as a horrible monument to man's brutality (ch. 36).

On the other side of Donnelly's pessimism we find George Allan England's *The Air Trust* (1915), which explores a sinister robber baron's attempt to privatize the air itself, provoking a socialist revolution to defend the right to breathe. Jack London, too, takes up the terrain pioneered by Bellamy with his socialist novel *The Iron Heel* (1908), depicting the revolution from the perspective of a historian annotating a twentieth-century manuscript called the "Everhard Manuscript" from the perspective of the year 419 BOM (Brotherhood of Man)—approximately 2600 A.D. London anticipates the fascist takeovers of the 1930s through his depiction of the Oligarchy, a union between business monopolists and the state that leads not to state socialism, as in Bellamy, but to widespread exploitation and misery under a newly asserted "divine right" of capitalists to rule (ch. 4). *The Iron Heel* is perhaps unique in the utopian subgenre for its relentless devotion to a long-term perspective (on *The Iron Heel* as dystopic science fiction, see Chapter 33 in this volume). The revolution takes approximately three hundred years, including not only the First and Second Revolts that appear in its pages, and "the tortuous and distorted evolution of the next three centuries would compel a Third Revolt and a Fourth Revolt, and many Revolts, all drowned in seas of blood, ere the world-movement of labor should come into its own" (foreword). The novel ultimately breaks off in the middle of a sentence, shortly before the moment its female narrator, Avis Everhard, is captured and killed by police. The final achievement of global justice may be a happy achievement, but the cost in blood and years is so dire as to shrivel hope itself.

More generally optimistic are the feminist utopias that arose in Bellamy's wake, the most widely read of which today is Charlotte Perkins Gilman's *Herland,* serialized in Gilman's magazine *Forerunner* beginning in 1915 and, largely forgotten before its rediscovery in the late 1970s, celebrated now as an anticipation of later, more explicitly science fictional feminist utopias. Such novels were generally preoccupied by the problem of what to do about childbearing and reproduction (especially once men have been eliminated). Gilman's approach is astounding: after a devastating series of wars, natural disasters, and gender revolts conspire to kill off every male and leave Herland permanently isolated from the surrounding world, the remaining Herlanders discover a woman who is able to reproduce by parthenogenesis, giving birth to five children, each of whom gives birth in turn to five more (ch. 5). The pattern holds until Herland has reached its optimum population, at which time (in defiance of Malthusian pessimism about the inevitability of overpopulation) the women come together and rationally decide to hold their population permanently steady: "With our best endeavors this country will support about so many people, with the standard of peace, comfort, health, beauty, and progress we demand. Very well. That is all the people we shall make" (ch. 6).

The three male explorers who discover Herland by chance find a nation lacking war, poverty and exploitation, and crime and punishment, as well as (naturally) the oppression of women—a point underscored in Gilman's rarely read sequel, *With Her in Ourland* (1916), in which one of the explorers brings his Herlandian wife to America to show her his home, only to see her spend the trip entirely aghast. The men begin *Herland* with open imperialist ambitions, and at least one of them still intends at the end to return to Herland with an expeditionary force despite a promise never to reveal its location. The Herlanders, for their part, likewise view the men with a colonizers' gaze, as seen in the report generated at the first sighting of the men: "From another country. Probably men. Evidently highly civilized. Doubtless possessed of much valuable knowledge. May be dangerous. *Catch them if possible; tame and train them if necessary.* This may be a chance to re-establish a bi-sexual state for our people" (ch. 8, emphasis added).

As is typical of such literary utopias, *Herland* is not an earnest proposal for alternative social organization, but an opportunity for satire and social critique, as when Herland's women discover that the explorers' beneficent claim that "We do not allow our women to work. Women are loved—idolized—honored—kept in the home to care for the children" is compromised by the fact that women "of the poorer sort" do work in America after all—a mere seven or eight million people at the time (ch. 5). Similar questions abound about gender relations, capitalism, politics, and religion, each serving to skewer the conventional wisdom of the day, particularly with respect to feminism and gender equality. "It is only in social relations that we are human," Gilman claimed elsewhere in her work: "To be human, women must share in the totality of humanity's common life" (qtd. in Lane [1979], xi). The narrative thrust of *Herland* is to raise the consciousness of at least one of the male explorers until he is finally able to view the inhabitants of Herland not as *women,* but as *people.*

In the face of feminist scholarship that has largely embraced *Herland* since its republication (and rediscovery) in 1970, Alys Eve Weinbaum takes up the unhappy task of demystifying the novel in her book *Wayward Reproductions*, calling attention to *Herland*'s erasure of race and violence in the colonial encounter, as well as its reinscription of eugenic thinking about white purity current at the time (2004). (The Herlanders are explicitly eugenic, both pressing on "the lowest types" of their population not to breed and aggressively removing custody from any woman deemed unfit to mother a child [1915, ch. 7].) This unfortunate tendency is much more obvious in *With Her in Ourland*, which sees its enlightened Herlandian heroine calling for assimilation for "tribal" Jews and noting that the presence of an "ill-assorted and unassimilable mass of human material"—unskilled immigrant workers—makes democracy impossible in America as "only some races—or some individuals in a given race—have reached the democratic stage." Such unfortunate episodes help explain why *Ourland* is less widely read than *Herland* today.

Science Fiction and Imperialism

The presence of colonialist, eugenicist, and racist themes lurking not only in *Herland*, but in so many of the utopias already discussed above, has helped motivate the recent "imperial turn" in science fiction studies, which significantly complicates the critical interest in utopia by calling attention to the historical relationship between science fiction and imperialist fantasies. In his essay "Science Fiction and Empire," Istvan Csicsery-Ronay, Jr., notes that "The dominant sf nations are precisely those that attempted to expand beyond their national borders in imperialist projects: Britain, France, Germany, Soviet Russia, Japan, and the US," with periods of most intense interest in science fiction coinciding with periods of expansion beyond the borders of the nation (2003, 231). Early science fiction registers the central importance of technology as a tool for imperial domination, with technological innovation serving as "not only a precondition for the physical expansion of the imperialist countries but an immanent driving force" that "facilitated the subjugation of less developed cultures, wove converging networks of technical administration, and established standards of 'objective measurement' that led inevitably to myths of racial and national supremacy" (233). Csicsery-Ronay notes too how "fantasies of physical mastery and engineering know-how" that accompanied this technological expertise dominated early science fiction (234), connecting these once again to the similar fantasies of mastery that structured the ideologies of imperialism and race war during the period.

In *Colonialism and the Emergence of Science Fiction*, John Rieder likewise finds colonial and imperial ideology at the heart of science fiction's imagination of other places and times, with power inevitably distributed along a rhetoric of "progress" that either places white Europeans at the culminating apex of human history or threatens them with supersession from either terrestrial or extraterrestrial competitors. Lost races, first contacts, alien invasions—such narratives draw not only from the history of colonial and imperial encounters, but also and perhaps most crucially from pseudo-Darwinian discourse about racial superiority and inferiority. The popularity of "Yellow Peril" fictions at the turn of the century—first depicting strategies by which the people of Asia might be wiped out by ever-more efficient military technology, and then turning inevitably to the threat that such weapons might someday be loosed on the US population instead—represent only the worst extremes of such virulent fantasies. So-called edisonades, dime-novel stories of fantastic inventions, likewise frequently hinged on the invention of fantastic superweapons, perhaps most vividly in Garrett Serviss's *Edison's Conquest of Mars* (1898), a sequel to Wells's *War of the Worlds* in which Thomas Edison himself develops both flying machines that can reach Mars and disintegrator rays to lay waste to the Martian population once human beings arrive. In Edgar Rice Burrough's Barsoom series (1912–64), the imperial encounter between East and West is similarly transposed to Mars, where Burroughs's Great White Hero John Carter encounters and subdues monstrous green- and red-skinned "savages" on the surface of Mars through ingenuity and physical superiority in stories that anticipate the adventures of his later hero, Tarzan. Even edisonades taking a less gung-ho attitude towards imperialism—such as the popular Franke Reade series of dime novels (1892–99) primarily authored by "Noname" Luis Senarens—frequently employed dual-use technologies of transportation and communication that were improved versions of those being employed in colonial and imperial wars.

From the perspective of the imperial turn, the best example of nineteenth-century American proto-science fiction may be not *Looking Backward* but rather Mark Twain in his quasi-reply, *A Connecticut Yankee in King Arthur's Court* (1889), which makes intriguingly literal the retemporalizing gesture that Johannes Fabian identified as a crucial strategy for the justification of imperial violence: the "assign[ing] to the conquered populations a different time" (1983, 30). In what is believed to be the first such time-travel story in English literature, Twain inverts and destabilizes the usual imperial narrative by having his "Connecticut Yankee" appear in the imperial West's own preindustrial past. (An interesting complement to Twain's gesture can be found in John Ames Mitchell's lesser-known *The Last American,* published the same year, which satirically recounts the discovery and excavation of the ruins of "Nhu-Yok," largest city of the lost Mehrikan empire, by Persian archaeologists in the year 2951.) Hit on the head with a crowbar during a fight with one of his subordinates, factory superintendent Hank Morgan (an engineer who has "learned to make everything—guns, revolvers, cannon, boilers, engines, all sorts of labour-saving machinery" [1889, "The Stranger's History"]) finds himself awakening in Arthurian England, transported in both space and time. With his advanced scientific and technical know-how (including the fortuitous knowledge of an impending total solar eclipse), Morgan quickly displaces the magician Merlin to take administrative control of Camelot, implementing a plan for modernization and development that rivals any attempted in actual imperial history.

A Connecticut Yankee seems at first as if it will conform to a familiar nineteenth-century narrative of progress; critics frequently begin their discussion of *A Connecticut Yankee* with Twain's dream that spawned the novel:

> Dream of being a knight errant in armor in the middle ages. Have the notions and habits of thought in the present day mixed with the necessities of that. No pockets in the armor. No way to manage certain requirements of nature. Can't scratch. Cold in the head—can't blow—can't get at handkerchief, can't use iron sleeve. Iron gets red hot in the sun—leaks in the rain, gets white with frost and freezes me solid in winter. Suffer from lice and fleas. Make disagreeable clatter when I enter church. Can't dress or undress myself. Always getting struck by lightning. Fall down, can't get up. (1889, preface)

The description of the dream—Twain's apparent first notes for the novel—suggests that it is the past that is the intended victim of his satire. And although Twain is not commonly associated with optimism about either the present or the future, optimistic attitudes can occasionally be found elsewhere in his work. He praised *Looking Backward,* notably, as "the latest and best of all the Bibles," and said Bellamy "has made the accepted heaven paltry by inventing a better one on Earth" (preface). The excitement of this benediction calls to mind Twain's unexpected (and uncharacteristic) optimism on the occasion of Walt Whitman's seventieth birthday in 1889, when he rhapsodized on the coming glories of the twentieth century. "Wait thirty years and then look out over the earth," he writes. "You shall see marvel upon marvels, added to those whose nativity you have witnessed; and conspicuous above them you shall see their formidable Result—Man at almost his full stature at last!—and still growing, visibly growing, while you look" (preface).

But despite these occasional flirtations with optimism, Twain seems constitutionally incapable of holding the feeling for very long. The meeting of the lost Arthurian past with contemporary scientific culture, while seeming to promise advancement, turns by the end of *A Connecticut Yankee* to utter ruin. The mechanisms of modernity and "progress" that Morgan devises and implements in his capacity as "Boss" of Camelot come to their natural conclusion in the form of a bloody massacre. After Arthur's death Morgan and his men attempt to retain their control of Camelot against the reactionary forces of the nobility and the Church that unite against the Yankee's attempt to establish a Republic. Now we see the other side of technology and progress: dynamite, mines, Gatling guns, and an electric fence quickly decimate a hopelessly outmatched opposing army. "Within ten short minutes after we had opened fire, armed resistance was totally annihilated, the campaign was ended, we fifty four were masters of England! Twenty-five thousand men lay dead around us" (ch. 43). Merlin—not a charlatan after all—soon uses his magic to send the Yankee home, and the Church conspires to cover up all the evidence of his experiment in the past, leaving only the Yankee to remember, and to be tortured until his death by horrible and unsettling dreams.

This climactic vision of mass death, facilitated by technologies both already in use and soon to be employed in imperial adventure overseas, is the culmination of a critique of imperialism that is hinted at throughout the novel. The first of Dan Beard's illustrations for the novel, immediately preceding chapter one, likewise suggests that the time travel at the center of the story is related somehow to a critique of global imperialism. The image of a giant statue of a lion, on which a man in a suit and bowler cap stands perched with one hand in his pocket, labeled on the pedestal "THE TALE OF THE LOST LAND," suggests not Arthurian England but Africa. Morgan's first view of Camelot's locals similarly points to questions of race and racialization that were on Twain's mind as his politics turned more and more anti-imperialist in his old age. The peasants of Camelot are "brawny men, with long, coarse, uncombed hair that hung down over their faces and made them look like animals." Many are naked, "but nobody seemed to know it" (ch. 1), suggesting both Eden and tropical locales like the Hawaii from which a young Twain reported for the *Sacramento Daily Union* at the start of his literary career in 1866. In fact, as Fred W. Lorch and Stephen H. Sumida have argued, Hank Morgan's story most likely has its origin in an unfinished novel about Hawaii on which Twain had been working at the time, a project he eventually abandoned in favor of *A Connecticut Yankee*. That story of a meeting of nineteenth-century industrial society with a preindustrial, pastoral past, beginning with notions of progress and uplift but ultimately culminating in an imperial disaster, turns out to be a closer match to Hawaiian history than Twain could have known at the time; the early violence of the 1887 and 1888 uprisings in Hawaii would culminate in a United States–led overthrow of the Hawaiian kingdom and final US annexation by 1893. Along the same lines, John Carlos Rowe convincingly links *A Connecticut Yankee* to Twain's history of growing anti-imperialism over the course of his adult life, a precursor to the anti-imperialist satires he would eventually write during the US military occupation of the Philippines.

While it may seem to contemporary readers "impossible that any reader of *A Connecticut Yankee* could fail to be disturbed by the violence of its ending," Stephen Railton notes with some surprise that in fact "no contemporary reviewer even mentioned it" (2004, 88), speculating that such reviewers may in fact have been unwilling or unable to see this aspect of the narrative. Paul K. Alkon, in contrast, suggests that it is *we* who are unable to read *A Connecticut Yankee* with proper objectivity, as the bleak, scorched-earth violence of the ending inevitably recalls for us such "twentieth-century nightmares" as trench warfare, aerial bombing, and nuclear weapons (2002, 133). Despite the book's comedy and ample satiric charms, the abrupt switch into total war at its conclusion makes it difficult for modern readers to see the novel as representing much more than "irreverence, the guillotine, a reign of terror, and a kind of generalized despair" (Kaplan 1991, 296). José Martí offered an exceptionally cogent description of *A Connecticut Yankee's* irresolvable dialectic between optimism and cynicism in his 1890 review, observing, "although it is humorous, as it is said to be, it was written after having cried" (2010, 55).

Science Fiction, Literature, and the Pulps

In *Metamorphoses of Science Fiction*, Darko Suvin bemoans the lost tradition of science fiction that might have begun with Twain had "certain fragmentary sketches" found among his papers been completed and published during his life, allowing Twain to eclipse H. G. Wells as "the major turning point in the tradition leading to modern SF" (1979, 201). But this was not to be—and instead American science fiction descended first into the edisonades and Edgar-Rice-Burroughs-influenced dime novels and then the pulp magazines from which, a century later, it is still in many ways trying to emerge. Hugo Gernsback's vision, not Bellamy's or Twain's, would ultimately shape science fiction's emergence as a genre.

Gernsback's editorial on page one of the first issue of *Amazing Stories* in 1926 breathlessly announces "a new sort of magazine." Our now-"intimate" relationship with science across all spheres of life from history-making conflicts to everyday domesticity, Gernsback claims, has created "an entirely new world" through which science fiction "blaze[s] a new trail" (1926, 3). This enthusiastic celebration of the new overlooks the fact that this novelty was most commonly expressed, throughout the earliest years of the magazine, in decades-old reprints. In the first six months, only six of the thirty-eight stories published by Gernsback were original to *Amazing*, and in his first attempt at defining science fiction he describes "the Jules Verne, H. G. Wells, and Edgar Allan Poe type of story—a charming romance intermingled with scientific fact and prophetic vision" (1926, 3).

To properly qualify as science fiction in the Gernsbackian mold is to hit each of these three marks: it must be a tale of adventure (often with a love interest) modeled on accurate scientific knowledge and predicting a likely course for technological and scientific advancement. Exemplifying this intersection is Gernsback's own contribution to the genre, *Ralph 124C 41+* ("one to foresee for one and more"), a "romance of the year 2660," then 750 years hence, which was published as a serial in Gernsback's magazine *Modern Electrics* (1911), long before the advent of *Amazing Stories*. The novel depicts the singular experiences of its title character as he explores the technoutopian world of 2660 until (in an almost perfunctory climax) he battles a Martian brute for the return of the woman he loves.

Contemporary science fiction criticism almost universally derides the novel as unreadable, reflecting the extent to which Gernsback's approach has fallen out of favor (and Gernsback himself is largely unremembered outside of scholarly circles). The novel embodies the worst of the science fiction that is to follow it, with a cardboard-cutout protagonist whose "physical superiority" (while ample) is "as nothing compared to his gigantic mind" (1911, ch. 1) and whose experiences, in lieu of a plot, careen from one expository science lesson to another. And yet Gernsback undoubtedly took great pride in the novel's successful predictions, among them (as outlined by the novel's 1950 forwards from Lee de Forest, the inventor of radio, and science fiction author Fletcher Pratt) television, microfilm, air and helicopter travel, lie detectors, talkie film, spaceflight, sleep-learning, night baseball, synthetic fibers, and radar, to name only a few (ch. 1).

Of course, science fiction's prognostications are only sporadically accurate, and it is worth noting that Gernsback's invention-oriented notion of science fiction was not the one best loved by the public even in his day. Most of his science-fiction publishing ventures failed, including *Amazing*, of which Gernsback lost control after declaring bankruptcy in 1929. Of the four science fiction magazines he founded afterwards, most folded or merged after just a single year. Adam Roberts notes that other magazines, like *Astounding* (founded in 1930), gained prominence in part by *rejecting* Gernsback's "insistence on didactic science" and instead focusing on "adventure, excitement, and exoticism" (2007, 177). Everett Bleiler, too, notes that Gernsback's preferred theme of technological optimism took a back seat to the unending cavalcade of disaster, catastrophe, and out-and-out apocalypse that actually dominates the science fiction of the period, a preoccupation Bleiler groups under the single evocative heading "Things Go Wrong" (1990, xv). Generally speaking the hegemony of the magazines in US science fiction history resulted from social conditions independent of any writer or editor's vision. As difficult as the Great Depression was for magazine publishers, it was far crueler for book publishers, with publication of original science fiction novels outside serial form essentially drying up until the Second World War. The best-remembered science fiction novelists of the era, like Burroughs, Jack Williamson, and E. E. "Doc" Smith of *Skylark of Space* fame, were all publishing their books serially in the pulps.

The increasing primacy of the pulps in the late 1920s and early 1930s established a situation in which science fiction was understood rightly to "belong" to the mass audience of the pulps, and writing in the genre consequently came to be seen as a commercial rather than artistic pursuit. The aura of disposability that accompanies magazines and their (admittedly often-deserved) reputation for low literary quality contributed to the growing popular perception in the United States that science fiction was a fundamentally unserious and unliterary endeavor—in stark contrast to critical reception in Britain, where science fiction novels from authors such as H. G. Wells, Aldous Huxley, George Orwell, Katharine Burdekin, and Olaf Stapledon were treated by reviewers and critics as "serious literature" as late as *Nineteen Eighty-Four* in 1949 (and even beyond).

This difference in critical reception is not totally unwarranted. Brooks Landon has noted, "Almost every study of science fiction in the twentieth century details an essential difference in 'seriousness' or 'purpose' between American SF and noteworthy strains of well-known SF from the United Kingdom, Eastern Europe, and the Former Soviet Union" (2002, 76–77). The chapter in Adam Roberts's *History of Science Fiction* titled "High Modernist Science Fiction" does not include a single American name, nor does Brian Aldiss's list of the "greater talents" who "most ably put the salt on the tail of the *zeitgeist* and, by capturing it, seem to defy it and live on." American pulp writers, he admits in contrast, "have by now lost what savour they possessed," telling us "less about the world and more about the tricks of their lowly trade" (1986, 201–202). Accordingly, Aldiss designates Hugo Gernsback "one of the worst disasters ever to hit the science fiction field" (1986, 202). Darko Suvin speaks for the many who agree with Aldiss when he notes that "the Gernsbacks keep SF alive at the cost of starving, stunting, and deforming it; comparing *The Iron Heel* with the output in the United States between the World Wars, one strongly suspects the cost is too high" (1979, 23).

But the imprint of Gernsback on the genre he helped found remains undeniable. As Gary Westfahl observes, the British and European models for science fiction that predated Gernsback were ultimately not able to survive him. "When [British and European science fiction critics] look at their native literatures in the period from 1890 to 1920, they find more than enough examples of works classifiable as science fiction that are far superior to anything produced in America at that time," Westfahl writes:

> but as they extend their chronological surveys past 1920, they watch their own traditions fade and fall apart, while American science fiction expands and grows stronger to the point that, by 1950, American writers and ideas dominated the world, and British and European authors were forced to imitate or respond to the American tradition. (1998, 27)

Westfahl even catches the Swedish critic Sam J. Lundwall bemoaning that science fiction was "stolen" by Americans from the Europeans (27)!

Perhaps, indeed, there was no such thing as science fiction before Gernsback at all. Although "science fiction" was first used as the name for stories that combine aesthetic pleasure and narrative interest with pedagogical instruction in the sciences in 1851, it was Gernsback who (after a brief flirtation with the infelicitous portmanteau "scientifiction") recoined and popularized the term early in his career as a magazine publisher. Consequently Westfahl has argued that the impulse to locate some origin-point for science fiction further and further back in time is fundamentally wrong-headed; the origin of science fiction should instead be located here, with Gernsback in the America of the 1920s, the first of the genre's author-editor-critics who, in the act of naming the genre, brought it about.

While frequent attempts have been made to locate the quintessential "American-ness" of post–First World War and especially post–Second World War science fiction in the history, ideology, or material conditions of late-nineteenth and mid-twentieth-century America, Westfahl assigns the credit to Gernsback himself, not as writer or editor but as *critic*, as the founder of a particular literary-critical discourse around which the genre was organized and galvanized. While we might be able to recognize relatives of the genre in retrospect, Westfahl argues, it took Gernsback's taxonomic innovation to bring those family resemblances to our attention. "What Gernsback provided," argues Westfahl,

> was not simply a set of marketing slogans or slick promotions; he offered a complete theory of science fiction which readers, editors, and writers understood and responded to. . . . Because of the stimulating and supportive atmosphere of the commentaries engendered by Gernsback, American science fiction steadily expanded and improved; because of the absence of such commentary, British and European traditions floundered. Simply put, literary criticism made American science fiction great, and that was Gernsback's great contribution to the field. (1998, 28–29)

The medium of the pulps allowed for a level of interactivity among writer, editor, and audience that far surpassed anything to be found in the one-way transmission of the novel; the fan essays, contests, prizes, and letters to the editor to be found in the pulp magazines of the Gernsback era are the earliest forerunners of fan clubs, fanzines, conventions, and Internet comment threads that are still a vital part of the field. Science fiction was conceived and executed as an ongoing, two-way dialogue between writers and readers from its earliest instances in the pulps—and this active reception would prove to be a crucial component for the establishment and growth of science fiction as a popular genre, not only in the pre–Second World War era but in the "Golden Age" and "New Wave" eras that would follow. "How good this magazine will be in the future is up to you," Gernsback writes in that first *Amazing Stories* editorial in 1926; "Read *Amazing Stories*—get your friends to read it and then write us what you think of it."

From the many fans influenced by Gernsback's call to community, who loosely organized themselves into "science clubs" to discuss the work, Bleiler identifies a core of one hundred of so "trufans"—those for whom science fiction was as much an ethos as an aesthetic pleasure—from whose list of members can be distilled a significant fraction of the writers and editors who would soon inaugurate what is commonly known as the Golden Age of Science Fiction, beginning around 1940: Isaac Asimov, James Blish, Arthur C. Clarke, John Wyndham Harris, Damon Knight, Judith Merril, Sam Moskowitz, and Donald Wollheim (1990, xxix–xxx). In the coming decades this group would take over the field, becoming the establishment that the writer-critic-fans of the "New Wave" of the 1960s and 1970s would in turn pit themselves against in both critique and homage.

Still, despite the advantages this critical community offered to the growth of science fiction, one cannot help but imagine an alternate history of science fiction that is organized not around Gernsback and the pulps but instead (as in the European tradition) around the "slipstream" novels that quietly deploy the science fictional imagination within the literary canon. The Afrofuturist school of literary criticism, beginning in the late 1990s, has already convincingly organized its intervention into literary history along these lines, arguing, in Greg Tate's formulation, that "Black people live the estrangement that science fiction writers imagine" (qtd. in Dery 1995, 208) and, in Isiah Lavender's, "the blunt thesis underlying Afrofuturism is that *all* black cultural production in the new world is SF" (2007, 187). Such a thesis need not look far to find its evidence. Pauline Hopkins's *Of One Blood* (1903) rewrites the popular "lost race" tale of early science fiction to describe an unknown Ethiopian kingdom from which all human civilization originated, anticipating not only the Africanist movement in historical studies, but also the science fictional cosmology of the Nation of Islam and 1970s Afrofuturism in music and film. Among Sutton E. Griggs's self-published novels, which were widely read among African Americans but "virtually unknown to white Americans of his time" (1899, "Preface"), *Imperium in Imperio* (1899) can be positioned at the intersection of political science fiction, conspiracy fiction, and utopianism in its depiction of an African American shadow government operating in secret in Washington, DC. W. E. B. Du Bois, too, borrows from science fiction's imagination of disaster in "The Comet," the short story that closes his 1920 book *Darkwater*. In that story the close pass of a comet apparently destroys all civilization on earth and leaves New York City populated by only two people, a black man and a white woman. The new Eden promised by this encounter, populated by a once-again united human race undivided against itself, is soon disrupted by the discovery that the disaster has only been local after all; soon other survivors appear, including white men who seek to lynch Jim for his presumption that racial inequality could be suspended even by the end of the world. George S. Schuyler's Harlem Renaissance novel *Black No More* (1931) similarly employs science fictional tropes—here, fantastic invention—to provide the grounding for his skewering of white racism (on Schuyler's *Black No More*, see Chapters 28 and 30 in this volume). The development of a skin-whitening treatment that can turn African Americans "whiter than white" (ch. 13) serves as a clever deconstruction of America's fantasies of race, culminating, at the end of the novel, in the entire population (white and black alike) turning to tanning creams to *darken* their skin, in order to prove to their peers the fantasy that their whiteness is genuine and *real*.

The science fictionalization of the canon need not stop there. The immigrant fiction of the turn of the century is surely a close cousin of the science fiction novel, with its characteristic cognitive estrangement originating not from the physical laws of science, but from the social laws of culture, language, and migration. These writers describe lives that have been transformed beyond imagination—and of disparate nations that stand in no closer relation to each other than distant planets. "I was born, I have lived, and I have been made over," begins Polotsk-born Mary Antin in her autobiography, *The Promised Land* (1912), in language that suggests the estranging experience of the immigrant is the same whether the ultimate destination is Manhattan or Mars: "Is it not time to write my life's story? I am just as much out of the way as if I were dead, for I am absolutely other than the person whose story I have to tell. Physical continuity with my earlier self is no disadvantage. I could speak in the third person and not feel that I was masquerading. I can analyze my subject, I can reveal everything; for *she*, and not *I*, is my real heroine. My life I have still to live; her life ended when mine began" (1912, introduction). Abraham Cahan's Russian-born David Levinsky (1917) likewise views his past in terms that suggest radical self-division and *ostranenie*, a "metamorphosis" that leaves a single human body forever divided between two warring halves (ch. 1), a past and a present that cannot be made to fit together again. Jerry Siegel and Joe Shuster translated the experiences of their immigrant parents into the origin story of the genre-establishing comic book hero Superman (1938), last son of a lost world to which he can never return—and it is surely no coincidence that the father of science fiction, Hugo Gernsback himself, was an immigrant from Luxembourg.

The aesthetics of cognitive estrangement—of realities that are pregnant with multiplicity and alterity, of individuals who are more than themselves, of pasts and futures that improbably meet somewhere in the middle—can give us fresh purchase on literary contexts as diverse as Yoknapatawpha County, West Egg, New York; Winesburg, Ohio; and expatriate Paris. What for that matter could be more manifestly science fictional than the alternate history that makes up Sinclair Lewis's *It Can't Happen Here* (1935), in which a Hitler-like populist becomes dictator of a fascist United States, or the haunting nightmare of Dalton Trumbo's antiwar classic *Johnny Got His Gun* (1938), whose tragic soldier-narrator is kept alive in alienated misery despite the loss of his arms, legs, eyes, ears, and tongue in the trenches of the First World War? The persistent discovery of deeper and deeper kinship between science fiction and the literary canon with which it is inevitably juxtaposed suggests there may be more than mere bravado behind the declaration of John W. Campbell (whose 1938 ascension to the editorship of *Astounding Science Fiction* marks both the end of the period covered by this book and the beginning of science fiction's "Golden Age") that "'mainstream literature' is actually a special subgroup of the field of science fiction—for science fiction deals with all places in the Universe, and all times in Eternity" (1963, xv). The law of genre, as Jacques Derrida famously observed, is as much a "principle of contamination" as it is a "line of demarcation" (1980, 57); one hundred years after and six hundred and fifty years before *Ralph 124C 41+*, science fiction, like some strange creature out of its own pages, still cannot be kept safely confined in its cage.

IV

THE NOVEL, 1915–1940

24

MODERNISM AND THE INTERNATIONAL NOVEL

BY MARK SCROGGINS

The intellectual backgrounds of modernism have been well charted, and involve a series of radical questionings of the entire Western worldview. By the latter half of the nineteenth century, Charles Darwin's evolutionary theory and the "higher criticism" of the Bible had already shaken literal belief in scripture among the educated classes. On their heels, a series of thinkers in various fields reconceived and undermined received pictures of reality. Karl Marx's works were important less for providing (in the *Communist Manifesto*) a point of crystallization for various revolutionary impulses, than for proposing that human consciousness and culture were determined by economic relationships, and that history itself was a narrative not of great men or redemptive upward progress, but of class struggle. Sigmund Freud's psychoanalysis proposed a similar hermeneutics of unmasking, arguing that the human consciousness—the self-conscious *psyche*, or soul—was to a large degree no more than a socially accreted shell over a core of animalistic and ungovernable drives. Einstein's Theory of Relativity demonstrated with mathematical rigor that science itself, a mainstay of Victorian faith in progress, was not the epistemological bulwark it had seemed, that it was "a construction of the human mind before it [was] a reflection of the world" (Bell 1999, 11). All of these intellectual developments were cast in a metaphysical key by Nietzsche, who had argued that the history of Western philosophy is but a series of systematic masks for the individual "will to power."

Western consciousness, the rhythms of people's apprehension of the world and their communication with one another, was itself in flux during the modernist period. Newly efficient systems of mass transit, the widespread sight of by no means rare but still unsettling flying machines, and the increasing availability of automobiles quickened the basic pace of life, and in some quarters—among the Italian futurists, for example—fostered veritable cults of speed. New technologies of communication, first the telephone and then the wireless, for the first time gave people the experience of *disembodied* voices, an experience crucial, it could be argued, to the verbal textures of poems like T. S. Eliot's *The Waste Land* (1922) and Ezra Pound's *Cantos* (1925) and novels such as James Joyce's *Ulysses* (1922). The rise of the cinema as mass entertainment and self-conscious artistic form provided a sharply provocative, "cool" yet technologically dazzling alternative to the established mimetic forms of opera and live theater.

Of course, mapping the precise connections of these technological and intellectual currents to the multifarious cultural ruptures that make up modernism is a maddeningly imprecise enterprise. At its outset, however, modernism was certainly a European phenomenon. While the United States, with its well-established representative democracy, its flourishing industry, and its hyper-capitalist public ethos, could claim to be the most vigorously *modernizing* nation on earth, American cultural production at the turn of the century was largely timid and conservative. The United States was introduced to international modernism, the conventional story goes, in February 1913 at the International Exhibition of Modern Art in New York—the infamous "Armory Show." The "lunatic fringe" was out in force, President Theodore Roosevelt grumbled in his review of the cubist, futurist, and "Near-Impressionist" works on display, and one waggish American commentator pronounced Marcel Duchamp's *Nude Descending a Staircase* "an explosion in a shingle factory" (Brown 1988, 145, 137). It was the European capitals that had been the most active centers of rupture with nineteenth-century artistic mores, especially Paris, which from the 1880s through the outbreak of the Second World War hosted a bewildering succession of movements in music, literature, and especially the visual arts.

Novelists were listening to the new music, and they were certainly looking at the new painting, and the influence is evident in some correlations between the various postimpressionist artistic movements and the modernist novel. For preimpressionist painters, easel painting was above all a representational art, a way of reproducing reality. The radicalism of impressionists' practice consisted in the degree to which they departed from accepted schemes of pictorial representation (their rejection of conventional color palettes, their disdain for "finish") in order to capture more accurately the impressions of visual phenomena, in the process (perhaps paradoxically) foregrounding the fact that their canvases were flat surfaces smeared with paint, rather than "windows" on the world. Cézanne and the painters that follow him manifested a new impulse toward abstraction, the valorization of geometrical shapes, color values, and patterns of light and shade, and a concomitant recognition of the aesthetic and tactile value of the painting *as medium*, irrespective of its representational value.

This is the classic narrative, most famously advanced by Clement Greenberg, of modernism as "purification" and "self-critique," within each artistic practice, of its "unique medium." One can see how the novel turns to self-examination and purification in the modernist period: in Franz Kafka's stripping back of narrative structures to their parabolic, fairy-tale roots and Joyce's reinvigoration of the novel's links to ancient epic; in a relentless exploration of the potentials of narrative *voice*, incorporating an unprecedented degree of self-consciousness concerning narrative point of view (interior monologue, polyphonic storytelling); and in an intentional foregrounding of prose *style*. As T. S. Eliot observes in his 1937 introduction to Djuna Barnes's *Nightwood* (1936), most novels "obtain what reality they have largely from an accurate rendering of the noises that human beings currently make in their daily simple needs of communication; and what part of a novel is not composed of these noises consists of a prose which is no more alive than that of a competent newspaper writer or government official."

The corrective to such dead, instrumental language is a prose that is "altogether alive," that is at all points consciously considered and stylistically intended. The French novelist Gustave Flaubert, painstaking stylist and relentless deflator of nineteenth-century bourgeois conventions, and the expatriate American Henry James, in whose late work plot and event, the very heartblood of the classic novelist form, are largely displaced by a relentless exploration of mood and implication, are obvious precursors to this type of modernist fiction. But it might be argued as well that in terms of style—whether the limpid clarities of Hemingway, the sonorous and tangled Jacobeanism of Barnes herself, or the oblique abstractions of Gertrude Stein—the modernist novelist wrote a prose that took on many of the qualities of poetry. The cross-fertilizations among the arts and the genres are exceptionally rich in the modernist moment, and while one might write of the "cubist" novel or the "cinematic" novel, one ought not to overlook the *lyric* novel, or the novel whose arrangement resembles less the story told than the poem *constructed*.

The American novel was from its very beginnings a transatlantic affair. American novelists had always been keenly influenced by developments in British fiction, if sometimes their relationship to British writing took the form of outright competition, and the American in Europe had become a standard plot device in American fiction well before Henry James made it the recurrent topos of his novels. James himself had been an expatriate since 1876, and in the first decades of the twentieth century there was a flourishing colony of American writers living in Paris. This Parisian expatriate colony, centered socially around such salons as those of Natalie Barney and Gertrude Stein, the cafés of Montparnasse, and the bookshop Shakespeare and Company (owned by the New Jerseyite Sylvia Beach, who published *Ulysses*), served as something of a conduit for modernist influences to enter American fiction. A number of African American writers found in Paris a cosmopolitan atmosphere largely free of the racism omnipresent in American society, and electric with connections to the global African diaspora. Other Americans came to Paris to partake of European culture, to escape American Prohibition, and to take advantage of favorable postwar exchange rates. While they were there, their own writings were influenced by the innovations roiling European culture, and when they returned to the United States, either for visits or permanently, they brought those innovations home with them.

If Paris was (in Walter Benjamin's phrase) the "capital of the nineteenth century," it also bid fair to be the capital of the modernist revolution, at least in painting. Gertrude Stein settled in Paris in 1903 at the age of twenty-nine, where she (along with her brother Leo) began collecting works by Cézanne, Matisse, Renoir, and the young Spaniard Pablo Picasso. Her salon at the rue de Fleurus eventually became a gathering place for Paris's avant-garde: Picasso, Georges Braque, Henri Rousseau, and such literary figures as Guillaume Apollinaire and Max Jacob were all regular visitors.

Stein is perhaps the most radical of the first generation of American modernists, and while several of her important works can be clearly categorized as "novels," her work as a whole manages to transcend genre and achieve the status of mere "writing." Her first attempt at full-scale narrative was the rather wan, Jamesian *Q. E. D.* (1903). That same year she had begun a family chronicle of undetermined scope, *The Making of Americans*, which she put aside when she sailed for France. In Paris during 1905 and 1906, Stein tried her hand at fiction on a more compact scale. The three long stories (or short novellas) of *Three Lives* (1909) were to a certain extent modeled on Flaubert's *Trois Contes* (1877), especially "Une Cœur Simple," although the middle story, "Melanctha," was a recasting of the Baltimore love affair that had inspired *Q. E. D. Three Lives* is Stein's most extensive excursion in conventional narrative fiction; the stories of three working-class women are rendered in a repetitive, lexically restrained idiom which proves almost hypnotic, narratively effective, and surprisingly moving. The African American dialect of "Melanctha," especially, was singled out by early readers such as Richard Wright as surprisingly "authentic." Some later readers would find Stein's language condescending, even racist (on Stein's appropriation of African American dialect, see Chapter 13 of this volume).

Stein resumed work on *The Making of Americans* in 1906, and finished the last chapters in 1911. (It was not published in full until 1925.) The completed work is a massive book of over nine hundred pages; Stein liked to compare it to Samuel Richardson's *Clarissa* (1749). *The Making of Americans* begins as an American family narrative, a chronicle of the Hersland and Dehning families. As the novel proceeds, however, Stein yields to her fascination with human character and psychology. (She had studied and researched under William James at Radcliffe, and entered medical school at Johns Hopkins intending to become a psychologist.) The novel, whose narrative line is at best tenuous and wandering, becomes a full-scale taxonomy of human character types. As she puts it in "The Making of the Making of Americans" (1935), "I was sure that in a kind of way the enigma of the universe could in this way be solved . . . if I went on and on and on enough I could describe every individual human being that could possibly exist" (142).

The basis of human character, Stein believes, can be discerned in repetition, in the ceaseless "repeating" of behavior and verbal traits that manifests the "rhythm" of each individual psychological type. *The Making of Americans* itself is an enormous exercise in repetition, in which words, phrases, and whole sentences are recycled at almost maddening length:

> Every one then sometime is a whole one to me, every one then sometimes is a whole one in me, some of these do not for long times make a whole one to me inside me. Some of them are a whole one in me and then they go to pieces again inside me, repeating instead comes out of them as pieces to me, pieces of a whole one that only sometimes is a whole one in me. ("Martha Hersland")

Stein aims to capture her characters, she explains in "Composition as Explanation" (1926), in a "continuous present" (524), a verbal idiom that relies on an almost deadening reiteration of the gerund, a continual barrage of "–ing" verbs, so that the individual figures of the novel (never more than shades) become well-nigh indistinguishable in their "living," "loving," "feeling," "being," and so forth. The true drama of *The Making of Americans*, as the passage above indicates, comes to reside not in the doings of its characters or even in the taxonomy of their "repeating," but in the writer's struggle with her Herculean self-imposed task of psychological classification.

After the publication of *Three Lives* in 1909 and the completion of *The Making of Americans* in 1911, deeply influenced by the multiplication of perspectives and the fragmentation of the picture space in the cubist paintings of her friends Picasso and Braque, Stein devoted herself to small-scale, often highly abstract "portraits." In 1914 she published one of the truly epochal modernist works, *Tender Buttons*, a series of "cubist" still lives of "food," "objects," and "rooms." Stein wrote incessantly for the rest of her life, focusing especially on what she called "operas" and "plays," but the various works of her last three decades which she labeled "novels"—*Lucy Church Amiably* (1930), *Ida: A Novel* (1941), *Mrs. Reynolds* (1941, published 1952), and others—are less novels in any recognizable sense than they are explorations into what effect might be gained by hanging the label "novel" upon a loose set of linguistic and narrative meditations. *Lucy Church Amiably*, perhaps the least novelistic of these works, subtitled "A Novel of Romantic beauty and nature and which Looks Like an Engraving," has the outward look of a novel—conventional paragraphing, sequentially numbered chapters—and introduces a number of characters ("Lucy Church," "John Mary," "Simon Therese") early on. But for the most part the book entirely sets aside character and plot in favor of word-play and description; it becomes something of a pastoral diary, more interested in "an appreciation of natural beauty or the beauty of nature hills valleys fields and birds" (ch. 1): "an engraving," as the "Advertisement" has it, "in which there are some people."

Stein's most demanding works—*The Making of Americans*, *Tender Buttons*, the long series of brief prose "portraits"—made her the center of cultish devotion in some limited avant-garde circles. Only later, after the publication of the engaging (and bestselling) *The Autobiography of Alice B. Toklas* (1933) and her triumphant 1934 lecture tour of her homeland, which resulted in *Lectures in America* (1935), did Stein become a media darling, at once derided in the popular press for her "difficult"

writing and celebrated as a kind of homespun idiot savant for her more straightforward pronouncements. During the 1920s, however, she had been a Parisian literary
destination for American writers second only to Joyce himself. Of the younger writers who frequented the house on the rue de Fleurus, Ernest Hemingway and Sherwood Anderson would go on to craft realist styles of exceptional clarity and lexical
simplicity, deeply influenced by Stein's *Three Lives* and by her active blue-penciling
of their manuscripts.

The American poet William Carlos Williams, who had visited Paris but who preferred his New Jersey home to a life of expatriation, would later claim that the
1922 publication of T. S. Eliot's *The Waste Land* had been an "atom bomb" that
destroyed the immediate possibility of a nativist American poetry. James Joyce's
Ulysses, published that same year, had a similarly epochal—if less negative—impact
on American fiction. Indeed, Joyce's immensely anticipated work (the subject of a
groundbreaking, intense, and sometimes unsubtle "underground" publicity campaign) was a novel with which every English-language writer seemed bound to come
to terms. Joyce's multiple narrative voices and narrative styles and his treatment of
fictive time deeply influenced William Faulkner, especially in *The Sound and the
Fury* (1929) and *As I Lay Dying* (1930; on Faulkner as modernist and hemispheric
writer, see Chapter 29 of this volume). Even more important was the technique of
"interior monologue" with which Joyce had experimented in *A Portrait of the Artist
as Young Man* (1916), and which he brought to a high pitch of depth and complexity
in *Ulysses*.

In *The Principles of Psychology* (1890), William James described the processes of
human thought as a "stream of consciousness," a continuous "flow" marked by "substantive" and "transitive" states: "Like a bird's life, it seems to be an alternation of
flights and perchings" (vol. 1, ch. 9). Conventional expository prose, then, as when
a realist author narrates what a character is thinking, is a radical simplification and
formalization of the actual "stream" of human consciousness, a misrepresentation of
the ever-shifting movements of the character's thought and perception. In contrast,
Joyce's "interior monologue" aims directly to present the "stream" of his character's
thoughts, unmediated by the streamlining and subordinating demands of traditional narration. In the most characteristic chapters of *Ulysses*, we are immersed in
the consciousness of Joyce's protagonist, Leopold Bloom, following his observations,
memories, anticipations, and reveries, with only very occasional sentences of third-
person narration indicating what he is actually *doing*.

Interior monologue can make for a strenuous reading experience, forcing the
reader constantly to make connections among the specificities of a character's
thought, to reconstruct the whole of a phenomenal world from an array of perceived particulars. But for many modernist writers, interior monologue carried the
promise of a thoroughgoing revolution in the representation of interiority, a new,
even more radical mimetic "realism," and there were few modernist novelists who
did not at least dabble in the technique. A Joycean interior monologue marks much

of Faulkner's greatest fiction, and was pursued as well by such Americans as John Dos Passos, in his *U. S. A.* trilogy (*The 42nd Parallel* [1930], *1919* [1932], and *The Big Money* [1936]), Henry Miller, in *Tropic of Cancer* (1934) and other works, and Henry Roth, in *Call It Sleep* (1934).

On its face, Dos Passos's *U. S. A.* is one of the most formally disparate and ostensibly innovative American modernist novels. As Dos Passos describes it in the overture to the trilogy's single-volume publication, the work aims to present a panoramic portrait of the nation as a whole, woven together in the language of its citizenry: "U. S. A. is the slice of a continent. U. S. A. is a group of holding companies, some aggregations of trade unions, a set of laws bound in calf, a radio network. . . . But mostly U. S. A. is the speech of its people." Dos Passos's earlier urban novel, *Manhattan Transfer* (1925), was clearly influenced by *Ulysses*, *The Waste Land*, and Sergei Eisenstein's cinematic montage, but the three novels of *U. S. A.* up the ante by alternating at least four radically different narrative modes: "newsreel" sections, which splice together in quick *Waste Land*–like collage newspaper headlines, texts from popular journalism, and fragments of popular songs; brief biographies, at times lineated like poetry, of such representative figures as socialist labor leaders Eugene Debs and Big Bill Haywood, economist Thorstein Veblen, Henry Ford, and film star Rudolph Valentino; "camera eye" sections, which trace the youth and maturation of a Dos Passos–like figure in second person interior monologue; and straightforwardly realistic narrative sections.

In the sharply polarized political climate of the Great Depression, Dos Passos's sympathies were decisively with the radical Left, whose literary organs had for some time been promoting an aesthetic of "Socialist Realism" as the only permissible idiom for the socially responsible artist. The modernist collision of modes that structures *U. S. A.* certainly presents a complication of the mode of classic socially engaged realism made familiar by Norris, Dreiser, and Upton Sinclair, and would seem to transcend not merely socialist realism but even the familiar boundaries of novelistic expression. The degree to which the "newsreel" and "camera eye" sections, despite their up-to-date monikers, actually adapt a cinematic vocabulary, however, is rather small: instead they exploit rather well-established modernist *literary* idioms, the collage and the interior monologue, respectively. And it is difficult to avoid the conclusion, by the end of the trilogy, that far more of Dos Passos's energy and literary passion has been invested in his various realist narrative sections than in the "newreels," "camera eyes," or capsule biographies. *U. S. A.* is less a genre-spanning modernist monument on the order of *Ulysses* than a series of realist novellas punctuated by various formally heterogeneous interludes.

Roth's *Call It Sleep*, greeted with considerable critical acclaim upon its publication in the depths of the Depression, explores a more thoroughgoing modernist idiom. In its narrative voice it frequently evokes *Ulysses*, and its plot reminds one of *Portrait of the Artist as a Young Man*, which like *Call It Sleep* draws on the traditions of the *Bildungsroman*. *Call It Sleep* follows the New York childhood of the Jewish immigrant boy David Schearl. Although a bright child, David is only dimly aware of the sources of the discord within his own family, the sexual tensions that make him, his long-suffering mother, and his half-mad father into a paradigmatic Oedipal triangle. David's childhood in the squalid tenements of Brooklyn and lower Manhattan is presented in a narrative voice that modulates between grimy realism and high lyricism, between precise visual description and muddled interior monologue. While David has known no other world than New York, he is caught between the worlds of his parents' Galician past and a larger American scene of which he has only glimpses.

Roth strikingly renders the immigrant child's linguistic and spiritual plight in a bravura scene set in David's Hebrew school, or cheder, where a whole range of linguistic registers struggle one with another: the rabbi's Yiddish, translated into a graceful, formal English; the boys' phonetically rendered, almost incomprehensible New York accents as they squabble among themselves, interspersed with their recitation of untranslated Hebrew (none of them can understand what they are reading); and David's own agonized interior monologue, as he tries to understand the import of a passage of Isaiah the rabbi has just paraphrased, in which the prophet's lips are purified by the touch of a red-hot coal (bk. 3, ch. 4). The scene represents a culmination of a whole genealogy of classroom moments, from *Hard Times's* (1854) Mr. Gradgrind, to *Jane Eyre's* (1847) Lowood School, down to Stephen Dedalus's schoolroom humiliation in the first chapter of *A Portrait of the Artist as a Young Man*. Like Stephen's, David's classroom ordeal ultimately ends in triumph, the rabbi praising him as having a "true Yiddish head," but Roth has vividly depicted how the boy's first awareness of transcendence, of avenging deity, has come about in a moment of chaotic linguistic conflict.

At the end of *Call It Sleep*, having brought all of the various conflicts of the novel to a tangled (and frankly rather far-fetched) climax—David has let an admired Gentile friend who has earlier given him a rosary abuse his cousin Esther; in panic, he has told Reb Yikel that he is not his parents' son, but the child of a deceased aunt and her Gentile lover; the rabbi brings this news to David's parents, just as his uncle arrives to confront them about Esther—David flees the apartment and, in search of some sort of escape or transcendence, electrocutes himself on a streetcar rail (obviously conflated in his mind with the Prophet Isaiah's burning coal). This long scene, frantic with emotion and activity, is narrated in a fragmentary, hallucinatory kaleidoscope of languages: the brutal and obscene banter of various barflies, workers, and other adult New Yorkers is juxtaposed to the urgent narrative prose of David's frantic flight and to his own inchoate thoughts and impulses, rendered in italicized, lineated verse lines. The final pages of the novel, as the family reaches a kind of rapprochement after David's electrical shock, settle back into free indirect discourse centered around the boy's own observations, his sense of triumph and satisfaction.

Call It Sleep spent three decades as a forgotten classic before it was reissued in 1964 (Roth himself ceased writing between the early 1940s and the late 1970s), but in the past half-century it has become increasingly recognized as a highly significant achievement in modernist fiction. Building on Joyce's depiction of Irish subjectivity under British political and cultural hegemony, *Call It Sleep* forcefully adapts the techniques of interior monologue and polyphonic montage to explore the first-generation Jewish American experience. If Roth's novel lacks the dazzling architectonics of *Ulysses*, it perhaps compensates for its occasional shapelessness with the intensity of cross-cut linguistic registers by which it represents David Schearl's experience of growing up between cultures and among languages.

Perhaps the greatest American modernist novelist was the Mississippi writer William Faulkner, who deployed all of the narrative techniques of Joyce and the verbal richness of William Butler Yeats and the French symbolics in a loving and pitiless examination of the most economically and culturally backward region of the States, the American South. In *The Sound and the Fury, As I Lay Dying, Light in August* (1932), and *Absalom, Absalom!* (1936), Faulkner produced a quartet of novels that bear comparison with the greatest works of Joyce, Marcel Proust, D. H. Lawrence, or Virginia Woolf. But he was by no means the only Southern American writer for whom modernism provided an idiom by which to address the cruel and tragic legacy of the South's "peculiar institution."

Evelyn Scott's *The Wave* (1929) was published the same year as *The Sound and The Fury*, and Scott, born and raised in Tennessee and by that point a well-established novelist and poet, contributed an essay on Faulkner's work that was circulated along with advance copies of his novel. While Faulkner dramatized the downfall of a family of Mississippi "gentry" through techniques of interior monologue that readers still find bewildering, Scott's *The Wave* aims to depict the whole of the American Civil War through a kaleidoscopic narrative which, in its details, remains largely realistic, but which in its larger structure is a work of radical modernist collage.

Scott describes the technique of her novel through an epigraph from a science textbook, Philip Lake's *Physical Geography*:

> The waves travel in some definite direction, but a cork thrown into the water does not travel with the waves. It moves up and down, to and fro, but unless it is blown by the wind or carried by a current it returns to the same position with each wave and does not permanently leave its place. . . . In deep water the motion of the particle at the surface [of the wave] is nearly circular.

The titular "wave" of Scott's novel is the Civil War, a violent and epochal disturbance that for four years had roiled American society from its highest to its lowest quarters. *The Wave* depicts the war from its very beginnings, the bombardment of Fort Sumter in April 1861, to its immediate aftermath, the "Grand Review" of the victorious Union armies in Washington in May 1865.

Scott clearly works with an awareness of the tradition of the historical novel from Walter Scott to Tolstoy, and like them her focus is not primarily on the "great men" of history but on the more "ordinary" folk caught up in the movement of great events. Where Evelyn Scott breaks radically with the tradition of the historical novel, and with novelist tradition in general, is in entirely renouncing continuity of plot and continuity of character. *The Wave* consists of some hundred-odd brief vignettes, ranging from two to fifteen pages, presented in chronological order: the order, that is, of their occurrence over the course of the war. But aside from a few prominent figures who appear in more than one section (General Ulysses Grant, President Abraham Lincoln), each vignette, no matter how fleeting, introduces a new character or set of characters.

The Wave is populated by an astonishing range of personages, black and white, slave and free, Northern and Southern, from all levels of society: enlisted men and officers from both Union and Confederate armies, as well as a number of deserters; the wives, fiancées, mothers, and other relatives of the men at the front; a pair of East Tennessee partisans hunting Confederate soldiers; a New Orleans streetwalker; a Jewish family in Vicksburg; a well-to-do Vermont businessman and his wife; a Polish laborer in an East River ironworks; and many, many more. The "wave" of the war sweeps all before it over its four-year course, but the narrative eye of Scott's *The Wave* focuses only briefly on each set of the individuals caught up in it, just as a physical wave momentarily displaces a given set of particles of water (or "a cork thrown in the water") before moving on.

The narrative technique of *The Wave*, taken vignette by vignette, is a more or less realist one, although there is a certain amount of interior monologue in many of the vignettes, and an odd use of quotation marks, by which the narrative voice sets off words or phrases characteristic of the character being followed. It is the novel's over-all structure that is strikingly radical. Scott certainly learned something of her shift-ing viewpoint from Leo Tolstoy (as in his tour-de-force multiviewed presentation of the Battle of Borodino in *War and Peace*), but the end-result is closer to Ezra Pound's *Cantos*, in which the poet builds up his larger structures by the mosaiclike juxta-position of disparate materials and scenes. The *New York Herald Tribune*'s reviewer keenly notes the element of cinematic montage in Scott's form; one is reminded of the crowd scenes in Eisenstein's *Battleship Potemkin*, where the camera lingers upon and shifts from character to character in order to build up a detailed impression of the whole.

Djuna Barnes's first novel, *Ryder* (1928), showed that its author had learned the lessons of *Ulysses* well, although Barnes, who had made a name as a journalist in New York and illustrated her early books with masterful drawings whose styles range from the decadence of Aubrey Beardsley to complex pastiches of French folk art, was no mere acolyte of Joyce's. *Ryder* treats, in a lightly veiled form, Barnes's own early life (like all of her major works, it is a roman à clef). Barnes's own stand-in in the novel is the young Julie Ryder, but its real center of interest is her father, Wendell Ryder, a polygamous artist and man of letters. The curve of the narrative is broad: *Ryder* begins by recounting the parentage of Wendell's mother, Sophia, and winds its way through three generations of the family, ending with the ambiguous breakup of the household Wendell has established with his wife, Amelia, his mistress, Kate, and the two women's eight children.

Ryder's plot is at once lurid and inconsequential, continually interrupted by divagations, emotional monologues, and quasi-philosophical dialogues. Indeed, one is not far into the book before it becomes clear that the forward movement of the narrative is of far less importance than the opportunities the characters' relationships provide for virtuosic displays of verbal *style*. In contrast to Hemingway or Anderson, who were forging styles of exceptional clarity, lucidity, and reticence, Barnes revels in the rich excess of Elizabethan and Jacobean prose—Thomas Nashe, Robert Burton, Sir Thomas Urquhart's Rabelais. The whole of the chapter "Rape and Repining!" is a prose lament for the loss of innocence: "'Sblood's Death! Is it right, m'Lords? Ravished, and the Cream not yet risen in the Pantry! Ravished, and the Weather Fork not turned twice upon its Vane! Ravished, and no Star pricked upon its point!" (ch. 5). Several chapters are written in pseudo-Chaucerian pentameter couplets, one (like *Ulysses*'s "Circe") is presented as a dramatic scene, and yet another is the direct transcript of Sophia Ryder's Last Will and Testament.

The baroque stylistic exercises of *Ryder* stand in sharp contrast to the novel's earthy, even sordid events, most of which involve the human being's necessary and painful embodiment, its entrapment within a fleshly vessel continually racked by physical desire and somatic enfeeblement. For the novel's female characters, in particular Amelia, Kate, and Wendell's mother, Sophia, embodiment consists of a hateful subjection to the demands of childbearing and motherhood, and to desire for an unworthy man. For Wendell himself, embodiment thwarts his higher aesthetic aspirations by making him a slave to carnal desire, a perpetual *fécondateur*. As Dr. Matthew O'Connor, the novel's only other significant male character, remarks, "a man's member is like a mighty bloodhound, and a man's body, forsooth, nothing but the staple it tugs at" (ch. 49). The effect of this sordid story's unfolding in the language of Nashe, Middleton, or Chaucer is striking, and twofold: on the one hand, Barnes is able to treat in detail physiological matters which, if addressed in contemporary English, would almost certainly have resulted in her being prosecuted for obscenity. (*Ulysses*, after all, was banned in both Great Britain and the United States, and several of Barnes's illustrations, as well as a few passages of text, were expurgated from the 1928 Liveright publication of *Ryder*.) On the other hand, while dealing with matters of the bathroom and bedroom in a highly wrought, archaic English might cast a "literary" obliquity upon them, it simultaneously serves to underline the distance between the beauties and complexities of the aesthetic intellect and the gritty, lubricious depths into which that intellect is drawn by the desires of the flesh.

Ladies Almanack (1928), published the same year as *Ryder*, is a mostly plotless series of vignettes and portraits of the expatriate lesbian community centered on Natalie Clifford Barney's Paris salon. If anything, its language—highly wrought, shot through with sexual double entendre, and remarkably Rabelaisian—is even more mannered than that of *Ryder*, but while *Ryder* makes one long, sustained howl at the indignities of somatic existence, *Ladies Almanack* is content to punctuate an enthusiastic celebration of feminine desire and female homosociality with occasional laments about the social condition of women. *Ladies Almanack* is a striking example of modernist stylistic pastiche, recasting the forms of early modern pamphlet literature to represent the experiences and attitudes of the most countercultural, forward-looking subculture of its own day.

Barnes's true triumph, however, is the haunting *Nightwood,* a novel of somewhat more restrained verbal texture than her earlier books, but of unusual power and emotional intensity. *Nightwood* narrates, in the relationship of the characters Nora Flood and Robin Vote, Barnes's own ill-fated love affair with the artist Thelma Wood. The novel's cast is compact but unforgettable: the factitious "Baron" Felix Volkbein, half-Jewish and obsequiously obsessed with European aristocracy; his American wife, Robin Vote, who bears him a child and abandons them both, moving in with the devoted Nora; the "squatter" Jenny Petherbridge, who battens upon other's loves and enthusiasms, and who steals Robin from Nora; and, reappearing from *Ryder,* the "gynecologist" Dr. Matthew O'Connor, whose long, anguished monologues make up most of the second half of *Nightwood.* (In *Ryder* Matthew is presented as an obstetrician, bringing Wendell's numerous children into the world; in *Nightwood* he seems to practice mostly as an abortionist.)

The text of *Nightwood* consists mostly of people talking, the baroque and extravagant outpourings of a set of characters in deep distress. Felix mourns his wife's abandonment, and frets over the future of their sickly and religiously fixated young son, "Mentally deficient and emotionally excessive, an addict to death" (1936, "Where the Tree Falls"). Nora grieves over Robin, who continually returns to the "night" of barrooms and random lovers, but who refuses entirely to sever the two women's relationship. "You've got to listen!" Nora tells the doctor,

> She would come back to me after a night all over the city and lie down beside me and she would say, "I want to make everyone happy," and her mouth was drawn down. "I want everyone to be gay, gay. Only you," she said, holding me, "only you, you mustn't be gay or happy, not like that it's not for you, only for everyone else in the world."

"Everything we can't bear in this world," Nora mourns, "some day we find it in one person, and love it all at once" ("Go Down, Matthew"). Matthew himself is perhaps the most miserable of all the characters: not merely is he the repository into which they pour their varied anguishes, but he is tormented by his own identity as a homosexual, his own homoerotic desire:

> *Misericordia,* am I not the girl to know of what I speak? We go to our Houses by our nature—and our nature, no matter how it is, we all have to stand—as for me, so God has made me, my house is the pissing port. ("Watchman, What of the Night?")

The only one of *Nightwood*'s characters who is immune to such lacerating despair is Robin, for Robin is beyond, or rather *before*, human morality: indeed, she is not entirely human. Time and again, she is represented in images of animality; she is a creature who knows affection, desire, and the need for companionship, but she has never entered the order of human morality. She knows neither self-consciousness nor guilt, and is no more responsible for her actions than a cat or dog.

In his preface to the first American edition of *Nightwood*, T. S. Eliot was anxious to dissociate the misery the novel's characters suffer from their homoerotic attachments: "the book," he writes, "is not a psychopathic study." Instead, Eliot argues, it is a study of "universal" "human misery and bondage": "It seems to me that all of us, so far as we attach ourselves to created objects and surrender our wills to temporal ends, are eaten by the same worm." While this universalizing "moral" reading, clearly in keeping with Eliot's Anglican Christianity (although quite Spinozan, as well), is to a certain degree plausible—there is as much misery to be found in heterosexual as in homosexual relationships—it has the effect of ironing out what is most striking in the characters' own self-diagnoses. While lesbian relationships are treated with a light, enthusiastic hand in *Ladies Almanack*, in *Nightwood* Nora and Matthew lament their own homoerotic desire as not a social, but an *ontological* paradox. "A man is another person," Nora tells the doctor, "a woman is yourself, caught as you turn in panic; on her mouth you kiss your own." When she tells him of Robin's destroying the doll she had given her, he replies, "The last doll, given to age, is the girl who should have been a boy, and the boy who should have been a girl." In the end, however, Nora's deepest pain lies in the realization that her wayward lover is not merely beyond gender, but beyond humanity itself: "I have been loved," she said, "by something strange, and it has forgotten me" ("Go Down, Matthew").

"Man was born damned and innocent from the start, and wretchedly—as he must—on these two themes—whistles his tune," the doctor tells Felix ("Where the Tree Falls"), a fair representation of *Nightwood*'s language at its strongest: a rhetoric wholly apart from conventional realism, but by no means laced with the archaisms of *Ryder* and *Ladies Almanack*; a language showing the same compressed metaphoricity as late Shakespeare or Thomas Middleton. In his preface, Eliot claims that the novel "will appeal primarily to readers of poetry"; this "does not mean that it is not a novel, but that it is so good a novel that only sensibilities trained on poetry can wholly appreciate it." By this Eliot implies that *Nightwood*, in contrast to most prose fiction, is thoroughly "written," is composed in language raised to "the first intensity." But Eliot's remark that the novel's final chapter, which he had initially thought "superfluous," is actually "essential, both dramatically and *musically*," suggests that *Nightwood*'s affinities to modernist poetry might be as much *formal* as they are linguistic—a suggestion pursued by Joseph Frank in his influential essay "Spatial Form in Modern Literature."

The logic of the novel has traditionally been one of *time*, of the forward temporal movement of progressive narrative; according to Frank, in such modernist novels as *Ulysses*, Proust's *À la Recherche du Temps Perdu*, and preeminently *Nightwood*, temporal progression has been displaced by the "spatial" organization of internal elements—an organizational mode pioneered in such modernist poems as *The Waste Land* and *The Cantos*. The work is to be experienced not as a narrative that unfolds over time, but all at once, as a structure apprehended in a (ideal) single moment. (This is the import of Frank's famous comment that in *Ulysses* "Joyce cannot be read—he can only be reread" [1982, 52].) In Barnes's novel, significant plot is purposefully attenuated, is forwarded only in offhand moments; the real richness of the book lies in its cunning patterns of language, imagery, and symbol: "The eight chapters of *Nightwood* are like searchlights, probing the darkness each from a different direction yet ultimately illuminating the same entanglement of the human spirit" (59). Frank argues that "spatial form" in the novel is even analogous to the abstractions of cubist painting: "the naturalistic principle has lost its dominance" in Barnes's work; "We are asked only to accept the work of art as an autonomous structure giving us an individual vision of reality; and the question of the relation of this vision to an extra-artistic 'objective' world has ceased to have any fundamental importance" (57).

Barnes pressed the novel to an extreme of both painterly and poetic abstraction in *Nightwood*, but there were few Americans to accompany or follow her. Unsurprisingly, some of the more conventionally "lyrical" novels of the modern period were written by novelists who were themselves poets. The American poet H. D. (Hilda Doolittle) came to prominence in years before the First World War as a member of the "imagists," promoted by Ezra Pound; indeed, it was one of her short poems that inspired Pound to name and launch the "movement." From the early twenties on, however, H. D. devoted a large proportion of her creative energies to writing novels. Some of them, such as *Palimpsest* (1926) and *Hedylus* (1928), were set in the ancient world, following through on the classicism of H. D.'s earlier poetry. Others, such as the books collectively known as the "Madrigal" cycle—*Paint It Today* (1921, published 1992), *Asphodel* (1921–22, published 1992), *HER* (1927, published 1981), and *Bid Me To Live* (1939, 1949, published 1960)—were lightly veiled autobiography, vividly and impressionistically depicting the poet's struggles with her own ambiguous sexuality and with the influence of the men who would channel and claim her creativity.

The modernism of these novels lies in their language, H. D.'s "prosodies of otherness in the textures of prose," as Rachel Blau DuPlessis describes it (1986, 67). Action, activity, is presented only obliquely; the narrative's focus is upon the protagonist's impressions of and reactions to what happens. Indeed, as DuPlessis notes in reference to *HER*, the narrative voice at times becomes positively cinematic: "there are freeze frames, strange camera angles, intense close-ups of objects, fades, interesting montages or superimpositions of eyes, of pools, of concentric circles" (66–67). While its prose is rather more straightforward than that of the "Madrigal" works, *Palimpsest* is probably the most formally innovative of H. D.'s novels. A palimpsest is a piece of parchment that has been imperfectly erased and then overwritten, so that the earlier text is still faintly visible: an emblem of H. D.'s method in the three long narratives that make up *Palimpsest*— "Hipparchia," set in 75 B.C.E. Rome, "Murex," in London during and after the First World War, and "Secret Name," among Egyptian archaeological sites in 1926—in which the conquests and gender conflicts of classical antiquity are counterpointed to those of contemporary life (H. D.'s own version of Eliot's "mythic method"), and in which each story is in some sense a revision or overwriting of the others. All of them, that is, undertake the recovery of a font of feminine vitality and creativity beneath the aesthetic and political excrescences of male-centered history and culture.

If H. D., reared in Pennsylvania but spending most of her adult life in England and Switzerland, emblematizes the American expatriate modernist experience, the poet Mina Loy represents modernist internationalism in its purest form. Born in London to a Jewish father and a Gentile mother, she moved to Paris in 1903, spent time in Stein's circle, then migrated to Italy, where she associated closely with the futurists. She was in New York for several long stretches, becoming an integral member of that city's art world, and spent the last decades of her life in Aspen, Colorado. She is as "stateless" an artist as could be imagined, at home only in a cosmopolitan urban environment (whether Paris, New York, Berlin, or Florence), in language itself, and in the visual and plastic arts.

While Loy is best known for her emotionally charged but intellectually dense poems (Pound considered her a prime example of "logopœia," "the dance of the intellect among words" ["Others," 1918]), like Wyndham Lewis she considered herself as much an artist as a writer, producing drawings, paintings, sculpture, and collages, and designing lampshades and other decorative items. Her only novel, *Insel* (composed in the late 1930s, published 1991), takes place in the Parisian art world of the 1930s, and centers upon the character Insel, whom Loy models upon the impoverished German surrealist painter Richard Oelze. The novel documents the struggle for creativity, for identity even, between the narrator (Loy herself) and the spectacularly needy, parasitic Insel, an artist whose radical surrealism of manner and outlook seem inborn and go well beyond any of the programmatic aesthetics of the "official" French group headed by André Breton: as the narrator quips, "he's too surrealistic for the surrealists" (ch. 16).

Insel's narrative voice is for the most part measured and tightly controlled, but at times slides vertiginously into surrealist territory:

> The glare in Capoulards Café grew dim. Insel's brain floated up from his head, unraveled, projected its convolutions. They straightened in endless lines across a limitless canvas, a map of imminent directions. On the whole of space were only a few signboards on which grew hands, alive and beckoning. (ch. 25)

The narrator, herself an artist and writer, must defend herself against Insel's misogynist, antinomian surrealisms, and the surrealism her narrative voice takes on is at once an incursion of Insel's aesthetic into her language and a kind of defensive measure, an outbidding of the artist on his own terms. In part, the novel represents Loy's rejection of the surrealist movement (*Insel*'s editor, Elizabeth Arnold, points out that the novel may well be to some degree modeled on Breton's *Nadja* [1928]), as she had earlier rejected the futurists—not a rejection of the psychological insights of surrealism, or of futurism's vision of the velocity of the present, but of the subordinate place into which both of those movements relegated women. When *Insel*'s narrator decisively casts off the painter and his influence in the novel's last pages, it marks a final moment in Loy's successive rejections of the "movements" by which much of international modernism had structured itself, a declaration of independence of the individual, internationalist, feminine creative intelligence.

Loy's *Insel*, like *The Making of Americans*, *U. S. A.*, *The Wave*, *Nightwood*, and any number of other American modernist novels, is sui generis. The modernist novel in the hands of American writers, like American modernism in all the arts, is less a participation in some coordinated avant-garde than a series of scrappy, individualistic, ad hoc interventions in the larger international discourse of the early twentieth century: less a matter of programmatic experimentation than of finding, in the words of Wallace Stevens's "Of Modern Poetry" (1942), "what will suffice." The American modernist novelists seized upon and extended the experiments in language and form they found already fomenting in European writing, they initiated some pathbreaking experiments themselves, and they broke important ground in the representation of history, of social struggle, of the experience of ethnic minorities, and of female and queer subjectivity. Theirs was in many ways a series of isolated achievements: it is arguable whether they began any coherent or continuous "tradition" in American writing. But it is clear that they produced a number of enormously impressive works.

25

THE NOVEL AND THE RISE OF SOCIAL SCIENCE

BY SUSAN HEGEMAN

Although the social sciences—the field of inquiry shared by such diverse disciplines as anthropology, sociology, economics, political science, and psychology—seem to be extremely heterogeneous in terms of methods and objects of study, they could all be described as having their origin in a common pursuit: the study of modernity and its others, including peasants, women, and virtually all non-European peoples. Or, more precisely, this was the central uniting effort of such discursive founders of the social sciences as Adam Smith, J. G. Herder, Emile Durkheim, Max Weber, Georg Simmel, Sigmund Freud, and Karl Marx. These and other European thinkers developed the central narratives for describing what they took to be the very special state of modern society, the complex behavior of modern people, and the emergence of modernity from presumably more primitive and fundamental ways of life.

One might imagine that America—a modern society formed in the cauldrons of New World encounter, the slave ship, and the global push and pull of labor in the development of industrial capitalism—would be the perfect laboratory for developing this narrative. Indeed, it would become so in some small ways. Karl Marx was fascinated by the early ethnographic work of Lewis Henry Morgan, whose close description of the cultures of the Indians of upstate New York helped Marx conceptualize the historical development of complex civilizations out of more basic social states. Somewhat later, Max Weber would use his close knowledge of Protestant religious communities in the United States to aid him in theorizing the relationship between religion and the transition from feudalism to capitalism. But it is notable that throughout the nineteenth century especially, American social scientists themselves left the issue of modernity largely to the Europeans. Instead, they were busy constructing what is arguably a divergent tradition, less historicist than the Europeans and more heavily marked by both scientism and liberal individualism.

In *The Origins of American Social Science,* Dorothy Ross has explained this difference, especially in the years before the Civil War, by way of the influence of the idea of American exceptionalism, the widespread belief that America had a providential place in history that set it apart from the standard story of modernity embedded in the struggles and turmoil of old Europe (1991). However, another factor was certainly the American obsession with race. Understood as an innate property of individuals, race served as a catchall concept that helped explain and naturalize the social hierarchy. Historical facts such as African slavery and the Indian genocide as well as social problems like poverty, criminality, and sexual deviance were all understood to be artifacts of the different capacities of the various races of humanity, which included not only blacks and indigenous people, but also various types that subsequently came to be considered white, including Jews, Sicilians, Bohemians, and the Irish. This preoccupation with racial theory also inclined American social scientists not towards theorizations of modernity and its dramatic histories, but to inquiry modeled on the tools and suppositions of the natural sciences, especially anatomy, physiology, and natural history. Nineteenth-century American social science characteristically accounted for differences, divisions, and conflicts as facts written on the human body, and sought immutable scientistic laws to account for the apparent epiphenomena of historical change.

As the nineteenth century drew to a close, however, both the American social sciences and the novel changed in ways so that their interests and approaches converged. Most generally, in this moment of profound social instability and change, it became increasingly difficult for Americans to understand themselves in the nineteenth century's exceptionalist mode as a nation of yeomen farmers or pioneers. From the perspective of, say, Lower Manhattan, in 1900 the most densely populated place on earth, the models of old Europe—as exemplified, for example, by the urban tumult of Paris or London—seemed more relevant than ever. America, too, was finally and widely understood to be in the grips of the heretofore European narrative of modernity. As Gertrude Stein was fond of saying, America was not a new land, but rather "the oldest country in the world," because it had reached twentieth-century modernity first. America would soon become modernity's exemplary case.

The Novel, the Social Sciences, and the Theme of Modernity

The decades around the turn of the twentieth century, a period of formation and transition into what would eventually be recognizable as the modern academic social scientific disciplines, saw a great deal of activity devoted to the basic project of information gathering. With the closure of the frontier and the subjection of indigenous populations, it was now possible to see American Indians and other indigenes not as military threats, but as inevitable victims in the story of modernity's advance. Moreover, the dispirited existences of many "pacified" Indians in the early reservation era suggested to many that American Indians and their ways of life were rapidly dying out. The task, therefore, of "collecting" and "salvaging" the remains of Indian traditions—rich troves of indigenous artifacts, folklore, language, and aesthetic practices—was considered an urgent project. In another way, the story of American modernity required a new factual investigation of a host of its more unsavory consequences, including urban poverty, vice, and crime, immigration and immigrant communities, interracial conflict, labor and housing conditions, and much more.

The fieldworkers of the late-nineteenth century—from such diverse institutional sites as the US Geological Survey, the Bureau of American Ethnology, the Bureau of Indian Affairs, the various fledgling natural history museums, the urban anti-vice committees, and the settlement house movement—were often subsequently displaced and derided in histories of the social sciences as "amateur" ethnographers, adventurers, journalists, memoirists, and social housekeepers. Yet their work often formed both the database and methodology of the modern American social sciences. Notable figures here include Jacob Riis, John Wesley Powell, James Mooney, Frank Hamilton Cushing, Charles Eastman, Frances Densmore, Francis La Flesche, and Alice Fletcher. But the preeminent example in this respect is Jane Addams, founder of the American settlement house movement, and arguably one of the most important early figures in American sociology. In particular, *Hull-House Maps and Papers* (1895), written in collaboration with other Hull-House residents, established many of the central concerns of twentieth century American sociology, including the study of immigrant communities and urban poverty. Moreover, it represents a very early instantiation of the systemic and spatial study of urban areas—a method that would later come to be associated with the United States' most prominent sociology department at Addams's neighboring University of Chicago.

Unsurprisingly, many literary and journalistic writers shared the general thematic interest in American modernity with these social scientific writers. Charles Chesnutt, Mark Twain, and George Washington Cable delineated the paradoxes and absurdities of the "color line." Stephen Crane and Theodore Dreiser tracked the figure of the working girl, and Jack London that of the hobo: twin obsessions of the decades around the turn of the century that served as gendered figures for conceptualizing industrialization, urbanization, and the proletarianization of vast populations from the rural peripheries of Europe and North America. Frank Norris's unfinished "Epic of the Wheat" (*The Octopus* [1901], and *The Pit* [1903]) promised a synoptic look at the ways a basic food product was subject to the ever-more complicated systems of corporate farming, transportation, and commodification. Harold Frederic's *The Damnation of Theron Ware* (1896) addressed the challenges to traditional Protestant communities by ethnic diversity and new scientific and philosophical beliefs.

As the twentieth century dawned, this confluence between the social sciences and the novel became ever more pronounced. New ideas and trends in both the arts and social sciences were heavily influenced by ideas emanating from Europe.

In the academic social sciences, this European influence came via the prestige of the German university system, where many of the most prominent founding figures in the American academic social sciences received at least some of their training. Meanwhile, it was hard not to see that European artists were involved in something altogether new and exciting: a spirit of innovation and experimentation that would go under the collective rubric of modernism. As the term suggests, modernism was also involved in the project of apprehending modernity. Indeed, its experimental drive emerged from a new sense of the difficulty of this very project. Whereas for the realists and naturalists there was some sense of the possibility of grasping and conveying the social totality, the modernists were more impressed by the ineffable nature of modern life's disruptions, not only of experience, but also of the very possibility of representation. Experimentation in modes of representation naturally followed suit, as modernist artists attempted to find new ways to get at the complexity and confusion of modern existence. It is in this sense most generally that American social scientists and modernist artists found their common ground (on experimentation and the modernist novel, see Chapter 24 of this volume).

There was also a more literal common ground to be found between the writers and social scientists of the early twentieth century. Because of their proximity to two of the most significant, and distinctively American, social scientific institutions—the Sociology Department at the University of Chicago, and the Anthropology Department at Columbia University—the vibrant bohemian enclaves of New York and Chicago became especially important sites for intellectual exchanges between the worlds of letters and the social sciences. It was here that a new kind of intellectual also emerged, for whom the generic boundaries of journalism, fiction, memoir, political pamphlet, exposé, ethnography, and social theory were increasingly fluid.

New York and Boasian Anthropology

For the assorted radicals, artists, and intellectuals who congregated there, one of the attractions of the bohemian colony in Greenwich Village was its proximity to the city's immigrant neighborhoods. As the radical journalist John Reed would put it, "Within a block of my house was all the adventure in the world; within a mile was every foreign country" (qtd. in Kazin 1995, 170). In other words, those who found their way to the polyglot world of lower Manhattan often had a touristic, if not fully ethnographic, curiosity about their neighbors. Hutchins Hapgood, a journalist from the Midwest who would go on to help found the Provincetown Players, wrote a number of books that offered journalistic forays into New York's subcultures, including *Autobiography of a Thief* (1903) and more famously, *The Spirit of the Ghetto* (1902), which offered a survey of the Jewish neighborhood of Manhattan's

Lower East Side. Illustrated by Jacob Epstein (later to become an important modernist sculptor) and significantly aided in its research by the immigrant novelist and socialist newspaperman Abraham Cahan, *The Spirit of the Ghetto* went well beyond a typical muckraking account of an impoverished and overcrowded corner of the city. Instead, it focused on the cultural and intellectual life of immigrants who had brought with them not only Jewish religious traditions and scholarship, but also a wealth of modern ideas and attitudes developed in the capitals of Eastern Europe. Hapgood described a community as passionately invested in the newer ideas (embodied in such writers as Henrik Ibsen and Fyodor Dostoyevsky) as the bohemians, and yet also culturally alien to the middle class Protestants who made up Greenwich Village's "advanced" cultural and artistic circles. As such, the Jewish ghetto also seemed to offer both spiritual and cultural resources to the bohemians that promised to help destabilize the conventional attitudes of the dominant society. Not much later, a number of Villagers—notably Hapgood's close associate Mabel Dodge Luhan—would transfer this desire for cultural alterity onto American Indians. She, and a significant handful of writers, painters, and free thinkers including the painters Georgia O'Keeffe and John Sloan and the British novelist D. H. Lawrence would decamp to Taos, New Mexico, where they could take inspiration from the desert scenery and the rich cultural resources of the proximate Pueblo Indians.

Meanwhile, a new cadre of young anthropologists—many of them immigrants and the products of the ethnic neighborhoods that the bohemians found so enchanting—were discovering bohemia. One such figure, Robert Lowie, who studied with the eminent Franz Boas at Columbia University, described the deliriously theatrical scene at one of the bohemian Village literary clubs as follows:

> [At the Liberal Club] one met a motley crew of poets, authors, journalists, editors, publishers, reformers, and radicals—some of them members, many of them guests. Dr Grant introduced Carl [Gustav] Jung on the latter's first American visit, and we heard an enthralling talk on folklore from a psychological point of view. Robert Henri enlightened us about the first American exhibition of modernist painting and sculpture. Edna St. Vincent Millay and Amy Lowell read from their poems. Jacques Loeb expounded the latest advances in physical science. The notorious Frank Harris thrilled an audience with a two-hour lecture on Shakespeare. In the basement restaurant of the Greenwich Village headquarters one might dine at the same table with Bill Haywood of the Industrial Workers of the World or with Jim Larkin, the Irish labor leader. Upstairs during the dance craze of the period members even learned the latest tango steps to the tune of "Maurice Irrésistible."
> (1984, 122)

This exciting intermingling of people and ideas led to the kind of diverse and interesting careers that in retrospect only seem possible in such moments of intellectual ferment. Several anthropologists, including Ruth Benedict, Edward Sapir, and

Margaret Mead, published poetry in the modern free verse style, and several others, including Boas himself, were active contributors to magazines such as the *New Republic*, the *Masses*, and *The Dial*, which served as bohemia's intellectual core.

No one better exemplified this intersection of bohemia and academic anthropology than Elsie Clews Parsons. With a Columbia PhD in sociology, Parsons somehow managed to live a double life as the proper wife of Congressman Henry Parsons and a bohemian feminist author. Parsons wrote a series of books (sometimes pseudonymously) with titles such as *Old Fashioned Woman* (1913) and *Fear and Conventionality* (1914) that wittily, and often scandalously, used social scientific evidence to skewer the absurdities of traditional American class hierarchies and arrangements of gender and sexuality. She was widely published in the little magazines and radical press, and was most closely associated with the *New Republic*, to which she was a frequent contributor. Later, under the guidance of Boas and Benedict, Parsons turned her interests to academic anthropology. But even with this new vocational direction, Parsons retained a foot in bohemia: a central site of her important ethnographic work in the American Southwest was in northern New Mexico, the environs of the artists' colony of former Greenwich Villagers.

Another figure who embodies the complexity of the intellectual life of this scene—and indeed, of the early twentieth century United States—is W. E. B. Du Bois. Trained in history at Fisk and Harvard, and then sociology in Berlin, the epicenter of the most advanced social scientific learning, Du Bois's professional life was divided between academia and advocacy for African Americans. His writing was similarly diverse, encompassing sociological projects (most notably his Settlement House-inspired study, *The Philadelphia Negro* [1899]), novels (*The Quest for the Silver Fleece* [1911]; and *Dark Princess* [1928]), poetry, essays, and histories. His most famous work, *The Souls of Black Folk* (1903), combined many of these genres to present a lyrical picture of the struggles and the cultural "gifts" of African Americans. A founder of the NAACP, Du Bois served as the editor of its Harlem-based magazine, the *Crisis*, for twenty-four years (1910–34). Though his relationship with the magazine and the NAACP was often contentious, the *Crisis* was nevertheless a central organ of progressive African American thought and cultural expression, and hence a focal point of Harlem's own bohemia, latterly described as the "Harlem Renaissance." Du Bois had long been influenced by Boasian anthropology—particularly its critiques of scientific racism and its positive assessments of African cultural achievements—and he and the magazine became natural conduits between the intellectuals of Harlem and of Columbia University. As George Hutchinson and others have pointed out, Boas in turn not only published in the *Crisis* and actively supported projects to study and promote African American history and heritage, he encouraged the careers of African American anthropologists, most famously, Zora Neale Hurston.

While bohemian New Yorkers were attracted to anthropology for its ability to present an exotic other to urban modernity, Boasian anthropology could be said to have developed something like an aesthetic sensibility. In the earlier decades of his long career, Boas was particularly focused on challenging the pseudoscientific theorizations of race that characterized most American anthropology of his day and developing a database of native American life ways before what he perceived to be their inevitable decay and loss. These two imperatives led to a methodology that came to be known as "historical particularism," an emphasis on the gathering and interpretation of culturally and temporally contextualized information that could be deployed as counterinstances against the sweeping generalizations of scientific racism.

The name "historical particularism" gives some sense of the comprehensiveness and detail Boas demanded of himself and his students, but it does not capture another striking aspect of Boasian anthropology: its strong emphasis on the intangible elements of cultures, including language, oral and graphic expression, thought and belief systems, and even psychological and emotional characteristics. Importantly, the Boasians saw languages, oral traditions, beliefs, and philosophical systems as central parts of any given cultural context: indeed, as the media through which human beings made sense of and organized their world. Culture for the Boasians was never just an assemblage of elements—whether tools or rituals or dictionaries of words— but a process by which human beings collectively created and understood their lives. In articulating the complex interrelationships between language, thought, tradition, individuals, and collectivities, Boas and his students not only created a distinctively American anthropology but also became important founders of and contributors to the emergent academic fields of folklore, linguistics, and psychology.

Subsequent generations of anthropologists and historians would find fault with the Boasian concept of culture. For them, it implied something too rigid: a spatially and temporally bounded entity that served to reify differences between peoples. They believed that the earlier Boasian mode of historical particularism was often more attractive, in that it helped ground a view of culture that was subject to processes of change and encounter among peoples. This critique can be partially accounted for in the difference between modernist and postmodernist sensibilities. From a postmodern perspective, it has become especially important to emphasize the agency of actors; in other words, the performative and improvisational elements of culture. But for the Boasians and their contemporaries, the central problem was one of defining the terms by which to conceptualize the social totality.

Just as literary modernism could be defined as an experimental attempt to come to terms with the increasingly complex social totality of modern life, so could Boasian anthropology, in its largest lineaments, be said to be a series of experiments in describing the social totalities of so-called primitive peoples—often in the service of providing a mirror for more complex societies. In exploring this issue, the anthropologists arrived at some philosophical dilemmas that we may also characterize as quintessentially modernist. A number of Boasians were strongly impressed with the idea of the relativity of perception and belief based on cultural context.

Some (notably Edward Sapir and Benjamin Whorf) would go so far as to propose a linguistic corollary that held that speakers of different languages thought and perceived the world in different, and perhaps even incommensurate, ways. Another related concern was that of the relationship between a given social context and the individual: what was the relationship between society and the misfit or the genius? To what extent was one individual or one creative act capable of causing cultural change? What, indeed, was creativity?

These kinds of questions were motivated not only by the anthropological project of understanding the "primitive" other; they emanated equally from observations and concerns about modern society and its subjects. Indeed, many of Boasian anthropology's best-known works, including Margaret Mead's *Coming of Age in Samoa* (1928), Benedict's *Patterns of Culture* (1934), and Boas's own *The Mind of Primitive Man* (1911) and *Anthropology and Modern Life* (1928) drew direct analogies between the lives of those in exotic cultures and modern existence. Often, as with Parsons's earlier critiques, these comparisons were not flattering to modern Americans. While Mead's book was devoted to studying why young Samoans made the transition to sexual and social maturity without all the stress and anxiety of modern American teenagers, Benedict's *Patterns of Culture* compared different cultures to show how the very same behavior in different cultural contexts can be seen either as the quintessence of normality or grotesque maladjustment. The result of this comparison is a powerful attack on behavioral normativity—an issue of personal importance to Benedict, who felt a need to defend her own homosexuality against stereotypes of illness and dysfunction. Benedict concluded, "Those who function inadequately in any society are not those with certain fixed 'abnormal' traits, but may well be those whose responses have received no support in the institutions of their culture" (1959, 270). Concerns about the multifarious possible clashes between the individual and society were also amply represented in modernist fiction: in the small-town "grotesques" of Sherwood Anderson's *Winesburg, Ohio* (1919); in the stories of compromised masculine prerogative in much of Ernest Hemingway's work; in Faulkner's complex novels of Southerners struggling within a society deformed by its very history.

Chicago Sociology

Like Boasian anthropology, the unique brand of academic sociology associated with the University of Chicago was the product of the convergence of genres and communities. Like the Boasians, the Chicago School sociologists had strong ties to the bohemian enclaves and immigrant and migrant neighborhoods of its city. Perhaps even more obviously than Boasian anthropology, they also participated in a lively cross-pollination with journalism, progressive era reformism, and experimental literature.

Several of the department of sociology's early luminaries, including Robert E. Park, Ernest W. Burgess, and W. I. Thomas, had strong literary and journalistic backgrounds and inclinations. Thomas had once taught literature at Oberlin College, while Park had been a journalist, drama critic, novelist, and playwright before going on to study philosophy and sociology with, among others, William James, Josiah Royce, George Santayana, John Dewey, and Georg Simmel. Subsequent to receiving his PhD, Park worked as Booker T. Washington's personal secretary and speechwriter, an experience that gave him a strong interest in issues relating to African Americans. While Thomas and Burgess explicitly compared their brand of sociological methodology to the kind of nuanced literary portrayals of urban life by naturalist writers such as Émile Zola and the Chicagoan Theodore Dreiser, Park admonished his students to "write down only what you see, hear, and know, like a newspaper reporter" (Bulmer 1984, 98). The result was a distinctively narrative approach to social science that drew on a diversity of forms and genres for its information, including epistolary sources and life narratives. Given this novelistic form of sociology, it should come as no surprise that the sociologists, in turn, attracted the attention of fiction writers. James T. Farrell, to take but one well-known example, began his *Studs Lonigan* trilogy (1932–35), set in the Chicago Irish South Side, while taking sociology classes at the University of Chicago.

Indeed, the most profound intersection between Chicago School sociology and the modern novel was probably the setting of Chicago itself, both a fertile literary ground in the early twentieth century and the Chicago School's primary object of inquiry. The sociologists were preceded in their investigations of Chicago not only by the extremely influential figure of Jane Addams, but by some of the most famous muckrakers and reformers of the Progressive Era, including Upton Sinclair, whose novel *The Jungle* (1906), a fictional exposé of the meatpacking industry in Chicago, contributed to the institution of government oversight into the manufacture and processing of food and medicines.

A few neighborhoods in particular became important sites for the kind of intermixing of the arts and social sciences also found in New York. In the 1930s and '40s, the South Side African American neighborhood would prove to be a fertile meeting ground between the sociologists and the neighborhood's literary and political intelligentsia. But in some senses the character of Chicago School sociology was established decades earlier in the model Addams established at Hull-House, in which researchers and informants lived and worked together in close proximity. This practice would soon be transferred by the academic sociologists to the ragged bohemian district around Chicago's "Bughouse Square" (a nickname for the city's Washington Square Park, across from the Newberry Library).

This neighborhood was already an interesting meeting point of "hobohemia"— the cheap hotels, employment offices, and speakeasies that catered to a significant population of largely male transient workers—and literary Chicago. The Near North Side neighborhood was also home to the Newberry Library, several radical

bookstores, and the famous Dill Pickle Club, which served as an unofficial head-
quarters for members of the "Chicago Renaissance" including Carl Sandburg,
Sherwood Anderson, Floyd Dell, and Theodore Dreiser and hosted lectures and
performances similar to those offered in the Greenwich Village literary clubs. Here,
the young social scientists of the University of Chicago found a site for direct interaction with artists, radical political figures, journalists, reformers, hoboes, gangsters,
immigrants, and demimondaines. Interaction between these communities was facilitated by the colorful Ben Reitman, an anarchist and former hobo turned medical
doctor and neighborhood organizer. Under his aegis, members of his community
and those of Chicago's sociology department met quite formally: they gave and listened to each other give lectures, and even competed against each other in debating
competitions.

From these kinds of exchanges, the ideas were crystallized and informants located
for a number of important Chicago School projects. A characteristic product of this
close exchange was Nels Anderson's *The Hobo* (1923), the first publication in the
University of Chicago Press's groundbreaking series in sociology. Funded in part by
a grant from the Chicago Public Health Department (obtained through Reitman's
intercession), Anderson's book in many ways crystallized the developing methodology of the Chicago School by combining data obtained from external sources with
interviews and firsthand observation.

Participant Observation and the Spyglass of Social Science

In the degree of proximity between informants and researchers, the Chicago School
of sociology converged with the Columbia anthropologists, who had also been developing a distinctive research strategy that helped to define their emerging academic discipline. This research strategy eventually came to share a common name
in both disciplines: participant observation. This method required the researcher to
spend a significant period of time in close proximity with the communities under investigation and to immerse him or herself in local languages and customs. Anderson
(who would later write a popular work, *The Milk and Honey Route: A Handbook for
Hoboes* [1938], under the hobo alias Dean Stiff) lived among and strongly identified
with the men who were his research subjects. Although the barriers to participant
observation were often greater for the Boasian anthropologists, they too sought to
immerse themselves insofar as it was possible in the languages, customs, and lives of
the Native Americans who were their primary objects of study.

Participant observation (also associated with the British anthropologist Broni-
slaw Malinowski) inevitably encouraged the emergence of a new kind of researcher:
the social scientist who was also a native informant. Quite simply, the researcher
who already had access to difficult native languages or closely held local knowledge was seen as having a rare advantage. This was the logic that first brought

Anderson, an occasional rail-rider, to the attention of his mentors: who better to study the sometimes-secretive world of the hoboes? A similar logic helped explain the number of prominent women among Boasian anthropologists: Boas believed that women researchers had special access to certain kinds of information that were off limits to men. It also contributed to Boas's support for the anthropological work of such native informant ethnographers as Zora Neale Hurston, whose roots were in the defensively secretive African American communities of rural Florida, and Ella Cara Deloria, a Yankton Sioux (Dakota) Indian and perhaps the preeminent ethnographer of her people, and translator, linguist, and interpreter of D/N/Lakota language.

It is tempting to see the strange position of being both a researcher and native informant as somehow inspiring the impulse toward fiction. Both Deloria and Hurston turned toward novel writing, and both struggled in their own ways with their complex mediating position between objectivity and subjectivity, and between scientific authority and the ignorance of the inquiring outsider. Hurston famously found in anthropology the "spy-glass" through which to see herself and her home community (1935, introduction). Yet much of her ethnographic work in *Mules and Men* (1935) and elsewhere is preoccupied not so much with the optics of truth-seeing as with the complicated social dynamics of lying, concealing, and revealing knowledge. Similarly, Deloria seems to have fretted over the way her inquiries as an anthropologist went against the grain of Sioux conceptions of acceptable behavior. For both, one solution was to turn to the narrative devices of fiction (such as *Their Eyes Were Watching God* [1937] for Hurston and *Waterlily* [1988] for Deloria) that emphasized a particular, and distinctively feminine, viewpoint on their worlds. Although both writers entered the mid-century largely unappreciated (*Waterlily* only found posthumous publication), they were recovered in part because of the way their works complexly registered problems of feminine agency and authority, issues especially resonant in the wake of feminism and postmodern approaches to culture.

This combination of social science and fiction is equally, if differently, visible in the work of Richard Wright (on Richard Wright's combination of social science and fiction, see Chapter 32 of this volume). Although he was never formally trained in sociology, Wright acknowledged a significant debt to the work of the Chicago School. In an introduction to *Black Metropolis* (1945), St. Clair Drake and Horace R. Cayton's magisterial sociological study of African American Chicago, Wright mirrored Hurston's account of finding in social science a new perspective on lived experience: "I did not know what my story was, and it was not until I stumbled upon [social] science that I discovered some of the meanings of the environment that battered me" (xvii). The "story," it turned out, was that of modernity itself.

More precisely, Wright's central explanatory story was that of the Great Migration: the transformation of a Southern black peasantry into a Northern industrial proletariat. It was the explanatory narrative that helped give shape and a sense of broader meaning to his major works, including *Native Son* (1940) and the auto-biographical *Black Boy* (1945). But it also offered a solution to the problem of black "invisibility" in the racist United States that he documented in much of his work, and that would prove to be such an important theme for African American writers who drew inspiration from Wright. Nowhere was this clearer than in *12 Million Black Voices* (1941), a documentary book of photographs from the Farm Security Administration archives for which Wright wrote the text with the aid of Horace Cayton. While the photographs of black sharecroppers, maids, preachers, and children served for Wright as direct responses to the problem of the social invisibility of African Americans, the larger historical narrative the images illustrated was clear. Wright concluded,

> Imagine European history from the days of Christ to the present telescoped into three hundred years and you can comprehend the drama which our consciousness has experienced! Brutal, bloody, crowded with suffering and abrupt transitions, the lives of us black folk represent the most magical and meaningful picture of human experience in the Western world. Hurled from our native African homes into the very center of the most complex and highly industrialized civilization the world has ever known, we stand today with a consciousness and memory such as few people possess. We black folk, our history and our present being, are a mirror of all the manifold experiences of America. (pt. 4)

For Wright, black people required white recognition precisely because they figured as important subjects for understanding the conditions and processes of modernity. But still more dramatically, "hundreds of thousands of us are moving into the sphere of conscious history" (pt. 4). As such, Wright could argue, African Americans were more than a "mirror" for the American experience; they were *the* subjects of a dramatic and unfolding history.

Social Engineering

At this point in his career, Wright was working under the influence not only of sociological theory, but also of Marxism. In that intellectual tradition, the juxtaposition of disparate social situations—the convergence of peasantry and proletariat, for example—was the seedbed for revolution: the context in which the contradictions of the present could be recognized and addressed. However, many American social scientists of this period saw things differently. For them, the persistence of old ways of thinking and behaving in the context of modern life was seen not as part of the contradictions that produced change, but as maladjustment, a faulty response to changing conditions, a "cultural lag." Over the course of the period before the Second World War, many social scientists saw their work as not only identifying such conditions of maladjustment, but also curing it. Such a project promised a vast expansion of the power and significance of social scientific research. Thus, sociologist W. I. Thomas wrote. "If we learn the laws of human behavior as we have learned the laws of mathematics, physics, and chemistry, if we establish what are the fundamental attitudes, how they can be converted into other more socially desirable attitudes, how the world of values is created and modified in the operation of these attitudes, then we can establish any attitudes and values whatever" (1921, 196).

In this project, Thomas would be joined by a diversity of other thinkers, including the philosopher John Dewey, who called for nothing less than a second "great scientific revolution" of social science to combat the "entrenched and stubborn institutions of the past [that] stand in the way of our thinking scientifically about human relations and social issues" (1968, 328). Such a revolution "will ensue when men [*sic*] collectively and cooperatively organize their knowledge for application to achieve and make secure social values; when they systematically use scientific procedures for the control of human relationships and the direction of the social effects of our vast technological machinery" (329–30). Even Ruth Benedict, whose work was at least in part directed against the false imputation of norms to the wide diversity of human behavior, found herself arguing that the perception of abnormality may be a result of its failure to adapt its norms and moralities to new social conditions. Noting that "no society has yet attempted a self-conscious direction of the processes by which its new normalities are created in the next generation," Benedict concludes *Patterns of Culture* in favor of what she calls "social engineering," by which "traditional arrangements" could either be done away with or "adapt[ed] . . . to rationally selected goals" (1959, 270–71).

As alarming, even dystopian, as this call for the social engineering of "new normalities" may seem now, in its time this view was both widespread and utopian. The deep political and cultural conflicts between north and south, rural and urban, center and periphery that characterized American society in the interwar years were generally seen by intellectual elites as thoroughgoing failures of rationality. The application of some scientific rationality was thus often held to be both explanatory and almost magically transformative; as Benedict herself optimistically put it, "As soon as the new opinion is embraced as customary belief, it will be another trusted bulwark of the good life" (278). It was a kind of social scientific version of revolutionary optimism: a faith in the radically transformative possibilities inherent in the practical application of social scientific knowledge. This faith in the possibility of radical change represents one further way in which the social scientists and artists of this period may be said to have converged, in that the artists of this moment also often subscribed to a modernist aesthetic philosophy that placed artistic practices within a total transformation of human life. With the approach of the Second World War, this kind of enthusiasm for social engineering would come to an abrupt end as it came increasingly to resemble ideas espoused by the European fascists. But this faith was only one of many grand ideas that lost their luster in the wake of horrifying and disillusioning events including the Moscow show trials, the Hitler-Stalin pact, bureaucratized mass murder in Nazi Germany, and the incineration of Hiroshima and Nagasaki.

The Second World War and After

The Second World War represented a watershed in the prestige of American social science. For decades, social scientists had struggled to establish themselves institutionally by creating academic fields with identifiable methodologies and theories. But when social scientists were mustered into government and military service, they found that their expertise had applications on a wide range of fronts. Academic social scientists helped, for example, to administer domestic food rations, provide intelligence research on the cultures of US enemies (Benedict's famous study of Japan, *The Chrysanthemum and the Sword* [1946], was a product of her war work), and, notoriously, aid in the administration of the Japanese interment camps. Although social scientists had also been involved in the prosecution of the First World War, the duration of the Second World War and its close supersession by the Cold War meant that social scientists' wartime influence in government would persist for decades. It also brought about a new project for the social sciences. In the postwar twentieth century, social science would become a tool for the organization of social structures and resources and for the disposition of norms and values. No longer just a discourse about modernity, it would become its instrument.

The Cold War and the maintenance of American hegemony brought with it the urgent political priority of containing the spread of communism and winning newly postcolonial countries over to US influence. Out of the desire to accumulate knowledge of other countries, particularly the Soviet Union, a new academic configuration of "area studies" was born, along with the quasi-governmental fields of foreign aid and development. On the domestic front, issues of race relations and poverty also had important implications for the prosecution of the Cold War, for they both represented ideological limits to US claims to a morally superior social system. In what was often a revolving door between academia and government, social scientists were deployed to address all these areas. In other words, social scientists helped to shore up a new narrative of modernity, one that in effect put the United States at its apex, as the culmination and ideal of the long narrative of Western history.

At the same time, social science was also experiencing an unprecedented degree of public prestige. Margaret Mead, Gunnar Myrdal, Alfred Kinsey, Vance Packard, David Riesman, Benjamin Spock, John Kenneth Galbraith, Oscar Lewis, E. Franklin Frazier, Nathan Glazer, and Daniel Patrick Moynihan all became household names, gracing bestseller lists, the mastheads of popular magazines, and, to a remarkable degree, occupying the public consciousness. They were the experts in a cultural moment that craved expertise; indeed, in a moment that placed a high value on social conformity, they helped to define Cold War social normativity.

But perhaps because of the new prestige of the social sciences, the moment of the convergence between American fiction writers and the social sciences was largely over. Just when the social scientists were seeing their moment of greatest public influence, many artists found themselves retreating from the public sphere in the wake of the crisis in modernist utopianism. In the context of broken prewar hopes and enthusiasms, formal considerations and an individualistic and ethical perspective consistent with Cold War ideologies took on a new significance. Explicit social and political content, in turn, became associated with propaganda, antiart, and "kitsch." Meanwhile, it would take the emergence of new avant-gardes and political movements to begin nibbling away at the stifling conformity of Cold War America. The normativities propagated by Cold War American social science would come to be seen by the Beats and their heirs, and by the new recruits to the civil rights, feminist, and gay liberation movements as part and parcel of the oppressiveness of midcentury society.

Conclusion: "The Bitter Drink"

No account of the convergence of the novel and the social sciences in the early twentieth century would be complete without some substantial attention to Thorstein Veblen. A major interdisciplinary figure in the American social sciences, Veblen not only strongly influenced the literary intelligentsia of his moment, he also became a literary character in his own right. Moreover, his story nicely draws together some of the major figures, locales, and themes of this essay.

Like so many of the social scientists of this period, Veblen was the product of an immigrant community—in his case, the rural Norwegian enclaves of the upper Midwest. But rather than turning (like Boas or Lowie) to the study of exotic others, or becoming (like Hurston, Deloria, or Anderson) a native informant, Veblen turned his outsider's gaze on the dominant formations of American society. Like Du Bois and Wright, he became, in effect, a participant observer of modernity. Thus, Veblen famously investigated the American social elite in *The Theory of the Leisure Class* (1899) and entrepreneurs and businessmen in *The Theory of Business Enterprise* (1904). Also notable is Veblen's *The Higher Learning in America: A Memorandum on the Conduct of Universities by Businessmen*. Published in 1918, at the height of a witch-hunt against academics who had expressed pacifist sympathies during the First World War, this book was both a political critique of his current moment and a participant-observer study of Veblen's time at the University of Chicago shortly after its founding, in 1890, by oil magnate John D. Rockefeller. As its subtitle suggests, the work is a scathing indictment of the modern American university, which he diagnosed as not only too immersed in the interests of money, but also too inclined toward rarified specialization.

Writers as diverse as Alfred Kazin and David Riesman have made much of Veblen's difficult relationship to academic institutions. Drawing on an early and apparently flawed biography of Veblen, many have portrayed him as a grouchy, neurotic outsider, an atheist and a womanizer, too brilliantly idiosyncratic to keep an academic job. But as recent scholars, including Stephen Edgell and Rick Tilman, have shown, Veblen was neither personally nor intellectually the marginal "man from Mars" he is often made out to be. Thus, while *The Higher Learning* has often been seen as evidence of Veblen's alienation, I think it is instead possible to take Veblen at his word, and see it as a systemic, and often alarmingly prescient, study of a representative institution in American life. Veblen, in other words, may have disliked the strictures of academia with good reason, and what seems to many commentators as his perversity may instead signal something else about the man: that Veblen was both a scholar *and* a bohemian.

While a professor and editor of the *Journal of Political Economy* at the University of Chicago, Veblen crossed paths with Boas (then affiliated with the Field Museum), the eminent biologist Jacques Loeb, philosophers George Herbert Mead and John Dewey, and of course many of the Chicago School sociologists, including Albion Small and W. I. Thomas. All of these figures would have an influence on his work. But at the time, he also lived among the artists and intellectuals of Chicago's bohemian scene. Veblen's central research topics, which included feminism and the status of labor, in a sense bridged these worlds, speaking to both the radical ideas of the diverse free thinkers of bohemia and to the more scholarly social scientific preoccupations with the larger topic of modernity. Indeed, at its heart *The Theory of the Leisure Class*, written during Veblen's years at Chicago, was part of the larger Marxian inquiry of its day into the nature of the historical conditions that would produce socialism. Beyond identifying competition and envy as driving social and psychological components of class status, Veblen's larger concern was in addressing how consumerism influenced class consciousness: did it inspire class conflict, or did it, on the other hand, mollify political anger? In addressing the complexities of this question, Veblen can be understood, as Ross argues, as "the American Gramsci, drawn by the problem of false consciousness . . . into a revision of Marx's theory of history" (1991, 207). This work drew Veblen significant academic recognition across a diversity of fields, while outside the academy, William Dean Howells cemented its reputation by praising it as a brilliant work of social satire.

Later in his career, Veblen became editor of *The Dial Magazine,* in its brief incarnation as an antiwar political journal. Not only did this immerse Veblen in the vibrant New York bohemian scene, but it also established him as a popular intellectual figure. This was the Veblen that the conservative H. L. Mencken felt compelled to ridicule, and that Sinclair Lewis's restless highbrow Carol Kennicott attempted to read from her isolation in Gopher Prairie (*Main Street* [1920]). And yet, even at this moment of his greatest public acclaim, Veblen clearly longed for participation in a different kind of academic project. Along with other major figures in the Greenwich Village scene, including Parsons, Veblen helped to found the New School for Social Research, an institution that, it was hoped, would provide a context for intellectual life free from the constraints of political and business interests.

About a decade after his death, Veblen would become immortalized in a novel: John Dos Passos's *The Big Money* (1936), part three of his massive trilogy, *U. S. A.* "The Bitter Drink," one of the short biographical sketches deployed throughout the trilogy, obviously draws on the same flawed biography that influenced so many of Veblen's interpreters. It portrays him as a fundamentally tragic figure: an incisive and ironic dissector of the hypocritical moneyed interests that control the United States, a frustrated witness to history, and a man with a congenital inability to say yes to the routines and petty politics of university life, conventional morality, religious piety, and the niceties of small talk. Dos Passos portrays Veblen's life story as a scandal-ridden passage from one academic position to another. Indeed, he is nothing less than a modern Socrates, who because of "the sharp clear prism of his mind" must ultimately drink "the bitter drink" of obscurity for telling truths "etched in irony" ("The Bitter Drink").

In a fairly common interpretation that goes back at least as far as Kazin, this Veblen becomes a kind of key to the whole *U. S. A.* trilogy. Dos Passos's work as a whole is likened to Veblen, itself interpreted as a lonely, cantankerous, and ironic refusal of an America dominated by moneyed interests and moral hypocrisy. This reading is also, of course, highly complimentary to Dos Passos in that it implicates him in this deeply romantic representation of the lonely and alienated teller of in-convenient truths. And in fact, Dos Passos was becoming just such a figure. By the time his much-anticipated final volume of the trilogy was complete, he had dramatically shifted his political outlook away from his former leftist views, thus turning his back not only on his faith in society's radical transformation, but on the leftist literati and intellectuals who considered him their most important novelist. In this sense, the almost laughable hyperbole of equating Veblen with Socrates is nothing more than a self-flattering fantasy of Dos Passos's own isolation from the communities and ideas of leftist politics in general.

It is easy to see why such a figure might appeal to a writer in the midst of a political conversion. This stubbornly defiant Veblen can easily stand not only for a critical stance against contemporary society, but against faddish thought of any kind. But as my account of the brief convergence of social science and the novel should make clear, Dos Passos's fantasy of a project convergent in its very alienation and marginality is really less indicative of the complex intersections of social science and the novel in the period between the wars than anticipatory of the antipolitical stances characteristic of writers of the Cold War era. Dos Passos imagines writers and social scientists together as critical outsiders, left to the job of rendering the story ("etched in irony") of the failed potential of a radical vision of modernity, as "the last puffs of the ozone of revolt went stale/in the whisper of speakeasy arguments" ("The Bitter Drink"). The "irony" that Dos Passos attributes to Veblen's criticism is a compliment only in the sense that it resembles that most fetishized trope of the new critical interpreter and the sophisticated, postideological writer.

Veblen, on the other hand, apparently bristled at suggestions that his work was satirical in nature, and doubtless would have chalked up any "ironies" found therein to the more classically Marxist idea of the contradictions of capitalism. But I'd like to think he would have also been perplexed by the representation of himself as an alienated outsider. Rather, he partook of a particular kind of modernist utopia, the complex form of intellectual sociability also called bohemia. Its alternative, the "highly sterilized, germ-proof system of knowledge" that he identified in the modern academy (Veblen 1918, 6), anticipated the kind of disciplinary specialization that would ultimately make the world of arts and the disciplines of the humanities and interpretive social sciences seem so far apart—and render Veblen himself an obscure and cantankerous curiosity of literary and intellectual history.

26

THE NATIVE NOVEL

BY SEAN KICUMMAH TEUTON

In 1854 Cherokee outlaw John Rollin Ridge wrote *The Life and Adventures of Joaquin Murieta: The Celebrated California Bandit*, the first novel by a Native American. Ridge's father John Ridge and others had gathered covertly to sign away Cherokee title to ancestral homelands in the east and to move the Cherokees west. For selling Cherokee land without consent of the nation, in 1839 a band of traditionalists gathered one night at the Ridge house and brutally assassinated the father before the eyes of the son. For the rest of his youth John Rollin Ridge avowed revenge and one day killed a man he suspected to be one of his father's murderers. Fleeing to the California gold fields, John Rollin Ridge endured his banishment perhaps through an imaginative association with the California bandit Joaquin Murieta, the Hispanic folk hero who, upon family murder and stolen claim, robs the wealthy to support the weak throughout the land.

Not all Native American novels bear such complex histories but, since *Joaquin Murieta*, many Indigenous authors have sought through the structure of the novel to confront histories that recover solutions to current crises, to develop characters that raise social consciousness, and to create plots that allow Natives to depart and then return to replenish community and land. As the Acoma Pueblo writer Simon Ortiz observed in his important 1981 essay, "Towards a National Indian Literature," throughout this tradition, Native novelists transform the genre to meet the intellectual and social needs of Indigenous communities. Whether masquerading or assimilating, resisting or recovering, the Native American novel persists, ironically, not only by preserving but in fact by rewriting narrative traditions.

From the advent of this first American Indian novel, the Native novel has engaged these traditions with the pressure to meet the demands of a mainstream audience often harboring inaccurate views of Native Americans. Even though American Indians since the seventeenth century have enrolled in American colleges, where they learned to read and write Latin and Greek as well as English, the concept of a Native American intellectual has historically seemed almost an oxymoron in the American mainstream. Indeed, colonialist constructions of North American savagery specifically invoke Natives' supposed lack of sophisticated languages and, more specifically, their lack of writing. Thus, for many mainstream critics from the seventeenth century onward, to see an Indian writing is to see neither savage nor civilized, but an aberration of each, and so no one at all. Even as the colonialist project destroyed Native Americans, the colonial imagination assuaged resulting guilt through the image of the Vanishing Indian who, though he must die, dies beautifully to yield to the flowering of Western civilization across America. While that image has been exposed and decried in the American novel, it nonetheless persists in the Native American novel, well into the twentieth century.

Today, colonial desire for cultural authenticity, or corresponding repulsion at perceived cultural corruption, remains less in the image of the Native intellectual and more in that of the Native literary work, particularly of the novel, in part because readers so generally associate the genre itself with European rather than with Native literary traditions. Perhaps for this reason, Native writers to this day face additional pressure to appropriate the confines of the novel in a way that best serves its Native characters and audience. Some critics contend that Sherman Alexie portrays poverty and disfunction in *Reservation Blues* (1995), for example, as the unexamined and unlucky consequence of being American Indian in the world today. Such other contemporary Native novels as Blackfeet writer James Welch's *Death of Jim Loney* (1979), Chippewa writer Louise Erdrich's *Love Medicine* (1984), and Cherokee writer Thomas King's *Truth and Bright Water* (1994), present Indians who similarly self-destruct, but in ways that allow readers to better understand that destruction in its broader colonial context. As mainstream American readers come more to confront the nation's colonial history, Indian novelists may be able to put away the Vanishing Indian once and for all, to deal honestly with this history of cross-colonial relations.

Nearer its beginning, on the other hand, the Native American novel often negotiated the arduous psychological demands of readers' colonial imagination by envisioning ancient connections between Indigenous people on a hemispheric level. As Louis Owens explained in his pathbreaking book on the American Indian Novel, *Other Destinies*, while Native authors have always faced pressure to accept and market the image of the Vanishing Indian, they have always found alternatives in novelistic expression: assimilation to the dominant mainstream and, more subversively, masquerading or disguising an Indigenous narrative within a more acceptable allegory of the ethnic other.

The Life and Adventures of Joaquin Murieta, for example, is based on a true story. Murieta really did mine a claim during the California gold rush. His family apparently actually suffered the attack of white miners jealous of his success, and he really did become an outlaw bent on revenge. At this point in the story, however, fact becomes difficult to disentangle from legend. Murieta's mother was rumored to be Cherokee, which may have inspired Ridge to identify with this particular rebel among other legendary characters in early California. Equal numbers of Californians viewed Murieta as a bandit and as a hero during his own lifetime, which explains why, even as the California State Rangers exhibited his supposed head at the price of one dollar per view, new reports of Murieta's heroic deeds continued to surface. As these stories grew, Murieta became known as "the Mexican Robin Hood," and eventually took on the legendary name with which his stories became most associated: Zorro. Our first novelist, John Rollin Ridge, thus set a bold standard in writing *Joaquin Murieta*, a work that became the creative space for Ridge to declare his outrage for layers of injustice: the ongoing theft of Cherokee lands in the southeast, the rape and murder of Cherokee citizens at the hands of the Georgia Guard, the refusal of the federal government to enforce its 1832 Supreme Court decision upholding Cherokee sovereignty, and of course the assassination of his father. As a fugitive with fair skin and a Western education, Ridge could easily have assimilated into the American mainstream as a journalist in northern California. Instead, he wrote behind his Indian name of Yellow Bird to perform two contradictory tasks: to disguise his identity and to declare his Indianness. Readers can sometimes imagine through the words of Murieta Ridge's own fantasy of revenge, escape into the sunset, and ensuing legend:

> He dashed along that fearful trail as he had been mounted upon a spirit-steed, shouting as he passed:
> "I am Joaquin! kill me if you can!"
> Shot after shot came clanging around his head, and bullet after bullet flattened on the wall of slate at his right. In the midst of the first firing, his hat was knocked from his head, and left his long black hair streaming behind him (ch. 6).

Here Murieta might particularly resemble romantic portrayals of the noble savage, galloping astride a "spirit-steed," immune to bullets, his long black hair flowing in the wind. Yellow Bird resourcefully adapts what we might call a radical romance, but in imagining and exploiting a transnational connection with Indigenous Mexico he perhaps began a trend in Cherokee and other Native novels to come. Indeed, Ridge's first novel informs Native historical novels in general, which often plumb oral traditions and tribal histories to engage current crises on a hemispheric scale. For this reason, we might direct our close attention to this early impulse.

With the passing of the Removal Act in 1830, Americans had finally set the course to send Indian nations west to make cotton rich land in the south available for plantations. Fearing the doom of Indian removal, on March 5, 1835, John Ross, the chief of the Cherokee Nation, penned an unusual letter to a diplomat in Washington, in which he declares it "desirable to explore some of the provinces of Mexico for settling a colony within its sovereign jurisdiction." (1985, 330). Chief John Ross's desperate plan may surprise those who have come to believe that he rejected any form of removal of the Cherokee Nation from the southeast. It seems here, however, that faced with the threat of removal, Ross sought alternatives outside the claimed jurisdiction of the Unites States.

Perhaps Mesoamerica was not all that foreign to Cherokees, even before Ross's ideas for transnational migration. Indeed, as early as 1807 Cherokees were trading in Spanish Texas and, by 1819, the first Cherokees led by Chief Duwali Bowl, had settled permanently south of the Red River, and soon into the region north of Nacogdoches. In 1822, Bowl sent a delegation under Chief Richard Fields to Mexico City, where they received a treaty and title to their new lands. Bowl himself spoke Spanish but no English, but nonetheless remained at the colony. While the junta that formed the Texas Republic in 1836 kept this treaty from being fully ratified, adoptive Cherokee Sam Houston negotiated another treaty for the Texas Cherokees. To Houston's ire, in 1839 Texas President Mirabeau Lamar nonetheless ordered the Cherokees routed from Texas when the Texas militia killed Bowl, scalped him, and cut strips of skin from his back to make bridle reins. Some hundreds of destitute Cherokees fled south, deep into the tribe's unknown reaches of Mexico, and these people came to be called the "Lost Cherokees." Years later white settlers reported finding the region's trees carved with intricate animal shapes and geometric designs.

We might productively imagine the first Native novel then, not only in the context of Ridge's personal history, but also within textual histories seeking deeper Indigenous hemispheric connections: say, between the documented record of Cherokees in the Texas borderlands and the legend of the Lost Cherokees in Mexico imagined in their totemic tree carvings. Such connections challenge Western conventions of historical evidence, and might be dismissed as Indian folklore or myth. But not to take such mythic knowledge into account is to miss some of the story, and perhaps to deny what Wai Chee Dimock has called "deep time." Such readings offer a more planetary scope for human history and so productively invoke oral histories that impinge on our graphic worlds to emerge from the "deep waters" of our myth-making unconscious. Literary scholars may do justice to that Indian story by heeding these complementary modes, the historicist and the myth-critical. Such a mode will enable us better to understand such Cherokee works as Ridge's *Joaquin Murieta*, as well as such literary progeny as John Milton Oskison's *Singing Bird* (composed in the 1930s, published in 2007) and Robert Conley's *Captain Dutch* (1995), which seek to connect Native people on a hemispheric level via history as well as myth.

In the midst of the removal crisis, Cherokees might have turned their national imaginations to these mythic pan-Indigenous similarities, noting that both Cherokee and Mesoamerican traditions have corn-mother stories, that both southeastern and Mexican prehistoric cultures built earthen or stone pyramids, and that winged serpents were said to live in the waters around both peoples. Within this mythic structure, Cherokees could recover agency to seize control of their forced migration by imagining earlier hemispheric connections as part of their destiny. After all, in Ross's Cherokee universe migration to Mexico might have made more symbolic sense than removal to Arkansas; the west was the

Darkening Land, the place of the dead, whereas the south was associated with the color white, the hue of universal harmony. Such free-range speculation might enable more transnational readings of Cherokee oral and written literature. Perhaps the more mythic life of the Native American-Mesoamerican relationship enabled uprooted Cherokee authors to ground themselves in a more empowered Indigenous past.

This background returns us to Ridge and the first Indian novel, *Joaquin Murieta*. While this well-known text is often understood by such critics as Louis Owens as a "masquerade" through which Ridge imagined revenge for the theft of Cherokee lands, it is most interesting that Ridge chose to use the myth of this Mexican folk hero for his cause. No doubt Ridge was an opportunist and, living in California, the story and audience were close at hand. At one point in this rollicking adventure, the narrator juxtaposes the literate Mexican Murieta to the non-literate and uncivilized "Digger" Indians who, he says, make good foot messengers precisely because of their lack of letters:

> They are exceedingly faithful in this business, having a superstitious dread of that mysterious power which makes a paper talk without a mouth. The digger got himself a small stick about two feet long, and splitting the end to the depth of an inch or two, stuck the letter into it, and holding it out in front of him, started off in a fast trot (ch. 9).

Fearing literacy, this southwest Indian, with whom readers might at first assume Ridge would empathetically identify, in fact appears clownish compared to Ridge's Mexican character, his white readers, and, we might infer, his Native author alike. He arrives and stands petrified before the lettered Mexican revolutionary Murieta, with whom critics have suggested Ridge most identifies.

This spectacle of literacy and its sovereign guarantees perhaps draws other Native writers into the transnational imaginary. As recently as 1995, in Cherokee author Robert Conley's *Captain Dutch*, the narrator takes us back to the Texas Cherokees in Mexico in the 1820s. In this historical novel, the author educates Cherokees in their tribal history, but especially in the power of literacy to gain treaties and assert tribal sovereignty. Here, not the Indians but the whites are without a treaty and, by suggestion, literacy, both of which derive their power from none other than Mexico. Conley's fictionalized Chief Bowl says:

> There are lots of white Texans. They're all around us. More come every day. They want our land, too, because it's good land, but they can't get it. We had elections. Our new chief here is Richard Fields, and Richard has papers from Mexico City that give us this land to live on. When white men come to Texas, they have to get permission from Mexico before they can settle on land, just like we did. We already have the papers for this, so they can't have our land, no matter how badly they want it. (ch. 19)

This fabled homeland for the safeguard of tribal literacy and sovereignty, however, is best imagined in Cherokee author John Oskison's posthumously published 1930s novel, *The Singing Bird*. The novel portrays life in the 1820s at the Dwight Mission School for the Western Cherokees, one of the first Protestant missions established west of the Mississippi. The Presbyterian Church established Dwight Mission near Russellville, Arkansas, a few years after the Western Cherokee removed to the Ozarks to escape mounting pressures within the eastern Cherokee Nation in the years before the Removal Act. Oskison draws much of his story from *Reminiscences of the Indians* (1869) by Reverend Cephas Washburn, a missionary to the Cherokee in Georgia who transferred to Arkansas to head the Dwight Mission anticipating removal, and who then moved with the mission to Oklahoma Indian Territory when the Cherokee lost their Arkansas land. The novel takes a dramatic turn from its portrayal of mission school life when, in chapter four, in steps the fascinating character of Sequoyah, the famous inventor of the Cherokee written language. The frame narrative of the mission project recedes to an emerging subplot surrounding Sequoyah's actions, and much of the novel's story depicting Sequoyah is historically accurate. It was the Western Cherokees in Arkansas who first accepted Sequoya's syllabary, and it was a speech written from a Western tribal leader to the eastern Cherokee in their written language that convinced the eastern Cherokee to adopt his script. In 1843, Sequoyah actually left the Western Cherokee for Mexico in search of the Lost Cherokee, where he died and was buried in a cave. In the novel, however, Oskison imagines that Sequoyah hopes to find in Mexico the "sacred symbols" that record ancient Cherokee history. Here Oskison's missionary character Dan Wear writes about Sequoyah's deepening scholarly immersion:

> I guessed that it was a history of his people, and that he could not complete it without the material he hoped to find in Mexico. This is pure speculation, but I believe it has to do with the theft, long ago, of certain sacred symbols of the Cherokees. I recalled what an old chief once told me, that after their loss there was unrest and spiritual discontent amongst the people. Perhaps Sequoyah believes these sacred symbols are somewhere in Mexico, and that he may be able to recover them. I have felt that a reunion in peace of all the tribes dominates him. It is believable that he hopes to restore the faith of the Cherokees in their old god. (ch. 16)

Again, Oskison invokes nonfiction. Ethnographer James Mooney also records the myth of the Lost Cherokees, who had, in some distant primordial past, left the homeland, either west or south, and gradually lost touch. And he also documents an oral account of an Ark of Covenant—a wooden box wrapped in furs—in which Cherokees kept their sacred symbols. One day this ark was stolen, and the Cherokees soon weakened in collective spirit. Most exciting, however, Oskison, like Sequoyah and Ridge, again looks to Mesoamerica for the origin and recovery of a lost Cherokee history and concomitant sovereignty. For as Sequoyah knew, that sovereignty is best protected in a sacred text that unites a people with their ancient land and charts its destiny.

In their introduction to *The Singing Bird*, Timothy Powell and Melinda Mulliken suggest that Oskinson's novel offers a Native form of historiography to challenge Western history by including oral traditions, much the way Arnold Krupat questions the centrality of historical fact to see historical truth. I would add that *The Singing Bird* might even model the alternative methodology here described. In the telling passage above, the author himself, through the character of the missionary, engages in "pure speculation" about his tribe, against the limits of Western history, to better connect Cherokees with their past, each other, and a shared future. In so doing, Native writers and scholars immerse themselves in what scholars such as Ramón Saldívar call the "transnational imaginary," that space where national commitments are undone and new communities discovered. Such wanderings across geography and time might well discover a transnational Black Atlantic for the Americas, a "Red Atlantis" to trace the many departures and arrivals that unite and distinguish the greater Indigenous hemisphere.

As early as the late nineteenth century, in novels such as Creek writer Alice Callahan's *Wynema, A Child of the Forest* (1891)—the first Indian novel by a woman—the American Indian novel has also sought to express Indigenous realities not through disguise and invocation of a mythic pan-Indigenous past, but rather through assimilation to what it views as an increasingly European-American future. In *Wynema*, the white Methodist teacher Genevieve Weir, working in the Creek Nation, finds in the young traditional Creek woman Wynema all the promise of a wealthy Southern lady. Genevieve remains largely at the cultural center of this sentimental novel of women's rights, and Wynema herself dreams of matching Genevieve's suffragette virtues: "we are waiting for our more civilized white sisters to gain their liberty, and thus set us an example which we shall not be slow to follow" (ch. 11). In fact, in invoking Indian mission work for the cause of women's rights, *Wynema* overlooks the fact that the Muscogee nation is itself traditionally matrilineal; in many ways, the "liberty" the title character awaits at the hands of her civilizers constitutes a major step backwards for Indian women.

The turn of the twentieth century is critically recognized as the nadir of Indian populations and cultural vitality in North America. After repeated federally sponsored removals and massacres, corrupt financial dealings with Indian subsistence on reservations, and the division of communal lands through the 1887 General Allotment Act, Native communities and their governments had been reduced to utter dependence on the federal government and its social planners, who saw the traditional ways of Indian people as impossible to maintain and even the cause of their malaise. By the early twentieth century, white and Native leaders in Indian "uplift," in organizations such as the Society of American Indians, sought to prepare Native Americans for citizenship by eradicating the last of their traditional cultures. Such an answer to the "Indian problem" was at that time viewed as progressive. Writing within these times, Indian novelists often offered plots that placed white American culture at the center toward which marginalized traditional American Indians aspired.

Wynema thus remains a painful though instructive novel dramatizing not only the economic but also the psychological effects of assimilation on Native people. Throughout, Methodist missionaries silence or puppet Creek voices, reject Creek traditions, and misrepresent Creek culture and politics, especially regarding the crisis of the Allotment Act. On this question Wynema speaks her mind, but it is a colonized Indian mind that has internalized the dominant colonial narrative. Wynema argues to Genevieve that because Native people are shiftless, they must be made to value work through personal property and its improvement. But in an ironic reversal, her teacher opposes allotment—because Indians are not competent to oversee their property and will thus be cheated out of it. Wynema is ashamed of her ignorant error: "Oh, I am so sorry, dear Mihia [her teacher]—so sorry I was so foolish! Pray, forgive me! It is always the way with me, and I dare say I should be one of the first to sell myself out of house and home," and the girl hung her head, looking the picture of humiliation" (ch. 13). The assimilation debate thus begins with the assumption that Indigenous people are backward and slowly educable, entertaining only the question of their best preservation in the long road to citizenship.

Other novels by John Milton Oskison perhaps best exemplify the Native novel of assimilation. Educated at Stanford and Harvard, editor and feature writer of *Collier's Magazine*, and an active member of the Society of American Indians, Oskison wrote novels, such as *Wild Harvest* (1925), and *Black Jack Davy* (1926), set in Indian Territory—before Oklahoma statehood—that posit the arrival of white settlers as a pivotal moment to negotiate cultural changes. The most developed of these is *Brothers Three* (1935), which uses the struggle of three brothers to keep the family farm as an emblem of the cultural challenges facing Natives. The terms of assimilation that characterize *Wynema* are evident as well when the autobiographical third son returns from New York as a writer and investor to help save the farm. But *Brothers Three* provides an Indian character equally at home writing in the urbane city or farming among the rural people around whom he lived years before. The novel meditates on the social and economic history of Oklahoma to weave Native characters into its concern with a larger historicist and regionalist perspective. Of course, saving the farm has shaped many plots in the American novel, perhaps especially rural plots of Oklahoma and the larger West and Midwest in the first half of the twentieth century. This plotline allows the central Native characters to appeal to wider audiences as they promote the more generally understood values of hard work and integrity in hard times. As if to engage American Indian cultural issues, Oskison allows minor traditional Native characters to make occasional entrances. To trace a similar trend today, one might consider the recent novels of Louise Erdrich, such as *The Last Report on the Miracles at Little No Horse* (2002).

By the 1930s, American lawmakers became aware of the disastrous consequences of allotment and reservation bureaucracy as exposed by the 1928 Meriam
Report. As Commissioner of Indian Affairs during the Roosevelt administration,
John Collier introduced the Indian New Deal, the 1934 Wheeler-Howard Indian
Reorganization Act (IRA) to restore self-government on reservations. While assimilationist novels such as those by Oskison continued to present literary realist
plots and characters, other Indian writers began to employ modernist techniques to
question the necessity or even the possibility of Natives entering the mainstream.
Osage writer John Joseph Mathews studied at the University of Oklahoma and at
Oxford University, and trained pilots during the First World War before developing a writing career self-consciously dedicated to advocacy for Osage and Native
peoples. Mathews's *Sundown* (1934) is a semiautobiographical novel that straddles
these two literary and cultural trends in the Indigenous novel. The young protagonist, Challenge Windzer, lives in his Osage community that has recently experienced an oil boom, in which great new wealth offers to Westernize or destroy
Osage life—depending on whether Chal is listening to his assimilationist father or
his traditionalist mother. Mathews employs both realist and modernist devices to
tell the story of Chal, drawing on each literary movement at key moments. When
Chal is with his mother or gazing at Osage lands, all is presented with realistic clarity. However, when Chal must head to college, rush a fraternity, or deal with the
destructive power of alcohol, modernist fragmentation and internalized narrative
memories gain full expression:

> "Well," said Marie, eagerly, "Whatta we waitin' on?"
> He pulled the bottle from the car pocket then uncapped the soda water.
> Chal drove home carefully that night. He could remember the black derricks
> against the red afterglow, and he could remember the glazed look in Marie's eyes.
> He remembered her cigarette-stained fingers and that she seemed to be constantly
> looking for a cigarette she had dropped. He remembered that she was careless about
> her skirts, but the rest of the time they spent there was a haze. (ch. 13)

The well-crafted prose, using strategic repetition and visual images of blurry colors,
mirrors the internal psychological state of a young Native man struggling to negotiate colonial change in his hometown and to maintain cultural memory, which
threatens to dissipate with his own dissipation. Mathews's invocation of emerging
modernist style and imagery distinguish this from other Native novels, as well as
from other novel genres engaging the pressures of assimilation—the immigrant
novel, for example—by invoking the alienation of a young man who, through the
education he embraces, begins to feel distanced, not only from his family, culture,
and land, but from his former self.

Mathews's contemporary, Cree anthropologist and writer D'Arcy McNickle,
completed two fine novels to explore the often hopeless predicament of American Indians, which editors described as "wandering between two generations, two

cultures" (Parker 1992, 43). With *The Surrounded* (1936), McNickle set the prototype of the Native novel most recognized by contemporary audiences, complete with the serious treatment of colonialism and the power of oral traditions to resist it. Unlike earlier American Indian novels such as Okinagan writer Mourning Dove's *Cogewea, the Half-Blood* (1927), which offered protagonists of mixed Indian and white ancestry as "low born" or "poor breeds" both emotionally and psychologically ill-formed, McNickle's novels develop protagonists with mixed ancestry with great complexity to ask difficult questions about Native American ancestral knowledge, cultural identity, and colonial change. Ultimately, however, McNickle shows great doubts about whether American Indian people can successfully negotiate that change. Instead, McNickle suggests, Natives will either exist in flux, torn between the demands of both white and Indigenous cultures, or simply self-destruct. In *The Surrounded*, Archilde Leon arrives home to his Flathead reservation from wandering abroad to visit his parents, a Spanish father and an Indian mother. He is estranged from his father and suspicious of his recommendations that Archilde end his travels and pick up the plow. But when Archilde visits with his mother's family and Modeste the elder and observes a traditional dance, there too he feels somehow embarrassed and out of place:

> Actually, in the way he was learning the world, neither Modeste nor his mother was important. They were not real people. Buffaloes were not real to him either, yet he could go and look at buffaloes everyday if he wished, behind the wire enclosure of the Biological Survey reserve. . . . To him they were just fenced up animals that couldn't be shot, though you could take photographs of them. (ch. 6)

Readers will detect the comparison of Native Americans to bison, both tied to the land yet exploited and captured in a static image. Archilde heads to the mountains with his brother Elise, who plays the stereotypical Indian renegade, only to see his mother and his girlfriend murder a white police officer. In this fateful ending, Archilde has thrown off his Western culture but can find no comfort or protection on his Indigenous road that leads only deeper into the mountains.

For decades McNickle worked on his most complex novel, *Wind from an Enemy Sky*, published posthumously in 1978. Two elder Indian brothers, one a revered chief camped on traditional mountain lands, the other an assimilated farmer working in the nearby town, have grown apart over the years but are now brought together by a terrible event. The government has suddenly dammed up the river that has sustained the Little Elk people for generations and, in reprisal, a young member of the tribe has shot and killed a worker at the dam. Later, a well-meaning white anthropologist claims to have located in a museum the Little Elk people's invaluable beaver medicine, the power of which promises to save the people. The anthropologist, however, discovers that the beaver medicine had been left to rot in a basement warehouse and so offers the Little Elks a Peruvian artifact instead. Such absurdly sad miscommunications between the Indians and the settlers continue a chain of tragic events in

Wind from an Enemy Sky, through which McNickle again shares his conclusion that Western and Indigenous worldviews are ultimately irreconcilable.

Like Oskison, McNickle also turned to the Mesoamerican historical novel. Reared on the early hope of John Collier to return tribal autonomy to Natives under the Indian Reorganization Act, McNickle spent the years 1936–52 working for the Bureau of Indian Affairs (BIA). On seeing the federal government begin to terminate tribes with the 1953 House Concurrent Resolution 108, McNickle resigned. His sense of betrayal and pessimism is hardly masked in the above two novels, and perhaps explains his wish to write historical fiction. A year later, McNickle published *Runner in the Sun: A Story of Indian Maize* (1954), a delightful novel written for a young adult audience. The author takes us back to a pre-Columbian time in the cliff-dwelling southwest, when Indians faced a similar yet different threat to their environments and governments, cultures and societies. The novel's hero is a young man named Salt who is chastised by elders for seeking scientific explanations for the worsening drought and for suggesting that tribal understandings of perceived threats are superstitious. The banished Holy One sends Salt on a journey to Mesoamerica to discover a solution to the crisis, where Salt finds a new strain of corn and a new religious symbol to ensure their survival. In any assessment of McNickle's literary work, one cannot neglect *Runner in the Sun*. In what is probably his last novel, the author offers a positive vision of crisis, change, and renewal to Indian communities. While one could argue that such a work of historical fiction is escapist, here McNickle leads Native youth to an earlier time when Western invasions were not the source of their crisis. Instead, Indian people are shown a community that challenges those who corrupt sacred knowledge through fear mongering and intimidation, and are shown Natives using their scientific minds to deduce and solve problems, seeking answers through hemispheric collaboration.

From Ridge's early historical experiment with Murieta, such historical fiction has gained Indigenous audiences, and perhaps for the same reasons then as today. Also writing during McNickle's time and also drawing upon training in anthropology, Sioux author Ella Deloria wrote *Waterlily*, drafted in 1944 and published posthumously in 1988, to return to nineteenth-century Sioux life for a richly detailed account of camps, kinship, and religious and social customs (on Ella Deloria's blend of fiction and anthropology, see Chapter 25 in this volume). The recovery and interpretation of the past would continue to be important to Native American fiction through the late twentieth century. On the one hand, the increased visibility of American Indian fiction resulted in several Native novels that were published posthumously in the 1970s and 1980s. Novels written during these decades, moreover, often return to the Native history of previous eras. In Blackfeet and Gros Ventre author James Welch's *Fools Crow* (1986), set in the 1870s, Blackfeet contend with the new moral crises of encroaching soldiers and disease, but also with the time-honored generational differences and gender relations. Chickasaw writer Linda Hogan's novel *Mean Spirit* (1990) engages corruption during the Osage oil boom of the 1930s.

As early as 1927, with the publication of Mourning Dove's *Cogewea, the Half-Blood*, Native American authors have harnessed the novel to engage the problem of maintaining an Indigenous identity in the face of European colonization. Born Christine Quintasket, Mourning Dove was a migrant farm worker in Washington state, where, after years of writing in her tent on evenings after laboring, she finally completed *Cogewea*. An Indian enthusiast named Lucullus McWhorter stepped in to edit her manuscript, eventually helping her publish the novel with his embellishments and in a very different form. McWhorter probably had much to do with changing Mourning Dove's work into a popular western romance, complete with villains and the woeful pleas of halfbreeds in distress, and by adding epigraphs to each chapter taken from Henry Wadsworth Longfellow's "Hiawatha," among other works. From this fascinating and complicated origin, the novel opens on a Montana cattle ranch on the Flathead reservation, where cowboys are Indians with mixed white and Native ancestry. The young woman Cogewea lives with her Indian family—her white father has left for good to the Alaska gold fields—and she must decide between white and American Indian suitors: the dastardly villain, Easterner Densmore, or the silent hero, "breed" James LaGrinder. While this boisterous novel bears all the inconsistencies of an invasive editor at odds with the author, *Cogewea, the Half-Blood* displays the actual challenges facing mixed-race Natives barred from either culture, when, for example, Cogewea enters as a rider in a horse race dressed as a white woman and wins. On being discovered she loses her prize, the judge calling her a "squaw." Yet on entering a race for Native girls, there too she is told it is a race for Indians, not "breeds." It seems however that McWhorter, in the interest of plot conflict, wished to exaggerate what he perhaps saw as the sad psychological predicament of the halfbreed. After all, Cogewea, though of mixed racial heritage, has been reared almost entirely by her Native American mother, and clearly identifies solely with her Indigenous side; one assumes such character developments to be the work of Mourning Dove. Interjected within this character development, however, are what are most likely the editor's confusing shifts, with lamenting refrains such as, "Regarded with suspicion by the Indian; shunned by the Caucasian; where was there any place for the despised breed!" (ch. 1).

Of course, McWhorter, as editor, operates from a particular though lingering moment in our colonial history, when the carefully constructed and policed confines of race-ranked society forbade miscegenation. From such a view, indeed he likely saw no possible place for the "despised breed." Yet, immersed in the same society, Mourning Dove writes with surprising resistance to that purported reality of her time. Courageously, Cogewea dares to imagine entering both "races": "I'm part Injun and can participate in that as well as in the ladies race. They can't stop me from riding in both races, can they? If there's any difference between a squaw and a lady, I want to know it. I am going to pose as both for this day" (ch. 6). Strikingly, Cogewea perceives her Native identity less as a fixed biological fact than as a shifting performance. Here, identity is not who you are but what you do. She insists on consciously "posing" within a more freely defined social space that enables the kind of "mixed blood" identity not to be openly celebrated for decades.

By the 1960s, Native American authors had begun to make the question—but also the recovery and the renewal—of Indigenous cultural identity the central theoretical and literary task in the Indian novel. While earlier writers such as Mourning Dove and McNickle at times saw the problem of mixed ancestry as important to understanding cultural erosion, the new writers saw Native identity and even mixed ancestry as the embodiment, the cause, and the solution to their colonial situation. American Indians writing during the Indian movement, and those influenced by it, understand the crucial place of tribal knowledge, identity, and experience in the decolonization of Indigenous peoples. Such well-known Native writers as N. Scott Momaday, Leslie Marmon Silko, and James Welch elucidate just how American Indian people can awaken politically, reclaim a history, and build a community, and often through a historical, transnational process that hearkens to the earlier Indigenous writers who founded the Native novel.

27

THE NOVEL AFTER THE GREAT WAR

BY PAUL GILES

In "Within the Rim" (1917), an essay first published the year after his death, Henry James portrays himself walking along the coast near the "high-perched Sussex town" where he used to live and "staring" out "at the bright mystery" across the English Channel: "Just on the other side of that finest of horizon-lines history was raging at a pitch new under the sun." In the same way that James in *The American Scene* (1907) represents himself as a displaced observer perturbed by the processes of modernization, so "Within the Rim" evokes an image of the author perplexed and disoriented by the prospect of change. He compares his sentiments to how a "quiet dweller in a tenement" might feel "when the question of 'structural improvements' is thrust upon him." James, with his typical candor and artistic openness to the unpredictable nature of experience, does not simply resist what he calls "the shock of events." Instead, he depicts himself as being disturbed by "the history of the hour addressing itself to the individual mind," along with the "degree of pain attached to the ploughed-up state it implied."

James's response was not untypical of that of American writers to the First World War, an event known simply as the "Great War" until the outbreak of the Second World War in 1939. However much they were appalled by the scenes of carnage and suffering, American writers also at some level tended to regard the war as an emblem of modernity, a necessary disruption of that state of ossified gentility which, by the second decade of the twentieth century, appeared to have become thoroughly anachronistic. Paul Fussell has written of how for English writers the First World War operated as a kind of apocalyptic caesura, with the period before August 4, 1914, appearing in legend as a timeless Edwardian idyll, and the "Time After" a regrettable collapse into twentieth-century modernity (2000, 80). But Fussell's observation that "the Great War was perhaps the last to be conceived as taking place within a seamless, purposeful 'history' involving a coherent stream of time running from past through present to future" (21) is an argument more readily applicable to English than to American writers: Rupert Brooke, for example, was nostalgically attached to a notion of "purposeful" tradition and "coherent" history in a way that John Dos

Passos and Ernest Hemingway never were. In this sense, as in many others, James's intellectual allegiance oscillates between different sides of the Atlantic, since his final essays imply a loyalty to the British fight against what he calls "the huge Prussian fist," while at the same time acknowledging, as do Dos Passos and Hemingway more explicitly, the various subtle ways in which contemporary conditions have the effect of "overscoring the image as a whole or causing the old accepted synthesis to bristle with accents" ("Within the Rim," 1917). There is an elegiac tone in James's farewell here to the "old accepted synthesis" of Edwardian Britain, but also an understanding that new "accents" have become inevitable.

Another difference between English and American cultural responses to the war derived from their discrepancies in their contributions to active military service. Woodrow Wilson held back from entering the conflict in 1915, when the British ship Lusitania was torpedoed with the loss of over a hundred American lives, and it was only in April 1917, after significantly increased submarine warfare in the Atlantic, that the United States declared war against Germany. Since the Armistice was concluded in November 1918, this meant that American soldiers were engaged for only nineteenth months, as opposed to forty-eight months for troops from Britain and the Empire. Consequently, the fatality toll in America was 126,000 out of a total population of one hundred million, a figure that in terms of brute statistics was quite small when compared with Britain's losses of 908,000 out of a population of forty-three million. In addition, the forced centralization and increases in manufacturing technology associated with the war effort caused the US economy to forge ahead during the First World War, while the economies of Europe, which experienced the kind of widespread destruction of physical plants from which America was exempt, conversely lost ground and were significantly worse off than they had been at the start of the conflict. In light of such anomalies, it is not altogether surprising that American writers were able to take what Malcolm Cowley in *Exile's Return* (1934) called a more "spectatorial attitude" towards wartime events (47). Most American soldiers in 1917 were involved in peripheral military activities—training, driving ambulances and so on, rather than being caught up on the front line—so that the comment of Fred Summers, in John Dos Passos's novel *1919*, about how "this ain't a war, it's a goddam Cook's tour" would have had a particular relevance to the situation of American servicemen in Europe ("Newsreel 26"). Cowley's later description in *A Second Flowering* of the Great War as "the greatest spectacle in history" (1974, 9) is oddly reminiscent of Jean Baudrillard's description of the Gulf War in 1990–91 as marked by simulacra and an absence of direct conflict. While there might be an element of intellectual truth in both cases, such curiously estranged, lop-sided perspectives tend to overlook how things often appeared quite differently from particular vantage points on the ground.

For American writers, nevertheless, the Great War was at least in part bound up with travel and exploration, the excitement of discovering Europe for the first time. For Americans at the beginning of the twentieth century, Europe was associated with the allure of transgression in a way that is difficult to reconstitute fully within the media-saturated environment of a hundred years later, when transcontinental travel has become much more commonplace. For Lambert Strether in James's novel *The Ambassadors* (1903), it is Paris itself that operates as the prime agent of the hero's increasing involvement in a field of moral ambiguity, a dangerous swerve away from the staid business values with which he had been surrounded in his home town of Woollett, Massachusetts. Similarly in E. E. Cummings's *The Enormous Room* (1922) there is a distinct focus on the French environment itself as opening the doors to perceptions of a new aesthetic modernity. A war memoir which is related in the first person, with characters and events being dramatized in fictional terms, *The Enormous Room* was published some years after its author's wartime experiences, when he had been interned along with his friend William Slater Brown in a French military camp at La Ferté-Macé, a detention center for "undesirables" and suspected "spies." These somewhat farcical events are fused in Cummings's narrative into a kaleidoscopic portrayal of the military prison as an embryonic scene of modernity, with this picture of a world in a state of enforced immobility allowing the author to introduce weirdly oblique perspectives. In prison, Cummings remarks, events appear to exist independently of time: when an inmate realizes that no "speculation as to when he will regain his liberty" can hasten his release, he forgets the oppressive concept of "Time" altogether. In this sense, Cummings's representation through the French prison of an "actual Present—without future and past," where "each happening is self-sufficient" (ch. 5), resembles his poetry of the interwar period, which similarly seeks to identify Neoplatonic patterns underlying the more positivistic concerns of human history. *The Enormous Room* thus recasts the French prison camp in the shape of modernist art, using caricature to frame its depictions of dehumanization within what the book calls a "somewhat cubist wilderness" (ch. 2), while redescribing the French landscape in painterly, impressionist terms: he mentions, for example, "a very flourishing sumach bush . . . whose berries shocked the stunned eye with a savage splash of vermillion" (ch. 8). Gertrude Stein, in *The Autobiography of Alice B. Toklas* (1933), remarked on how she was "much impressed" by *The Enormous Room* (ch. 7), and while Cummings here certainly ridicules authoritarian military structures, the book is also a notable example of the way in which American writers in the 1920s were seeking to requisition wartime landscapes as a harbinger of cultural modernism.

In "The Ideology of Modernism," the Hungarian Marxist critic György Lukács argued that modernist aesthetics involved a betrayal of the realist principles that had informed social consciousness in nineteenth-century literature, since modernism's fetishization of the eccentric and the abnormal caused it to lose sight of the broader historical dynamic linked to human agency. According to Lukács, the preference of modernist writers for focusing on the solitary, alienated condition of man tended to reify external reality as unalterable and thus to preclude the possibility of cultural or political change. It is true that American writers largely represent the First World War as an instrument of fate, but it would also be true to say that it is through the techniques of formal dislocation and strategic irony that they seek to reflect in narrative forms the historical conditions of wartime within their texts. In this sense, the Great War operated as what J. Gerald Kennedy has called an "enabling exercise" for American modernity (1993, 28), not only exposing writers to the machinery of technological conflict but also displacing them from familiar home surroundings and assumptions. Modernism itself was, in George Steiner's term, "extraterritorial," in that artists made a point of moving around among different locations to avoid provincial enclosure, and Paris, a locus of artistic experimentation for émigrés such as Igor Stravinsky, Pablo Picasso, and James Joyce during the first quarter of the twentieth century, was also a site of initiation for American writers such as Cummings and Dos Passos, who first encountered the city through the exigencies of war (on extraterritoriality and modernism, see Chapters 24 and 29 in this volume). Just as African American modernism, as Brent Hayes Edwards has shown, was formed by artistic experimentation in Paris as much as Harlem, so the masculine novel by white Americans in the early-twentieth century rotated upon a transatlantic axis that operated, either literally or subliminally, as a memento of military conflict.

Metaphorical equations between personal and cultural maturity are made explicit in Dos Passos's first novel, *One Man's Initiation: 1917*, which was first published in 1920. The book starts with an epigraph testifying to the authenticity of its narrative: "To the memory of those with whom I saw rockets in the sky, on the road between Erize-la-Petite and Erize-la-Grande, in that early August twilight in the summer of 1917." The hero, Martin Howe, says that he "never used to think that at nineteen I'd be crossing the Atlantic to go to a war in France." He continues, however, by stating that he has "never been so happy in his life" (ch. 1), since for Martin the "initiation" of the book's title involves discovering the charms of French women as well as the chaos of the battlefield. Various overtly sexual references were censored when the book was first published in America, and one key theme of the work involves a turning away from ossified conventions and an embrace of modernity in all of its confusions: one of Martin's fellow soldiers says that "life was so dull in America that anything seems better" (ch. 7). At the same time, through one of the paradoxes of modernism in general, such an avant-garde sensibility also involves cultural regression, the acknowledgement of how contemporary events often echo ritualistic patterns of the past. Martin, in a nod to Dante's *Divine Comedy*, says he wants "to be initiated in all the circles of hell"—his colleague admits he would "play the part of Virgil pretty well" (ch. 6)—while Martin also links the danse macabre of the Great War to the way "the people in Boccaccio managed to enjoy themselves while the plague was at Florence" (ch. 9). Such a forced integration of the New World into medieval cycles serves to challenge the old idea of American exceptionalism, the notion that the United States enjoyed a sense of "freedom" from "the gangrened ghost of the past." Martin here specifically observes how his native country "has turned traitor to all that . . . now we're a military nation, an organised pirate like France and England and Germany" (ch. 9). In this sense, Dos Passos conscripts American literature into the wider conceptual framework of modernism, where, as in T. S. Eliot's *The Waste Land* or James Joyce's *Ulysses* (both published in 1922), aesthetic modernity betokens a conscious attempt to reclaim the classical past, to disinter the archaeological or atavistic framework underlying the superficial modernity of twentieth-century life.

Dos Passos's next novel, *Three Soldiers* (1921), extends this wartime scene into a more elaborate consideration of limitations on human freedom. The book again turns upon a transatlantic axis, starting off in San Francisco before following the fortunes of three American servicemen in France. Initially, Fuseli, like Martin Howe, enjoys the opportunities afforded by war—he says "It's great to be a soldier. . . . Ye kin do anything ye goddam please" (pt. 1, ch. 4)—but as the narrative progresses the forces of mechanization appear ever more brutalizing, and the romance of war is suppressed in favour of its "interminable monotony," with Fuseli coming to feel "full of hopeless anger against this vast treadmill to which he was bound" (pt. 2, ch. 4). In *Three Soldiers*, war is presented not so much as a site of physical carnage but as a gargantuan bureaucracy, a way of constraining human individuality "into the rigid attitudes of automatons in uniforms," all of which betokens "the hideous farce of making men into machines" (pt. 5, ch. 3). The leading character in this novel, John Andrews, is a composer who comes to feel that serving his country in battle resembles the older forms of "slavery" that have disfigured history, and when he deserts from the army towards the end of the book he gives his name to a police officer as "John Brown," thereby deliberately affiliating himself with the nineteenth-century abolitionist, "a madman who wanted to free people" (pt. 6, ch. 4). In this way, Dos Passos extends his specific critique of war into a more general indictment of the coercive, corporate aspects of twentieth-century life. There is in this novel a deep romanticization of art as an antidote to such forms of dehumanization: Andrews himself idealizes Paris as a place "where one can find out things about music" (pt. 5, ch. 4), while the book pays homage to composers Claude Debussy and Robert Schumann and to the writer Gustave Flaubert, whose "gorgeously modulated sentences" Andrews much admires (pt. 4, ch. 1). At the same time, the landscapes of Paris are frequently projected within an Impressionist aesthetic: "the plane trees splotched with brown and cream color along the quais[,] . . . the Eiffel Tower with a drift of mist athwart it, like a section of spider web spun between the city and the clouds" (pt. 5, ch. 3).

Three Soldiers is characteristic of early Dos Passos in the way it sets up a binary opposition between artistic ideals and mechanized routines, an opposition that the later novels tend to disallow. By the time of *Manhattan Transfer* (1922), the author is more concerned with how the revolving glass doors of modern urban life create their own machine aesthetic, while in his *USA* trilogy of the 1930s we witness what Michael Denning has called "a Tayloring of the novel" (1996, 177), where narrative scenes are organized in standardized typographic and media formats, rather than merely following the world, as in the more traditional picaresque idiom of *One Man's Initiation*, through the eyes of an individual narrator. *1919*, the second novel in this *USA* trilogy and first published in 1932, takes the Great War as one aspect of its global remit, but it also juxtaposes the events of war with other historical markers of the time: with Lenin and the Russian Revolution; with the Seattle general strike; and with the work of radicals in the art world such as Picasso and Stravinsky in Europe and Charlie Chaplin in the United States. In this way, *1919* moves away from the more sentimental dimensions of *Three Soldiers* by inscribing a global aesthetic where the shocks of war become analogous to the shocks of modernity in other cultural fields.

From James to Dos Passos, American novelists who wrote about the Great War pondered how its violence shaped a new aesthetic world. But the question of how that world reverberated in the sphere of American letters, and in particular the relationship between cultural modernity and aesthetic modernism, has remained a vexed one for literary studies. When the journal *American Quarterly* ran a special issue in 1987 on "Modernist Culture in America," the very idea of such a phenomenon appeared controversial, since the traditional narrative of literary history institutionalized by Alfred Kazin and others after the Second World War had been that European modernism developed in an abstruse and etiolated manner while American novelists responded in a more robust, realistic fashion to changes they saw unfolding in the world around them. The attempts to define American literature as a separate field of study during the Cold War era often had the regrettable side-effect of marginalizing European or transnational contexts, and in his contribution to this special issue of *American Quarterly*, Malcolm Bradbury specifically took issue with Hugh Kenner's version of American modernism as "a homemade world," which Bradbury described as an act of intellectual "appropriation" that underestimated the involvement of American writers in more cosmopolitan artistic ventures (1987, 28). For example, the first version of F. Scott Fitzgerald's *The Great Gatsby* (1925) was organized self-consciously around classical parallels with ancient Rome—the author had in mind here the Homeric parallels of Joyce's *Ulysses* (1922)—before Fitzgerald's editor at Scribner's, Max Perkins, persuaded him that a slimmed-down version of the Trimalchio myth would appeal more directly to an American readership. On one level, recognition of Gatsby's palimpsestic textual construction would speak to what Frank Lentricchia has described as the typically "ambidextrous" quality of American modernism (1994, 107), where highbrow and lowbrow, mythology and realism, are conflated in an often unobtrusive manner: unlike Eliot or Virginia Woolf, who flaunt their modernist complexities, Robert Frost presents his poem "After Apple Picking," from *North of Boston* (1915), as a much more oblique, down-home version of *Paradise Lost*. But more recent critical work has suggested ways in which artistic modernism in general was not, as Lukács suggested, a principled rejection of historical modernity by its antagonists, but was rather enmeshed in complicated ways within it. In *Modernism, Technology, and the Body*, Tim Armstrong, for instance, has written of how the arts of modernism were implicated in numerous ways with the scientific, technological, and political shifts that characterize the modern era (1998).

In this broader sense, one of the important legacies of the Great War was to raise awareness among American writers of the ethics and aesthetics of the machine. "When everything is done by machines," asks Clara Butterworth in Sherwood Anderson's novel *Poor White* (1920), "what are people to do?" (ch. 8). Industrial development in the aftermath of the First World War introduced the same kind of anxieties that were to be seen at the end of the twentieth century around issues of information technology, and many writers of this earlier era address the issues of displacement, both psychic and geographic, that were associated with a general shift from an agrarian to an urban economy. Some of these tensions were played out in the often hostile reception accorded in the United States to the alien figures of high modernist art, with the 1913 Armory Show in New York being the most egregious example of Americans accustomed to more traditional styles of representation finding it difficult to come to terms with Picasso paintings where human beings might be portrayed with two heads. But, as Paul K. Saint-Amour has shown, this kind of "syntax of rupture" (2003, 349), where observers cannot give credence to the object that appears before their eyes, was not just a feature of cubist art but was also developed in common wartime technologies such as wireless telegraphy and aerial photography. Edward Steichen, who finished the war as chief of the US Air Service Photographic Section, was instrumental in developing the practice of overlapping aerial photographs for reconnaissance purposes, a technological shift which implicitly revealed the spatial and temporal contingency of human vision by emphasizing instead the kind of "vertigo of scale" associated with a stereoscope (Saint-Amour 2003, 368). Dos Passos's aesthetic idiom in *1919*, which is similarly designed to construct overlapping scenes so as to build up a "stereoscopic" vision of America's place in the world, might in this sense be linked to the kinds of reorganization of perceptual circuits that wartime technologies had helped to bring about.

There is also a more familiar equation between writing from the First World War and the aesthetic strategies of modernist art, a link signaled by Ernest Hemingway in a 1922 newspaper article where he recalled looking down from an airplane on a field outside Paris: "It looked cut into brown squares, yellow squares, green squares and big flat blotches of green where there was a forest. I began to understand cubist painting" (1967, 42–43). Gertrude Stein, who was one of Hemingway's mentors in Paris, wrote in *The Autobiography of Alice B. Toklas* of the Great War as a specifically modern and American event, although in *Wars I Have Seen* (1945) she describes war as a form of compulsive repetition, where primordial national characteristics are brought to light. In this sense, war for Stein is a conceptual equivalent to her understanding of abstract art, a historical correlative to the aesthetics of Cézanne where ornamental superfluity is stripped away and the essential nature of man revealed. It was Hemingway's similar elimination of the fustian associations of British literary tradition, along with his deliberate attempt to focus upon objects uncluttered by any kind of superfluous rhetoric, that first attracted Stein's attention. *In Our Time* (1924), which D. H. Lawrence called a "fragmentary novel" (1982, 73), is a series of linked short stories that intercuts narratives set in America with scenes from the battlefront, with the book's title implying not only the hollowness of the prayer book's injunction—"give us peace in our time, O Lord"—but also ways in which the psychic disorientations of war extend across different times and places. The author himself compared the dual perspective of *In Our Time* to watching the coastline from a ship first with the naked eye and then with binoculars, and this metaphor speaks again to the multilateral dimensions of American writing in the wake of the Great War, its attempt self-consciously to encompass more than was ordinarily grasped within one particular person's field of vision.

Much of Hemingway's later work similarly seeks to understand the Great War not only journalistically but also within a larger framework of cultural modernism. *The Sun Also Rises* (1926), which John McCormick described as "the finest war novel we have" (1971, 58), is actually set not on the front but in postwar Paris and Spain, with its hero, Jake Barnes, seeking to recover from the legacy of his wartime injuries by attending carefully to the present moment. Jake insists on what he actually does think and feel, rather than what he is supposed to think and feel, and the novel harshly undercuts every kind of false sentiment in its effort to achieve a state of psychological integrity. Hemingway at a late stage lopped off the first fifteen typed pages of *The Sun Also Rises*, omitting the biographies of Barnes and Lady Brett Ashley in an attempt to eliminate the cluttered verbiage of the old-fashioned novel of manners and to achieve instead a kind of minimalist grace. The bullfighting scenes in *The Sun Also Rises* also testify to ways in which wartime violence becomes sublimated for Hemingway's characters into other forms of ritualistic practice, while *A Farewell to Arms* (1929) treats this theme of First World War violence more explicitly, being set on the Italian front and told largely through the eyes of Lieutenant Frederic Henry, an American serving as an ambulance driver in the Italian army. Henry is wounded in the knee and sent to a hospital in Milan, and the subsequent development of his romance with Catherine Barkley, a nurse in the military hospital, is set against the backdrop of war. Part of the book's force involves its interrogation of patriotic clichés and its emphasis instead upon a phenomenological authenticity through which the facts of war come in themselves to attract a luminous aesthetic force: "Abstract words such as glory, honour, courage, or hallow were obscene beside the concrete names of villages, the numbers of roads the names of rivers, the numbers of regiments and the dates" (ch. 27). As biographer Carlos Baker recounts, Hemingway himself was very critical of what he took to be the "fake" aspects of Willa Cather's war story "One of Ours" (1923)—he claimed Cather's war scenes were all "stolen" from D. W. Griffith's film *The Birth of a Nation*

(1915)—and the dominant effect of *A Farewell to Arms* is of a laconic knowingness, of characters in the modern world unsurprised by the violent events that surround them (Baker 1969, 153).

At the same time, the belatedness that is endemic to Hemingway's war writing— as suggested by the title *A Farewell to Arms*—implies how elements of parody are inherent within Hemingway's literary project. In his attempt to achieve the emotional purity of "a clean well-lighted place," his work compulsively parodies what it takes to be the calcified conditions of a superannuated culture. Just as Hemingway mocked the style of Sherwood Anderson and other modernist writers in *The Torrents of Spring* (1926) and spoofed the jargon of psychoanalysis in *The Sun Also Rises*, so the story "Soldier's Home," from *In Our Time*, turns upon a language of intertextual inversion and negativity: "There is a picture which shows him on the Rhine with two German girls and another corporal. Krebs and the corporal look too big for their uniforms. The German girls are not beautiful. The Rhine does not show in the picture." In the same way that he indicts Cather for recycling wartime clichés, Hemingway also seems to express impatience toward his own narratives for the ways in which they are inevitably incarcerated in a metaphorical prison where the inherently reflexive quality of language always denies access to simple experiential truth. Hemingway's notorious violence, in other words, is incorporated into a psychological and philosophical world of self-immolation; for all of the author's stylistic innovations, his texts are haunted by specters of absence, by the wounds not only of wartime but also of ontological duality and a categorical loss of innocence. One of the reasons Hemingway was obsessed by wars and their "moral equivalents," as Harry Levin observed (1951, 606), was that his fiction came to represent life as being all about the fight to capture a state of plenitude or authenticity, something that for his narrators remains always elusive. Consequently, the power of Hemingway's writing lies in its rhythms of perpetual anticlimax and disillusionment. He recapitulates the turbulence of the Great War that is explicit in his early writing in other kinds of conflict in his later work, whether in other military scenarios, such as the Spanish Civil War in *For Whom the Bell Tolls* (1940), or through more oblique forms of violent engagement, such as the scenes of big game hunting in *The Green Hills of Africa* (1935).

No group in America before 1918 had called itself a generation, and one of the impacts made by the Great War was to identify people born at a certain point in history as shaped more by large-scale national or international trends rather than by older traditions of family or region. One of the authors who echoed Stein's observation that the First World War marked a generational shift was Edith Wharton, who wrote in her autobiography *A Backward Glance* (1934) how American social life had been changed abruptly by the United States entry into the war in 1917, when "what had seemed unalterable rules of conduct became of a sudden observances as quaintly arbitrary as the domestic rites of the Pharaohs" (ch. 1). Stein herself expresses admiration in *The Autobiography of Alice B. Toklas* for Fitzgerald's very successful first novel,

This Side of Paradise (1920), which she described as the "book that really created for the public the new generation" (1933, ch. 7), and which sold almost fifty thousand copies in its first year. Fitzgerald was fascinated by the structure of interpolated sketches that Hemingway devised for *In Our Time*, which he saw as characterizing the effects of war across a broad geographical spectrum, and his own fiction similarly embodies a choric quality, in the way it is designed self-consciously to tell the story of its era rather than just that of individual people within it. Amory Blaine in *This Side of Paradise* highlights this theme of temporal zones by describing how the war "certainly ruined the old backgrounds, sort of killed individualism out of our generation," and the novel suggests how in this new twentieth-century era even Leonardo da Vinci or Lorenzo de Medici could not have attained heroic status, since now "Life is too huge and complex" (bk. 2, ch. 2). During his time at Princeton, Amory Blaine cannot be bothered with the war: "Beyond a sporting interest in the German dash for Paris the whole affair failed either to thrill or interest him" (bk. 1, ch. 2). Nevertheless, the war's cultural ramifications are said to condition the lives of Amory's "generation" in both profound and superficial ways: for example, Cecilia Connage, sister of Amory's girlfriend, remarks here that a general loosening of morals among the young—more smoking, more drinking, more frequent kissing—is "one of the effects of the war" (bk. 2, ch. 1).

Fitzgerald himself was just too young to see active military service, but Nick Carraway, narrator of *The Great Gatsby*, says that he enjoyed the war and came back restless, feeling that his native Midwest now appeared to be "the ragged edge of the universe" rather than, as formerly, its "warm centre." Carraway has been unsettled by the war, saying that he "wanted the world to be in uniform and at a sort of moral attention forever" (ch. 1), and *The Great Gatsby* is thus a book about displacement at all levels. Jay Gatsby himself, like Carraway, has moved from the Midwest to the East Coast, and he is also said to be a war veteran, with the years spent travelling with the army initially bringing him into contact with Daisy Buchanan but also causing him to miss his initial opportunity with her. In this sense, Stein's famous remark to Hemingway about how his was a "lost generation," which the latter recalled in *A Moveable Feast* (1964), has a particular resonance for Fitzgerald's work as well. Ann Douglas has suggested there is a theological implication behind Stein's notion of a "lost" generation (1995, 42), and aspects of this postlapsarian sensibility are more obviously applicable to the work of Fitzgerald and Hemingway than to the writing of Stein herself. In *Tender is the Night* (1934), Dick Diver's professional occupation as a psychiatrist offers an opportunity for the traumatic effects of the Great War to be discussed by his colleague, Dr. Gregorovius, who says that even though Diver lacks direct experience of war that does not mean he may not have been "changed like the rest" (bk. 2, ch. 2). Later in the book, Diver has "a long dream of war," and when he wakes up he speaks in a "half-ironic" way of "Non-combatant's shell-shock" (bk. 2, ch. 14). Most of this novel is set on the French Riviera, but there is also a scene where Diver visits the battlefields of the Somme with his friends, Abe North and Rosemary

Hoyt, and exclaims: "All my beautiful lovely safe world blew itself up here with a great gust of high explosive love" (bk. 1, ch. 13). *Tender is the Night* thus allegorically associates Dick Diver's own "crack up" with what Fitzgerald takes to be the increasingly shell-shocked condition of the twentieth-century world.

Whereas Fitzgerald and Hemingway both represent the Great War as an epitome of modernist fate, there were other writers, particularly during the early war years, who fiercely opposed American involvement in it on political grounds. H. L. Mencken, of German ancestry himself, was one of the most prominent of these, while various other Greenwich Village radicals, including Max Eastman and Randolph Bourne, campaigned against the prospect of war before 1917. After the war, however, these oppositional voices became harder to find. Such quiescence was not simply a consequence of the war itself: as Neil Smith has remarked, it was the Russian Revolution and labor unrest at home that helped to bring about at this time a "deglobalization of sorts" (2003, 454), with the US Senate in 1919 rejecting membership in the League of Nations, and Congress rescinding most of the progressive measures that had been passed during the war. One consequence of this increased political conservatism was that questions of "taste and cultural value," as Susan Hegeman has observed, came to be articulated during the 1920s as never before or since in "geographical terms" (1999, 23). There was increased antagonism between country and city, with traditional rural communities expressing horror over social changes wrought through processes of modernization, while in turn Mencken and others in New York openly disdained the South and Midwest as primitive and backward. Sinclair Lewis's *Main Street* (1920), with its conflict between the values of Gopher Prairie, Minnesota, and modernization—Blodgett College, which the novel's inquisitive heroine Carol Kennicott attends, is said to be "still combating the recent heresies of Voltaire, Darwin, and Robert Ingersoll" (ch. 1)—foreshadowed a series of novels in the 1920s where isolated and backward-looking communities were played off against the allure of progressive, free-thinking big cities. This trend, in turn, fed into the demonization of the Midwest by the likes of Mencken, and it also contributed to the sense of restlessness that was endemic to fiction of the 1920s, where, as in Sherwood Anderson's *Winesburg, Ohio* (1919), the hero eventually feels compelled to abandon his provincial past in search of the riches of modern life.

Repression, then, was one of the general themes of fiction of the 1920s: not just the institutional repression of small-town life, but also the psychic repression arising out of sensibilities shaped by the First World War. Sigmund Freud, who gave a series of lectures in Massachusetts in 1909, was very well-known in America by the 1920s, and though of course his theories of psychoanalysis were often reworked into popular self-help narratives, the United States generally welcomed his work more readily than did traditional Europe, where the very notion of an unconscious was often considered suspect. Freud in 1915 suggested that wartime can last beyond the end of hostilities, and, as Marianna Torgovnick has written (2005, 1), this sense of the "cultural memory" of war is one of the starting points for *The Great Gatsby*, where Nick Carraway recalls at the beginning how he "participated in that delayed Teutonic migration known as the Great War" (ch. 1). A more systematic use of Freudian motifs manifests itself in Ludwig Lewisohn's novel *The Island Within* (1928), whose very narrative trajectory, chronicling a Jewish genealogy from nineteenth-century Prussia to twentieth-century America, might be seen in itself as an extended form of therapy, an attempt to delve back into the past so as to establish cultural identity more securely in the present. "Until the other day we Americans lived as though we had no past," says the narrator on the book's first page (bk. 1, ch. 1), but *The Island Within* then moves on deliberately to trace the contours of the past in order to excavate and explain the idea of ethnic difference. The notion of psychoanalysis is foregrounded in the narrative through Arthur Levy's professional practice as a therapist, and the whole structure of the novel is that of a man talking to himself, or perhaps a patient on a couch working through issues associated with the "inferiority complex" frequently cited here. After graduating from Columbia in 1914, Levy feels perturbed by the outbreak of European war, which he feels "to be something irrational—a hiatus in the march of civilization" (bk. 5, ch. 2), but as the book goes on this sense of "irrational" agents in human affairs appears to be increasingly validated, with the hero drawn back towards his own Jewish heritage that he feels has left "an indelible stamp" on him (bk. 7, ch. 4). Arthur's marriage to his non-Jewish wife, Elizabeth, consequently falls apart, with the compulsive though not entirely rational business of "reidentifying oneself with one's own people or group or clan" coming to supersede what are perceived to be the illusory freedoms of secular thought (bk. 8, ch. 6): "You didn't know you were going to resurrect the Jew in you," concludes Elizabeth plaintively at the end of the novel (bk. 9). For Levy, then, the traumatic disruptions of the Great War, which is said to have "loosened the taut strain of Puritan morals" (bk. 6, ch. 3), shift his attention away from his narrow medical studies and expose him to the more uncomfortable aspects of "a barbarous world" (bk. 8, ch. 5), where rationalizations of all kinds appear shallow when set against the atavistic nature of human instincts.

These kinds of "herd prejudices," as *The Island Within* describes them (bk. 4, ch. 8), were not just found within the latent structures of psychoanalysis but also circulated more widely on the American political scene at this time. The entry of America into the First World War in 1917 sparked a wave of intense nationalism, fuelled not only by the normal jingoistic rhetoric of wartime but also by a determined effort on the part of political leaders to consolidate the official position of English by suppressing the teaching of other immigrant languages. It was this kind of nationalism that helped to push the subject of American literature into a more prominent place on high school curricula. The 1920s was also the decade when American literature began fully to establish itself as an academic subject at university level. In his introduction to *The Reinterpretation of American Literature*, a collaborative book published by the newly-formed American literature section of the Modern

Language Association, Norman Foerster declared there was a new need in the wake of the First World War to know what America "really is" (1928, vii). Whereas the field of American history had become professionalized, said Foerster, questions of American literature had so far been left to "facile journalists and ignorant dilettanti" (viii). But the events of war had served to focus attention on the United States as an independent powerful nation rather than merely a series of local cultures: "Throwing our nineteenth century into clearer perspective, the Great War removed from large numbers of Americans the sectional spectacles that had distorted their vision" (24). It would hardly be going too far to say that it was this "Great War" that effectively invented the idea of "American literature," not only in an institutional sense, as Foerster suggests here, but also conceptually. As Walter Benn Michaels has argued, the intense concern among writers of the 1920s with "nativism" as an ineradicable marker of cultural identity—the obsession in Hemingway, William Carlos Williams, and other American modernists with "America" itself as a sign of racial authenticity—produced an intellectual framework within which American literature, simply because of its Americanness, could be categorized as inherently different from other national idioms.

While the American novel of the early twentieth century has become widely associated with the "Jazz Age" through the texts of Fitzgerald, Hemingway, and others, it is important to recognize how the traumatic violence of the Great War was also an important contributory factor to this formative moment of cultural nationalism. The early novels of William Faulkner also testify in interesting ways to the manner in which the shadow of the First World War hovers over "Jazz Age" literature. Faulkner himself had minimal exposure to military activity: keen to be a pilot, he joined the Royal Air Force in Canada and was posted to Toronto to be trained, but found his ambitions thwarted when the war finished before his training was complete. Although discharged as a cadet, Faulkner nevertheless purchased an officer's uniform, which he wore on the train home to Mississippi, where he subsequently regaled his old friends with tall tales of the wounds he had suffered in air conflict. More important than this, however, is the way in which Faulkner's first novel, *Soldiers' Pay* (1926), recasts his native South in the light of the Great War. Set mostly in Georgia rather than in Faulkner's mythological Mississippi, and noticeably oriented more toward the contemporary in its evocation of recent historical events, *Soldiers' Pay* chronicles the return home of Donald Mahon, a pilot who has been shot down in Flanders and who now wears a permanent scar on his face. The rupture and transformation of war are epitomized in the figure of Mahon, of whom a local doctor says: the "man that was wounded is dead and this is another person, a grown child" (ch. 3). This notion of a "grown child" anticipates Faulkner's later novel *The Sound and the Fury* (1929), where Benjy is an adult of thirty-three who is said to have a mental age of three, and it suggests ways in which Faulkner was attracted to the war partly as a way of approaching one of the key thematic concerns throughout his work: the disruption and reorganization of chronological sequence.

In *Soldiers' Pay*, people once considered too young to marry now find that "war makes you older" (ch. 7), the reverse of the grown child syndrome, while the scope of the conflict also effectively remaps the spatial coordinates that link the rural country to national events. "To feel provincial," says the narrator, involves "finding that a certain conventional state of behavior has become inexplicably obsolete overnight" (ch. 5).

Soldiers' Pay thus repositions the American South in the aftermath of the Great War, reconfiguring nature itself through metaphors of battle—"The stars swam on like the masthead lights of squadrons" (ch. 6)—and contemplating "the hang-over of warfare in a society tired of warfare" (ch. 5). More realist in its style than most of Faulkner's later fiction, *Soldiers' Pay* could be seen as his Jazz Age novel, since it describes the appearance of flappers and comments on how new social mores have brought about "physical freedom" for women, with a girl's "young, uncorseted body" seeming to be "flat as a boy's, and, like a boy's, pleasuring in freedom and motion" (ch. 5). Many of the novels written in the shadow of the Great War react self-consciously against traditional gender codes associated with military life, with fictional characters such as Jake Barnes in *The Sun Also Rises* and Dick Diver in *Tender is the Night* represented as having lost their masculinity in various ways, and in this sense *Soldiers' Pay* touches on a theme fairly common to war novels of this era. The plot of Faulkner's novel revolves around whether Cecily Saunders will fulfill her promise to marry Mahon despite his war injury, or whether instead she will take off with her able-bodied suitor, George Carr. There is a veiled discussion here of Mahon's possible impotence—whether, as Mrs Powers puts it, he is "all right . . . for marriage," since she says "a man ain't no right to palm himself off on a woman if he ain't" (ch. 7)—and the idea of sexual relations here is presented in the kind of brutal, unsentimental way that later attracted censure to Faulkner for *Sanctuary* (1929). What is more striking, though, is the strong emphasis in Faulkner's narrative on sexuality in general, along with a tone that often verges toward the cynical; such features were characteristic of iconoclastic writing in the 1920s, but they caused such outrage in Faulkner's home state that the book was initially banned at the University of Mississippi. The particularly provocative dimension of *Soldiers' Pay* lies in the way sexuality is associated implicitly not with spirit but with a world of matter, as if to align the narrative with the controversies of the Scopes trial which had taken place in Tennessee the year before, a trial that set Christian fundamentalists against those who advocated the teaching of evolution in high schools. College teacher Januarius Jones, for example, scrutinizes Cecily here as if she were an embodiment of Darwinian principles—"Her long legs, not for locomotion, but for the studied completion of a rhythm carried to its *nth*: compulsion of progress, movement; her body created for all men to dream after" (ch. 6)—with the implication that his scholarly interests in Latin play second fiddle here to his frustrated sexual urges. In addition, the frequent references in *Soldiers' Pay* to icons of the Decadent movement (Charles Algernon Swinburne, Aubrey Beardsley, and so on) enhance the reader's impression of a world where conventional moral values have fallen into disrepair and where a wider sense of degeneration—what Margaret Powers, thinking of Jones, describes as "an impression of aped intelligence imposed on an innate viciousness" (ch. 7)—has become the order of the day.

It was Sherwood Anderson who helped to get *Soldiers' Pay* published, and Faulkner dedicated to Anderson one of his subsequent novels, *Sartoris* (1929), which bridges the Jazz Age qualities of *Soldiers' Pay* with an immersion in the cyclic history of Mississippi that was to become Faulkner's authorial trademark. *Sartoris* is the first Faulkner work to be set in Jefferson, and it features a wartime aviator, Bayard Sartoris, returning home to the changing South. The old housekeeper Miss Jenny is generally unsympathetic to the idea of men going off to "play soldier," and in particular to Bayard's decision to come back to America in the middle of the war to get married. She compares Bayard unfavorably to his twin brother John, who "at least had consideration enough, after he'd gone and gotten himself into something where he had no business, not to come back and worry everybody to distraction" (ch. 2). But John is killed in the war, whereas Bayard eventually returns to Mississippi with a taste for speed, machinery, and accidents; he buys an automobile, kills his grandfather in a car crash, then flees to South America, where he meets an airman in a bar and, unable to resist the allure of flying again, subsequently dies in an aviation experiment at the age of twenty-seven.

Faulkner thus portrays Bayard as caught up within a cycle of obsessive behavior, compelled to repeat the violence of war to a point of self-destruction. These psychopathological repetitions also merge here into Faulkner's more general view of the South, where the fate of young Bayard mirrors the self-immolation of his namesake in the American Civil War fifty years earlier. In this sense, the trauma of the Great War for the Sartoris clan introduces a larger Faulkner theme, "the perverse necessity of his family doom" (ch. 4), the ways in which ancestral bonds circumscribe individual destiny, a theme we see developed in relation to the Compson family in Faulkner's most famous novels. The prospect of social change is generally viewed askance by the characters in *Sartoris*. The black soldier Caspey claims he "don't take nothin' fum no white folks no mo'," saying that "War done changed all dat. If us cullud folks is good enough ter save France fum de Germans, der us is good enough ter have de same rights de Germans is." But Simon, a fellow African American, is less open to new ideas, insisting that he still prefers horses to automobiles, and appealing to the "arrogant shade" of "Marse John" Sartoris to rebuke Caspey's uppity notions (ch. 2). Later in the book we are told that "Caspey had more or less returned to normalcy" (ch. 3), but the question of what is "normalcy," and the ways in which the representation of Caspey's speech as a form of dialect serves effectively to marginalize him within this world, epitomizes both the power and the problems of Faulkner's writing. The problematic nature of Faulkner's work lies in the way it conflates racial stereotypes and hierarchies with a state of nature, as if such differentiations arose out of the cycles of the earth; its strength, though, lies in its radically inchoate character, the way it textually evokes opposing forces without seeking to impose any kind of premature closure upon them. *Sartoris* brings European war and American pastoral, modernity and Mississippi, into violent juxtaposition, but rather than seeking any kind of sentimental resolution it allows these divergent pressures to work themselves out in circuitous ways. Although the lawyer Horace Benbow returns from the European front to idealize his Jefferson home in "a golden Arcadian drowse," saying that "the reason for wars" is "[t]he meaning of peace" (ch. 3), Faulkner's complex, multivalent novel does not altogether endorse such a regressive view of domestic bliss. Indeed, it is the burden of Faulkner's modernist rhetoric to bring alternative discourses and interpretations of the world into conflict, so that characters with different views on law and race are implicitly at war with each other. Unlike in the more emollient world of postmodernist narrative, where different worldviews are allowed to operate harmoniously alongside each other, Faulkner's personae exist within the more fraught circumstances of modernism, where they find themselves tormented by an impulse to achieve states of purity and truth. In this sense the figure of the Great War comes for Faulkner to have a wider metaphorical resonance, since violence, conflict, and rupture are the dynamics upon which his fictional world turns.

In the twenty-first-century world of high-tech warfare, when international conflict has become a highly specialized operation, it is sometimes difficult to reconstitute the very different twentieth-century mind set, when world war involved the threat of universal conscription. War in the early years of the twentieth century was a labor intensive occupation where lives were easily expendable and where the prospect of lay people being drawn into the conflict was much more evident. Although the United States itself was never a theatre of conflict and did not have to endure mass bombing, the traumas suffered by servicemen on behalf of the country as a whole helped to shape the direction of the American novel throughout the 1920s. Faulkner published *Sartoris* in January 1929, just a few months before *The Sound and the Fury* appeared in October of that year, but even in Faulkner's later novels the echoes of war still reverberate, and the ways in which he often imaginatively conflates the First World War with the US Civil War suggests how this wartime aesthetic had a durable effect on his fiction. Indeed, whereas from the synoptic retrospective gaze of the second half of the twentieth century the First World War was often regarded as merely a prelude to the Second World War, for Faulkner, as for other writers of this period, it was the comparisons with the US Civil War that were more pressing. Henry James similarly begins his essay "Within the Rim" by evoking the shade of this earlier conflict: "The first sense of it all to me after the first shock and horror was that of a sudden leap back into life of the violence with which the American Civil War broke upon us, at the North, fifty-four years ago, when I had a consciousness of youth which perhaps equaled in vivacity my present consciousness of age." While James recognizes the similarity of these historical situations in terms of their conditions of violence, he is also astute enough to acknowledge the "illusion" of the "analogy," and part of the disorienting aspect of the First World War for American writers was precisely that this new kind of war pulled them out of their familiar and accustomed national orbits. For Faulkner, as for many other Americans of this era, the issue of active military engagement was ultimately less significant than the ways in which the country appeared to be drawn into more extensive social and political circuits, with the circumference of world war positioning US culture differently in relation to the march of global events.

28

THE HARLEM RENAISSANCE NOVEL

BY ZITA NUNES

"The Harlem Renaissance" names a period of unprecedented artistic production lasting from the early 1920s to the mid-1930s, in which black writers, artists, and intellectuals sought to counter racism by focusing on the cultural sphere to advocate social and political change. What we now prefer to call the Harlem Renaissance was also known at the time as the Negro Renaissance and coincided with the New Negro Movement. The phrase "New Negro" had been in use at least since the end of the nineteenth century and was popularized by Hubert H. Harrison, journalist, editor, and author of the 1920 study, *When Africa Wakes: The "Inside Story" of the New Negro in the Western World*. While not the first to embrace the term, Alain LeRoy Locke, writer, philosopher, Howard University professor, and patron of the arts, is most closely associated with it. Locke is often credited with launching the Renaissance when he accepted the first invitation ever extended to an African American to edit a special issue of the periodical *Survey Graphic*, a mainstream journal focused on sociological and political concerns. The special issue coincided with the sixty-year anniversary of the ratification of the Thirteenth Amendment abolishing slavery, and Locke titled it: "Harlem: Mecca of the New Negro." Extraordinary sales prompted its release in an expanded form as the celebrated anthology, *The New Negro* (1925). This publication brought together those who would become known as the leading figures of the Harlem Renaissance.

In "The New Negro," his much-discussed centerpiece contribution to the anthology, Locke proclaimed that, unlike the *Old Negro*, who was the object of another's gaze and analysis, the *New Negro* would look out on the world and represent it as "he" saw and experienced it; the New Negro would not accept, through mimicry, the role assigned to him as a screen for projected fears and desires:

> In the last decade something beyond the watch and guard of statistics has happened in the life of the American Negro and the three norns who have traditionally presided over the Negro problem have a changeling in their laps. The Sociologist, the Philanthropist, the Race-leader are not unaware of the New Negro, but they are at a loss to account for him. He simply cannot be swathed in their formulae. For the

younger generation is vibrant with a new psychology; the new spirit is awake in the masses, and under the very eyes of the professional observers is transforming what has been a perennial problem into the progressive phases of contemporary Negro life (1925).

In the same collection, W. E. B. Du Bois, among the most prominent and influential intellectuals of the past century and a half, argued that claiming the right to self-representation brought with it the responsibility to understand art as propaganda (by which he meant all art necessarily has a point of view), which would have specific effects on its audience. Writers continued the debate long past the publication of this collection. While agreeing with Du Bois in his assessment of art as propaganda, the poet, translator, and activist Langston Hughes, in his 1926 essay, "The Negro Artist and the Racial Mountain," maintained it was not the responsibility of artists to take the audience's reaction into account if it prevented artists from expressing their true racial selves. In subsequent essays, the anthropologist and novelist Zora Neale Hurston and the journalist and novelist George Schuyler demurred on the question of the artist's responsibility in favor of the question of what constituted Negro art. While Schuyler rejected the idea of a "black art" in his 1926 essay, "The Negro Art Hokum," Hurston outlined a distinct black aesthetic in her 1934 essay "Characteristics of Negro Expression."

In the midst of all of these passionate debates, those associated with the Harlem Renaissance agreed about the importance of art and culture in advancing the condition of black people. In answer to the question, "what is the knowledge which the New Negro needs most?" Hubert H. Harrison explained:

> He needs above all else a knowledge of the wider world and of the long past. But that is history, modern and ancient. . . . The Negro needs also the knowledge of the best thought; but that is literature as conceived, not as a collection of flowers from the tree of life, but as its garnered fruit. And, finally, the Negro needs a knowledge of his own kind. (133)

The name "Harlem Renaissance" links the revival of "the best thought" of this "long past" to the celebration of a New York City neighborhood that had shifted from predominately white to black by the first decade of the twentieth century. The 1920s witnessed Harlem's rapid growth as waves of black immigration from the United States South during the Great Migration and from the Caribbean, South America, and Africa, forged networks linking black people worldwide. These migrations contributed to the creation of groups of writers, artists, activists, and intellectuals in Harlem that inspired others throughout the country and beyond. Black Americans circulated, furthermore, as soldiers in the First World War stationed in Europe and Africa; as laborers on the Panama Canal; as emigrants to Europe, South America, and Africa seeking to escape the racism of the United States that impeded their access to wealth, education, or opportunities to practice a profession; as dockworkers and sailors throughout the world; as dancers and entertainers in Europe, where they could capitalize on the vogue for the exotic primitive; as activists protesting the United States' invasion of Haiti, fighting in the Spanish Civil War, or joining anticolonial and workers' struggles in many nations; as participants in meetings such as the Pan-African Congresses fostered by W. E. B. Du Bois or the International Conventions of Marcus Garvey's Universal Negro Improvement Association. International and domestic concerns intertwined in the writings of many Harlem Renaissance writers, contributing to plots and themes.

The Harlem Renaissance was preceded by a period that the historian Rayford Logan has controversially described as "the nadir" of American race relations. The period from the late 1870s through the first decades of the twentieth century was marked by antiblack violence, lynchings, segregation, racial discrimination, race riots, and other expressions of white supremacy, including the circulation of vicious stereotypes of black people in popular culture. Legal means had failed to address the second-class status of black citizens, and in 1896, the Supreme Court ruling in *Plessy v. Ferguson* upheld a doctrine of legal segregation in the United States. If equal representation for black people as citizens could not be achieved through the institutions of law and government, reasoned Harlem Renaissance writers, perhaps art and culture could provide better results. In describing his goals for the New Negro, Alain Locke claimed,

> The great social gain in this [becoming an active collaborator and participant in American civilization] is the releasing of our talented group from the fields of controversy and debate to the productive fields of creative expression. The especially cultural recognition they win should in turn prove the key to that revaluation of the Negro which must precede or accompany any considerable further betterment of race relationships. (1925)

There were some challenges to the idea that the New Negro would gain social, political, and economic representation equal to that of whites by taking charge of his or her representation in the cultural sphere; A. Philip Randolph and Chandler Owens had argued, for example, for the need for New Negro voters to focus on a new form of political representation by putting forth candidates rather than merely choosing among those proposed by the white establishment. Despite this view, the general consensus was with Claude McKay, who suggested, in his 1932 essay "The Negro Writer to His Critics," that "art might [do] better than society."

Agreement on this point, however, introduced disagreements about how to proceed and gave rise to a series of important questions: What kind of art and culture would do better? Would it be found in drumming, spirituals, the blues, jazz, a classical symphony, or a mixture of all of the above? Would it be in the novel, in folktales, signifying, poetry, sermons, or in a mixture of different forms? Who should produce this art and who would judge it? Would it be white people or black people? The bourgeoisie or working people? What would constitute authentic black art? Would this art reflect ties to Africa, the culture forged during slavery in the South, or an international federation of black working people? Should it be conveyed in Standard English or in dialect? Could it be conveyed in French, Spanish, Portuguese, or any number of African languages? Should the idea of a distinct black culture be embraced or rejected? Should this art project a unified black identity or should it address potentially divisive issues of gender, class, sexuality, and nationality? Should the goal of black art be integration or a separate cultural, if not political and economic, sphere for black people in the United States, and, if not in the United States, then in another area of the world? Should this art counter negative stereotypes and only be positive and uplifting or should it convey unseemly truths? The politics of representation was debated in the press and other publications, in salons, and in public gatherings. The searching attitude toward these ultimately unresolvable questions rather than any particular answer characterizes the enduring relevance of the Renaissance and influenced the form and content of the writing associated with it. The novel gained a particularly prominent position, and even authors who were better known as poets, including Countee Cullen and Langston Hughes, or as essayists, such as W. E. B. Du Bois, attempted the form at least once.

In a 1928 essay, "The Dilemma of the Negro Author," James Weldon Johnson, lawyer, diplomat, critic, poet, songwriter, and novelist, described some of the issues the black author encounters in taking on the novel form:

> It is known that art—literature in particular, unless it be sheer fantasy—must be based on more or less well established conventions. . . . It is this that gives it verisimilitude and finality. Even revolutionary literature, if it is to have any convincing power, must start from a basis of conventions, regardless of how unconventional its objective may be. These conventions are changed by slow and gradual process—except they be changed in a flash. The conventions held by white America will be changed. Actually they are being changed, but they have not yet sufficiently changed to lessen to any great extent the dilemma of the Negro author.

Concern with the limited representations of black people in literature found expression in the novels of the Harlem Renaissance with a range of formal experimentation, which significantly coincided with modernist aesthetics. New technologies of representation—photography, film, recordings—and the speed of reporting on the violence and achievements of the modern world, facilitated by airplanes, automobiles, telephones, and the telegraph, gave fresh tools and perspectives to writers and readers who were disenchanted with modes of storytelling that imagined the world as a coherent and logical place where the center of meaning emanated from a transcendent figure.

For the writers of the Harlem Renaissance, the violence of racism, the experience of dislocation—physical and psychological—and the challenge involved in making use of language, literary and artistic conventions previously employed to denigrate black people, made it impossible to adopt any form, especially the novel form, without contending with this history. Formal strategies, including fragmentation, multiple points of view, a focus on psychology and interiority, the incorporation of multiple genres into a single text or the breaking down of genres, the incorporation of song, sermon, images, ethnography, the use of shocking imagery and inclusion of morally ambiguous situations reinforced thematic elements that addressed the complexity of black experience. Writers experimented with these strategies as they attempted to represent a world that did not make sense morally—how, for example, could one account for the violence of lynching, of race riots, of segregation?—or to imagine a new one that was frightening, exciting, dangerous, promising. A range of works emerged from the engagement with the novel form, including McKay's *Home to Harlem* (1927) and *Banjo* (1929); Jessie Redmon Fauset's *Plum Bun* (1928); Nella Larsen's *Quicksand* (1928) and *Passing* (1929); Rudolph Fisher's *The Conjure-Man Dies* (1932); Du Bois's *Dark Princess* (1928); Hughes's *Not Without Laughter* (1930); George Schuyler's *Black No More* (1931) and *Black Empire* (1938); Wallace Thurman's *Infants of the Spring* (1932); Countee Cullen's *One Way to Heaven* (1932); and Zora Neale Hurston's *Their Eyes Were Watching God* (1937).

Often identified as the first Harlem Renaissance novel, Jean Toomer's *Cane* (1923) is sufficiently experimental to defy easy classification. A series of vignettes in prose, poetry, song, and dialogue, the novel contains fragmented points of view and shifts in reader identification, both important strategies for challenging received ideas about history and identity in the interest of a more comprehensive understanding of each. *Cane* confounds clear distinctions between oppressed and oppressor, as well as the neat distinctions between love and hate, desire and repulsion, the beautiful and the ugly, past and present, white and black, North and South. The relationship between the poem "Portrait in Georgia" and the story that follows it, "Blood-Burning Moon," illustrates this point. "Portrait in Georgia" points to a racial boundary only to undo it by merging the image of a white woman and of a lynched black man burned to death in a terrifying yet intimate embrace:

> Hair—braided chestnut, coiled like a lyncher's rope,
> Eyes—fagots,
> Lips—old scars, or the first red blisters,
> Breach—the last sweet scent of cane,
> And her slim body, white as the ash of black flesh after flame.

The layered images of the white woman, the lynching pyre, and the burning body of the black man graphically demonstrate the coupling of the man and woman and show how the discourse of white supremacy depends on and yet punishes even the specter of that coupling to maintain an illusion of racial separation that the poem undermines, especially when read in the context of the novel as a whole. The poem suggests that racial segregation is created and violently enforced to produce and protect the idea of white superiority and to deny the extent to which the intertwining of black and white is central, indeed foundational, to Americanness. The theme of the poem and the commingled images of terror and beauty expressed in part through the emphasis on the color purple and the sweet scent of cane, a reference to the crop worked by enslaved people, link the poem to "Blood Burning Moon," the story that follows it.

The story, which takes up, revises, and extends this representation of lynching, complicates its usual justification, which scapegoats the black man as predator and threat, by positing a black woman rather than a white woman as object of desire and contestation. Both Bob Stone, the scion of the former slaveholders, and Tom Burwell, the descendant of the enslaved people who worked the land, want Louisa. Bob feels shame that he has to woo her, a sign of the change from the past, when she would have been his by right; Tom loves her, but as a fieldworker, he cannot be sure that he can claim a right to her. Metaphors linking Louisa to the landscape—"Her skin was the color of oak leaves[,] . . . her breasts . . . like ripe acorns[,] . . . her singing had the low murmur of winds in fig trees"—invite us to read her as a stand-in for the South. But Tom, Bob, and the townspeople are all similarly situated: Tom, the cane cutter, rooted to the soil by his dream of farming his own land; Bob Stone, son of the former plantation owner, through the imagery suggested by his name; the "white men like ants upon a forage" as they rush to prepare the lynching. All of the characters have some connection, a natural or, at least, proprietary claim, to this land. Allegorically, the battle between Bob and Tom in the canefield becomes a battle between representatives of blacks and whites, workers and bosses, the agricultural past and the industrialized future, for who gets to claim the South.

The imagery of the story, however, confounds any possibility of a clear victory in that battle. For Toomer, black and white, master and slave, human and earth, past, present, and future are too inextricably linked to allow for the survival or destruction of one without the other. Repetition of the word "jumble," and the jumbling of images initially associated with one character, reinforces the point. Bob and Tom "jumbled when [Louisa's] eyes gazed vacantly at the rising moon. And from the jumble came the stir that was strangely within her." Neither man wins, and at the end of the story, after Tom kills Bob and is in turn lynched, the description of Tom's "stony" eyes and "head, erect, lean, like blackened stone" suggests his merging with his nemesis, Bob Stone. Stone, then, is Bob's name, an indicator of his whiteness, the set of Tom's eyes as he is lynched, and the color of the flesh of each. The "jumbling" that is the relation of black and white is evident as well in the description of the crowd and the environment in relation to the word "stone" when "the mob's yell echoe[s] against the skeleton stone walls" of the factory before which Tom is lynched and burned. The technique of layering an image to suggest the inseparability of all in the South and the inevitable tragedy of attempts at segregation and division is a hallmark of *Cane*. The color purple is similarly significant. It is the color of Louisa's desired dress, promised to her by Tom, as well as of the clouds at dusk, and of Bob Stone's flushed cheeks when he contemplates the loss of white supremacy. The color purple appears throughout *Cane* to apply equally to black and white characters and, in this story, as an alternative to the binary of black and white, as a "jumble" of all colors. The "jumbling" suggests the futility of the fight for white supremacy manifested in the lynching. The image of a crucified Tom (the blood moon of the title of the story augers the crucifixion), which suggests the enduring spirit that survives, reinforces not only the horror and self-destructiveness of the lynching for blacks, for whites, for the South, but also the resilience of black people and culture.

Toomer invents a form and language for *Cane* to accommodate a refusal of the binaries—oppressed and oppressor, love and hate, desire and repulsion, beautiful and ugly, past and present, white and black, North and South—that have underpinned conventional representations and reception of the narratives of black experience. For all of its newness associated with its modernist form, *Cane* has been described as an elegy, which binds it nostalgically to the past, accounting for the arc of the narrative's back and forth movement. As Farah Jasmine Griffin has argued in *"Who Set You Flowin'?"* Toomer mourns a South, which, for all of its violence and horror, is also the home of the ancestors of black people and, therefore, to be venerated and appreciated as such. This attachment to the ancestors must be experienced at a distance since it is tied in with the experience of migration—spurred, in part, by lynching. Textual emphasis on the unfinished and fragmenting nature of this experience finds expression not only in the form of the narration, but also in a drawing of a broken arc that precedes each section of the text, the representation of a circle that never closes because a return to the South is no longer possible except, perhaps, in an imagined literary world.

Unlike *Cane*, which was met with favorable reviews and a small readership, Carl Van Vechten's *Nigger Heaven* (1926) sparked controversy and quickly sold out its first printing. After nine printings in four months, it became the best-selling Harlem Renaissance novel. Much of the public reacted negatively to its provocative title, a reference to the balcony where black theater patrons were forced to sit, which served in the novel as a metaphor for Harlem's relationship to the rest of New York City. While a number of white reviewers praised the novel for providing a window onto an otherwise inaccessible world, many black reviewers lamented that the unusual access the white Van Vechten had to the social and literary world of Harlem, facilitated through his promotion of black writers, had led him, particularly in the preface, to feed the prurient interests of white readers and reinforce the demeaning stereotypes of blacks. Others, including Charles Chesnutt, Eric Walrond, and Paul Robeson, enthusiastically praised the novel, and Nella Larsen wondered, "Why, oh, why, couldn't we have done something as big as this for ourselves?" (qtd. in Hutchinson 1995, 210). Even some of Van Vechten's supporters, who were, like Langston Hughes (who eventually wrote blues lyrics to substitute the ones illegally used in the early edition of the novel) and Alain Locke, ambivalent about the title, ultimately aligned themselves with James Weldon Johnson's assessment that "the book and not the title is the thing" (2007, 393).

Like Wallace Thurman's *Infants of the Spring* and Countee Cullen's underappreciated *One Way to Heaven*, both published in 1932, *Nigger Heaven* is a roman à clef featuring thinly veiled versions of prominent Harlem Renaissance figures. Collectively, these novels reveal the self-awareness of the movement and the ways in which its debates influenced novelists' aesthetic and narrative choices. These novels rehearse the questions that opened this chapter about the role of art in addressing the second-class citizenship of African Americans and the extent to which art can bridge the hierarchies of class, color, nationality, and religion within the black community. *Nigger Heaven* brings together two plots: the first involves salacious aspects of Harlem's night world and the second, a romance between two middle-class main characters, Mary Love, a librarian, and Byron Kasson, an aspiring Harlem Renaissance writer. In his withering review of the novel, Du Bois criticized Van Vechten for his inability to produce an aesthetically coherent work of art. Mary's response to Byron's presentation of a story idea suggests Van Vechten's awareness that he ran the risk of not successfully integrating plots involving various Harlem communities: "These propaganda subjects are very difficult," she tells him, "difficult, that is, to make human. It is hard to keep them from becoming melodramatic, cheap even. Unless such a story is written with exquisite skill, it will read like a meretricious appeal to the emotions arising out of race prejudice" (bk. 2, ch. 3). The novel ends without resolving questions about who should represent the Negro and how it should be done.

Infants of the Spring, which also takes in place in 1920s Harlem, is a scathing critique of the Renaissance. Published as the Renaissance was waning following the 1929 crash of the stock market and the ensuing Depression, Thurman's novel reproduces the conflicts of the movement at its height in order to satirize it. The novel opens with a description of "Niggeratti Manor," the sardonic name given by Zora Neale Hurston to the residence that she and Thurman shared with the writers Langston Hughes and Bruce Nugent, and the painter Rex Gorleigh, among others. Like their real-life counterparts, the fictionalized residents "live a free, bohemian life which brings down upon them the wrath of the 'respectable elements,'" but they also dissipate their political energy in parties and debates.

During the summer of 1926, the actual inhabitants of the house, with the addition of the artist Aaron Douglas, the writer Gwendolyn Bennett, and John P. Davis, a lawyer who had substituted for Du Bois as the literary editor of the *Crisis*, had produced a new journal titled, *FIRE!! Devoted to Younger Negro Artists*. Frustrated by the constraints placed on artists, who were to uplift the race through example and promote the ideals of the educated elite identified by Du Bois as the "Talented Tenth," their work, influenced in part by the frank treatment of sexuality and popular culture in *Nigger Heaven*, was a response and provocation to the more conservative leaders of the Renaissance, among them Du Bois. It indeed scandalized them, and the journal did not survive its initial publication. *Infants of the Spring* ends with the irony that a brilliant manuscript produced by one of the members of this group is rendered illegible by the water overflowing the bathtub in which he has committed suicide. Like Van Vechten, Thurman can neither produce, nor imagine, a work produced during the Renaissance that will fulfill its goals.

Many critics have dismissed Van Vechten's and Thurman's novels as well as Countée Cullen's roman à clef, *One Way to Heaven*, for their structural flaws. They argue that each has two barely related plots where the characters of the literary elite are more developed than the characters of the popular classes, who are types or caricatures. This "flaw," however, may result from the reality of a class divide that could not be bridged even imaginatively in the novels that take on the Renaissance movement. In his 1940 memoir, *The Big Sea*, Langston Hughes assessed the Renaissance retrospectively from his perspective as a participant:

> I was there. I had a swell time while it lasted. . . . But some Harlemites thought the millennium had come. They thought the race problem had at last been solved through Art plus Gladys Bentley [the famous lesbian Blues singer]. They were sure the New Negro would need a new life from then on in the green pastures of tolerance. . . . I don't know what made any Negroes think that—except that they were mainly intellectuals doing the thinking. The ordinary Negroes hadn't heard of the Negro Renaissance. And if they had, it hadn't raised their wages any. ("When the Negro Was in Vogue")

In his assessment of the movement, Hughes notes that intellectuals sought to create an African American art that combined high "Art" and popular culture. Whether any of the novelists were able to achieve this balance is debatable, but, according to Hughes, the social changes that intellectuals envisioned as coming about through activity in the cultural sphere were difficult to identify. The inability to merge plots concerning intellectuals on the one hand and the "ordinary Negroes" on the other, therefore, enacts a general conflict characteristic of the Renaissance between a desire to account for the range of ways of being black and the implications of representing that range to white and black readers.

It is not unusual for that conflict to turn on depictions of sex and sexuality in Harlem Renaissance novels. Scholars have suggested, for example, that *Nigger Heaven* paved the way for the frank explorations of sex and sexuality in novels by Nella Larsen and Claude McKay in particular. Like Toomer, Larsen experimented with the form of the novel to address debates about representation in the New Negro movement. But equally important for her were the gendered implications of its program, especially in relation to women's intellectual, artistic, and sexual desires. In *Quicksand*, for example, Larsen employed the conventions of the "tragic mulatto" plot, but while the novel certainly takes on this theme, it is important to remember that Helga cannot pass for white. Larsen suggests that Helga was illegitimate—her parents may not have been married as a result of antimiscegenation laws—and her social status, as a result, was precarious. Larsen uses the conventions of the "tragic mulatto" plot as a foil that permits a more controversial critique of the limits on the representation of black women and of the masculinist bias of the

New Negro movement. By focusing on Helga's pursuit of beauty and on the extent to which she turns herself into a work of art, Larsen confronts what it means to seek social and political change through art and the cultural sphere specifically for black women.

Helga's struggle in *Quicksand* is an ultimately unsuccessful attempt to embrace the New Negro agenda, which is to move from the object of someone else's gaze and desires to being the author of one's own narrative. Seeing herself as someone who "could neither conform, nor be happy in her unconformity" (ch. 1), Helga cannot settle into any established community. She moves from "Naxos," a Southern institution based on Tuskegee University, because of the school's conservative racial uplift philosophy, to Chicago and subsequently, shunned by her white relatives, to New York to embrace the vibrant black community of Harlem. Quickly disillusioned by the snobbery and hypocrisy of Harlem's middle class, however, she seeks respite from American racism with her aunt in Copenhagen, but is soon dismayed by her exoticization and eroticization as a mixed-race woman in Denmark. Her restlessness takes her back to New York, and eventually to the South as a preacher's wife. The novel ends on an unsettled note, with Helga, trapped and weak from an extended illness, about to give birth to her fifth child, against her doctor's strong recommendation.

The narratives that trap her as a woman are exemplified by the celebration of the good, useful, sexually repressed woman in a patriarchal setting that promotes black self-sufficiency and "uplift" (the women of Naxos), by the embrace of the aesthetics and ideals of a white world transposed to a black world (Anne Grey), by the exoticizing of the ostensibly primitive (Helga during her Denmark sojourn), and finally by the religious helpmate, wife, and mother (Helga as the minister's wife). Although Helga is fascinated by Audrey Denney, the one example of a woman who eschews predetermined roles, she ultimately finds her daring untenable. Audrey's disappearance midway through the novel underscores her insufficiency as a viable alternative. The novel documents Helga's struggle to for self-expression as a black woman whose existence transcends conventional binaries—good/bad, white/black, repressed/wanton. Each attempt she makes to turn herself from an object to a subject by moving to a new environment fails. The novel manifests the tension of Helga's struggle in its narrative form, which is neither entirely in the third person, which would wholly objectify Helga, nor in the first person, which would make Helga the subject and center. This narrative hybridity represents Helga's awareness and cultivation of being looked at, but inability to speak fully in her own voice. Through Helga's failure to speak fully in her own voice, Larsen offers a critique of the limited range of possibilities available for the representation of black women during the New Negro Movement.

In an extreme and literal version of the goals of the New Negro Movement, Larsen has Helga attempt to turn herself into a work of art, even as others, especially the men she encounters, try to make her a muse. Larsen thereby reveals not only the masculinist bias of the New Negro aesthetic agenda, but also the dangers inherent in a commodification of blackness that she links to primitivism. Primitivism refers to the idea that primitive cultures offered an antidote to contemporary cultural malaise because they had not suffered the stultifying effects of a Western civilization in decline, and the energy of their art and culture heralded a better future. These ideas caught the attention of many, including some Harlem Renaissance figures, because of the influence of African art on European artists, such as Pablo Picasso and Amedeo Modigliani; others encountered them through the explorations of Sigmund Freud and the anthropologist Franz Boas. Although influential, the primitivist strain gave rise to ambivalence when it was marshaled in the description of black music, dance, and art, particularly because it was associated with sexual abandon. Whereas Helga's sexual seductiveness had been a source of anxiety and shame at Naxos and even in Harlem, in Copenhagen she is incited to be seductive, to stage the sensuality of her body, and to highlight her primitive side, which includes feigning an inability to speak Danish correctly, but in the process she becomes a commodity—circulated for its social value to her aunt and uncle, a value that increases as she embodies savagery and primitiveness, especially through her sexuality. The novel stages the impossibility of choices for self-expression and growth available to Helga in a world that has no place for her. Her struggle encapsulates a social critique that was familiar to Larsen's cohort and recurs in their work.

If, in his reviews of their work, Du Bois praised both Toomer and Larsen for their novels and particularly their representations of black sexuality, he famously did not do the same for Claude McKay. Of Toomer, Du Bois wrote in his essay, "The Younger Literary Movement":

> The world of black folk will some day arise and point to Jean Toomer as a writer who first dared to emancipate the colored world from the conventions of sex. It is quite impossible for most Americans to realize how straightlaced and conventional thought is within the Negro world, despite the very unconventional acts of the group. Yet this contradiction is true. And Jean Toomer is the first of our writers to hurl his pen across the very face of our sex conventionality (1924).

In "Two Novels," a review published in the June 1928 issue of the *Crisis*, Du Bois similarly praised Larsen's handling of the main character's attempts to deal with her sexuality: "I think that . . . Nella Larsen . . . has done a fine, thoughtful, and courageous piece of work in her novel." Hailing Helga as "typical of the new, honest, young, fighting, Negro woman," he claims: "White folks will not like this book. It is not near nasty enough."

This praise for *Quicksand* is interwoven with Du Bois's notorious scorn for Claude McKay's controversial novel, *Home to Harlem*, which had made the New York best-seller lists. The novel traces the adventures of Jake Brown, who had deserted his First World War army unit in France, as he tries to find the woman he had spent the night with on his return to Harlem. Responding to the novel's frank depictions of Harlem nightlife, Du Bois asserted that *Home to Harlem* "nauseates me, and after the dirtier parts of its filth I feel distinctly like taking a bath." It is important to note, however, that Du Bois's praise of Larsen and his dismissal of McKay is couched in terms of McKay's seeming mishandling of the novel form as much as its sexual content:

> [McKay] has used every art and emphasis to paint drunkenness, fighting, lascivious sexual promiscuity and utter absence of restraint in as bold and bright colors as he can. If this had been done in the course of a well-conceived plot or with any artistic unity, it might have been understood if not excused. . . . Nella Larsen on the other hand has seized an interesting character and fitted her into a close yet delicately woven plot.

Du Bois's approbation notwithstanding, Helga's proposed but unrealized "Plea for Color," in which she imagined the embrace of aesthetic appreciation for color and excess as a response to those who advocate the dullness and repression of social uplift, may suggest more common points between the two works than Du Bois acknowledges. In fact, subsequent critics have identified in the works of Larsen and McKay a shared interest in the exploration of same-sex desire, transnational blackness, and the limits of the novel form for the representation of complex black identity. The subtitle of McKay's second novel, *Banjo: A Novel without a Plot*, apparently takes on Du Bois's criticism. Brent Hayes Edwards notes that *Banjo*'s full title "immediately raises a question of literary form, in other words—a question of the relation between its apparent 'plotlessness' and its portrait of a transnational community of black drifters and dockers in Marseilles." He argues that questions about the suitability of the designation of *Banjo* as a novel has led many baffled critics to use other tropes to describe it, often drawing from music, which suggests that "even if the book does not aim directly to imitate musical form—in *Banjo*, a black transnational community is defined more than anything else by a certain relation to music" (2003, 190; on *Banjo* and black diasporic proletarianism, see Chapter 33 in this volume).

Years after Du Bois's 1928 review of *Home to Harlem*, McKay would muse, in "A Negro Writer to His Critics,"

> I did not grow up in the fear of skeletons in the closet whether they were family, national or racial, sacred cows and the washing of dirty clothes in public. And I have often wondered why many subjects that seemed to me most beautiful and suitable for literature and by which art might have done better than society—subjects that intellectual persons of both sexes discuss over the dinner table and the salon and that people in the street gossip about, should be publicly shocking in print and taboo in art. (2007 [1932], 392)

The expressed hope that art may do "better than society" explains why, according to yet another of his essays, "The New Negro in Paris" (1937), McKay declined an invitation to travel from Morocco to Paris: "I wondered after all whether it would be better for me to return to the new *milieu* of Harlem. Much as my sympathy was with the Negro group and the idea of a Negro renaissance, I doubted if going back to Harlem would be an advantage. I had done my best Harlem stuff when I was abroad, seeing it from a long perspective."

Many Harlem Renaissance novelists were as intrigued as McKay by the idea of "a long perspective" when it came to the Negro. This long perspective was thematized in novels that had characters from or traveling to locations outside the United States, including *Quicksand* and Larsen's other novel, *Passing* (1929), McKay's *Home to Harlem* (1928) and *Banjo* (1930), and Jesse Redmon Fauset's *Plum Bun* (1928). In other cases, this long perspective was expressed through formal experiments with time in order to raise questions about the present by imagining other times and realities in novels such as George Schuyler's *Black Empire* and *Black No More*, W. E. B. Du Bois's *Dark Princess*, and Rudolph Fisher's *The Conjure Man Dies*. These novels collectively explore a range of ideas about citizenship and national belonging.

Much of the scholarship on *Quicksand* and Larsen's other novel, *Passing*, McKay's *Home to Harlem* and *Banjo*, and Fauset's *Plum Bun* (1928) has focused on conceptions of race and racial passing as well as of sexuality and same-sex desire. Recently, however, attention has turned to another aspect of these novels, which involves the relationship between being black and American that is explored through comparisons of the United States to Brazil and Europe. While some characters see foreign spaces as havens or even as proof that non-racist societies could be reproduced in the United States, other characters insist on their right to full American citizenship and belonging. Irene Redfield, one of the main characters of *Passing*, rejects her husband's desire to leave New York to escape the specter of racial violence: "She would not go to Brazil. She belonged in this land of rising towers. She was an American. She grew from this soil, and would not be uprooted" (pt. 2, ch. 4). These varying positions reenact debates within the Renaissance about the relative merits of uplift and integration within the United States, elite cosmopolitanism, black nationalism, and a return to Africa as articulated by figures such as Garvey, or Pan-Africanism as articulated by Du Bois as the means to articulating a new black identity.

Like the self-consciously transnational novels mentioned above, W. E. B. Du Bois's *Dark Princess*, Rudolph Fisher's *The Conjure Man Dies*, and George Schuyler's *Black No More* and *Black Empire* explore a solution to the "race problem" through their depiction of other places, times, and realities. *Dark Princess*, published in 1928, at the apex of the Renaissance, can be paired with *Black Empire*, which originally appeared in two parts, " Black Internationale" and "Black Empire" in sixty-two weekly installments in the *Pittsburgh Courier* between November 1936 and April 1938, as the Renaissance was coming to an end. Although their political paths would diverge after the Thirties, with Du Bois moving to the left and Schuyler to the right, their novels projected an international revolutionary black movement that is articulated in relation to communism, positively for Du Bois, ironically for Schuyler. Du Bois frames his novel, one of his favorite writings, as a romance, which, through its main characters, links Pan-Africa and Pan-Asia in the fight against racial and colonial oppression. According to William J. Maxwell, "the eccentric, synthetic pomp of Du Bois's marriage scene [which culminates the novel]—futurist-Orientalist in aesthetics, royalist-communist in politics, and Hindic-Christian in religion—celebrates the union between the 'red-black South and the yellow-brown East' that he [Du Bois] had earlier summoned in his contribution to Locke's *New Negro* anthology" (1999, 180). The union between the "red-black South" embodied in Matthew Townes and the "yellow-brown East" embodied in Princess Kautilya promises a transnational and anti-imperialist liberation led by the Talented Tenth, which is guaranteed and projected into the future in the form of Matthew and Kautilya's child, the "Messenger and Messiah to all the Darker Worlds!" (pt. 4, ch. 19; on this child as advocate for social justice, see Chapter 19 of this volume).

Although inspired by *Dark Princess*, Schuyler's novel is a satire—not romance—and therefore offers a critical rather than idealized vision of radical transnational politics. Schuyler interweaves imaginative mechanical inventions, futurist notions of time and space, and mythic formulations derived from religion and psychology with social commentary on racial segregation in the United States, black leadership, the Italian colonization of Ethiopia, black slavery in Liberia, the inequalities inherent in capitalism, and various definitions of race. Like *Dark Princess*, *Black Empire* celebrates the possibilities suggested by science fiction, if not science itself, for addressing issues of racism and provides the means to imagine and present a world with greater rights and representation for black people.

If these two novels harnessed the promise of new technologies in transportation, medicine, manufacturing, and communication, as well as the mysteries associated with sexuality, religion, and spirituality to explore the possibility of transnational black networks, two others took up this promise to explore issues in their Harlem setting. Schuyler's *Black No More* is a biting satire of black color consciousness that makes use of the conventions of the science fiction novel in its premise of a machine that can make black people white (on *Black No More* as science fiction, see Chapter 23 in this volume). The sensational success of this machine brings wealth and fame to its black inventors. The novel focuses on Max Disher, one of the first men to be made white, who, as Matthew Fisher, marries a white woman who had spurned his advances and infiltrates a white supremacist organization resembling the Ku Klux Klan. The plot, which turns on the erosion of the apparent foundation of the color line, satirizes the obsession with skin color among blacks, the illogic of biological conceptions of race, and the ways capitalism functions in tandem with racism. The description of the social upheaval created by the machine includes a send-up of many of the figures associated with the Renaissance, including Garvey and Du Bois. The novel ends ironically when whites, no longer able to distinguish themselves from altered blacks, begin tanning themselves to maintain their distinctive privileges. *Black No More* explores the tenacity of the color line and the difficulty of overcoming it through art or science.

Science fiction was not the only genre fiction with which Harlem Renaissance writers experimented. In an inscription to Carl Van Vechten, Rudolph Fisher describes his 1932 novel, *The Conjure-Man Dies: A Mystery Tale of Dark Harlem,* the first known detective novel written by an African American, as an "experiment with technique" (qtd. in Tignor 1982, 17). Fisher uses the conventions of the detective novel to reflect on issues of defining race by exploring how to understand what is not seen. The events of the novel are set in motion by the apparent murder of N'Gana Frimbo, a psychic and the conjure man of the title, who consults with clients in his office on West 130th Street in Harlem. Forensic science intersects with mysticism in the novel, as the decoding of folk beliefs and spiritual signs figures prominently in arriving at the story of the crime. The use of the genre of detective fiction allows the author to unfold and explore the mystery of the relationship between Africa and America and what it is, beyond visible markers, that joins black people together, from the perspective of black people.

These novels use the extended imaginative space of the novel to project into the future a different reality for the resolution of contemporary issues. There are, however, two novels by arguably the most widely read writers associated with the Renaissance, Langston Hughes and Zora Neale Hurston, that stage the debates of the Renaissance through their often nostalgic depictions of the lives of ordinary black folk. While Hughes's semi-autobiographical first novel, *Not Without Laughter,* rehearses the divisions between the accommodationist ideology of Booker T. Washington and the assimilationist ideology of Du Bois through the character of a young boy in a small Kansas town in 1910, Hurston's, *Their Eyes Were Watching God* is set in small-town Florida during the time of the Harlem Renaissance, although there is no direct reference to the movement.

Hurston participated actively in the Renaissance and any history of the period could not ignore her; nevertheless, she did not publish her most famous novel until 1937 when the movement was all but over. The second of her three novels (*Jonah's Gourd Vine* was published in 1934), *Their Eyes Were Watching God* was not generally well received at the time, as many critics reacted negatively to the use of dialect and accused her of promoting stereotypes. They also faulted her for idealizing black Southern life and not giving attention to the effects of white racism. Hurston had prepared the way for the novel, however, in her 1934 essay, "The Characteristics of Negro Expression." Drawing on her extensive anthropological research in the South, she argued for the existence of a specific black aesthetic rooted in a dramatic use of figurative language, storytelling, folklore, and dialect (on Hurston's anthropological research and *Their Eyes Were Watching God*, see Chapter 25 in this volume). The novel, nevertheless, languished until 1973, when the novelist Alice Walker revived interest in her work, claiming her as an important black female literary progenitor. Since then, it has been perennially popular in classrooms, reading groups, and on the screen. The novel tells the story of Janie Crawford's journey of self-discovery through three marriages to find contentment in herself when she learns that people, "got tuh find out about livin' fuh theyselves" (ch. 20). The majority of the scholarship on the novel has focused of Janie's self-realization as a woman and on Hurston's treatment of the South and folk culture. Recent work, such as that by Martyn Bone, however, links the concerns of the novel to some of the earlier transnational ones discussed earlier in this chapter. He argues that the South depicted in the novel is not as isolated as critics have described and that transnational flows particularly from the Caribbean figure significantly.

The reception of *Their Eyes Were Watching God* is a measure of how the appreciation of the novels of the Harlem Renaissance has varied over the past eight decades. By the mid-1930s, critics and writers as diverse as Hughes and Schuyler were already announcing the end of the Harlem Renaissance. While critics in the United States largely dismissed the period in the decades following the publication of *Their Eyes Were Watching God*, this was not the case in other parts of the world. Translations of the novels of McKay and Hughes, among others, had an important influence on black literary movements in the Caribbean, Europe, Latin America, and Africa. By the 1980s, motivated by the attention to Hurston's novel, critics reevaluated the period, the canon, and the scholarship on the novels of the Harlem Renaissance. Classroom syllabi and the pages of academic journals register a literary canon expanded to include out of print and neglected texts from the movement, particularly by women. This process continues to this day with the recent publication of *When Washington Was in Vogue*, a serialized fiction that appeared in the *Messenger* between January 1925 and June 1926. Critical reception of these novels has also been enhanced by readings based on theories and methods drawn from feminist, queer, critical race, and postcolonial studies and by work that highlights the connections between the Harlem Renaissance and Négritude and the Black Arts Movements in the United States, Africa, South America, and the Caribbean. While much has changed in the critical treatment of the novels of the Harlem Renaissance, what remains consistent is the thorny question of the relationship of the novel as an aesthetic form to its function as an act of political representation—the very question that so engaged the writers of these fictions.

29

FAULKNER AND THE WORLD CULTURE OF THE GLOBAL SOUTH

BY RAMÓN SALDÍVAR

I wish to begin my discussion of the relationship between William Faulkner and the category of the "global South" with a word about terminology. The first observation worth making about the current state of American literary studies is that a new vocabulary for naming and studying what we used to call "the Third World" has emerged in the last twenty years or so, representing a battery of interesting alternatives for us to consider. Why these vocabularies, arising primarily from the social sciences and from mid-twentieth-century postimperialist critical traditions, are of significance to students of literature is evident when one considers the continuing importance of nation-based literary history, of the kind that organizes the *Oxford History of the Novel*. In what follows, I consider Faulkner in the context of what we might term the world culture of the global South.

Noticing that a trans-American context is both implicitly and explicitly relevant to many of Faulkner's fictions allows us to read him as a different kind of regionalist— the kind who crosses national boundaries majestically, even as he stays firmly rooted within his own bounded territory of Yoknapatawpha County, Mississippi. Like other prominent US modernists—William Carlos Williams, Hart Crane, Langston Hughes perhaps most prominently, all of whom had family connections to the Caribbean—Faulkner participated in transnational crossings without actually doing much traveling. The concentration in literary studies on the trans-Atlantic aspects of modernism have typically prevented critics from seeing the connections between modernisms and modernists in the Americas, keeping them oddly separated from each other, and from political and cultural events in the hemispheric Americas. In particular, the eurocentric focus has tended to obscure the numerous ways that Faulkner's connection with the issues of coloniality and postcoloniality mark as well much Latin American literature of the pre– and post–Second World War years and thus link Faulkner to another South, the global South—especially to Latin America and its cultural history. By contrast, Latin American writers have often been clear about their Faulknerian connection. Chief among the themes Faulkner addresses that make his fictions of such moment to Latin America are those having to do with subject formation in relation to racial and social ideologies and the frightening pressures emerging from the colonized world as it begins to throw off its colonial burden.

The idea of the "global South" first emerged following World War II out of the recognition that, with few exceptions, practically all of the world's industrially developed countries lay to the north of the so-called developing countries. According to sociologist Saskia Sassen, at the beginning of the twenty-first century the term "global South" refers to a new phase of global capital; it designates primarily the territories that have been subjected to a post-Keynesian financial logic of land grabs, the imposition of debt as a disciplining regime, the extraction of value, and the massive expulsion of persons from middle-class status into abject poverty (2010, 24). The key word here is "expulsion." The underdevelopment of countries at a peripheral remove from the core of metropolitan economic power did not just happen—underdevelopment occurred as the result of active forces shaping its underdevelopment. For this reason, it is fair to say that the various southern economies and cultures share comparable experiences of marginalization and unequal access to the resources of globalization that differentiate them from fully developed and hegemonic cultures in their respective locations.

I wish to add one more idea to this mix: dependency theory, which as philosopher Eduardo Mendieta has argued, provided "the fundamental conceptual framework within which Latin American under-development and dependency could be understood" in a world system built on relations of impoverishment and enrichment (1999, xxi). Born from a critique of theories of modernization, dependency theory proposed that it is the manner of the integration of countries at the periphery into the world system of economic of power that perpetuates their dependence. The US sociologist Immanuel Wallerstein, in refining the theory, has called the process of dependency the "world-system." When allied to the emergence of dependency and world-systems theory, then, the concept of the global South offers a new direction for understanding the relations between the underdeveloped periphery and developed metropolitan societies. More than a geographical marker, the global South refers to the process of "growing immiseration of governments and economies . . . [that] launches a new phase of global migration and people trafficking, strategies, which function both as survival mechanisms and profit-making activities" (Sassen 2010, 32). The term does not imply that all developing countries are similar and can therefore be lumped together in one category. What it does usefully suggest is that although developing countries range across the spectrum in every economic, social, and political attribute one can imagine, they nevertheless share a set of vulnerabilities and challenges. These vulnerabilities and challenges constitute an identifiable category of shared sociopolitical realities and fates that make the notion of the "global South" more than an empty abstraction.

What does all this have to do with Faulkner and the history of the American novel? In the context of issues concerning the mid-twentieth-century era of de-colonization and the emergence of a postcolonial global South, Faulkner's Southern reach is of great importance. Focusing attention to the modernizing processes of the South and of the southern portions of the Americas, Faulkner helped initiate the transnational and globalizing themes that are of such concern to humanities and social science scholars today. He did so by focusing on the dependency of the South to the processes of modernization and by shaping his fiction as a formal response to and expression of those processes of dependency.

As Susan Willis has accurately noted, "what makes dependency theory so useful for literary analysis is that it defines the historical contradictions of domination in terms which can then be related to the form and language of the literary text" (1979, 82). This is the crucial point from Willis's analysis: dependency theory as formalized by the idea of the global South allows us to see how the economic and racial politics of our time are enmeshed with *the form and language* of the literary texts that de-scribe the modern world.

While I will also discuss *The Sound and the Fury* (1929) and *Light in August* (1932) in terms of their representation of historical contradictions of domination relating to the form and language of the literary text, I take Faulkner's *Absalom, Absalom!* (1936) as my primary textual instance of these relations among history, form, and literary language. *Absalom, Absalom!* is the novel in which Faulkner most dramati-cally situates the history of US cultural and narrative forms in the context of the larger histories of the hemispheric Americas. Consider the powerful conclusion of *Absalom, Absalom!* There, Shreve McCannon, Quentin Compson's Canadian room-mate at Harvard, insinuates himself into Quentin's final and desperate attempt at self-creation, which includes his efforts to forge a Southern heritage with which he can live. It is 1910, traditionally the moment of the purported emergence of the "modernist" era. We find Quentin attempting to construct his modern Southern self by looking backward in time. Through his reconstruction of the story of Thomas Sutpen's rise and fall—from his poor white roots through his amassing of a fortune in the Caribbean to his building of a plantation in Mississippi—Quentin seeks the validation of history and historical narrative. Shreve wants to mythologize that nar-rative. Quentin is struggling with the relation (in the double sense of telling and association) of histories such as Sutpen's at a time (modern 1910) and in a place (the US North) in which a white Southerner's ways reveal that white Southern identity is overdetermined as myth and history. In what amounts for Quentin to a life and death effort to achieve the peace of understanding, for Shreve what is at stake is mainly the aesthetic satisfaction of a completed story. Their shared storytelling em-phasizes how Quentin's sense of self arises in part through a defense of the South against the stereotypes of the South that Shreve marshals in trying to understand the stories that he hears from Quentin. And in the midst of the most dramatic moment in this most dramatic of novels, we think we begin to understand Sutpen's motivations as a Southerner when he is turned away as a child from the big house. Just at that point, the story veers even further South, to the south of the South: toward Haiti and the Caribbean.

It is immensely significant that the climactic ending of Faulkner's masterpiece stages this confrontation between American hemispheric North (Canada) and South (the United States) as a way of understanding the multiple ways "South" means and how it means in the novel. *Absalom, Absalom!* is framed by a larger sense of the conflict between North and South than scholars have traditionally addressed. This larger frame is especially evident in Quentin's own depictions of, and efforts to grapple with, the connections between that conflict and the story he is attempting to tell about the South. Quentin, in fact, is himself a different kind of double-consciousness or hybrid subjectivity from those Faulkner typically represents. As he grapples with the multiple alternatives that offer an explanation to the mysteries embroiled in Thomas Sutpen's life and its significance for his own fate, Quentin feels that he has no place to just be, North or South, for he is always determined by others' locations in time and place. We see this sense of dislocation from the very opening of *Absalom, Absalom!*, as Quentin is split in trying to reconcile the stories he is hearing: "two separate Quentins[,] . . . still too young to deserve yet to be a ghost but nevertheless having to be one for all that, since he was born and bred in the deep South," and "the two separate Quentins now talking to one another in the long silence of notpeople in not-language" (ch. 1).

One of the most striking features of the Sutpen saga in *Absalom, Absalom!* is its insistently trans-American reach: the novel's imaginary geography extends hemispherically, northward to Canada and southward to the Caribbean. It is the Americas broadly speaking, then, not just the southern parts of the United States, that constitute Faulkner's literary and cultural "region." In turn, the perspectives and claims of this larger hemispheric territory construct Sutpen as a symbolic "American" figure of national rather than merely regional—Southern—import. For this reason, I think it is important to ask, what happens if we pay attention to these inter-American connections? How does our recognition of these connection affect our understanding of American (literary) modernisms and, hence, of contemporary literary production in the Americas? And especially, what emerges from a view of Faulkner in relation to the global South?

Sutpen's destiny, the outcome of his master plan and design to refashion himself as an active agent of his own fate after the episode that General Compson will later describe as the "boy-symbol at the door" is to wander into the south of the South (ch. 7). Wandering and migration are important motifs in Faulkner's novels, conferring upon his characters a set of contradictions and inconsistencies, allowing them to be both part of and yet not part of their communities, and thus being able to criticize them. The most foreign city that is often the goal of Faulkner's wanderers is New Orleans, a portal to the global South. In *Absalom, Absalom!*, the American

South is pulled into the Caribbean in ways that undermine, even reverse, US imperialist ambitions that are part of the historical record: here "the South" is part of the
Caribbean, not vice-versa. Faulkner's Yoknapatawpha County is thus linked in fundamental ways to its immediate surroundings, the Caribbean and Latin America, by
commerce, migration, and diaspora, and particularly, by the effects of miscegenation born of rape and bondage.

The first motive that Sutpen espouses in his Haitian adventure is a commercial
one, the wish to make economic profit: he "had decided to go to the West Indies and
become rich" (ch. 7). In pursuit of that motive, however, he meets a class of people
unlike those of the antagonistic worlds of both his own Scottish mountain people
and the plantation owners of Tidewater whom he has fled. He enters instead into
a colonial social structure explicitly built upon suppressed relations of interlocking
racial articulations.

Haiti, the first locale in the Americas to receive African slaves (in 1517), was the
first to set the example of African slave revolt and revolution and liberty (in 1791) and
independence from France (in 1804). This is the history that Faulkner, notoriously,
gets wrong. What Faulkner gets right, however, is that in Haiti, Sutpen experiences
a social world where race does not constitute an absolute category of psychological
identity or ethical performance, where one might indeed elect to identify, or act, as if
race were not a constitutive, essential category. This is what the narrative of *Absalom*
calls a "speculative antagonism" between white and black people (ch. 7). Sutpen's
experience prior to his voyage to Haiti had shown that both Virginian mountain
and Tidewater cultures were awesomely static and dichotomized in their construction and enactment of categories of difference based on race and class. He finds
Haitian colonial society also structured on racial difference but enacting that difference differently. Haiti offers the possibility of a more intricate expression of racial
difference and of the understanding of that difference. For the young Sutpen, his
venture into the world of the Caribbean is like stepping into an alternate universe.
In this alternate world, the contingencies of Caribbean history, with its ebb and flow
of successive European dominant cultures, including those regarded as suspect from
the Anglo-Saxon perspective, namely the Mediterranean cultures of Spain and to a
lesser extent of France and Portugal, allow something Sutpen has never imagined:
the possibility that gradations of white and black might exist between the absolute
binaries of the US racial order of the nineteenth century.

From the seventeenth century on, the racial chromograph in Latin (Spanish,
Portuguese and French) America had been a much more complex thing than in
North America. Over sixty different castes had been chronicled by writers, philoso-
phers, painters, and historians of the region. In both Afro- and Hispano-Caribbean
colonial societies of the period, the category of the racially mixed *mulatto* (African
and European) and the many other gradations of mixed race *mestizaje* (American
Indian and European), problematic as it remains for both Afro- and Hispano-
Caribbean colonial society, historically represented classes of racialized identity that

were neither black nor white but distinct, even if determined in the last instance by their racial pedigree.

No such distinction holds in the context of American Southern racism, where under Virginia law by 1822 a person was defined as "mulatto," that is to say black, if he or she had at least one-quarter African ancestry. Sutpen's actions in Haiti run exactly counter to the implications of the Southern racial ideologies of his times. While American slavery and class structures effectively create identities formed on the basis of the dividing lines between black and white, master and slave, or land-lord and tenant, Haitian colonial society acts *as if* racial divisions were precise, all the while living the experiential blur between the two. At least in some instances, notably in the legitimation of the mixed-blood mulatto through the legalisms of marriage and property rights, Haitian colonial society, for all of its real limitations, allowed for the complicated experiential reality of racial difference. To his lifelong sorrow, Sutpen will experience the difference in the real effects of the long history of English, French, Spanish, Portuguese, indigenous American, and African rela-tions on the island, relations that remove questions of class and race from the simple binary configurations of black and white or rich and poor on the mainland. These relations, experienced as processes of cultural transcoding and racial revaluation, constitute the core of the uniquely colonial ideology Sutpen encounters in Haiti. To his and his family's full misfortune, he fails tragically, however, to respond to the features of this process in the colonial Caribbean and is incapable of translating it to the white supremacist world of Yoknapatawpha County. His formative migration to Haiti thus crucially signals a missed possible alternative to his later American tragedy.

Quentin's own later abject speculation in *The Sound and the Fury* that "a nigger is not so much a person as a form of behavior; a sort of obverse reflection of the white people he lives among" is a parallel intuitive insight to the social quality of appar-ently essential racial forms ("June Second, 1910"). In *Absalom, Absalom!*, Haiti serves as the site of the elusive possible insight that it is not the truth of race antagonism (or of class conflict for that matter) that is at issue in the elaboration of an identity. Rather, it is the transcription, the enactment of identity, by an act of ethical commit-ment and subjective assignment, of a strategic *design* upon race and class difference that is the key to it all. From Sutpen's account of his Haitian adventure to Quentin's grandfather, General Compson, Quentin and Shreve hypothesize that the clear and distinct dichotomy between racial and class motivations figured in the "boy-symbol at the door" episode is decisively shattered for Sutpen in Haiti, especially after he learns that he has been deceived into thinking that his first wife's mother "*had been a Spanish woman*" when in fact she "*was part negro*" (ch. 8). The historical facticity of that distinction is one that the young Sutpen initially was not capable of appreci-ating. After the disclosure of his wife's racial background, however, Sutpen is com-pelled with a vengeance to reformulate racial identity as a *real*, and no longer merely a "speculative," antagonism. The construction of this "reality" in opposition to its "speculative" possibilities is the central concern of the novel and of the relationship between the United States and the global South.

In the aftermath of the discovery that his Haitian wife, Eulalia Bon, is a mulatta, Sutpen rejects her and his child by this woman, Charles Bon, because of their racial identity. However, if in the figure of Charles Bon we have the most obvious instance of the racial continuum that disrupts the unproblematic purity of whiteness, Bon's son by an "octoroon mistress," Charles Etienne de Saint Valery Bon, with his "sixteenth part" black blood (ch. 4), makes the point even more starkly. He emphasizes "the tension surrounding the various shades of color found in Mississippi reality and the community's insistence on trying to push these shades back into black and white," as Hosam Aboul-Ela has correctly noted (2007, 156). The shock of this reality will reverberate backward and forward in time in Sutpen's story, with dreadful consequences for all.

Sutpen's rejection of Eulalia and Charles Bon on the basis of their racial identity is the paradigmatic moment of Faulknerian fiction. It represents the foundational instance of a scene that is played out over and over again not just in *Absalom, Absalom!* but also in *The Sound and the Fury*, *Light in August*, and all of his major novels. It points to racial hybridity as what John T. Matthews has identified as "the open secret of southern racism" (2004, 218). The secret of racial hybridity, like the "unspoken assumptions" that Cleanth Brooks once described as undergirding the false basis of southern community (1963, 52), defines and disrupts the core of white supremacy. In the wake of the calamitous revelation of Eulalia's and Charles's racial hybridity, Sutpen rejects the ideology of Haitian colonial society. Instead, he embraces and accepts as real with apparent equanimity the very racial polarities and "speculative antagonisms" of the slave-owning South that will ultimately destroy him and his design.

In *Absalom, Absalom!*, Faulkner is acutely conscious of the ramifications of this double bind of white supremacist ideology. But this awareness is explicit in other novels as well, particularly so in his earlier masterpieces, *The Sound and the Fury* and *Light in August*. Both novels offer exemplary instances of the formation of the racial subject in reactive structures of mutual codependence, the hallmark of Sutpen's experience in the global South.

The Sound and the Fury is particularly significant in this regard, especially if we join together aspects of the novel that, until very recently in the history of American literary studies, usually have not been linked: its experiments with narrative form on the one hand and racial formation on the other. Comprised of four sections, each narrated by a member or close associate of the Compson family, the novel draws heavily on stream of consciousness to capture the perspectives and prejudices of each of its narrators. And it is worth asking both why experimental narrative and racial formation have not typically been linked—and what happens to our understanding of Faulkner's novelistic experiments when we do link them, as does, for example, Edouard Glissant in *Faulkner, Mississippi*.

We may get at these questions first by examining the poetics of genre and the power of generic hybridity in Faulknerian narrative forms. Such an examination yields insight into how differing aesthetics as well as differing conceptions of racial formation are linked to the American novel in its modern forms. What is more, it shows as well how the processes of modernization and globalization in the American global South formally reshape the novel. In the American social and cultural context, race has traditionally referred to the social and legal patterns of hierarchy and domination characterizing the relations between groups of blacks and whites. Certainly Faulkner's novels powerfully represent the ways that this racial dynamic has shaped modern American life. Less obviously, however, it is also the case that *The Sound and the Fury, Absalom, Absalom!, Light in August*, and other Faulkner novels gesture toward a more complicated racial narrative. This narrative posits race and racialization as a *doing*, a communal ongoing system of processes that, as Paula M. L. Moya and Hazel Markus have convincingly argued in their introduction to *Doing Race: 21 Essays for the 21ˢᵗ Century*, "always involves creating groups based on perceived physical and behavioral characteristics, associating differential power and privilege with these characteristics, and then justifying the resulting inequalities" (2010, x). In these novels, the *multi*racial realities characteristic of the racialization of ethnicity in the United States are represented as an active doing that creates social structures and discourses that articulate a dialogical narrative of American social life based on multiplicity, heterogeneity, and difference, the latter of which then become rigidly hierarchical states of social and political existence. Unlike the processes of class formation, which do allow for the transformation of the classed subject from a position of relative powerlessness and limited agency into a fully active social agent, the object of racial doing does not enjoy that benefit. Wealth, social agency, and social standing are always fully liable to the color of subjectivity. A working-man in Faulkner's South may acquire wealth and power, as Sutpen so effectively does. A black man may do so only to the degree that his identity as a person of color is essentially mitigated.

In *The Sound and the Fury*, this matter of a multiracial *doing* emerges in each of the four sections of the novel. It appears, however, in a diffuse manner, sometimes thematically in its depiction of the ways that transnational circuits of migration, circulation, and intercultural exchange between the global North and South brought about by diasporic history shape American modernity. In other instances, narrative form itself works to further the representation of the racial structures of the global South.

As implausible as it may seem, the complex quality of this contact with the global South emerges most unambiguously in the Jason section of the novel, "April Sixth, 1928," replete as it is with a vile sort of dark comedic satire, focused mainly on Jason's ugly perceptions of race and sexuality. The celebrated experiments with stream of consciousness, spatial/temporal dislocations, decentered focalizations, and further modernist techniques of other sections of *The Sound and the Fury* give way here to more traditional realist narrative, but with a difference. An elegant experiment with a form of satire that verges on the Menippean, Jason's narrative offsets in its own right the more self-consciously avant-garde modernist techniques of the Benjy and Quentin chapters with what we may describe as a *formal* parody, an *image*, of realist narrative. The Jason section of the narrative, like Menippean satire, attacks attitudes of mind rather than the specific individuals who hold those points of view: "Pedants, bigots, cranks, parvenus, virtuosi, enthusiasts, rapacious and incompetent professional men of all kinds," as Northrop Frye explains this satiric mode in *Anatomy of Criticism* (1957, 309).

That the Jason section speaks from the vocal vantage point of the Menippean satirist makes his narrative all the more deliciously parodic and ironic. For here, Faulkner uses narrative *voice* rather than narrative *structure* to modernize the form of traditional realism, blending the form of the critique of social ills with the Menippean critique of the intellect that rationalizes those ills. Jason's celebrated unreliability as a narrator stems from this doubling of narrative modes. He scorns everyone around him who holds what he presumes to be insipidly simple understandings of the real social world. And yet in the end all of his scorn redounds on him with an ironic and comic vengeance. Moreover, this blending of generic forms—satire, irony, comic, and realistic narrative—underscores Mikhail Bakhtin's proposition in "From the Prehistory of Novelistic Discourse" that a narrative structured in parody ceases to be that form—sonnet, elegy, sermon, or epic, as the case may be—and becomes instead the *image* of a form (1981). For this reason, Menippean satire plays a special role in Bakhtin's theory of the novel. In *Problems of Dostoevsky's Poetics*, Bakhtin treats Menippean satire as one of the classical "serio-comic" genres that are united by a "carnival sense of the world," wherein "Carnival is the past millennia's way of sensing the world as one great communal performance" and is "opposed to that one-sided and gloomy official seriousness which is dogmatic and hostile to evolution and change" (1984, 160).

From Jason's perspective, pedants, bigots, cranks, and parvenus abound in the world around him, especially in the high comedic and carnivalesque scenes of his encounter with the carny showmen, with one of whom Caddy's daughter, Quentin, absconds with the money that Jason has stolen from her. From the perspective of Menippean satire, however, Jason's failed attempt to retrieve either Quentin or the doubly stolen money renders him the comic buffoon of the tale. This blend of parody, satire, and irony produces a grotesque realism and is the vehicle with which Faulkner drives his narrative of racism and desire in the context of the global South. As in classic Menippean satire, the butt of the ridicule is as much a social structure and its enabling ideological attitudes as any individual person or point of view. Here, Jason's grotesque realism is structurally not unlike the "speculative antagonism"— mediating between real and imaginary forms of racial formation—that, as we have seen, guides formations of race and racism in *Absalom, Absalom!* and governs the enactment of race in Faulkner's novels generally. So while Jason is indeed the object of satire, the force of the ridicule is not muted by his personal idiosyncrasies so much as those idiosyncracies channel the prevailing ideas of Yoknapatawpha and the South generally.

Matters of race emerge obviously in Jason's narrative in his relation to one of the family's servants, Dilsey, and her family, and to Jason's unyielding certainty of his superiority as a white heir to the still-functioning hierarchy of slavery—his cruelty to Dilsey's grandson Luster over a pair of show tickets manifests this most vividly. It is also evident, however, in the context of the speculative financial markets that link Yoknapatawpha County by telephone and telegraph to global commodity exchanges, through which, by exploiting others, Jason balances his accounts and thus proves his moral superiority as a self-made man.

Even though composed predominantly in the first-person realist mode, Jason's section cannot avoid the disruptions of time and space that we get in the Benjy and Quentin sections of *The Sound and the Fury*. Yet Jason seems the character most in sync with the modernist present, as a schemer and cotton speculator on "April Sixth, 1928," a few months before Faulkner actually published *The Sound and the Fury* in 1929, and a year and a half before the stock market crash of October 1929. Jason's narrative is a low comedy of sustained lack of self-knowledge. He complains that "fellows . . . sit up there in New York and trim the sucker gamblers" who do not have "inside information" about the speculative financial futures markets ("April Sixth, 1928"), underscoring his sense of Yoknapatawpha as the site of an internal colonialism, of the South colonized by the North, within the global economies. His sense of divestment from this economy, his distance from his own family, and his sadistic entitlement to racial superiority are all evidence in different registers of his bitter working understanding of how contrivance and privilege govern his local world's participation in global economic exchanges about to be played out by the Crash of 1929.

The point of the scenes in the country store where he works as a clerk is directly counter to the ethos of "white labor" and agrarian industry, which Jason scorns. Instead, while scheming to profit from "those eastern jews" by speculating with the money he has embezzled from his mother and his sister, he nevertheless fumes at the thought that it has "come to a pretty pass when any dam foreigner that cant make a living in the country where God put him, can come to this one and take money right out of an American's pockets" ("April Sixth, 1928").

It is worth noting that a version of this blend of the satiric, ironic, and high comedic modes of Jason's story unexpectedly characterizes parts of Quentin's narrative, "June Second, 1910," too. The thematic link between the global South and the grotesque realism of the Menippean satire of Jason's narrative affects the extended scene of Quentin's comically inept attempts to evade the company of "a little dirty child with eyes like a toy bear's and two patent-leather pigtails" on the day of his suicide in Boston. In these scenes, as Quentin ironically observes, the global South penetrates deep into the heart of America, "Land of the kike home of the wop" ("June Second, 1910"). Like Jason's "eastern jews," these "foreigners," immigrants who now indiscriminately populate New England— "Them furriners. I cant tell one from another," says the bakery shopkeeper—stand in as the racial other. Here, the "furriners" are "the obverse reflection of the white people" ("June Second, 1910") they live among, without whom the certainty of white identity is shaken.

Quentin's view of blacks as "the obverse reflection of white people" is the process of racialization, the doing of race, that in Sutpen's story in *Absalom, Absalom!* is named "speculative antagonism." Now, the obverse reflection and speculative antagonism extend to the Latin cultures of the Mediterranean and southern Europe, Spanish, French, Italian, in particular, transposed to the Americas. When after wandering the countryside with the little Italian child, repeatedly failing to get rid of her, and finally being assaulted by the child's brother, Julio, who assumes the worst from Quentin's ambiguous demeanor toward the little girl, the full circle joining satire and comedy to tragedy is completed. Encompassed within the circle are the fundamental themes of *The Sound and the Fury*—racial, ethnic, national, and sexual identity. When the credibility of Julio's suspicions about Quentin's intentions toward the child are challenged and dismissed because he is one of "them durn furriners," Julio counters by insisting "I American. . . . I gotta da pape" ("June Second, 1910"). He proposes, in other words, that his trustworthiness and whiteness are underwritten by the documentation of citizenship. In defense of Julio's suspicions of Quentin and his passionate defense of his sister's honor, it is worth noting that Quentin's last glimpse of the child is the narrative transition to thoughts of Caddy, virginity and sexuality, and his own ambiguous desires: "so many of them walking along in the shadows and whispering with their soft girlvoices lingering in the shadowy places and the words coming out and perfume and eyes you feel not see" ("June Second, 1910"). As is almost always the case in *The Sound and the Fury*, contact with the global South is pervasive, disruptive, and unavoidable. It forms the unexpected core of the Compson story.

Matters having to do with the disruptive nature of sexuality appear more obliquely than do questions of race in Jason's section. Here, the obsessive quality of Quentin's own concern for Caddy's sexuality is displaced onto the figure of Caddy's daughter, Quentin, the center of Jason's simmering financial problems and moral outrage. Joining in her name as she does Quentin's incestuous desires for Caddy with Caddy's own attempts to break the bonds imposed on her sexual desires, Caddy's daughter repeats the unresolved contradictory desires that drive the Compson family as a whole. In the context of a novel that mixes the narrative modes of extreme temporal and spatial dislocations of Benjy's and Quentin's stories, Jason's fraudulent schemes require a narrative mode that blends comedy, satire, and irony to produce a distinctive kind of modernist, satirical, realism. Hence readers' impression of the narrative of *The Sound and the Fury* having become overpopulated with meanings that do not cohere around a single, comprehending gaze. Like Benjy's and Quentin's narratives, this is exactly what Jason's narrative unravels as well: an objective world independent of subjective personal perspective.

Faulkner is acutely conscious of the ramifications of the pervasiveness of the global South and its intrusion into the American North in *Absalom, Absalom!* and *The Sound and the Fury*. But this awareness is explicit in other novels as well, particularly in *Light in August,* where the racial subject is formed explicitly in a reactive structure of mutual co-dependence, the hallmark of Sutpen's experience in Haiti and clearly discernable in Quentin's passage into the racialized immigrant spaces of early twentieth-century New England. In *Light in August*, racial confusion also figures prominently, especially in Joe Christmas and Joanna Burden's shared relations to another site of the American global South, namely, Texas with its history of crossed relationship to Mexico. Joanna Burden's "halfbrother" Calvin, is part Mexican and "dark like father's mother's people and like his mother" (ch. 11), while Joe Christmas's mother, Milly Hines, had claimed that "the fellow with the circus" who has fathered her baby "was a Mexican" (ch. 16). In the Mexican racialized subjectivity that figures in Joe Christmas's and Joanna Burden's respective racial histories, shaded in Joanna's case with "Huguenot stock" (ch. 11)—that is, Mediterranean Latin French ancestry—Faulkner's incessant observation of the complexity of racial hybridity in the Americas emerges as a sign of this relation. Thus, in *Light in August*, Joanna Burden, whose namesake, Juana, her father's Mexican wife, accedes to her eventual sorrow with her father's racial view that the black race is the "white race's doom and curse for its sins." Describing the merciless image of this doom to Joe Christmas, Joanna says:

> I seemed to see [negroes] for the first time not as people, but as a thing, a shadow in which I lived, we lived, all white people, all other people. I thought of all the children coming forever and ever into the world, white, with the black shadow already falling upon them before they drew breath. And I seemed to see the black shadow in the shape of a cross. And it seemed like the white babies were struggling, even before they drew breath, to escape from the shadow that was not only upon them but beneath them too, flung out like their arms were flung out, as if they were nailed to the cross. I saw all the little babies that would ever be in the world, the ones not yet even born—a long line of them with their arms spread, on the black crosses. (ch. 11)

Sorrowfully, implacably, the babies envisioned here by Joanna all bear the marks of their own defining racially crossed fate. The crossing relates in Joanna's case to what Joe Christmas early on in their affair ascribes to her "dual personality" (ch. 11), her security in pleasure and strength of awareness as a woman. The doubling, however, is particularly true of the centrally crossed sacrificial figure of the novel, Joe Christmas. His father, unnamed but identified by his mother, Milly Hines, as "a Mexican" (ch. 16), bequeaths to Joe Christmas the mestizo double ambiguity of being neither black nor white, essentially but born of the crossed ancestries of the Latin world. In fact, Joe Christmas's identity as a "white nigger" (ch. 15), that is, as someone who obscurely inhabits the color spectrum between white and black, stands on the far side of Sutpen's refusal to acknowledge his own mixed race son, Charles Bon, by his Haitian wife, Eulalia. These figures "Threatening white supremacy" (ch. 11), and the constructed nature of racial and class identity live and suffer the consequences of their actions. Their fates reflect what Edouard Glissant describes as the "contradictory atavistic" nature of the "composite cultures" created with European colonialism: "What is Yoknapatawpha? A composite culture that suffers from wanting to become an atavistic one and suffers in not being able to achieve that goal" (1999, 115).

Even if Thomas Sutpen had embraced his mulatto son, Charles Bon, and his grandson, Charles Etienne de Saint Valery Bon, finding atavistic homogeneity across generations and racial divides, all still would not have been well in Yoknapatawpha County. For *Absalom, Absalom!* is not just a narrative of the family romance gone south. Nor is Faulkner's novel simply an American imperialist representation of the Caribbean in which the foreign-born son, Charles Bon, plays the role of the Caribbean homeless son, desiring to naturalize, and being prevented from doing so and thus being legally assimilated into the US American body politic.

Affiliation is a much more complicated affair than either of those alternative designs in Sutpen's story might allow, as Quentin and Shreve attempt to figure out. For in Faulkner, the family, and with it the nation-state in all of its romantic certitude, is very much representative of a doomed order or design, one marked by rejection, vengeance, and fratricide. The problem of this American novel is ultimately the difficulty of accepting the existence of others, aliens, strangers within the self. All of which makes *Absalom, Absalom!* a timely and difficult novel. For if *Absalom, Absalom!* is a novel about the failure of self-sufficiency, it is also a novel about the failure of romantic individualism's denial of the role of the life of strangers in the self. One additional result of Faulkner's thematic foray into the global South, then, is, unexpectedly, a formally generic one, resulting in a blend of historical fiction, Menippean satire, and literary realism, in Faulkner's representation of the fate of racial identity in the South.

To (re)admit strangers, especially racial strangers, into constructions of both individual and communal selves, Faulkner's novels have to negotiate the relationship between what is narrated and what is unsayable especially as they attempt to establish historical veracity for their accounts of the fate of the American nation. As a result of this negotiation, literary realism comes to acknowledge the roles of fantasy, the uncanny (the *unheimlich*), the marvelous, and the imaginary in historical reality as integral aspects of the internal makeup of American history.

In his celebrated essay "The Marvelous Real in America," the prologue to his 1949 novel *El reino de este mundo* (*The Kingdom of this World*), Cuban novelist Alejo Carpentier offers an alternate, but related, explanation for the nature of American narrative and American reality. Carpentier claims that in the Americas, a modern perception of reality resulted from a unique fusion of the beliefs and superstitions of different cultural groups that included the European conqueror, his Euro-American criollo (creole) and Westernized mestizo descendants, the native peoples of the Americas, and the descendants of Africans carried into bondage in the New World.

Historically, the shared experiences and the misconceptions arising from the often conflicted contact among these groups colored the accounts of America's discovery and colonization by both native and European chroniclers. The early European chroniclers in the Americas not only brought with them erroneous preconceptions and utopian images of the New World, they also brought patterns for their narratives, particularly the *libros de caballerías* (books of chivalry), which related fantastic and incredible feats realized by fictional heroes. Little distinction was made between fact and fiction within the traditions of European Renaissance historiography and rhetoric. Similarly, by relying on the oral storytelling traditions of their ancestors' fables and myths as the primary source for their history, native chroniclers also combined truth and fantasy. For these reasons having to do with the experience of reality in the Americas and the consequent attempt to narrate it, Carpentier says in his essay, a new narrative mode emerged in the New World as an attempt to adequate the real and the marvelous, resulting in a mode he called *lo real maravilloso*, the marvelous real. In the Americas the reality of history is so strange as to appear fictional. "After all," Carpentier concludes, "what is the entire history of America if not the chronicle of the marvelous real?" (qtd. in Zamora and Faris 1995, 88).

Magical realism has had a phenomenally successful reception in the United States, even if that reception has been one based on a misconception of *lo real maravilloso* as a literary form and a historical event. In an essay entitled "Latin America in the U. S. Imaginary: Postcolonialism, Translation and the Magic Realist Imperative," Sylvia Molloy decries the stereotyping of Latin America conducted by the US literary establishments in what she terms the "fabrication of a Latin American 'South'" that resembles all too reprehensibly the parallel construction of an invented "Orient" (2005, 190). By adding temporal and spatial distance between the United States and Latin America, this version of magical realism keeps the Americas safely separate and distinct.

As apt as Molloy's accounts of the reception of magical realism in the United States is, it is possible to find a different version of the place of fantasy, the marvelous, and the imaginary in their relationship to United States history. Thinking proleptically, one may find a great deal of common ground between the role of *lo real maravilloso* in the narratives of the American global South and Faulkner. The basis for that common ground is their shared concern with the social and cultural legacies of colonialism, slavery, and political dependency in the Americas. As distinct as the outcome of each of these American experiences has been in the various regions of the American hemisphere, those differences nevertheless share identifiable genetic traits.

Let us take the instance of Alejo Carpentier, a fluent bilingual speaker and writer of French and Spanish, whose earliest writings from the 1930s make him a near exact contemporary of Faulkner. As Stephen Henighan remarks in "Two Paths to the Boom: Carpentier, Asturias, and the Performative Split," Carpentier's custom of asserting the predominance of whatever language he was *not* speaking at the moment indicated ongoing personal and artistic negotiations between his Franco- and Hispano-phone Caribbean identities. Equally, it represented the formative fissures within his creative personality and linguistic and discursive hybridity. In his own attempts to explain the fissures within American histories and their historiographical patterns, Faulkner too finds that discursive hybridity, in this case a blending of history and the real, fantasy and the imaginary, unavoidably form the warp and woof of new world narratives, extending north *and* south of the border between Latin and Anglo America. The South of this border, however, is not an exotic counterpoint without real contact with the world of historical significance. On the contrary, Faulkner's global South extends across this imaginary divide of the Americas, acknowledging their real historical kinship and difference.

This geography is one reason Glissant, thinking hemispherically, claims in an essay entitled "The Novel of the Americas," that he can identify "themes common to the concerns of those whom we classify as American writers" (1989, 144). Chief among these themes are time and history, space and landscape, and language and representational style. Glissant adds that a "tortured sense of time [produces] in the works of the American novelist . . . a struggle against time in order to reconstitute the past . . . in order to deny it better or reconstruct it." By dramatizing time, the American novelist is able to bring it to bear on the other aspect of the novel of the Americas, "the inescapable *shaping force* of our production of literature," namely, "the language of landscape" (145).

Concerning representational style from Faulkner to Carpentier, Glissant concludes that time and space in the American novel are consistently rent, shattered, and torn out of shape, requiring different forms of representational style to reshape them into a properly American form. "This is why," Glissant concludes, "realism—that is, the logical and rational attitude toward the visible world—more than anywhere else would in our case betray the true meaning of things" (145). When we put Faulkner in the context of the global South, his realism turns into something very much akin to *magical* realism. This is precisely the context in which Carpentier, Jorge Luis Borges, Guillermo Cabrera Infante, Carlos Fuentes, Gabriel García Márquez, and the other great novelists of mid-twentieth-century Latin America encounter him: as a chronicler of the world culture of the global South.

30

THE DEPRESSION AND THE NOVEL

BY SONNET RETMAN

From the vantage of the present, we might recall the Great Depression through a series of iconic images: The black-and-white photographs taken by Walker Evans and Dorothea Lange, for instance, of breadlines, sharecroppers tending fallow fields, and gaunt migrant mothers clutching their children close; or the homespun tenacity of Ma Joad and the budding radicalism of Tom Joad—the protagonists of John Steinbeck's bestselling novel, *The Grapes of Wrath* (1939). In the massive economic and social upheaval of the '30s when the American Way of Life was increasingly perceived to be nothing more than a ruse, artists such as Evans, Lange, and Steinbeck focused on the lives of poor and working-class people left out of its socially mobile trajectory. In literary critic Morris Dickstein's words, "The crisis kindled America's social imagination, firing enormous interest in how ordinary people lived, how they suffered, interacted, took pleasure in one another and endured" (2010, xiv). Such ordinary people were presumed to be "real" and representative by virtue of their economic disenfranchisement. They functioned as a powerful resource for both marking and resolving the crisis, for envisioning new and old figures of enduring national personhood in the form of the common man, the proletariat, and the folk.

In these popular depictions, we witness the makings of the "Great Depression narrative," a 1930s paradigm of social suffering and survival, collective life and resistance. This paradigm organizes and authorizes specific understandings of the subject of suffering and the project of representation itself through the concept of authenticity. It encompasses social realism, documentary, and ethnography, texts that promise a transparent and immediate encounter with "authentic" peoples—in cultural historian William Stott's words, "the worker, the poor, the jobless, the ethnic minorities, the farmer, the sharecropper, the Negro, the immigrant, the Indian, the oppressed and the outlaw" (1986, 53). Indeed, these "raw" subjects and realist modes of representation are so intertwined that they are barely recognizable without one another. In this version of the '30s, realism rules the day as it petitions for social reform on behalf of "[society's] most deprived and powerless subjects" (56). Underpinning these subjects were the folk and their premodern authenticity. The folk provided what Van Wyck Brooks had once called, in another context, a "usable past" for an uncertain present (1968, 219).

Much of the criticism about the novel in the 1930s has conformed to the Great Depression narrative, yet this pervasive paradigm excludes important modes of cultural representation from the era such as modernism, satire, and parody. This chapter briefly surveys the conventional Great Depression narrative to locate alternatives within and beyond its literary canon. While it might be tempting to situate modernism, satire, and parody as fictional opposites of realism and its variants, that account forecloses the messy complexity of the novel in this moment. It largely ignores the presence of hybrid genres perhaps more difficult to categorize, modes that cohered specifically around the populist figure of the folk to lodge a form of social protest. Seizing upon the insurgent energies of these combinations, I argue that the hybrid genres of *modernist burlesque* and *signifying ethnography* illuminate other powerful, often progressive formations of the novel within the cultural politics of the period. These hybrid genres promote a reflexive reading practice, which allows us to perceive the seductions of the real and the authentic in narratives of self, community, and nation.

Such seductions might include our memories of the 1930s themselves. As we see once again in our own Great Recession, the Great Depression is routinely called upon to authenticate moments of economic crisis and resistance. It has come to represent the standard by which every subsequent economic crisis has been measured. Yet there is irony in the fact that the "authenticity" now routinely assigned the '30s was, in fact, an invention of that era, one that was promoted, marketed, and contested by those who lived during the years of the Depression itself.

In the wake of the stock market's collapse in 1929, the search for authenticity gained new urgency, shape, and direction. Amidst skyrocketing unemployment and spiraling deflation, novelists, ethnographers, documentarians, filmmakers, politicians, and reformers sought out something real, something genuine, with which to ground an increasingly tenuous sense of national identity. At the forefront of their efforts lay the thorny problem of how to represent "the people." Ideological battles over "the people" were fought vociferously on the right and the left by the likes of crooked populist Huey Long, fascist Father Coughlin, liberal centrist President Franklin D. Roosevelt, and progressive labor leader John L. Lewis.

Writers, too, wrestled with conceptions of "the people." Alfred Kazin observed that the '30s produced a "literature of nationhood . . . largely the story of the American people as they came to understand it for themselves in a period of unprecedented crisis" (1995, 485). Seeking to represent "the people" within the "American tradition," many writers posited the folk as a particularly resonant and resilient character type. The folk were not synonymous with the people; rather, they were construed as regionally located ancestors or native others in competing conceptions of the people. Starting in the late nineteenth century, American folklorists, collectors, and local-color writers envisioned the folk primarily as white Americans of

"Anglo-Saxon" descent, African Americans, and Native Americans. Different racial formations of the folk were featured in different national stories depending upon the politics and the region. In some of these stories, the folk embodied a purportedly precapitalist way of life, an enduring stoicism in the face of the erratic excesses of the marketplace. In other accounts, they represented an embattled group in need of government intervention—"pseudo-peasants" on the verge of vanishing because of the ravages of capitalism and unpredictable forces of nature (Smith 1993, 298). Viewed either as relics worthy of preservation or as victims deserving of aid, the folk were perceived as a pastoral resource integral to the nation's healing and crucial to the brokering of new deals.

The folk's rural, artisanal know-how seemed to comprise the "raw stuff" with which to remake American identity (Kazin 1995, 489). Within the standardized products of assembly-line culture, or Fordism, the folk were positioned as unique artifacts, their difference commodified and made "real" through modernized media on a national scale. Cultural loss and its preindustrial folk iconography thus became the occasion for a lucrative nostalgia, which ironically fortified capitalism, the very agent of "authentic" culture's demise. Four out of the five bestselling novels of the '30s explored the search for security in history or on the land, with repressive gender and racial hierarchies firmly in place: *The Good Earth* (1931), *God's Little Acre* (1933), *Gone With the Wind* (1936), and *The Grapes of Wrath*. Historian Robert McElvaine observes, "The past, like the ownership of a piece of land, offered a refuge for people distressed with the present and fearful of the future" (1993, 221). Many were seduced by this strain of nostalgia, fixating on a stability that never was. Embracing mythical figures of authenticity and realist forms of representation, the most well-known chroniclers of the '30s created a self-conscious "literature of nationhood," a reserve with which to revitalize conceptions of the nation and its citizenry.

In conventional literary histories of the 1930s, the novels that have come to sum up this "literature of nationhood" unfailingly represent versions of social realism, the fictional vehicle of the authentic commonly associated with the left, such as Erskine Caldwell's *Tobacco Road* (1932), John Dos Passos's *U. S. A.* trilogy (1930–36), Mike Gold's *Jews Without Money* (1930), Josephine Herbst's *Rope of Gold* trilogy (1933–39), John Steinbeck's *Grapes of Wrath*, and Richard Wright's *Native Son* (1940). These texts are often categorized more particularly as subgenres of social realism, such as the proletarian novel, the strike novel, the populist novel, the road novel, the migrant novel, and the documentary novel. These realist variants share a purported fidelity to the facts, to the quotidian textures, rhythms and hardships of life lived by oppressed peoples, whether they are the rural poor, the urban industrial working class, or the racially and economically disenfranchised. The subjects of social realism—in Franklin D. Roosevelt's words, the "ill-housed, ill-clothed, [and] ill-fed"—were cast as "the salt of the earth," authentic by virtue of their marginalization and their representativeness. As the radical '30s literary critic Granville Hicks would suggest of

Dos Passos in an April 12, 1933, article for the *New Republic,* many of these writers made the "fundamental discovery . . . that American life is a battleground, and that arrayed on one side are the exploiters and on the other the exploited." Though not all of these writers were Communists, many were left leaning, adopting Marxist and socialist political perspectives in their work. They hoped to use their writing as a means of instigating social reform, if not revolution: social realism was intended to have real-world effects.

No novel synthesizes these aspects of social realism more cohesively than *The Grapes of Wrath.* Steinbeck began to draft the novel in 1938 after writing a series of articles for the *San Francisco News* about the dire living conditions of migrants from the Midwest who were unsuccessfully trying to find work within California's agriculture industry and also after reporting at the behest of the Farm Security Administration on flooding and starvation in Visalia, California. Drawing upon this journalism, Steinbeck's Dust Bowl novel charts the migration of the Joad family, poor white sharecroppers or in the novel's parlance, "Okies," as they are evicted from their home in Oklahoma and travel to California looking for work, only to be disillusioned by the exploitive labor and living conditions they find in this promised land. As Ma Joad strives to keep the family together, her eldest son Tom becomes a class-conscious fugitive, after joining a strike that becomes violent and killing the murderer of his mentor, Preacher Casy. Steinbeck documents the Joad family's survival skills, their grit and gumption out on the road as they leave their old way of life for something new. He offers us a migrant and road novel wrapped in one, the forward motion of individuals, a family, a mass movement, finally, as Dickstein suggests, the abstraction of "the People," rendered murkily through the contradictory rhetoric of individualism and collectivism, naturalism and proletarianism (2009, 135). In Kazin's words, the Joads "became a living and challenging part of the forgotten American procession," resilient populist types in an unfolding national drama (1995, 397). The Joad's story of dispossession and migration, "the Okie exodus," ironically displaces the many other stories of dispossession we might know the '30s by—the stories of migrant Mexican, Filipino, Chinese, and Japanese farmworkers, African American sharecroppers among them. Surely, part of the Joad's representativeness has to do with their folksy whiteness rendered in the broad strokes of social realism (Denning 1996, 267).

It is no accident that the term "folksiness, the state or quality of being 'folksy,' " originated in the United States around 1931, at the end of the Hoover Administration (*OED*). Or that we have come to remember the tumultuous '30s through near-iconic iterations of the folk and the folksy, such as Ma Joad. Bearing the weight of so much consequence in politics and popular culture, the rhetoric of the folk not unexpectedly became "folksy." Nathanael West would remark upon Ma Joad's folksy quality in a letter addressed to Popular Front writer and journalist Malcolm Cowley in 1939: "Take the 'mother' in Steinbeck's swell novel—I want to believe in her and yet inside myself, I honestly can't" (qtd. in Martin 1970, 335–36). Considering Ma

Joad from West's perspective, we begin to see how the folk were frequently transformed into populist, regional clichés of "real" Americans and "real" America. We
also glean West's and other novelists' resistance to this mode by way of more experimental, hybridized forms.

When social realism is invoked as *the* genre of the 1930s, in Michael Denning's
observation, it "has come to mean three things: the documentary aesthetic, a rear-
guard opposition to modernism, and a relatively straightforward representational-
ism in the arts" (1996, 118). But Denning, Barbara Foley, Paula Rabinowitz, and
other scholars have demonstrated the degree to which these residual understandings of the period obscure and ignore the innovative revolutionary aesthetics that
emerged within the radical culture of the Depression, what might be described as an
overtly politicized social modernism that was, by definition, oxymoronic, hybrid,
and unstable. Furthermore, in this persistent focus on realism, the satirical energies
of the '30s have been largely overlooked, an omission that has rendered the work of
George Schuyler, Nathanael West, and others at best anomalous and at worst inscrutable. In fact, these writings were by no means anomalies, but instead responses to
the Depression era's representational crisis and its corresponding recourse to icons of
working class and rural authenticity.

Attention to the decade's convergent satirical and documentary genres challenges
social realism's hold on the '30s and brings to light alternative forms of cultural
production and social critique around the figure of the folk in texts such as George
Schuyler's *Black No More* (1931), Nathanael West's *A Cool Million* (1934), Zora Neale
Hurston's *Mules and Men* (1935), and James Agee and Walker Evans's *Let Us Now
Praise Famous Men* (1941). During the '30s, such authors fashioned hybrid forms of
satire and documentary through which to stage and query conventional racialized
and gendered epistemologies of the folk. As evident in the example of *The Grapes of
Wrath*, it would be easy to set up documentary and social realism as earnest purveyors
of the folk and satire as their wayward foil. Yet that opposition does not acknowledge
the many works of documentary, ethnography, and social realism that undermined
the authentic aura of the folk they set out to represent. Nor does it allow for the ways
that the satires often delivered their final punch through the reportorial straight face
of documentary. Such an opposition between documentary and satire ignores the
methods of social persuasion shared by these genres, their live wire of irony and their
delight in overturning the presumed spatio-temporal distance that structures the
gaze of the ethnographer, the middle-class observer, and the folk. Something more
incongruous is afoot. Both documentary and satire are dependent upon realism for
their articulation and authority, documentary presumed to be a transparent transcription of non-fictional reality and truth, and satire, a deeply exaggerated, fictional
representation of reality that nevertheless conveys a highly mediated commentary
on the status of the truth. Although strikingly different in tone and style, they are
each fundamentally propelled by the enunciation of a set of truth-claims, however
provisional and incomplete.

The readings that follow are organized around two variations of this hybrid genre, which I call *modernist burlesque* and *signifying ethnography*. The first, modernist burlesque, emerges as a highly theatrical form of satire that draws upon popular vaude-villian aesthetics and technologies of mass reproduction to dismantle the authentic aura that surrounds the folk and the self-made man within the sustaining myths of the American Way of Life. The second variation I analyze is signifying ethnography, a deeply intertextual and subversive form of documentation that implicates the ethnographer and the reader as participants in creating notions of "the authentic." Each of these literary modes exposes the ways the folk were called upon to evoke a precapitalist past and exploited (in the form of nostalgic "folk authenticity") to sell goods, including the idea of the nation itself. The folk are thus revealed to be an anxious product *of* corporate capitalism—not an antidote *external* or *prior* to commercial culture. Modernist burlesque and signifying ethnography encourage readers to acknowledge their desire for authenticity. By looking at the ways that satire and documentary hybridize each other in this period, we see at once how the folk were constituted within a nostalgic story of corporate capitalism and also how such hybridized forms of cultural expression issued a vigorous critique of that constitution. From this angle, then, the Thirties' "literature of nationhood" is far more irreverent, incendiary, and self-critical than the Great Depression narrative and other accounts have allowed.

The Modernist Burlesque

The modernist burlesque novels of the 1930s would seize upon the "impossible purity" of the folk. There are no better examples of this hybrid genre than George Schuyler's and Nathanael West's respective novels about the myth of class mobility, *Black No More* and *A Cool Million*. Both Schuyler and West deploy modernist burlesque to reveal how the clichéd story of American class ascension—the boot strap myth—depends upon impersonation, a performative making of the self into the upwardly mobile, white, and masculine rugged individual. Their texts thus expose the gendered workings of "racial capitalism," political theorist Cedric Robinson's formulation for the ways race is always a foundational structure within the operation of capitalism in the United States (2000, 2). Each character enacts this performative self-making on stage in front of large audiences. The reader witnesses how the audience that consumes the performance wholesale becomes reified, incorporated as white supremacist and/or fascist cogs in a mass-produced nationalist script. In this way, Schuyler and West disturb the dynamics of identification central to the rags-to-riches plot. By providing examples of all-consuming spectatorship and their violent outcomes in the voice of documentary, they distance readers from the audience depicted within the text. The critical capacity that emerges when readers divest themselves from these narratives of authentic personhood and nation forms the basis for other progressive political configurations and possibilities.

Given the antiracist, socialist critique of *Black No More,* it might come as a surprise that Schuyler's novel has been so steadfastly ignored in literary accounts of the 1930s. If we read about Schuyler at all, he is usually posited as a minor writer within the Harlem Renaissance, an account in part resulting from his own retrospective narration as an arch conservative later in life. Yet throughout the 1920s and 1930s, Schuyler was a prominent progressive black intellectual, sometime activist, a socialist for whom antiracist and class struggles were inseparable endeavors. Indeed, as biographies by Jeffrey Ferguson and George Peplow show, Schuyler began his career as a journalist writing for an array of liberal and radical publications, including A. Philip Randolph and Chandler Owner's journal *The Messenger, The Crisis, Opportunity, The Nation,* H. L. Mencken's *American Mercury,* and Mike Gold's *New Masses.*

Schuyler's early satirical writings in these publications allowed him to hone the political bite of his best-known novel, *Black No More: Being an Account of the Strange and Wonderful Workings of Science in the Land of the Free, A.D. 1933–1940,* published in 1931 and at the apex of his long, strange career. Schuyler's novel is at once a work of science fiction and a burlesque of the novel of racial passing, a genre that emerged at the turn of the century in response to legalized segregation, the separation and elevation of white people above black people within public and private spaces. These novels usually featured a black protagonist who successfully "passed" as a white person to access the privileges accorded whiteness and in the process, undermined this codification of racial hierarchy. In Schuyler's novel, we see how notions of racial authenticity and purity are capitalized upon and produced within mass consumer culture. *Black No More* deploys a literal "mechanics of passing." The novel begins with Dr. Junius Crookman's invention of a machine called Black-No-More that turns black people phenotypically white. The first Black-No-More sanitariums open in African American neighborhoods and the procedure costs an affordable fifty dollars. Of a piece with market culture, especially commodities such as skin lighteners and hair straighteners, Dr. Crookman's invention packages and sells whiteness, reproducing the singular black body that is able to pass for white on a massive scale. In this way, Crookman both usurps and eludes the central role of maternal labor in the reproduction of race. As the nation's black population disappears, the novel explores the ensuing hysteria over identity brought about by the standard-issue whiteness of the country's complexion and the possibility that every white citizen may have once been black. This violent demographic shift provides an occasion for lucrative nostalgia, an appeal to consumer desire for a folksy blackness that never existed in the first place: popular minstrel songs lament the "vanishing" of the black man, while dime museums exhibit the last few remaining black people who refused the whitening process and are desperate for work.

Against this backdrop, we follow Max Disher, our self-interested black protagonist, the first American consumer of Crookman's product. Once equipped with a "pork-colored skin," Max occupies the privileged position of white masculinity. He infiltrates the reigning white supremacist organization of the South, the Knights of Nordica, for personal gain. This outrageous plotline enables Schuyler to explore America's bootstrap myths of prosperity and democratic citizenship against the stark realities of racial segregation. Along the way, Schuyler skewers the racial populisms that prevented interracial working-class solidarity in his day. Moreover, he anticipates the mass production of the folk, joining a diverse range of writers from the period who questioned that construction, such as James Agee, Erskine Caldwell, Langston Hughes, Zora Neale Hurston, Nella Larsen, Tillie Olsen, and Nathanael West.

The cynical trickster Max realizes that one really profits from whiteness by producing and selling it, not simply owning it. If Dr. Crookman profits from his black consumers' desires to be white, a desire occasioned by their acute experiences of racial oppression and violence, Max schemes to profit from white people's anxieties about the security of their racial privilege in the wake of Black-No-More, when almost everyone has become "white." He understands, moreover, that without black laborers to occupy the role of scapegoat, workers might actually organize around class interests instead of false notions of racial purity. Max preempts this potential class-consciousness by reinventing race as an invisible but nonetheless marketable entity. Addressing the Knights of Nordica's membership "composed of the lower stratum of white working people" (ch. 4), he pitches to workers the notion of the subversive and undetectable "white Negro" in their midst who "[takes] their jobs and [undermines] their American standard of living" (ch. 6). Paradoxically, the workers' fear of incorporation with a communist, black, Catholic other guarantees that they are subsumed in a pervasive capitalist machine, much in the way that the protagonist of West's *A Cool Million* will meet his catastrophic end.

In the novel's conclusion, Dr. Crookman, now the acting Surgeon General, discovers that the black subjects he turned white are a few shades paler than the average Nordic, which leads the general populace to conclude that "surely it were not so well to be white!" (ch. 13). A new chapter in racial hysteria is marked by the advent of sun-tanning and darkening products. Schuyler sets this final section off in the text with the all-capped words "AND SO ON AND SO ON," so as to underscore the absurdly cyclical pattern at work here: "dusky" skin may appear to be a more inclusive skin color but the capitalist foundation that undergirds America's color-struck society has not changed (ch. 13). The novel's last vignette depicts Crookman smiling wearily at a newspaper photograph of Max's family—including his "very, very dark" son—playing on the beaches of Cannes, the truth-claim of the image and its reportorial setting delivering the novel's final irony (ch. 12). Even as the novel wrenches whiteness from its supposedly stable meanings by way of racial passing and miscegenation, it insists that the capitalist structures of racial oppression consolidated in white supremacy remain.

Black No More makes for uneasy reading. Far from romanticizing the folk or the masses, Schuyler depicts white workers as pathetic dupes and potential lynchers. The black working class fares somewhat better but is still castigated for the quickness with which they put aside notions of race pride to purchase Black-No-More. In this damning portrait of the folk, Schuyler rejects appeals to populism in any shape or form and, in the same breath, predicts the ways that particular racial and ethnic identities would be produced as marketable entities in the service of a nation in crisis. For Schuyler's critique to be effective, readers must separate themselves from the hegemonic majority who "buy into" the ideological system under review and also the novel's opportunistic protagonist, Max. Instead, the novel aligns the reader's perspective with the critical perspective of the novel's marginalized in-group, the few black women characters that refuse the incorporated whiteness of Black-No-More. The reader's insider/outsider position within these triangulated, ideological theatrics anticipates the performative strategies, an "aesthetics of anti-fascism," used by West and many artists of the 1930s to implicate their readers and viewers (Denning 1996, 380). Ultimately, by asking us to disidentify with "the great majority," *Black No More* directs us to resist our own conscription as actors in this national drama of racial capitalism and its violent ends.

Published three years after *Black No More*, *A Cool Million: or, The Dismantling of Lemuel Pitkin* (1934) has often been disparaged as Nathanael West's least successful novel. But it, like *Black No More*, should be recognized as a key novel of the literary left for its scathing burlesque of the myth of class mobility and its populist appeals, what might be described, following Jonathan Veitch, as a pernicious Thirties' folklore of racial capitalism. The novel's mixed reception may have had something to do with its banal and offensive literary sources, among them, Adolph Hitler's *Mein Kampf* (1926) and the Horatio Alger stories, the formulaic juvenile novels from the nineteenth century that depicted poor boys who rose from "rags to respectability" through "pluck and luck." (As Rita Barnard has noted, West cribs over one-fifth of his novel from actual Alger texts.) Perhaps critics could not accept the book's obvious satire: the novel must be read as a brutal denunciation of the American Dream for it to make any sense at all.

What remains abundantly clear is that West's modernist burlesque was distinct from the most recognizable proletarian representations of the era. In contrast with the sentimentally-inclined social realist novels that explored the plight of the proletariat within a network of capitalist exploitation, West examined the vagaries of commodity culture and the working-class consumer's role within it. West was not alone: a range of writers such as Dos Passos, Chester Himes, Hughes, Larsen, Sinclair Lewis, Olsen, and Schuyler used satire, invective, and parody to explore the consequences of Fordism's bodily, psychic, and economic incorporation. Indeed, West and these other writers might expand our conception of the fiction of the left. As Daniel Aaron suggests by way of novelist Edward Dahlberg, "there was another kind of writing . . . Dahlberg called it 'implication literature' tinged with 'just as deep radical dye.' West belonged to that select company of socially committed writers in the Depression Decade who drew revolutionary conclusions in highly idiosyncratic and undoctrinaire ways" (1971, 162). *A Cool Million* is West's most overtly political effort and no less compelling for it. The novel illuminates the radical ideas that drove West's day-to-day activism as part of the "Hollywood Popular Front" and his other satirical novels, *The Dream Life of Balso Snell* (1931), *Miss Lonelyhearts* (1933), and *The Day of the Locust* (1939).

In *A Cool Million*, West limns the many entanglements of "a pioneer people," drawing upon the frontier and bootstrap myths and their attendant constellations of the folk to consider the rise of fascism in America. Riffing on the Horatio Alger novels of the nineteenth century and their increased popularity as collectibles and moral touchstones in the 1910s and '20s, West's surreal tale unveils the myth of class mobility and the violent economics of propertied white patriarchy at the heart of the American Dream and Depression-era visions of "a usable past." *A Cool Million* follows the descent—not ascent—of our plucky American boy hero, Lemuel Pitkin, within the troubled marketplace of 1934. Upon the threat of foreclosure of his grandmother's house, Lem follows the advice of his small town's most prominent citizen, the former president and future fascist leader of the United States, Mr. Shagpoke Whipple, who urges him to "go out into the world and win [his] way" (ch. 2). On his failed quest, Lem repeatedly encounters the conniving Whipple and also his childhood sweetheart, Betty, who is brutalized, exploited, and raped throughout the book.

Throughout *A Cool Million*, opportunists capitalize upon and reinvent Lem's and Betty's increasingly desecrated bodies, making them representatives of the American folk. As Lem attempts to make his millions in New York City and instead faces police brutality, incarceration, and the extraction of all of his teeth by the prison dentist, Betty is captured by white slavers and taken to a themed whorehouse nearby. Following its original incarnation as "The House of Nations," the brothel is redesigned as a "one hundred per centum American place" in keeping with the nation's patriotic turn: it boasts a series of interiors styled after "Pennsylvania Dutch, Old South, Log Cabin Pioneer, Victorian New York, Western Cattle Days" (ch. 18), and other decors, better to market Betty as a "real American girl" (ch. 8)—another piece of Americana. She is the vessel through whom enfranchised and disenfranchised men alike hope to claim and assert the privilege of white masculine birthright. Unlike Lem, Betty has no birthright to claim herself in the world of business, and her capacity for self-making is never in question—rather, as a white woman, she exists in the novel only to be claimed as a guarantor of whiteness, an accessory to white patriarchy. Fittingly, by the book's conclusion, Betty has become Mr. Whipple's personal secretary within his fascist party.

While Betty is made into a desirable collectible, a representative of "genuine native stock" (ch. 18), Lem is made to be a unique folk exemplar of his failed "inalienable birthright" (ch. 13)—that access to social mobility and self-invention which constitutes his white masculine inheritance. With Lem, West centers the figure of "the little guy" or "the forgotten man" as his duped protagonist, inquiring after the meanings of the white male worker—the nation's most protected class of laborers—who is unable to claim his birthright both in the public sphere and the sphere of labor. *In spite of* Lem's white, masculine privilege, he cannot overturn the strictures of the American class system. With each effort to gain employment and earn "an honest cool million," Lem loses another body part—his teeth, an eye, a thumb, a leg, his scalp, and so on. The more Lem emulates the fictional model of Horatio Alger and fails, the more his broken body is capitalized upon, enabling his stage career as a spectacular freak. Throughout the narrative, he is displayed in a series of tawdry exhibits, as "Our young hero" in the novel itself; as "the last man to have been scalped by Indians" in the "Chamber of American Horrors" dime museum (ch. 27); as a stooge in the Riley and Robins's traveling burlesque; and finally as a martyr to the fascist National Revolutionary Party. West thus demonstrates the Alger stories' disingenuous populist overtures to the hard-working poor. He also predicts the ways that Alger plotlines would shape the populist rhetoric that cohered around particular configurations of the folk in the Depression era's discourse of national recovery.

Assassinated by undercover fascists in need of a martyr, Lem's demise represents the tragic ending of a thwarted all-American boy. He becomes a symbol for the triumph of fascism, the figure around which the country rallies under the National Revolutionary Party. The novel's humor drops away as if to say, a year before the publication of Sinclair Lewis's novel, *It Can't Happen Here* (1935), "it *has* happened here and it can and will happen here again." With this alarming turn, West shows how the American Dream works through stereotypical figures of success—the conventional Horatio Alger tales—and also *figures of failure*, such as Lem. For Whipple and his followers attribute Lem's failure not to the inequities of capitalism, but rather to the scheming of "sophisticated aliens," an external enemy of "the people" (Zizek 2006, 559). West reveals the intimate proximity between the Alger folk hero and fascist folk martyr, exposing the bankruptcy of racial capitalism and its fascist possibilities. In this way, West illuminates a seeming paradox of the Depression—the continued popularity of the bootstrap myth rejuvenated through populist depictions of hard-working folk when those same images might have served as a powerful counterexample of the ways capitalism failed so many people, *no matter how hard they tried*. Homing in on the 1930s' folk revival, West demonstrates with cruel precision the different ways in which particular racial bodies become fetishized, incorporated, and commodified as figures of the folk within a modernist culture of collecting. In this way, he creates a grotesque fictional burlesque of the documentary collections so popular in the '30s.

Signifying Ethnography

The signifying ethnographies of the period subverted the period's documentary impulse and praxis from another angle by both invoking and refusing the promise of the authentic folk. In different but exemplary ways, Zora Neale Hurston and

James Agee boldly embraced this strategy. Given the fact that signifying ethnography pertains primarily to works of non-fiction, the genre might appear to have little relevance to the Depression-era novel. However, signifying ethnography comprises a significant strain of Thirties' literary production, encompassing the period's documentary novel and its impure fiction/non-fiction blend. For this reason, I turn to Hurston's work of folklore, *Mules and Men*, and I conclude with a reading of Agee's documentary novel, *Let Us Now Praise Famous Men*, to map the parameters of signifying ethnography.

Like modernist burlesque, signifying ethnography cites and inhabits that which it means to question in order to instill in its readers a self-conscious critical reading practice. Whereas modernist burlesque implicates the performing protagonist and his or her multiple audiences in the perpetuation of insidious nationalist dramas, signifying ethnography implicates the ethnographer and the reader in the activity of searching for the authentic folk. In so doing, it shows the folk to be fluid, ephemeral, and impure. My use of "signifying" draws upon Hurston's definition of "to show off" found in *Mules and Men* and Henry Louis Gates's elaboration wherein signifying deploys the "use of repetition and reversal" to launch "an implicit parody of a subject's own complicity in illusion" (1987, 240). The signifying ethnographies of the period, such as B.A. Botkin's interregional Folk-Say anthologies (1929–32), Ella Deloria's *Speaking of Indians* (1944), Hurston's *Mules and Men* and *Tell My Horse* (1938), and Richard Wright's *12 Million Black Voices* (1941), make the reader aware of her own potential investment in the fiction of nonfiction's unmediated status.

Hurston's first book of folklore, *Mules and Men*, published in 1935, is a tour de force of signifying ethnography. As such, it deserves a central place in the literary histories of the '30s. Yet, like the work of Faulkner, West, and other Thirties' writers who have been awarded the halo of individual genius in the past century, Hurston's oeuvre has frequently been severed from her Depression-era context, assigned to other periodizations such as the Harlem Renaissance and modernism. Such demarcations prevent us from seeing how her work as an anthropologist, a folklorist, a dramatist, a performer, and a novelist consistently illuminates the manufacture of the folk and the primitive crucial not only to anthropological practice but also to the cultural capital of high modernism, the Harlem Renaissance, and the New Deal (on the relation of Hurston's anthropological work to her fiction, see Chapters 25 and 28 in this volume).

In *Mules and Men*, Hurston plays herself as an anthropologist outsider and a folk insider, entwining these stock roles into a Mobius strip of authenticity and performativity. The collection includes seventy southern African American folktales, together with hoodoo rites, folksongs, and other folkways drawn from Hurston's expeditions to the South, mainly to Eatonville, Florida, neighboring Polk County, and parts of Alabama and Louisiana. An intermediary between her subject and her audience, Hurston signifies on the colonial and imperialist entanglements of anthropology and her readers' concomitant expectations of a pre-industrial folk, real in their simplicity, out of time, and removed from the circuits of modernity. Referring to her subjects sometimes as "these people" and "the Negro" and at other times with an inclusive "we," Hurston subtly situates herself in the text both as a Columbia-trained folklorist and as an Eatonville-born representative of the "folk." As Daphne Lamothe argues, Hurston and other "native ethnographers" like her deploy "a black modernist gaze"; they insist upon "a way of seeing that dislocates ways of [anthropological] knowing" (2008, 2, 3). In this regard, folktales are the perfect slippery ethnographic subject. By designating fictional tales as the real artifacts of her fieldwork, Hurston asserts the centrality of the imaginary within the ethnographic endeavor, a perspective that challenges the shared insistence within modernist anthropology and the documentary movement upon objective truth and factuality— "the communication, not of imagined things but of real things only" (Stott 1986, xi). By the book's end, her readers become most conscious of Hurston's performance in staging the folk and their own press for authenticity. They are complicit in this process of commodification. She thus joins Schuyler, Hughes, Wallace Thurman, West, and others in foregrounding a central paradox of the period: that although the primitive and the folk were defined as entities outside of the commerce of the modern nation, they were nevertheless situated thoroughly within it. Each of these writers reveals the primitive and the folk to be nothing less but sometimes more than nationally-vested, market-driven formations of authentic identity.

Agee's epic *Let Us Now Praise Famous Men* intersects with *Mules and Men* in its focus on the southern folk, its centering of the ethnographer as a protagonist within the narrative, and its subversion of the documentary method so frequently used to capture "the folk." Ever intriguing for its aggressively genre-defying form, *Let Us Now Praise* is considered by some critics, such as Barbara Foley, to be a documentary novel on the grounds that it uses "the techniques and materials of fiction to reveal a truth about American society that is essentially historical" (1980, 390). Though Agee's political commitments were complex and often contradictory, *Praise* demonstrates the ways many writers within the orbit of the Popular Front pushed genre into excess as a vehicle for individual and collective protest, burlesqueing, dismantling and refiguring typical narrative formulas and codes to shake their readers and viewers loose from a practice of passive reception (Denning 1996, 122–23). This strategy of disillusion through illusion moves away from populist oversimplification, towards a critical reading practice and in some texts—not necessarily Agee's—a possible re-conception of progressive politics.

The documentary book was well established in 1936 when Agee and Evans traveled to Alabama to write an article illustrated with photographs about the life of an average white sharecropping family for *Fortune* magazine's "Life and Circumstances" series. The project eventually became *Let Us Now Praise Famous Men*, its publication delayed until 1941. At this point, the popularity of the genre was in decline, the most popular documentary works of the period having preceded it, books such as Margaret Bourke-White and Erskine Caldwell's *You Have Seen Their*

Faces (1937), Archibald Macleish's *The Land of the Free* (1938) and Dorothea Lange and Paul Taylor's *American Exodus* (1939). Emblematic of "the ethnographic and literary convergence of the [T]hirties," each of these works represents a different style—epic, grotesque, sentimental, lyrical, and scholarly—yet they all aim to recollect an "authentic," mythologized piece of America through a visual and textual accumulation of "real" evidence and detail (Hegeman 1999, 178). As T. V. Reed argues, Agee and Evans's book departs from these works, unrelentingly questioning its own representational practices: it cites and upends the most significant tropes of documentary and journalistic reportage, and in the manner of modernist fiction, it adopts an exceedingly self-conscious, berating first-person perspective that achieves omniscience by way of imagination, empathy, and closely observed detail. Much like the New Deal-sponsored collecting projects, the text attempts to exhaustively collect its tenant subjects, but it does so by taking inventory of their objects, traversing the divide between the person and the thing, a strategy not unlike *Mules and Men*'s blurring of the divide between teller and tale.

Distinct from Hurston's "black modernist gaze," where she looks back at the discipline of anthropology from the inside and outside as a "native ethnographer" (Lamothe 2008, 2), Agee's practice of signifying ethnography issues from his own white liberal guilt regarding his privilege as a southern-born, Harvard educated writer ensconced in the East Coast literary scene. Agee fears he will betray the tenants by not sufficiently representing their "great weight, mystery and dignity" (preamble). Yet the closer he comes to representing the tenants fully, the more he exposes them to the surveillance of others: "they are now being looked into by . . . others, who have picked up their living as casually as if it were a book." The tenants are "innocents" while all "observers" are "monstrously alien human beings" (preamble). Distancing himself from his role as documentarian, Agee contemplates his actions in the passive voice and in the third person. The sharecroppers' lives are commodified and consumed like the book that depicts them, and he is the agent of that exchange. While Agee aims his diatribe at the voyeurism of his former employers at *Fortune*, along with complacent readers, New Dealers and liberals everywhere, he also underscores his own conscious complicity in the project. Like most documentarians of the period, Agee believed in the conjoint aesthetic and political potential of their "truth-telling": if he and Evans could communicate the ravages of poverty to middle-class readers, then they might advance their disenfranchised subjects' interests on the nation's political agenda. However, he is distrustful of New Deal reformism, and even more anxious about depicting his subjects in a manner that reduces them to "the folk" in the form of a sentimental generalization or a government statistic.

To elude such generalizations, Agee deploys a number of narrative strategies, none more explicitly working in a mode of signifying ethnography than his use of descriptive excess. Agee focuses on the sharecroppers' objects, spending seventy-five pages cataloguing their houses, in a taxonomic scheme gone mad. When he explains his reasons for discursively turning the Gudgers's house inside out, he posits his desire to get at its fine "particularities" ("Colon"). Soon, his desires become more ambiguous, overtaken by voyeurism's stealthy pleasures: "They are gone. . . . I shall move as they would trust me not to, and as I could not, were they here. I shall touch nothing but as I would touch the most delicate wounds, the most dedicated objects. . . . [T]his house itself, in each of its objects, is one lens" ("Shelter"). Like Evans's camera, he promises to see and reproduce these objects through "one lens" with the precision of a mechanical instrument. He remembers times in "hot early puberty" when alone in his grandfather's "large unsentineled home," he would wander from room to room permitting "nothing to escape the fingering of [his] senses," his furtive search eventually leading to masturbation. In this house, he claims "it is not entirely other-wise . . . yet it differs somewhat: for there is no open sexual desire . . . but the quietly triumphant vigilance of the extended senses before an intricate task of surgery . . . a knowledge of being at work" ("Shelter"). The house is a body, replete with delicate wounds, and he is the surgeon. It is as if his scopic excision will restore these injuries through a process of apperception.

Yet as Agee moves about the house, he feels a pang of shame, imagining its renter, George Gudger, working in the cotton field at that same moment. The implicit jux-taposition of different kinds of labor designates the act of "observation" as a middle-class occupation. As a bourgeois spy investigating the internal corpus of the tenant underclass, Agee must transform Gudger's work and the fruits of his labor into a spectacle for the reader. Observation here is what Mark Seltzer calls "the process of production itself" (1992, 51). If Agee gives himself one narrative task in this section, it is to order things and allot them power. This he does with exactitude and a tinge of nostalgia. As he surveys the mantel, for example, he finds "A cracked roseflowered china shaving mug, broken along the edge. A much worn, inchwide varnish brush stands in it. Also in the mug are eleven rusty nails, one blue composition button, one pearl headed pin (imitation), three dirty kitchen matches, a lump of toilet soap. . . ." ("Shelter"). We know by now that it is not the Gudgers but Agee who is the collector: call it a labor of love. He experiences the objects in the house aestheti-cally, arranging them according to the layout ("the hallway, structure of four rooms"; "odors: bareness and space"; "the front bedroom: general placement of furniture," and so on). Every item is used and worn, a fragment of its initial size and an emblem of its owner's economic class (the pearl headed pin is an imitation). Through his exhaustive inscription, even the objects' worn features become valuable as they are made to actively represent and bear evidence to the collective narrative of the family, as Agee constructs it. Each object functions as a metonym for the whole. Indeed, the household is not a formal collection until he imposes this narrative structure upon it, part of his middle-class labor as an observer.

Agee's collecting technique attempts to restore the context of the object's origin, the Gudger household. In fact, it signals the creation of a new "context standing in a metaphorical, rather than a contiguous, relation to the world of everyday life"—the context of his documentary novel (Stewart 1984, 151–52). Later comparing himself to an archaeologist, Agee invigorates the objects and imbues them with interiority by putting them in circulation within the context of his incantatory narrative. These anthropomorphized object-relations finally testify to Agee's formulation of himself: his intense identifications with the tenants' things permit him to figuratively undo the barrier between subject and object in order to gain an intimate and illusory understanding of the tenants. In the end, as Susan Hegeman observes, this endeavor amounts to a personal representation of his own angst-ridden, desirous, middle-class, bohemian, intellectual self.

It is only a short leap from this strategy of taxonomy as narrative to Agee's later deployment of "types" and "variants." Agee states, "from any set of particulars it is possible and perhaps useful to generalize" ("On the Porch: 2"). In the "Clothing" chapter, for example, Agee details "categories of body covering," making differentiations according to race, labor, and class. Yet, after so many pages of particularities, Agee generalizes: "there seems to be such deep classicism in 'peasant' clothing in all places and in differing times that, for instance, a Russian and a southern women of this country, of a deep enough class, would be indistinguishable by their clothing[,] . . . backward and forward in time." We confront the timeless, feminized (proletariat?) folk, "undistinguishable from a woman of her class five hundred years ago." While Agee alternates between his intimate recollections and this detached reportage, his invocation of "types" and "variants" precariously approximates the government-sponsored documentary projects he so despises in the preamble of his book. Agee states: "failure is almost as strongly an obligation as an inevitability[,] . . . the deadliest trap of an exhausted conscience" ("On the Porch: 2"). *Praise*'s failures are as illuminating as its successes for exposing the workings and desires of the documentary gaze.

When we turn to Schuyler and West, to Hurston and Agee as exemplars of literary production during the 1930s, we see a powerful form of social commentary located in the performative dimensions and reading practices of the hybrid genres of documentary and satire: we see how they reveal the manufacture of the folk in a narrative of commercial capitalism's progress; how they expose the inner-workings of populist and fascist ideology; and how these hybrid forms undercut the folk revival's claims of authenticity. By harnessing the force of the performative in the hybrid genres of modernist burlesque and signifying ethnography, these writers set out to raze America's folklore of racial capitalism.

All the while, these writers proceed from a question succinctly posed in *Let Us Now Praise Famous Men*: "How was it we were caught?" ("Part One: A Country Letter"). Agee repeatedly asks this question, first in the voice of one of his female subjects and then as a rhetorical mantra, transforming it into an existentialist plaint. As we see in the work of Schuyler, West, Hurston, and others, each of these artists begins with the assumption that they and their readers are caught—they are implicated—just as surely as the characters that populate their works and the folk who took center stage in the populist rhetorics of the Depression era. Enjoining their readers to ask "How was it we were caught?," they call for a reflexive reading practice that perceives the seductions of the real and the authentic in narratives of self, community, and nation, and the possibility that radical truths may be found in the most outrageous of fictions. It is this reading practice and its potential that might redirect our understanding of the novel in the Depression era.

31

HOLLYWOOD AND THE AMERICAN NOVEL

BY PATRICK JAGODA

F. Scott Fitzgerald's final, unfinished Hollywood novel, *The Love of the Last Tycoon* (1941), follows Monroe Stahr, a young film producer who embodies the American Dream and closely resembles MGM's actual 1930s boy wonder, Irving Thalberg. While Fitzgerald was unable to complete the manuscript before his death on December 21, 1940, the existing pages include an extended set piece in which the narrator, Cecelia Brady, the daughter of Stahr's boss, chronicles several episodes of "A Producer's Day." These glimpses into Hollywood focus on Stahr as he manages a novelist, an actor, and a team of writers, performs script edits, discusses film profits with investors, replaces an incompetent director, and shares creative notes in a projection room. The episodes depict a Hollywood frenzy in which "minutes were precious most days" (ch. 4). In fragments of dialogue, which appear without a fuller context of the movie projects that are being discussed, Fitzgerald represents Hollywood as a well-tuned if incomprehensible machine—a complex system that cannot be grasped by outsiders or even those employees who contribute to its success. This organization seems even to elude the ordering form of Fitzgerald's novel itself. As Cecelia reflects early in the novel, Hollywood "can be understood too, but only dimly and in flashes" (ch. 1).

This chapter examines the expansion of Hollywood as a major cultural industry in the interwar period during which American cinema rose to worldwide prominence. The studio system that emerged in these years had a significant influence on both the national imaginary and the perception of the United States around the world. In addition to its effects on film art, the fledgling movie business altered the American novel and the lives of many of America's most prominent novelists. Through the early decades of the twentieth century, writers including F. Scott Fitzgerald, William Faulkner, Nathanael West, Daniel Fuchs, Anzia Yezierska, and Budd Schulberg contributed to filmmaking through their literary works and screenplays. In turn, a number of writers were sustained financially through screenwriting and, still more, inspired by what was arguably the most influential new medium of the period. The effects of cinema were evident even in the work of experimental modernists such as Gertrude Stein. As she explained in "Portraits and Repetition," one of her American lectures from 1935:

> I was doing what the cinema was doing. . . . I of course did not think of it in terms of the cinema, in fact I doubt whether at that time I had ever seen a cinema, but, and I cannot repeat this too often any one is of one's period and this our period was undoubtedly the period of the cinema and series production. And each of us in our own way are bound to express what the world in which we are living is doing.

In a fundamental way, Hollywood constructed an American "subject" both through its characters and plots. Its fantasies of an American subject became an early and important cultural commodity that circulated within an expanding world market of the 1920s and 1930s. Film changed the way modern people, including American novelists, thought about and inhabited the world. While the mutual effects of literature and cinema can be studied through film adaptations of prominent novels, the relationship between these art forms extends beyond such translations. It entails simultaneously parallel and incompatible processes of world making.

The study of the Hollywood system, including its relation to other artistic forms, promises a fuller understanding of American modernism across different media. Critical interest in the bidirectional effects of literature and film has prospered only in recent years. While the mutual influence of Hollywood film and the American novel is now discussed in analyses of the conventions of both artistic forms, literary texts were long privileged over the products of popular or mass culture or, at best, the two areas were compartmentalized. Many critics considered the universal accessibility of the cinematic image to be incommensurable with the realm of literature, which was understood to be more demanding and specialized. Recent scholarship has been more attentive to the numerous effects that these cultural forms have had on each other. Between the 1920s and the 1940s, a key moment in their coevolution, films were influenced by American novels, just as the formal parameters of prose narratives changed in response to cinema. Critics have often emphasized the differences between novels and films in the context of modernist literature with its experimental styles. However, the careful study of the novel and cinema in early twentieth-century America also reveals aesthetic and formal convergences that offer insight into modernism as a cultural practice that spans various media.

The American Studio System and the International Space of Hollywood

The nascent film industry made a significant move from New York City to Southern California in the early years of the twentieth century. By 1915, the Los Angeles area was the leading American motion picture production center. Most of the major studios, which continued to rely on East Coast financing, were already established by the early 1920s. Through this relocation, the film industry recapitulated broader American expansionist tendencies of westward movement. In these years, movie-making increasingly took the form of a factory system and, consequently, studios required space to expand the scale of their productions. The Southern California location had the advantages, as Aida A. Hozic observes, of "stable weather; cheap, non-unionized, and abundant labor; equally cheap and abundant land; and a great variety of landscapes" (2001, 56). Carl Laemmle, the president of the Universal Film Manufacturing Company, explained that he selected Southern California as the central site of his movie production empire because he believed "the best way of having men, women, birds, beasts, buildings, lakes, rivers, mountains, and so forth in pictures was to build a city and put some of each in it" (1915, 90). Universal City offered a diversity of sets that could quickly be overhauled and transformed into others depending on the needs of a particular project. A perceived abundance of space spurred the construction of massive movie studios that largely replaced independent film production. Between roughly 1915 and 1960, Hollywood studios adopted a labor model that resembled that of Ford automobile factories in their promotion of mass production, efficient work, and profit maximization. While maintaining room for creative collaboration, these plants privileged the standardization of production processes and interchangeability of workers in order to create hundreds of feature films annually.

The transfer of the American movie industry to Southern California was both economically and culturally significant. By taking control of production, distribution, and exhibition of films, Hollywood metamorphosed into a key sector of the American economy. During its "golden years," in the classical period of American cinema, Hollywood was functionally an oligopoly made of the "Big Five" production powers: Warner Brothers, Paramount, Twentieth-Century Fox, RKO, and Loew's/MGM. At their height, in the 1930s and 1940s, a handful of major companies based in Los Angeles combined to produce 90 percent of American films. Studios were self-contained worlds that minimized dependency on external production resources. Through careful control of both moviemaking and distribution, they employed vertical integration to maximize profit. It was not until the 1948 landmark Supreme Court decision of *United States v. Paramount Pictures Inc.* that this monopolistic organizational model was dissolved and the studio system began its gradual decline.

The Fordist economic model of mass production adopted by major Hollywood studios involved more than the rapid creation of entertainment. The assembly line, with its repetition and specialization, also produced a particular type of worker subjectivity. The discipline necessary for this model's success led to "an increased need for the surveillance of workers' private lives and to the development of institutions that could perform that task—personnel departments, welfare offices, and state-sponsored behavioral regulations such as prohibition" (Hozic 2001, 50). Like Ford factories, Hollywood studios maintained a tight grip on their workforce. When, for example, the reformist, anti-Hollywood writer Upton Sinclair ran for governor of

California on the Democratic ticket in 1933, Hollywood launched a successful smear campaign against his candidacy that was funded by substantial mandatory contributions from its workers, regardless of their political beliefs.

Along with the direct control that Hollywood held over writers, directors, set designers, and other workers whom it employed, the industry also exerted an indirect influence over the growing population of moviegoers, both in the United States and, increasingly, abroad. The financial success of the studio system transformed Hollywood into one of the most powerful American cultural institutions of the twentieth century. With its newly established production base, Hollywood studios could create and feed a host of desires through the production of excessively elaborate phantasmatic spaces. At once a microcosm of American capitalism and a factory for the production of US mythologies, Hollywood served a critical ideological function in constructing celluloid visions of American national identity and expanding its international appeal. As pioneering Soviet film director Sergei Eisenstein observed, "We know the inseparable link between the cinema and the industrial development of America. We know how production, art and literature reflect the capitalist breadth and construction of the United States of America. And we also know that American capitalism finds its sharpest and most expressive reflection in the American cinema" (1957, 196).

In the early decades of the twentieth century, Hollywood films represented various aspects of America, from capitalist competition to democratic egalitarianism. Even before the rise of the studio system, Vachel Lindsay presciently declared, in his 1915 book *The Art of the Moving Picture*,

> The possibility of showing the entire American population its own face in the Mirror Screen has at last come. Whitman brought the idea of democracy to our sophisticated literati, but did not persuade the democracy itself to read his democratic poems. Sooner or later the kinetoscope will do what he could not, bring the nobler side of the equality idea to the people who are so crassly equal. (57–58; on Vachel Lindsay and the democratic potential of film, see Chapter 16 in this volume)

From the earliest short films and travelogues to feature films such as D. W. Griffith's *The Birth of a Nation* (1915) and *America* (1924), the idea of American national identity was a central focus of the movies. As a major culture industry, Hollywood packaged the national divisions that followed the Civil War, propped up the myth of American exceptionalism, popularized stories of westward migration, and explored facets of ethnic assimilation in an increasingly multicultural country.

The American film industry developed against the backdrop of significant southern European and Asian immigration to the United States, conflicts such as the Spanish-American War and the First World War, and profound changes in race relations. National identity was a remarkably fraught concept in the United States during the early decades of the twentieth century and yet mainstream cinema remained fairly narrow in its depiction of the shifting American social landscape. Shaped, by a wide range of immigrants, especially prominent Jewish Americans such as Samuel Goldwyn, Adolph Zukor, and the Warner Brothers, Hollywood itself modeled the American ideal of a melting pot, and many films registered that vision. Ruth Vasey explains, "Hollywood *constituted* its audiences as 'American' in a remarkably literal fashion. By involving audiences in its particular vision, which was characterized by bourgeois and consumerist behavior, it influenced attitudes and behavior both inside the United States and abroad" (1997, 227–28). Most films featured easily recognizable stars playing white, middle-class American characters that were made even more glamorous by elaborate cinematography. Specific racial, ethnic, and cultural differences, which exerted a strong influence on American life, were rarely explored in Hollywood films. Popular movies more often settled for a generalized otherness. As with characters, representations of foreign locations in films such as *The Bad One* (1930) and *Morocco* (1932) were often predicated on ethnic stereotypes and cultural exoticism that appealed to a mainstream American audience.

Along with Hollywood's cinematic examinations and distortions of American national identities, there were many types of experiences that this system outright excluded or failed to imagine. The classical Hollywood style that characterized cinema from the late 1920s to the late 1950s, during the studio period, conformed to conventions of chronological plotting, economically structured narrative, conventional genres, glamorous stars, extravagant set designs, and thrilling camera techniques. As David Bordwell explains, "the principles which Hollywood claims as its own rely on notions of decorum, proportion, formal harmony, respect for tradition, mimesis, self-effacing craftsmanship, and cool control of the perceiver's response" (1985, 3). The very elements that comprised the classical style and its particular form of realism also severely limited the production and distribution of films that adopted more socially subversive aesthetics. Films with socially and politically radical material, such as Erich von Stroheim's *Greed* (1924), Charlie Chaplin's *The Gold Rush* (1925), and King Vidor's *The Crowd* (1928), still entered mass circulation in the 1920s. By the time the "talkies" became dominant, however, controversial content became increasingly uncommon, limited primarily to independent, regional, or avant-garde productions.

The national space produced by major Southern California studios was, at once, demarcated by sharply drawn boundaries and expansive in its reach. Despite its geographical basis in Southern California and its representational concern with American life, Hollywood was an international, even proto-global, space. The Hollywood studios of the early twentieth century "were cities within cities, industries within industries, worlds within a world" (Hozic 2001, 58). These worlds, self-sustaining as they were, were also major hubs in the network of worldwide capitalism that strengthened the image of America as an emerging power. As with domestic American audiences, Hollywood served as a factory of fantasy for international audiences. While it cannot be characterized as a simple propaganda machine, the industry exported powerful concepts about American life through aggressive distribution and the development of the classical Hollywood style. Indeed, the classical style, with its representational standards and alleged ideological neutrality, was shaped in large part through the pursuit of new filmgoers. As Vasey observes, "Hollywood had to formulate a recipe for movies that could play in the North and the South, on the West Coast and in the East, and from Capetown to Capri" (1997, 4).

Following the First World War, the strength of the domestic film industry allowed Hollywood to engage in rapid international expansion. For instance, while French films claimed significant international market share early in the century, by 1919, the majority of films shown in European theaters came from the United States. As Richard Maltby observes, "By the late 1920s, American movies occupied as much as 80 percent of the screen time in those countries that had not established quotas on American imports to protect their own film production industries" (2003, 126). Even as film culture in the 1920s and 1930s remained thoroughly international, Hollywood increased its foreign distribution of American national films in order to tighten its grip on the emerging transnational market. The growing habit of moviegoing facilitated other forms of trade and laid the groundwork for global Americanization. Miriam Hansen contends, "Hollywood did not just circulate images and sounds; it produced and globalized a new sensorium; it constituted, or tried to constitute, new subjectivities and subjects" (1999, 71). Thus, in its attempt to construct a universalist narrative, Hollywood cinema both shaped a new mass market by actively transforming American middle-class consumerism into a desired norm and created a variety of novel subjects.

American Novelists in Hollywood

As the major cultural industry of the first half of the twentieth century, Hollywood attracted a number of prominent American novelists. In the early years of cinema, writers did not produce detailed scripts but, instead, provided basic concepts and plot synopses. The introduction of narrative and dialogue intertitles imbued film with a more literary quality. Cinematic storytelling, however, was discussed as an art only after the creation of the first narrative films, beginning with Edwin S. Porter's *The Great Train Robbery* (1903). Within a decade, these early cinematic narratives inspired the production of epic stories with multi-dimensional characters and subplots, such as D. W. Griffith's breakthrough film, *The Birth of a Nation*. As film narratives developed in the early 1920s, producers such as Samuel Goldwyn began to experiment with hiring contemporary novelists to facilitate the production of artistic films that would appeal to a more refined audience. These intersections between Hollywood and the literary establishment were not always successful, giving rise to feuds between writers and film production bureaucracies. However, by the mid-1920s, when the movie business was growing immensely successful and generating inter-studio competition, more sophisticated plots often yielded stronger box office returns. Studio producers saw the quality of intertitles as having an effect on cinematic storytelling. "There was new talk of the need for titles that could 'hit the back wall,' that could induce laughs and tears all by themselves" (Hamilton 1990, 28). Instead of simply shaping overarching narratives, writers began to influence the mood and flow of films through their descriptions and dialogue.

The introduction of sound to movies in 1927 produced an even more competitive climate and led to the serious recruitment of novelists as screenwriters. Describing the addition of sound to the movies, Hollywood insider Budd Schulberg later wrote, "An S.O.S. was beamed to the East, a hurry-up call for what was then described as *real* writers, to distinguish them from the continuity boys, the gag-men, the ideas men and the rest of the colorful if illiterate silent continent" (1959, 133). The influx of new writers to Hollywood in the 1930s included not only novelists, but also vaude-villians, playwrights, and newspaper writers desperate for work in the midst of the Depression. In order to improve the quality of movies and draw in larger audiences, studios were especially interested in hiring America's great literary figures as screen-writers. They used substantial contracts to lure novelists such as F. Scott Fitzgerald, William Faulkner, and Raymond Chandler to Hollywood in these years.

For many prose writers, the transition from writing novels to screenplays was far from seamless, requiring a level of collaboration and artistic subordination to which many prominent literary figures were not accustomed. Even as the need for more immersive narratives grew, the role of writers remained circumscribed in the studio system. "It was normal studio practice to employ several writers on a given movie, often working independently of each other at the same time. Writers were seen as technical staff, many of them employed for particular specialist skills" (Maltby 2003, 139). Writers might compose portions of dialogue or design a subplot, but were rarely given creative control over an entire project. For Hollywood producers, the release schedule was usually more important than the quality of the scripts. Most novelists lacked the abilities to negotiate the subtleties of the factory system in the manner of more seasoned Hollywood screenwriters. In the end, the names of literary writers were more often used to add value to a film production than to instill the film with substantial literary qualities. Compared to novelists, career screenwriters such as Ben Hecht and Dudley Nichols tended to be more successful in Hollywood and exerted greater influence on the shape of finished films. Despite countless failed attempts by novelists who sought to adapt to the film industry, there were exceptions. Writers such as William Faulkner and James Agee contributed to screenplays for well-received films, including *The Big Sleep* (1946) and *The Bride Comes to Yellow Sky* (1952).

The tense relationship between the Hollywood system and American novelists is effectively illustrated by the experiences of F. Scott Fitzgerald. In 1927, Fitzgerald, who was considered by many at the time to be the greatest contemporary American popular novelist, first arrived in Southern California to work for MGM. During this trip, he wrote the script for *Lipstick*, which similarly to most screenplays in the studio system, was never filmed. Despite his overall failure as a screenwriter, Fitzger-ald and his wife Zelda made a social splash in Hollywood with their participation in star-studded parties during their short stay. Later, in the 1930s, Fitzgerald returned to Hollywood where he wrote his own fiction and scripts for MGM up to his death in 1940. In his final years, he worked on a number of projects but earned only a single screen credit for the film *Three Comrades* (1938). Fitzgerald failed to thrive in Hollywood in part because he was unable to translate his novelistic talents to film. Producer Joseph Mankiewicz recalled, in a 1967 interview, "I personally have been attacked as if I had spat on the American flag because it happened once that I rewrote some dialogue by F. Scott Fitzgerald. . . . It was very literary dialogue, novelistic dialogue that lacked all the qualities required for screen dialogue. The latter must be 'spoken' " (qtd. in Bontemps 1967, 31). Although he never quite adapted his talents to the new medium, Fitzgerald was paid as much as $1,250 per week for his efforts—a significant sum in 1938.

While Fitzgerald had only a minor creative influence on Hollywood, this cultural space had a more significant effect on his thinking. Fitzgerald is often characterized as suffering from a creative decline following the publication of *Tender Is the Night* in 1934, yet he continued during his final years to write short stories and essays, a number of which were directly inspired by his Hollywood experience. Through tales about a struggling screenwriter named Pat Hobby, Fitzgerald aired his views about hack writers and the Hollywood life. A character in Fitzgerald's *The Love of the Last Tycoon*, a British writer named George Boxley, similarly voices the author's own frustrations about writing for the new medium. During a consultation, Boxley acknowledges his unsuitability for the job and complains to producer Monroe Stahr about the "two hacks you've teamed me with [who] listen to what I say but . . . spoil it—they seem to have a vocabulary of about a hundred words" (ch. 3). Fitzgerald's reflections on Hollywood were captured even more explicitly in posthumously published essays. In "The Crack-Up" (1945), he muses about the debasement in artistic expression represented by film: "I saw that the novel, which at my maturity was the strongest and supplest medium for conveying thought and emotion from one human being to another, was becoming subordinated to a communal art that . . . was capable of reflecting only the tritest thought, the most obvious emotion." For Fitzgerald, moving pictures could not capture ideas and affects as effectively as prose, nor could the collaboration necessary for film production equal the force and focus of an individual novelist's vision.

In 1932, five years after Fitzgerald first came to Hollywood, MGM employed another great American novelist, William Faulkner, as a screenwriter (on Faulkner in Hollywood, see chapter 22 in this volume). As Hamilton explains, Faulkner "had gone to Hollywood because he could not live on earnings from his six novels—two thousand copies was his average sale" (1990, 196). Faulkner became notorious for his excessive drinking, unreliability, disinterest in film, and an affair with Howard Hawks's script girl, Meta Carpenter. He commuted between his hometown of Oxford, Mississippi and Hollywood until he was told that he would have to work exclusively from California if he wished to continue in the business. He left Hollywood shortly afterward only to return in 1935 as a contract writer for Twentieth-Century Fox—prompted by debts to his publisher and poor sales on his novel *Pylon* (1935). Along with a screenplay for the First World War romance *The Road to Glory* (1936), Faulkner completed the manuscript of his novel *Absalom, Absalom!* (1936) in his Beverley Hills hotel room. Like Fitzgerald, he struggled with the transition between media, producing a number of treatments that never reached the screen. The speeches he wrote for films such as *Banjo on My Knee* (1936), for example, were cut because they were considered too literary and too difficult for actors to deliver. In 1938, Faulkner managed to sell the screen rights for *The Unvanquished* (1938) for $25,000. While this money kept him comfortable for a couple of years, his support of extended family eventually left him broke again. In the 1940s, Faulkner returned to Hollywood to work for Warner Brothers, his film career revived by director Howard Hawks who remained one of his greatest fans. His circumstances, however, led him to sign an unfortunate contract that committed him to seven years of work at a salary that was considerably lower than the one he had negotiated a decade earlier. Ian Hamilton explains that Faulkner eventually managed to slip out of his contract quietly in 1945 and, except for work on the screenplay of the 1955 film *Land of the Pharaohs*, done as a favor to Hawks, he never returned to screenwriting.

While initially commissioned to adapt his own short story "Turn About" (1932) into the film *Today We Live* (1933), Faulkner worked primarily on films that were not based on his fiction. Despite their shared aversion to the medium, he was ultimately more successful as a screenwriter than Fitzgerald, receiving screenplay credits for films such as *To Have and Have Not* (1944) and *The Big Sleep* (1946), which were based on novels by Ernest Hemingway and Raymond Chandler, respectively. In the late 1940s and 1950s, some of Faulkner's own works were eventually adapted to film, but for the most part, producers were wary of his modernist texts. Faulkner declined an offer to adapt some of his own works in the 1950s by Twentieth- Century Fox, observing, "I have never learned how to write movies, nor even to take them very seriously" (Dardis 1976, 149). One of the few eventual adaptations of Faulkner's experimental writing, *The Sound and the Fury* (1959), circumvented the source material's disorienting perspectival shifts, psychological complexity, and novelistic interiority, opting instead for the narrative continuity and economy that characterized the classical Hollywood style. While Faulkner never wrote his own Hollywood novel, the West Coast appears peripherally in texts such as *Pylon* and *The Wild Palms* (1939), and Faulkner's work on war films such as *The Road to Glory* (1936) also influenced his own allegorical novel *A Fable* (1954).

Nathanael West, who befriended Faulkner in the 1930s, had an even more difficult time in Hollywood. Unlike Fitzgerald and Faulkner, West was not a known literary name during his years in the film industry and depended entirely on screenwriting to make a living. During the early 1930s, he worked as a contract writer and sold the screen rights to his second novel, *Miss Lonelyhearts* (1933), which allowed him to survive as a full-time writer. By the mid-1930s, however, West could not find work in Hollywood and his novels were deemed commercial failures. In 1936, he bounced back with a weekly contract with Republic Pictures, a minor studio at which he contributed to a dozen films, including the political drama *The President's Mystery* (1936). West eventually signed a contract with RKO, but he did not gain renown for his screenwriting until his work in 1938, for Universal, on *The Spirit of Culver* and *I Stole a Million*. Shortly before his early death in 1940, West and his associate Boris Ingster convinced Columbia to buy a comic adaptation of West's *A Cool Million* (1934) for $10,000 and sold a treatment for a film titled *Bird in Hand* for $25,000 to RKO.

Working on genre films at such studios as Republic eventually inspired West's most renowned novel, *The Day of the Locust* (1939). West's literary language paints a grim portrait of the darker side of Hollywood and the violent dissolution of the American Dream during the Great Depression. While Fitzgerald's *The Love of the Last Tycoon* is comparatively balanced in its depiction of the Hollywood movie-making process, *The Day of the Locust* more closely resembles the scathing critique of Hollywood culture in novels such as Horace McCoy's *They Shoot Horses, Don't They?* (1935). Tod Hackett, the protagonist, is a talented artist recruited by a National Films talent scout and brought to the West coast "to learn set and costume designing" (ch. 1). Along the way, he encounters an extensive cast of Hollywood characters, some of whom derive from the B-movies of the 1930s, including Faye Greener (a young actress unable to break into the movies), Audrey Jenning (a once-prominent star of silent films), Harry Greener (an ex-vaudevillian), Earle Shoop (an Arizona cowboy who now frequents Sunset Boulevard), and Maybelle Loomis (an ambitious stage mother). Drawing from West's years of experience, the novel depicts an entire generation that is ruined by the false fantasies that Hollywood has propagated: "They realize that they've been tricked and burn with resentment. Every day of their lives they read the newspapers and went to the movies. Both fed them on lynchings, murder, sex crimes, explosions, wrecks, love nests, fires, miracles, revolutions, wars. . . . Nothing can ever be violent enough to make taut their slack minds and bodies. They have been cheated and betrayed" (ch. 27). West's novel draws aesthetically on cinematic techniques and descriptions while condemning classical Hollywood film and the America that it produced in its image.

While the Hollywood stories of Fitzgerald, Faulkner, and West are filled with personal failures, studios frequently used the literary successes of these American writers to garner additional publicity for their films. This promotional strategy was introduced as early as 1921 when Samuel Goldwyn bought the rights to Anzia Yezierska's collection of stories, *Hungry Hearts* (1920), for $10,000 and brought the writer to Hollywood to adapt her collection into a feature film. The book's depiction of the difficulties of the Jewish immigrant experience and the life lived in New York's lower East Side tenements made it a great success. Yezierska moved to Hollywood and became an instant celebrity. She was immediately dubbed the "Cinderella of the Tenements" (Botshon 2000, 306). Despite her success, few of Yezierska's scenes and intertitles were used in the final production of *Hungry Hearts*. The film concluded

with a typical Hollywood happy ending, ignoring the tragic sense of loss and frustration evoked by the original tales. Finding it difficult to work in Hollywood, Yezierska returned to writing fiction full time. Her novel *Salome of the Tenements* (1923)
was eventually adapted into a film, but she did not contribute to the screenplay.

Most serious writers found the transition from page to screen to be a struggle, and
many refused the temptation of significant paychecks. Even established screenwriters found it difficult to translate the most ambitious novels into films, and other
novels presented challenges that Hollywood could not overcome. Theodore Dreiser's *An American Tragedy* (1925), for example, for all of its literary importance, encountered studio resistance in the adaptation process because it contained material
openly critical of American society. When the film was eventually produced, Dreiser
did not approve of and even attempted to block its distribution. Upton Sinclair
had an even more conflicted relationship with Hollywood. Although he sold the
film rights to several of his books, he was generally mistrusted because of his radical political leanings and suspicion of Hollywood. Irving Thalberg famously said of
one of Sinclair's books, "Buy it but keep that Bolshevik out of the studio" (qtd. in
Hamilton 1990, 86).

No American novelist earned more notoriety in Hollywood or generated more
antagonism than Budd Schulberg. His controversial first novel, *What Makes Sammy
Run?* (1941), depicts Sammy Glick, a poor yet ambitious Jewish boy who grows up
on New York's Lower East Side and rises from a newspaper copy boy to an all-pow-
erful studio producer. When Schulberg presented his publisher, Bennett Cerf, with
the manuscript, he was told that there was no market for the novel, given the recent
commercial failure of *The Day of the Locust*. Cerf published an initial run of two
thousand five hundred copies, but he predicted that, despite advance praise from
writers such as John O'Hara and Fitzgerald, the novel would not sell. He told Schulberg, "The problem is that people who read novels have no interest in Hollywood,
and the people who go to movies don't read books" (Schulberg, *What Makes Sammy
Run?*, afterword). Cerf was wrong; the novel became a runaway bestseller, serving
as an accessible exposé of the American dream and the Hollywood myth. Schulberg
continued his exploration of Hollywood with numerous essays and novels such as
The Disenchanted (1950), which offers a fictional portrait of Fitzgerald's final years in
Hollywood, but none of his other works achieved comparable popularity.

The narrator of *What Makes Sammy Run*—Al Mannheim, a newspaper reporter
who becomes a Hollywood screenwriter—captures the Old World fantasy of America's Hollywood when he admits, "I had wanted to go for all the usual reasons: I was
anxious to investigate the persistent rumors that the 'streets paved with gold' which
the early Spanish explorers had hunted in vain had suddenly appeared in the vicinity
of Hollywood and Vine. I was half convinced that Southern California was really the
modern Garden of Eden its press agents claimed it to be" (ch. 3). When Mannheim
arrives in Hollywood, however, he realizes the incongruity between his expectations
and the reality of the situation. Describing writer Julian Blumberg, whom Sammy

repeatedly exploits, Mannheim notes, "His Hollywood wasn't that exclusive night club where everyone knew everybody else. He learned that Hollywood extended from Warner Brothers at Burbank, in the valley beyond the northern hills, to Metro-Goldwyn-Mayer, twenty-five miles southwest in Culver City. He found a new side of Hollywood, the ten-man-for-every-job side, the seasonal unemployment, the call-again-next-month side. The factory side" (ch. 7). The film industry functionally blacklisted Schulberg for writing an insider's novel and betraying his Hollywood origins, but the text is equally about the larger issues of American capitalism and the forms of individualism that it enabled in the 1930s.

Hollywood's particular investment in constructing a strong image of American life and culture came inevitably at the expense of a diversity of creative styles and alternative social perspectives. Given its international aspirations, however, the industry also lured in British novelists such as Aldous Huxley, P. G. Wodehouse, Christopher Isherwood, and R. C. Sherriff with sizable contracts. Huxley, who admitted to the use of certain cinematic devices in his prose while simultaneously expressing a growing disdain toward film, agreed to adapt several of his novels to screenplays in exchange for quick earnings. Along with adaptations of his own fiction, Huxley contributed to a film biography of Madame Curie, which eventually fell apart and was taken up by other writers including Fitzgerald, and a successful adaptation of *Pride and Prejudice* in 1940. Huxley's experience was not uncommon. Between the 1920s and 1940s, a number of British novelists were commissioned by Hollywood and paid substantial sums for writing they rarely found engaging. As with American novelists, they were often hired primarily for the prestige that their names would bring to motion pictures.

The American Novel, Film, and Modernism

It is important to acknowledge that novels and films rely on distinct semiotic systems that are made up of different signs, grammars, and formal qualities. Moreover, as David Trotter contends, simple analogies between cinema and literature cannot hold up because "literature is a representational medium, film a recording medium" (2007, 3). Despite inherent differences between their respective media, however, novels and films also share countless "formal techniques, audiences, values, sources, archetypes, narrative strategies, and contexts" (Elliott 2003, 1). In other words, while these forms rely on varied technologies, they make use of similar stories and overlapping methods to construct their narrative worlds.

In one of the most detailed early analyses of film adaptation, Dudley Andrew argues, "Well over half of all commercial films have come from literary originals" (1984, 98). Hollywood films of the 1920s and 1930s would faithfully recreate, loosely borrow from, or in some cases, radically transform literary subject matter and novelistic form (for more on the topic of adaptation, see Chapter 16 in this volume). One of the earliest practitioners and theorists of the influence of literary novels on the emerging art of cinema was director Sergei Eisenstein. In a 1951 essay, Eisenstein contends that the work of writers such as Charles Dickens and Walt Whitman heavily influenced not only particular films, but also the classical Hollywood style as such. Linking the novel and the film, Eisenstein observes, "for me personally it is always pleasing to recognize again and again the fact that our cinema is not altogether without parents, without pedigree, without a past, without the traditions and rich cultural heritage of the past epochs" (1957, 232). In particular, Eisenstein tracks the influence of Dickens's proto-cinematic eye and parallel narrative style on the films of pioneering American filmmaker D. W. Griffith (217). The cinematic techniques that he developed in the process of reading novels, including montage, parallel editing, the close-up, the flashback, and the dissolve transition, enabled films to cut through time and space in a way that theatrical stage productions, for example, could not.

Eisenstein focuses primarily on the influence of Dickens, Thackeray, Eliot, Trollope, and other British writers on the art of film. The influence of the nineteenth-century British novel on early cinema frequently enters film scholarship, as does the Americanness of the film industry as such. However, the relationship between the American novel and cinema is less frequently taken up in these discussions. Nevertheless, numerous American novels were equally influential on the classical film style and Hollywood productions. As Timothy Corrigan points out, the number of adaptations of both British and American novels increased beginning in the late 1920s, with the introduction of sound and, consequently, the possibility of extended dialogue. Even so, Hollywood conventions and industry censorship standards (especially those introduced by the Motion Picture Production Code or Hays Code, as it was popularly known) resulted in many movies that departed dramatically from their source material. Such restrictions affected film adaptations of numerous American novels. For example, John Steinbeck's novel *The Grapes of Wrath* (1939) was evacuated of many of its political references when it made the transition to the screen in 1940. While the first half of the film served as a faithful adaptation, Twentieth-Century Fox softened the ending by replacing the dissolution of the Joad family in the novel with an optimistic sense of the family's changing fortunes. Faulkner, in his work as a screenwriter, also encountered censorship limits on several occasions. The racial themes from his fiction gradually found their way into his treatments, including an adaptation of Belamy Partridge's *Country Lawyer* (1939), written for Warner Brothers, which was never produced. Throughout his time in Hollywood, Faulkner's racially charged scripts remained untouched. In particular, he was unable to sell a screenplay of his own novel *Absalom, Absalom!* because of its ultimate narrative disclosure of miscegenation.

As I have noted, the influence of American film and novels was mutual. While novelists such as Frank Norris (*McTeague* [1899]), Jack London (*Before Adam* [1906–7]), and Henry James ("Crapy Cornelia" [1909]) explored the space of the cinema and drew metaphors from early film, this new form did not influence the formal structures of their novels (Trotter 2007, 22). Modernist writers were perhaps the first to be influenced more substantially by cinematic form and technology. Studying machinic repetition and montage, these writers developed literary techniques that paralleled their filmic counterparts and facilitated explorations of modern American life. Both the technology of film and the techniques of modernist language can be said to emerge from similar concerns with representation, consciousness, and industrial machinery that were prominent in the late nineteenth and early twentieth century. Poets such as Gertrude Stein and William Carlos Williams were interested in film's recording capacities. The focused attention to things in imagist poetry, for instance, closely resembled the photographic realism and visual grammar, especially the close-up, that belonged to cinematographic conventions. Novelists such as Fitzgerald and West similarly appropriated a cinematic grammar into texts that explicitly focused on Hollywood as a setting of dramatic action. Fitzgerald's *The Love of the Last Tycoon* even included detailed descriptions of shot sequences as when film director John Broaca muses during a production meeting: "I'll shoot up at him. . . . Let him go away from the camera. Just a fixed shot from quite a distance—let him go away from the camera. Don't follow him. Pick him up in a close shot and let him go away again. No attention on him except against the whole roof and the sky" (ch. 3).

In his *U. S. A.* trilogy (1930–36), John Dos Passos went further by integrating cinematic techniques even more intricately at the level of literary form. He used, for instance, autobiographical, stream-of-consciousness sections titled "The Camera Eye" and montage-style "Newsreel" segments. Visually rich cinematic details fill the pages, ranging from omniscient descriptions of the era to vivid subjective observations that are reminiscent of Expressionist films. As one "Camera Eye" section reads: "suddenly I've been asleep and it's black dark and the blue tassel bobs on the edge of the dark shade shaped like a melon and everywhere there are pointed curved shadows" (1938, "Newsreel II"). Stream-of-consciousness styles developed by Dos Passos and other modernist writers, in turn, influenced impressionist films in the 1920s and psychological thrillers of the 1930s and 1940s, including Hollywood film noir. Dos Passos, like the film techniques that he explored, sought to record reality, to reproduce it aesthetically rather than merely to represent it. In order to capture the scope of America in the early twentieth century, he turned to various forms, including biography, newspapers, poetry, novelistic prose, and cinema. Mixed media enabled him to interlink personal experiences and macro-political events. The *U. S. A.* trilogy, in particular, relied on forms as diverse as the American novel and Hollywood cinema to forge connections between different scales of twentieth-century experience—concrete modern individuals and the more abstract totality of American capitalism.

While modernist texts adopted film grammar and cinematic ways of seeing the world, movie adaptations of modernist novels were extremely rare in the 1920s and 1930s. Halliwell explains, "Historically the solution to the problems of adapting modernist texts has been the tactic of general avoidance, with the nineteenth-century realist novel, naturalistic drama, and genre-based fiction offering easier routes to adaptation" (2007, 91). Modernist novels clashed formally with the classical style. For the most part, they were deemed difficult to consume, opposed to dominant sociopolitical norms, and (as a result) commercially unviable. Despite these incompatibilities, both modernist novels and Hollywood films shared an interest in urban life and an American landscape transformed by industrial technology. Moreover, Hollywood studios hired American modernists such as Faulkner and West as screenwriters for more conventional projects.

Modernism is a useful category for thinking about both the elite and experimental literature of the early twentieth century, and the response of the filmic arts to the modern world order and its social, political, and technological developments. Cinema was emblematic of many of the spatial, perspectival, and technological shifts of modernity. More precisely, as filtered through Hollywood, beginning in the 1920s, film was the medium that forged an inextricable link between the general phenomenon of modernity and the more specific form of Americanization. Film became an art form that reproduced the rhythms of modern America but, unlike high literary modernism, remained largely accessible to the mass public. At its height, the studio system privileged American stories and themes, thereby narrowing the gap between the phenomena of American global aspirations and modernity as such. Moreover, film more than any other early twentieth-century form allowed culture to be concretized as a commodity.

While experimental modernist literary works may appear categorically opposed to the popular films produced by the Hollywood studio system, critics have suggested that these forms share a common history. Miriam Hansen, in particular, has argued influentially that popular media culture and new technologies are frequently ignored in studies of modernism that solely privilege experimental poetry and the novel. Redefining modernism to include popular productions, such as early Hollywood films, Hansen writes:

> While the spread of urban-industrial technology, the large-scale disembedding of social (and gender) relations, and the shift to mass consumption entailed processes of real destruction and loss, there also emerged new modes of organizing vision and sensory perception, a new relationship with "things," different forms of mimetic experience and expression, of affectivity, temporality, and reflexivity, a changing fabric of everyday life, sociability, and leisure. From this perspective, I take the study of modernist aesthetics to encompass cultural practices that both articulated and mediated the experience of modernity, such as the mass-produced and mass-consumed phenomena of fashion, design, advertising, architecture and urban environment, of photography, radio, and cinema. (1999, 60)

Hansen uses the term "vernacular modernism" to complicate the opposition between high literature and low cinema. This concept suggests that any serious study of American modernism must account for American literature and film in both their mutual influences and divergences. The gradual global dominance of Holly-wood cinema, in fact, derived not from its unyielding homogeneity but rather from its flexible capacity to negotiate heterogeneous formal categories and audiences. As Hansen adds, "by forging a mass market out of an ethnically and culturally heteroge-neous society, if often at the expense of racial others, American classical cinema had developed an idiom, or idioms, that travelled more easily than its national-popular rivals" (68). Hollywood studios succeeded, in other words, by incorporating and recasting a diverse viewership in the United States and abroad.

"A Distinctly American Institution"

Fitzgerald noted in a 1939 letter to *Collier's* editor Kenneth Littauer that Cecelia, the narrator of his in-progress novel *The Love of the Last Tycoon*, "is *of* the movies but not *in* them. She probably was born the day 'The Birth of the Nation' was pre-viewed." (1994, 414). As Cecilia puts it in the novel's opening line, "Though I haven't ever been on the screen I was brought up in pictures" (ch. 1). With Cecilia's voice, Fitzgerald sought to channel the experience of many Americans who came of age in the 1920s and 1930s. Consciousness, during this period, was shaped by countless social, political, and economic sources. Yet few cultural institutions had as great an influence as Hollywood. The studio system, with its considerable popularity, played an important role in the way that American and international audiences engaged with images of "the world" in the first half of the twentieth century. Film did not merely alter the content of modern art but transformed its dominant forms. It did not simply influence the ideas of audiences but affected their sensorium and shaped their consciousness.

William Fox, the founder of Fox Pictures, once described the cinema as "a dis-tinctly American institution" and observed that "movies breathe the spirit in which the country was founded, freedom and equality" (qtd. in Maltby 2003, 120–21). Fox's optimistic language emphasizes the links between American political ideals of the film industry. Indeed, Hollywood was shaped by an immigrant, especially Jewish, sensibility and gave rise to an unprecedentedly far-reaching and distinctly American mass culture. Nevertheless, Fox's characterization, through its blatant disregard for the exclusions that defined the classical period of cinema, lays bare the aporia implicit in Hollywood's universalist notion of America. The cinema, if indeed "distinctly American," conveys many of this nation's contradictions and complexities. It lacks political but also formal purity. Without painting, theatri-cal melodrama, the American novel, and other forms, American films would not have acquired the conventions that they developed in the interwar period. A careful study of the interanimating relations among any of these forms—especially between Hollywood classical cinema and the modern American novel—reveals a complex of effects that are at once social, political, and aesthetic.

32

NATIVE SON AND DIASPORIC MODERNITY

BY MIKKO TUHKANEN

It has become commonplace to regard *Native Son*'s famous opening—the "*Brrrrr-rriiiiiiiiiiiiiiiiiiinng!*" of the alarm clock (bk. 1)—as a wake-up call for the novel's audiences, particularly its white readership. This reading points out that, on its publication in 1940, the novel constituted something of a traumatic break in the culture of the United States. Its story unfolds as a series of tragicomic accidents and misunderstandings bred by deeply ingrained racial ideologies. No sooner is Bigger Thomas, the novel's protagonist, employed as a chauffeur by the white, liberal Daltons than he accidentally kills Mary, the daughter of the family; to keep her from revealing his presence, he suffocates her with a pillow when her blind mother chances upon the pair in the girl's darkened bedroom. Having dismembered and incinerated her body, he craftily frames Mary Dalton's communist boyfriend for her disappearance, but is exposed when her remains are discovered. After a brief escape, he is caught, tried, and, at the end of the narrative, sentenced to death.

Whether correctly or incorrectly, Richard Wright's debut novel is often credited as the first widely read African American text that ostentatiously refused to stage the scripts of minstrel buffoonery or bourgeois assimilationism, spectacles that had assuaged white audiences' unease when dealing with racial difference. "In a sense," Henry Louis Gates, Jr. writes, "the book performed a public, ritualized unveiling— the removal of the very mask of our blackness itself. Certainly the effect was like nothing before in the history of American letters" (1993, xii–xiii). In the annals of American literature, *Native Son* is frequently dubbed an event "from which there was no going back" (Scruggs 1993, 69): its stark scenes of poverty, resentment, and violence produced a shock that reverberated beyond the literary scene.

As much as the ringing of an alarm clock imposes a consciousness of time on the waking subject, the novel's opening not only constituted a call for its readers to wake up but also announced the necessity for a new chrononomy—a new regime of telling time—for the slumbering peoples of the United States. Most immediately, the impact of Wright's novel, its "harsh and unpalatable truth" (Kinnamon 1993, 124), consisted of its demand that the white audience acknowledge the ongoing reality of race prejudice, which, rather than undone by the events of Emancipation and Reconstruction, had been fossilized into the stubborn structures of exploitative labor arrangements, segregationist urban geographies, ever-present threats of physical violence, substandard education, and routine disfranchisement. White Americans, Wright argues, need to reset their timekeepers by realizing that, in terms of racial politics, the time of the nation had stalled somewhere around 1877, the year of Reconstruction's failure and the ascendancy of white supremacy in the postbellum United States. Conceptualizing the time of the nation in this way, Wright is part of an African American intellectual tradition, stretching from Pauline Hopkins to James Baldwin and Toni Morrison, that has depicted the United States as a land of an uncanny temporal disjointedness, a land where the ghosts of slavery, supposedly laid to rest, return to haunt the present.

Apart from addressing issues specific to the histories and cultures of the United States, the concern with the vagaries of time also situates Wright's work in the intellectual tradition of theorizing Western modernity. This less frequently discussed dimension of *Native Son* renders Wright's novel an important text for contemporary scholarship that seeks to rethink the study of literatures in global, rather than national, terms. As Wendy Walters suggests, African diasporic writing "often look[s] beyond the nation-state, demanding reading strategies that see connections in other frameworks" (2005, vii). Wright's transnational allegiances became more pronounced in the work he produced after his expatriation to France in 1946, particularly his three travel narratives—*Black Power* (1954), *The Color Curtain* (1956), and *Pagan Spain* (1957)—and the essays on decolonization that were collected in *White Man, Listen!* (1957). Unsurprisingly, given the reception of literary texts through national canons and imaginaries, these texts, where he seemed to abandon the themes with which he, an African American, was supposedly most familiar, have been little discussed and often dismissed. While recent years have witnessed the welcome emergence of scholarly interest in Wright's postcolonial, transnational work, *Native Son* already contextualized the American tragicomedy of racial relations in the larger histories of industrialization, colonization, and the slave trade—more succinctly, the constellation of Western modernity.

Western modernity itself remains a disputed concept. While some theorists locate its beginnings in the Enlightenment—the era of "reason" that arguably commenced with the seventeenth-century philosophy of René Descartes—many suggest that its most distinctive and far-ranging upheavals occurred in the nineteenth century, when rapid industrialization resulted in massive waves of urbanization and the concomitant disintegration of feudal communities. According to the latter concept of modernity, the transformations of the nineteenth century precipitated a loss of belief in the ability of the Cartesian "light of reason" to orient the individual in an ever-expanding, complex world. Rather than rational, self-possessed agents, the subjects of modernity became insignificant placeholders in the super-individual movements of labor, production, and migration. One of the most influential theorists of modernity's fallout, Sigmund Freud, writes of the modern people's "helplessness and . . . insignificance in the machinery of the universe; they can no longer be the center of creation, no longer the object of tender care on the part of a beneficent Providence. They will be in the same position as a child who has left the parental house where he was so warm and comfortable" (1985, 233). Having left behind their allegedly harmonious and integrated lives in premodern, feudal communities, the Western subjects lost the moorings that had supposedly secured their existence.

If industrialization, with its technological breakthroughs, is the crucial event in modernity, one can see how modernity precipitated a radical reordering of people's experience of time, a phenomenon to which Wright's work gives a peculiar inflection. In his groundbreaking essay, "Time, Work-Discipline, and Industrial Capitalism," E. P. Thompson argues that the regime of labor, necessitated by capitalist production, imposed a new form of time consciousness on workers: production demanded that rules and conventions be adhered to when measuring time; laborers needed to adjust to a strict ordering of their daily activities—all of which had specific consequences for the kinds of wage labor that African Americans performed. With the further technological advances of the last quarter of the nineteenth century, there also emerged what one fin-de-siècle commentator called modernity's (and, in cultural terms, modernism's) "cult of speed" (qtd. in Kern 2003, 111). Modernity necessitated one's coming to terms with a "ceaseless process of temporal differentiation" (Osborne 1995, 8): expanding markets demanded people's adjustment to new timetables and frequent changes in everyday routines. Consequently, as David Harvey writes, "[m]odernization entails . . . the perpetual disruption of temporal and spatial rhythms" (1996, 216). Such experiences were reflected also in cultural production. While turn-of-the-century modernist literature responded to "the rapidity with which ideas and opinions were exchanged across national frontiers" (McFarlane 1991, 78), in the United States such musical innovations as ragtime and jazz expressed the volatile pace of modern life: "The new rhythms were not simply faster; indeed, some innovations delayed or even stopped the beat unexpectedly, but the mixture of syncopation, irregularity, and new percussive textures gave an overall impression of the hurry and unpredictability of contemporary life" (Kern 2003, 123).

From his earliest work onwards, Wright illustrates the unease, and particularly the temporal disorientation, that characterizes the "careening juggernaut" of modernity (Giddens 1990, 53). In "How 'Bigger' Was Born" (1940), he writes of his attempts to embody the experience of modern alienation in *Native Son*'s protagonist. He sought to depict "men and women living in a world whose fundamental assumptions could no longer be taken for granted: a world ridden with national and class strife; a world whose metaphysical meanings had vanished; a world in which God no longer existed as a daily focal point of men's lives; a world in which men could no longer retain their faith in an ultimate hereafter" (446). He envisioned, in other words, lives whose deeply entrenched, seemingly natural traditions and beliefs ("metaphysical meanings") had been destabilized, had even evaporated, in the turmoil of the industrializing world. Five years later, in an introduction to St. Clair Drake and Horace R. Cayton's *Black Metropolis* (1945), a sociological study of African American life in the ghettos of Chicago, Wright reiterates this conceptualization. Offering the study as scientific corroboration of the phenomena he had depicted in *Native Son* and the autobiographical *Black Boy* (1945), he writes of the changes precipitated by modernization: "The advent of machine production altered [man's] relationship to the earth, to his family, to his fellow men, and even to himself. Under feudalism the family had been the unit of production, the nexus of emotional relations, a symbol of the moral order of the universe." He locates life's lost groundings in the patriarchal traditions of feudal communities: "The eternal and temporal orders of existence coalesced and formed one vivid, timeless moment of meaning, justification, and redemption. Man and earth and heaven formed a unit." With industrialization, "men became atoms crowding great industrial cities, bewildered as to their duties and meaning. . . . Holy days became holidays; clocks replaced the sun as a symbolic measurement of time." In the nineteenth century, Wright argues, the pace of feudal life—the steady clocking of its seemingly natural tempo—was replaced by the temporal ordering of capitalist work discipline. This abrupt leap had released the uprooted human being into a vortex of forces over which he had no control.

Wright thus identifies *timekeeping* as the crucial question that haunts American culture and produces the typologies of characters we find in *Native Son*. The modern world is suffering from a kind of a jetlag: having recently left behind the temporal order of feudal societies, the modern subjects are unable to adjust to the newly emergent time zone, the disjunctive pace with which modernity moves. Introducing *Black Metropolis*, Wright argues that the task of pragmatist thinkers like William James and John Dewey has been to readjust the disoriented American consciousness to the flows of modern time. "The best philosophic energy of American thought," he writes, "has gone into trying to 'tell what time it is,' how far we have strayed from the feudal home, or how close we have come to making ourselves feel secure in an arid and senseless world." While *Native Son*'s urgent call for a renewed time-consciousness seeks to awaken the nation to the ways in which ghosts of the past—the unfinished business of race—meddle with the present, Wright also suggests that this temporal disorientation is the result of industrialized peoples' having been wrenched out of their securely organized feudal cultures into the fast-spinning vortex of modern life. He situates the problem in the transnational context of Western modernity: the cultures of the United States, he suggests, cannot be understood in isolation but need to be contextualized in global trends of long duration.

Bigger Thomas is Wright's emblem of the individual's disorientation amidst the jarring shifts of modern life, as well as the racial hierarchies that have ossified into structural features of modernity, an aspect of the industrialized West to which I'll return in more depth shortly. In an early, often discussed scene of *Native Son*, Bigger and his friend Gus gaze longingly at an airplane as it writes a commercial message onto the sky. They pensively recognize the contrast between their boredom and immobility—Bigger "was restless and had time on his hands"—and the speedy movements of the plane:

> "Them white boys sure can fly," Gus said.
> "Yeah," Bigger said, wistfully. "They get a chance to do everything." (bk. 1)

This scene alludes to an African-American cultural tradition in which the ability to fly offers an escape from the restricted geographies of the slave plantation (the myths of flying slaves, represented, for example, by Sapphira Wade in Gloria Naylor's *Mama Day* [1988]) or poverty-ridden urban ghettos (suggested by the airplane in the opening shot, and its continuous, off-screen droning in the soundscape, of John Singleton's film *Boyz n the Hood* [1991]). Wright rewrites this tradition by grafting it onto the experience of industrial modernity. As much as the airplane exemplifies the technologies that, destabilizing traditional ways of living, have produced alienated lives such as Bigger's, the skywriter's advertising message— "USE SPEED GASOLINE"—succinctly encapsulates the characteristically temporal demands of modern life. As Henri Lefebvre observes, modernity required "the ability to move fast" (1995, 158).

This contrast between rapid movements and stagnant racial hierarchies is anticipated in *Lawd Today!* (1963), the posthumously published novel that Wright completed before *Native Son*. Its protagonist, Jake—who, like Bigger, dreams of becoming a pilot—observes the fast-paced circuits of commerce that are unavailable to him as an African American man. Working as a clerk at the post office, he looks at his white colleagues; closely echoing Bigger and Gus's exchange, the text focalizes him: *"Them white boys always in a hurry to get somewhere. And soon's they get out of school they's going to be bigshots. But a nigger just stays a nigger"* (pt. 2, ch. 1). As in *Native Son*'s skywriting scene, here too the mobility that modernity seems to have granted white folks is figured in terms of avian potential: " 'They rush about like bees,' " Jake says to a black colleague, who responds:

> "Yeah, but ain't no use of a black man rushing."
> "Naw, 'cause we ain't going nowhere." (pt. 2, ch. 1)

Contrasting white speeds to his stunted existence, Jake here names what *Native Son* calls "the narrow orbit of [one's] life" (bk. 2), to which urban economies confine the likes of Bigger and his girlfriend Bessie.

The velocities generated by modern technologies similarly guarantee Bigger's eventual entrapment after his involvement in Mary Dalton's disappearance has been exposed and he has momentarily escaped into the derelict buildings of the city's decrepit ghetto. As he gazes at a photograph of his employers in a newspaper he has stolen, he anxiously anticipates his capture: "Here was a picture of Mr and Mrs Dalton standing upon the basement steps. That the image of Mr and Mrs Dalton which he had seen but two hours ago should be seen again *so soon* made him feel that *this whole vague white world which could do things this quickly was more than a match for him*, that soon it would track him down and have it out with him" (bk. 2, emphasis added). The newspaper represents the machinery of modern technologies, whose superior speed is bound to defeat Bigger.

Bigger's experience in Western modernity is determined by the racial hierarchies that circumscribe his life. His rhetorical question to Gus bespeaks his awareness of his segregated, marginalized position in modernity: "Why they make us live in one corner of the city? Why don't they let us fly planes and run ships[?]" (bk. 1). As numerous African American artists and intellectuals have argued, the practices of racial prejudice in the twentieth-century United States constitute a continuation of those ideologies that characterized the enslavement of African Americans of earlier centuries. From this perspective, *Native Son*'s opening alarm appears as a call for readers to recognize how the time of slavery lives on, in mutated forms, in the contemporary United States. Yet Wright's depiction of life in Jim Crow America includes also a further, transnational aspect, one that posits the global histories of colonialism and the slave trade, as well as their concomitant racial ideologies, at the very core of post-eighteenth-century European and American lives.

The constitutive role that the histories of global modernity and the African diaspora play in Bigger's life is suggested in a scene where the protagonist and his friend Jack spend an afternoon in a movie theater. The scene has the two men captivated by newsreel "images of smiling, dark-haired white girls lolling on the gleaming sands of a beach." The film's voiceover enjoins the audience to gawk at "*the daughters of the rich taking sunbaths in the sands of Florida! This little collection of debutantes represents over four billion of America's wealth and over fifty of America's leading families. . . .*" (bk. 1). By an unlikely coincidence, one of the girls is identified as Mary Dalton, the daughter of Bigger's soon-to-be employers. The newsreel continues with scenes of the young woman frolicking on the beach with a man who, by another fluke, turns out to be Jan Erlone, the communist activist whom Bigger later frames as responsible for Mary's disappearance. The gossip reporter describes her parents' dismay at the company she keeps: they "*summoned Mary home by wire from her winter vacation and denounced her Communist friend.*" "What's a Communist?" Bigger asks his friend (bk. 1).

As his ignorance indicates, the scene depicts Bigger as an unselfconscious consumer of capitalist ideology and its representations, exemplified by the seductive images of white affluence that flash across the screen. His gullibility leads to his identification with the interests of wealthy white people and loathing of poor whites:

> [R]ich white people were not so hard on Negroes [Bigger thought]; it was the poor whites who hated Negroes. They hated Negroes because they didn't have their share of the money. His mother had always told him that rich white people liked Negroes better than they did poor whites. He felt that if he were a poor white and did not

get his share of the money, then he would deserve to be kicked. Poor white people were stupid. It was the rich white people who were smart and who knew how to treat people. (bk. 1)

Wright depicts his protagonist as a subject in thrall of *ideology* in the precise Marxist sense: fascinated by representations of success, he misrecognizes the true conditions of his social existence. In this respect, Wright anticipates the work of such scholars as the labor historian David Roediger, who argues, in *The Wages of Whiteness,* that the fantasies elicited by representations of racial difference have functioned in the service of a hegemonic bourgeoisie in the United States. He suggests that, to compensate for their poverty and exploitation, white workers have accepted the consolation of "the wages of whiteness": their limited lives have seemingly gained value by their ability to identify with whiteness as opposed to the degraded category of blackness. Such a mechanism has expediently discouraged them from joining black workers in political action against the white bourgeoisie. Watching the newsreel, Bigger is guilty of a parallel misrecognition in aligning himself with the interests of white wealth rather than those of the economically disenfranchised people. Here, too, representations accomplish their ideological work successfully by neutralizing the threat of a joint challenge by the disenfranchised classes.

Such depictions of Bigger's manipulability, his helplessness in "the stifling embrace of an invisible force" (bk. 2), have inspired many to categorize *Native Son* as a naturalist novel. Like Theodore Dreiser's and Frank Norris's protagonists, Bigger finds himself "caught up in a vast but delicate machine whose wheels would whir no matter what was pitted against them"; he is "being turned here and there by a surge of strange forces he could not understand" (bk. 3)—forces designated by the umbrella term *modernity*. Yet it is important to note that, for Wright, the processes and consequences of modernization as they are played out in the West are always connected to global histories, particularly those of the African diaspora. For example, in *12 Million Black Voices* (1941), a photo essay that delineates the socioeconomic contexts from which the characters of *Native Son* emerge, Wright follows the massive population shift of African Americans from the agrarian South to the industrialized North during what has become known as the Great Migration of 1910–40. However, he also carefully situates this seemingly nation-specific history in a larger, transnational context: at stake is not only the migration of citizens from one part of the country to the other, but a movement that recapitulates global patterns of conquest and migration where peoples were "[h]urled from [their] native African homes into the very center of the most complex and highly industrialized civilization the world has ever known." Long before he observed and wrote about the processes of decolonization in Africa, Wright emerges in his early work as a diasporic thinker: for him, twentieth-century life in the United States cannot be understood outside the larger transnational frames that bring into focus the histories of colonization, imperialism, and the slave trade.

That urban African-American life, exemplified by Bigger and his friends, is also connected to diasporic modernity in *Native Son* becomes clear as the scene in the movie theater proceeds. Lost in fantasies provoked by the cinematic images of prosperity, Bigger resurfaces when he "hear[s] the roll of tom-toms and the screams of black men and women dancing free and wild, men and women who were *adjusted to their soil and at home in their world, secure from fear and hysteria*" (bk. 1, emphasis added): he finds himself watching a scene that purportedly depicts life in an African village. The villagers' supposed "adjust[ment]" and "secur[ity]," as well as their freedom from "fear and hysteria," function as foils to the experiences of anxiety and rootlessness that characterize black and white lives in the post-eighteenth-century West and that lead to the series of misunderstandings behind Mary Dalton's brutal murder. Notably, the term "hysteria" returns in *Native Son*'s courtroom scene: speaking of the white mob outside the courthouse that calls for the defendant's lynching, Bigger's lawyer, Boris Max, observes that "'Bigger Thomas acted *as hysterically as those people are acting at this moment in that mob outdoors*'" (bk. 3, emphasis added). In the novel, both black and white Americans are driven by the "fear and hysteria" from which the "premodern" Africans, their lives firmly rooted in their long traditions, supposedly do not suffer.

The skywriter and cinema scenes suggest that, having been banished from their past locales and excluded from modern life in the West, the likes of Bigger Thomas have become homeless exiles, suspended between time zones. According to Wright, in the introduction to the *Black Metropolis*, this condition characterizes every jet-lagged modern subject, regardless of race: "Men still cling to the emotional basis of life that the feudal order gave them, while living and striving in a world whose every turn of wheel, throb of engine, and conquest of space deny its validity. This dual aspect of living is our riven consciousness, our tension, our anxiety." He nevertheless suggests that the situation is particularly acute for African diasporic peoples. With the exile, as Wright notes in *12 Million Black Voices*, there emerges "[a] paradoxical cleavage in our lives": "we have never been allowed to become an organic part of this civilization; we have yet to share its ultimate hopes and expectations." As W. E. B. Du Bois puts it in the introduction to *Darkwater* (1920), the "double-conscious" African-American subject is "in . . . but not of" Western civilization. Bigger's lack of access to modernity—represented by the airplanes and the ships—has left him stranded in a "No Man's Land," a phrase deployed by Boris Max in *Native Son* (bk. 3), as well as by Wright in "How 'Bigger' Was Born."

Wright utilizes the binary pair of *premodern-modern* (or *agrarian-industrial,* or *rural-urban*) elsewhere, too, in describing life in the capitalist, globalized world. The best-known examples of this are the observations of the narrator of *Black Power,* Wright's travel narrative of the Gold Coast (later Ghana), who describes tribal Africans as incapable of responding to modernization's irreversible changes, brought on by British colonization. Instead, the Africans are paralyzed by a kind of inert slumber— "tribal dreams," as the narrator calls it—from which they cannot awake to the time of the present. This state is strictly analogous to the premodern existence that Wright in *Black Metropolis* calls "the feudal dream"; with modernization, the subject "awaken[s]" to time's progression and the future's uncertainty. Yet, as Mary Louise Pratt has suggested, delineating Western modernity by juxtaposing it with the supposedly lost innocence and harmony of premodern (and often non-Western) life may bespeak nothing but a nostalgic yearning for the imagined comfort of a rooted existence. Such schemas depend upon what Leo Bersani has called "the pastoral view of alienation as a peculiarly modern loss of cultural wholeness and harmony" (1978, 49). While Wright seems to rely on such ideas in *Black Metropolis*, he undermines their simplicity in *Native Son*. We should observe, after all, that the representations of the Africans' rootedness in their communities are the work of the same ideological machinery that elicits Bigger's mistaken identification with white capitalist interests: mass culture. As Wright is careful to point out, the scenes of African life that the black men witness come from *Trader Horn*, a 1931 Hollywood jungle adventure. These are manipulated images meant for the consumption of the Western subject of modernity; they do not provide any unmediated access to life outside the urban world that envelops Bigger. Implicitly casting doubts on the veracity of the representations of Africa, *Native Son*'s cinema scene not only undermines Wright's subsequent, seemingly earnest descriptions of premodern life in *Black Metropolis* and *Black Power*, but also anticipates the influential anticolonial activist and theorist Frantz Fanon's problematization, in *Black Skin, White Masks* (1952) and *The Wretched of the Earth* (1961), of the idealization of the African past that he saw in the work of négritude writers Aimé Césaire and Léopold Senghor.

However we judge his delineation of modernization's trajectory, it is clear that Wright adds to his theory of contemporary Western life an important dimension, one that, until very recently, has all but escaped commentary in scholarship on modernity and its cultural phenomena, such as literary modernism. According to Wright in *Native Son*, the disorientation of the Western subject is the result not only of his exile from the security of feudal communities; the white Westerner is also haunted by "[f]ear and hate and guilt" (bk. 3), affects whose origins Wright locates in the histories of colonization and the slave trade. Synthesizing the arguments of existential philosophy, Marxism, and the Chicago School of Sociology, he considers industrialization an opening to a future unlike anything that had been available for European and American cultures of previous centuries: as a radical rupture in collective experience, industrialization enabled experimentation with new forms of life heretofore unimaginable. Yet this unguaranteed future induced a vertigo that the Westerner tried to alleviate by "snatch[ing] millions of black men out of Africa and enslave[ing] them to serve him," according to Wright in his introduction to *Black Metropolis*. While lubricating the machinery of modernity, the unprecedented, forced migration of peoples of color to the Western hemisphere also generated a syndrome in those who were supposed to benefit from colonization and the slave trade: the white Westerner was henceforth plagued by guilt for the obvious injustice of slavery and fear for an impending retaliation. Wright thus suggests that what subsequent theorists of modernity have called the "overwhelming sense of fragmentation, ephemerality, and chaotic change" in post-eighteenth-century life in the West must be linked to diasporic experience (Harvey 1996, 11).

Already in his early work, then, Wright articulates a theory of diasporic modernity, which in late-twentieth-century Anglo American scholarship is most frequently associated with the work of Paul Gilroy. As Gilroy writes in his influential study *The Black Atlantic: Modernity and Double Consciousness*, "the history of the African diaspora and a reassessment of the relationship between modernity and slavery may require a more complete revision of the terms in which the modernity debates have been constructed than any of its academic participants may be willing to concede" (1993, 46). When rendered only in terms of Enlightenment reason and the challenges it faced as waves of industrialization and class revolutions swept across Europe in the nineteenth century, conceptualizations of Western modernity yield an incomplete picture. Rather, we need "to rethink modernity via the history of the black Atlantic and the African diaspora into the western hemisphere" (1993, 17). More recently exemplified by the work of Arjun Appadurai, Dipesh Chakrabarty, David Scott, and Michelle Wright, this approach recognizes not only that "the concentrated intensity of the slave experience is something that marked out blacks as the first truly modern people" (Gilroy 1993, 221), but also that the formations of Western modernity are unthinkable—despite their having been insistently theorized thus—without an acknowledgment of their diasporic dimension.

The diasporic context of (African) American modernity is most clearly—some say, didactically—articulated by Boris Max in the third and final section of *Native Son*. While, as numerous critics have noted, Bigger's white lawyer misses his client's singularity as a human being, he does offer a self-conscious articulation of diasporic modernity, a reading that Wright repeats in the introduction to *Black Metropolis*. During his lengthy address to the court, Max sees the audience's "fear" and "hate"—which drive the proceedings to the foregone conclusion of Bigger's death sentence—as symptoms of its members' disavowed knowledge of the consequences of African peoples' forced migration and enslavement in previous centuries. He observes the unconscious determinations that influence the proceedings: "There is guilt in the rage that demands that this man's life be snuffed out quickly!" he says, pointing to his client. "There is fear in the hate and impatience which impels the action of the mob congregated upon the streets beyond that window!" He suggests that the calls for Bigger's speedy execution are informed by "the long trailing black sense of guilt" that stems from Western modernity's "first wrong": "[the] dislocation of life involving millions of people, a dislocation so vast as to stagger the imagination." "Each [member] of [the white mob]," the lawyer says, "know and feel that their lives are built upon a historical deed of wrong against many people, people from whose lives they have bled their leisure and their luxury! . . . Fear and hate and guilt are the keynotes of this drama!" (bk. 3)

Speaking of the participants' complex of "fear-guilt," Max locates US racial formations in the same transnational context of diasporic modernity that Wright discerns behind the realities of Chicago's ghettos depicted in *Black Metropolis*: the inadmissible catastrophes of colonialism and the slave trade, which lie, in his words, at "the foundations of our civilization." In hastening the modernization of their world with slave labor, Western men "shut their eyes to the humanity of other men, men whose lives were necessary for [the] building [of modern nations]." Max locates abolitionism's primary rationale not in any concern for the humanity of African peoples but in the changing realities of the market: "the invention and widespread use of machines made the further direct enslavement of men economically impossible, and so slavery ended" (bk. 3). Even after slavery was abolished, its symptoms lingered, hardening into the patterns of life whose representative example one finds in Bigger.

In locating the "hysteria" that plagues modernity not only in black but also in white citizens, Wright identifies a syndrome that Gilroy, writing of late-twentieth-century Britain, calls postcolonial (or postimperial) melancholia. This is a condition whose symptoms include "the guilt-ridden loathing and depression that have come to characterize Britain's xenophobic responses to the strangers who have intruded upon it more recently" (2005, 90). According to Gilroy, white British attitudes toward immigrants from the country's former colonies—a movement that the Jamaican poet Louise Bennett famously calls "colonization in reverse"—are informed by an often unacknowledged unease stemming from the country's historical debt to these countries. As Gilroy continues,

> Repressed and buried knowledge of the cruelty and injustice that recur in diverse accounts of imperial administration can only be denied at a considerable moral and psychological cost. That knowledge creates a discomfiting complicity. Both are active in shaping the hostile responses to strangers and settlers and in constructing the intractable political problems that flow from understanding immigration as being akin to war and invasion" (2005, 94).

Echoing Wright's argument, Gilroy insists that not only colonized and enslaved peoples but also white Westerners are subject to the condition of diasporic modernity, its legacies of violence, and maladjustment. Both black and white are caught in what Boris Max in *Native Son* calls "the delicate and unconscious machinery of race relations" (bk. 3); "dominance," Gilroy observes, "can carry its own wounds" (2005, 52).

One symptom is the form of temporal disorientation to which *Native Son*'s opening calls attention. The ineradicable fact of the slave trade, its "gigantic wrong accomplished by a nation through three hundred long years" (bk. 3), rendered modernity's time out of joint. This temporal dislocation is lived as an experience of haunting, of the past's inappropriate return in the present, the irrational palimpsest of overlapping time zones. Ventriloquizing the white citizenry, Max notes that the presence of diasporic peoples in the West has become "this thing that haunts me"; he states that people like Bigger Thomas "glide through our complex civilization like wailing ghosts" (bk. 3). Thus, while Karl Marx and Friedrich Engels famously open *The Communist Manifesto* by suggesting that nineteenth-century Europe is "haunt[ed]" by "the spectre of Communism" (1848, 473), Wright redefines the argument: he insists on the diasporic perspective by highlighting the consequences of the slave trade for contemporary Western societies. It is to an acknowledgement of modernity's temporal disjointedness—linked not only to industrialization but also the histories of race and racism—that *Native Son*'s opening seeks to awaken its audiences.

From the very beginning of his work, then, Wright is a theorist of diasporic modernity: he traces the instabilities of post-eighteenth-century Western life not only to industrialization and the rise of capitalism (as Marx and Engels did, followed by an army of subsequent commentators), to the existential angst about the contingency and meaninglessness of human life (provoked by Charles Darwin's discoveries), or to the unconscious complexities of libidinal drives (explored by Freud and his followers), but also to the slave trade and the intellectual justifications that its obvious injustice necessitated across Western cultures. Read in the context of diasporic modernity, *Native Son*, as well as Wright's subsequent work, traces for us "the transnational path of the story of race in America" (Dudziak 2000, 17). Arguing that the discontent and splitting of Western life are symptoms of the betrayal of its ethical and philosophical groundings, Wright's entire oeuvre works towards the "revised account of European [and U. S.] modernisms" that Gilroy calls for, one that proceeds from a consideration of "their complex relationship with colonial and imperial experiences at home and abroad" (2005, 147). It is to an acknowledgment of the consequences of this history, willfully forgotten and disavowed, that the alarm clock in *Native Son* seeks to wake its audience.

Concomitantly, *Native Son* is also an untimely reminder of the artificial constraints imposed upon the literary field when one insists on framing it in terms of what is called American literature. Not only is "American literature" a notoriously imprecise appellation, potentially including literatures—those of "the Americas"—beyond the boundaries of the United States; as a perspective, it also eclipses the ineradicable ties that the culture of any nation-state has to the global, transnational stage. Wai Chee Dimock has recently made this point in her argument for a "planetary" scope in literary studies. "For too long," she writes, "American literature has been seen as a world apart, sufficient unto itself, not burdened by the chronology and geography outside the nation, and not making any intellectual demands on that score" (2006, 2–3). She suggests that, "[r]ather than taking the nation as a default position, the totality we automatically reach, we come up with alternate geographies that deny it this totalizing function" (2007, 3). In his diasporic orientation, Wright offers one way to make "[t]he planet . . . a single unit of analysis" (Dimock 2006, 143). This widened frame enriches the discipline of literary studies by expanding its categories beyond the culture of the nation-state: "African-American literature is infinitely richer when it is seen not as nation-based, self-contained within the United States, but as a diasporic formation, a literature of the two Americas with arcs reaching back to Africa. And American literature is infinitely richer when it takes its cue from this extended corpus, embracing a map of the world that commingles languages and cultures" (2006, 163). If, as Paul Giles writes, the study of American literature (re-) entered a postnational, globalized era around 1980, Wright's work constitutes an untimely meditation on the "deterritorialization" of national culture. Wright suggests that the histories of the United States cannot be fully understood if their intelligibility is circumscribed by the borders of the nation-state and national culture. While he is not the first African American writer to argue this—the earlier work of David Walker, Alexander Crummell, Pauline Hopkins, Claude McKay, and W. E. B. Du Bois come to mind—over his active writing career of twenty-odd years (until his death in 1960), he produced a compelling oeuvre whose transnational, diasporic range can guide contemporary literary scholars seeking to rethink the disciplinary boundaries, and unlearn the actively exclusionary practices, of their fields.

V
CRITICAL UNDERSTANDINGS

33

MASS CULTURE, THE NOVEL, AND THE AMERICAN LEFT

BY BENJAMIN BALTHASER AND SHELLEY STREEBY

To understand how writers and critics on the left understood the relationship of mass culture to the novel in the first four decades of the twentieth century, we need to subject each of these keywords to critical scrutiny—left, mass culture, novel—and determine why these three terms belong together. The "left" during this period encompasses a wide variety of changing movements of black nationalists and internationalists, anarchists, socialists, communists, and other radicals who sought fundamentally to change the future of the United States and the world. We focus on leftists because they envisioned alternative worlds in literature and mass culture during these years, especially during the Thirties, a decade of radicalism that won lasting victories through and pinned hopes on the production of a mass culture that fused canonical and pulp genres. Because so many prominent progressive US writers in the nineteenth and twentieth centuries hoped the novel might offer ways of mobilizing various publics within and outside of the United States, that form developed a self-conscious relationship with left politics and mass culture. That relationship was not without difficulty. Since the novel emerged as a form particularly attuned to middle-class life and the reconciliation of the individual with society, it was a challenge to use it for more radical purposes. The same was true, for different reasons, of the category of mass culture, which was imagined by some as an obstacle to fundamental change and by others as a crucial tool in revolutionary world-building.

At the end of the nineteenth century, William Dean Howells, Theodore Dreiser, Mark Twain, and other writers defined the project of literary realism in relation to other modes of representation and against emergent forms of mass media. In *A Hazard of New Fortunes* (1890), Howells delineates the changing contours of the literary field by distinguishing the business of the illustrated literary magazine *Every Other Week* from other popular and mass forms, such as "female fiction" (pt. 2, ch. 6) and ballads about the "wrongs of the working man" (pt. 2, ch. 11) and by considering its vexed relationship to capitalism's hierarchies and contradictions through the character of Dryfoos, the wealthy investor who is the magazine's main source of financial support. As Amy Kaplan suggests in the *Social Construction of American Realism*, nineteenth-century progressive authors imagined realism as competing with the dime novels, sentimental romances, and emergent consumer culture that dominated the marketplace. They hoped that realist novels might serve as a democratic alternative that could render truthfully the lives of ordinary people for an educated reading public. Realism derives its authority by acting as a social mediator, against which was posed the class differentiations of a mass publishing market that Howells, Dreiser, Twain, and other authors of realist novels believed typically insulted the very audience that consumed its products.

With its dense descriptions, complex and individuated characters, and long, slowly evolving plots, the realist novel sought to confound the speed and simplicity of the more plot-driven genre novel. As Kaplan points out, reading the lengthy realist text was supposed to be "work," intellectually and socially productive, thus aligning the cultural producer politically with its working class subject. Culture was not an escape but rather a productive enterprise in its own right. In *Sister Carrie* (1900), for example, Carrie chooses to be a consumer rather than producer of commodities and in doing so both loses her moral bearings and contributes to the death of her lover. In contrast, Lindau, the philosophy-reading German immigrant laborer of Howells's *A Hazard*, who loses his arm in the Civil War, represents just the sort of moral values that Howells believed the dime novel could not represent. March's position as an editor and his friendship with Lindau might be seen as the promise of the new alliance realism proposed. Indeed, March literally brings all the classes to the table for one very uncomfortable but provocative dinner—a scene that can be read as a metonym for the kind of discomforting labor the realist novel produced.

Kaplan suggests that realists such as Howells sought to balance and mediate the violent, disruptive forces in US society and politics through the "narrative construction of common ground among classes," a strategy that both effaced and affirmed social hierarchies (1988, 11). In *A Hazard of New Fortunes*, Howells struggled to imagine such a common ground in the wake of the 1887 execution of the Chicago Haymarket anarchists, a miscarriage of justice that he protested and that shook his faith in the US legal system. But as Kaplan shows, the class conflict that the realist novel attempted to contain keeps erupting in the novel's foreground, especially in Lindau's words and acts and in the violence of the suppression of the streetcar strike at its climax.

Howells's decision to use the realist novel to respond to the Haymarket affair was an unusual one. The German, English, and native-born anarchists and leaders of the international proletariat of Chicago who were found guilty of inciting an unknown person to throw a bomb at Haymarket Square would be remembered in the years to come in songs, poetry, speeches, journalism, posters, and other cultural forms, but only rarely in novels. Mass culture, on the other hand, was both a foe and a friend to the anarchists. During their trial, in the months leading up to their execution and in its aftermath, they were demonized in mass-circulation daily newspapers, the illustrated press, the crime gazettes, and in dime novels such as *The Red Flag: Or the Anarchists of Chicago* (1886) and *Deadwood Dick Jr. in Chicago: Or, the Anarchist's Daughter* (1888). But the anarchists' writings, speeches, biographies, portraits, and photographs also circulated through mass culture, both within texts in which they were imagined as a foreign, threatening, violent element and in those produced by participants in movements that sympathized with them. The literature of Haymarket includes labor newspapers in English, German, and Bohemian; Haymarket widow Lucy Parsons's compilations of the anarchists' speeches in court and her husband Albert's life, speeches, and writings; a slim volume of August Spies's writings and life story published by his widow Nina Van Zandt, and the lives of the anarchists, which were narrated to a journalist for the Chicago *Knights of Labor* and subsequently repackaged and excerpted in a wide range of publications and cultural forms. Howells's efforts to model a literary realism that would "make the comfortable people understand how the uncomfortable people live" remain at some distance from this kind of material (pt. 2, ch. 7), despite his sympathies for the anarchists: Basil March even compares Lindau's "violent" words to those published in "blatant labor newspapers" and to the "frenzied," "tasteless" rhetoric of speakers at strikers' meetings (pt. 2, ch. 12). In these ways, Howells tried to mediate and balance what he saw as the violent excesses of working-class rhetoric and mass culture.

Sentiment, Sensation, and the Radical Novel in an Age of Revolution

In the United States, writers such as Upton Sinclair were more closely connected to the world of mass journalism, professional muckraking, and the socialist press. Sinclair and other naturalists emphasized class conflict more than common ground in their efforts to extend representation and give voice to radical and working-class perspectives. *The Jungle* (1906) was initially serialized in Julius Wayland's *Appeal to Reason* (1897–1922), the socialist newspaper published in Girard, Kansas, that by 1910 would achieve a circulation of over five hundred thousand, making it one of the most popular weeklies of the period. Supported by a $500 advance from Wayland, Sinclair, who had been "converted" to socialism in 1902, went to Chicago to learn more about the meatpacking industry and within several weeks had finished *The Jungle: A Story of Chicago*, which the paper ran serially for almost a year in 1905. During the previous year, Sinclair had written articles for the *Appeal* about the strike in Chicago's Union Stockyards. His great novel of immigrant working-class struggle and the horrors of capitalism, which the paper promised readers would "stir the nation," emerged from this sphere of mass-circulation, muckraking, and socialist literature. A year later, Doubleday, Page, and Company published an abbreviated version of *The Jungle*, which had a different ending and contained fewer passages about the evil rich and the systemic aspects of the problem, after several other publishers had rejected it.

Sinclair's interest in popular and mass culture was evident from the beginning of his literary career as a writer of dime novels. After *The Jungle* became an international sensation and was translated into several languages, he participated in its film adaptation, playing the part of the socialist orator who converts the Lithuanian immigrant Jurgis to the cause. Sinclair also embraced his connections to literary sentimentalism. In a March 4, 1905, letter published in the *Appeal*, he described his novel as "fundamentally identical with" Stowe's *Uncle Tom's Cabin* (1852), despite the lack of "superficial resemblance," for it "set forth the breaking of human hearts by a system which exploits the labor of men and women for profits." In a letter from February 11, 1905, Sinclair described the effect he was aiming for in the language of sentiment and sensation, promising to "shake the popular heart and blow the top off the industrial tea kettle," unlike the balancing act to which Howells aspired.

While his heartbreaking scenes of labor exploitation designed to provoke an intense emotional response in readers connects him to Stowe and the sentimental tradition, his interest in the crimes of the rich and in class conflicts in the industrial city also links him to the sensational "mysteries of the city" literature written in an earlier era by writers such as Ned Buntline and George Lippard, who had connections to the mass-circulation press and to the labor movements of their period. Sinclair's focus on bodies in pain that narrate injustice and on melodramatic trios of villains, victims, and heroes also signaled his participation in the cultures of sentiment and sensation.

The Iron Heel (1908) was similarly shaped by Jack London's involvement in the growing Socialist movement and interest in mass culture, in this case dystopian science fiction. Interest in socialism increased in the United States at this time, peaking around 1912, when Socialist presidential candidate Eugene Debs received almost a million votes, before declining in the wake of the state's clampdown on radicals during the First World War. This was also an era of revolution: an unsuccessful one had just taken place in Russia in 1905, and another was about to begin in Mexico in 1910. Amid this leap of radical optimism, London imagines a revolutionary near future (1912–32), culminating in a utopian socialist society, the Brotherhood of Man, seven centuries later.

In a foreword to the novel, a narrator from the future, the historian Anthony Mann, looks back across the centuries and judges the "Everhard manuscript" especially "valuable in communicating to us the *feel* of those terrible times" (on *The Iron Heel* as dystopic science fiction, see Chapter 23 in this volume). Emphasizing feelings and foregrounding scenes of bodily suffering and class tension, London draws on sentimental and sensational conventions as he uses a female narrator and a love plot to tell the story of near future revolutionary transformation. Avis Everhard, the daughter of a Berkeley science professor who becomes a revolutionary, writes the manuscript after falling in love with Ernest, the socialist "superman" all "aflame with democracy" (ch. 1), who helps to lead the struggle against the Oligarchy, the wealthy class of capitalists who vow to "grind" the "revolutionists down under our heel" and "walk upon" their "faces" (ch. 5). London manifests his debt to those conventions in the third chapter, entitled "Jackson's Arm," in which a worker who loses his arm after it is caught in a machine is cheated and vilified by the company, Sierra Mills, in which Avis and her father are stockholders. The story of Jackson's injured body and his losses inspires Avis's conversion by moving her to join the socialist cause, thereby provoking the action motivated by affect that sentimental protest novels such as Stowe's *Uncle Tom's Cabin* sought to elicit.

London uses the device of the found manuscript and a narrator from the future to envision a utopian horizon in which the Socialist Brotherhood of Man has triumphed, but much of the novel is a bleak dystopia in which naturalist elements that emphasize lost agency and entrapment in various machines compete with sentimental and melodramatic scenes of the recognition and correction of injustice and inequalities. While literary naturalism manifested interest in workers, capitalists, and corporations as new subjects, moving beyond the boundaries of a genteel realism to engage "contemporary contradictions of global expansion," as Colleen Lye puts it, it also "facilitated a more persuasive picture of the social domination of monopoly capitalism than its political overturning," especially because of the naturalists' emphasis on "lost autonomy" and "mass degradation" (2005, 51, 70–71). London's novel ends abruptly, in the wake of a disastrous, abortive uprising in Chicago that is brutally suppressed by the Iron Heel just before Avis is presumably captured by the Mercenaries, the vicious military class that serves the Oligarchy. The mourning of lost agency, the focus on multiple forms of entrapment, and especially the representation of the revolutionary masses as the debased, ugly, and beastly "people of the abyss" mark the failure of socialist transformation. However, the "enclave of resistance" (in Tom Moylan's words) that widens into revolution, and London's efforts to adapt a popular genre to move people to act and participate in revolutionary movements, make this novel a critical dystopia that is open to the future rather than an anti-utopian text cynically rejecting the possibility of another world.

By imagining "an international revolution wide as the world is wide" (ch. 1), *The Iron Heel* negotiates some of the challenges confronted by other writers on the left in the early twentieth century who struggled, as Michael Denning suggests, to use the form of the novel, which had historically privileged middle-class individuals and values, to "create a public, agitational work in a form that, unlike drama, depended on private, often domestic consumption" and to "create a vision of revolutionary social change in a form almost inherently committed to the solidity of society and history" (2004, 59). Here Denning is thinking of late 1920s and 1930s proletarian novels such as Mike Gold's *Jews Without Money* (1929), Agnes Smedley's *Daughter of Earth* (1929), and John Dos Passos's *The 42nd Parallel* (1930), but similar struggles are evident in other early twentieth-century radical novels, including those by Sinclair and London.

Black nationalists and internationalists during this period, such as Cyril Briggs, Romeo Dougherty, W. E. B. Du Bois, and Claude McKay, similarly struggled to adapt the novel to depict the possibility of revolutionary change. Briggs, an immigrant from Saint Kitts and Nevis, worked as a journalist for the *Amsterdam News* in New York before beginning his own radical monthly magazine, the *Crusader* (1918–22), which originally aimed to publish "authoritative articles about Africa" and the possibilities for black nation-building in "the South American and West Indian republics." Following the First World War, the resurgence of race riots and lynchings, and the limits of Woodrow Wilson's internationalism, Briggs emphasized the need to "wake up the masses" (1921, vol. 3), and turned the *Crusader* into the official organ of the African Blood Brotherhood, a transnational organization that aspired to create a "world-wide Negro Federation" (1921, vol. 2). The *Crusader* featured political commentary by Briggs, including spirited defenses of the Bolshevik Revolution, a women's section, and serialized stories with titles such as "The Ray of Fear: A Thrilling Story of Love War, Race, Patriotism, Revolutionary Inventions, and the Liberation of Africa," "Secret Service," and "Punta, Revolutionist." While the first two were written by Briggs himself under the pseudonym "C. Valentine," the last and longest was written by Romeo Dougherty, who was also a movie programmer, the sports editor of the *New York News*, and a member of a prominent New York City basketball team. Dougherty understood the *Crusader*'s purpose to be the "intelligent agitation for a real true and unvarnished democracy for the darker peoples of the world" (1918, vol. 1.1), and both he and Briggs used sensational stories of adventure, inventions, and political intrigue modeled on dime novels to agitate for anticolonial struggle and worldwide revolutionary transformations.

Briggs's and Dougherty's adaptations of popular genres and forms reveal some of the limitations of mass culture at this moment as well as its uses for radicals. Dougherty's "Punta, Revolutionist," which was serialized in the *Crusader* in 1918 and 1919, is especially noteworthy for its explicit reflections on the culture of sensation and its efforts to connect anticolonial struggles of the Spanish-American War era with black radical movements in Dougherty's present. The protagonist, Harry Lonsdale, has migrated from Savannah, Georgia, to New York City and is passing for white as he works first as a newsboy and then as a reporter for the "sensational" newspaper the *New York Thunderer*. Londsdale educates himself by reading books of the "blood and thunder variety," such as Old Sleuth, Jesse James, and Nick Carter dime novels, and eventually "graduates" to "stories of love and adventure" by Laura Jean Libbey, E. D. E. N. Southworth, Eugene Sue, Dumas, and others. This crash course in sensational novel-reading prepares him to give his "imagination full play" as a newspaper writer and to make up "wonderful tales" about the Rough Riders that help to "swing public opinion" in support of the war (vol. 1, issue 5). But once Lonsdale is sent to an island called Santo Amalia to write stories about the activities of the troops in Cuba, he falls in with a crowd of "young Spanish-West Indians" (vol. 1, issue 6) and soon becomes a part of "the most drastic plan for Negro freedom ever conceived" (vol. 2, issue 1). By developing a secret weapon, a deadly aerial bomb, and building a giant wireless station "to communicate with far-off Africa," the revolutionaries hope to "launch the 'Black Revolution'" twenty years in the future. The novel ends abruptly, just as Lonsdale enters "the fight for justice for my people" and begins to travel around the world recruiting black people to the movement, despite the "to be continued" notice that followed the final excerpt (vol. 2, issue 3). But Dougherty's critique of the connections between sensational literature and US empire building comes through clearly.

Dougherty's "Punta, Revolutionist" as well as Briggs's "The Ray of Fear" and "Secret Service" are all examples of what Michelle Stephens calls "black empire narratives," which attempt to "imagine some version of an international revolutionary black state" and thereby reveal "the tension of a cultural politics constituted by both radical and reactionary impulses—impulses toward racial revolution, movement, and freedom, and impulses towards militarism, statehood, and empire" (2005, 38). This tension also shapes Du Bois's novel, *Dark Princess: A Romance* (1928), which was published towards the end of his editorship of *The Crisis* (1910–34), the NAACP's official publication. Throughout his long lifetime, Du Bois experimented with form and genre, including adaptations of mass cultural ones. His short story "The Comet," for instance, which was incorporated into the multiform text *Darkwater* (1920), resonates with the early science fiction of the dime novels and pulp magazines of his era. *Dark Princess* shares many elements with Dougherty's and Briggs's sensational fiction, especially in its emphasis on internationalism, secret networks of resistance, world revolution, and transnational romance (on *Dark Princess* and international social justice movements, see Chapters 19 and 28 in this volume). These works feature peripatetic heroes who move from place to place in response to racism, organizing resistance movements. The novel begins in Berlin as Du Bois's hero, the disillusioned former medical student and self-proclaimed exile Matthew Townes, meets the beautiful Princess Kautilya from India in a café after he punches a racist white American who makes advances on her. In what follows, Du Bois tries to imagine how a successful racial revolution might happen and maps transnational connections and disconnections among people of color all over the world in a sensational story of love and adventure that unsettles racial and national hierarchies partly through hierarchical narratives of gender, sexuality, and class.

Although this plot of international romantic adventure is similar to those of Dougherty and Briggs, Du Bois's language is both more ornate and frankly erotic, at some distance from the breezy, dime novel style of *The Crusader* writers. In *Dark Princess*, transnational romance is the main motor of change, since it results in the birth of the child who will lead the world revolution. This conclusion permits Du Bois to swerve away from questions about the role of violence in revolutionary movements that he raises in the middle of the novel. While Dougherty's and Briggs's heroes experiment with new inventions to find weapons for the black revolution, in Du Bois's novel change comes through romance and heterosexual reproduction. Kautilya makes the pragmatics of the latter clear when she tells Matthew that had their child "been a girl child," she would have left them both, since her country

"needs not a princess, but a King" (pt. 4, ch. 19). The novel's impulses toward statehood and counterempire, then, depend upon deep primary narratives of gender and
heterosexuality, culminating in a kind of repro-futurism that imagines the transformation of the world through the figure of the male child.

As the mother of the racial messiah, Kautilya plays a more important role than
other heroines, but she is also one of the leaders of an international "movement
looking toward righting the present racial inequalities in the world, especially along
the color line" (pt. 1, ch. 7). This movement "looked frankly forward to raising
not all the dead, sluggish, brutalized masses of men, but discovering among them
genius, gift, and ability in far larger number than among the privileged and ruling
classes," thereby using "democracy" as a "method of aristocracy" (pt. 4, ch. 2).
Ambivalence about the "masses" pervades *Dark Princess*, and despite Du Bois's
borrowing of mass cultural genres and conventions, the novel was not a popular
success. Most contemporary critics judged the novel by the standard of modernist
realism and were therefore baffled by Du Bois's literary experiment with antirealist,
fantastic forms.

In many ways, we can think of Claude McKay's novel of transnational vagabonds
in Marseille, *Banjo* (1929), as a proletarian answer to the aristocracy of the "darker
races" presented by Du Bois's *Dark Princess* (on *Banjo* and black diasporic proletarianism, see Chapter 28 in this volume). In this "novel without a plot," as McKay
described it, music rather than narrative serves as the foundational cultural matrix of
a black diaspora. While the black nationalist Goosey condemns the banjo as "Dixie"
and "bondage," it is clear that Banjo's orchestra is the centrifugal force that brings
the African-descended people of Marseille together (ch. 7). In the Café African "all
shades of Negroes came together" to listen to Banjo's orchestra play the "money
stuff" of "saxophone jazzing" and the "wheedle-whine blues": "British West African
blacks, Portuguese blacks, American blacks" who lose their national and even class
distinctions in the "sweet dancing thing of primitive joy" of Banjo's music (ch. 5).
Yet it is Ray, the writer and intellectual of the vagabond crowd, who articulates the
political undercurrents of Banjo's embrace of black popular culture. Arguing with
a West Indian student who believes the Senegalese are "savages," unlike those from
Martinique who are educated and speak a "pure French," Ray insists that only "by
finding your roots" in "black culture" can there be a "racial renaissance." By contrast,
the student believes "the greatest glory of the island was that Empress Josephine was
born there" (ch. 16). Rejecting the classist implications of both Du Bois's "talented
tenth" and the racial uplift programs of Marcus Garvey, Ray comes to believe Banjo's
transnational black aesthetic of music, wine, and beach life "possessed more potential power for racial salvation than the Negro *literati*, whose poverty of mind and
purpose showed never any signs of enrichment" (ch. 25). Rather than signaling the
end of the earlier era of revolutionary internationalism and the Harlem Renaissance,
however, *Banjo* bridged the 1920s and the 1930s in its efforts to imagine a black international proletarian culture.

Culture for the (New) Masses: The Radical Novel and the Rise of the Cultural Apparatus in the 1930s

In James T. Farrell's 1930s epic of the working-class Irish on Chicago's South Side, the *Studs Lonigan* trilogy (1932–35), we follow Studs as a grown man through what might be his only true moment of empathy: watching the Hollywood gangster film *Doomed Victory*. Studs's mind "became like a double exposure, with two reels running through it[;] . . . he saw himself in Joey Gallagher's boots, and Studs Lonigan and Joey Gallagher together leaped up the career of gangdom's adventurous ladder to fame" (bk. 3, ch. 3). This identification inspires him to be a "risk-taker" like the fictionalized gangster Joey Gallagher, hence the investment of his life savings in junk-stock, and his desire to do "things that might have happened in a movie," which prompts him to rape and ultimately impregnate his girlfriend Catherine. Every leap towards the life of masculine rebellion embodied by Gallagher only deepens the fatal logic of the novel: saddled with impending fatherhood and in need of a job, Studs's final act of defiance, smoking in a cold winter rain instead of looking for work, lands him on his death bed with the flu.

It would be tempting to conflate Farrell's critique of Hollywood with the judgments of nineteenth-century realists such as Howells or Dreiser. Indeed, realism was said to have returned in the 1930s as the dominant literary mode, thus placing the radical critiques of film, radio, and tabloids leveled by 1930s novelists within a definite lineage. John Dos Passos's great epic of the 1930s, *The Big Money* (1933), one of the most critically celebrated novels of the decade on its release, is as much a critique of Wall Street as it is a critique of newsreels, Hearst journalists, advertisers, movie stars, and songwriters. Like other radical novels of the decade, such as Robert Cantwell's *Land of Plenty* (1935), John Steinbeck's *The Grapes of Wrath* (1939), and Nelson Algren's *Somebody in Boots* (1935), the fictitious capital represented by the "big money" of Wall Street finds its allegorical double in the fictitious lives Hollywood and Madison Avenue present for US Americans to consume. The big money that lures Charley Anderson from his honest work as an inventor and mechanic is no different from the life in motion pictures that lures and then destroys Margo Dowling, who cannot move from silent pictures to "talkies" because her working-class Brooklyn accent is deemed unsuitable for a national stage: no voice in the text can overshadow "the colorless glare of klieg lights" that both illuminates and obscures them (bk. 3, sec. 5). It seems telling that the final character to whom we are introduced is an advertising man who most cleanly articulates the logic of the machine, someone who will not let "acquaintance stand in the way of efficiency at the office": mass culture is fully integrated into the "great imperial steamroller of American finance" that destroys everything it touches (Dos Passos 1926, "The *New Masses* I'd Like").

Despite such scathing critiques, as well as a political and formal inheritance from their predecessors, the novelists of the 1930s experienced a far greater intimacy with mass culture than the writers of the late nineteenth and early twentieth centuries.

By the late 1920s, mass culture was ubiquitous and penetrated spaces previously thought immune to its influence. The radio and phonograph replaced the concert and the live band in the same way the movie theater replaced vaudeville and the minstrel show. The 1930s and 1940s were the heyday of the motion picture industry, with over half of all Americans seeing at least one film per week. At its peak, the film industry could boast that two-thirds of Americans consumed as many as three to four features in a month. The historian Warren Susman calls "the Progressives . . . people of the book" and "the children of the 1930s . . . people of the picture and the radio" (1984, 161). Unlike the world of the turn of the century, the novel could no longer be thought of as a form that could compete with the blockbuster or the radio show. Henry Luce, the archconservative who invented modern news coverage with his flashy photography magazines *Time* and *Life,* articulated this new relationship with mass culture in an influential essay, "The American Century": "American jazz, Hollywood movies, American slang, American machines and patented products, are in fact the only things that every community in the world . . . recognizes in common" (qtd. in Denning 1998, 44). As much as progressives may have reviled him, Luce was correct to say that Americans in the 1930s experienced a shared mass culture.

But it was an expanded mass culture, no longer targeting the genteel sensibilities of the middle-class. As scholars such as Lizabeth Cohen, Michael Denning, Roland Marchand, and David Stowe point out, the new "CIO working class" were themselves the mass audience of the emerging entertainment industries (Denning 1998, 39). The urban, multiethnic working class who formed the new militant Congress of Industrial Organizations (CIO) was seen as the primary consumers of the new cultural apparatus of radio, swing music, photojournalism, and film. As a result or perhaps as a cause of this shift, working-class ethnic Americans for the first time saw themselves not only as the objects but also the subjects of the new culture industries. The gangster film, the mass marketing of jazz, comic books, and mass spectacle sports like baseball often featured Americans who themselves played plebeian characters and/or had plebeian roots: Humphrey Bogart, Paul Robeson, E. G. Robinson, James Cagney, John Garfield, Cab Calloway, Benny Goodman, Duke Ellington and Barbara Stanwyck changed the face and the voice of national culture in the 1930s by starring in glamorous working-class roles and popularizing working-class music. Many of the most popular films of the 1930s and early '40s—*The Public Enemy* (1931), *Little Caesar* (1931), *Kid Galahad* (1937), *The Grapes of Wrath* (1940), *The Wizard of Oz* (1939), *Tom Sawyer* (1930), *Jesse James* (1939), *Golden Boy* (1939), *High Sierra* (1941), and others—featured not only working-class characters but a working-class identity and working-class grievances as central concerns of the film. Despite its conservative message and racist depictions of black jazz performers, even *Dumbo* (1941) features the working-class Brooklyn accent of Timothy Q. Mouse, has clowns that protest for a raise, and projects the media as the central avenue by which Dumbo will escape his fate as an outcast.

This new relationship between class and mass culture is perhaps best revealed in Clifford Odets's famous agitprop play about a New York City taxi cab strike

"Waiting for Lefty" (1935), which now stands as shorthand for the entire field of radical cultural movements in the 1930s. The strikers croon radio songs, dance to the phonograph, imitate Mickey Rooney, and go on strike not in order to be able to afford a house in the suburbs or to fund a revolutionary party, but rather to promote a Hollywood romance. The entire presentation of the union and the drama depends less on what we think of as the "realism" of an earlier generation than on a kind of pop culture grotesque: the presence of the cigar smoking gangster, the vaudeville figure of "Fatts," the two brothers on opposing sides in the "Labor Spy Episode," the forbidden lovers, even the "Communist salute" comprise a sort of Bug's Bunny "upper-cut to the chin." "Lefty" is not a critique of mass culture so much as a full-scale absorption of it into a strike play, taking as its material established character, story, and plot types from pulp magazines and radio. Indeed, the saccharine promises of romance and plenty promoted by mass culture spur the working-class characters into action. Thus to understand the cinema scene in the *Studs Lonigan* trilogy, we can think of 1930s literature as if it were not about, but rather told through the point of view of, Dreiser's Carrie Meeber, a working-class subjectivity that is fully embedded within mass culture as its central frame of reference.

As historian Lizabeth Cohen writes, young, working-class children of immigrants like Odets "used mass culture to create a second generation ethnic working-class culture" that allowed them to feel located in the fragmented and often alienating environment of the urban United States (1990, 357). Many of these second-generation working-class ethnic writers like Odets also experienced class advancement through the new culture industries, as Hollywood, magazines such as *Life* and *Time*, and the Works Progress Administration art projects hired hundreds of thousands of new workers who had not previously expected to produce culture for wages. One signal of the change in perspective came as the Communist Party newspapers the *New Masses* and the *Daily Worker* began covering Hollywood films with increased seriousness and expectations in their film review section, although only seldom with unguarded approval. While Odets seems to celebrate the revolutionary potential of mass culture and Farrell satirizes his failed character's worship of it, there is no critical vantage point from which these characters—or the writers—can operate outside of it. Thus what brings Dos Passos and Odets together is a shared assumption that writers must engage with mass culture if they expect to be relevant to a politicized readership.

From the Brown Bomber to Bigger Thomas: The Devolution of a Celebrity Icon

Several years before the 1940 publication of *Native Son*, Richard Wright penned a number of short essays and articles about the African American heavyweight-boxing champion Joe Louis for the Communist Party's two main journals, the *New Masses* and the *Daily Worker*. Nicknamed "the Brown Bomber," Louis was hailed as a celebrity among African Americans for defeating the white heavyweight champion Max Baer and among antifascists for defeating Germany's Max Schmeling, the German boxer promoted by the Nazis as an example of the superiority of the Aryan race. Louis's nickname served as a metonym for the military struggle against fascism as well as a racial struggle for equality, thereby fusing the domestic politics of antiracism with the international fight against fascism in one pop-culture celebrity moniker. Wright opens his first article, "Joe Louis Uncovers Dynamite," in the October 8, 1935, issue of the *New Masses,* with the spontaneous "tidal wave" of joy in Chicago's black South Side after the 1935 defeat of Baer by Louis for the heavyweight championship. Describing the "explosion" of working-class black men from "beer taverns, pool rooms, barber shops, rooming houses and dingy flats" into the streets, Wright explains the meaning of Louis's victory in political terms: experienced through radio broadcasts, it "ripped loose" the racial unconscious of the city, as both blacks and whites understood Louis as "a consciously felt symbol[,] . . . the triumph of black over white."

To the extent that Louis was a celebrity icon and a media spectacle, Wright suggests that mass culture can play a crucial role in tapping a "pent up folk consciousness" for political, even revolutionary goals. As critic Christopher Vials points out, Wright refuses to focus on the media icon as a celebrity rather than the Brown Bomber's impact "on ordinary people and their political consciousness" (2009, 11). Mass culture for Wright becomes the central way that people experience politics, engage in collective acts, and "*feel*" racially as well as politically (on Richard Wright and the racialization of mass media, see chapter 32 in this volume). The notion that mass culture could play a positive role in democratic movements links it to earlier sentimental protest texts through the emphasis on feeling, yet removes it from the world of the literary altogether, creating a radical text out of a media event. As Cohen points out, mass culture in the 1930s created a shared cultural terrain by which workers otherwise separated by class, race, gender, or geographical difference could find common ground. Indeed, Cohen reports a different racial matrix created by the Baer-Louis fight, as both white and black workers, during a CIO organizing drive, supported Louis and even listened to the boxing march while attending a membership meeting. And either way the fight is interpreted, Cohen shares with Wright the assumption that mass culture created a crucial symbolic matrix within which the fight for working-class political change occurred.

Yet as Vials and others point out, Wright's celebratory portrait of mass culture and sports stands in sharp contrast to his portrait of Bigger Thomas in *Native Son.* If the Brown Bomber served as a site of racial pride and progressive political change, Wright's portrait of Bigger reminds us that mass culture remained a key force in maintaining a racial formation of white dominance, which relied on repeated images of black perversion and pathology to retain its hegemony. Much like Studs Lonigan, Bigger's entire imaginative field is a product of mass culture, as he unconsciously models himself on dime-magazines, films, and newspapers in order to project a tough-guy gangster persona. Bigger expresses a physiological desire for media images: "He wanted to see a movie; his senses hungered for it" (bk. 1). His constant search for stimuli to distract him from a desperate sense of being trapped is temporarily relieved only by "swing music," "movies," sex, or in "violent action," which often mimics the gangster films and sensational tabloids he reads. Bigger's relationship to whites and his understanding of the Daltons is also mediated through cinematic images of white wealth and power. Viewing the Daltons on a newsreel before he is to report to work, he is seduced by their near-celebrity fame, convinced he is going on to "something big" (bk. 1). Indeed, Bigger borrows the entire ransom-plot from a detective novel and, as Vials points out, spends his last "two cents" on a tabloid to read about "his story" (bk. 3).

Yet unlike Studs, Bigger has no way to imagine himself a hero: there is no black equivalent of Gallagher on which to model himself. As much as his ransom plot is ripped out of detective magazines, his attempt at mastery does not simply end in an anonymous death as it does for Studs. Rather, he ends up as part of the mass culture spectacle that he attempts to master. In an amazing scene in which Wright displays how images of race are constructed through the mobilization of black bodies, journalists lead Bigger back to Mary's bedroom to photograph him reenacting what they believe to be his murder of Mary: "Bigger's lips pulled back, showing his white teeth. Then he blinked his eyes; the flashlights went off and he knew in the instant of their flashing that they had taken his picture showing him with his back against the wall, his teeth bared in a snarl" (bk. 3). As critic Joseph Entin suggests, the flashbulbs are "analogous to pistols," literally framing Bigger within a fatal entanglement of media images and carceral violence that close around him ever more tightly despite, or rather because of, his efforts to resist (2007, 242). As Wright lifted racist lines directly from the sensational crime reporting of a young African American accused of murdering a white woman, he revealed how African Americans are conscripted into media narratives that serve to further their subjugation. One could frame Bigger's entire series of actions, from his plot to rob Blum's cafeteria to his attempt to extort ransom from the Daltons, as a commentary on how the same visibility hungered for by Studs Lonigan is a literal trap for African Americans.

So how do we square the space between Wright's readings of Joe Louis and Bigger Thomas? As Entin points out, the one media image Bigger most resembled was not a tabloid murder suspect but another sensational figure that crashed astride a major US metropolis: the 1933 King Kong. Bigger's very name implies a kind of giantism, a resemblance to Kong furthered by the accusation leveled against both: the illicit sexual liaison with a white woman. Kong's death atop the Empire State Building is reproduced as Bigger's fall from the water tower—in the same way the airplane emerges in both texts as an image of white modernity. Entin suggests, though, a crucial difference between Kong and the tabloid stories of black depravity, for Kong is both an object of both fear and sympathy. Indeed, the film reproduces white fears about blackness as much as it slyly challenges them. King Kong's ambivalence about the meaning of its monster marks him as an intriguing figure for Wright, resembling *Native Son*'s own ambivalence about its protagonist.

As Wright biographer Michel Fabré reports, Wright himself was an avid consumer of sensational horror and detective films and magazines. Indeed, *Native Son* is as much a critique of the racialization of the mass media as an homage to the very genres of horror and detective fiction that Bigger "hungers after." Wright poses the question to readers that he refuses to answer: do we derive social insight or titillation from the fast-paced litany of crimes committed in the novel by and against Bigger? As much as we can think of *Native Son* as a critique of mass culture, we must acknowledge that it is also a strategic redeployment of a system that produces sympathetic black monsters and racial heroes. As Nelson Algren wrote to Wright after *Native Son*'s publication, "it is the best detective story I've ever read" (qtd. in Entin 2007, 237).

Tom Joad Goes to Hollywood: Folk Culture for the Silver Screen

Few cultural icons of the 1930s were as well known as John Steinbeck's Joad family, the protagonists from his 1939 novel, *The Grapes of Wrath*. An immediate success upon its publication, *The Grapes* is the second-best-selling novel in US history, and the plight of the Okies in California stands as a metonym for the entire era. Many elements of the novel account for its shaping of the cultural memory of the late 1930s—its linking of class struggle with the national origin myth of the yeoman farmer, its celebration of populist and often socially conservative values, its embrace of the New Deal. Yet its endurance results in part from its massive proliferation, its position within an entire field of 1930s cultural production. Dorothea Lange's images for the Farm Security Administration, including her famous "Migrant Mother," Margaret-Bourke White's and Erskine Caldwell's bestselling photo essay *You Have Seen Their Faces* (1937), James Agee's and Walker Evans's *Let Us Now Praise Famous Men* (1941), Roy Styker's documentary film *The Plow That Broke the Plains* (1936), Woody Guthrie's *Dust Bowl Ballads* (1940), and of course, John Ford's film adaptation of Steinbeck's novel placed the white farmer at the center of debates around the causes of the Depression and fixed the perception that the vanishing yeoman was synonymous with the economic and social collapse of the country. The Joad story gestures to ways in which the left-wing writers not only incorporated mass cultural forms into their work but were themselves integral parts of larger mass culture narratives.

There is some irony in the rise of *The Grapes of Wrath* as a sensation, since the novel is highly critical of mass culture. Bing Crosby, movie stars, and picture magazines appear sparsely, and when they do, they belong to the artificial world of truck stops, resort towns, and other "mechanistic" elements that, like the tractor, conspire to make the Joads strangers in their own land (ch. 15). The only film to emerge in the novel in its entirety is recounted contemptuously by a pair of migrant farm-workers, who narrate the story of a "rich fella" who "makes like he's poor" and "this rich girl" who "purtends like she's poor too" until they "got married" (ch. 23). The absurdity of Hollywood conceits as well as Hollywood subject matter—rich people feigning poverty in the midst of a Depression—is exposed by the migrants who, because of their lack of familiarity with genres like romantic comedy, can see the class bias of the film for what it is. This small exchange between two migrants informs the cultural logic of the text: the retention of an organic folk culture by the Joads and their insight into the conceits of capitalism exist precisely because of their distance from its forms and institutions. The Joads are attached to the land, and in their attachment are both vulnerable and resistant to the mechanical culture set on replacing them. Unlike the film that mocks the migrants' poverty, the dances held at the Weedpatch camp are "decent" and grant the migrants "respect" (ch. 23). The mechanical arm of the juke box at a truck stop is contrasted with the harmonica "you can mold with curved hands" and the "deep strings of the guitar beating like a heart" the migrants play for themselves. And unlike the movie stars who have "pills, powders, fluids, jellies" to make "their sexual intercourse safe, odorless, and unproductive," an anonymous "Texas boy and girl" walk out into a moonlit night in a field together after a migrant square dance (chs. 15, 23).

It is not surprising that the greatest success of the left in the arena of mass culture bore little resemblance to the urban, ethnic, working-class cultural politics of the era. As historian James Gregory notes in *An American Exodus*, the massive labor strikes in California in the 1930s and the culture of solidarity that extended to Los Angeles and San Francisco from the Central Valley were largely based in Mexican and Filipino American communities, not those of white migrants from the South and Southwest. Arguably what made the *Grapes* narrative so commercially successful and available for mass distribution was not that it represented this new social movement, but rather that it staged popular class conflict within the comfortable terrain of already existing Hollywood genres: the Western, the outlaw, and the pioneer narrative. *The Grapes*'s narrative cut across so many of the emergent culture industries of the 1930s, from Hollywood to federal agencies to slick magazines like *Life* to the recording industries, because it managed to fuse genres that a studio executive system already understood and adopted.

In Denning's crucial distinction, we can think of *The Grapes*'s narrative less as an example of left-wing mass culture than as mass culture "enabled" by the left wing (1998, 268). While the left manifested ambivalence toward mass culture in the 1930s, much of the left's role in theater, film, radio, and music involved the artists' negotiating the medium within the confines of the studio or government system. Clifford Odets's transition from Group Theater to Hollywood involved great compromises on his part, such as his somewhat unsuccessful attempt to make the Yellow Peril film *The General Died at Dawn* (1936) into an allegory for the Spanish Civil War, yet he was ultimately in charge of which words appeared in the final script. Ford's filmic rendition of *The Grapes* was neither written nor acted by anyone even vaguely associated with the left. Nor does Steinbeck's iconoclastic role as an author resemble the emergence of Odet, Wright, or Dos Passos to nationwide fame within left-wing institutions. Unlike the rise of film noir, which often entailed a bitter struggle between executives and left-wing directors and writers, the most emblematic film of the Popular Front was not a Popular Front production. And despite the engagement, savvy, and sophistication of 1930s radical writers about mass culture, the success of *The Grapes* suggests that the studio and news media system, not left-wing cultural producers, ultimately decided the forms through which progressive class struggle could be represented on the national stage.

The complex relationship between the left and mass culture in the 1930s and 1940s was resolved, ultimately, by the dawn of the Cold War in 1948. The toll the red scare took within the culture industries cannot be underestimated. Not only were countless individuals hounded out of film, book publishing, journalism, and music, but the organizations that supported the sustained presence of the left within them were banned or collapsed under the weight of anticommunist hysteria. The shutdown of organizations such as the left-wing Conference of Studio Unions, the Screen Cartoonists' Guild, the Hollywood Anti-Nazi League (renamed Hollywood League for Democratic Action), the American Writers' Congress, and the Hollywood Peace Mobilization, together with the anticommunist closure of the Federal Theater and Federal Writers' Project, hampered the left's ability to intervene in cultural production, let alone produce an alternative. The one attempt to do so, Herbert Biberman's and Michael Wilson's collaboration with a left-led miners' union to produce *Salt of the Earth* (1954), was blacklisted in the United States and the legal challenges to its censorship bankrupted Biberman's fledgling film company. Yet despite the crackdown on left cultural production, the influence the left had in shaping the culture industries has left an indelible imprint on American culture. As Denning notes, the introduction of working-class subjects into film, music, and theater remains a marker of "American" culture, as plebian accents in everything from rock n' roll to political advertisements can trace their lineage to the cultural transformations of the 1930s. Likewise, as Vials writes, the advance of realism in American cinema as its dominant mode reflects the influence of the left on cinema's golden age of the 1930s. And although the nineteenth- and twentieth-century novel was often critical of mass culture, its development was inseparable from the constitution of both popular culture and popular political movements.

34

THE MAKING OF AMERICAN LITERATURE

BY ELIZABETH RENKER

The chronological framework of this volume provides a useful lens through which to examine the curricular history of the subject area we call "American literature," which made its initial inroads in college and university curricula during these decades. Most studies of the canon to date have focused on the status of particular authors and books, a focus that, while enormously valuable, has nevertheless obscured the important history of school subjects themselves as a distinct knowledge category. Since school subjects provide the broader knowledge categories that justify the inclusion of individual authors and texts in the curriculum, they serve as a crucial mechanism of canonical transmission. As in the case of authors and books, subject areas are not transhistorical; they must also negotiate their value and place in the broader social arena through complex social mechanisms. As Richard Hofstadter and C. DeWitt Hardy point out, the evolving historical incarnations of the curriculum serve as "a barometer by which we may measure the cultural pressures that operate upon the school" (1952, 11). John Guillory's pathbreaking work on canon-formation points out that "the debate over the canon concerns what texts should be taught in the schools, [but] what remains invisible within this debate—too large to be seen at all—is the school itself" (1993: 8, 38).

My focus in these pages is how the subject that we call "American literature" negotiated the transformation from noncanonical to canonical within the school system. I will show that American literature's image as a school subject was tied, for specific material reasons, to lower-level and non-elite kinds of schools, teachers, and students. These forms of social inferiority were in turn ascribed to the nominal content of "American literature" as a body of texts. We might consider this phenomenon to be an instance of social metonymy, by which I mean that American literature's alleged inferior "intellectual" status derived from its initial connections with the nonelite school populations to and by whom it had primarily been taught—not from the inherent quality of its books. This social metonymy blocked the subject's ascent up the curricular ladder into the realms of higher scholarship in colleges and universities. In short, the alleged inferiority of American literature to more serious forms of knowledge, which hampered its rise into college and university curricula until at least World War II, arose from the specific material factors that shaped its life as a school subject in the broader fabric of nineteenth-century America.

A changing university culture arose in the United States in the 1870s, shaped by the new phenomena of the research university and the PhD credential. As American literature tried to establish a place in this new culture, it met resistance for two reasons: on the one hand, its relation to lower-level schools, including their social functions and specific student and teacher populations; and, on the other, its relation to the still very new field of college- and university-level "English." (For ease of reference, I will use the term "lower schools" to refer to all schools teaching at or below the secondary level, and "higher schools" to designate colleges and universities.) Departments of English would become the primary (but not exclusive) curricular home for American literature in the new world of higher education, and those same departments would also become its primary antagonists.

In 1870, American literature had not yet entered college and university curricula in the United States. Half a century later, in the 1920s, a professional field began to consolidate, establishing academic journals, graduate programs, and professional organizations; producing a growing body of published research; and solidifying a canon. By 1940, the subject was on the brink of acquiring a regular curricular place across the nation, a result of the nationalism arising from World War II. My concern in these pages is not these important hallmarks of field formation, which have been covered in able detail by scholars like Kermit Vanderbilt's *American Literature and the Academy: the Roots, Growth, and Maturity of a Profession* (1986), Gerald Graff's *Professing Literature: An Institutional History* (1987), and David R. Shumway's *Creating American Civilization: A Genealogy of American Literature as an Academic Discipline* (1994). Instead, I will focus on the earliest decades during which the field was making its way into college and university curricula, a period not of consolidation and curricular gains like those of the 1920s, but of irregular status, curricular fluctuation, and setbacks.

Some colleges and universities routinely offered American literature beginning around 1880, but it was more typically the case that the subject was marginalized or omitted entirely. Marginalization took many forms. Curricular offerings often restricted American literature classes to lower-level undergraduates, for example; in many other cases, they placed American literature in remedial or nonacademic programs. Space constrains me from exploring the extensive and surprising alternate curricular locations quite typical for American literature during this period of uncertain identity, which include such domains as the scientific schools, agricultural schools, and normal schools, all of which served very different social purposes from postsecondary English at this time. American literature found space in such programs even when "English" was keeping it out. Even at the individual colleges and universities that taught American literature, its status was often erratic. It might, for example, enter the curriculum for a year or two, only then to vanish, often when an individual faculty member teaching the subject left or was fired.

Standard accounts of the field tend to obscure the meaning of this bumpy and erratic history by reinterpreting it teleologically from the standpoint of the post–World War II era's gains. Often written by the field's own advocates and practitioners, such accounts tend to comb the history for "pioneers," celebrating their forward thinking without trying to assess the omissions, failures, false starts, partial successes, and other fluctuations that were characteristic of American literature's status within the broader curricular fabric of the emergent school system. But it is in the particular contours of this uneven history that we see the new subject area negotiating its image problem; the bumps, failures, and false starts reveal many of the points of cultural anxiety, uncertainty, and pressure that progressive histories leave out.

American Literature and Lower Schools

The school subject called "American literature" found its earliest homes in secondary and grammar schools. As William J. Reese shows in *The Origins of the American High School* (1995), high schools, first established in Boston in 1820 as a practical educational alternative to the classical college preparatory academies, regularly offered American literature classes by 1870. While the classical academies trained students in Latin and Greek to prepare them for college, the high schools instead offered curricula for students—radically, including girls—who were not college bound. Educational parlance of the day called this non-classical curriculum "the English branches." Today we have utterly lost touch with what "English" meant in the nineteenth century. At that time, "English" denoted modern rather than classical subjects, including the modern languages (English, French, German, and Spanish) rather than ancient ones, and included practical subjects like bookkeeping, business correspondence, and penmanship. All these curricular areas were parts of "the English branches." This new, practical form of education was very popular with parents and students. From their standpoint, the English branches educated students for real, modern life, which the antiquated classical curriculum failed to do.

The fact that American literature occupied a growing space in high school curricula, when it received no attention in colleges, established a cultural semiotic by which the subject area itself became affiliated with the social populations and functions attached to the high schools. Remember that high schoolers were nonscholars seeking terminal education and then headed for practical pursuits, rather than higher study. Female high school graduates mostly moved into homemaking or lower-level teaching, and male graduates headed to business. American literature's place in this school system gave rise to its image as a practical, easy, and nonscholarly subject. This material dynamic was the origin of American literature's curricular inferiority as it tried to move up in level, an inferiority ascribed by its opponents to the content of the subject rather than to the history of its social functions in American schools.

Even advocates of American literature defined it as suited to lower levels of education. The influential Boston author and editor Horace Scudder, a prominent educational theorist with a special interest in the place of literature in primary and secondary schools, vigorously advocated a curricular role for American literature—but in lower schools only. In his editorial role at Houghton, Mifflin & Company, a major textbook publisher of American literature for lower schools, his Riverside Literature Series (begun in 1882) made unabridged American classics available in cheap school editions, selling for fifteen cents apiece. By 1888, according to Ellen Ballou in *The Building of the House*, the series had sold one hundred thousand copies. In his lecture "The Place of Literature in Common School Education" delivered before the National Education Association in July 1888, Scudder extolled the men he considered the great American writers: Bryant, Emerson, Longfellow, Whittier, Holmes, Lowell, Hawthorne, Irving, and Cooper. In keeping with the relative status of genres in relation to "greatness" at this time in history, note that most of these greats are poets, for complex reasons I can touch on only briefly here. They include both the higher genre status of poetry at this time and the relative youth of novels, the latter of which troubled mechanisms of literary judgment as the era understood them.

Arguing passionately for the inclusion of literature in the school curriculum, and specifically for the inclusion of works by these American authors, Scudder carefully stipulates that he construes American authors as appropriate material for lower-school children *only*. "I am not arguing for the critical study of our great authors in the higher grades of our schools," Scudder explained. "They are not the best subjects for critical scholarship; criticism demands greater remoteness, greater foreignness of nature. . . . I am arguing for the free, generous use of these authors in the principal years of school life" (1888, "Place," 27–28). Scudder's address thus defined American literature as a body of texts suited to the work of elementary instruction rather than advanced "critical scholarship," at least in part because it lacked "remoteness" and "foreignness of nature." We cannot overstate the importance of such a definition of American literature as inherently elementary, and, indeed, inappropriate to higher levels of schooling, coming from an influential figure like Scudder, under the imprimatur of Houghton, Mifflin. Houghton, Mifflin was not only a major textbook publisher of American literature for lower schools, but also the publishing house that controlled the copyright for the leading American authors of the day and most influenced the shape of the national literary canon of the latter nineteenth century. Scudder would become editor of the leading literary magazine the *Atlantic Monthly* in 1890, which was owned by Houghton, Mifflin, meanwhile maintaining his role as a senior editor in their trade division.

We must set Scudder's remarks to the National Education Association in the context of the troubled school system at this time. In the closing decades of the nineteenth century, that system faced tremendous and complex pressures: handling a rapidly expanding student body; stratifying itself into effective grades and levels; working out the relations among levels of the system, for example, between grammar schools and secondary schools, and, in turn, between secondary schools and colleges; and standardizing pedagogies and curricula. In 1892, the National Education Association appointed a Committee on Secondary School Studies, which came to be widely known as the Committee of Ten, to address what Frederick Rudolph calls the "curricular disarray" troubling relations between secondary schools and colleges (Rudolph 1962, 165). Led by President Charles William Eliot of Harvard, in 1893 the committee established national protocols for public secondary schools, directing that they spend more time on "English" than any other subject, with 60 percent of that time, in turn, spent on "literature." The committee allotted composition only half as much time. The new rules also called for reading whole works rather than manuals of literary history. The manuals typically presented rosters of names and dates, and often included only excerpts or perhaps no texts at all, a pedagogy that had become outdated. Rhetoric, oratory, elocution, and old-style recitation, the previously dominant pedagogical uses of vernacular literature in schoolrooms (and a curricular place where American texts might appear prior to the establishment of "American literature" as such), were all facing the pressure of modern pedagogy. As Witt shows, during a time of rapid and thorough educational change, all these classroom staples came to connote empty practices leading to mindless memorization without comprehension. A new approach via "literature" appeared to offer a hopeful prospect for pedagogical improvement.

"Literature" textbooks like Scudder's responded to these new pressures and promises. Textbooks often drove what transpired in actual classrooms, just as, reciprocally, what the schools needed drove decisions by publishers who wanted to tap into an increasingly gigantic market. William Charvat notes that, between 1850 and 1870, "the population of the country increased about 68 percent, but attendance at public schools almost doubled—to six and one-quarter million" (1992, 303). The growing school system at the precollegiate level was a far greater influence on the literary market than were the colleges. By Charvat's estimate, the academies alone admitted ten times the number of students in the colleges. The colleges were also retrograde in orientation, still largely adhering to the classical curriculum. Curricular innovations occurred much more frequently at lower levels of the system, where "modern" subjects found earlier space. As Scudder points out, "It would be hard to compute the literary force which has found a field for exercise in the construction of school textbooks in America" (Scudder, "Place," 19).

But American literature's place in the lower-level schools and their textbooks would create particular obstacles to its curricular rise into the realm of knowledge as the new university culture defined it. For example, the Riverside Literature Series successfully marketed a particular American canon at a time when no such thing existed at the college level. We must stress the importance of the fact that the earliest American canon was one tailored specifically for the lower-school textbook market.

The Riverside canon included such works as Longfellow's "Evangeline" (which was the first number in the series) and "The Courtship of Miles Standish," Whittier's "Snow-Bound," Benjamin Franklin's *Autobiography*, Lowell's "Vision of Sir Launfal," Emerson's essays, and Irving's *The Sketch Book*. When American literature first appeared on college entrance exams, it did so by way of exactly these texts. They had trickled up from Riverside and similar textbooks and from the lower curricula they helped to shape. Between 1906 and 1911, for example, the required texts for the entrance exams to Smith College included "The Vision of Sir Launfal," Franklin's *Autobiography*, *The Sketch Book*, "The Courtship of Miles Standish," Emerson's essays, and other texts from the Riverside canon. Simply put, the American literature canon at the *precollegiate* levels became the earliest college and university canon.

Early College Classes in American Literature

American literature's inferiority in English departments had its origins in this social dynamic. Some empirical data about early American literature college classes will exemplify their lingering ties to a lower-school legacy. In 1893–94, Ella Adelaide Knapp taught an advanced course at Mount Holyoke College that offered a "critical study of the principal writers of America" (Annual Catalogue, 1893–94, 15–16, The Mount Holyoke College Archives and Special Collections, South Hadley, MA). Albert H. Smyth's 1889 *American Literature* was the textbook. A detailed student notebook reveals Knapp's heavy reliance on Smyth's book for the content of her lectures, common practice for teachers at this time. Classes that taught the textbook were a hallmark of an increasingly obsolete model of pedagogy, signaling a non-"expert" teacher—that is, a college teacher without an advanced degree. The student notes provide revealing data about what transpired in an early American literature classroom (notebook, "American Literature," 1893, Frances W. French, The Mount Holyoke College Archives and Special Collections, South Hadley, MA). Fred Lewis Pattee of Penn State, one of the earliest university-level professors of American literature, would lament in 1928, at the distance of almost thirty years from having published his own textbook, that what American literature needed most was to liberate itself from the "classroom thinking" represented by just such books (Pattee, 1928, 6).

Both Smyth's book and Knapp's class based on it focused on biographical and historical facts. Indeed, although Knapp both lectured and assigned textbook reading about authors, the students read relatively few of the primary texts. Instead, they learned contextual facts. When Knapp's student took notes about *Wieland*, for example, which she had clearly not read or been expected to read, she (presumably) transcribed from Knapp's lecture that it was "A horrible story drawn out to a great length just as the novel[s] in Eng[land] were at that time." In cases in which the class actually did read the works discussed, neither the lecture nor the student's notes interpreted the reading; they merely listed facts about it.

Knapp assigned five stories from Hawthorne's *Twice-Told Tales* and nine from *Mosses from an Old Manse*, but the lecture did not discuss any of this reading. Interpreting the content of the texts as we do today was simply not part of classroom work. It is additionally notable that almost none of the assigned tales remains in today's Hawthorne canon. The assigned stories were "Little Annie's Ramble," "Sunday at Home," "The Gentle Boy," "A Rill from the Town Pump," and "The Village Uncle" (from *Twice-Told Tales*) and "The Fire Worship," "A Select Party," "Birds and Bird Voices," "Drowne's Wooden Image," "The Intelligence Officer," "Skeletons from Memory," "The Old Apple Dealer," "The Artist of the Beautiful," and "A Virtuoso's Collection" (from *Mosses from an Old Manse*). Thus although Hawthorne, perhaps the first canonical American author, remains a canonical author today, his individual texts have an alternative canonical history. Meanwhile, although the students did not read *The Scarlet Letter* for the class, Knapp briefly touched on it in her lecture. She summarized its importance by saying that it records "soul conflict" and that "Hester closes her life in great usefulness to others"; however, Knapp added, "Would not advise anyone to read Scarlet-Letter before 25 years old" (notebook, "American Literature," 1893, Frances W. French, The Mount Holyoke College Archives and Special Collections, South Hadley, MA). The seventy-one numbers published in the Riverside Literature Series by this time included eleven Hawthorne issues; they did not include any of his romances, but did include plenty of his tales and writings for children. When we talk about Hawthorne as one of the earliest canonical American authors from the vantage of modern terms, we do so only at the cost of eliding the actual use to which he was put in classrooms.

Knapp's class focused on packaging authors biographically as the textbooks had traditionally done. Washington Irving "was not good at books + not very obedient to his mother" and "One can get a knowledge of him from his books." Cooper, the second novelist most extolled in early American literature textbooks, "is the Sea novelist of America." Indeed, the class traces the lives and personalities of one author after another, particularly Poe, Emerson, and Hawthorne, who receive more attention than any other authors or periods. Of Emerson, the student writes: "He voices thoughts that awaken us fifty years later. He had blue eyes, dark brown hair, fair complexion, six feet tall, neither fleshy nor slim, voice like Wendell Phillips." The student notes, "We place Hawthorne at the head of letters" and goes on to express Knapp's rueful classroom remarks that the house he was born in "is now occupied by people who do not appreciate it." Poe, on the other hand, "inherited his love for drink," which, no doubt, in keeping with stereotypes of the day, follows from her earlier remark that "His father was Irish." Additionally, we learn that Hawthorne "Was not at all exclusive at College" but "Got in to as many scrapes as are good for a student." At the same time as the class records a biography-based assessment of American literature in keeping with an increasingly outdated pedagogy, one also finds a glancing awareness of emergent alternative criteria in English studies. The student reports of Thomas Jefferson: "He not only displayed his literary power in his private letters but also introduced the study of Anglo Saxon," a teacherly point that showed Knapp's awareness of English department preoccupations with philology at the time, however glancingly acknowledged in her own class (notebook, "American Literature," 1893, Frances W. French, The Mount Holyoke College Archives and Special Collections, South Hadley, MA).

A few years later, in 1896, the American literature textbook at the University of Washington was *Masterpieces of American Literature*, an 1891 volume that Riverside published at the request of "Boston school authorities for a collection of productions from American authors of distinction, especially suitable for use in the most advanced class of the grammar schools." The Boston school board "planned the book and approved every selection" (preface [iii]). Its contents derived mostly from the Riverside Literature Series, including selections by thirteen authors, along with biographical sketches: Irving, Bryant, Franklin, Holmes, Hawthorne, Whittier, Thoreau, Lowell, Emerson, Webster, Edward Everett (presented, like Webster, as a distinguished orator), Longfellow, and John Boyle O'Reilly.

The surprising inclusion of O'Reilly among an otherwise very typical list of American greats at this time merits attention. The biographical sketch of O'Reilly represents him as an Irish patriot, born in Ireland in 1844, naturalized in the United States in 1869, and a reporter and writer of "many noble poems," including the long poem included in this volume, "The Pilgrim Fathers" (*Masterpieces* 199–211). As Nina Baym shows in "Early Histories of American Literature: A Chapter in the Institution of New England," American literature textbooks published between 1882 and 1912 created a civic narrative founded on a portrait of New England, Anglo-Saxon origins, and the embrace of spiritual ideals, all part of a program to school immigrant and lower-class populations in compliance with the social system that disadvantaged them. Peter David Witt explains that the first Massachusetts compulsory education law, passed in 1852, led to an influx of immigrant children, especially Irish children, in school. Both the new industrialists and the older gentry "thought of the schools as an instrument of social control," equipping the working classes with practical skills while discouraging political agitation (Witt 67–68). The New England poets suited this program well; they functioned as reflective patriarchs imparting ideals and moral clarity. Adding a poem by an Irish immigrant lauding the Pilgrim heritage to the school textbook both acknowledged the particular "ethnic" population of the schools (a diversity gesture of its time) and kept even the Irishman consistent with the larger ideological message to be driven home.

The lower-level textbook was not the only problem with the 1896 American literature class at Washington. Both the institution itself and the teacher of the class connoted elementary status in the emergent culture of higher education. Indeed, my previous example from Mount Holyoke, of a woman's college class taught by a woman without an advanced degree, signaled the same marginal knowledge status. When the Territorial University of Washington opened in 1861, according to Charles M. Gates's *The First Century at the University of Washington 1861–1961*, one student was enrolled. The first two instructors at this "university" taught the primary, grammar, and high school grades. It was common for new universities, particularly in remote areas, to offer such remedial lower-level education, a necessity at a time when secondary education was erratic and unsystematized. By 1869, none of the thirty-eight students enrolled at Washington was yet taking collegiate-level classes. In 1886–87, the collegiate courses enrolled only three or four students in each class. The region was concerned primarily with the utilitarian business of its own rapid development rather than with sending its youth to college. The university faced a chronic lack of students, teachers, and resources. It closed twice for lack of money. It cobbled together the resources it could muster, including students and faculty with scant training. The fact that "American literature" showed up in curricula at such institutions helps us to understand why the subject had a reputation as elementary, unspecialized, and suited to less rigorous academic programs, even when taught at the college level. Here we can usefully oppose the curricular image of Greek at this time, the school subject of consummate difficulty, one to which concessions of ill-preparedness simply could not be made. The curricular presumption with American literature, on the other hand, was that anybody who could read English could either take it or teach it.

It was very important to the status of college and university-level English to ensure that the same could not be said of its own subject area. Here it is worth considering fluctuating relationships between English literature and American literature in these early decades. The teacher in charge of the English classes at the University of Washington at this time was Ellen J. Chamberlin, who actively taught American literature there. She had come to Washington in 1889 with a Mistress of English Literature degree (MEL) from Willamette University and with experience teaching at the elementary and secondary levels. As I show in " 'American Literature' in the College Curriculum: Three Case Studies, 1890–1910" (2000), she would be forced out of her job in 1897, when Washington replaced her with the English Department's first PhD hire, the Anglo-Saxonist Alfred F. Bechdolt (851–53).

The tale at Washington is emblematic of the larger institutional problem American literature faced. It was a regular course offering at a "university" still heavily tied to lower-level students, lower-level teachers, and remedial training, feeding the perception, from the standpoint of established universities, that it was part of more generally dumbed-down curricula for badly prepared students and taught by (female) teachers without advanced training. It is thus not at all surprising that, after Bechdolt took over English at Washington, he transformed the curriculum into a heavily philological one. American literature remained briefly as a no-credit class, then was entirely demoted to the university's secondary division, the University Preparatory School, and eliminated from the English Department entirely. Bechdolt's scientific approach to English broke the curricular connection Chamberlin had sustained between "English literature" and "American literature" as parts of a related study. Bechdolt the Anglo-Saxonist sustained no place at all in the English

Department for American literature. This particular kind of curricular demotion for American literature repeated itself across the United States as the PhD credential came increasingly to structure both higher education and English studies.

Obstacles from the Top Down: Status in English Departments

The emblematic case at Washington points to the problematic status of American literature within the new bureaucratic entity called the English Department. While English had itself percolated up from lower and non-elite schools, where, as noted earlier, the "English branches" first stood for all that was not classical and derived their popularity from that practical social function, by the mid-1880s, English had won its upward curricular battle for status against the reigning classical curriculum. By the 1890s, establishing one of the fancy newfangled "departments" of higher English was a hot fashion trend across the United States. "American literature" ran into two primary problems in the eyes of English, one of language and one of age.

As Guillory (2002) emphasizes, English departments at this time were departments of *language,* not of literature; they were part of the new knowledge culture of "modern languages" that increasingly replaced Latin and Greek. The force of this institutional fact, as well as its many residues in current practice, is one that our profession has mostly forgotten. The early English scholars, as historians of the profession have widely noted, built their professional status as experts on the practice of philology. As a scientific method that mapped the history of the English language, philology did not concern itself with literature as such, but with historical linguistics, particularly in the historically remote form of Anglo-Saxon. Its method was to explore textual artifacts as evidence of linguistic phenomena such as Teutonic vowel change. Although, as Gerald Graff has pointed out in *Professing Literature*, philology as a critical mode coexisted with other practices in these new departments, including the appreciative practices associated with belles lettres, the academic profession of English built its credibility in these early years on its claims to the scientific method by way of philology.

One charge from the standpoint of English departments was that the term "American literature" was meaningless *a priori*, an accusation we can only understand when we remember the linguistic orientation on which the field established its expertise. From this standpoint, the term "English literature" described writing in the English language, and therefore categorically included all writing in English, rendering the term "American literature" simply inadmissible. It is only by grasping this important element of the field history that we can comprehend the recurrent phenomenon whereby one textbook after another tries to establish working definitions of the terms "English," "English literature," and "American literature," crucial issues of credibility at the time.

In her 1897 *American Literature*, a widely used textbook targeted to high schools and colleges, Katharine Lee Bates of Wellesley College, an early advocate of American literature, wrote that "our literature, while in one aspect a branch of the noble parent literature of England, is rightly viewed also as the individual expression of an independent nation" (preface). Pattee strikes the same note in his 1896 *A History of American Literature: with a View to the Fundamental Principles Underlying Its Development, A Text-Book for Schools and Colleges*:

> The term *a literature* may be defined as "all the literary productions in a given language."
>
> By this definition English literature would embrace all the writings that have emanated from the race speaking the English language. The writings of America would, therefore, be only a branch drawing life from the great trunk of English letters (introduction).

Pattee's definition of "English literature" and his explanation of why "American literature" is a categorically illogical term are standard in such discussions. Having first granted that "American literature" is written in English, and therefore part of "English literature," he now stresses that, nevertheless, "American literature" is an independent category, in fact, "an exception, and the only exception, to the rule given above." "In no other case in all history," he writes, "have there been two distinct literatures written in the same language" (introduction).

Pattee's conceptually shaky attempt here to cede the point about language families, and yet simultaneously to carve out literary "independence," mixes political, cultural, and linguistic issues, finally asserting the "independence" of American literature as a category because of its political independence as a nation. This conceptual muddle is characteristic of his era. The confusion about the term "American literature" was only exacerbated by confusion adhering to the bureaucratically more powerful term "English," which also connoted mixed designations of a "race" (as the term was used at this time), a nation, and a language. But English was by now the site of bureaucratic power, and American literature had to try to respond to the way English managed its own professional terminology. As Guillory points out, the philologists determined the direction and orientation of the new university language departments, even though philology was not the only mode they practiced, and the "coincidence of bureaucratic reorganization with a moment of heightened prestige for science" enhanced their position (2002, 31).

A second foundational problem for American literature was the problem of age, or what Scudder called "remoteness" and "foreignness of nature." Specimens of the English language offered by this putative thing called American literature weren't old enough to invite the kind of philological investigation that the new English scholars prized. We must remember that higher English had wrested its own credibility from Classics, and its definitions of the idea of the "classic," as predicated or not predicated on age, would evolve over time. Scudder simply presumed the value of the idea of antiquity as a criterion when he commented that American authors "are not the best subjects for critical scholarship," since scholarship "demands greater remoteness, greater foreignness of nature." Importantly, "foreignness of nature," leveled on the ground of English as such, would have to inhere in older forms of the English language itself, rather than in productions of a so-called "foreign language."

We can see an anxiety in the early textbooks that nineteenth-century American literature, even if it existed, was simply too recent for adequate commentary. With its focus on historically remote materials, higher English certainly did not treat contemporary authors. In what becomes a nearly generic element of their introductions, American literature textbook authors address or sidestep the problem of assigning value to recent literature. William P. Trent opens his 1903 textbook *A History of American Literature 1607–1865* already hampered by this problem:

> For the period from 1830 to 1865 I have acknowledged to myself, and the reader will soon convince himself, that it is impossible to treat otherwise than tentatively and to a certain extent in impressionist fashion authors who have seemed almost a part of our own generation. Holmes and Lowell are not fitter subjects for the historian and critic as opposed to the appreciator than Tennyson and Browning are. Yet, as every one knows, the task of assigning the British poets their relatively proper places in their country's literature is one that must in the main be left to later generations. Nearly half the present volume, then, is not and cannot be a history of literature in the strictest sense of the term. (preface)

Brander Matthews' 1896 *An Introduction to the Study of American Literature* carefully explains that he concludes his volume with a chapter "devoted to the summary consideration of the condition of our literature at the end of the nineteenth century," but stipulates, "No living author is named in the text" (prefatory note). The chapter identifies two "noteworthy" "developments of fiction," "the international novel" and the "local short story" (ch. 18), and indeed does not name their practitioners—although the illustrations depict William Dean Howells and Samuel Clemens.

Demand from the Bottom-Up: Popularity

Scholars might have worried that American literature was not remote enough in age or language to warrant advanced study, but undergraduates found it vastly appealing on both counts. It was not written in a foreign language, not Greek, not Latin, not even Anglo-Saxon, the early English professor's compensatory response to the inferior image that English held in the minds of professors of Classics. It was not historically remote, but a part of recent history. It was, as later generations of college students might say, *relevant*. American literature was in fact consistently popular with undergraduates. For example, the third most heavily enrolled class at The Ohio State University in 1901–2 was the elective "American Authors." The most heavily enrolled class, the Introduction to English Literature, drew such numbers because it was a requirement. But the second and third most heavily enrolled were electives, "American Authors" and "Modern Novel" (Annual Report, 1902, The Ohio State University, 42, The Ohio State University Archives, Columbus, OH).

Indeed, one active strain of discussion defending American literature justified it as a subject not because it was "American" but because it was "modern," tactically turning the charge of historical youth into a virtue. This particular element of American literature's popularity is not the same as the nationalistic or civic model that Baym has usefully elucidated. Two world wars eventually consolidated the nationalistic rationale for American literature's curricular place, but the competing "modern literature" narrative coexisted with it in the nineteenth century, and the history of American literature studies has mostly lost sight of this justification. In this sense, American literature was modern literature before Modernism. N. K. Royse's *A Manual of American Literature. Designed For the Use of Schools of Advanced Grades* (1872) presents one such defense. Royse frames his textbook—yet another American literature mixed-level textbook—as a succinct overview of one of "the leading modern literatures" (preface). He defines "literature" as "works of taste and sentiment, such as poetry, romance, oratory, the essay, and history" ("General View"). Guillory (2002) points out that competing models of literary study in the nineteenth century include nation-based conceptions as well as genre-based conceptions like those we find in Royse, indices to an array of chaotic and frequently groundless attempts to determine the precise nature of the value of literary study in an age of scientific criteria. Utterly rejecting the criterion of historical remoteness, Royse includes only nineteenth-century materials. He argues that America's earlier literary productions were inferior, either because they were not genuinely literary (such as Puritan writings) or because they were "slavishly English" (such as seventeenth- and eighteenth-century poetry) ("General View").

Royse characterized his textbook as "a repository from which to draw selections either for reading or for declamation," marking it as the kind of textbook that was standard in the old-style classroom (preface). It was these kinds of textbooks that Pattee later, in 1928, insisted that American literature needed to replace with real scholarship if it was ever to become a serious college subject. Kate Sanborn of Smith College used Royse's textbook when she taught one of the very first college-level classes in American literature, in 1880 (Official Circular 8, 1881, Smith College, 11, Smith College Archives, Northampton, MA). In her 1915 memoir, *Memories and Anecdotes*, Sanborn noted that she considered the classical curriculum to be "brain-wearying," and that she energetically opposed her own teaching to it (96). In addition to using the Royse text, Sanborn's teaching methods were also increasingly dated. Her pedagogy was rooted in the lecture and the recitation method, the standard antebellum classroom fare now under pressure. The recitation consisted in a daily oral quiz throughout the academic year to test whether each student had memorized the lesson. Sanborn showed her ambivalence about the recitation method when she recalled proudly that during her years teaching at Smith she took questions from the class "for ten minutes at the close of every recitation" (Sanborn 1915, 116).

So although Sanborn embraced American literature as modern, she herself was a soon-to-be obsolete model of the teacher. As was the case at Washington, the entire profile of the Smith College class, one of the earliest in the nation, presents a crisp snapshot of American literature's image problem from the standpoint of the nascent culture of English departments and their PhD experts: a woman's college; a teacher without graduate-level training; a textbook for lower-level schools. Chamberlin and Sanborn were members of a corps of teachers eventually rendered obsolete by the new labor model of the PhD credential that increasingly defined the profession of college teaching.

The Emblematic Case of Albert H. Smyth

Albert H. Smyth, Professor of English Literature at the Central High School of Philadelphia and the author of Knapp's Mount Holyoke textbook, took on both the problems of language and age directly when he asked at the Modern Language Association Convention in 1887, "Is it because it is so *perilously modern* that we shrink from making of our literature a theme for public instruction? Is it because its language offers no peculiar attraction to the grammarian that certain learned and successful masters of English pronounce the subject to be 'so unsatisfactory'?" (Smyth 1888, 238; emphasis in original). Smyth's polemic that American literature was "highly serviceable in education because it admits of a complete severance of literature from philology" was in keeping with other forms of faculty resistance against philology at Central High School (Smyth 1888, 240). When, in 1880, the High School Committee of the Board of Public Education recommended that Central add to its teaching of English literature "the study of empiric and scientific etymology," and to change the name of the department to reflect that addition, the faculty refused ("Minute Book C.H.S. III 1872–1897," minutes of April 8, 1880 and April 22, 1880 meetings, The Central High School Archives, Philadelphia, PA).

The discussion that followed Smyth's MLA talk was preoccupied not with the American literature canon, but with the *level* of schooling at which American literature should be taught. Smyth polemically recommended its full inclusion at all levels of the curriculum: schools, colleges, and university seminaries. ("Seminary" was the original form of today's term "seminar." The Johns Hopkins University inaugurated the term in the United States, using it to designate its most advanced graduate classes. The term then spread both to other schools and downward to the undergraduate level. Departments adopted "seminaries" as a trendy mark of intellectual prestige, although in many cases it was simply a form of pretension that indicated nothing about classroom practice). Professor A. H. Tolman of Ripon College commented, "In the high-school and in the academy American literature has an important place . . . In the intermediate class-room, in the college class-room, which is where I teach,—into my class-room, American literature has not entered." The famous Hopkins philologist James W. Bright remarked that Smyth had "clearly marked the distinction between the various classes in which American literature could be studied, and the corresponding differences of aim and method in that instruction" (Bright and Tolman, qtd. in Smyth 1888, "American" 238, 240).

When Smyth spoke at MLA, as a fellow "Professor" to his college-level colleagues, Central High still conceived of itself as a school with advanced scholarly status. (The title "Professor," common in secondary schools in this era, applied only to male teachers.) One Central graduate of 1879, Thomas J. Van Ness, reported from the Harvard Divinity School that President Eliot of Harvard had "decided" that his Central degree was equal "with that of any other college or university of the land . . . It establishes a precedent which can be quoted, if need be, and may be of use to other graduates of the 'C.H.S.' who desire to enter this or any other of our great educational institutions" (letter from Thomas J. Van Ness, qtd. in the faculty minutes of December 8, 1881, The Central High School of Philadelphia Archives, Philadelphia, PA). Although at this time Central classified its teachers as "Professors," the Philadelphia school system would later strip this title from them as part of its program to standardize the public schools. It would concertedly try to bring Central into line with the rest of the secondary schools, efforts that Central faculty fought with passion, recognizing, correctly, that their own professional status in this highly transitional era was at stake (Minutes of faculty meeting, January 31, 1933, *Faculty Minutes From September 1931 to February 1939*, The Central High School Archives, Philadelphia, PA).

Smyth was not only a secondary schoolteacher but an early distinguished scholar of American literature, a meaningful conjunction in this era of mixed labor models and disciplinary transition. The PhD octopus, to use William James' memorable phrase, had not yet entirely altered the landscape, but was on the verge of doing so, and it rendered Smyth one of a vanishing breed. He published the already-noted American literature textbook, an excellent study of Philadelphia magazines, a biography of Bayard Taylor, and a distinguished edition of the works of Benjamin Franklin. He was a graduate of the institution at which he taught. David F. Labaree's *The Making of an American High School: The Credentials Market & the Central High School of Philadelphia, 1838-1939* (1988) points out that it was the second-oldest public high school in the United States; an all-male public school with a rigorous policy of competitive admissions; and a school widely known in its own time for providing outstanding education. It awarded degrees of BA by disposition of its charter. In addition to the BA Smyth earned at Central in 1882, Hopkins conferred an honorary AB on him in February 1887 (student file, Albert H. Smyth, The Ferdinand Hamburger, Jr. Archives, The Johns Hopkins University, Baltimore, MD). As biographers Albert Mordell and Franklin Spencer Edmonds point out, Smyth was a desperately impoverished student working in the Hopkins library while attending seminars in

English, including one taught by philologist Bright. His diary notes that he lived on hot chocolate and bread for long periods of time as he struggled to acquire an advanced education (Smyth, "Selections from the Diary of Albert H. Smyth," in Edmonds, 57; Albert Mordell, "Albert Henry Smyth: A Memoir," *The Barnwell Bulletin* 15.59 (1937), The Central High School Archives, Philadelphia, PA; Franklin Spencer Edmonds, *The Early Life of Albert Henry Smyth*, Philadelphia, PA: Associated Alumni of the Central High School, 1912, The Central High School Archives, Philadelphia, PA). Yet with his Central BA and his honorary AB, he still lacked a higher degree of the kind the new research culture valued.

Smyth exemplifies the cross currents of this age of transition. He was an early American literature scholar and a "Professor" in the subject, but he worked at a secondary school; he built a regular American literature curriculum at his own institution, but its status as a "college," as well as his as a "Professor," was changing. He had only an honorary university degree and therefore did not suit the labor model of new and growing PhD culture, and he stressed that American literature was not a philological subject, which he saw as its great promise in the classroom. In 1887, with complex battles of status in progress, Smyth's argument would not win the day—nor would the teachers like him. His credentials were soon entirely outdated.

Conclusion

Seen from the largest historical vantage, these irregularities and fluctuations in American literature's curricular status would only be resolved by the nationalism generated by two world wars, a potent force that would finally push American literature into a regular place in college and university curricula. While it would not earn the equivalent curricular space of the literature of Great Britain, American literature would become a standard offering across the nation. Yet we must remember that this partial resolution was a function of historical accident. And while the specific disciplinary formations that blocked the entry of American literature into the higher curiculum would change over time, American schooling and curricula would continue to evolve. The reign of philology, for example, would end, and modern literature assume its place as the focus of higher study in the discipline. Bias against "American literature," however, would persist under other guises even though the original grounds for such devaluation had vanished.

Guillory has traced what he calls the "residual effect" of early disciplinary forms, specifically the early and unresolved conflicts between language and literature that "trouble all subsequent versions of literary study" (2002: 19, 36). Even after the professional consolidations of the 1920s, Howard Mumford Jones would title a 1936 essay about American literature in *The English Journal* "The Orphan Child of the Curriculum." Scholars of American literature continued to cite persistent prejudice against American literature, especially in schools that had been shaped by a strong philological tradition. Even well after the curricular gains produced by World

War II, the inferior status of American literature would linger. J. Hillis Miller, to cite only one example, recently observed that, during his years at The Johns Hopkins University from 1953 to 1972, "American literature was marginalized, even scorned. Neither I, nor my colleagues, reflected that English literature is the cultural expression of a foreign country, a country moreover that we had defeated in a war of independence" (2009, 78). Such disciplinary residues would be based upon, even as they forgot, American literature's complex past in the social fabric of American schools.

35

THE FUTURE OF THE NOVEL AND PUBLIC CRITICISM IN MID-CENTURY AMERICA

BY PAULA RABINOWITZ

In his 1899 essay on "The Future of the Novel," Henry James declared the "prolonged prose fable" to be the most supple, malleable, capacious vehicle for conveying "impressions." Anticipating Mikhail Bakhtin's contention that the novel could give voice to competing and varied discourses, James claimed for the novel a preeminent place of "all pictures [as] the most comprehensive and the most elastic. It will stretch anywhere—it will take in absolutely anything. All it needs is a subject and a painter. But for its subject, magnificently, it has the whole human consciousness." James also understood that the novel was fundamental in its physical manifestation as a book: a technology that "is almost everywhere, and it is in the form of the voluminous prose fable that we see it penetrate easiest and farthest. Penetration appears really to be directly aided by mere mass and bulk." James saw how the "flare of railway bookstalls, . . . the shop-fronts of most booksellers[,] . . . the advertisements of the weekly newspapers and[,] . . . fifty places besides" would spread the book and its most "elastic" form, the novel, ensuring a new social compact among readers as the mass production and consumption of books opened areas previously closeted off from public scrutiny. With new readers—particularly the young and women of all ages—came new writers, "so we may very well yet see the female elbow itself, kept in increasing activity by the play of the pen, smash with final resonance the window all this time most superstitiously closed."

In this brief polemic, written at century's end, Henry James anticipated the shape of the twentieth-century novel. He also outlined the forms of its criticism, attending to ways in which "the future of fiction is intimately bound up with the future of the society that produces and consumes it." During the early years of the twentieth century, both the novel and its critics in America pushed its generic constraints to new limits by understanding the close link between formal innovations and social structures. Critics of the twentieth-century American novel restlessly sought clues to the future of society in the vibrant languages of the streets that were reconstructing American places in contemporary fiction. Paradoxically, they often did this through an obsessive return to diverse nineteenth-century writers only recently disinterred from critical neglect. This oscillation between currency and originality, on the one hand, and the curious need to resuscitate the nineteenth century as a continuous present, on the other, marked the varied approaches of mid-twentieth-century critics. It was language—vital talk—that connected experimentalism to realism.

For instance, in *Axel's Castle*, written in 1931, Edmund Wilson finds in Gertrude Stein's writing a wholly new method of novelistic realism, one indebted to Symbolism. Noting the original style of her 1909 novella, *Three Lives*, Wilson claims that Stein has

> caught the very rhythms and accents of the minds of her heroines: we find ourselves sharing the lives of the Good Anna and Gentle Lena so intimately that we forget about their position and see the world limited to their range, just as in Melanctha's case—and this is what makes her story one of the best as well as one of the earliest attempts of a white American novelist to understand the mind of the modern Americanized negro—we become so immersed in Melanctha's world that we quite forget its inhabitants are black (237–38).

While Wilson seems to be praising Stein's effacement of class and racial differences in her uncanny channeling of these three women's speech and sensibilities, what he also finds is that Stein has pioneered a new form of observation, one not interested in a "view of social conditions" from the outside in; rather she is interested in expressing interiority (on Stein's experimentation as a response to modernity, see Chapter 24 in this volume). She uses speech patterns, "the rhythmic repetitions[,] . . . the gradual unwinding of life" of "three fundamental types of women" (239, 238). Thus Stein has succeeded in making women's lives into a social category worthy of the novel—nothing new there as James Joyce, Henry James, or even John Cleland, author of the erotic 1748 novel *Fanny Hill,* knew—but in altering the terms of sexual difference, by aligning it as a social category dependent upon inner states of consciousness, she exploded the novel's content; her form became her content.

In *Three Lives* and *The Making of Americans* (written, in part, about her German-Jewish immigrant ancestors between 1902 and 1911, but not published until 1925), attention to the ordinary and quotidian, made strange through her "ruminative self-hypnosis" allows readers "to feel life as her people feel it, to take for granted just as they do the whole complex of conditions of which they are part" (Wilson 1931, 239; on Stein and interethnicity, see Chapter 13 in this volume). In so doing, Stein made possible, Wilson argues, the entire gamut of modern American literature by framing social formations as linguistic constructs:

> [w]e are still always aware of her presence in the background of contemporary literature—and we picture her as the great pyramidal Buddha of Jo Davidson's

statue of her, eternally and placidly ruminating the gradual developments of the processes of being, registering the vibrations of a psychological country like some august human seismograph whose charts we haven't the training to read. And whenever we pick up her writings, however unintelligible we may find them, we are aware of a literary personality of unmistakable originality and distinction. (252–53)

Wilson's recognition of Stein as a giant among modern American writers at the beginning of the 1930s, a decade that would see the rise of the social novel as the Depression refocused writers' attention to the structures of class relations, suggests that one must remember that even the most formulaic of proletarian novels was indebted to Stein's outlining of America as "a psychological country" forged in the linguistic innovations of its diverse population. His argument ran against the grain of critical assumptions that Stein's aesthetics forestalled social documentary. But Stein's imaginative attention to speech as a nonlinear mode *was* a form of close documentation of the social real. Stein herself provided a fitting outline of "How to Write" this new American novel the same year that Wilson celebrated her earlier works. A work of magnificent humor and insight, *How to Write* (1931) completely upends the grammar of the novel, in fact of literature in general, indeed of consciousness itself. This very personal exploration of the nature of composition—how to write quite literally—delves into the expressive evocation of words as they sonically, phonically, and philosophically interact with each other in sentences and paragraphs to make narrative, description, and conversation appear on the page and sing in the ear. In her succinct assessment, Stein exclaims, "A Sentence is not emotional a paragraph is" (ch. 2). She later insisted that this simple declaration was among her most important insights into writing: "Paragraphs are emotional not because they express an emotion but because they register or limit an emotion," she noted in her 1934 lecture on "Poetry and Grammar," published in 1935 as part of *Lectures in America*. Stein continues the lecture by pointing to a "fundamental" discovery within her graphic theory: "I found out about language that paragraphs are emotional and sentences are not and I found out something else about it. I found out that this difference was not a contradiction but a combination and that this combination causes one to think endlessly about sentences and paragraphs because the emotional paragraphs are made up of unemotional sentences."

Stein's interest in the limits of the paragraph and in their combinatory qualities offers an astute assessment of how American language and its novels work: with the oceanic borders of America setting geographical limits and the Americans themselves coming into being through a "making," literature needed to hear this simultaneous tension between enclosure and production, between the limit and the self-observant cast of linguistic making that tinkers with words endlessly. Those who make themselves make up as Americans. In "Arthur: A Grammar" (1931), for instance, the sheer exuberance of alliteration connects King Arthur to the author herself, asserting linguistic sovereignty as play, but also as political critique of militaristic presidential powers:

So good so beautiful but is it a grammar in chief.
From here to here in from there to there.
From here.
From here from here to from here to there.
Frown.
First time.
And obeyed here.
From here to here. Add obeyed to from here to from there to here.
Add obeyed to from here.

The ricochets of language—between, *here* and *there*, *frown* and *first*—could come from the pages of Dr. Seuss, who would begin his career as a cartoonist for the left-leaning daily, *PM,* a decade later. Stein's volume concludes with a nod towards that all-American genre, detective fiction, with "Forensics": "Forensics is in the state." In short, "Grammar is a conditional expanse," she posits of the space of American prosody. *How to Write* is hardly a work of "public" criticism, printed in a private edition of one thousand by Plain Edition published by Alice B. Toklas, Stein's partner, in Paris. Still, within years of its publication, Stein was delivering her popular "Lectures in America" and citing the insights of *How to Write* as foundational to her system of thinking America, thinking its system of narration, sounding the voices of its players.

If Wilson could discern in Stein's writing a curious amalgam of European influences—cubism and symbolism—and American idioms, he also understood that her writing "makes us laugh" because of both her humor and readers' scorn (1931, 244). "Widely ridiculed and seldom enjoyed, she has yet played an important role in connection with other writers who have become popular," he notes (252). Her musicality and attention to speech blurred distinctions between the literary and the critical, and, in such works as *Tender Buttons* (1914), which attends to nouns "as prose still-lifes" (Wilson 1931, 242), paved the way for the experiments in vernacular typical of novelists from Dashiell Hammett to Sherwood Anderson, and of course, most famously, Ernest Hemingway. Her work conveyed quotidian interior monologue as utterance, as sound, establishing the interconnection between private and public language so crucial to later developments in American social movements. She was writing at the dawn of radio, which moved public voices into domestic interiors, blurring the boundaries between the "grammar in chief" and the voices swirling in one's head.

The sounds of speech, especially the variegated accents of a country swelling with new immigrants, destabilized America as a nation, splintering it into incoherence, a state mirrored in new psychological theories of the individual. In his evocative assessment of Sherwood Anderson in his book on the Stieglitz circle, *Port of New York,* Paul Rosenfeld commands us to look closely at the ways in which mundane language, "the thin vocabulary of his inarticulate fellows" (1924, 186), induces a trancelike experience of "a gray and driven throng" (175). Like the crowd in T. S. Eliot's *The Waste Land* (1922) blindly "flow[ing] over London Bridge," American words, in Rosenfield's account, march forth in dull procession: "In the thick ranks of the newspapers they go drab and indistinct as miners trooping by grim factory walls in the latest dusk. Men's lips form them wherever in all the land talk is, but we mark their shapes no more than we mark those of the individual passengers in the subway press, the arm and overcoat jumble, each tired night at six" (175). Rosenfeld notes that Anderson's peculiar gift as an American writer—"The man's feeling for words, present always in him, reinforced one casual day when some one, expecting to produce a raw ha-ha, showed him *Tender Buttons* . . . "—is like "no fiction in America" (188–89). "[I]mpregnated with the inarticulate American," Anderson's prose builds a fragile world out of the inaudible; he forces us to hear as a public gesture the private silences of passivity, sickness, and loneliness and in so doing makes tangible and material the language of daily life and its myriad locations. The incursion of "demotic" speech (chided by Eliot) into American literature pushed the street vernacular of various regions into a national form with a distinctive history that foreground placing voices spatially.

Nothing declared this reconnection of language as material substrate of the terrain of America more clearly than the twin texts by two key modernists—D. H. Lawrence's *Studies in Classic American Literature* (1923) and William Carlos Williams's *In the American Grain* (1925)—which established through a methodology of citation and improvisation the form of criticism that would dominate the interwar years: a return to the source of American Letters. D. H. Lawrence, in his *Studies*, a wild quasipsychoanalytic investigation into the inner demons lurking amid American letters, discerned precisely the connection between American language—with its veneer of awkward simplicity—and what he called "the spirit of place." Written in the midst of the First World War, but not published until its aftermath, Lawrence's *Studies* understood the emerging power of American "reality," in his famous phrase: "Telephone, tinned meat, Charlie Chaplin, water-taps, and World Salvation, presumably. Some insisting on the plumbing, and some on saving the world: these being the two great American specialties" (1923, foreword). Commenting on this astute book during the horrors of the next World War, Edmund Wilson remarked, in his sweeping survey of American culture, *The Shock of Recognition*, on Lawrence's uncanny ability, born of his insider/outsider status as a sort of tourist of the bohemian Southwest, to see the nation as a location *within*, not separated from, the Western world as a whole. Of course, since Mark Twain (and even before, if only coyly and falsely, according to Lawrence, as in Hector de Crevecour's *Letters from an American Farmer* [1782]), vernacular speech had been the hallmark of an American literary language of place. What becomes clear, however, in the 1920s, the moment when modernism comes to America—a modern nation only finding modernism after the fact—is how modernism needed to be rethought retrospectively "in the American grain." As William Carlos Williams indicated in 1925, when he noted in the introduction to his idiosyncratic work of historiography by that name: "In these studies I have sought to re-name the things seen. . . . I have recognized new contours suggested by old words so that new names were constituted."

In his *Studies in Classic American Literature,* Lawrence, too, keenly felt the anachronism of America as a modernist nation: "The furthest frenzies of French modernism or futurism have not yet reached the pitch of extreme consciousness that Poe, Melville, Hawthorne, Whitman reached." The "old weird America," as Greil Marcus has called it, a deeply strange and dissociative sound that gestures toward atemporality, was augured by Lawrence: "The European moderns are all *trying* to be extreme. The Great Americans I mention just were it" (1923, foreword).

Williams's *In the American Grain*—which inspired Hart Crane to write *The Bridge* (1930)—does for "history" what Lawrence did for "literature": It listens to the sounds of the words uttered in print and orally by Puritans and their descendants as well as descendants of French and Spanish immigrants (such as his parents) and conquerors, slaves and indigenous peoples. For instance, Williams concludes his survey with Edgar Allan Poe (who bisects Lawrence's account at midpoint) by pointing to Poe's description of "America, the first great burst through to expression of a re-awakened genius of *place*" ("Edgar Allan Poe"). Like many American modernists—from the French-born filmmaker Robert Florey to expatriate Ezra Pound—Williams reanimates Poe as a modernist: "Sometimes he used words so playfully his sentences seem to fly away from sense, the destructive! with the conserving abandon, foreshadowed, of a Gertrude Stein. The particles of language must be clear as sand." Williams gives Poe the penultimate words in the American grain. (Lincoln gets final pride of place.) "On him is FOUNDED A LITERATURE," Williams declares ("Edgar Allan Poe"). He gives Poe this priority because, through a precision of mathematical elegance, Poe plumbed, in Lawrence's terms, "KNOWLEDGE." Where Lawrence finds Poe an "adventurer into vaults and cellars and horrible underground passages of the human soul," Williams extends the terrain: "The language of his essays is a remarkable HISTORY of the locality he springs from. . . . Seldom a long or sensuous sentence, but with frequent reduplication upon itself as if holding itself up by itself." America's originality is a construct of language—and this language paradoxically is reiterative and spatial, though not a "copy" of "the hard, sardonic, truculent mass of the New World, hot, angry": "Poe conceived the possibility, the sullen, volcanic inevitability of the *place*." No ideas but in things! And thingness tellingly is rock hard (sand, volcanic) words: "He counsels writers to *borrow nothing* from the scene, but to put all the weight of effort into the WRITING. Put aside the GRAND scene and get to work to express yourself. Method, punctuation, grammar—" What Williams declares, then, is that contrary to the sense, found in James Fenimore Cooper, for instance, that scenery and its description manifests place within American literature, it is the abstraction of language and its method as form that limns the landscape and reveals its history: "The whole period, America 1840, could be rebuilt, psychologically (phrenologically) from Poe's 'method'": a method that is essentially baroque and allegorical. Williams's attention to Poe's method calls for recognition of the method of *In the American Grain*, a method tellingly devoted to copying swaths of prose.

Williams wants us to see and hear the timbre and shape of the American language, how it names place, through extensive quotation—mirroring *avant la lettre* the methodology of exiled German philosopher Walter Benjamin's modernist critique *The Arcades Project* (written from 1924 to 1940, published in English in 2002)—and thus, like Benjamin, to walk through a place touching its fragmentary existence:

> Method of this project: literary montage. I needn't *say* anything. Merely show. I shall purloin no valuables, appropriate no ingenious formulations. But the rags, the refuse—these I will not inventory but allow, in the only way possible, to come into their own: by making use of them.
>
> How this work was written: rung by rung, according as chance would offer a narrow foothold, and always like someone who scales dangerous heights and never allows himself a moment to look around, for fear of becoming dizzy (but also because he would save for the end the full force of the panorama opening out to him). (Benjamin 2002, 460)

By collecting quotations, Benjamin attempted to create a form of surrealist scholarship responding to cinema by attention to the "art of citing without quotation marks. Its theory is intimately related to that of montage" (458). In so doing, he demonstrates the international spread of this form of citational criticism (and literary writing if one includes *The Waste Land* and James Joyce's *Ulysses* [1922] also) and reinforces Williams's identification of locations, words, and objects. My use of extended quotations throughout this essay sustains this process: if we are to take seriously the contributions of critics to American fiction, we must follow their words as closely as they followed American authors' prose.

In advocating the materiality of language, Williams and the other followers of Stein, The Mother of Us All (as she called Susan B. Anthony in the libretto to the opera she cowrote with Virgil Thomson in 1947), veered close to the theories of literary language developed by the Russian Mikhail Bahktin. Not entirely such a surprising connection: John Reed's *Ten Days That Shook the World* (1919) made clear, at least rhetorically, that the Russian revolution was directly connected to the American; Lawrence too connected the great Russian writers to those of Americans; each had produced a literature that had "come to a real verge" (1923, "Foreword"). This parallel was also elaborated in *Exile's Return: A Literary Odyssey of the 1920s* (1934), Malcolm Cowley's memoir/history of the "Lost Generation." Signaling Stein as origin, the second sentence of *Exile's Return* recalls her comment to Hemingway—"You are all a lost generation"—which Hemingway used as an epigraph for his first novel, *The Sun Also Rises* (1926). Yet the few references to Stein scattered throughout Cowley's book repeat what was by the mid-1930s clichéd, because she, with James Joyce, had become "popular authors, best-sellers in New York" (1934, 286), suggesting that her influence—like that of all mothers of wayward sons—was waning. She had become a convention, a shorthand, practically a joke, or at least a riddle. Stein "seemed, indeed, to be writing pure nonsense, and yet it was not quite pure: one felt uneasily that much of it could be deciphered if only one had the key" (148). Cowley's nod to Stein's influence is dwarfed by his attention to the eerie, but not quite similar, homologies between Fyodor Dostoyevsky, writing his preeminently Russian novel *The Possessed* (1872) while in exile, and America's first Nobel prize-winning author, Sinclair Lewis: "Change the names to Perkins or Schmaltz, change 'Russia' to 'America' or 'the Middle West,' and it might have been written by Sinclair Lewis. Change the style to something more colloquial, objective, and it might almost have been written by a young American in Montparnasse as he leaned his elbows on a café table of imitation marble ringed with coffee stains" (91). Who needs modernism? It's so old hat. "It is not Paris we want; it is more New York, more Chicago, more Kalamazoo, Omaha, Kenosha, more loop, more gumbo and gravel, more armature spiders," declares Paul Rosenfeld, speaking of Carl Sandburg's "emphatic and cruel phrases, raging and gorgeous slang of the American streets" (1924, 80, 72).

As these critics wander amid the forgotten texts of America, retrieving its lost tales, America appears haunted, populated by ghosts who cannot fully forget, though neither can they directly express, a past: Puritan repression (*The Scarlet Letter* [1850]), Indian removal (*The Last of the Mohicans* [1826]), African captivity and enslavement (*Moby-Dick* [1851]), everything is shrouded—as Europe itself is in the work of Poe, for instance, replaced by an incantatory longing for the places one seeks to escape. "Was he a ghost, with all his physicality?" asks Lawrence of Whitman, noting a "certain ghoulish insistency . . . about his beatitudes" (1923, "Whitman"). In his melancholy reconsideration of postbellum America, which he called *The Brown Decades* (1931), Mumford points to the abrupt transformation of the nation after the Civil War—slavery's end, of course, but also "the growth of steel mills, the mechanization of agriculture, the substitution of petroleum for whale oil, the development of the trade union movement, and the concentration of great fortunes, built up by graft, speculation, war-profits, or the outright donation of priceless lands to great railway corporations, acquisitions which were not called theft . . . only because the sums involved were so huge and the recipients so rich" (5–6).

This wholesale shift in its economic and social contours meant the "nation not merely worked differently after the Civil War: the country *looked* different—darker, sadder, soberer. The Brown Decades had begun. Dead men were everywhere" (6). These shades—which for Mumford registered as "mediocre drabs, dingy chocolate browns, sooty browns that merged into black"—were "present in memory," clouding the senses of those at work to refashion the Republic during Reconstruction (5, 6). If a few years earlier, his contemporaries thought of Whitman, Hawthorne, Melville as trafficking in corpses, Mumford argued that their literary and artistic successors were even more ghoulish, "the Buried Renaissance," he called this cohort. These living dead held a fascination for such contemporary painters as Edward Hopper, intent on recording the evacuated landscapes of America's lonely towns, by focusing on details like mansard roofs and dingy period facades. These shades lingered in what appeared to be an American limbo—modernism not yet realized. After all, as Mumford noted during the "Brown Decades," "three American translations of the Divine Comedy appeared" (6). In Mumford's revisionist history, the new century needed to reckon with the ghosts of the immediate past; modernism was haunted.

By the 1920s, contemplating all these ghosts could veer towards the "nostalgic," according to Cowley: "In Paris or Pamplona, writing, drinking, watching bullfights or making love, they continued to desire a Kentucky hill cabin, a farmhouse in Iowa or Wisconsin, the Michigan woods, the blue Juniata, a country they had 'lost, ah, lost,' as Thomas Wolfe kept saying; a home to which they couldn't go back" (1934, 9). Because if you want to be a writer, write novels in the secret imagined places of America, you'd better get out of them. No lightin' out for the territories; rather get to Greenwich Village and beyond, to Paris—carrying "our most essential baggage . . . home . . . but does it exist outside your memory?" (14). This unsettling of America, a failure to reckon itself as other than a loss, of a past that was unredeemable except through its language, which could not be fully learned until it was out of earshot, sent these critics back to retrace the steps of the dead. These ghosts were deeply strange; they were modernism's shadows arriving too soon. Off the deep end, modern before modernism, situated and structured through a language spread across vast space: this was how American literature looked to critics in the 1920s.

So it would seem farfetched at that time to contemplate the vast shift in focus that would follow the Great Depression, when the exiles would return from Paris and Berlin fleeing a rising fascism and inflation, lacking money, to discover the collapse of "this metallic landscape," into a "the shapeless, polyphonic, nascent thing America" (Rosenfeld 1924, 76, 68). The America of memory that Cowley claimed the exiles carted with them had sunk into a dire economic morass, and the ecstatic renderings of place and objects through language which seemed to make America out of its texts, as a text, stumbled onto the breadlines. Actually, the critics of the 1920s had foreseen it all—an architecture of pure invention—but their energies appeared misplaced: now looking back from "the trough of the depression," workers' bodies and their hungers needed attention, according to Cowley in 1934 (11). In 1930, a brash critic named Michael Gold, who would publish his proletarian novel *Jews without Money* the same year, smashed his way into liberal middle-class living rooms with his denunciation, in the *New Republic*, of "Wilder: Prophet of the Genteel Christ." It is not as if leftists and Bohemians had not heard Gold's and the other literary radicals' scolds already; what had changed for Cowley was that this missile was aimed at a wider audience (1934, 303–4). In fact, Cowley notes that Bohemia was ideally suited for a new consumer culture that replaced "the *production* ethic" with a "*consumption* ethic" rapidly being taking up by such middlebrow bastions of conservative values as the *Saturday Evening Post*, not to mention the *New Republic* (1934, 60–62).

With the economy in collapse, though recognized at first only by those already on the margins—immigrants, African Americans, farmers suffering ongoing droughts—the edges of social distinction between regions and classes were apparently fraying. In fact as early as February 1921, in the wake of the October Revolution, *The Liberator* had sent writers and critics like Gold "Towards Proletarian Art." Gold's lyrical editorial under that title heralded "the bright forms that stir at the heart of all this confusion, and that shall rise out of the debris and cover the ruins of capitalism with beauty." This exclamation was the easy part; far more difficult for the artist—even one such as himself "born in a tenement"—was to "consent to the suicide of our souls" and allow the "cultural upheaval that must come." Gold acknowledged what Lawrence and Williams, Wilson and Rosenfeld, were later to chart: that the "Social Revolution" was long and difficult because it meant "baffled solitaries" needed to connect with the "masses," always a difficult endeavor in Puritan-rooted America, and especially one only recently experimenting with what Cowley called "the idea of self-expression." Still, "The Revolution, in its secular manifestations of strike, boycott, mass-meeting, imprisonment, sacrifice, agitation, martyrdom, organization, is thereby worthy of the religious devotion of the artist" (Gold, "Towards Proletarian Art"). Replacing the abstraction of "America" with that of "Revolution," Gold nevertheless maintained the primacy of language (and other arts) in etching new spaces for those forgotten within the national borders: "When there is singing and music rising in every American street, when in every American factory there is a drama-group of workers, when mechanics paint in their leisure, and farmers write sonnets, the great art will grow and only then." Once again, America must see its direct connection to Russia where Prolet-Kult was "forming its grand outlines against the sky" ("Towards Proletarian Art"). Gold's call verges on the messianic (a theme reiterated in the final passage of his novel a decade later) but it was extremely prescient, indicating the emergence of a literary radicalism that would reroute the discourse about American fiction from its focus on the specters of place to one structured by labor and class differences. Yet each dynamic continued to foreground language, the vernacular of American speech, as central to the production of American fiction.

With their joint histories of slavery and serfdom only recently abolished; with their revolutionary links; with their colonial relationship to Europe, Russia and America were twins for many 1920s literary critics. With the crisis of capitalism spurred by the 1929 Crash and the disasters of the ensuing Great Depression, with fascism in ascendancy in Germany, Spain, and Italy, the Soviet Union, as a workers' state, appeared as a new model for America. Or perhaps not so new. Since the "discovery" of an American literary heritage based on the street ramblings of Walt Whitman and the ship crewing of Herman Melville, by such scholars in and out of the academy as Joseph Warren Beach, Matthew Josephson, Lewis Mumford, and H. L Mencken, working people and the labor they perform were clearly at the heart of an "American Renaissance"; one could learn how to whale, it seemed, just from reading *Moby-Dick*. But the how-to aspects were overlaid with huge metaphysical sentiments. The Open Road and Doom in Lawrence's calculus—democracy and collective love; violence and white death: the rest "Post mortem effect" (1923, "Whitman"). Yes, if one sees only symbolism, a national literature is over. But literary radicals were looking for something else. As Gold put it in a 1929 article for the journal *New Masses,* writers of the left should record "the lumber camps, coal mines, steel mills, harvest fields and mountain camps of America." He sought "a new writer[,] . . . the son of working-class parents" who "writes because he must" (1929, "Go Left, Young Writers!").

Cowley remarked on the class affiliations of his "lost" generation: few writers were wealthy, fewer still from "the slums. Most of them were the children of doctors, small lawyers, prosperous farmers or struggling businessmen," whose bright sons attended Harvard or Princeton; he described T. S. Eliot as a "local-boy-makes-good[,] . . . a St. Louis boy[,] . . . a Harvard boy" (1934, 5, 116). Gold had also spent some time at Harvard, but his allegiance was to the tenements. Still, most writing about the working-class and about the Depression was not written by "the son of working-class parents." Despite groups such as the John Reed Clubs or the Affiliated School for Working Women that sponsored classes and workshops, despite myriad little magazines springing up in union halls to nurture new talent, and despite successes like Richard Wright and Tillie Olsen, few novelists—or their critics—came from the working class. Rather, as novelist Edward Dahlberg noted in his 1935 discussion of Waldo Frank's novel, *Death and Birth of David Markand* (1934), it was disaffected middle-class intellectuals who offered "the representation fluxional emotions and doubts of the social conscience of an entire class and era" during the transformative years of the Depression. Frank, who had "been a voice of the middle class, the intelligentsia, the students, the teachers, for a decade or more," crafted a novel about a character fleeing his past—in typical American literary fashion. "His relentless peregrinations, industrial, social, erotic, are continental. Markand, tortured, mazed, starves, works as itinerant laborer in the Chicago stockyards, as coal stoker and as bartender in New Orleans. He meets up with Georgia crackers, Negro sharecroppers, chambermaids, Wobblies and Marxists." Dahlberg argued that unlike most proletarian fiction—from Dreiser's *An American Tragedy* (1925) to Dos Passos's *U. S. A.* trilogy (1930–36)—Frank's novel did not send characters "from place to place but [who] never evolve . . . [and] are from the point of view of creative energy and will, horizontal." Instead Frank's "swan song of the American bourgeoisie," a portrait of alienation, presents "picture, pigment and social insight compressed into violent and fragmentary imagery . . . varied in tone and texture" (Dahlberg, "Waldo Frank and the Left").

Dahlberg's commentary acknowledges Frank's writing, its "tone and texture," as fundamentally what makes this work a "major novel," one that doesn't rely on "reporting, a doggerel slangy prose[,] . . . a method of chronicling[,] . . . a stenographic record of surface relations and tabloid events." While "the use of the Americanese is often highly effective," this work insists on its literariness ("Waldo Frank and the Left"). Frank's novel has long since disappeared into the dustbin of literary history, along with Dahlberg's criticism (though Dahlberg's 1929 proletarian novel *Bottom Dogs*, with an introduction by D. H. Lawrence, helped inaugurate Depression fiction). Dahlberg cogently understands the ways in which contemporary writers had failed to limn place through language—had become merely "horizontal." The public criticism by the *New Masses* could be full of prescriptive invective about how lacking in true proletarian sensibility or how despairing and "febrile," as Henry Roth's *Call It Sleep* (1934) was tagged, a work might be. Yet Dahlberg discerned a continuity in Frank's novel, owing to his history within the "intelligentsia," with the critical perspective of his contemporaries.

Frank was a link to the linguistic play made possible by Stein, but, by 1937, when Dorothy Van Ghent contributed an essay to the Works Progress Administration volume, *American Stuff,* entitled "Gertrude Stein and the Solid World," she was chastised in a review by Jack Conroy for taking up valuable publishing real estate. "Interest in Miss Stein, shipped up by her vaudeville stunts of two or three years ago, is scarcely enough to warrant this usurpation of a great deal of space" in the anthology (1939, "Review and Comment"). In Conroy's reading the specter of Stein that had haunted authors and critics only a decade before needed to be exorcised. As Cowley put it in surveying the obsessions of "lost generation" writers, "What is the Joyce solution to these problems (or the Eliot, the Pound, the Gertrude Stein, the Paul Valéry solution)?" However, Stein's words still created a "Solid World" for many writers (1934, 110). For the proletarian novelist, like Conroy (author of the landmark 1933 novel, *The Disinherited*), Stein has been replaced by the apparently far more solid world of Richard Wright confronting "The Ethics of Living Jim Crow," which also appeared in *American Stuff* and which propelled experience—in this case of Southern racism—to the forefront of American letters. Whitman's legacy—"Stay in the flesh. Stay in the limbs and lips and in the belly," says Lawrence (1923, "Whitman")—was to concretize American morality plays into accounts of living on the earth. Whitman's influence on literary radicals meant that the allegorical romance of American literature, understood so subversively by Stein as a daring linguistic practice, needed to acquire tangibility as a form of documentation. Where the truth of America seemed to need a form of mythology for the generation before, the Depression altered this sensibility by focusing on the people and their locations within a class and racial system. Writing needed to become a camera, what James Agee called "the central instrument of our time," to convey the Depression's devastating effects on the landscape and its psychic toll on the American population.

Cowley had signaled this transformation by concluding *Exile's Return* with a description of the controversy spurred in 1930, on the one hand, by Allen Tate and others' excoriation of Harvard Humanism, paving the way for the Southern Fugitives, whose politics veered Right and whose aesthetics ushered in New Criticism, and, on the other, by Michael Gold's scathing review of Thornton Wilder's novels

in the *New Republic* that inaugurated a decade of Left literary radicalism. Denouncing Wilder as "a Prophet of a Genteel Christ," whose allegorical novels, such as
The Bridge of San Luis Rey (1927), fed escapist fantasies that cloaked morality in
romance, Gold was definitively turning his back on the very work of the weird
nineteenth-century writers so recently exhumed and reexamined. Hundreds of letters poured into the editor of *New Republic* decrying Gold's attack on the ideology
of Wilder's novels, rather than simply doing the critic's job and providing a description of what they were about. Wilder's method, Gold argued, left no room for "the
modern streets of New York, Chicago and New Orleans[,] . . . the cotton mills, and
the murder of Ella May and her songs[,] . . . the child slaves of the beet fields[,] . . .
the stockbrokers' suicides, the labor racketeers or the passion and death of the coal
miners." Gold charged much more, depicting, in his notorious words, Wilder's "literary religion . . . [as] a pastel, pastiche, dilettante religion, without the true neurotic
blood and fire, a daydream of homosexual figures in graceful gowns moving archai-
cally among the lilies. . . . Prick it and it will bleed violet ink and *aperitif*" (1930,
"Wilder: Prophet of a Genteel Christ"). Gold's homophobia suggested that this was
not the bold pan-eroticism of Whitman, whose good grey gay desires incorporated
all. Instead Wilder epitomized for him Thorstein Veblen's leisure class of "conspicuous inutility." Attention to facts and to the class and racial formations of social relations: this was essential for the new literature of hard times.

   In his introduction to *The Anthology of American Negro Literature* (1929), Alain
Locke extended his conclusions about the "New Negro" to demonstrate that in the
twentieth century, American culture *was* black culture (on the New Negro, Locke
and Du Bois, see Chapter 28 in this volume). W. E. B Du Bois had already argued
as much in 1903. *The Souls of Black Folk* laid out a devastating analysis of black consciousness as ever a "two-ness—an American, a Negro: two souls, two thoughts, two
unreconciled strivings; two warring ideals in one dark body." His notion of "double
consciousness" and of living behind "a vast veil" described more than "the history of
the American Negro" (ch. 1). As a student of modern psychology and philosophy,
Du Bois had, in delving into the African-American "double self," laid out the psychic terrain of modern subjectivity. Thus he implicitly argued that black subjecthood
was the model for modern subjectivity; developments within psychology, from his
(and Stein's) professor at Harvard, William James, to Sigmund Freud, would only
confirm this sense of a "warring" identity endlessly seeking reconciliation. Locke
focused this insight on culture: "Some of the most characteristic American things
are Negro or Negroid, derivatives of the folk life of this darker tenth of the population, and America at home basks in their influence, thrives upon their consumptions
and vulgarization, and abroad at least must accept their national representativeness.
This because these are among the most distinctive products of the American soil"
(1925, introduction). Locke notes the impact of black experience on contemporary
white novelists, pointing negatively to the sensationalist fiction of Carl Van Vechten
(*Nigger Heaven* [1926]) in contrast to the astute realisms about the Southern racial

caste system in works by Ellen Glasgow (*Barren Ground* [1925]). But the most significant new trend was the emergence of black novelists, like Claude McKay, who "have
given new values and fresh momentum to the contemporary cultural self-expression
of America" (1925, introduction). A decade later, Richard Wright's explosive 1940
novel *Native Son*, whose very title insists on claiming blackness as intrinsically native
to the nation, would secure this assessment.

Wright had outlined his "Blueprint for Negro Writing" in 1937, and it too focused
on the aspects of African American culture that most palpably rendered black life
cohesive: not only the various institutions of Jim Crow segregation, such as the
black press or churches, but rather the underground flow of oral culture. It was, he
suggested, in "folklore moulded out of rigorous and inhuman conditions of life that
the Negro achieved his most indigenous expression. Blues, spirituals, and folk tales
recounted from mouth to mouth, the whispered words of a black mother to her
black daughter on the ways of men, the confidential wisdom of a black father to his
black son, the swapping of sex experiences on street corners from boy to boy in the
deepest vernacular, work songs sung under blazing suns." This submerged culture
was not designed for a white audience yet had more in common with modernist
literature than the "bloodless, petulant, mannered and neurotic" efforts of most
bourgeois African American writers. "One of the great tasks of Negro writers of the
future will be to show the Negro to himself; it will be, paraphrasing the language
of James Joyce, to forge in the smithy of our souls the uncreated conscience of our
race." Making this subterranean stream of jokes, jazz, and talk visible, putting oral
culture onto the page, thus giving it legibility in visual form, was for Wright the
fundamental task of modernist writers from the "oppressed minorities." In other
words, black writers had much to learn from the Irish modernist Joyce and from
Stein's attention to the speech of the poor immigrant women—black and white—
whom she attended as a medical student in Baltimore before composing *Three Lives*.
In calling for a return to folk vernacular, Wright was also stressing the position of
Lenin and the Communist Party that Black America constituted an oppressed national minority. The work of black writers, argued Wright, needed an acute "social
consciousness." "To borrow a phrase from the Russians, it should have a *complex
simplicity*. Eliot, Stein, Joyce, Proust, Hemingway, and Anderson; Gorky, Barbusse,
Nexo, and Jack London no less than the folklore of the Negro himself form the heritage of Negro writers. Every iota of gain in human sensibility and thought should
be ready grist for their mill, no matter how far-fetched they may seem in their immediate implications" (1937, "Blueprint"). Where Jack Conroy chastised the editors
of *American Stuff* for including a tribute to Stein—and implicitly suggesting that
its pages might be better spent on work by such writers as Wright—Wright was
simultaneously acknowledging the significance of Stein and the other modernists
usually trounced by *New Masses* critics. In the pages of an African American left-
wing journal (again, like Stein's venues, hardly very public, if by that term one
means popular), Wright offered another take on the suggestions of Williams and

Lawrence—to see American literature in its fullest sense as an effort to record the sounds of American—all Americans'—speech. Thus in the same issue of the *New Challenge*, Henry Lee Moon, echoing Gold, praises the Works Progress Administration volume *American Stuff* for offering a "New Song of America" but one that harked back to Whitman's nineteenth-century rendering through "the lusty voice of America singing throughout the vastness which is this country. . . . It is a song sometimes bitter, but seldom despairing; sometimes vibrant with soul-stiffing joy, but seldom gay with laughter. A song of all the peoples of America: seafaring folk of New England, black peasants in the cotton fields of Dixie, Anglo-Saxon mountaineers in the uplands of West Virginia, European immigrants seeking a new life; Mexicans in the Southwest fostering the ancient culture of old Spain" (1937).

Despite writing from within the Communist literary movement, Gold diverges from Wright and the *New Challenge* editors in his insistence that these new writers do more than record experiences. For Wright, the new African American novel needed a "complex simplicity," it needed "perspective," that is, it needed to both record and analyze the social world through form "approached from a thousand angles, with no limit to technical and stylistic freedom. But at the core of the life of a people is one theme, one historic sense of life, one prismatic consciousness refracting aesthetic effort in a whirlwind of color" (1937, "Blueprint").

This ecstatic vision of writing that is close to the people also informed William Carlos Williams's 1937 *New Masses* review of the proletarian poet H. H. Lewis. Commenting on Lewis's vernacular verse, as the "beginning of a definitely new sort in American literary history," he notes, harking back to Henry James, the significance of the "cheaply printed, paper-covered booklets" comprising Lewis's four volumes. These are "closest to word of mouth, next to Homeric singing and a stage" and given the ten cents Lewis charges for his chapbooks, "Woolworth is the logical medium" for sales ("An American Poet"). Unlike Southern Agrarian Donald Davidson, who was horrified by the "industrialism" of mass-marketed publishing, Williams exalts in this democratic mode of transmission. He demurs, however, from judging the quality of the poetry itself; he is interested in the means of its distribution and in the Americanness of "the content of the poems." Echoing connections drawn by Cowley and Lawrence, Williams hears "pure American revolutionary stuff" in Lewis's passion for Russia: "When he speaks of Russia, it is precisely then that he is most American, most solidly in the tradition[,] . . . directly express[ing] the mind of the United States . . . in this second quarter of the twentieth century." For, as Williams makes clear, the poems of the lost generation "constituted a revolt in the form of the poetic matter[,] . . . a preparation for Lewis and the second quarter of the century!" One clear borrowing from "the first quarter of the century" (by which he means Stein): "dialect." Lewis writes colloquially, with "the natural ease of a native speaking his own language as he hears it spoken in his own place and day" ("An American Poet").

This slangy, quotidian language grounds Lewis in precisely the shift so many critics noticed occurring within the 1930s' literary practices: what had been a recourse to the vernacular as allegorical in nineteenth-century prose, akin to the kinds of cultural work or representation that Walter Benjamin noted occurred in German *Trauerspiel* two centuries earlier, is now put to the service of recording. Williams outlines a new documentary edge to recorded speech. Benjamin developed his theories about Baroque drama during the intense years of modernist experimentation and the spread of radio and film between 1915 and 1925. Seeking to redeem a debased form, Benjamin argued that these extravagant works, especially paintings and drama, brought into relief the contaminations of the past on the present. His astute reading of the "allegorical mode of expression" as fundamentally a "strange combination of nature and history" is also at the heart of interwar readings of nineteenth-century American literature (1998, 161). For instance, the magisterial effort of Harvard literature professor F. O. Matthiessen to codify the *American Renaissance* places the richly symbolic writings of Hawthorne and Melville at the center of his story of "Art and Expression in the Age of Emerson and Whitman."

The 1930s novels' attention to recording labor with their long passages recounting various jobs, what Michael Denning calls "the laboring of American" during the Popular Front, had reframed the national panorama away from nature and its "idea" and towards the machine and its history (Denning 1996, 118). Depression-era writers were thus returning to Whitman, who Matthiessen declared had used "the English tongue in America . . . in the whole range of American facts" (1941, 517). Citing a never-delivered lecture entitled *An American Primer* (whose form synchronizes the alphabet with an object or action), Matthiessen shows how Whitman outlined, a century before literary radicals' interests, that "a perfect user of words uses things[,] . . . miracles from his hands—miracles from his mouth[,] . . . things, whirled like chain-shot rocks, defiance, compulsion, houses, iron, locomotives, the oak, the pine, the keen eye, the hairy breast, the Texan ranger, the Boston truckman, the woman that arouses a man, the man that arouses a woman" (517–18). Whitman culminates almost all of the left-wing considerations of American literary history. He is seen as the "greatest" by Vernon L. Parrington (1927, 86), the "founder" by Granville Hicks (1935, 30), the "first genuine force" by V. F. Calverton (1932, 276) in American literature. Foundational, because he relied on American vernacular to catalogue daily working life, Whitman allowed 1930s critics to claim America for revolution. Williams culls from H.H. Lewis's work an attention to the lived experiences of the "farmer." "He might fall into simple allegory, but it is so plain that it goes for fact simply. He has picked up from Joyce—or out of his own head—the valuable, time-saving trick of inventing words. Compressing them to give a new twist to meaning: Joyce Killer, flagrags, daily-bathism, demockratism, dogmatrix, Rusevelt " (1937, "An American Poet"). Thus Williams shows that, even the language of labor, supposedly so wedded to description, returns to subversive play of Stein's "grammar."

When Henry James noticed that the future of fiction would be found in the shards of the smashed windows separating women from all that the novel might encompass—that is, life—he might already have been picturing the words of his brother William's brilliant student, Gertrude Stein. In gesturing towards a new readership of young people, he also implied that others confined by class or race or ethnicity or age would also break into prose to produce their images in the mirror of fiction. Writing in the midst of the explosion of documentary forms—reportage, photography, film—Matthiessen looked back to the half-century that preceded James and saw smashed windows. Filmmaker John Grierson had coined the term "documentary" in 1926 to describe the kinds of moving pictures that relayed actuality, people's daily acts of survival. Matthiessen saw a precedent in the forgotten works of the 1850s; he argued that two important "facts" affected the work of his five authors: "when these writers began their careers, the one branch of literature in which America had a developed tradition was oratory; the effect of the nineteenth century's stress on seeing[,] . . . the emphasis on vision and that put on light by the advancing arts of photography and open-air painting" (1941, xiv). The voice and the image—sound and allegory—the speech of Stein's gentle immigrant maids and daring black girls: this was what Matthiessen would find in his retrospective look at the American Renaissance. Stein's project to write fiction from the quotidian through a language of idiosyncratic speech patterns generated an enormous range of writing in the decades following the publication of *Three Lives*. Black writers, working-class writers joined the avant-garde modernists and sent American fiction back to its nineteenth-century roots in the simple sounds of a place.

SECONDARY BIBLIOGRAPHY: QUOTED SOURCES

AARON, DANIEL (1971). "Late Thoughts on Nathanael West," in Jay Martin (ed.), *Nathanael West: A Collection of Critical Essays.* Englewood Cliffs, NJ: Prentice, 161–69.

ABBOTT, MEGAN E. (2002). *The Street Was Mine: White Masculinity in Hardboiled Fiction and Film Noir.* Basingstoke, UK: Palgrave Macmillan.

ABOUL-ELA, HOSAM M. (2007). *Other South: Faulkner, Coloniality, and the Mariátegui Tradition.* Pittsburgh, PA: University of Pittsburgh Press.

ADAMS, HENRY (1872). "Review of *Their Wedding Journey.*" *North American Review* 114, 444–45.

ALDISS, BRIAN (1986). *Trillion Year Spree: The History of Science Fiction.* New York: Atheneum Books.

ALKON, PAUL K. (2002). *Science Fiction before 1900: Imagination Discovers Technology.* New York: Routledge.

ANDERSON, CAROLYN (1988). "Film and Literature," in Gary R. Edgerton (ed.), *Film and the Arts in Symbiosis.* New York: Greenwood Press, 97–134.

ANDERSON, ERIC GARY (1999). *American Indian Literature and the Southwest: Contexts and Dispositions.* Austin, TX: University of Texas Press.

ANDREW, DUDLEY (1984). *Concepts in Film Theory.* Oxford, UK: Oxford University Press.

ANDREWS, WILLIAM L. (1976). "William Dean Howells and Charles W. Chesnutt: Criticism and Race Fiction in the Age of Booker T. Washington." *American Literature* 48, 327–39.

ANGENOT, MARC (2000). "Society after the Revolution: The Blueprints for the Forthcoming Socialist Society Published by the Leaders of the Second International," in Patrick Parrinder (ed.), *Learning from Other Worlds.* Liverpool: Liverpool University Press, 98–117.

APTER, EMILY (2006), *The Translation Zone: A New Comparative Literature.* Princeton: Princeton University Press.

ARMSTRONG, TIM (1998). *Modernism, Technology, and the Body: A Cultural Study.* Cambridge, UK: Cambridge University Press.

ARONSON, MARC (1994). "Wharton and the House of Scribner: The Novelist as a Pain in the Neck." *New York Times*, January 2.

ASBURY, BRET D. (2009). "Law as Palimpsest: Conceptualizing Contingency in Judicial Opinions." *Alabama Law Review* 61, 121–63.

AUERBACH, JONATHAN (1996). *Male Call: Becoming Jack London*. Durham: Duke University Press.

AUGST, THOMAS (2001). "Introduction: American Libraries and Agencies of Culture." *American Studies* 42.3, 5–22.

AYRES, HARRY MORGAN (1921). "The English Language in America," in William Peterfield Trent et al. (eds.), *The Cambridge History of American Literature: Later National Literature: Part III*. New York: G.P. Putnam's Sons, 554–71.

BAKER, CARLOS (1969). *Hemingway: A Life Story*. London: Collins.

BAKHTIN, M. M. (1981). "From the Prehistory of Novelistic Discourse," in Michael Holquist (ed.), *The Dialogic Imagination: Four Essays*. (trans.) Michael Holquist and Caryl Emerson. Austin, TX: University of Texas Press, 41–83.

BAKHTIN, M. M. (1984). *Problems of Dostoevsky's Poetics*. (trans.) Caryl Emerson. Minneapolis, MN: University of Minnesota Press.

BALDWIN, JAMES MARK (1897). *The Mental Development in the Child and the Race*. New York: The Macmillan Company.

BALL, ERIC L. (2006). "Literary Criticism for Places," *symploke* 14:1–2, 232–51.

BARNARD, RITA (1995). *The Great Depression and the Culture of Abundance: Kenneth Fearing, Nathanael West, and Mass Culture in the 1930s*. New York: Cambridge University Press.

BECKER, GEORGE (ed.) (1963). *Documents of Modern Literary Realism*. Princeton, NJ: Princeton University Press.

BECKER, STEPHEN (1959). *Comic Art in America*. New York: Simon and Schuster.

BECNEL, KIM (2008). *The Rise of Corporate Publishing and Its Effects on Authorship in Early Twentieth-Century America*. New York: Routledge.

BELL, MICHAEL (1999). "The Metaphysics of Modernism," in Michael Levenson (ed.), *The Cambridge Companion to Modernism*. Cambridge, UK: Cambridge University Press, 9–32.

BELL, MICHAEL DAVITT (2001). *Culture, Genre, and Literary Vocation: Selected Essays on American Literature*. Chicago: University of Chicago Press.

BENEDICT, RUTH (1959). *Patterns of Culture: With a New Preface by Margaret Mead*. Boston: Houghton Mifflin.

BENJAMIN, WALTER (1968), "The Work of Art in the Age of Mechanical Reproduction," in Hannah Arendt (ed.), *Illuminations: Essays and Reflection*. New York: Harcourt, Brace and Janovich, 217–51.

BENJAMIN, WALTER (1998). *The Origins of German Tragic Drama*. (trans.) John Osborne. New York: Verso.

BENJAMIN, WALTER (2002). *The Arcades Project*. (trans.) Rolf Tiedemann. Cambridge, MA: Belknap Press of Harvard University Press.

BENSTOCK, SHARI (2003). " 'The Word Which Made All Clear': The Silent Close of the House of Mirth," in Carol Singley (ed.), *Edith Wharton's the House of Mirth: A Casebook*. New York: Oxford University Press, 131–62.

BENTLEY, NANCY (2008). "The Fourth Dimension: Kinlessness and African American Narrative." *Critical Inquiry* 35, 270–92.

BENTLEY, NANCY (2009). *Frantic Panoramas: American Literature and Mass Culture, 1870–1920*. Philadelphia: University of Pennsylvania Press.

BERMAN, MARSHALL (1988). *All That Is Solid Melts into Air: The Experience of Modernity*. New York: Penguin Books.

BERSANI, LEO (1978). "The Other Freud." *Humanities in Society* 1.1, 35–49.

BEST, STEPHEN (2004). *The Fugitive's Properties: Law and the Poetics of Possession*. Chicago: University of Chicago Press.

BINGGELI, ELIZABETH (2009). "Worse than Bad: *Sanctuary*, the Hays Office and the Genre of Abjection." *Arizona Quarterly* 65.3, 87–116.

BISHOP, W. H. (1879). "Story-Paper Literature." *Atlantic Monthly* 44.263, 383.

BLAKE, DAVID HAVEN (2006). *Walt Whitman and the Culture of American Celebrity*. New Haven: Yale University Press.

BLEILER, EVERETT F. (1990). *Science Fiction: The Early Years*. Kent, OH: Kent State University Press.

BLIGHT, DAVID W. (2001). *Race and Reunion: The Civil War in American Memory*. Cambridge, MA and London: Belknap Press of Harvard University Press.

BLODGETT, JAN (1997). *Protestant Evangelical Literary Culture and Contemporary Society*. Westport, CT: Greenwood Press.

BLOTNER, JOSEPH (1974). *Faulkner: A Biography, Vol. 1*. New York: Random House.

BLOUSTEIN, EDWARD J. (1964). "Privacy as an Aspect of Human Dignity: An Answer to Dean Prosser." *New York University Law Review* 39, 962–1007.

BLUMENTHAL, SUSANNA L. (2008). "Metaphysics, Moral Sense, and the Pragmatism of the Law." *Law and History Review* 26.1, 177–85.

BOK, EDWARD W. (1892). "Literary Factories." *Publishers' Weekly* 1072, 231.

BONTEMPS, JACQUES and RICHARD OVERSTREET (1967). "'Measure for Measure': Interviews with Joseph Mankiewicz." *Cahiers du Cinema in English* 18, 28–41.

BORDWELL, DAVID, JANET STAIGER, and KRISTIN THOMPSON (1985). *The Classical Hollywood Cinema: Film Style & Mode of Production to 1960*. New York: Columbia University Press.

BOTSHON, LISA (2000). "Anzia Yezierska and the Marketing of the Jewish Immigrant in 1920s Hollywood." *JNT: Journal of Narrative Theory* 30.3, 287–312.

BRADBURY, MALCOLM (1987). "The Nonhomemade World: European and American Modernism." *American Quarterly* 39.1, 27–36.

BRADBURY, MALCOLM, and JAMES MCFARLANE (eds.) (1991). *Modernism: A Guide to European Literature 1890–1930*. London: Penguin.

BRENNER, JACK (1966). "Howells and Ade." *American Literature* 38.2, 198–207.

BREU, CHRISTOPHER (2005). *Hard-Boiled Masculinities*. Minneapolis: University of Minnesota Press.

BRODHEAD, RICHARD (1993). *Cultures of Letters: Scenes of Reading and Writing in Nineteenth-Century America*. Chicago: University of Chicago Press.

BRODHEAD, RICHARD H. (1988a). "Literature and Culture," in Emory Elliott et al. (eds.), *Columbia Literary History of the United States*. New York: Columbia University Press, 467–81.

BRODHEAD, RICHARD (1988b). "Sparing the Rod: Discipline and Fiction in Antebellum America." *Representations* 21.21, 67–96.

BROOKS, CLEANTH (1963). *William Faulkner: The Yoknapatawpha Country*. New Haven: Yale University Press.

BROOKS, PETER (1977). *The Melodramatic Imagination: Balzac, Henry James, Melodrama and the Mode of Excess*. New Haven: Yale University Press.

BROOKS, VAN WYCK (1968). "On Creating a Usable Past," in Claire Sprague (ed.), *The Early Years*. New York: Harper & Row, 219–26.

BROWN, BILL (ed.), (1997). *Reading the West: An Anthology of Dime Westerns*. Boston: Bedford/St. Martin's.

BROWN, MILTON W. (1988). *The Story of the Armory Show*. New York: Abbeville.

BRUMBERG, STEPHAN F. (1986). *Going to America, Going to School: The Jewish Immigrant Public School Encounter in Turn-of-the-Century New York City*. New York: Praeger.

BUELL, LAWRENCE (2005). *The Future of Environmental Criticism: Environmental Crisis and Literary Imagination*. Oxford, UK: Blackwell.

BULMER, MARTIN (1984). *The Chicago School of Sociology: Institutionalization, Diversity, and the Rise of Sociological Research*. Chicago: University of Chicago Press.

CALVERTON, V. F. (1932). *The Liberation of American Literature*. New York: Charles Scribner's Sons.

CAMPBELL, JR., JOHN W. (1963). "Introduction," in Campbell (ed.), *Analog 1*. Garden City: Doubleday, xv–xviii.

CAREY, RALPH ALLISON (1971). *Best Selling Religion: A History of Popular Religious Thought in American as Reflected in Religious Best Sellers, 1850–1960*. Dissertation. Michigan State University.

CARPENTIER, ALEJO (1995 [1949]). "On the Marvelous Real in America," in Lois Parkinson Zamora and Wendy B. Faris (eds.), *Magical Realism: Theory, History, Community*. Durham: Duke University Press, 75–88.

CARTER, PAUL A. (1991). *The Spiritual Crisis of the Gilded Age*. DeKalb, IL: Northern Illinois University Press.

CASSUTO, LEONARD (2009). *Hard-Boiled Sentimentality: The Secret History of American Crime Stories*. New York: Columbia University Press.

CASTRONOVO, RUSS (2007). *Beautiful Democracy: Aesthetics and Anarchy in a Global Age*. Chicago: University of Chicago Press.

CHAMETZKY, JULES (1972). "Our Decentralized Literature: A Consideration of Regional, Ethnic, Racial, and Sexual Factors." *Jahrbuch für Amerikastudien* 17, 56–72.

CHANDLER, RAYMOND (1945). Letter to Charles Morton. The Raymond Chandler Papers. October 13.

CHARTIER, JEAN PIERRE (1996 [1946]). "The Americans Are Making Dark Films Too," in R. Barton Palmer (ed.), *Perspectives on Film Noir*. New York: G. K. Hall and Co., 25–27.

CHARVAT, WILLIAM (1968). *The Profession of Authorship in America, 1800–1870.* Matthew J. Bruccoli (ed.). New York: Columbia University Press.

CHATMAN, SEYMOUR (1980), "What Novels Can Do That Films Can't (and Vice Versa)," *Critical Inquiry* 7:1, 121–40.

CHENEY, O. H. (1930). *Economic Survey of the Book Industry, 1930–1931.* New York: Bowker.

CHEUNG, FLOYD (2003). "Introduction," in *And China Has Hands.* New York: Ironweed Press.

CHILES, KATY (2008). "Within and Without Raced Nations: Intratextuality, Martin Delany, and *Blake; Or the Huts of* America." *American Literature* 80, 323–52.

CHIN, GABRIEL (2008). "Unexplainable on Grounds of Race: Doubts about *Yick Wo.*" *University of Illinois Law Review*, 2008, 1359–91.

CODY, PHIL (1926). "Editorial," *Black Mask Magazine* (January).

COHEN, LIZABETH (1990). *Making a New Deal: Industrial Workers in Chicago, 1919–1939.* Cambridge, UK: Cambridge University Press.

COHEN, ROSE (1995 [1918]). *Out of the Shadow.* Ithaca, New York: Cornell University Press.

COOPER, LYDIA R. (2009). "Human Voices: Language and Conscience in Twain's *A Connecticut Yankee in King Arthur's Court.*" *Canadian Review of American Studies* 39, 65–84.

COWLEY, MALCOLM (1934). *Exile's Return: A Narrative of Ideas.* New York: Norton.

COWLEY, MALCOLM (1973). *A Second Flowering: Works and Days of the Lost Generation.* New York: Viking Press.

CRISLER, JESSE, ROBERT C. LEITZ, III, and JOSEPH R. McELRATH, JR. (eds.) (2002). *An Exemplary Citizen: The Letters of Charles W. Chesnutt, 1906–1932.* Stanford: Stanford University Press.

CSICSERY-RONAY, JR., ISTVAN (2003). "Science Fiction and Empire." *Science Fiction Studies* 30, 231–45.

DANIELS, ROGER (2002). *Coming to America: A History of Immigration and Ethnicity in American Life.* New York: HarperCollins.

DARDIS, TOM (1976). *Some Time in the Sun.* New York: Scribner's.

DARROW, CLARENCE (1899 [1893]). *Realism in Literature and Art.* Chicago: C. H. Kerr & Company.

DENNING, MICHAEL (1996). *The Cultural Front: The Laboring of American Culture in the Twentieth Century.* London: Verso.

DENNING, MICHAEL (1998 [1987]). *Mechanic Accents: Dime Novels and Working-Class Culture in America.* London: Verso.

DENNING, MICHAEL (2004). *Culture in the Age of Three Worlds.* London: Verso.

DERRIDA, JACQUES (1980). "The Law of Genre." (trans.) Avital Ronell. *Critical Inquiry* 7.1, 55–81.

DEWEY, JOHN (1968 [1931]). *Philosophy and Civilization.* Gloucester MA: Peter Smith.

SECONDARY BIBLIOGRAPHY: QUOTED SOURCES

Dery, Mark (1995). "Black to the Future: Interviews with Samuel R. Delany, Greg Tate, and Tricia Rose," in Mark Dery (ed.), *Flame Wars*. Durham: Duke University Press, 179–222.

Dickstein, Morris (2010). *Dancing in the Dark: A Cultural History of the Great Depression*. New York: W.W. Norton & Co.

DiMaggio, Paul (1982). "Cultural Entrepreneurship in Nineteenth-Century Boston: The Creation of an Organizational Base for High Culture in America." *Media, Culture & Society* 4, 33–50.

Dimock, Wai Chee (1997). *Residues of Justice: Literature, Law, Philosophy*. Berkeley: University of California Press.

Dimock, Wai Chee (2006). *Through Other Continents: American Literature Across Deep Time*. Princeton: Princeton University Press.

Dimock, Wai Chee, and Lawrence Buell (2007). "Planet and America, Set and Subset," in Dimock and Buell (eds.), *Shades of the Planet: American Literature as World Literature*. Princeton: Princeton University Press.

Dobson, Joanne (1997). "Reclaiming Sentimental Literature." *American Literature* 69.2, 263–88.

Douglas, Ann (1995). *Terrible Honesty: Mongrel Manhattan in the 1920s*. New York: Farrar, Straus, and Giroux.

Duyckinck, Evert (1847). "Nationality in Literature," *The United States Magazine and Democratic Review*. 20.105 (March), 264–72.

Dudziak, Mary L. (2000). *Cold War Civil Rights: Race and the Image of American Democracy*. Princeton: Princeton University Press.

DuPlessis, Rachel Blau (1986). *H. D.: The Career of that Struggle*. Bloomington, IN: Indiana University Press.

Eby, Clare Virginia (2001). "Slouching toward Beastliness: Richard Wright's Anatomy of Thomas Dixon." African American Review 35:3 (Fall), 439–58.

Edgell, Stephen (2001). *Veblen in Perspective: His Life and Thought*. Armonk, NY: M.E. Sharpe.

Edwards, Brent Hayes (2003). *The Practice of Diaspora: Literature, Translation, and the Rise of Black Internationalism*. Cambridge: Harvard University Press.

Eisenstein, Sergei (1957). *Film Form [and] The Film Sense; Two Complete and Unabridged Works*. (trans.) Jay Leydan. New York: Meridian Books.

Eisenstein, Sergei (1977). "Dickens, Griffith, and the Film Today," in Jay Leyda (ed.), *Sergei Eisenstein: Essays in Film Theory: Film Forum*. New York: Harcourt.

Elliott, Kamilla (2003). *Rethinking the Novel/Film Debate*. Cambridge, UK: Cambridge University Press.

Elliott, Mark (2006). *Color-Blind Justice: Albion Tourgée and the Quest for Racial Equality from the Civil War to* Plessy v. Ferguson. Oxford, UK: Oxford University Press.

Empson, William (1974 [1935]). *Some Versions of Pastoral*. New York: New Directions.

ENTIN, JOSEPH (2007). *Sensational Modernism: Experimental Fiction and Photography in Thirties America*. Chapel Hill: University of North Carolina Press.

ESCARPIT, ROBERT (1966). *The Book Revolution*. London: George G. Harrap.

EVERETT, ANNA (2001). *Returning the Gaze: A Genealogy of Black Film Criticism, 1909–1949*. Durham: Duke University Press.

FABIAN, JOHANNES (1983). *Time and the Other*. New York: Columbia University Press.

FERGUSON, JEFFREY B. (2005). *The Sage of Sugar Hill: George S. Schuyler and the Harlem Renaissance*. New Haven: Yale University Press.

FETTERLEY, JUDITH (1994). "'Not in the Least American': Nineteenth-Century Literary Regionalism." *College English* 56, 877–95.

FISHKIN, SHELLEY FISHER (1985). *From Fact to Fiction*. Baltimore: Johns Hopkins University Press.

FLUCK, WINFRIED, and WERNER SOLLORS (eds.) (2002). *German? American? Literature?: New Directions in German-American Studies 2*. New York: Peter Lang.

FOERSTER, NORMAN (ed.) (1928). *The Reinterpretation of American Literature: Some Contributions toward the Understanding of Its Historical Development*. New York: Harcourt, Brace and Company.

FOLEY, BARBARA (1980). "History, Fiction, and the Ground Between: The Uses of Documentary Modes in Black Fiction." *PMLA* 95.3, 389–403.

FOUCAULT, MICHEL (1989 [1963]). *The Birth of the Clinic: An Archaeology of Medical Perception*. (trans.) Sheridan, A.M. London: Routledge.

FRANK, JOSEPH (1982). "Spatial Form in Modern Literature," in Richard Kostelanetz (ed.), *The Avant-Garde Tradition in Literature*. Buffalo, NY: Prometheus Books.

FREUD, SIGMUND (1919 [1920]). "A Child Is Being Beaten: A Contribution to the Study of the Origin of Sexual Perversion." *The International Journal of Psychoanalysis* 1, 371–95.

FREUD, SIGMUND (1985 [1927]). "The Future of an Illusion," in James Strachey and Albert Dickson (eds. and trans.), *The Pelican Freud Library, Vol. 12: Civilization, Society and Religion*, 179–241.

FRYE, NORTHROP (1957). *Anatomy of Criticism*. Princeton: Princeton University Press.

FUSSELL, PAUL (2000). *The Great War and Modern Memory*. New York: Oxford University Press.

GASKILL, NICHOLAS (2009). "Red Cars with Red Lights and Red Drivers: Color, Crane, and Qualia." *American Literature* 81.4, 719–45.

GATES, JR., HENRY LOUIS (1987). *Figures in Black: Words, Signs, and the "Racial" Self*. New York: Oxford University Press.

GATES, JR., HENRY LOUIS (1993). "Preface," in Gates, Jr. and Kwame Anthony Appiah (eds.), *Richard Wright: Critical Perspectives Past and Present*. New York: Amistad.

GATEWOOD, WILLARD (1975). *Black Americans and the White Man's Burden, 1898–1903*. Urbana: University of Illinois Press.

GEHERIN, DAVID (1985). *The American Private Eye: The Image in Fiction*. New York: Ungar.

GERNSBACK, HUGO (1926). "A New Sort of Magazine." *Amazing Stories* 1.1: 1.

GIDDENS, ANTHONY (1990). *The Consequences of Modernity*. Stanford, CA: Stanford University Press.

GILLMAN, SUSAN and FORREST G. ROBINSON (1990). *Mark Twain's* Pudd'nhead Wilson: *Race, Conflict and Culture*. Durham: Duke University Press.

GILROY, PAUL (1993). *The Black Atlantic: Modernity and Double Consciousness*. Cambridge: Harvard University Press.

GILROY, PAUL (2005). *Postcolonial Melancholia*. New York: Columbia University Press.

GLASS, LOREN (2004). *Authors Inc.: Literary Celebrity in the Modern United States, 1880–1980*. New York: New York University Press.

GLAZENER, NANCY (1997). *Reading for Realism: The History of a U. S. Literary Institution, 1850–1910*. Durham: Duke University Press.

GLAZENER, NANCY (2011). "The Novel in Postbellum Print Culture," in Leonard Cassuto, Clare Eby, and Benjamin Reiss (eds.), *The Cambridge History of the American Novel*. Cambridge UK: Cambridge University Press, 337–64.

GLISSANT, EDOUARD (1989). *Caribbean Discourse: Selected Essays*. (trans.) J. Michael Dash. Charlottesville, VA: University Press of Virginia.

GLISSANT, EDOUARD (1999). *Faulkner, Mississippi*. (trans.) Barbara Lewis and Thomas C. Spear. New York: Farrar, Straus and Giroux.

GOLDSTEIN, NANCY (2008). *Jackie Ormes: The First African American Woman Cartoonist*. Ann Arbor, MI: University of Michigan Press.

GOODMAN, NAN (1998). *Shifting the Blame: Literature, Law, and the Theory of Accidents in Nineteenth-Century America*. Princeton: Princeton University Press.

GOTANDA, NEIL. (1991) "A Critique of 'Our Constitution is Color-Blind,'" *Stanford Law Review* 44.1 (November), 1–68.

THE GREAT BOOKS FOUNDATION. June 20, 2012. http://www.greatbooks.org.

GUILLORY, JOHN (1993). *Cultural Capital: The Problem of Literary Canon Formation*. Chicago: University of Chicago Press.

GUILLORY, JOHN (2002). "Literary Study and the Modern System of the Disciplines," in Amanda Anderson and Joseph Valente (eds.), *Disciplinarity at the Fin de Siecle*. Princeton: Princeton University Press, 20–43.

GUNNING, TOM (2006). "The Cinema of Attraction[s]: Early Film, Its Spectator and the Avant-Garde," in Wanda Strauven (ed.), *The Cinema of Attractions Reloaded*. Amsterdam: Amersterdam University Press.

GUNNING, TOM (2009). "Narrative Discourse and the Narrator System," in Leo Braudy and Marshall Cohen (eds.), *Film Theory and Criticism*. New York: Oxford University Press.

HALL, GRANVILLE STANLEY (1893). *The Contents of Children's Minds on Entering School.* New York: E.L. Kellogg & Co.

HALL, GRANVILLE STANLEY (1904). *Adolescence: Its Psychology and Its Relation to Physiology, Anthropology, Sociology, Sex, Crime, Religion, and Education. Vol 1.* New York: Appleton.

HALLIWELL, MARTIN (2007). "Modernism and Adaptation," in Deborah Cartmell and Imelda Whelehan (eds.), *The Cambridge Companion to Literature on Screen.* Cambridge, UK: Cambridge University Press.

HAMILTON, IAN (1990). *Writers in Hollywood 1915–1951.* London: Heinemann.

HANSEN, MARCUS LEE (1964). "Immigration and American Culture," in *The Immigrant in American History.* New York: Harper Row.

HANSEN, MIRIAM (1999). "The Mass Production of the Senses: Classical Cinema as Vernacular Modernism." *Modernism/modernity* 6.2, 59–77.

HARPER, DONNA AKIBA SULLIVAN (1995). *Not So Simple: The "Simple" Stories by Langston Hughes.* Columbia, MO: University of Missouri Press.

HARRIS, CHERYL (1993). "Whiteness as Property." *Harvard Law Review* 106, 1707–91.

HARRISON, HUBERT H. (1991 [1920]). *When Africa Wakes: The "Inside Story" of the New Negro in the Western World.* Chesapeake, VA: ECA Association Press.

HART, JAMES D. (1963). *The Popular Book: A History of America's Literary Taste.* Berkeley: University of California Press.

HARTMAN, SAIDIYA V. (1997). *Scenes of Subjection: Terror, Slavery, and Self-Making in Nineteenth-Century America.* New York: Oxford University Press.

HARVEY, DAVID (1996 [1990]). *The Condition of Postmodernity: An Enquiry into the Origins of Cultural Change.* Cambridge, UK: Blackwell.

HARVEY, ROBERT C. (1994). *The Art of the Funnies: An Aesthetic History.* Jackson, MS: University Press of Mississippi.

HEGEMAN, SUSAN (1999). *Patterns for America: Modernism and the Concept of Culture.* Princeton: Princeton University Press.

HENIGHAN, STEPHEN (1999). "Two Paths to the Boom: Carpentier, Asturias, and the Performative Split." *Modern Language Review* 94, 1009–24.

HEYDRICK, BENJAMIN A. (ed.) (1920). *Americans All: Stories of American Life of To-day.* New York: Harcourt.

HICKS, GRANVILLE (1933). "American Fiction: Realism." *The New Republic* 74, 238–41.

HICKS, GRANVILLE (1935). *The Great Tradition: An Interpretation of American Literature Since the Civil War.* New York: Biblo and Tannen.

HIGGINSON, THOMAS WENTWORTH (1892). "The Local Short Story." *The Independent* 44, 4–5.

HINEY, TOM (1998). *Raymond Chandler: A Biography.* London: Vintage.

HOFSTADTER, RICHARD and C. DEWITT HARDY (1952). *The Development and Scope of Higher Education in the United States.* New York: Columbia University Press.

HOFSTADTER, RICHARD (1952). "Manifest Destiny and the Philippines," in Daniel Aaron (ed.), *America in Crisis: Fourteen Crucial Episodes in American History*. New York: Knopf.

HOGANSON, KRISTEN. (1998). *Fighting for American Manhood: How Gender Politics Provoked the Spanish-American and Philippine-American Wars*. New Haven: Yale University Press.

HOLT, HENRY (1923). *Garrulities of an Octogenarian Editor*. Boston: Houghton Mifflin.

HOOPES, ROY (1982). *Cain: The Biography of James M. Cain*. New York: Holt, Rinehart and Winston.

HORWITZ, MORTON J. (1992). *The Transformation of American Law, 1870–1960*. New York: Oxford University Press.

HOWELLS, WILLIAM DEAN (1882). "Henry James, Jr." *Century* XXV. 25–29.

HOWELLS, WILLIAM DEAN (1887). "Editor's Study," *Harper's New Monthly Magazine*, 983–87.

HOWELLS, WILLIAM DEAN (1889). "Editor's Study," *Harper's New Monthly Magazine* (November), 966.

HOWELLS, WILLIAM DEAN (1896). "Life and Letters," *Harper's Weekly*, 630.

HOWELLS, WILLIAM DEAN (1901). "Psychological Counter-Current in Recent Fiction." *North American Review* 173, 872–88.

HOZIC, AIDA A. (2001). *Hollyworld: Space, Power, and Fantasy in the American Economy*. Ithaca, NY: Cornell University Press.

HUNTZICKER, WILLIAM (1999). *The Popular Press, 1833–1865*. Westport, CT: Greenwood Press.

HUTCHINSON, GEORGE (1995). *The Harlem Renaissance in Black and White*. Cambridge, MA: Harvard University Press.

HUTCHINSON, GEORGE (2006). *In Search of Nella Larsen: A Biography of the Color Line*. Cambridge, MA: Harvard University Press.

HUTNER, GORDON (2009). *What America Read: Taste Class, and the Novel, 1920–1960*. Chapel Hill: University of North Carolina Press.

INGE, M. THOMAS (1986). "Faulkner Reads the Funny Papers," in Doreen Fowler and Ann J. Abadie (eds.), *Faulkner and Humor*. Jackson, MS: University Press of Mississippi.

JAMES, HENRY (1897). "James Russell Lowell," in Charles Dudley Warner (ed.), *Library of the World's Best Literature, vol. XXIII*, New York: International Society, p. 9229.

JAMES, W. P. (1897). "On the Theory and Practice of Local Colour," *Macmillan's Magazine* 76 (May): 16–22.

JAMES, WILLIAM (1890). *The Principles of Psychology*. 2 vols. New York: Henry Holt.

JENKINS, THOMAS E. (1997). *The Character of God: Recovering the Lost Literary Power of American Protestantism*. New York: Oxford University Press.

JOHANNINGSMEIER, CHARLES A. (1997). *Fiction and the American Literary Marketplace: The Role of Newspaper Syndicates in America, 1860–1900*. New York: Cambridge University Press.

Joo, Thomas Wuil (1995). "New 'Conspiracy Theory' of the Fourteenth Amendment: Nineteenth Century Chinese Civil Rights Cases and the Development of Substantive Due Process Jurisprudence." *University of San Francisco Law Review* 29, 353–88.

Joo, Thomas Wuil (2008). "*Yick Wo* Re-revisited: Nonblack Nonwhites and Fourteenth Amendment History." *University of Illinois Law Review*, 2008, 1427–40.

Kallen, Horace (1915). "Democracy Versus the Melting-Pot," *Nation*, 100.2509-91 February, 18 and 25, 190–94, 217–20.

Kaestle, Carl F. (2009). "Seeing the Sites: Readers, Publishers, and Local Print Cultures in 1880," in Kaestle and Radway (eds.), *A History of the Book in America, Volume 4. Print in Motion: The Expansion of Publishing and Reading in the United States, 1880–1940*. Chapel Hill: University of North Carolina Press, 22–45.

Kaestle, Carl F., and Janice A. Radway (2009). "A Framework for the History of Publishing and Reading in the United States, 1880–1940," in Kaestle and Radway (eds.), *A History of the Book in America, Volume 4. Print in Motion: The Expansion of Publishing and Reading in the United States, 1880–1940*. Chapel Hill: University of North Carolina Press, 8–21.

Kahn, Jonathan (1996). "Enslaving the Image: The Origins of the Tort of Appropriation of Identity Reconsidered." *Legal Theory* 2, 301–24.

Kahn, Jonathan (2003). "Privacy as a Legal Principle of Identity Maintenance." *Seton Hall Law Review* 33, 371–410.

Kanellos, Nicolás (2005). *Hispanic Literature of the United States: A Comprehensive Reference*. Westport, CT: Greenwood Press.

Kanellos, Nicolás (2007). "Recovering and Re-constructing Early Twentieth-Century Hispanic Immigrant Print Culture in the US." *American Literary History* 19.2, 438–55.

Kaplan, Amy (1988). *The Social Construction of American Realism*. Chicago: University of Chicago Press.

Kaplan, Amy (2002). *The Anarchy of Empire in the Making of U.S. Culture*. Cambridge: Harvard University Press.

Kaplan, Justin (1991). *Mr. Clemens and Mark Twain: A Biography*. New York: Simon and Schuster.

Kazin, Alfred (1995 [1942]). *On Native Grounds: An Interpretation of Modern American Prose Literature*. New York: Harcourt, Brace & Company.

Kennedy, J. Gerald (1993). *Imagining Paris: Exile, Writing, and American Identity*. New Haven, CT: Yale University Press.

Kern, Stephen (2003 [1983]). *The Culture of Time and Space, 1880–1910*. Cambridge: Harvard University Press.

Kessler, Carol Farley (1982). *Elizabeth Stuart Phelps*. Boston: Twayne Publishers.

Ketterer, David (1974). *New Worlds for Old: The Apocalyptic Imagination, Science Fiction, and American Literature*. New York: Anchor Books.

Kim, Elaine H. (1994). *Asian American Literature: An Introduction to the Writings and Their Social Context*. Philadelphia: Temple University Press.

KIMMEL, MICHAEL S. (2006). *Manhood in America: A Cultural History*. New York: Oxford University Press.

"THE KINGDOMS OF VANITY" (1905). *Kansas City Star*, October 22, 3.

KINNAMON, KENETH (1993). "How *Native Son* Was Born," in Henry Louis Gates, Jr. and Kwame Anthony Appiah (eds.), *Richard Wright: Critical Perspectives Past and Present*. New York: Amistad.

KITTLER, FRIEDRICH (1999 [1986]). *Gramophone, Film, Typewriter*. Stanford: Stanford University Press.

KORDA, MICHAEL (2001). *Making the List: A Cultural History of the American Bestseller 1900–1999*. New York: Barnes and Noble.

KNIGHT, STEPHEN (2004). *Crime Fiction, 1800–2000: Detection, Death, Diversity*. Basingstoke, UK: Palgrave Macmillan.

KRAMNICK, JONATHAN (2007). "Empiricism, Cognitive Science, and the Novel." *The Eighteenth Century* 48.3, 263–85.

LAEMMLE, CARL (1915). "Universal City Starts Housekeeping: The Complete Municipality That Produces Ten Miles of Film Per Week." *Photoplay*.

LAMOTHE, DAPHNE (2008). *Inventing the New Negro: Narrative, Culture, and Ethnography*. Philadelphia: University of Pennsylvania Press.

LANDON, BROOKS (2002). *Science Fiction after 1900: From the Steam Man to the Stars*. New York: Routledge.

LANE, ANN J. (1979). "Introduction," in Charlotte Perkins Gilman (ed.), *Herland*. New York: Pantheon.

LAVENDER III, ISIAH (2007). "Ethnoscapes: Environment and Language in Ishmael Reed's *Mumbo Jumbo*, Colson Whitehead's *The Intuitionist*, and Samuel R. Delany's *Babel-17*." *Science Fiction Studies* 34, 187–200.

LEE, CHARLES (1939). *How to Enjoy Reading*. Boston: Waverly House.

LEFEBVRE, HENRI (1995 [1962]). *Introduction to Modernity*. (trans.) John Moore. London: Verso.

LEFF, LEONARD J. (1997). *Hemingway and His Conspirators: Hollywood, Scribners, and the Making of American Celebrity Culture*. Lanham, MD: Rowman and Littlefield.

LEICK, KAREN (2009). *Gertrude Stein and the Making of an American Celebrity*. New York: Routledge.

LENTRICCHIA, FRANK (1994). *Modernist Quartet*. Cambridge, UK: Cambridge University Press.

LEVIN, HARRY (1951). "Observations on the Style of Ernest Hemingway." *Kenyon Review* 13.4, 581–609.

LEWIS, R. W. B. (1975). *Edith Wharton: A Biography*. New York: Harper and Row.

LEHMAN, CHRISTOPHER P. (2007). *The Colored Cartoon: Black Representation in American Animated Short Films, 1907–1954*. Amherst: University of Massachusetts Press.

LESLIE, ESTHER (2002). *Hollywood Flatlands: Animation, Critical Theory and the Avant-Garde*. New York: Verso.

LINDSAY, VACHEL (1970). *The Art of the Moving Picture*. New York: Liveright.

LOEFFLER, JAMES (2002). "'Neither the King's English nor the Rebbetzin's Yiddish': Yinglish Literature in the United States," in Marc Shell (ed.), *American Babel: Literatures of the United States from Abnaki to Zuni*. Cambridge: Harvard University Press.

LOFGREN, CHARLES (1987). *The Plessy Case: A Legal-Historical Interpretation*. New York: Oxford University Press.

LONG, ELIZABETH (2009). "Aflame With Culture: Reading and Social Mission in the Nineteenth-Century White Women's Literary Club Movement," in Kaestle and Radway (eds.), *A History of the Book in America, Volume 4. Print in Motion: The Expansion of Publishing and Reading in the United States, 1880–1940*. Chapel Hill: University of North Carolina Press, 476–90.

LOWELL, JAMES RUSSELL (1849). "Editorial." *North American Review* 69, 209.

LOWIE, ROBERT H. (1984). "Comments on Edward Sapir, His Personality and Scholarship," in Konrad Koerner (ed.), *Edward Sapir: Appraisals of His Life and Work, Amsterdam Studies in the Theory and History of Linguistic Science, vol. 36*. Philadelphia: John Benjamins Publishing Company, 121–30.

LYE, COLLEEN (2005). *America's Asia: Racial Form and American Literature, 1893–1945*. Princeton: Princeton University Press.

LYND, ROBERT S., and HELEN MERRILL LYND (1957 [1929]). *Middletown: A Study in Contemporary American Culture*. New York: Harcourt Brace Jovanovich.

LYND, ROBERT S., and HELEN MERRILL LYND (1965 [1935]). *Middletown in Transition: A Study in Cultural Conflicts*. New York: Harcourt Brace Jovanovich.

MACPHERSON, C. B. (1962). *The Political Theory of Possessive Individualism, Hobbes to Locke*. New York: Oxford University Press.

MAFFI, MARIO (1998). "The Strange Case of Luigi Donato Ventura's *Peppino*," in Werner Sollors (ed.), *Multilingual America: Transnationalism, Ethnicity, and the Languages of American Literature*. New York: New York University Press, 166–75.

"Magazine Novels" (1869). *The Galaxy* 7, 130–32.

MAJEWSKI, KAREN (2001). "The Politics of Polishness in the United States: American Literature in Polish before World War II," in Orm Øverland (ed.), *Not English Only: Redefining "American" in American Studies*. Amsterdam: VU University Press, 112–18.

MALTBY, RICHARD (2003). *Hollywood Cinema*. Malden, MA: Blackwell.

MARTIN, JAY (1970). *Nathanael West: The Art of His Life*. New York: Farrar, Straus and Giroux.

MARTIN, RONALD E. (1981). *American Literature and the Universe of Force*. Durham: Duke University Press.

MARTIN, TERENCE (1957). "Social Institutions in the Early American Novel." *American Quarterly* 9.1, 72–84.

"Martyrdom of Evangelina Cisneros." *New York Journal*. August 19, 1897.

MARX, KARL, and FRIEDRICH ENGELS (1978 [1948]). *Manifesto of the Communist Party*, in Robert C. Tucker (ed.), *The Marx-Engels Reader*. New York: W. W. Norton.

MATTHEWS, BRANDER (1889). *American Authors and British Pirates*. New York: American Copyright League.

MATTHEWS, BRANDER (1901). *The Philosophy of the Short-Story*. New York: Longmans, Green, and Co.

MATTHEWS, JOHN T. (2004). "This Race Which Is Not One: The 'More Inextricable Compositeness' of William Faulkner's South," in Jon Smith and Deborah N. Cohn (eds.), *Look Away!: The U.S. South in New World Studies*. Durham: Duke University Press, 201–26.

MATTHIESSEN, F. O. (1941). *American Renaissance: Art and Expression in the Age of Emerson and Whitman*. New York: Oxford University Press.

MAXWELL, WILLIAM (1999). *New Negro, Old Left: African-American Writing and Communism Between the Wars*. New York: Columbia University Press.

McCANN, SEAN (2001). *Gumshoe America: Hard-Boiled Crime Fiction and the Rise and Fall of New Deal Liberalism*. Durham: Duke University Press.

McCORMICK, JOHN (1971). *American Literature 1919–1932: A Comparative History*. London: Routledge and Kegan Paul.

McDONNELL, PATRICK, KAREN O' CONNELL, and GEORGIA RILEY DE HAVENON (eds.), (1999). *Krazy Kat: The Comic Art of George Herriman*. New York: Harry N. Abrams.

McELVAINE, ROBERT S. (1993). *The Great Depression: America, 1929–1941*. New York: Times Books.

McFARLANE, JAMES (1991 [1976]). "The Mind of Modernism," in Malcolm Bradbury and Mc Farlane (eds.), *Modernism: A Guide To European Literature 1890–1930*. New York: Penguin, 71–93.

McGILLIGAN, PAT (1986). *Backstory*. Berkeley: University of California Press.

McHENRY, ELIZABETH (2002). *Forgotten Readers: Recovering the Lost History of African American Literary Societies*. Durham: Duke University Press.

McHENRY, ELIZABETH (2009). "Reading and Race Pride: The Literary Activism of Black Clubwomen," in Kaestle and Radway (eds.), *A History of the Book in America, Volume 4. Print in Motion: The Expansion of Publishing and Reading in the United States, 1880–1940*. Chapel Hill, NC: University of North Carolina Press, 491–510.

McKEE, IRVING (1947). *"Ben-Hur" Wallace: The Life of General Lew Wallace*. Berkeley: University of California Press.

McLEOD, ELIZABETH (2005). *The Original Amos 'n' Andy*. Jefferson NC: McFarland.

McLUHAN, MARSHALL (1967). *Medium is the Massage*. New York: Random House.

MENAND, LOUIS (2001). *The Metaphysical Club: A Story of Ideas in America*. New York: Farrar, Straus, and Giroux.

MENDIETA, EDUARDO (ed.) (1999). *The Underside of Modernity: Apel, Ricoeur, Rorty, Taylor, and the Philosophy of Liberation*. (trans.) Enrique D. Dussell. Amherst, New York: Humanity Books.

MENCKEN, H. L. (1919). *The American Language: An Enquiry into the Development of English in the United States.* New York: A. A. Knopf.

METCALFE, JAMES (1926). "What the Movies Do to Classics." *The Wall Street Journal.* August 12.

MEYERS, JEFFREY (1997). *Ernest Hemingway: The Critical Heritage.* New York: Routledge.

MICHAELS, WALTER BENN (1995). *Our America: Nativism, Modernism, and Pluralism.* Durham: Duke University Press.

MILLER, J. HILLIS (2009). "The University, with Conditions," in Gary A. Olson and John W. Presley (eds.), *The Future of Higher Education: Perspectives from America's Leaders.* Boulder, CO: Paradigm, 5–81.

MITCHELL, LEE CLARK (1989). *Determined Fictions: American Literary Naturalism.* New York: Columbia University Press.

MITCHELL, LEE CLARK (1996). *Westerns: Making the Man in Fiction and Film.* Chicago: The University of Chicago Press.

MOLLOY, SYLVIA (2005). "Latin America in the U.S. Imaginary: Postcolonialism, Translation and the Magic Realist Imperative," in Mabel Moraña (ed.), *Ideologies of Hispanism.* Nashville, TN: Vanderbilt University Press, 189–200.

"MONTHLIES AND WEEKLIES" (1874). *Every Saturday* 1, 475.

MOORE, CHARLES H. (1870). *What to Read, and How to Read.* New York: D. Appleton and Company.

MORETTI, FRANCO (2005). *Graphs, Maps, and Trees: Abstract Models for a Literary History.* New York: Verso.

MOTT, FRANK LUTHER (1947). *Golden Multitudes: The Story of Best Sellers in the United States.* New York: R. R. Bowker.

MOYA, PAULA M. L., and HAZEL MARKUS (2010). "An Introduction," in Moya and Markus (eds.), *Doing Race: 21 Essays for the 21st Century.* New York: W.W. Norton & Co., 1–102.

MUMFORD, LEWIS (1931). *The Brown Decades: A Study of the Arts in America, 1865–1895.* New York: Harcourt, Brace and Company.

MURPHY, GRETCHEN (2011). "The Hemispheric Novel in the Post-Revolutionary Era," in Leonard Cassuto, Clare Eby, and Benjamin Reiss (eds.), *The Cambridge History of the American Novel.* Cambridge, UK: Cambridge University Press, 553–70.

MURPHY, GRETCHEN (2007). "How the Irish Became Japanese: Winnifred Eaton's Racial Reconstructions in a Transnational Context." *American Literature* 79, 29–56.

NABERS, DEAK (2006). *Victory of Law: The Fourteenth Amendment, the Civil War, and American Literature, 1852–1867.* Baltimore: Johns Hopkins University Press.

NARANJO-HUEBL, LINDA (2006). "The Road to Perdition: E. D. E. N. Southworth and the Critics." *American Periodicals* 16, 123–50.

NEVINS, JESS (2010). "Where Did Science Fiction Come From? A Primer on the Pulps." io9.com. November 4, 2010. http://io9.com/#!5680191.

NOLAN, WILLIAM F. (1985). *The Black Mask Boys: Masters in the Hard-Boiled School of Detective Fiction*. New York: William Morrow & Co.

NORD, DAVID PAUL (2004). *Faith in Reading: Religious Publishing and the Birth of Mass Media in America*. New York: Oxford University Press.

NISSEN, AXEL (2009). *Manly Love Romantic Friendship in American Fiction*. Chicago: Chicago University Press.

OKINA, KYUIN (1923), *Ishokuju*. Transplanted Tree: Oakland, CA.

OSBORNE, PETER (1995). *The Politics of Time: Modernity and Avant-Garde*. London: Verso.

O'SULLIVAN, JOHN (1842). "Democracy and Literature." *Democratic Review*. August. 196–200.

ØVERLAND, ORM (1996). *The Western Home: A Literary History of Norwegian America*. Northfield, MN: Norwegian-American Historical Association.

Oxford English Dictionary (1991). 2nd ed. Oxford: Clarendon Press.

PARINS, JAMES W. (1991). *John Rollin Ridge: His Life and Works*. Lincoln, NE: University of Nebraska Press.

PARKER, DOROTHY R. (1992). *Singing and Indian Song: A Biography of D'Arcy McNickle*. Lincoln, NE: University of Nebraska Press.

PARKER, ROBERT DALE (2003). *The Invention of Native American Literature*. Ithaca, NY: Cornell University Press.

PARRINGTON, VERNON (1927). *Main Currents in American Thought, Vol. 3*. New York: Harcourt, Brace and Company.

PATTEE, FRED LEWIS (1928). "A Call for a Literary Historian," in Norman Foerster (ed.), *The Reinterpretation of American Literature*. New York: Harcourt Brace, 3–22.

PECK, HARRY THURSTON (1897). "Automatic Authorship. A Protest." *New York Times*. December 11, BR4.

PHAN, HOANG GIA (2006). "Imagined Territories: Comparative Racialization and the Accident of History in Wong Kim Ark." *Genre* 39, 21–38.

PHILES, GEORGE P. (1873). *How to Read a Book in the Best Way*. New York: Printed for George P. Philes.

PORTER, CHARLOTTE (1885). "The Serial Story." *The Century* 30, 812–13.

POSNER, RICHARD A. (1978). "The Right of Privacy." *Georgia Law Review* 12, 393–422.

POST, ROBERT C. (1991). "Rereading Warren and Brandeis: Privacy, Property, and Appropriation." *Case Western Reserve Law Review* 41, 647–80.

POST, ROBERT C. (1989). "The Social Foundations of Privacy: Community and Self in the Common Law Tort." *California Law Review* 77, 957–1009.

PRONZINI, BILL, and JACK ADRIAN (eds.) (1995). *Hard-Boiled: An Anthology of American Crime Stories*. Oxford, UK: Oxford University Press.

PULITZER, JOSEPH (1891). *New York World*. October 11.

PUTNEY, CLIFFORD (2001). *Muscular Christianity: Manhood and Sports in Protestant America, 1880–1920*. Cambridge: Harvard University Press.

RADWAY, JANICE (1997). *A Feeling for Books: the Book-of-the-Month Club, Literary Taste, and Middle-Class Desire*. Chapel Hill: University of North Carolina Press.

RAILTON, STEPHEN (2004). *Mark Twain: A Short Introduction*. Malden, MA: Blackwell Publishing.

RANDEL, WILLIAM PEIRCE (1962). *Edward Eggleston*. Gloucester, MA: Peter Smith.

RICHARDSON, ROBERT D. (2006). *William James: In the Maelstrom of American Modernism: A Biography*. New York: Houghton Mifflin Co.

RIESMAN, DAVID (1975). *Thorstein Veblen: A Critical Interpretation*. New York: Seabury Press.

ROBERTSON, MICHAEL (1997). *Stephen Crane, Journalism, and the Making of Modern American Literature*. New York: Columbia University Press.

ROBINSON, CEDRIC (2000 [1983]). *Black Marxism: The Making of the Black Radical Tradition*. Chapel Hill: University of North Carolina Press.

ROGGENKAMP, KAREN (2002). *Narrating the News: New Journalism and Literary Genre in Late Nineteenth-Century American Newspapers and Fiction*. Kent, OH: Kent State University Press.

ROGIN, MICHAEL (1991). "'The Sword Became a Flashing Vision': D. W. Griffith's *Birth of a Nation*," in Philip Fisher (ed.), *The New American Studies: Essays from Representations*. Berkeley: University of California Press.

ROSENFELD, PAUL (1924). *Port of New York: Essays on Fourteen American Moderns*. New York: Harcourt, Brace and Company.

ROSS, DOROTHY (1991). *The Origins of American Social Science*. New York: Cambridge University Press.

ROSS, JOHN (1985). *The Papers of Chief John Ross, 1807–1839*, in Gary E. Moulton (ed.), Norman, OK: University of Oklahoma Press.

ROTHFIELD, LAWRENCE (1994). *Vital Signs: Medical Realism in Nineteenth-Century Fiction*. Princeton: Princeton University Press.

RØLVAAG, OLE EDVART (1920). "Review of Simon Johnson, *Fire Fortellinger*." *Kvartalskrift* 16, 16–18.

ROHRBACH, AUGUSTA (1999). "To Be Continued: Double Identity, Multiplicity and Antigenealogy as Narrative Strategies in Pauline Hopkins' Magazine Fiction." *Callaloo* 22.2, 483–98.

ROWE, JOHN CARLOS (1995). "How the Boss Played the Game: Twain's Critique of Imperialism in *A Connecticut Yankee in King Arthur's Court*," in Forrest G. Robinson (ed.), *The Cambridge Companion to Mark Twain*. Cambridge, UK: Cambridge University Press, 175–92.

RUBIN, JOAN SHELLEY (1992). *The Making of Middlebrow Culture*. Chapel Hill: University of North Carolina Press.

RUDOLPH, FREDERICK (1962). *The American College and University: A History*. New York: Alfred A. Knopf.

RUHM, HERBERT (ed.) (1977). *The Hard-Boiled Detective: Stories from "Black Mask" Magazine 1920–1951*. New York: Random House.

SAINT-AMOUR, PAUL K. (2003). "Modernist Reconnaissance." *Modernism/Modernity* 10.2, 349–80.

SALDÍVAR, RAMÓN (2006). *The Borderlands of Culture: Américo Paredes and the Transnational Imaginary.* Durham: Duke University Press.

SAMMOND, NICHOLAS (2012). "'Gentlemen, Please Be Seated': Racial Masquerades and Sadomasochism in 1930s Animation," in Stephen Johnson (ed.), *Burnt Cork: Traditions and Legacies of Blackface Minstrelsy.* Amherst: University of Massachusetts Press, 164–71.

SANDERSON, MARK (ed.) (1980). *Mark Twain's Notebooks and Journals 3.* Berkeley: University of California Press.

SASSEN, SASKIA (2010). "A Savage Sorting of Winners and Losers: Contemporary Versions of Primitive Accumulation." *Globalizations* 7.1–2, 23–50.

SATTERFIELD, JAY (2002). *"The World's Best Books": Taste Culture and the Modern Library.* Amherst: University of Massachusetts Press.

SCHICKEL, RICHARD (1992). *Double Indemnity.* London: British Film Institute.

SCRUGGS, CHARLES (1993). *Sweet Home: Invisible Cities in the Afro-American Novel.* Baltimore, MD: Johns Hopkins University Press.

SCHUDSON, MICHAEL (1978). *Discovering the News: A Social History of American Newspapers.* New York: Basic Books.

SEDGWICK, ELLERY (1994). *The Atlantic Monthly, 1857–1909: Yankee Humanism at High Tide and Ebb.* Amherst: University of Massachusetts Press.

SELDES, GILBERT [1924] (2001). *The Seven Lively Arts.* Mineola, NY: Dover Publications.

SELTZER, MARK (1992). *Bodies and Machines.* New York: Routledge.

SERVER, LEE (1993). *Danger is My Business: An Illustrated History of the Fabulous Pulp Magazines 1896–1953.* San Francisco: Chronicle Books.

SERVER, LEE (2002). *Encyclopedia of Pulp Fiction Writers: The Essential Guide to More Than 200 Pulp Pioneers and Mass-market Masters.* New York: Facts on File Inc.

SHADOIAN, JACK (1977). *Dreams and Dead Ends: The American Gangster Film.* Cambridge: MIT Press.

SHAMIR, MILETTE (2006). *Inexpressible Privacy: The Interior Life of Antebellum Literature.* Philadelphia: University of Pennsylvania Press.

SHAW, JOSEPH T. (1930). "Letter to the Editor," *Writer's Digest,* September.

SHEEHAN, DONALD (1952). *This Was Publishing: A Chronicle of the Book Trade in the Gilded Age.* Bloomington: Indiana University Press.

SHIFFMAN, DANIEL (1999). "Ethnic Competitors in *Studs Lonigan.*" *MELUS* 24.3, 67–79.

SHKLAR, JUDITH N. (1991). *American Citizenship: The Quest for Inclusion.* Cambridge: Harvard University Press.

SHOVE, RAYMOND (1937). *Cheap Book Production in the United States, 1870–1891.* Urbana, IL: University of Illinois Library.

SHUMAN, EDWIN L. (1903). *Practical Journalism: A Complete Manual of the Best Newspaper Methods.* New York: D. Appleton.

SICHERMAN, BARBARA (2010). *Well-Read Lives: How Books Inspired a Generation of American Women.* Chapel Hill: University of North Carolina Press.

SILBER, NINA. (1993). *Romances of Reunion: Northerners and the South, 1865–1900.* Chapel Hill: University of North Carolina Press.

SMALL, A. W. (1895). "The Era of Sociology," *American Journal of Sociology* 1, 1–15.

SMITH, ANNA TOLMAN (1897). "A Study in Race Psychology." *Popular Science Monthly* 50, 355–62.

SMITH, ERIN A. (2000). *Hard-Boiled: Working-Class Readers and Pulp Magazines.* Philadelphia: Temple University Press.

SMITH, NEIL (2003). *American Empire: Roosevelt's Geographer and the Prelude to Globalization.* Berkeley: University of California Press.

SMITH, ROGERS M. (1997). *Civic Ideals: Conflicting Visions of Citizenship in U.S. History.* New Haven: Yale University Press.

SMITH, TERRY (1993). *Making the Modern: Industry, Art, and Design in America.* Chicago: University of Chicago.

SMYTH, ALBERT H. (1888). "American Literature in the Class-room." *Transactions and Proceedings of the Modern Language Association of America, 1887* 3, 238–44.

"THE SOCIALIST IN FICTION" (1893). *The Critic* 601, 133.

SOIFER, AVIAM (1987). "The Paradox of Paternalism and Laissez-Faire Constitutionalism: United States Supreme Court, 1888–1921." *Law and History Review* 5, 249–79.

STAM, ROBERT (2005). *Literature Through Film: Realism, Magic, and the Art of Adaptation.* Malden, MA: Blackwell Publishing.

STEPHENS, MICHELLE (2005). *Black Empire: The Masculine Global Imaginary of Caribbean Intellectuals in the United States, 1914–1962.* Durham: Duke University Press.

STEVENS, JOHN D. (1991). *Sensationalism and the New York Press.* New York: Columbia University Press.

STEWART, SUSAN (1984). *On Longing: Narratives of the Miniature, the Gigantic, the Souvenir, the Collection.* Durham: Duke University Press.

STOTT, WILLIAM (1986 [1983]). *Documentary Expression and Thirties America.* Chicago: University of Chicago Press.

STREEBY, SHELLEY (2002). *American Sensations: Class, Empire, and the Production of Popular Culture.* Berkeley: University of California Press.

STREEBY, SHELLEY (2004). "Sensational Fiction," in Shirley Samuels (ed.), *A Companion to American Fiction, 1780–1865,* Malden, Mass.: Blackwell.

STEMPEL, TOM (1988). *A History of Screenwriting in the American Film.* New York: Continuum

SUNDQUIST, ERIC. J. (1982). "The Country of the Blue," in Eric J. Sundquist (ed.), *American Realism: New Essays.* Baltimore: Johns Hopkins University Press.

SUNDQUIST, ERIC (1993). *To Wake the Nations: Race in the Making of American Literature.* Cambridge: Belknap.

SUSMAN, WARREN I. (1984). *Culture as History: The Transformation of American Society in the Twentieth Century*. New York: Pantheon Books.

STEMPEL, TOM (1988). *A History of Screenwriting in the American Film*. New York: Continuum.

SUVIN, DARKO (2010). *Defined by a Hollow: Essays on Utopia, Science Fiction, and Political Epistemology. Ralahine Utopian Studies, Vol. 6*. New York: Peter Lang.

SUVIN, DARKO (1979). *Metamorphoses of Science Fiction*. New Haven: Yale University Press.

SZALAY, MICHAEL (2000). *New Deal Modernism: American Literature and the Invention of the Welfare State*. Durham: Duke University Press.

SZASZ, FERENC MORTON (1982). *The Divided Mind of Protestant America, 1880–1930*. Tuscaloosa: University of Alabama Press.

TAUBENFELD, AVIVA (1998). " 'Only an "L" ': Linguistic Borders and the Immigrant Author in Abraham Cahan's *Yekl* and *Yankel der Yankee*," in Werner Sollors (ed.), *Multilingual America: Transnationalism, Ethnicity, and the Languages of American Literature*. New York: New York University Press, 144–65.

TEBBEL, JOHN (1972). *A History of Book Publishing in the United States, Volume 2: The Expansion of an Industry, 1865–1919*. New York: R. R. Bowker.

TEBBEL, JOHN (1978). *A History of Book Publishing in the United States, Volume 3: The Golden Age Between Two Wars: 1920–1940*. New York: R.R. Bowker.

THAYER, WILLIAM ROSCOE (1915). *The Life and Letters of John Hay, Vol II*. New York: Houghton Mifflin.

THOMAS, BROOK (1997a). Plessy v. Ferguson: *A Brief History with Documents*. Boston: Bedford/St. Martin's.

THOMAS, BROOK (1997b). "Plessy v. Ferguson and the Literary Imagination." *Cardozo Studies in Law & Literature* 9, 45–65.

THOMAS, BROOK (1997c). *American Literary Realism and the Failed Promise of Contract*. Berkeley: University of California Press.

THOMAS, WILLIAM ISAAC (1921). "The Persistence of Primary-Group Norms in Present-Day Society and their Influence in our Educational System," in Herbert S. Jennings, J. B. Watson, Adolf Meyer, and William I. Thomas (eds.), *Suggestions of Modern Science Concerning Education*. New York: Macmillan.

THORP, WILLARD (1961). "The Religious Novel as Best Seller in America," in James Ward Smith and A. Leland Jamison (eds.), *Religious Perspectives in American Culture*. Princeton: Princeton University Press, 195–241.

TIGNOR, ELEANOR Q. (1982). "Rudolph Fisher: Harlem Novelist." *Langston Hughes Review* 1.1, 13–22.

TILMAN, RICK (1996). *The Intellectual Legacy of Thorstein Veblen: Unresolved Issues*. Westport, CT: Greenwood Press.

TOMPKINS, JANE (1985). *Sensational Designs: The Cultural Work of American Fiction 1790–1860*. New York: Oxford University Press.

TOMPKINS, JANE (1992). *West of Everything: The Inner Life of Westerns*. New York and Oxford: Oxford University Press.

"Topics of the Times: Copyright at Home and Abroad" (1881). *Scribners Monthly* 22.1, 142–47.

TORGOVNICK, MARIANNA (2005). *The War Complex: World War II in Our Time*. Chicago: University of Chicago Press.

TRACHTENBERG, ALAN (1982). *The Incorporation of America: Culture and Society in the Gilded Age*. New York: Hill and Wang.

TRAVIS, JENNIFER (2005). *Wounded Hearts: Masculinity, Law, and Literature in American Culture*. Chapel Hill: University of North Carolina Press.

TROTTER, DAVID (2007). *Cinema and Modernism*. Malden MA: Blackwell.

TURIM, MAUREEN (2009). *American Cinema of the 1920s: Themes and Variations*. New Brunswick: Rutgers University Press.

TWAIN, MARK (1974). "Notebook 27" in Anderson, Frederick, Frank, Michael B. and Kenneth M.

VAN DOREN, CARL (1921). *The American Novel*. New York: Macmillan.

VASEY, RUTH (1997). *The World According to Hollywood, 1918–1939*. Madison, WI: University of Wisconsin Press.

VEBLEN, THORSTEIN (1918). *The Higher Learning in America: A Memorandum on the Conduct of Universities by Business Men*. New York: Huebsch.

VIALS, CHRISTOPHER (2009). *Realism for the Masses: Aesthetics, Popular Front Pluralism, and U.S. Culture 1935–47*. Jackson, MS: University Press of Mississippi.

WALD, PRISCILLA. (1995). *Constituting Americans: Cultural Anxiety and Narrative Form*. Durham, NC: Duke University Press.

WALTERS, WENDY W. (2005). *At Home in Diaspora: Black International Writing*. Minneapolis, MN: University of Minnesota Press.

WANN, LOUIS (1925). "The 'Revolt From the Village' in American Fiction." *Overland Monthly and Out West Magazine* 83.8, 299.

WARREN, KENNETH W. (1993). *Black and White Strangers: Race and American Literary Realism*. Chicago: Chicago University Press.

WEBSTER, NOAH (1953). *Letters of Noah Webster*. Harry R. Warfel (ed.), New York: Library Publications.

WEINBAUM, ALYS EVE (2004). *Wayward Reproductions: Genealogies of Race and Nation in Transatlantic Modern Thought*. Durham: Duke University Press.

WEINSTEIN, CINDY (1995). *The Literature of Labor and the Labors of Literature: Allegory in Nineteenth-century American Fiction*. New York: Cambridge University Press.

WELKE, BARBARA YOUNG (2001). *Recasting American Liberty: Gender, Race, Law, and the Railroad Revolution, 1865–1920*. Cambridge: Cambridge University Press.

WESTFAHL, GARY (1998). *The Mechanics of Wonder: The Creation of the Idea of Science Fiction*. Liverpool, UK: Liverpool University Press.

WHITE, G. EDWARD (2003). *Tort Law in America: An Intellectual History*. Expanded ed. Oxford: Oxford University Press.

WIEGAND, WAYNE A. (1986). *The Politics of an Emerging Profession*. New York: Greenwood Press.

WIEGAND, WAYNE A. (2009). "The American Public Library: Construction of a Community Reading Institution," in Kaestle and Radway (eds.), *A History of the Book in America, Volume 4. Print in Motion: The Expansion of Publishing and Reading in the United States, 1880–1940*. Chapel Hill: University of North Carolina Press, 431–51.

WILLIAMS, RAYMOND (2010). "Utopia and Science Fiction," in Andrew Milner (ed.), *Tenses of Imagination: Raymond Williams on Science Fiction, Utopia, and Dystopia. Ralahine Utopian Studies Vol. 7*. New York: Peter Lang, 93–112.

WILLIAMS, RAYMOND. (1973). *The Country and The City*. New York: Oxford University Press.

WILLIAMS, RAYMOND (1976). *Keywords: A Vocabulary of Culture and Society*. New York: Oxford University Press.

WILLIS, SUSAN (1979). "Aesthetics of the Rural Slum: Contradictions and Dependency in 'The Bear'." *Social Text* 2, 82–103.

WILSON, CHRISTOPHER P. (1992). *White Collar Fictions: Class and Social Representation in American Literature, 1885–1925*. Athens GA: University of Georgia Press.

WILSON, EDMUND (1931). *Axel's Castle: A Study in the Imaginative Literature of 1870–1930*. New York: Charles Scribner's Sons.

WISTER, OWEN (1988 [1928]). "A Best Seller," in Wister (ed.), *The Virginian*. New York: Penguin, xxxi–xxxviii.

WISTER, OWEN (1988 [1911]). "Re-Dedication and Preface," in Wister (ed.), *The Virginian*. New York: Penguin, xliii.

WITT, PETER DAVID (1968). "The Beginnings of the Teaching of Verncular Literature in the Secondary Schools of Massachusetts." Diss., Harvard University.

WONHAM, HENRY B. (2004). *Playing the Races: Ethnic Caricature and American Literary Realism*. New York: Oxford University Press.

WRIGHT, CARROLL D. (1901). *A Report on the Effect of the International Copyright Law in the United States*. Washington: Government Printing Office.

WU, CYNTHIA (2008). "The Siamese Twins in Late-Nineteenth-Century Narratives of Conflict and Resolution." *American Literature* 80, 29–55.

XIAO-HUANG, YIN (2000). *Chinese American Literature Since the 1850s*. Urbana: University of Illinois Press.

ZIZEK, SLAVOJ (2006). "Against the Populist Temptation." *Critical Inquiry* 32.3, 551–74.

ZUNSHINE, LISA (2006). *Why We Read Fiction: Theory of Mind and the Novel*. Columbus: Ohio State University Press.

INDEX OF AMERICAN NOVELISTS, 1870–1940

Note: Page numbers in *italics* refer to illustrations.

GENERAL INDEX

Printed in the USA/Agawam, MA
March 14, 2016

631983.035